Books by Oscar Lewis

ON THE EDGE OF THE BLACK WAXY

LIFE IN A MEXICAN VILLAGE: *Tepoztlán Restudied*

VILLAGE LIFE IN NORTHERN INDIA

FIVE FAMILIES: *Mexican Case Studies in the Culture of Poverty*

THE CHILDREN OF SÁNCHEZ: *Autobiography of a Mexican Family*

PEDRO MARTÍNEZ: *A Mexican Peasant and His Family*

PEDRO MARTÍNEZ

A Mexican Peasant and His Family

PEDRO MARTÍNEZ

A Mexican Peasant and His Family

OSCAR LEWIS

DRAWINGS BY ALBERTO BELTRÁN

Random House
NEW YORK

TO *Ruth*

ACKNOWLEDGMENTS

Because the field research and the writing of this book have been spread over a twenty year period, from 1943 to 1963, I have incurred many obligations. I am grateful to the American Philosophical Society for summer research grants in 1947 and 1948; to Washington University for a summer grant in 1947; to the Wenner-Gren Foundation for Anthropological Research for grants in 1943 and 1956; to the Behavioral Sciences Division of the Ford Foundation for a grant-in-aid in 1952; to the Guggenheim Foundation for a fellowship in 1956; and finally, to the Research Board of the University of Illinois for their continued support of my Mexican research since 1948.

To Asa Zatz I am indebted for his fine translation of the greater portion of the field data upon which this volume is based. Mr. Zatz was also of great assistance to me in translating data for my earlier book *The Children of Sánchez.*

To Mrs. Caroline Luján, Mexican psychologist, who gave generously of her time and talent, I am grateful for administering the Rorschach test to Pedro Martínez and for her insightful analysis of the Rorschach and Thematic Apperception Test protocols of Pedro and his wife. I also want to thank two American psychologists, Mrs. Ethel D. Kardiner and Professor William E. Henry, for their able analyses of the same materials. The test protocols, the psychologists' analyses, and my own evaluation of the test data will be published separately at a later time.

I am grateful to the late Manuel Gamio, who was Mexico's elder statesman among social scientists, for his sponsorship of the study during its first year in 1943. I am also grateful to Angélica Castro de la Fuente and Dr. Alejandro D. Marroquín for their assistance in the early phase of the field work on the village culture. To Alberto Beltrán I am grateful for his fine drawings which illustrate this book. His intimate knowledge of Mexico and his first-hand familiarity with the people of Azteca give his drawings a unique authenticity.

A number of my friends and colleagues have read and commented upon the manuscript at various stages of its growth. I especially want to thank Joseph Alvarez, Professor Joseph B. Casagrande, Dr. Howard F. Cline, Irving Dilliard, Jason Epstein, Jules Feiffer, Professor Irving Goldman, Professor William E. Henry, Berenice Hoffman, Helen Kuypers, Lourdes Marín, Professor Margaret Mead, Professor Robert E. Scott, Tad Szulc, Professor Charles Shattuck, Dr. William Vogt, and my son, Gene L. Lewis.

To my wife, Ruth M. Lewis, I am grateful for her untiring collaboration in all phases of the preparation of this book. She has given me invaluable assistance in organizing, editing, and translating from the Spanish vast quantities of my field notes and taped interviews. Her work has been a major contribution to this book. I also want to thank my wife and my daughter Judy for sharing with me the hardships of anthropological field research.

To the Martínez family, whose true identity must remain anonymous, I am grateful for their co-operation and friendship over these many years.

GLOSSARY
of Spanish Words and Political Figures

---

acabada, the termination of the cultivation of corn, which is celebrated by a fiesta in the fields and at home.

ahuatle (*ahuautli, aguautle*), larvae of an unknown species of fly.

los aires, mysterious forces, winds, spirits or little people that inhabit stream beds, ravines, stagnant pools and high hills and that are believed to cause sores, pimples, paralysis and other illnesses.

alcahuete, a go-between or a procurer.

barrio, a subdivision of the village.

caciques, an elite group who owned most of the privately held land and who controlled the local government and the communal lands.

calzones, pajama-like pants of coarse white cotton cloth, tied with a string at the waist and ankles. These were generally made at home by the women of the family.

Cárdenas, Lázaro, President of the Republic from 1934-40. His administration is remembered for the expropriation of Mexican oil from foreign owners, for the acceleration of land distribution, the establishment of agricultural schools and for the encouragement of co-operative farming.

carga, a sack of 100 *cuartillos* of grain, usually corn or beans; corn measure containing 4 *fanegas* or 6.40 bushels.

Carranza, Venustiano (1859-1920), well-to-do landowner from the north who supported the Madero Revolution against Díaz in 1910. After the murder of Madero, Carranza headed the Constitutional Revolution against Huerta. Carranza acted as de facto President of Mexico in 1915 and as the elected President from 1917-20. He was opposed by Zapata, Pancho Villa and later by Obregón and de la

Huerta. Deserted and betrayed by most of his followers, Carranza fled in 1920 and was finally murdered by a local *cacique* in a small town in Puebla. (Followers of Carranza were called *carrancistas*.)

comal, clay griddle for toasting *tortillas*.

compadrazgo, a system of relationship between godparents (*padrinos*) and godchildren (*ahijados*) and between godparents and parents.

corral, enclosed yard where animals are kept.

Cristeros, name given to militant Catholics who combatted the government anticlerical policy by burning schools, murdering schoolteachers and committing acts of banditry. Their slogan was *Cristo Rey*, Christ is King. The revolt lasted from 1927 to 1930 and took place chiefly in Jalisco, Colima and Michoacán.

CROM (*Confederación Regional de Obreros Mexicanos*), national federation of labor unions founded in Saltillo in 1918, under the leadership of Luis Morones. It was organized on a craft-union basis, modeled after the American Federation of Labor. The CROM organized a Mexican Labor Party and supported Obregón for President in 1920. In 1928, when Portes Gil was the President, the CROM was smashed by the government with the help of rival independent unions. Its successor was the *Confederación General de Obreros y Campesinos* (CGOC), organized in 1932 by Lombardo Toledano, long a member of the old CROM. The CGOC was succeeded in 1936 by the *Confederación de Trabajadores de Mexico* (CTM), also under Toledano.

cuartillo, approximately two dry quarts. The size of a corn plot is measured by the amount of seed corn that can be planted on it. On the average, it takes ten *cuartillos* of corn to plant one hectare or 2.2 acres of land.

Díaz, Porfirio (1830-1915), was elected President in 1876 to fill out the unexpired term of President Lerdo, whom Díaz had helped overthrow. Re-elected in 1884, Díaz managed to stay in power until May, 1911, when he was forced to resign and go into exile in Europe.

ejido, communal lands expropriated by *haciendas* before the Revolution and later returned to the *municipios*. These lands were placed under the National Ejido program and were administered by specially elected local officials rather than by the regular municipal authorities.

ética, a wasting disease characterized by chronic diarrhea and a swollen abdomen.

huaraches, Mexican sandals.

Huerta, Victoriano (1845-1916), Mexican general who opposed Zapata and who betrayed Madero. After Madero's murder, Huerta was President from 1913 to 1914.

Juárez, Benito (1806-1872), provisional President in 1858-60 and elected President from 1861-65. He was the leader of the independence movement against the French. When Maximilian was captured and shot, Juárez was again elected President and served from 1867-1872. He was responsible for many reforms, the most important of which reduced the power of the army and the church.

Madero, Francisco I. (1873-1913), the son of a wealthy landowning family, a liberal idealist who opposed the re-election of Díaz in 1910 and who was elected President of Mexico in 1911. He was murdered in 1913.

mayordomo, the administrator or chief in a *barrio* or on an *hacienda.*

mestizo, the offspring of a marriage between an Indian and a white. In Azteca it referred to an acculturated Indian.

mexicano, refers to the Nahuatl language.

mezcal (mexcal), an alcoholic drink distilled from the maguey plant.

milpa, a cornfield.

nahual (nagual), a sorcerer or witch with the power to change into an animal such as a dog or a pig for the purpose of stealing or doing mischief.

Obregón, Álvaro (1880-1928), served as President of Mexico from 1920-24, initiating the distribution of land to the peasants and supporting organized labor and the CROM. Calles succeeded him to the Presidency in 1924 but Obregón was re-elected in 1928. He was assassinated by a religious fanatic shortly thereafter.

padrino, godfather.

petate, mat woven of straw.

PRI (*Partido Revolucionario Institucional*), the official government party which dominates the political scene in Mexico.

rebozo, Mexican shawl.

regidor, councilman responsible for the financial operations of the *municipio.*

síndico, councilman responsible for the communal natural resources, that is, the land, forests and water. He also inspects cattle to be slaughtered and acts as attorney general.

temazcal (temascal, temaxcal), pre-Hispanic Indian steambath or sweathouse.

texcal, hillside land covered with volcanic rock and a thorny scrub forest.

tlacolol, a type of agriculture in which planting is done with a primitive hoe on land which is steep, rocky and wooded.

Villa, Pancho (1877-1923), leader of the northern forces in the Madero Revolution in 1910. After the murder of Madero, he fought against Huerta and Carranza. U.S. troops under Pershing fought against Villa in 1916. Villa continued guerrilla warfare until defeated by Obregón. Later he was bribed into submission by a gift of an *hacienda* in Durango. Villa was assassinated in 1923.

Zapata, Emiliano (1880-1919), peasant leader of Revolutionary forces in the southern states of Morelos, Guerrero and Puebla. He demanded land for the peasants and withdrew his support from Madero when the latter failed to carry out his promise to institute land reforms. With Villa, Zapata captured Mexico City in 1914 and fought bitterly against Carranza and Huerta. Led into a trap by Guajardo, a *carrancista* officer, Zapata was assassinated in 1919. (His followers were called *zapatistas*.)

A SYNCHRONIC RECORD

OF

SOME MAJOR EVENTS

IN THE

MEXICAN NATION, IN AZTECA

AND IN

THE MARTÍNEZ FAMILY

A Synchronic Record of Some Major Events in the

YEAR	MEXICO
1810–1821	War of Independence against Spain.
1857	Benito Juárez and the Reform Laws imposing separation of Church and State.
1876–1880; 1884–1911	Regime of Porfirio Díaz.
1910	Mexican Revolution begins, Pancho Villa rises in the north.
1911	Emiliano Zapata rises in the south. Porfirio Díaz goes into exile. Francisco I. Madero proclaims Plan of San Luis. Madero becomes President. Zapata proclaims Plan of Ayala.
1913	Madero assassinated. Victoriano Huerta becomes President.
1914	Venustiano Carranza becomes President.
1917	Article 27 of Mexican Constitution establishes Land Reform.
1918	The CROM (*Confederación Regional de Obreros Mexicanos*) is founded.

Mexican Nation, in Azteca, and in the Martínez Family

AZTECA	THE MARTÍNEZ FAMILY
Church land taken over by some leading village families.	
Attempted revolt by landless men. *Cacique* Felipe Galindo murdered. Railroad built through the *municipio* [1897]. *Caciques* control village.	Birth of Pedro [1889]. Birth of Esperanza [about 1891]. Pedro lives in Yautepec [1897–1904].
	Pedro's mother dies. Pedro marries Esperanza.
Revolutionaries enter the village. *Caciques* flee to Mexico City. Aztecan leaders kill each other.	The first child, María, born to Pedro and Esperanza.
Typhus epidemic; villages burned; martial law declared; villagers flee.	Second child, Manuel, born and dies.
Martial law.	Third child, Gonzalo, born. Pedro joins Zapata's army.
Hunger widespread.	Pedro deserts the army and flees with his family to Guerrero. Gonzalo and María die. Fourth child, Conchita, born.
Village almost deserted.	

YEAR	MEXICO
1919	Zapata assassinated by Guajardo.
1920	Carranza assassinated. Guajardo executed. Álvaro Obregón becomes President.
1921	CGT (*Confederación General de Trabajadores*) founded.
1922	
1923	Pancho Villa assassinated.
1924	Plutarco Elías Calles becomes President.
1925	
1926	The Forestry Department given control over nation's forests. The Archbishop of Mexico declares policy of resistance to the government. Priests close churches.
1927	Armed Catholics, the *cristeros*, actively oppose government.

AZTECA

Peace re-established in village. *Zapatistas* in hiding.

Carrancista soldiers leave. Jesús Montoya sent by Governor to be president.
Ex-*zapatistas* now confident.

The Union of Aztecan Peasants is organized with the help of the CROM.

Jesús Montoya thrown out by the ex-*caciques*. Struggle for power between the *centrales* and the Union.

The Union gains control and is given arms for Civil Defense.

The Union is in control.

The Union in control.
First corn mill established in the village.

Aztecans must get permit from Forestry Department to cut or burn wood in the communal forest. Church and *barrio* chapels close and priest leaves for Mexico City.

Small group of *cristeros* enters Azteca but is defeated by the Civil Defense. First Protestant missionary appears. Valentín Quiroz is killed by Herrera. Sereno Hidalgo forms Civil Defense against the Union.

THE MARTÍNEZ FAMILY

Pedro leaves Guerrero and returns with Esperanza and Conchita to Azteca.

Pedro is *mayordomo* of his *barrio*. Pedro appointed president of voting booth.

Pedro joins the Union and the struggle to protect the forests.

The fifth child, Rufina, born. Pedro imprisoned for twenty-two days.

The sixth child, Felipe, born.

The seventh child, Martín, born. Pedro becomes a councilman (second *regidor*).

Eighth child, Macrina, born. Pedro is second *regidor*. Pedro imprisoned for second time. Pedro flees to Yautepec.

YEAR	MEXICO
1928	Obregón re-elected President. Obregón assassinated. Emilio Portes Gil is President. CROM dissolves.
1929	Formation of the Partido Nacional Revolucionario (PNR) as the official party of the Revolution.
1930	Pascual Ortiz Rubio is President.
1932	Abelardo Rodríguez is President.
1934	Lázaro Cárdenas is President.
1935	Formation of the Confederación de Trabajadores Mexicanos (CTM)
1936	
1937	Organization of the Partido de la Revolución Mexicana (PMR) to replace the PNR.
1938	
1939	
1940	Manuel Avila Camacho is President.
1941	
1942	

AZTECA	THE MARTÍNEZ FAMILY
Massacre of ex-*caciques* in the plaza by the Herrera brothers. Union members flee. Conservatives now control village.	Pedro flees to Mexico City.
2,100 hectares of *ejido* land distributed to Aztecan families. Church reopened. The Union of Aztecan Peasants reorganized as *fraternales*.	Pedro returns to Azteca. Ninth child, Ricardo, born. Daughter Rufina dies.
Forestry Co-operative under Sereno Hidalgo organized.	Pedro converts to Seventh Day Adventism.
	Tenth child, Mauricio, born and dies.
Road to Cuernavaca is begun.	Felipe loses an eye.
Sereno Hidalgo killed. President Cárdenas visits village.	Eleventh child, Moisés, born. Conchita goes to school in Huaxtepec.
Road to Cuernavaca completed.	
Second *ejido* grant and distribution of land.	Conchita attempts suicide.
	Conchita goes to school in Coyoacán.
	Twelfth child, Sara, born and dies.
Third *ejido* grant and distribution of land.	Pedro becomes a judge.
	Conchita becomes a schoolteacher.
	Conchita's son, Germán, born.

YEAR	MEXICO
1943	
1945	
1946	Miguel Alemán is President. Organization of the Partido Revolucionario Institucional (PRI) to replace PMR.
1947	
1949	
1950	
1952	Adolfo Ruiz Cortines is President.
1955	
1956	
1960	Adolfo López Mateos is President.
1961	
1963	

AZTECA	THE MARTÍNEZ FAMILY
	Conchita, age 26, marries Juan.
	Pedro becomes a councilman (*síndico procurador*).
New primary school is built.	Pedro is a councilman.
	Pedro and Esperanza ill. Pedro has an operation in the hospital. Conchita's baby dies.
	Macrina elopes at age 22.
New secondary school is opened.	Moisés enters secondary school in village.
	Ricardo leaves home. Moisés becomes a schoolteacher.
	Esperanza dies.
Electricity installed in center *barrios*.	Felipe marries at age 37.
	Martín marries at age 36. Germán graduates from secondary school and enters normal school.
	Germán becomes a schoolteacher.

CONTENTS

Acknowledgments   ix

Glossary   xi

Synchronic Record   xvi

Introduction   xxvii

PART ONE

Prologue: PEDRO   3

Chapter I   PEDRO: *Childhood and Youth*   6

Chapter II   PEDRO: *Marriage*   39

Chapter III   ESPERANZA: *Youth and Marriage*   48

Chapter IV   PEDRO: *Becoming Independent*   54

PART TWO

Chapter V   PEDRO: *The Revolution Begins*   73

Chapter VI   ESPERANZA: *The Revolution*   92

Chapter VII   PEDRO: *Fighting with Zapata*   97

Chapter VIII   ESPERANZA: *Three Years in Guerrero*   111

PART THREE

Chapter IX   PEDRO: *Village Politics*   119

Chapter X   ESPERANZA: *On Politics*   153

Chapter XI   PEDRO: *In Mexico City*   162

Chapter XII   ESPERANZA: *In Mexico City*   173

PART FOUR

Chapter XIII   PEDRO: *Conversion to Protestanism*   181

Chapter XIV   ESPERANZA: *Conversion*   213

Chapter XV   FELIPE: *Childhood*   218

PART FIVE

Chapter XVI   PEDRO: *On Conchita*   249

Chapter XVII   PEDRO: *Back to Politics*   260

Chapter XVIII PEDRO: *The PRI and Village Politics*   284

Chapter XIX   FELIPE: *Youth and Courtship*   306

PART SIX

Chapter XX   PEDRO: *Conchita and Family Problems*   331

Chapter XXI   ESPERANZA: *Family Problems*   353

Chapter XXII   FELIPE: *Problems at Home*   360

PART SEVEN

Chapter XXIII PEDRO: *Esperanza's Death*   391

Chapter XXIV   FELIPE: *Leaves for Mexico City*   402

Chapter XXV   PEDRO: *Old Age*   439

               Epilogue: PEDRO   454

               APPENDIX

    I   *Division of Labor and Family Budget*   461

    II   *More on Pedro's Children*   470

    III   *The Village Background*   485

INTRODUCTION

———

In this tape-recorded story of a Mexican peasant family as told by three of its members*—Pedro Martínez, the father; Esperanza, his wife; and Felipe, the eldest son—I hope to convey to the reader what it means to be a peasant in a nation undergoing rapid cultural change: how peasants feel, how they think, and how they express themselves.

Although peasantry is as old as civilization itself and constitutes the bulk of the population in the underdeveloped countries and in the world, we still have much to learn about peasants, their values, problems and aspirations, the intimate details of family living, the effects upon their lives of Western technology and culture and their potential for participation and leadership in the modern world.

We in the United States have never had our own peasantry, and our popular image of peasants is based upon European novels, especially the French, English, Italian and Russian. We sometimes forget that a large portion of the 200 millions of people in Latin America are peasants, a great many of them of Indian background. It is these very people who will have to be understood and reached if programs of economic and social improvement, including those of the Alliance for Progress, are to be successful.

* Except for historical figures, the characters in this book have been given fictitious names, to protect their anonymity.

It has commonly been held that peasants are essentially a stabilizing and conservative force in human history. The events of our own century, however, throw some doubt on this comfortable stereotype. Peasants have had an important, if not a crucial role, in at least four major revolutions—the Mexican Revolution of 1910, the Russian Revolution of 1917, the Chinese Communist Revolution, and the Cuban Revolution under Fidel Castro.

The story of Pedro Martínez is of special interest because it gives us one of the few first-hand accounts of a great revolution as seen by a peasant who not only lived through it but actively participated and identified with its ideals. It is a tribute to the Mexican Revolution that it imbued poor and illiterate peasants like Pedro with ideals of social justice which gave meaning to their lives. In doing this, the Revolution, particularly in the early *zapatista* phase, attempted to reawaken the ancient village traditions of collective action which had been repressed during the long regime of Porfirio Díaz.

It is difficult for most of us in the United States to view revolutions with equanimity, much less with sympathy; indeed, we have a deep-seated dread of revolutions. Our own revolution occurred so long ago that it is no longer an integral part of our contemporary ideology. This puts us at a tremendous disadvantage in understanding and in providing leadership for the many countries that are now or that will soon be living through their revolutions.

It is particularly important for us in the United States to have a better understanding of Mexican history and culture, its people and its revolution. Mexico, after all, is our next-door neighbor, and a few million American citizens are of Mexican descent. Moreover, it is one of the most advanced, progressive, and prestigeful nations in Latin America and continues to play a key role in inter-American affairs. One cannot understand Mexico without understanding its revolution, for out of it have grown many of the basic institutions of contemporary Mexico. The very term revolution has great positive content, and almost every major government proposal or innovation is put forth in the sacred name of the Revolution. Indeed, the official government party, the PRI, is the Institutional Revolutionary Party.

In the United States, the Mexican Revolution was maligned for many years as a dangerous, atheistic and even Communist movement. However, faced with the threat of Castroism, many of our leaders, including President Kennedy, have now hailed the Mexican Revolution as a progressive movement in the history of mankind and have suggested it may serve as a model for the rest of Latin America.

The Mexican Revolution was truly one of the great social, economic and political upheavals of the twentieth century. The Revolution had three distinctive phases. In the first or military phase, which lasted from 1910 to 1920, the country was in the throes of civil war. It was violent, bloody and disruptive and cost Mexico a million lives, reducing the total population from fifteen to fourteen million. During this period and extending into the second phase, most of the leaders of the Revolution, including generals, presidents, and senators, were assassinated. Among the outstanding victims were Francisco I. Madero (1913), Emiliano Zapata (1919), Venustiano Carranza (1920), Pancho Villa (1923), and Álvaro Obregón (1928). (See Glossary.)

The second phase of the Revolution, which can be dated roughly from 1920 to 1940, came to a close with the end of the Cárdenas administration. In this period important basic institutional changes were brought about. The semifeudal agrarian economy was transformed and the way was prepared for the industrial revolution, which has been going on since 1940. Large landholdings were broken up and distributed to the peasants through the *ejido* system; the power of organized labor was strengthened, foreign participation in, and control over, the economy was reduced, and public education was expanded.

During the third phase, from 1940 to 1960, the tempo of social change and land distribution slowed down appreciably and there was a definite shift in government policy. The major emphasis was upon industrialization, increased production and the encouragement of foreign investment. The Catholic Church regained much of the influence it had lost during the Revolution; the United States became predominant in the field of foreign investments and greatly expanded its cultural influence. Although the total wealth of the Mexican nation increased and standards of living improved, the wealth distribution heavily favored the upper brackets, and the great majority of the Mexican population continued to live at an impoverished level.

Pedro's life story illustrates some of the achievements and shortcomings of the Mexican Revolution on the village level. Today in Azteca, Pedro's village, there is no longer the pawning of children, no beating of *peones* on neighboring *haciendas*, no monopoly of the local government and the land resources by the *caciques*. At the same time there has been a tremendous increase in the facilities of public education; in the Martínez family the parents and most of their relatives among the older generation were illiterate, but Pedro educated two of his children and his grandson to be schoolteachers. Peasants like Pedro now had the opportunity to participate in the local government, in elections and in the political life generally. A striking feature of Pedro's account is that it reveals the intense participation of peasants in community affairs immediately after the Revolution. Indeed, Pedro, with only one year of formal schooling, was more in touch with national agencies and events during the twenties and thirties than are his more educated children at present.

Few men have undergone greater changes within a lifetime. Pedro has changed from an Indian to a *mestizo* way of life, from speaking Nahuatl to Spanish, from an illiterate to a "half-lawyer," from a *peón* to a village politician, from a Catholic to a Seventh Day Adventist. Compared to many Aztecan peasants, Pedro has shown great personal and social development. He relates more easily to others, has more friends outside the village, is more knowledgeable, has a wider range of experience and considerable prestige in the village despite his poverty.

Pedro's life has been a search for ideals and causes with which to identify: Catholicism, *zapatismo*, village politics, education, and most recently, Adventism and religious evangelism. He tried them all and was disillusioned with them all. His meager educational background and the effects of severe deprivation on his character made him unable to absorb and to integrate meaningfully the many new ideas to which he was subject during his lifetime. He had taken literally the slogans and catchwords to which he was exposed, hoping that each would lead him to a better life, and he was inevitably disappointed. He was not attuned to the underlying middle-class values of post-Revolutionary Mexico and did not adapt quickly enough to the realities of the growing money economy. Time and money were of little importance to him; a higher standard of living and status-through-wealth were not his goals. He hoped to achieve recognition and respect through "good works" and communal effort, but was only partially successful. Moreover, as the Revolution took an increasingly conservative turn, he found himself on the losing side. In politics, Pedro ends up a disillusioned and confused man. He gave lip service to the democratic ideals of the Revolution but could not truly understand them, particularly as they operated on the village and state level. By the time he was an old man, Pedro was nostalgically admiring the strong monolithic character of the Díaz regime which he had fought against in his youth.

Despite Pedro's relative sophistication and wide range of experience, he remains, first and foremost, a peasant. He shares many classic peasant values—a love of the land, a reverence for nature, a strong belief in the intrinsic good of agricultural labor, and a restraint on individual self-seeking in favor of family and community. Like most peasants, he is also authoritarian, fatalistic, suspicious, concrete-minded and ambivalent in his attitudes toward city people.

There is a tendency among all of us, even anthropologists, to idealize the past and to think of Mexican Indian villages prior to the Mexican Revolution of 1910 as relatively stable, well-ordered, smoothly functioning and harmonious communities. Pedro's story, however, reveals social disorganization, sharp class cleavages, widespread poverty, and the proletarianization of the landless segment of the population. It also shows the existence of many of the traits of the culture of poverty—consensual unions, the abandonment of women and children, child labor, adultery and a feeling of alienation. One of the major accomplishments of the Revolution for villages like Azteca was to return to the villagers the privilege of utilizing their communal lands. This slowed down or stopped the process of proletarianization and eliminated many of the traits of the culture of poverty.

However, poverty itself has remained. The description of village conditions after the Revolution hardly encourages a Rousseauan view of peasant life. The stories of Pedro, Esperanza and Felipe reveal the persistence of poverty, hunger, ignorance, disease, suspicion, suffering, cruelty, corruption, and a pervading quality of fear, envy and distrust in interpersonal relations.

※   ※   ※

I first met Pedro Martínez in 1943, shortly after I arrived in Azteca to begin a study of the community. His name was given to me by local officials who suggested that he could tell me a great deal about his *barrio*, San José, and about the village.

The *barrio* of San José, one of the four smaller, poorer *barrios* of Azteca, was located on a slope, halfway between the highest and lowest points in the village. Pedro's street began at the asphalt highway and extended up the slope for several blocks, some of which were unpaved and no more than gullies strewn with large boulders. The block on which Pedro's house was situated, however, was nicely paved and lined on both sides by small tile-roofed, one-story adobe houses, each with a yard containing semitropical plants and trees set behind low walls of volcanic rock.

Pedro himself answered my greeting, coming out of the low doorway and standing inside his log gate while I explained the purpose of my visit. He questioned me suspiciously for about a half-hour without opening the gate. This was the only house where I had not been politely ushered in and seated on a hastily dusted chair. Others had listened to me quietly and had agreeably answered my questions. Pedro was different. He stood there, short, stocky, and round about the middle, aggressively asking me about my religion, my politics, my government and my motives for coming to the village.

When I told him we were there to study the customs of his people, he was unimpressed. "Many cultured persons have come to study us, but not one has helped us," he said. I told him we were trying to understand their problems and he answered that the villagers knew their problems only too well: the lands were becoming more sterile; the yields were lower; because of lack of rainfall they had only one crop a year, and insects destroyed part of that; they needed a new school, a doctor, water and electricity. Only when I said we hoped to get the Mexican government to help the village, did he show some interest. But he said promises were easy to make and the government was not to be trusted.

Pedro looked shrewd rather than hostile, and he spoke with a half-smile which crinkled up the corners of his small, round dark eyes. He seemed to be telling me he was no simple peasant to be taken in by a foreigner. His independence and his spirited conversation were refreshing, and I hoped he would become one of my informants and friends.

It was not until eight days later that I saw him again. This time we passed in the street and he stopped me. He said he had made inquiries and had heard good things about us and I could count on his assistance. Pedro became one of several paid informants who worked with me at intervals during my study of the village. The prospect of earning money was only a minor factor in his decision to co-operate. His early motives were basically those of a *político*, that is, he believed we would be a useful "contact," that he would be participating in something important to the village, and that his own history and civic contributions would be recorded for others to read. Pedro also had an inherent sociability, a lively curiosity and an interest in intellectual matters which could find only little outlet in village relationships and which were stimulated by discussions with us. In 1944, Pedro agreed to allow us to begin a formal study of his family and we came to know his wife, Esperanza, his six children, and his grandson who lived with them.*

Pedro was pleased when I asked him to tell me the story of his life, and he readily launched into an account of his activities as a *zapatista* and political leader. He could reminisce at length about these past events, but when I pressed for more personal details of his life, of his relations with the people who were close to him, of his emotional experiences and early childhood, his memory failed and he became uncomfortable and almost speechless. It took patience and prodding to get a more or less coherent account of this aspect of his life.

His life history was obtained at intervals from 1943 to 1948, through conversations, questioning, and systematic interviews. About ten years later, when I began to use the tape recorder in my field work, I reinterviewed Pedro and several members of the family to get lengthier, more detailed autobiographies in their exact words. Unfortunately, by that time his wife had died, and her original story could not be expanded.

* A day in the life of the Martínez family appeared in my earlier volume *Five Families* (Basic Books, New York, 1959).

The agreement, and at times the word-for-word similarity, between Pedro's earlier and later versions of many incidents was quite remarkable and convinced me that I was getting his true, unwavering image of his life.

Pedro's story illustrates clearly the effects of severe deprivation upon the development of his personality. Pedro's earliest memories are quite explicit about his sense of abandonment, his mistreatment, hunger, beatings, and his resentment of his mother's love affairs. At the age of three months he lost his father and at eighteen months he was abandoned by his mother. She left him with a poor grandmother and an aunt, who in turn gave him away, for a time, to a godmother in the village. In summing up his childhood, Pedro says, "I suffered completely."

To all of this he reacted with anger, an anger which has never left him and which has colored his reaction to his family, to his fellow villagers, to ideological causes and to the Catholic Church. It was this anger and related negativism that helps to explain his great readiness to be critical of others, his railings against the folk-Catholicism in which he was raised, and his eventual conversion to Seventh Day Adventism. In short, Pedro was an angry young man back in 1900.

However, Pedro's mother never totally abandoned him and was far from an entirely negative figure in his life. She defended him against his uncle, against his stepfather and against his harsh teacher during his one year at school. Pedro admired his mother, particularly as she grew older and became more competent and more independent of her husband. She helped Pedro to buy a house and to get a wife. Pedro admired her energy and her discipline and at age twenty he still feared her punishment. Even as an old man he clings tenaciously to a positive image of his mother, emphasizing her warmth and her love for him.

In his early years, Pedro saw his mother as an oppressed woman. He strongly identified with her sufferings, her anxieties about food and shelter and the threat of being beaten, jailed or abandoned by her husband. She was ignorant and poor and all her insecurities became Pedro's. His desire for social justice was probably derived in part from his relationship with his mother.

As a child and as a young man, Pedro had no adequate male figure with whom to identify. He pictures his stepfather and his uncles as weak, selfish, cruel, poor or good-for-nothing. It is significant that it was the Mexican Revolution which gave Pedro the first positive male figure with whom he could identify—Emiliano Zapata. Of Zapata's murder, Pedro says, "It was as if they had killed my own father."

The lack of identification with a strong male figure and his close attachment to his mother may have created in Pedro some feelings of ambivalence about his own masculinity and led to some passive, dependent feelings at a deep unconscious level. But if this is so, he has been quite successful in struggling against these feelings. He was one of the most active men in the village, a dominant and, at times, a tyrannical husband and father and, by village standards, he had a successful marriage which lasted forty-five years. The absence of a father and of a strong father substitute gave him more freedom as a child and reduced his Oedipal conflicts; there were no models for him to emulate and no devils for him to conquer. Indeed, for all of his verbal aggressiveness, Pedro was not a man of extreme violence or profound hatreds. In a village with a very high homicide rate, he has never killed anyone.

At this point it may be helpful to comment on the sharp dichotomy between Pedro's public and private personality. In public, Pedro was soft-spoken, cautious, reserved, and he usually treated villagers with respect and dignity. If he criticized someone, it was indirectly. But in the privacy of his home, Pedro was often domineering, impulsive, arbitrary, punitive, and even cruel to his wife and children.

This contrast in Pedro's public and private behavior must be understood in the light of a striking paradox in Aztecan village culture. The people are quiet, well mannered, even gentle, in dealing with neighbors and friends. Boisterousness, aggressiveness, fist fighting, wrestling or rowdiness in the streets are disapproved of. There are relatively few socially approved outlets for the expression of anger in public. According to village belief, anger is dangerous and may cause one to fall victim to the illness of anger, which leads to death unless the proper taboos are followed. To threaten, humiliate or dominate a fellow villager is also considered dangerous and to be avoided. Underlying this blandness in public behavior is a fear of reprisal which may come in the form of secret sorcery or sudden attack. Revenge by ambush and murder is a pattern not only in Azteca but throughout the state of Morelos, which has one of the highest homicide rates in the nation. Pedro, therefore, like other villagers, felt free to express his bitterness and frustrations only in the privacy and relative security of his home.

Pedro shows an inordinate need to be in control of his family. He always kept his wife under the closest supervision and even went so far as to buy her clothing. He allowed his sons very little freedom and was reluctant to give his eldest son the authority an elder son expected to have over younger brothers and sisters. Pedro seemed to have a strong fear of rebellion and of insubordination.

Pedro Martínez is not introspective and has little insight into his own character. He rarely questions his own motives and actions although he is quite critical of others. In general, he has a positive self-image. He sees himself as a good husband and father, an upright civic-minded citizen, a man of ideals. He believes he is almost a hero because he placed the interests of his village above the interests of his family. He has little sense of guilt, and shows a sometimes disconcerting unawareness of his inconsistencies and contradictions. He boasts of his honesty but admits to accepting bribes; he claims to have been "a *zapatista* down to the marrow" but tells of deserting Zapata's forces. He speaks ardently of the need for justice but uses connections, bribes and trickery to get his nephew out of jail. He says he admires democracy but is fundamentally authoritarian. He is for the poor and the downtrodden but is scornful of the illiterate peasants and backward Indians. Although proud of speaking Nahuatl, he has little knowledge of or interest in his pre-Hispanic Indian background. He views the Spanish conquest as a positive thing for Mexico because it abolished paganism and brought Catholicism, the Spanish language and science.

Pedro lacks empathy and sensitivity toward others and shows a typical Mexican peasant tendency to mask his feelings and restrain the expression of sentiment. His narrative is packed with action, violence, death and destruction, but he tells it with such understatement and matter-of-factness that it has a quality of impersonality. What is essentially tragic and dramatic emerges as relatively flat in emotional tone. The full impact of Pedro's story builds up slowly from the sheer quantity of data rather than from any feelings expressed by him.

By U.S. middle-class standards, Pedro may seem a loveless, selfish and dishonest man, perhaps even a scoundrel. However, his character and morality must be seen in the light of Mexican village culture. In this peasant society a man expresses love and affection by providing the basic necessities of food, clothing and shelter for his family. Pedro was a hard worker for many years and never abandoned his wife and children; indeed, he was very much concerned about them. He has shown himself capable of real affection, kindness, self-sacrifice and, occasionally, even tenderness.

Pedro's dishonesty is also a relative matter. By village standards, with its familistic morality, Pedro was an upright man and a good citizen. Indeed, the only criticism of Pedro I heard during my many years in the village was that he was a fool not to have taken greater advantage of his years in politics to enrich himself. The acceptance of bribes by officials is considered by most villagers as normal behavior.

Of course, familism, with its definition of morality in terms of family interests, is not the only value in Aztecan culture. There is also much emphasis, at least on the verbal level, upon civic-mindedness, upon doing something for the community. However, the poor peasant who dedicates himself to village interests must inevitably do so at the cost of his own family. Because of the low productivity and the absence of surplus, most peasants must devote their full time to subsistence needs. During my stay in the village, Pedro never harvested enough corn to last for more than three or four months, after which time his wife was continually worried about getting enough food. The wages paid to local government officials were lower than those paid to field hands. Thus, while Pedro dedicated himself to the village, his family suffered. Pedro's explanation of his motives in terms of his ideals and his desire for social justice is only part of the story. Politics also served to satisfy his deep personal needs for recognition, for belonging, for warmth and male companionship. In politics, Pedro sought to repair the damage wrought to his ego by his early experiences.

For over twenty years Pedro was a Catholic prayer leader but at age forty-two he shocked the villagers by becoming a Seventh Day Adventist and by converting a number of other families. In appraising the motives and circumstances which led Pedro to become a Protestant, we find a combination of social, political and psychological factors, all of which were intimately intertwined. Pedro's early interest in religion, his curiosity and thirst for knowledge, and his keen enjoyment of debate and religious criticism, made the discovery of the Bible one of the great revelations of his life. This experience, as well as his earliest contacts with Protestant missionaries, happened to coincide with his defeat in the post-Revolutionary political struggles in Azteca and with his growing disillusionment in the Mexican Revolution which had left him as poor and landless as before. Pedro's turn to Protestantism may therefore be seen as a reaction against the established order and as a search for a new ideal which would serve as an outlet for his great energy and aggression and desire for leadership. It also represented a revolt against the uncle who had been a cruel authoritarian figure in Pedro's youth.

Certainly his conversion was as much an emotionally charged act as a matter of intellectual or doctrinal conviction. Because the conversion occurred in middle age rather than in his youth, and was not the result of a revelation or of a mystic experience, the usual psychological explanation for conversion as a rebellion against parental figures seems to be somewhat tenuous here. It may be that Pedro's psychological development was slow, in which case his conversion may have been symbolic of his ambivalent image of his mother, who was both a "good mother" and a "bad mother" to him. In rejecting the Catholic Church, he was rejecting his "bad mother." One might also speculate that he viewed the Church as his weak stepfather whom he tried to love but could not. By contrast, Seventh Day Adventism, with its austere and rigid moral code, represented the strong father figure he had never had and to whom he wished to submit, at least temporarily. As Pedro became aware of the weaknesses of his adopted church, he became more tolerant of the Catholicism he had rejected and to which he later partially returned.

Some of the positive results of the conversion for Pedro may be summarized as follows: it led, for a period of years, to a cessation of drinking and the wasting of his resources; it strengthened the unity of the family by increasing Pedro's interaction with his wife and children through prayer and study; it provided opportunity for regular reading, thereby making Pedro's self-taught literacy functional; it broadened his world view by introducing him to the rich lore of the Old and New Testament. In a sense, becoming a Protestant made Pedro a modern, Western man. As a Protestant he became a Christian in a more universal sense, because the folk-Catholicism of the Mexican peasant represents an amalgam of pre-Hispanic pagan and Christian beliefs; becoming a Protestant provided Pedro with a new avenue of leadership and brotherhood after his failure in village politics; and, finally, it tended to sharpen Pedro's critical faculties and channelize his rebelliousness into the religious sphere. On the other hand, Pedro was much more of a revolutionary as a Catholic than as a Seventh Day Adventist. Although always fatalistic, his fatalism became stronger, more rigid and overwhelming after his conversion. His conversion, in a sense, represented a coming to terms with the status quo and a slackening in his efforts to change the village.

Important changes have occurred in Pedro's character during the twenty-year period that I have known and worked with him. He seemed to become less suspicious and aggressive, kindlier toward his children, and generally more mature. These impressions are supported by a comparison of the results of psychological tests (the Rorschach and the TAT) which were given to him in 1945 and again in 1960. The tests clearly showed that he had better mental health as an older man. This pattern of change is unusual in the village where, also according to test results, most men over fifty tend to become more insecure and disturbed about their waning physical and sexual powers.

It seemed to me that the greatest change in Pedro occurred after the death of his wife in the summer of 1956, when, as he said, he almost died of grief. I was impressed by the difference in his evaluation of his wife before and after her death. Prior to her death, he stressed her limitations and weaknesses; after her death he emphasized her strengths—her dedication to their home, her love for him and her faithfulness to him.

I believe that my work with and my friendship for Pedro has contributed to his increased strength as an old man. He has often told me that we are "brothers," and, although I am about twenty-five years his junior, he sometimes says, "You have been like a father to me." Because he has frequently asked my advice on family matters, I have been able to help the family through illnesses and emotional and economic crises.

❀   ❀   ❀

In 1943, Pedro was a vigorous man of fifty-four, dressed in typical Mexican peasant clothing of coarse white cotton cloth, cut in traditional pattern by his wife and stitched by a village seamstress. He wore *cal-zones*—pajama-like pants tied with a string at the waist and ankles—a loosely hanging collarless shirt, and a collarless jacket knotted together in front. His clothes were generally patched and dirty, except on Saturdays, when he bathed and changed. His straw *sombrero* was worn tipped low over his forehead at a rather cocky angle for a man of his age; his blackened, calloused feet were shod in heavy *huaraches* or sandals, cut from old rubber tires. The only pair of shoes he had ever owned were those he bought for his wedding. On cold or rainy days he wrapped himself in his wool *sarape,* and when he went to the fields he carried the blanket neatly folded lengthwise over one shoulder.

A sparse, untrimmed mustache covered his upper lip, and he was almost always unshaven. He rarely went to the barber more than once a month. His hands were brown, gnarled, cut and scarred, the hands of a man who did rough work in the fields. His sunburned face and neck, with their network of fine lines and deep creases, also suggested the outdoors. As the years went by, Pedro's hair began to gray. His general appearance, however, did not change very much although he later began to wear dark trousers and collared shirts which he bought in Cuernavaca or Mexico City. In 1945, when he held his last political office, he gained weight and developed a paunch which caused some sarcastic comment among the villagers. It was gossiped that Pedro was accepting bribes and eating well.

Esperanza, Pedro's wife, was about his age, as short and stocky, and with the same medium-dark complexion. Her black hair was parted in the middle, combed straight back, and worn in a single braid. Her clothing consisted of a slip and an ill-fitting cotton dress. Like most women in the village, she went barefoot, but she owned one pair of shoes for occasional trips to Cuernavaca. A dark-blue cotton shawl, or *rebozo,* of the most inexpensive quality completed her costume. When Pedro was in office he bought her a rose-colored rayon dress which aroused some envious comment in the village.

Esperanza was a slow-moving unspirited woman with a rather drawn, sad face. When her husband or her children upset her, she tended to cry and become ill. Because of her "colic," she began to drink heavily and would sometimes cry so loudly that the neighbors heard her, but for the most part, she was quiet and pleasant and often used endearing terms with her children and visitors.

The three elder sons—Felipe, 18; Martín, 17; and Ricardo, 13—resembled their father in appearance. They were all short and wore the same type of clothing. They worked hard in the fields and were served by the women of the family.

The youngest son, Moisés, was a thin white-faced boy of eight when we first saw him. Pedro had already decided that this son was not physically fit for peasant's work and would have to be educated instead. Like most village schoolboys at that time, Moisés went barefoot and wore village-style clothing. The other male child in the family was a grandson, Germán, the illegitimate son of the eldest daughter, Conchita, who was married and living with her husband not far from her father's house. In 1943, Germán was a dark, silent child of almost two. While his mother taught school, he had a few simple toys and was kept well-dressed in store-bought suits and shoes; later he went barefoot and wore the same type of clothing as Moisés.

Macrina, at fifteen, was a plump short girl with a round face and a pretty smile. With her dark hair in two braids, her bare feet and her plain, faded cotton dress, covered by a dark-blue cotton shawl, she looked like a typical Aztecan girl.

Six other children, three boys and three girls, had been born to Pedro and Esperanza but had died. Esperanza spoke of her "dead little ones" more readily and with more emotion than did Pedro and was much more shaken by their deaths. Their first child, María, died at eight "of the stomach." The second, Manuel, died at eight months of smallpox. Gonzalo, the third, died at two of a scorpion bite. Rufina, born five years after Conchita, died at seven "of the stomach," and the last child, Sara, born in 1940, died at ten months of "bronchitis."

The Martínez family was a tight, cohesive organization, held together by common economic strivings, by a village tradition of family loyalty and parental authority, by the stability of the marriage, by a deep mutual dependence and by the absence of other social groups to which the family might turn in time of need. It was one of the poor, landless families of the lowest economic group, which constituted about 80 percent of all families in Azteca. The Martínez exemplified those who, having no land of their own, planted corn with a hoe and other primitive tools on the steep, hilly communal land called *tlacolol*. In 1943, the "wealth" of the family consisted of one mule, seventeen plum trees, the house site on which they lived, ten small turkeys, four egg-laying hens, some hand tools such as *machetes* and hoes for working hillside plots, tools for ropemaking, fifty-eight crates for marketing plums, and some simple house furnishings.

The family was monolithic and authoritarian, with the father at the head and the mother carrying out his orders and supporting his authority. Pedro and Esperanza believed the children should give unquestioned obedience to the parents because of the latter's great sacrifices in rearing them and because of the urgent need to act as a unit. Pedro was extremely jealous of his prerogatives as head of the family, and his wife and children recognized his right to control because he was the father, the strongest, most skilled, and knowledgeable person in the family, and because for many years he alone had supported them. All this was in accord with Aztecan tradition.

The continual need for respect, particularly on the part of the father, acted as a barrier between the parents and children. This, as well as Aztecan emphasis upon reserve and decorum, curbed spontaneity and self-expression in the family.

The atmosphere in the home tended to be "dry" and undemonstrative. Even quarrels were carried on without shouting and gesturing, cursing or insulting. Pedro, the most expressive person in the family, never used "bad" words and when angry would often simply warn the offender or lecture him in a moral tone. Only when furious did he raise his voice and use such terms as "pig," "hog," "lazy," or "beggar." He might slap a son about the head or face, and in extreme cases take a rope and beat the boy on the back and thighs. When the children were small, Esperanza would occasionally hit or whip them hard, but later she limited herself to scolding or slapping them. She herself was frequently scolded by her husband and, at times, beaten. The children remember having seen their mother being beaten by their father, especially before his conversion and again about ten years later when his interest in Adventism waned. However, Pedro managed to control his wife quite effectively without the use of force, and compared to many Azetecan husbands, he beat her very little.

Although there were deep bonds of affection and loyalty among the Martínez, there was little display of tenderness, except on the part of the mother, who expressed it chiefly in connection with feeding her children and caring for them when they were ill. Both parents considered it immoral to show loving behavior to each other in the presence of their children; the furthest they went was to occasionally tease and joke together. More often they were serious and quiet.

Pedro showed affection for his children when they were small by caressing them or holding them (kissing was not common in Azetca until recently), but by the time they were five years old all such demonstrations stopped. After that "he taught his children not to come near him," as Esperanza observed. They were allowed to kiss his hand respectfully in greeting or to embrace him after a long separation. The children carried this over to their mother, and she sometimes complained that they were too "distant." There was even less demonstration of affection between the brothers and sisters, although they were usually ready to help each other when the need arose.

To all appearances, the father was in complete control of the family, but on a deeper psychological level it was the mother who held it together. Esperanza was a self-sacrificing, protective mother who bound her children to her by playing upon their dependence and their need for affection and by containing their latent and manifest resentment toward their father. At times she acted as a buffer to protect them from his excessive punishment, but she, too, believed they had to be kept under strict parental control.

Esperanza had a weak ego and depressive tendencies; she related to her environment by submitting to it and by renouncing all self-assertion. She accepted the sordidness of life as natural and inevitable, with death as the only way out. Lacking hope and pervaded by a sense of futility and resignation, she did not try to make up for her own deprivation by living through her children. She was self-punishing, nonreactive, inarticulate, conciliatory and fearfully respectful of her husband. Threatened by change and modernization, and particularly by the loss of those who were dependent upon her, she was satisfied to accept the status quo, poor as it was.

Esperanza's weakness was in a sense her strength, for she was able to subsist and raise a family on the meager spiritual and physical nourishment offered her by her husband. His demanding personality also helped to keep her in contact with the outside world and, in this sense, was therapeutic for her. In the long run, however, her ability to take punishment without resistance was self-destructive and also damaging to her children. In emphasizing submission and family unity, Esperanza inadvertently sacrificed her children's development and kept them from becoming independent. With a stronger mother, they might have stood up to their father and liberated themselves or forced him to be more positive toward them. They were much less fearful of their father's disapproval than of hurting their mother and losing her love.

We see this most clearly in Felipe, the eldest son and the third narrator in our story. Strongly tied to his mother and in subdued conflict with his father, Felipe was unable to assert his independence or even to express his feelings. He would lapse into fits of bad temper or into long stubborn silences or he would become ill. He was sensitive to slight and jealous of his rights as the elder brother. Authoritarian by nature, he was submissive to his father but domineering toward his sisters and the younger boys in the family. Even well into adulthood, Felipe showed feelings of sibling rivalry, especially toward Martín and Moisés. His parents and brothers and sisters considered him to be the most difficult in the family to get along with.

Felipe's life story, although related when he was thirty-seven, has an ingenuous childish quality. One is struck by his overwhelming sense of self-pity and dependency, by his immaturity and by the slowness of his development. It wasn't until after the death of his mother in 1956 and after a series of illnesses that Felipe was able to overcome his fear of the outside world and to leave home. It was at this time, while he was living in Mexico City, that he became more communicative and was able to tell me his life story.

❊   ❊   ❊

The Martínez family lived in a modest two-room house, little different from those of their neighbors. When Pedro and his mother built it in 1905, five years before his marriage, it had consisted of one tile-roofed, adobe room, approximately twelve feet wide and twenty feet long, built on one corner of the house site, close to the street. It was to this windowless, dirt-floored house that Pedro brought his bride and here they cooked, ate, slept on straw mats and reared their children.

The rest of the lot extended about one hundred feet to the rear of the house. At first Pedro used this land to plant corn, but later he slowly converted it into a small garden in the front and an orchard and yard for animals in the back. It was not until 1946 that Pedro made another

major improvement. With the help of his two older sons, he added a tile-roofed, cane-walled kitchen to the adobe room. He moved the simple hearth of three large stones into the airy new room where the smoke could filter through the spaces between the cane stalks and thus permit the family to cook and eat in greater comfort.

Pedro also bought a low table, one yard long and half a yard wide, at which he and his three older sons took their meals. Before that, the entire family ate seated on the floor or on stools, holding their *tacos* or their plates in their hands. Normally they did not eat all at once; the men were served first, then the younger children and the women. There were only five plates and eight cups for daily use, four blackened, dented soup spoons, one sharp knife and seven glasses. Three dozen other glasses and two dozen small clay jars, tied together by their handles and hung on a nail, were reserved for serving coffee or *ponche* at the *barrio* fiesta, on Pedro's Saint's Day or at a wedding or wake. Another dozen white cups and saucers purchased by Pedro in Mexico City were kept in a wooden chest, although on occasion a few were hung on the wall for display. They were used only when a politician from Cuernavaca or some other prominent person came to call.

Other kitchen equipment, the clay *comal*, or griddle, for making *tortillas*, two or three clay pots, a clay jar to cook beans, a wooden mixing spoon, and a few tin cans were kept near the hearth. Here, too, were the three-legged stone *metate* and stone rolling pin used for grinding corn. They were given to Esperanza by her mother when she married. A large clay jug, partly buried in the earthen floor, held the drinking water. The jug was sometimes covered with a wooden board to keep out the dust and insects, but most of the time it was left uncovered. Because of spilling and seepage from the clay, the ground around the jug was always muddy and slippery.

The adobe room in the front was the main room of the house. The earth-colored walls, papered here and there with old newspapers, religious posters and calendars, had nails jutting out to hold extra clothes, *sombreros,* gourds, rope, and odds and ends. Hanging high near the doorway was a large glass-covered, framed photo of Pedro and Esperanza taken in the early years of their marriage. Against the back wall stood an unpainted wooden table that had served as an altar when the family was Catholic. It now held small piles of old, worn school texts, some religious pamphlets, a booklet on recent labor legislation published by the Labor Secretariat, a few paperback novels, comic books and a notebook or two. There was a special pile of six Bibles, one for each member of the family who could read. In addition, Pedro had other, more highly prized books which he kept in the wooden chest next to the table. There were one or two religious books, a copy of the Constitution of Mexico, and the Civil Code of Morelos, to which he referred when neighbors consulted him about legal problems. Here, too, he kept important papers, birth and baptismal certificates, letters and records connected with his political activities, and photos. Esperanza also used the chest to hold her best dress, her one pair of shoes, and other valued articles.

A narrow cot stood against each side wall, and the remaining space was taken up by seven low unpainted stools and two reed chairs, all of which Pedro had purchased in the past few years. In addition, there were three small benches made by Martín in a carpentry class conducted by a visiting government cultural mission. Formerly the family sat on the floor or on plum crates made of rough twigs. Several rolled-up straw mats stood in one corner and in another, a sack of shelled corn.

For a time, the entire family continued to sleep in the adobe room. When Conchita had trouble with her husband and came to live with her parents, she slept with her children on the dirt floor in the kitchen. However, late in 1947, after her last reconciliation with her husband and her estrangement from her father, Pedro decided to move his and Esperanza's new bed into the kitchen. Pedro had bought the battered but comparatively fine metal bedstead for one *peso,* fifty *centavos* from a fellow patient he met during a brief stay in the hospital. The bed was more imposing than comfortable, for it lacked a spring and mattress. In their place, a straw mat supported by cane stalks was laid over the bed frame.

Pedro explained the moving of the bed by saying it embarrassed him to lie down with his wife in the presence of his grown children. But no sooner did he make the change than his daughter Macrina insisted upon moving her little *tepexco,* a native cot made of cane and wood, into the opposite corner of the kitchen. She argued that it was not nice for a girl to sleep alone with all her brothers. This her parents could not contest, for they had always required Macrina to sleep at their cousin's house when they were away from home. So Macrina and little Germán moved into the kitchen, despite the fact that the only corner available for their bed was particularly cold and drafty. The cane walls were poor protection, and during the rainy season Macrina often awoke in the morning to find her pillow and blanket quite wet.

The four sons of the family slept in the adobe room. For many years they had slept on straw mats on the ground, but as the family accumulated beds the boys were raised up one by one. Felipe, the eldest, was the first to have a bed. His opportunity came when Conchita went away to teach, leaving behind the metal cot her father had bought for her when she was in boarding school. It had long since lost its spring, mattress and coat of paint, but Felipe, who had always slept with his elder sister, was delighted when she gave it to him. At first he was required to share the cot with Ricardo, but Felipe made it so unpleasant for his younger brother that Ricardo finally began to sleep on some empty plum crates. The other two boys, Martín and Moisés, peacefully shared one blanket and a straw mat, later a wooden cot, on the other side of the room.

Eventually, the two metal beds became hopelessly broken and had to be discarded; on one of my return visits some members of the family were once again sleeping on the floor. The native cots of wood and cane were more easily repaired or replaced, and the family used them until much later, when Moisés became a schoolteacher and bought a modernistic, blond-finished wooden bedstead with a spring and mattress for himself and a new cot for his father.

Moisés also bought bed linen for the new beds. Before that, there were no sheets in the Martínez home except for one which was sometimes used by Macrina because her blanket was very worn. The five pillows made by Esperanza were used without covers. When they became very soiled, she ripped open the casings, removed the rag stuffing, washed them, and remade the pillows. While in school, Macrina had embroidered a pillowcase as a gift for her parents. It was kept in the wooden chest and used only on special occasions.

There were six blankets of coarse wool, one for each member of the family except the two younger boys, who had no beds of their own. The blankets cost about fifty *pesos* each and were the most expensive things in the house. The men's blankets, which were also used in the fields for protection against rain and cold, had to be replaced every three or four years. Old rags were used as towels; for drying hands and face, the women frequently used their shawls and the men their shirt tails.

Pedro and his three elder sons supported the family by carrying on a variety of economic activities. In addition to planting corn on the communal land, the men cut and sold firewood, worked as farm hands, made rope, marketed hog plums, and transported goods when they owned animals. The father also earned something as a legal adviser to villagers or as a political office holder, but he spent most of this money with his friends. The mother earned a little each day by selling produce. Because of Pedro's views on forest conservation, an important source of income from making and selling charcoal was ruled out for this family. Pedro made charcoal only once a year and then only for heating the family iron. Eventually, the federal government placed severe restrictions on the production of charcoal for commercial use, thus justifying Pedro's attitude.

Despite the presence of four working male adults, the Martínez family barely maintained itself at the subsistence level and was chronically in debt. Borrowing from Peter to pay Paul was a continual pattern. Pedro could not remember a year when he was not in debt; every step forward, every small expansion, every crisis, required a loan at high interest. When he was unable to borrow, he would be forced to sell something of value.

※   ※   ※

In this book I have tried to do for the Mexican village scene what my earlier volume *The Children of Sánchez* tried to do for the urban slum. Although the technique used in both volumes is similar, namely, multiple autobiographies in a single family, there are important differences in focus, in organization, in the time span covered, in the character of the people, and in the quality of their language and imagery. In both books, however, I have attempted to give voices to people who would otherwise not be heard.

In my earlier volume, the major emphasis was on the children, the eldest of whom was only thirty; their stories, therefore, had a quality of contemporaneity. In the present volume the emphasis is primarily upon the father, who was born in 1889 and who is now seventy-two. The Martínez story, therefore, covers a much longer time span and throws light on some of the most important aspects of recent Mexican history.

The setting of *The Children of Sánchez* was a slum in the heart of Mexico City. The Casa Grande where the Sánchez children lived was only about thirty years old. By contrast, Azteca has been continuously inhabited since the time of Christ. The villagers have a sense of stability, of local pride and of identification with their community, in sharp contrast to the feelings of marginality and alienation found among the urban slum dwellers. Even landless villagers like Pedro owned their house sites and had access to the communal lands, making for a deep sense of belonging. Most Aztecans were born in the village, married there, and will probably die there. By contrast, the people in the Casa Grande came from twenty of the thirty-two states of the Mexican nation, and although residence was stable because of the low fixed rental and housing shortage, it is likely that a large number of the families will move on to other slums.

The contrast between *The Children of Sánchez* and *Pedro Martínez* is a contrast between urban slum life with its crowding, its lack of privacy, its rapid pace, the early development of sexuality, the intense sociability and expressiveness of the people, and peasant village life, with its slower rhythms, its greater stability and traditionalism, its emphasis on privacy, and the reserved, withdrawn and suspicious nature of the people. The Martínez children, under the strict control of the father, had less freedom, fewer alternatives, fewer outside influences and fewer ways of escape than did the children of Sánchez. The Sánchez family shows a greater variety of moods, from exuberant joyousness and abandon to dark despair, from luxurious thoughtlessness to panicky self-criticism, from a mood of carnival to a mood of atonement. Pedro Martínez and his family are much more emotionally constricted. There is less flux, less color, less joy.

The world view of Pedro Martínez and his family is less familiar and less accessible to most American readers than that of the children of Sánchez. The values, language, imagery and way of thought of *The Children of Sánchez* reflect much more of modern Western culture. The Sánchez children, like most modern urban slum dwellers, are subject to the mass media: they listen to the radio, go to the movies, and are at least familiar with TV. The family of Pedro Martínez was, and is, more isolated and much less influenced by mass media. Even in language, these differences are reflected. In Azteca, most people are bilingual, speaking both Nahuatl (the language of the Aztecs) and Spanish, whereas in the Casa Grande only Spanish is spoken.

The difference between the Sánchez family and the Martínez family, however, is not only between urban and rural, between a slum and a traditional village, but also between a *mestizo* family and a family of Indian background. No one within living memory in the Sánchez family spoke an Indian language (although the family members look as Indian in physical type as the Martínez), whereas everyone in the Martínez family can still speak some Nahuatl and the father and mother were fluent in it because it was their first language. Although Pedro told his story in Spanish, he still thinks in Nahuatl, and his Spanish is a curious combination of pre-Hispanic Nahuatl and rural lower-class Spanish interspersed with biblical imagery.

❋   ❋   ❋

Azteca is an ancient highland village in the State of Morelos about sixty miles south of Mexico City. It is the administrative head of the *municipio* (county) of Azteca which embraces an area of 60,000 acres and consists of eight villages. The village of Azteca is centrally located within the *municipio* and nestles in a broad valley surrounded by beautiful buttes and cliffs which rise to 1,200 feet above the house sites. The cliffs form a natural fortress and at various times have served as a refuge for the villagers. Each butte is known by its ancient Nahuatl name and each has a legend associated with it. In Azteca, as in Mexico as a whole, there are contrasting elements of the primitive and the modern, the Spanish colonial and the contemporary. It has a strong Indian heritage; in 1940 most of the 3,500 inhabitants still spoke the indigenous Nahuatl in addition to Spanish. Side by side with pre-Hispanic cultural elements are items of modern industrial civilization. These include corn mills and sewing machines, clocks, poolrooms, patent medicines, powdered milk, battery radios, a few telephones and automobiles. Since 1960 the village has obtained electricity and now has a few television sets.

Azteca is large, sprawling, and roughly rectangular in shape, approximately a mile and a fourth in length and a mile in width. It is located on a slope, the northern or upper part of the village being several hundred feet higher than the southern part. During the rainy season many streets become cascading streams. To avoid erosion, some streets have been stone paved and terraced. Only the road and the plaza in the center are on a more or less level plane.

The village has a typical Mexican plaza complete with park, bandstand, shade trees and benches. Around the plaza are grouped the chief buildings: the courthouse; offices for the president, secretary and other local officials; the schoolhouse, the main church, some stores, a few corn mills and a small market place.

The streets off the center are uniformly rustic and quiet and stamp Azteca as a rural village. Only those nearest the plaza have name placards, house numbers and lighting. On nights when there is no moon, it is difficult, even dangerous, to walk through the village without a flashlight or candle, and most people do not venture out. The only sounds heard after dark are those of animals, the serenades of romantic youths, or the shout of an occasional drunken peasant being taken home. Even during the day the village is not noisy, except for the church bells, the motors of the corn mills and the buses racing and honking along the main road.

Most families live in tile-roofed, adobe houses, with one or two rooms, usually with earthen floors. The houses are separated from each other by gardens or yards, some with small orchards or cornfields. Low stone walls enclose the house sites and permit overhanging trees to shade the streets. Here and there in the poorer, outlying areas, some families still live in the more primitive *jacal*, built of cane and roofed with thatch. In the large center *barrios* are a few wealthier homes built in Spanish style. These have glass-paned windows and are enclosed by high, concealing walls.

At the beginning of our study in 1943, the great majority of houses in Azteca had no running water or sanitary facilities of any kind. By 1957, most of the houses in the center had water piped into their gardens or kitchens, a privilege for which they paid a small municipal tax. Toilets or outhouses were still not common. The new schoolhouse, however, had toilets and showers.

The village is divided into eight *barrios,* or named locality groupings, each with its own chapel, patron saint, and annual fiesta. The *barrio* is essentially a socio-religious organization with fixed boundaries and great stability; most of the present-day *barrios* were probably built up in the seventeenth and eighteenth centuries. Since the entire village is on a slope, the smaller *barrios* at the upper end are usually referred to as "those above" and the larger ones at the bottom as "those below." Some Aztecans refer to the paved road as the dividing line between the upper and lower halves of the village.

The *barrios* serve to break up the village into smaller communities. Kinship ties tend to be strongest within one's own *barrio* or with an adjoining one. As high as 42 percent of all marriages in a *barrio* occur among its own members; about 50 percent occur between persons of adjoining *barrios.*

Barrio membership is determined mainly by ownership of a house site in a *barrio* and by payment of a tax for the upkeep of the *barrio* chapel. A person usually belongs to the *barrio* in which he was born or raised, although a man may purchase a house site in another *barrio* and establish his home there. Upon marriage a woman becomes a member of her husband's *barrio.*

Each *barrio* has a *mayordomo* who is responsible for the collection of funds for the upkeep of the chapel and for the organization of *barrio* members into collective work parties to clean the churchyard, repair the chapel or the streets, and help cultivate and harvest the corn on the plot of land belonging to the chapel.

Preparing for the annual fiesta in honor of the *barrio* patron saint is the *mayordomo's* major function. He decides how the fiesta is to be celebrated, whether to have a Mass or sermon or both, and whether to invite the local priest or one from Cuernavaca. He arranges for the band of musicians, for the fireworks, for the ancient flute to be played on the chapel roof, for the sacred dances or for a bullfight. He appoints assistants and committees for specific assignments and sees that contributions pledged to the saint are collected from *barrio* residents. Frequently he spends his own funds to assure a successful fiesta, which lasts from one to seven days. *Barrio* esprit de corps is at its height at this time and everyone co-operates. The chapel is decorated and candles are brought in ceremonially and burned. Most families receive guests from other *barrios* during the fiesta and serve a festive meal of chicken with *mole* sauce, *tamales* and *ponche,* an alcoholic beverage.

Important economic and social characteristics differentiate the *barrios*. On the whole, the smaller *barrios* are poorer and have a higher proportion of families that depend upon the communal lands, a higher incidence of illiteracy, and a reputation of being more Indian. The larger *barrios* of the center, which show the widest extremes in poverty and wealth, have controlled the village politically: practically all the village presidents from 1922 to 1944 came from the three large *barrios*.

In pre-Hispanic times the village was subject to Olmec and Toltec influence and was conquered by the Aztecs in 1437. The villagers paid tribute to Moctezuma in the form of cotton mantles, cloth, paper, pottery, shields, warrior costumes and agricultural products. They worshiped Aztec gods and practiced the Aztec rites of human sacrifice, offering children to the rain god and the hearts of prisoners to the war god. The village was conquered in 1521 by Hernán Cortés, and remained under Spanish rule for three hundred years.

Although Mexico won its political independence from Spain in 1810, colonial forms of life in the village continued relatively unaltered. The first great change came with the Reforms of Benito Juárez in 1857 when the church and state were separated and church property was confiscated. The land belonging to the village church was distributed among a small group of landowners, who became the new local aristocracy, the *caciques*. The *caciques* controlled the local government, prohibited political parties and elections, and prevented the landless villagers from planting on the communal lands. For the poor, it was a time of suffering and exploitation. When Porfirio Díaz came to power as President of Mexico in 1877, the position of the *caciques* in Azteca was further strengthened. The repressive and authoritarian Díaz regime continued until 1910.

The Mexican Revolution of 1910-20 was a turning point in the history of the village. Azteca was in the heart of *zapatista* country and few villages in Mexico suffered greater upheavals. In 1911, more than a year before Zapata's call for revolt in Morelos, Azteca liberated itself by force from the rule of the local *caciques*. Later the village was the scene of repeated invasions, first by rebel troops and then by government forces, and it endured depredations at the hands of both. Cattle were killed, corn and other crops were requisitioned, women were raped or taken as hostages, and large areas of the village were burned. When the situation became even more dangerous, the villagers fled to the hills and lived there for as long as six months at a time, stealing back on occasion to pick some fruit or to bury their dead.

From the start, the villagers' sympathies were with the rebels, but only a handful understood the ideals of the Zapata movement and were motivated by them. The promise of land had great appeal, but most Aztecans tried to remain neutral and joined the conflict only when it became a matter of life or death. The lack of unity among the villagers became apparent in the early days of the revolt, when the ablest Aztecan leaders killed one another in their fierce rivalry for power.

During these bitter years, the religious life of the village came to a standstill. The priests and the *caciques* had fled for their lives, the church and chapels were abandoned and sacked, and the ancient monastery became troop headquarters and stables. Some functions of the absent priests were carried on by *rezanderos,* laymen who knew prayers from memory and who charged a fee for saying prayers for the dying, for difficult deliveries, and the like.

By late 1919, the State of Morelos again was peaceful and the village of Azteca began its struggle back to normalcy. When the dispersed villagers returned from the hills and nearby villages, they were without homes and in absolute poverty. Loss of life in battle and starvation and illness had caused a rapid decline in the population; in 1921, there were only 2,156 persons in the village and 3,000 in the *municipio.*

The Revolution transformed the social structure of Azteca. Some of the *caciques* or their sons returned to their battered, burned homes, but they had lost most of their wealth, particularly their cattle and their shops. It was necessary for all, rich and poor, to begin to build again. But the building took place in a new social framework. The participation by the villagers in the *zapatista* forces had left its imprint on the psychology of the people and had acted as a distinct leveling influence. The Revolutionary slogans of the *zapatistas* had been "land and liberty" and "down with the *caciques.*" Now the political dominance of the *caciques* was gone.

The political history of the village during the twenty-five years after the Revolution was intense, dramatic, and often tragic. It centered on the issue of the preservation of the forests and other resources. Because the neighboring *haciendas* had been destroyed, work was scarce and the villagers began cutting down the forests for the commerical production of charcoal. Two groups arose: one, chiefly ex-*zapatistas,* wanted to conserve the forest resources; the other, led by sons of former *caciques,* wanted to recoup their fortunes by continuing to exploit the communal forests. The former group became the Union of Aztecan Peasants and was affiliated with the CROM, a labor organization with headquarters in Mexico City. The other village faction, called the *centrales,* branded the Union as radical and it came to be known locally as the *bolcheviques* (later the *fraternales*). These two factions struggled for village control throughout the twenties and thirties, with assassinations, imprisonments, and even massacre marking their conflict. In 1930, a co-operative for producing charcoal was organized. At one time it numbered over five hundred members but by 1937, after many bitter political conflicts, it went into bankruptcy and was dissolved.

Because of its proximity to both state and national capitals, Azteca is particularly subject to outside influences, and almost every political current of national importance had some repercussions in the village. At various times in history, Aztecans have achieved positions of prominence in different fields and have had personal contacts with men in the highest political circles in the state and the nation. In the middle of the last century, many young men of the better-to-do peasant families left Azteca to become doctors, lawyers, teachers, engineers, priests and government officials. These men and their descendants kept in touch with one another and with their relatives in the village. In 1920, the Colonia Azteca, an organization of Aztecans living in Mexico City, was founded to eliminate illiteracy and to preserve the Nahuatl language in Azteca. This organization became a major outside political force in the village and a permanent, active, urbanizing influence.

After the Revolution, the position of the Church in Azteca went through several changes. When peace was first restored, the priest returned and village religious life was resumed, although without its former splendor. The new tranquility was shattered in 1926, however, when the Archbishop of Mexico ordered a policy of nonco-operation with the government. All priests were to close their churches and cease public religious services. Azteca's priest left the village and only clandestine services by lay prayer leaders were available for a time. Regular church services were again resumed in about 1929.

In the early thirties, Protestantism came to Azteca when about fifteen families, most of them poor, became Seventh Day Adventists. Those families were ostracized, their houses were stoned, and their children were the butt of jokes and abuses. In the face of such hostility their number dwindled. The Catholic Church waged successful propaganda campaigns against other Protestant projects and the villagers came to be suspicious of non-Catholic strangers.

Two technological innovations which reached Azteca in the 1920's made great changes in the lives of the women. In 1925, the first commercial mill for grinding corn was built, but soon closed because of opposition from the men. In 1927, however, another mill met with financial success through "the revolution of the women against the authority of the men," and by 1942 there were four mills in the village which all the women regularly patronized. From the mills they gained from four to six hours of freedom daily from the grinding stone, and their new leisure enabled them to undertake commercial ventures such as the raising of fruit and animals for marketing. The increased use of sewing machines also lightened the women's work.

An event of great importance in the history of the village was the completion in 1936 of an asphalt road connecting Azteca with the Mexico City–Cuernavaca highway. This road allowed more frequent and varied social contacts, it brought in the tourist trade, and it gave the village easy access to new markets for its fruit and other produce. Two bus lines were formed, both of them owned by Aztecans and operated as co-operatives. The bus lines not only improved means of communication but also became new economic and political factors in the village. The bitter competition between them divided the village into two factions. Their leaders took over political control from the peasants, and the employees constituted the first important group of nonfarmers in Azteca.

The school became another important agent of culture change in the village. Enrollment soared from less than 100 in 1926 to 611 in 1944. The school increased literacy, taught the children new standards of personal hygiene and cleanliness, and made it possible for many to go on to further education.

Azteca mirrors many national trends and brings into sharp focus some of the most pressing problems of Mexico. The changes which have occurred in Azteca since the Revolution—the distribution of land to some of the landless, the building of a modern highway, the establishment of bus service, the expansion of educational facilities—are typical of changes which are taking place over wide areas in Mexico. Similarly, many of the problems which continue to plague Azteca also exist in thousands of Mexican villages—for example, the poor agricultural resources, population pressure, the importance of forest and grazing lands in the agricultural economy, soil erosion, deforestation, the small size of land holdings, low yields, and the absence of adequate credit facilities.

❋   ❋   ❋

Because of the wide range of regional and ethnic differences in rural Mexico, no single village or family, no matter how rigorously selected, could be representative of Mexican peasantry as a whole. However, Azteca, typical primarily of the densely populated highland villages, reflects a great deal of Mexican rural culture and its people share many of the traits which students have described for Mexican national character. The Martínez family itself is in some ways a microcosm of rural Mexico in transition. Indeed, one of the advantages of a family study as compared to an individual autobiography is that the former gives us a variety of types and reflects age, sex and generation differences. Pedro represents the peasant who strives for modernization; his wife Esperanza represents the more traditional, conservative peasant woman; and Felipe and Martín, the eldest sons, because of their more limited opportunities, are in many ways closer to the traditional peasant mentality than their father. The eldest daughter, Conchita, is typical of peasant girls who, after an unsuccessful attempt at a teaching career, reject modernization and revert back to old village ways.

The youngest sons, Ricardo and Moisés, and the grandson, Germán, have gone furthest along the road of modernization. They have shown the greatest ability to take advantage of the opportunities opened up by the Revolution, and their life stories have an element of hopefulness—and even joyousness—which was lacking in the lives of their older brothers and sisters and of their parents. It seems to me extremely interesting that Germán, the grandson, identifies closely with the more positive values of his grandfather and particularly with Pedro's desire for social justice. The story of the Martínez family illustrates dramatically the differential effects of the Mexican Revolution on the older and the younger generations within one family.*

* The reader who would like to have some further background material on the culture of Azteca and on the Martínez family before beginning the story of Pedro Martínez, may turn to the Appendix.

PART ONE

PEDRO

Prologue

Anyone who is a man of ideas is that way from birth. Such a man is aware of what goes on. Others die just as they are born, still children. Some study, yet they are nothing—no better than the rest. At dawn, when God awakes, off they go to the fields, and from the fields, back home to supper, and from supper to bed . . . and that is all. These men are like dead ideas. They don't aspire to anything, they don't even have aspirations for their children. No! they have no ambition, neither for good nor for bad. In my judgment these men are absolutely dead. Here we call a man like that "a chunk of meat with eyes."

And I am not one of those. Ever since I was little, I have liked to study. But I was an orphan and poor. How could I? And even now that I am old, I still like to study. That is why I wanted to send my children to school. If I had had the means, my children would not have been peasants like me. I would like my children to know three times as much as I do. I keep saying to them, "I don't want you to be like me. I was illiterate. I didn't know anything, I couldn't read, I want you at least to know something."

I would rather they knew something than for them to be rich because there is one thing I see here in my village. There are several who are rich but as they don't know anything, what good is it? There is a rich fellow here who doesn't even know how to count. His wife has to watch everything he buys. They don't even know enough to be able to enjoy their money. As they know nothing, they are worth nothing in society.

Knowledge is worth more because things aren't always peaceful. Every once in a while these lawsuits come up and if one doesn't know anything, who devours him? The lawyers, of course! That is why I want my children to have their wealth in their heads, because money is of no help.

But I am a peasant and I love the country. Of course! Corn is life. Without corn, the peasant is in bad shape, he can never rest. Everything is dear today which is why I like to plant. What a pity I cannot work the way I used to. I would walk five hours to do my planting. Now I can't anymore. Now I am beginning to have a premonition, now my body feels too heavy for me to go on foot. But, still, here I am. When I get to the cornfield I feel the strength come back to my body. When I am at home in the shade, it does me harm, even to my stomach. In the corn-field, I am cured of everything. Naturally, being as old as I am I get tired, but it is not the work that does it, it is the long walk to get there. Once I get to the fields, I pull up any wild plant and *zas!* that is my meal. There are so many things there for a poor man to eat . . . sprouts, purslane, *papalo*, kale, violet, *chipile, pipiches* . . . and no cooking them, either. We eat them right where we find them or we would be spending the whole day cooking. The idea is to eat fast and *zas!* to work.

As I once said to one of our pastors who forbade us to drink alcohol, "Never compare yourselves to us because we are peasants. You are like the shade plants and we are like plants out in the sun. We seek the sun. If I went with you people to work in the shade, I would die, and if you were to go out into the sun with me, you would die. If we ate your food, it would kill us because we would waste away. Our food is different, our surroundings are different, our water is different. You even drink distilled water. Distilled water for us, indeed! We drink whatever we find in the ravine. You are brought up with fine diapers, but not us. Whatever is at hand for us! How can you compare yourselves to us? Why, if a decent doctor comes here, he cannot treat us because he does not understand the peasant's way of life."

I never complain to God. I have very little, but I do not go hungry. As I've often said, I am not covetous. I don't even have land because I don't covet it. My religion forbids greed, it forbids stealing, it forbids doing injustice. Yes, the poor should be resigned to their poverty, but they should work. According to the Bible, it is easier to convert the poor because they love God more. It is more difficult for the rich man because where his money is, there is his heart. The poor man puts his heart in God and that is all. More is taken from the one who doesn't have in order to prove his faith in God, while more is given to the one who has, to condemn him and send him to the depths once and for all because of his greed.

I always want to be poor. My thought has been to improve the village, not myself. No! The Lord came to struggle for the people, not for Himself! I fought with Zapata in the Revolution and since then I have been struggling for justice. That's why I have nothing and why my family suffered. To be a hero, a man cannot think of his home or of how his children or his wife or parents will suffer. They *must* suffer! There is no other way. A man who thinks first of his family is not a hero or a patriot. He is nothing.

I have suffered all along, for my village. In 1921, I worked to save the forest. Later, they even put me in prison. I fought with the Governor to defend our municipal boundaries, and I never stopped to say that my family had nothing to eat. No, because a hero never goes begging or complaining. He follows his path even if he must die. Vicente Guerrero, who fought for independence against Spain, is a model for us. When he was summoned by the Spanish Viceroy to defend himself, his father begged him on his knees to submit to the Viceroy, to save himself, but Vicente Guerrero said, "Father, you are very sacred to me, very, very sacred, but when my country is concerned, it is dearer to me than you are."

Of course, most men like comfort and try to get ahead and see what they can grab for themselves. They are men without spirit. But those who are born restless must die restless. Men like Hidalgo, Zapata and Madero are heroes because they defended the people and fought for justice. I, too, since I was young, had this idea of justice.

CHAPTER I

PEDRO

Childhood and Youth

My life as a child was much more bitter than it is now. I was very small when I was left orphaned by the death of my father. I was three months old and my mother was just a girl. That's why she gave me the breast for only eighteen months, no more. Being just a girl, you know, she got herself a boy, and as she was foolish besides, simple, like they were in those days, she went off to Yautepec with him, and me she left behind with my grandma and my aunt.

In those days they married very young. My mother was only twelve when my father asked for her, and he paid my grandma thirty-six *centavos* for his bride. The bride price was called *chichihualtomi*, which means money for the mother's milk. My *papá* was a little better off than my *mamá's* family. And he wasn't so ignorant; he knew how to write! They were married in church but after eight years he died. He had a disease, a kind of leprosy, and he left my mother and went to Cuernavaca. They say he had to beg in the streets there. After a time he came back and died at my mother's side. But while my *papá* was in Cuernavaca my *mamá* must have had lovers, because as soon as she was a widow she went off with another man.

And so my grandma and my mother's half-sister Paulina brought me up. And that is why I say to you that my life was more bitter then than now, because I suffered completely. They raised me on black-bean soup; beans were plentiful and on that alone they raised me. There was much hunger in those days because the rich didn't allow the poor to plant on the communal hillsides. The rich peasants who lived in the center were called *caciques* because they were the kings here. Only the *caciques* planted in the good valley land. When the destitute ones who had no land began to make clearings in the hills, the *caciques* said, "We mustn't allow the poor to have their own cornfields because then we won't have *peones* to work for us." And so they went and brought them back.

The big *caciques,* like *don* Vicente Ortiz and Felipe Galindo, had a lot of power. A poor person was looked upon as nothing and because there were many poor who didn't know any other place to go, naturally they offered themselves as servants. They earned miserable pay, and if they didn't get to work early the doors were shut and they were not accepted. On the *haciendas* the *peones* who came late were whipped, but in Azteca the *caciques* didn't dare do that. They had to treat their *peones* and servants with respect, but, of course, no one could speak up to the *caciques,* no one. If someone talked back, nothing was said to him at the moment, but when he least expected it, the troops came and *zas!* they took him away to be a soldier or a prisoner in Quintana Roo. That's the way it was in those days. If one did a small thing, or if the *caciques* were a little bit angry, he would be reported. That's why the people were frightened and didn't speak up. Why should they?

The *caciques* lent money to the poor before planting time, knowing that they couldn't pay back unless they worked. "Borrow, borrow," the rich men said. "You know you can pay back when you work for me." After the harvest, the poor would borrow again until the next season. They worked practically as serfs because they never finished paying off.

My father and his two brothers and my grandfather were tile makers. They spoke *mexicano* and only my father knew a little Spanish. They didn't plant because they had no land. I didn't know my father's parents because they died when he was a boy. My grandparents were legitimate Aztecans; I have no foreign blood in me. I cannot say what my mother's father did, but he was no more than a peasant. My mother's mother was called María Cristina; women had no last names at that time. I know only that she had a half-brother, Gumersindo Guerrera, because her mother had two husbands.

My grandma was just a little old lady and she and my aunt provided for me out of what they earned. It wasn't much because they were poor. Well, anyway, they brought me up.

When I opened my eyes I began to see, I began to understand. They gave me away to a godmother of mine. She was a little better off than my grandma so they gave me to her. I was three years old, but I was always sick, always ailing. You might say I was undernourished because they did not feed me well. For this reason I could not stand up, I couldn't walk. So my godmother of baptism comes and asks for me. She says, "I have a duty to my godson. I will take him in. Now that his mother has abandoned him, I better take him." So she took me, and I stayed at her house during the rainy season.

But you see, I was sickly, and every so often, diarrhea, diarrhea, diarrhea. I had no pants. They just dressed me in an old shirt, one of my godfather's castoffs. It hung down to here on me. They tied me up in it and that was that.

Well, perhaps my godmother noticed something because I was wanting to go to the toilet. And it was raining a downpour. The yard filled up with water. I was trying to get them to take me to the toilet, or something like that, but my godmother slapped my bottom. She was always beating me. She had children of her own and didn't like me at all.

But this time I got angry. I was only a little boy, but I got mad all the same. And so I went out in all that downpour, dragging myself through the water as best I could. I made my way down to the *corral* and did what I had to do. Then I come crawling back through the water again. I didn't go into the kitchen to my godmother any more but went through the yard and out to the street, up the cobblestone slope. The water reached about here on my chest because I was crawling along on my knees, crying.

Then, my sister's godmother, who lived on the opposite side of the street, comes out—to this day I don't know her name—but, anyway, she feels sorry for me. The poor woman got her shawl and went over to the yard of my house, my grandmother's house, that is. She went calling my grandma to come and see what I was doing out in the rain. My poor little grandmother, she was so old but she came running and found me in the middle of the street. I kept sitting down because I couldn't drag myself over the stones. And then there was the water, and me bathed in it, soaked through. And very angry! I was crying, but with a bit of rage, eh?

I had almost found my way home when my grandma saw me. She started to cry and picked me up and hugged me and hugged me and took me with her. Then my aunt, who had gone to the market just before the rain, came back. My grandmother tells her what happened and the two of them begin to cry. My aunt says, "Why do we have to go giving away this child? We mustn't give him away!"

Well, I just listened. They changed my clothes and steamed me with the leaves of *pericón* to warm me, and things like that. Then they began to care about me and supported me as well as they could.

My poor little grandmother had a hard life. Her first husband died, leaving her with two children, Rufelia and Crescenciano. After that she never married, but she must have had lovers because she had two children, my mother and her brother Adelaido, with a man named Gómez, and a daughter, my aunt Paulina, with a man named Flores. This is why my *mamá* had two half-sisters and one half-brother. She had another half-sister and half-brother through her father, who was married to another woman. My mother was the daughter of Gómez, but I can say she had no father because he attended only to his legitimate children. A natural child is almost always looked down upon.

My grandma suffered a lot with this Gómez because his lawful wife made up false stories about her. His wife told him my grandma stuck out her tongue at her, or insulted her, and then Gómez came and beat up my grandmother. She was very humble and bore it all. Once in a while this lover of hers would help her out with a little gift. But he didn't support her, and that's why my mother's brothers were always working as little servants. Many times my grandmother had to pawn them when she needed money. She would borrow three or four *pesos* from a rich family or from the priest and leave one of her sons to work there until she could pay it back. With the boy's work they paid off the interest. Sometimes it took her six months or a year, or even two years, to find the money to pay the debt and get back her son. My uncles Crescenciano and Adelaido didn't know how to work in the fields because they practically grew up as servants without pay in the priest's house. Later, they worked for a rich *cacique* who paid them twenty-five *centavos* a day.

The house we lived in belonged to my aunt Paulina. As she was young, an old man with his tail still wagging begins to make love to her. He had his little pile of money and promised her a house with a little store. All that! Because my aunt was poor, she got ambitious and accepted him as a husband. It turned out that the old man was married. He lived in Yautepec but he came to Azteca to go after the girl. He really did set up a little adobe house—one room and a kitchen—and put the papers in her name. Then he actually set up a little store for her and she began to do business. After she was all set, after she had her little house and everything, my aunt ran the old fellow out. She ran him out and was left with the house.

My aunt Paulina was going to marry a man named Buenaventura but they killed him and all she had was a child by him, a girl named Macedonia. Buenaventura had gone south to bring back cattle so he could get married but his own companion killed him!

My aunt worked very hard all the time. She would go to the mountains to gather mushrooms and whatever little thing she could pick up to sell. Later she learned to make rope and with this we managed to get along.

My grandma went around giving massages to pregnant women. She earned her living as a midwife and healer. She gave massages and ground other people's corn for *tortillas,* and sometimes she sent me to beg for food in the shops in the plaza. Yes, she had to, because we barely had enough to eat in those days. In addition to beans, all they gave me to eat was *ahuatle.* It was sold a lot on the streets and cost three *centavos* a quarter of a kilo. They say it is the dung [larvae] of a fly—who knows what fly?—but it's very tasty. It was like dough. They ground it and made it into *tortillas.* That was my food, *tortillas* of fly dung.

When my grandma went out to cure someone, I knew she would bring back special *tortillas* for me and mmmm! . . . I could taste the sweetness beforehand. What a feast! They would give me a great big *tortilla* and *zas!* even a *tortilla* tasted sweet to me! I never had enough to eat.

When I was little, I must have been about six years old, it was the custom for the people of San Pedro to invite children to dance at the fiesta of San Pedrito. If the fathers and mothers refused, then the child would get sick. It was just suggestion. That's what happened to me. They came to ask me to dance but I was not given permission. You had to dress up and as my guardians were poor, they couldn't afford it.

So then I got sick and went to bed right off with a fever. Fever, fever . . . I thought the house was falling in on me and I screamed with fear. I could see the house and the trees crashing on top of me and my body felt heavy. This frightened my grandmother and my aunt and they said that in that case I had better dance. So they came for me and, half-sick and all, they took me and . . . *zas, zas,* there I was holding a little arch of flowers, learning the dance.

Fiesta time came and they managed to borrow the crown, the plumage, the shoes and other adornments. They sent word to my mother to buy the suit of clothes. I was very happy because she got me the nicest cotton shirt I ever had and my first pair of pants. Before that, I wore only a long shirt that came down to my knees, and that was all. That was the way most of the poor orphans were dressed. I felt very proud the day I went to dance, and the fever left me.

At about that time I learned the story of El Azteco, the god of my ancestors. Before the Spaniards came, the Indians were backward so anything was called god. They called their leader, El Azteco, god, and

the lord of Cuernavaca was called god. There were many gods then, but of course we don't believe that any more.

According to the story, there was a maiden, an Indian, who had a child while she was still a virgin. She had the baby by the Winds. That's what they told me, that it was by the Winds. When the time came to give birth, her parents didn't want it to be known because she was a virgin and how could this happen? So they said, "We'd better kill him!" And they went and threw the baby inside a maguey plant where they left him to die. They came to see him the following day, but he didn't die. Then, in anger, they threw him in the middle of a swamp. There he stayed one day, and on the next day they went to see him and the baby boy was fine. No harm came to him. They wondered, "He doesn't die, how can this be?" So they took him back and they brought him up in secret and with difficulty. Then his mother died and the old grandparents were the ones who raised him.

At age seven he was full of curiosity. He made some arrows and shot them up into the air. He was only playing, but birds fell from above. That's the way he killed them and he brought them to his grandparents.

At that time there was a ferocious animal in Teclama, and old people over seventy were taken to be eaten by the animal. When the grandfather's turn came the youngster said, "You're not going, grandfather. No, I'd better go."

"But you're so young, you're a child, they won't accept you."

"No, I'm going."

Before leaving, he gave his grandparents a signal: "If you see a black cloud appear in the east, I have lost. But if you see a white cloud, then rejoice, for I have won."

Well, they took him prisoner so the monster could eat him, there in Teclama. On the way, he stopped in the fields and gathered obsidian flakes, sharp as knives. He put them into his shoulder bag. He kept collecting the flakes until they reached Teclama. And there they delivered him to the monster.

The animal was restless and hungry. When he saw the little boy, he said, "Throw him to me. He's only a morsel, but I'll eat him."

El Azteco held his hands together in front of him, and when the monster opened his mouth he ran into it, and the animal swallowed him whole. There, inside, El Azteco took out his obsidian knives, and *zas, zas,* he went to work and tore up all the intestines and the animal died. Then he cut it open and got out.

When El Azteco grew up he was very intelligent, very astute. It was then that he went to steal the sacred drum from the king of Cuernavaca. Cuernavaca was a kingdom, Azteca was a kingdom, Icapixtla was a kingdom, Tlayacapán, Tlalnepantla, all those places were kingdoms. Then he overthrew this kingdom of Cuernavaca. So he was persecuted like a bandit. They went after him, but as there were many hills around he escaped and they could not get him.

A long time went by. When he was old, the Spaniards came and conquered the village. He began to fight against them. But later he was the first to know the new religion and convert to Catholicism. He was so intelligent, he understood everything that was said in Spanish. They took him to Spain and he brought back the image of the Virgin, the one whose fiesta is still celebrated in the village. It was El Azteco who started this festival in her name. He said, "I am giving this fiesta for my Mother, María, who is great in Heaven. She has two stars on her head and two stars at her feet. Learn this religion, learn this wisdom." Well, he convinced them and they embraced it.

Once El Azteco came to Mexico City. It was he who placed the bell on the Cathedral. It was very big and no one could lift it. He came and everyone felt something like a wind blowing and they had to cover their eyes because of the dust. They couldn't see and when they wiped their eyes the bell was already ringing.

Then they gave him a treasure for Azteca, some doves in a small but very heavy box. He asked for this treasure and for nothing else. He called the Aztecans together and said to the little Indians, "Take this box and bury it in the middle of the village square. This has a meaning." He stayed there and eight people carried it away. But they were foolish people and on the way they opened the box to see what was in it. Well, the doves flew out and scattered all over the nearby towns, one went to Cuernavaca, another to Tlayacapán, one more to Yautepec; all were scattered. The only one left was a baby dove that could not fly. The doves signified virtue. Because the doves went to Cuernavaca and the other towns, they prospered. Azteca remained poor because the dove that was left could not fly, it had no wings, no feathers. Well, they still buried it, but it was of no use any more. My village remained small, absolutely insignificant. It is not included in the list of all the sciences. It is a forgotten town.

When I was seven, my uncle Agustín asked me to come and help him take care of the oxen. Agustín was my uncle Maximiano's son, and it was only on account of his age that I called him uncle. But he was still young; he wasn't married then. My uncle Maximiano was my mother's half-brother. Both were the children of Gómez but they had different mothers. Maximiano was married to another relative of mine, on my father's side. Maximiano's wife, my aunt Francisca, was my fa-

ther's father's sister and, as a matter of fact, she and Maximiano were
the ones who brought up my father when his parents died. And now
they were asking for me to come and work for them. They said they
would teach me to read.

My aunt Paulina went to Yautepec to tell my mother. "All right,"
says my mother, "because I want my son to learn something. Yes,
let him go."

So I went to live in my uncle's house. And then my sister followed
my example and also went, as a nursemaid, because my aunt Francisca
had just given birth to my cousin Rafaela. So my sister was a nursemaid and I looked after the oxen. I cried a lot in my uncle's house because of the oxen and because of Agustín. He was mean and beat me all
the time.

I got up at five in the morning, brought water from the fountain
and watered the hog-plum trees. Then I had to take the oxen out to
pasture, all the way to a place called Cuiquixtlán.

My uncle Agustín said, "Be back at eight o'clock because you are
going to study." If I didn't come back at that time, he would let me
have it. At night I also studied. My uncle didn't give me one moment
to play. I didn't get sick there, but I wanted to go back to my grandma's because I got tired of not playing. I even forgot how to play marbles! Once I rebelled and ran to my grandma's but my uncle came for
me and brought me back.

My uncle Maximiano did not beat me, he was the one who taught
me. But just think! If I didn't learn my lessons, *zas!* he would grab me
by an ear and dig his fingernail into it. That's what he would do to
me. But after that, he would tell my uncle Agustín and that one used
the whip. *Zas!* And that's the way it went, day in and day out for a
whole year. My sister was no better off, she worked very hard.

Then my uncle Maximiano's leg went bad. It was a tumor. That
was when he began to balk at the expense I caused him. He would say,
"*Carambas!* These children came here just to bother me, to spend my
money. Me with my bad leg and I have to support them!"

I heard all of that, all my uncle Maximiano's grumbling, and I go
and tell my grandmother and my aunt what he said. *Uuy!* and they
tell it to my mother.

My mother was very humble and my stepfather was very mean.
He beat my mother all the time and didn't like us kids at all. But that
was before my mother began to earn money. She still hadn't opened
her eyes. She was still young. Later my mother sold *tortillas* in Yautepec.
She began to work; she opened her eyes.

So when my aunt went to tell her everything that was happening
to us at my uncle's, she came immediately. She arrived well dressed,

with shoes and everything, because she was earning money by then. It seems that I am looking at her! It seems only yesterday that I saw her!

She comes and says, "Brother, what about this? What are you doing?"

"Nothing. Look, I am ill."

"Well, with your permission, I will take away my children."

"And why?"

"Because I left them so that they would learn something, but you are mistreating them. Why? I'm still alive! They may be orphaned by their father, but not by their mother. Here I am to prove it. I know that Agustín has hit my son a lot. You don't do that to teach someone. Look, brother, don't you go believing that I cannot support them. I am taking them right now, with your permission and many thanks. I'll be seeing you."

So she took me away. She took us to Yautepec. There we were better off. I was a little bigger then and knew how to read. My uncle Agustín did teach me . . . with the flat of his hand, but, yes, I did know how to read a little. That is, I could read but I couldn't speak Spanish. I didn't go out of the house for nine days because I didn't know how to speak.

They sent me to school. *Uuy!* That was another martyrdom. The professor hit me, and when we went out to recess the boys hit me because I spoke in *mexicano*. I used bad words because that's what I was accustomed to in *mexicano* and they hit me even more.

Well, I had to put up with a lot, but I liked the school. Things were always happening to me, but I remember one day in particular. All of us boys were sitting there at dismissal time, twelve o'clock. Ten minutes beforehand they had us there with our arms crossed without moving. The teacher just kept looking us up and down, waiting for somebody to misbehave. Well, all at once one of the boys began to call me "Indian" in a low voice. I just looked at him. Finally, the teacher went into the big boys' room and he began again, "Indian . . . Indian." I just lifted my elbow a little and let him have it right where it hurts. *Uuy!* did he begin to yell! *Caracoles!*

The teacher came running in. "What happened? What happened?" Everybody blamed me. "This one here hit him. Look, he drew blood!"

What blood! It looked more like water. So the teacher grabbed hold of me. They used to hit in those days. He came with the stick in his hand. *Zas!* He gave me twelve strokes. Poor little me! I was rolling around on the brick floor. He threw me down. I even wet my pants, if you'll pardon me for saying so. I couldn't explain or defend myself.

Then it got to be twelve o'clock, time for lunch, and everybody began to leave. They began to shut the doors and they took me to the tables in front of the fourth-year classroom. The tables were big and they made me kneel down on top of one of them with a stone in each hand. They were going to leave me locked up in there. They went to eat and me a prisoner there on the table!

All the boys had gone and only the teachers were left. Now they are going, too. Now they are gone and I am all alone! All alone and scared to death and just watching. Now the doors are closing. When the last teacher closed the last door to leave me locked in, I jumped off the desk. I began to scream and threw away the stones and ran out. They tried to catch me but didn't have a chance. I got out of there so fast I left my hat behind.

So there I went, screaming and screaming, running through the woods all the way home. When I came to the house, my mother said, "What's wrong with you? What is it?" My stepfather was there, too. Then I explained what happened and all the things they did to me. My mother may have been ignorant but she had plenty of spirit, and so she says, "We are going to take him to school this afternoon. I'll show them! What right have they got to make fun of my son! Bah!"

Uuy! was my mother furious with that teacher!

"Why are you doing this to my son? I am going to complain to the authorities that you mistreat him because he doesn't know how to talk Spanish. Instead of treating him justly, all you do is abuse him. Why? You have no consideration. Sure, we are Aztecans! Sure, we are Indians! But you should be more considerate."

Well, they bawled him out. That put an end to it. They never beat me again.

Then, once, my stepfather and my *mamá* had a big fight, who knows what it was about, and he had her put in jail. My stepfather had the backing of a lawyer from Azteca and that made him feel strong, so he put her in jail. I was little and no one told me anything, but I felt like an orphan again because my aunt took care of me. We went to the prison every day to see my *mamá*. That was all we could do, just see her. My stepfather missed her, too, and he himself got the lawyer to let her out. He took her back and they continued together again, but they had many fights.

They kept taking me out of school to work. I hardly ever stayed in school because my stepfather was ignorant, very ignorant, and made me work more and more often. It got worse when I began to earn money.

I went to work on the Atlihuayán *hacienda* when I was about ten years old. There were lots of boys working at different wages. I earned eighteen *centavos* a day; some earned as much as thirty-seven. I knew how to speak Spanish by then, and the older I got the more I improved.

The foreman was from Azteca. His name was Manuel Ponce. He had about eighty little boys working, gleaning after the harvest. He had the habit of warming us up with a whipping. We were in line and he started at one end, *zas, zas, zas!* he gave us each one lash with the same whip they used on the mules. He started at one end of the line and ended at the other. "That was just a warming," he said. When he was angry he gave about eight of those lashes. They knew how to whip then, there in Atlihuayán. Also in Oacalco. Well, at that time, everywhere.

In Oacalco, the foreman, *don* Bonifacio, once gave me a blow right here in the stomach. He hit hard and cut my breath. I fell down. I almost fainted. He got scared that time. He picked me up and started rubbing my stomach. Then I went to work at San Carlos. The second foreman, his name was *don* José, also carried a whip, and *zas!* We were just standing, not working, and they were in a hurry, and *zas!* the whip. In Temisco, *újule!* I was beaten there several times. We had to carry some big beams to the machine to be cut into boards. There were twelve of us and we had hooks, but even so it was heavy and we couldn't do it. We couldn't hold it any longer . . . and *zas!* we got a blow with a club. They hit us more in Temisco; they were all Spaniards there. We couldn't do anything about it then. That came later. At that time no one dared, they were afraid of the government, of *don* Porfirio, of all the officials who backed the *hacendados*.

My stepfather never beat me, never. But I don't owe him a thing. In some ways he was a good man but in others he wasn't. The thing that hurt him was to see us eat. He fought with my mother over that. My mother sold *tortillas* and earned more than he did. He earned thirty-seven *centavos* at the *hacienda* and she earned one and a half *pesos*.

We helped by delivering the *tortillas*. At eleven o'clock in the morning I went out with a basketful of *tortillas*. As I was always hungry I ate some of them on the sly. My mother didn't know how to count so I would tell her that there were two or three short. Then she would say, "That's all right, son. Tomorrow I will make more." I liked delivering *tortillas* because the people often gave me a *taco* to eat.

Afterward, I began to earn money myself and then my stepfather liked me. But at first he did not like us. He didn't even want us all to eat together. I liked him very much, but he didn't care for me, especially not at mealtimes. That is why my mother fed us first and then sent us to sit off to one side like orphans while he ate.

But later she fought for us right along. My mother used to say, "And why do you have to give them dirty looks if I am working for them? I make more than you. So what have you got to complain about? I am paying their way! Hmph!"

She got all my clothes for me then and was dressing me nicely, the same way you see me now, shirt and blouse, white cotton pants, of course, and *huaraches*. By that time my mother loved me a lot.

My sister took care of me and played with me. Yes, she was my companion. What I am going to say is not nice, but my sister was little and there was this older girl . . . Well, she made up things that weren't right. She needed a man already and well, she forced me. As for my sister who was younger, she was sent to guard the door and watch out for our mothers. So, I was violated by a girl. But I was a little fellow . . . what could I do? After that I got to like it because then when she would say, "Here they come, get going," and pushed me off quickly, I would begin to cry. I liked it now! Then she would run with me to the orchard and give me fruit and tell me not to tell our *mamás*.

In the *tortillería*, where my mother made *tortillas*, I noticed that many women, and men, too, came there and got together. They whispered to each other and made signs or stroked each other and then a couple would go to a room and lock the door, or they would go outside. I was already evil and understood what they were going to do.

After a while my mother sent my sister back to my aunt and my grandmother in Azteca, where we were brought up. She got married there. My sister was fourteen years old when they asked for her hand. I was little and used to sleep with her. When I woke up and did not find her, I began to cry. They had already taken her away. I missed my sister but she was gone. So what they did was give me a great big piece of bread. "Come on, come on . . . Look, your sister brought you this." With this they contented me! Then they gave me corn gruel. I was getting to be a big boy by then. I was nine years old, but I grew very slowly as I was undernourished.

By the time I was twelve years old I was working all the time. I never got beyond first year in school but I already knew how to read. When I was a little bigger, thirteen or fourteen years old, I began to open my eyes. I already liked the things of the world. I already liked the girls. Well, I'll tell you a bad thing I did.

I used to go around with another fellow. As a matter of fact, later on he was a colonel in the Revolution. His name was José. He was the first friend I ever had and we loved each other a lot, like brothers. That's why later we became *compadres* of baptism. I took his first child to be baptized. I didn't have another friend so intimate, so close, so brotherly, until much later in Azteca.

Well, we were still little then and José had a sister, María. We went around with another boy by the name of Joaquín, except that he was younger. So José says, "Look, my sister and these two girls are going to bathe in the gulley. Let's do it to them . . ."

So we followed the girls, sneaking up on them. When we got to where they were, José says, "Look, those are my sister's clothes. They are for you. I give you my sister. Go on, get moving! And those are so and so's clothes. They are for me. You, Joaquín, the little one is yours. Now you'll see what we are going to do to them."

Well, yes. In those days they didn't wear anything, no bathing suits, they went just as they were. Right after we spotted them, we ran for the clothes. I grabbed mine and off I ran. Everybody grabbed clothes, and there were the girls out in the middle of the lagoon with just their heads sticking up out of the water. Then the oldest one says, "All right, you roughnecks, why are you acting like this?"

So then we say, "Now you are going to have to give us what we want."

The girls did not answer. They just looked and looked and looked and laughed.

"And now what do we do?" There they were sitting in the water with just their heads showing. Finally, the big one thought it over and she says, "All right. Yes, we will give you what you want, but hand over our clothes."

"Really?"

"Yes, really." Poor things, they covered themselves with their hands like this and came out, huddled close together. They sat down. "Over here, eh! If you don't, we won't give you your clothes. Then what will you do, all naked!" So they kept sitting there and began to dress. Then, after they had their clothes on, wheee! They gave us each a shove and began to run. There they went running and running, with us after them.

Finally when we caught up with them at a place called Tronconada, they began to cry. But María says, "Shut up! Stop crying. Can't you see it will be a scandal?" Poor Joaquín is trying to make a grab for the other one, but he can't do anything as he is too little, and they end up punching each other. And us . . . we were off to one side rolling around in the bushes. Finally, they got tired and we did what we wanted.

That was my first experience. Yes, I was still a youngster . . . a boy . . . but that fellow José in Yautepec initiated us.

By then I could say everything in Spanish. And so we began to bum around together, that other boy and I. Then my mother began to beat me because I started to go out at night once in a while. My mother thought it over and she said to my stepfather, "Let's take this boy to Az-teca. Yautepec is very corrupt. They are going to spoil him, so we better get out of here."

So we came back to Azteca in 1904. I was fifteen years old. It was difficult to get used to the village because they didn't allow one to speak to the girls or to make love. In Yautepec the girls were much more free and I had already had several women.

When I was in Yautepec, I was called "Indian," and now in Azteca they called me *ladino*. They would say in *mexicano*, "This one here has turned into a *ladino*. He is a *xicolo* now." They would call me "*xicolo* . . . *xicolo*" and that would make me mad and I would hit them. *Xicolo* means that one is from Yautepec and knows how to speak Spanish. Everyone in Azteca spoke *mexicano;* only a few with schooling knew Spanish. But all the *caciques* in Azteca were *ladinos* by then. Yet they spoke to us in *mexicano* . . . they even taught us in *mexicano* in school. How were we going to learn Spanish if they didn't speak to us in Span-ish? It wasn't until about 1912, during the Revolution, that the people began to learn Spanish.

But I went to school for only a week. After that I went off again to the *hacienda* at Chiconcuac. I worked at watering crops. By then, I was earning fifty *centavos*. Well, there I was and there I stayed. I didn't get into mischief because there was nothing to do and temptation faded away. They treated me well at that place. Later on, my stepfather de-cided to bring me to the San Vicente *hacienda*. It was time to harvest the sugar cane, but I wasn't able to cut cane. My stepfather scolded me because I couldn't handle even a short *machete*. I was of no help to him. He scolded me plenty, like he always did. Also, when he taught me to plow with a team of oxen I was supposed to be able to do a job like a man, but I couldn't.

Later on, he says to me, "Look here, let's do this. I'm going to get customers for the hay and you can make the deliveries. You'll take two bundles with the mule. They sell at a *peseta* a bundle, so you'll make more money that way. Make two trips and you earn a *peso*." And *zas!* that's just what I did!

I would go to San Vicente for two-week stretches. One time I de-cided to get married there once and for all. I had a sweetheart already. She was my first sweetheart and I myself asked for her hand. We lodged at her house and the *señora* there liked me very much. Her name was *doña* Patricia and her husband was *don* Crispín. Well, the girl, Zenorina, was their daughter and she had her own cattle, but they liked me very much as I was a young fellow, you know what I mean? I was seventeen years old at the time, or something like that.

Doña Patricia was very fond of me. It was almost as if I was in my own home and they trusted me. Imagine, in the morning, for instance, Zenorina would take me milking. I didn't handle the cows, I just came along and helped. But I behaved properly. I never took advantage of the girl. So then I told the mother that I wanted to get married. *Don* Crispín liked me very much also. He says, "Very well. You are a young-ster. My daughter is a youngster. That's good, you're both youngsters." So I had my sweetheart.

For a time I stopped seeing my mother. I just quit going home to see her every two weeks because *doña* Patricia was giving me my meals. She wouldn't let me eat the *tortillas* they sent me from Azteca but gave me a hot meal there. She was giving me everything by then.

So then my mother sent for me and I went. She wouldn't let me go back to the *hacienda* any more. But a labor recruiter from Azteca comes over and says, "Let's go to work at San Gaspar." So I said to my mother, "I am going to San Gaspar." She thought that I was going to break off from San Vicente. Not on your life!

So I went to San Gaspar with the recruiter. But that recruiter turned out to be a bandit. I went along with him and he became a good friend of mine. One day the bandit invited me to go and steal with him . . . to rob the San Miguel *hacienda* because it was September and we couldn't work because there was too much rain. He says to me, "We are not earning a thing and look how poor we are. Let's make a killing. There's eight thousand *pesos* at the *hacienda* and there are eight of us. That's a thousand *pesos* a man."

Well, in those days money was in silver, real money! A *peso* then had about the value of a dollar now. So, like a fool I said, "Yes, let's go." He was about forty at the time . . . old, already.

We took the road, the broad highway, so we could go there on foot. The rain had stopped and the sun was out when we saw the manager of the San Gaspar *hacienda*. There he was galloping along on his old mule until he caught up with us. He says to the recruiter, "Go back. There's work here. Look, the sun is out now. In a little while you can start clearing the field, then at twelve o'clock yoke the oxen for plow-ing."

So the recruiter turns to me, "What do you say?"

"Whatever you say." I was a boy, a young kid, what else could I say to him?

"All right. We better go back. We'll go to this place some other day."

But my mother knew by then that I was going around with this bandit and the man had a bad reputation. So she sent a letter to him, this recruiter, because I did not go to my house any more. I hadn't been home in about a month. I hadn't even set eyes on Azteca.

So one Saturday he says to me, "Say, let's go to Azteca."

"Not I. My *mamá* will beat me because I didn't show up for two half-months in a row. I know what she is like. No. I'm going to San Vicente. They even wash my clothes for me there."

I hadn't put in an appearance at home but I did send my wages, four *pesos*, fifty *centavos* a week. I was still afraid of my mother. She was a short little thing but very strict.

"No, she won't hit you. You don't even have to go there. Come to my house. You can eat there and early Monday we come back here."

Finally he talked me into it. I said, "All right, but I won't go in the daytime."

The recruiter was tall and I am short and so he kept me hidden pretty well as we approached my house. He was covering me with his *sarape* but then he pushed me and said to me, "Go on, go leave your sack in your house."

"What are you talking about? Leave my sack! My *mamá* will kill me! No, not I. If that's what you brought me here for, I'd better get going."

He grabs hold of me. "No, man, look . . ." And he began to plead with me. "Go on in. Go ahead. Look, if they hit you, come running out and I'll be waiting for you."

Like an innocent kid, I believed him. After all, I was only a youngster. He lied to me. I guess he must have made an agreement with my mother. As soon as I appeared, she embraced me and began to cry. She wouldn't let go of me. She didn't hit me so I wasn't scared any more.

Then she says, "Come on, son, have some supper."

I wanted to leave right away on Monday again for the *hacienda* but she wouldn't let me now. "No, son. Don't go. There is the horse. You take him and go for wood." My stepfather was there too. "Don't go to the *hacienda*. I am working now. So you don't have to go." I guess they must have all gotten together. They knew what I was up to in San Vicente.

And so I was under my mother's orders again. I say to her, "But you'll give me my Sunday money, won't you, mother?" And she answers, "Yes, I will. Just so you won't leave, I'll let you have it."

I was satisfied. She didn't hit me or even say anything to me. On Monday, I went for wood and kept at it all week. Then, after the half-month, I say, "All right, *mamá*, now I am going."

So my stepfather says to me, "No, don't go there. Let's go over to Cuautla." Well, what could I do? I was under their orders. They took me with them. I didn't go to San Vicente for a month and a half. After that time, my mother let me go there with another recruiter. But when I arrived, my sweetheart was gone. She was married. Someone had gone off with her. It was good-bye! I got real angry and said to *doña* Patricia, "*Caray*, where is Zenorina?"

"Well, you see, you didn't come back and, well, some man deceived her . . . and, well, now he's taken her off with him. They live over in such-and-such a place."

I was furious and didn't work at San Vicente any more but took the road back to Azteca. What did I want her for now? I returned, and as it was a weekday, Monday by then, I took the horse and went for wood again. It wasn't until the next half-month that my mother says to me, "Why didn't you stay at San Vicente?"

"Because there was no work."

Well, the half-month was over and I say, "Now I'm going, but over that way. Now I'm going to work at the *hacienda* of the Hospital de Calderón." That's where I went and there I stayed until I got married.

Things went badly for my sister. I didn't really see for myself everything that happened because I was still a youngster when she got married. But I was able to judge things. Her husband deceived us completely; he fooled my mother. He managed it because he put on a big front—he carried a blanket and a *sombrero* and dressed . . . well, not badly. My aunts said, "No, he is a fine boy. According to the way he dresses, he must have his way of earning a living."

It was all a lie just to get the girl. He was a pauper without even a house of his own. The bit of land he had was his through his mother, but they sold it to get the money for him to get married. His *padrino* grabbed it up.

As we all worked, we did not lack for things in our house. When my sister got married she brought with her a new blanket, her sheets, a grinding stone and some irons. My mother gave her everything she could take along. In those days we didn't have beds or benches, chairs or tables. We ate on the ground and slept on straw mats.

Well, when this fellow started coming around he had a new blanket too, except that we didn't know whether it was his or not. In those days, there was a lot of buying on credit. There were a number of houses that would give out merchandise on trust. As his mother was a widow and he had no blanket, she took one out for him on credit, so he could get married.

Soon after they were married, the woman who had trusted them for the blanket came to collect. She came to collect but got nothing. Her name was *doña* Juana. Then one day, about two weeks after the marriage, she got angry. "For the last time, I had better take back my blanket, because they are not going to pay."

Naturally, she got there early . . . at dawn, before they were up. She just walked in, pulled the blanket off them, and left. What would they have done if my sister hadn't brought her own blanket? In what condition would they have been left? Since all of them were ignorant, naturally the woman thought of doing such a thing. She just grabbed the blanket, and *zas!* "I'll be seeing you." She says, "Your mother doesn't want to pay me. So with your permission, I am taking the blanket." And off she went with it.

As I was practically grown up, I judged that he really had nothing at all. Four days later it was discovered that not even the little house site was his. It now belonged to his *padrino,* his godfather of marriage. *Uuy!* So it wasn't his! Nothing was his!

I was working in Yautepec, and I would go back to Azteca for a visit every once in a while, about every week. I could see that my sister and her husband were absolutely poor. And lazy! All he did was poke around in squirrel holes trying to smoke them out. That was the work he was doing, while his poor mother was feeding them. I just observed; I was a big boy by then.

Their first child that lived was named José. He was very tiny as he did not eat. They didn't have food to give him. He didn't even have diapers. I just took note of these things. Finally, one day on a visit from Yautepec, I came there. The poor child was crying. I said to my sister, "What does he want?"

"He is crying because the neighbor has *chiltepín* and I always buy there but not this time."

"Why not?"

"I don't have anything to buy it with."

So I took out something. I had my little savings. I was working for the *hacienda,* clearing the fields. I had about two *reales.* I took out a half and said to my sister, "Go and buy. Run!"

My sister, poor little thing, began to cry.

According to her, my brother-in-law had gotten a job at the *hacienda* and had gone to work. She just made me laugh. It was a lie. Her husband never worked at the *hacienda.* He was a loafer.

I stayed there with her that night. At about nine o'clock, the "*hacienda* worker" came home carrying a battered can in his old net.

"Ah, you're back," said my sister.

"Yes, I'm back."

"Didn't you go to the *hacienda?*"

"No, they didn't take me on today. So I went into the fields. I brought back half a can of resin."

"Ah!" said my sister. "Then tomorrow I'll go and sell it, right away quick."

As resin brought a good price, this was enough to satisfy my sister, poor thing. It was worth seventy-five *centavos* a quart and he had brought in about three quarts. Well, he went out for two days getting resin so he wouldn't have to work the rest of the week. The following day he slept and the day after he brought in a handful of firewood while they ate on the two *pesos*, twenty-five *centavos* he earned. Do you call that working? He spent his days sleeping. He would bring in acacia pods or sweet potatoes from the fields and my sister would go and sell them. This meant two or three *pesos*, so he wouldn't have to work all week. He used to go into his *corral* and sit there on the stones like a lizard. How could he do it!

Suffice it to say he didn't even have a *petate*. Do you know what he did, my poor brother-in-law, may he rest in peace? He would cut the wide leaves from the banana trees and weave them into a mat, like a *petate* but very big, and he made it real nice. That's how he occupied his time. I said to myself, "*Caray!* this man doesn't even have a straw mat or a dish to serve food in." The grinding stone was gone by then, too. He sold the *metate* my mother gave them . . . and the irons, the dishes, the plates she gave them . . . all sold.

My sister had a mob of kids of all ages. She didn't work, other than help her godmother with the coffee harvest. She helped her grind the coffee and kept occupied in this way. Chico, her husband, didn't leave his godmother's side any more now . . . that was certain. When the lady saw that, as she had no family and was all alone, she gave him a little piece of ground.

She said, "Look, Chico, I am going to give you this little plot. It is ours, but I am giving it to you. Look, pay me twelve *pesos* for it."

He said, "All right."

My brother-in-law began to work on it right away, clearing it and planting little trees. Then the *señora* said, "Well, Chico, aren't you ever going to pay me for the plot? I told you the price was twelve *pesos*."

If he gave her three *pesos* in all his life, it was a lot. The *señora* was so good-hearted that she didn't try to collect and he in turn tried to earn a living by picking a little coffee, fixing a few things. That's the way he earned a living. She never again asked for the money. And so I know that the only piece of ground they had was a gift . . . they didn't buy it.

I was working at the Hospital *hacienda* with my stepfather when one of my cousins came to get us. He told us that my grandmother was dead. My stepfather wanted to leave me there. He says, "I'll go myself and you stay here."

I say, "No, what are you thinking of! I'll go. She brought me up. How could I not go to see her?"

So that is why I returned and that's when my mother had a meeting of her two brothers and her sisters, my aunt Paulina and my aunt Rufelia, and Rufelia's two older sons. They all lived on the same street, opposite my aunt Paulina's house, and they were all very poor.

Well, my *mamá* called them together and said, "Tell me, what contributions are you going to make? What are you going to give me toward expenses for the funeral?"

The blind brother, Crescenciano, says, "But what help do you expect from me, sister? I have nothing. I am blind. You know that. I can come and pray, that would be about the most I could do in the way of help."

"What about you, brother Adelaido?"

He began to cry. "But, sister . . . I . . . it's true I am still strong, I am not a cripple, but I don't have anything to work with and my wife supports me so that I am really unable to contribute."

My mother says, "What a pity! What's the good of you being a man?"

"Well, say what you like, but I have nothing to help you with."

Then my aunt Ceferina, his wife, spoke. "Look, sister-in-law, I have nothing to give you either, but I have a *rebozo*. Give us a loan on it."

My mother says, "No, Ceferina, not a loan! My brother won't pay me back. I know him. Whenever I give him a loan, he pays me back with blows. He beats me. That's why no loan!"

My aunt says, "No, sister-in-law, do not be distrustful. This time I am responsible, not my husband. I will answer for it. I have a *rebozo*. Pawn it for me for seven *pesos*. I can get the casket with that."

They agreed, and with that money they got the casket.

Then the nephews, my aunt Rufelia's sons, say, "All right, aunt, now it's our turn. Our mother has nothing to help you with, but we are here." One of them was named Tarcisio, the other, Fidencio. They say, "Look, aunt, choose your share of the funeral expense."

My mother says, "You choose first and I will take care of what you leave over. If you want to take on the wake, I'll pay the expenses during the day. Or leave the wake to me and you pay for the day."

"Agreed, aunt. We'll take the wake and you pay tomorrow's expenses."

"Agreed."

Do you know why it was like that? Because we were better off than they were. My *mamá* was a seamstress. I worked on the *hacienda* and so did my stepfather. That's why we had a little something. My aunt Rufelia and her two daughters were only servants and her sons were working but were still young. Her husband was a good man but he didn't count for much, poor thing. My uncles, Crescenciano and Adelaido, worked as servants for *don* Vicente Ortega until they were married and all they had to show for it was a house site he let them each have. As he was always a village official, he took some unoccupied land and gave it to them, titles and all, as though they had bought it. They were his servants, so, naturally, he helped them when they got married.

My uncle Crescenciano began to work for himself, selling firewood and a little charcoal. He had a horse and he had his son Lorenzo who helped him. But my uncle was very mean and that's why God punished him and made him blind. His eyes were just a little irritated, but the more he cured them the worse they became, until finally he lost his sight. He was so mean he didn't even like his own mother! If my poor little grandmother came to his house at mealtime, he would hide the food. He never gave her anything.

Whenever my grandma got angry with Crescenciano, he would accuse her. "You used up all the money I earned! You never bought me anything!" He had never worked in the fields but still he wanted her to give him money! He would throw it up to her and that's why my *mamá* was always fighting with him. His son Lorenzo was big and strong but he was as mean as his father, and when my uncle went blind, Lorenzo wouldn't help him any more. Then my uncle had to learn how to make rope to earn a living. He also learned to be a prayer leader. After he went blind, he changed a little. But what good did it do? My little grandma was already dead. Later, when the Revolution came, he finally paid attention to me and helped me learn to be a prayer leader. Before that, he did nothing for me. That man was mean, very mean. And now at his mother's funeral he washed his hands of the matter, but after all, he was blind. What else could he do but pray and eat?

My uncle Adelaido earned a miserable wage as a servant. He was a bit lazy about planting because he never had been a peasant. His wife, my aunt Ceferina, was a good woman, far better than my uncle, and she was a hard worker. She wove waistbands and raised pigs and did lots of other things to support their four children. My uncle had been married to another woman before I was born, and he had a daughter by her. They were married in church and all, but when the wife died he abandoned his daughter and who knows where she is now. In those days, and even now, the men with hard hearts didn't take care of their children, not even their legitimate ones. That's the kind of man my uncle was.

By the time my grandma died, my aunt Paulina had two more children with another man, and she had to work hard to support them. Besides, we were all living in her house, so my *mamá* didn't ask her to contribute. We took care of all the expenses of the day—bread, alcohol, sugar, cigarettes, the grave diggers, the benediction, and the music. In those days, they buried the dead to music. My cousins took care of the wake—the coffee, bread and alcohol. It didn't cost much. Living was cheap then. We buried her and that was that.

Later, my mother bought me a little house, the one I live in now, as a matter of fact. She was still working, so she bought a little pig. She says, "With this little pig I will get a house for my son." That year we bought the lot and it was really a mystery, too, because we also bought a sewing machine and the horses. The bill of sale for the machine was in my stepfather's name; one horse in his name, and one horse in mine. My mother was always dividing things up. She was backward, but not so dumb.

My mother says to my stepfather, "Look, be satisfied. The sewing machine and one horse will belong to you. The other horse is for my son, but don't forget that he works too. I saved his money so he could buy it. Now this little pig is to buy him a house."

As we were buying the sewing machine on payment for my stepfather, he was satisfied. The machine cost 140 *pesos,* a lot of money in those times. With the interest, it came to 240. The payments lasted two years, ten *pesos* a month.

My mother fattened up the little pig and sold it for twenty *pesos.* Well, just at that time *don* Apolinar offered me a house site for forty *pesos.* My mother says, "Go ahead. Grab it."

The man says, "Meanwhile, give me twenty *pesos* and you can use the *corral.* At the end of the year pay me the rest and the site will be the boy's."

That's the way it was. I went and paid the man the twenty *pesos.* Then my mother said to my stepfather, "Now, don't you go mixing into this. The site is my son's. We will earn another twenty *pesos* during the year to give to the man, and that will make up the forty. With forty *pesos* my son will be able to have his little parcel of land."

A year later the time was up on both the pledge for the house site and for the sewing machine, and my stepfather didn't want to help pay. The installment collector now had most of the money. Twenty *pesos* were still owing for the last two months. "It looks like we might lose the sewing machine. I haven't got the money to pay now." So my mother says, "Well, let it be lost then."

In those days there weren't more than three machines in the village. Nobody had one. That was why my mother was a seamstress. I had saved up another twenty *pesos* once again, to pay for the house site. Then my mother says to me, "You go ahead and get your house. It makes no difference if we lose the machine. Tell *don* Apolinar to make out the deed for the lot. Here are your twenty *pesos*."

So I went. I say to the man, "Listen, *don* Apolinar, here I am. I brought you the other twenty *pesos*."

So he says, "No. Look, now it costs forty-two *pesos*."

"*Uuy! Caray!* But why?"

"And I'm even going to take off two meters from you because they are not mine. The lot belongs to my brother. He is back now and does not agree to the deal. So, if you want it like this, all right. If not, not. Somebody else wants it, anyway."

I wanted it, but then there was the question of the sewing machine, too. So I say to him, "Well, listen, then it's not like we agreed!"

He says, "No. It was up to me at the time, but not now that my brother is back. If you want your money back, I'll give it to you in the afternoon."

When I got home, I found my mother and stepfather quarreling over the said twenty-*peso* debt on the sewing machine. We were about to lose it. So I say, "Listen, mother, stop quarreling. The man backed out. Here are the twenty *pesos*. Go and pay up the machine tomorrow once and for all and I'll buy my house later."

My stepfather liked that. "So now it's off, eh?" he says.

"Yes. He went back on his bargain."

So my mother says, "Look, Herminio, in that case, let's go pay up the machine tomorrow. But you realize that we are going to have to sacrifice ourselves to buy a house for my son."

"Don't worry about that. As soon as the machine is ours we can pawn it and buy the house for him."

They went to Yautepec to pay and brought back the bill of sale. Now there were twenty *pesos* left in reserve. My mother says, "Here are these twenty *pesos* left over. I am going to buy two pigs." But unfortunately one of them died and so she raised only one. We sold it a year later for twenty *pesos*. Then she says, "We didn't make anything . . . just got our twenty *pesos* back."

Then this man comes around, the one who sold me the house I live in now. He was my neighbor. He went to my mother to talk over a deal with her. Counting on us pawning the machine, he too asked forty *pesos* for a house site. So later my mother goes to the man and says, "Here, I brought you the money. Let's draw up the deed for the site."

"Well, it would be fine but *don* Germán was here and he offered me forty-eight *pesos*."

So that's how it was! My mother had a sharp tongue when she spoke *mexicano*. "Don't play around with me! Especially because I am a woman. You're a man and are you going to go back on your word? A real man doesn't do such things. You'll have to keep the agreement."

"Yes, but I already made the other deal."

"That doesn't matter. Arrange it any way you can, but you give me that site!"

"All right, then. Let me have the extra eight *pesos*."

"I am going to give you nine *pesos* more." My mother raised it another *peso!* After that she went to tell my stepfather. "Hurry up, run and borrow some money. We have to pay nine *pesos* more." He had his little pile tucked away but it was not very much. All he had was five *pesos*. They ran around all over the place getting together the other four *pesos*. I just looked on. The thing that interested me was that they were going to buy me a house.

Then, finally, my stepfather, poor little fellow, came back with the money. Who knows how far he had to go to get it?

"All right, get a move on. Come on, get going and draw up the paper," says my mother.

So my stepfather took me into the village to see a man by the name of *don* Ezequiel. He was a learned man, one who worked with his head. So my stepfather says to him, "I would like you to draw up a private paper."

"By all means. I can do that for you. In whose name shall I make it out?"

"The boy's."

"The law doesn't allow it. When the boy turns twenty, then, yes. Now, no. Better you."

"But it's not my money. It's his."

"Oh, I see. Well, in that case, this is what we'll do. The boy is seventeen, but we'll put him down for twenty. It won't hurt him to be a little older."

At last! Finally I had my piece of ground. I got to work right away, right there on that same site. But it was not a garden then, it had no trees or plants. It was only a *corral* for planting corn. I got to work clearing out all the small stones. I piled them up in the corners of the lot and began to plant maguey. The first thing was maguey for *pulque!* In one year we put up the house and then we went to live in it.

I was a jealous man by nature. That's how I was. I wanted my house unstained.

My mother enjoyed taking me with her to the towns every now and then. This time she said to me, "Let's go to Tepalcingo."

"Yes, *mamá*, let's go! We'll take just one horse because pasture is scarce in Tepalcingo."

One horse only, for her and me. I sat on the rump behind my mother and away we went. I suspected my mother was involved with another man. So while we were on the way, I said, "Look, mother, I love you a lot. You are my mother. But just one thing, I don't like to see such goings on, not at all, I don't. And even when my stepfather scolds you I don't want you to talk back because you are going to set a bad example for me. I'll be getting married and if my wife sees what goes on, then next thing I know she will be copying your ways. And I don't want that. I want my house unstained. That man I saw one time, well, I don't want him coming around here again, not at all, I don't!"

So she smiles and says, "Now what's wrong with you, son? Why get angry? You're always getting angry. Look, why don't you face it, the neighbor and even his children know what their mother is doing."

"Ah! You want me to be like that, too, don't you? Well, not I. I am not like them. No, that's out. Let other families live the way they want, but us, we're going to be different. I don't want to see any more of that stuff. And look, mother, another thing, if I do see any more of it, I am going to make it my business to kill one of them. It was one thing when I was a youngster, but now, that's out. Especially now that I have a house of my own, and even more, that I am getting married." And I say to her, "Just look at my aunt Rufelia. I am not going to let her in my house because I know what her behavior is like."

My aunt Rufelia was old already, but I could see how she did things. I could see her defects. She liked to drink and she had lovers even while her husband was alive. When he died she abandoned her children and went off with Rufino, my mother-in-law's brother. Rufelia took only the youngest child with her and left the rest. Her son Julio was still a boy but he didn't want to follow his mother and instead went with my *mamá* and my stepfather to Yautepec. He lived with us. My *mamá* treated him like a son. She loved him a lot; when he got sick she cured him. He and I went working on the *haciendas* together, like brothers.

While my aunt Rufelia was having a good time with her lover Rufino, her two elder sons, Tarcisio and Fidencio, became angry because she was neglecting them and her other children. They waylaid Rufino in the woods and gave him a beating and because of that both of them went to jail in Cuernavaca. When they got out, the boys had a fight with Rufino's son by his lawful wife and all three were put in jail. Then Rufino's wife had a fight with my aunt Rufelia and both of them were sent to jail. Finally, Rufino himself was put in jail for adultery. When they all got out, Rufino's wife left him and he and my aunt lived together in Rufino's house. My aunt's children continued to live in her house and things quieted down.

My cousin Julio remained with us until he was sixteen. Then all my relatives began saying he should get married because he needed someone to take care of him. He just laughed, but they pointed out Gloria to him and he liked her. They told him, "This girl is still young. She is thirteen and just right."

Well, it wasn't my aunt Rufelia who went to ask for Gloria, it was my *mamá* and my uncle Adelaido. Gloria's *mamá* said yes and the day came to get the girl for the wedding and even then my aunt Rufelia didn't go, nor did my grandmother. Again, the one who went to represent Julio's mother was my *mamá*. She brought them chocolate and bread and sugar and drinks in a basket, but because we didn't bring a turkey, Gloria's mother and grandmother and grandfather made a fuss and wouldn't let her go. They said, "No, she is not a widow for you to come like this. You might have at least brought an old buzzard!"

And my *mamá* said, "Yes, you are right. We didn't bring a turkey but I promise to bring one tomorrow without fail."

But it was no and no, my daughter is not a widow and all that. I was listening and all the people on the street were listening to what they were saying to my *mamá*. But by then my cousin Julio wanted to have the girl and what do you think he did? He began to shoot firecrackers and, according to the people in the village, that meant the girl was not a virgin. So then the parents and the grandparents said, "Oh, if she is no longer a girl then you had better take her. Take her without the turkey." But my mother promised to bring a turkey and she did and they were married.

They were still just children and Julio didn't know what to do with a wife and she didn't let him get close and so they got angry at each other. Gloria's sisters-in-law said, "Man! What does this mean? Lie with him! Go on and let him," but Gloria ran out of the house. One night she ran all the way to her grandparents house in the center *barrio,* and we chased her thinking some man was waiting to carry her off. Gloria didn't need a man then, so she ran away, but later, when she was older and began to get hot, *újule,* she couldn't stand it and she went with lots of men. She had plenty of children but not one was her husband's!

When Gloria's first child was born, the boy looked like the Arab who came to Azteca to sell clothing on credit. People used a lot of credit then and the Arab peddlers went from house to house. Right off, we could see that the child was not of our race and we said, "No, this child is not one of us. He is not from here." And my cousin Julio didn't want to accept the baby.

Then my aunt Rufelia began to say, "The child looks like my

mother-in-law, just like my mother-in-law. Yes, son, believe me, he is yours."

What mother-in-law? She didn't even have a mother-in-law! Then Gloria had a very pretty little girl who also looked like the Arab. After that, Gloria went with another cousin of mine, the son of Crescenciano, and she had a child with him. Then she went with another man and had a child with him. Gloria's husband didn't say anything. My aunt, his mother, kept coming and saying, "No, son, this is your child. You can recognize the brand right away." Even when Gloria went off with this man for a week, my cousin took her back. My cousin was a fool and my aunt always intervened, saying, "Take her back. She is your wife. She has no place to stay." Gloria was already carrying another child, but my cousin took her back!

Yes, my aunt was actually being a go-between for her daughters-in-law and also for her sons. She was wise to all the lovers and even brought them to her daughters-in-law behind the backs of her sons. That was the kind of character she had. In the first place, she was ignorant, and in addition she was just naturally evil. She earned money doing these things and that is why I dared to discuss it with my mother.

I said, "She may be my aunt and all, and we practically lived with her, but I don't care for her character."

So then my mother made me a promise, "No, son, get married, and you will never again see anything like that in your house."

And as a matter of fact I never did. My mother was more afraid of me than of my stepfather because I had changed. The thing is that I took after her, I was forceful too. She also was jealous by nature. And she beat me, too. After I grew up, by the time I was nineteen, I gathered more courage. I was capable by then, I earned as much as a man.

Well, being a man already, I had tasted the things of the world. I even had a child with a married woman, except that it didn't bear my name because the woman's husband was alive and he thought he was the child's father. We worked together on the *haciendas*, the husband and I, and as he was my friend, he would borrow money from me practically every day. He was always asking me to lend him one *peso*, two *pesos*, and even money each week for his wife's expenses.

His wife, Regina, happened to be a relative of mine, the daughter of my mother's mother's half-brother. She was married to her husband for ten years and never had children. As for me, ever since I was quite young I had a strong desire to have a child. Naturally, being a boy who was anxious to try everything, well, I asked her and she didn't say no.

The husband practically knew. They told him to his face, but he accepted it. He would even come to my house to get me, because he was a drinker. We would go together to the *hacienda* on Mondays. On Sundays he'd be drunk and sometimes would bring home his wages and sometimes he wouldn't. I would pay the week's expenses; that's why he liked me. He would stay drunk all day Sunday. But that's what I wanted. He would come and get me.

"Let's go to my house."

"Well, all right, let's go." Then once we were there, I would say, "Don't you want a drink?"

"That's why I went to fetch you," he would say.

"Well, go ahead. Take this." So I would give him six *centavos* to go and buy two *decilitros* . . . and *zas!* His own wife would send him into the village so we could enjoy it better. By then he knew why she was sending him, but he didn't care. He would come to get me because I gave him money. Regina liked me a lot, for after all, I was young. But I wasn't with her even a year, no, only about nine months.

I liked the girls and I went out a lot. My mother hit me and my step-father scolded me because I came home late at night. They said I ought to get married so that I wouldn't be in the streets so much.

I worked hard on the *haciendas* and gave all my money to my mother. But I said, "My *mamá* is not saving my money. I'd better get married." I liked a girl named Elpidia who came to do sewing at my house. Her mother would bring her around and I liked her and thought I would ask for her hand. One day, just before Carnival time, on a Saturday, I came home from the *hacienda* and ventured to go to her house. It was early, about seven o'clock in the evening. The girl was washing dishes and the mother was ironing. Well, just like that, I began talking and said I wanted her daughter's hand. The girl was a youngster, just thirteen years old.

So the mother says to me, "Well, who knows if she wants to?" But she was beginning to get angry! She says, "And what are you doing coming around here asking us questions? Aren't your father and mother alive? Let them come."

I say, "Yes, they have to come, I know. I only came to open the door for them. I just wanted you to tell me yes or no. If it's no, what's the use of their coming? But if you tell me that it's yes, then I'll send not only my parents, but my uncles and godfathers, too."

"Ah, so that's how it is! Then you came around in good faith," said the mother. "But I don't know if she wants to. Because so-and-so asked for her already, and she didn't want to. But now, who knows? She's still a little girl. She isn't staining yet. I can't tell you anything right now, neither yes or no."

Then the girl gets up and says, "Yes, *mamá*. I didn't want to marry that old one, but I like this one. Tell him yes."

So the mother got mad at her and says, "Keep quiet! Who was talking to you? He was talking to me, not you."

The girl kept quiet and went on washing the dishes. Well, after that the woman's attitude changed. She saw that her daughter favored me. So she said, "All right. We'll be expecting you when you come from the *hacienda*."

So I went back to work with the matter pending. When I came home a week later, my mother scolded me.

"Why did you go and do that? Aren't we still alive?"

I say to her, "Yes, but I don't want you to be going in vain. I want to make sure that when you go it's all arranged."

She says, "All right. Are you doing this in good faith?"

"I didn't go for anything else. I went for what I went. If they want to give her, let them give her. If not, then not. So what?"

I have always been very frank, ever since I was a youngster. I was never timid. Well, then, in truth, the next day my mother took me there, to the girl's house. We exchanged greetings and were well received. Even the girl's stepfather received us well.

We spoke to them. I said, "Well, yes, it is true that it was I who came, but not to do anything wrong, or with any bad intentions. The proof is that I came alone, and not only that, I came early. Just like you see me now, with no bad ideas in mind. I just came for what I came. I didn't come for the *señora*, I came for the girl."

The man says, "Well, if that's how it is, boy, well then, all right. Come back a week from today and we'll see what the girl says."

This time my parents went with my uncles and aunts. And that was it! Everybody said yes. Two weeks after that they went again. Now it was definite and they discussed the wedding and when it should be. Then my people began to bring her little presents. Well, so now I was really going to get married! I was nineteen years old.

Then the time drew close for the presentation in church. Everything was ready. All the requirements they ask you for were fulfilled. I was at the *hacienda* and Saturday came around when I found a piece of paper, a sheet of paper, a clean new one that they threw into the house. It attracted my attention and I picked it up and read it.

"It must be her ex-sweetheart," I thought. Now I was beginning to realize who it was because others had said to me, "The bed is going to be too narrow for the three of you."

I began to think, "Well, if I let that stand in my way this so-and-so will say I am a coward. I'm a young man, I'm not afraid. If he says anything, well, he'll be seeing me."

I kept the piece of paper. But this happened toward the end, when we were about going to present ourselves in church. In those days nobody used the civil ceremony.

I was very Catholic, see? It was my *barrio* fiesta and that week it was my turn to do vigil in the chapel. It is the custom here to bring your little candle and incense burner in the mornings. I got there early on Saturday and early on Sunday, at five o'clock in the morning, with my incense burner. I walked on my knees from the door of the little chapel all the way in as far as the altar. I got there with my little candle. Filled with the faith I had in my heart, I asked God that if He knew this woman was going to be good for me, to give her to me, and if not, to take her away and give me another one that would be better for me, for my life. That was all I asked, there in that little chapel. I lit the little candle. It filled the altar with smoke. I closed the chapel and went to the tower to ring the bells. That was all.

The next day was Monday and I went back to the *hacienda*. When I got home the following Saturday I found my mother all broken up, crying and crying.

"What happened, *mamá?* Why are you crying?"

"Why shouldn't I cry? I am filled with grief."

"What for?"

"Well, because your bride . . . she herself gave me notice that it was off. She doesn't want to any more, and that's all. Why did you go and send her a letter?"

The thing was that I had sent her a letter asking her, "If you want to, all right. I'm not trying to back out. I just want to know who he is so I can be on my guard." That was all I said to her, but it made her mother mad because she read the letter. And so, when my *mamá* went to notify them that we were ready to present ourselves, she came right out and said that it was off, that her daughter was angry.

"All right, then," I say. "*Ay, mamá,* and you let a thing like that upset you?"

"That's right. Because I want to see you married once and for all. Tomorrow or the next day I might die. And you? What then?"

I said, "Pssht! What do you mean you're going to die? No, man! No! As for me, it's better this way. I'm even glad. Now that I got this rope off my neck I'm going to enjoy the world. So what! I am still young. Stop worrying! Give me supper and forget about it."

Well, after that she was happy again and all. But inside me I knew what I had done in the little chapel. Me, with all that faith I had, I said to myself, "So it was fulfilled! God took her away from me, as I asked."

About two weeks later when I came home from the *hacienda,* there was the woman, the one who was going to be my mother-in-law.

My mother said, "She came to pay for the presents we gave. She **is** worried that one day you'll be passing by in the street and you might meet her daughter and carry her off. That's what's on her mind because now she is obligated to us."

"Me? Carry her off? I'm not one of that kind. What's spilled is spilled. I'm going to look for another, a better one if possible. So let's forget it, now. It's over, it's over! I gave the presents because I wanted to. When I get drunk with my friends, do you suppose I ask them to pay me back what I spend? No, all that is lost and done with. It doesn't mean a thing to me any more."

The woman says, "Then you won't accept it, Pedro? But don't go carrying her off somewhere, I beg you."

"That all depends. If she gives me the opportunity, why not? But not for marriage, any more. I tell you that plainly. Not any more! There are lots of girls around. The world is a garden filled with flowers and I will pick the prettiest for myself."

So that blew over. Elpidia married the same one who sent me that paper. I was even thinking of killing him, but that was later when I was older and more of a man.

When I wasn't working I didn't go home to sleep. I was always out. That's what I learned from that bandit. I liked to go out and get drunk and sing.

Once in Elotepec when there was a fiesta, I had one too many. There I was, going up the street with a cousin of mine helping me along. And who do we bump into but him, her husband! He was a musician and went around at night playing. So there I had him in front of me. If not for my cousin, I would have killed him. I had a great big knife on me. I stared him right in the face and grabbed his instrument and I said, "So that's what you go around doing, eh? I'll show you how men settle things. Don't be going around with little pieces of paper, eh! I'll teach you a lesson right this minute."

And so I pulled out my knife. *Uuy!* Did he jump! But he didn't let go of his guitar. He dragged me along and I didn't let go. My relative had me around the waist and was pulling, too. He wouldn't let go of me and kept saying to the other fellow, "Let go of your instrument. Go on, get out of here. Run, or I'll let him loose." I was drunk. He pulled and pulled and finally ran off.

PEDRO

Marriage

In 1910, I began to look for a bride. I said to my mother, "Now is the time. I have five candidates, eh? Now, I am going to get married for sure."

"Really? Go ahead, so you'll give up being a carouser."

I started on the first candidate. Then I went on to the second one. Finally, I made it with the third one—Esperanza, who happened to be my second cousin because her grandfather and my father's father were brothers.

But what bad luck! The very same year, exactly on the fifteenth of March, my mother died. I was left all alone, without father or mother, without anyone. My stepfather? Bah! He was just a stepfather! After my mother's death, whom could I count on? While she was alive, he was my stepfather. After she died, it was over. Then he was nothing to me.

But my mother had left everything arranged with my mother-in-law before she died. They had already talked it over, and my mother and I were waiting for the family to decide. The Tepalcingo fair came around, and we took twenty ropes to sell there. We met Esperanza's godmother and she says, "Be confident. The girl is willing." So then my *mamá* says to me, "Let us buy something for your wife because it looks favorable."

We bought a *rebozo* and shoes and yard goods and lots of dried codfish to give to my bride. After that, we came back, but with the sickness this time. My *mamá* was already ill. She wanted me to go to the fiesta of Tlayacapán but I said, "No, I am going to work on the *tlacolol*."

My stepfather and I were planting our own corn for the first time, on a hillside belonging to the *hacienda* of Atlihuayán. Many of us who worked as *peones* on the *hacienda* asked to be allowed to plant on the unused land. The custodian of the land was a man from a village in this *municipio* and he gave us permission. But it was eight hours walk from Azteca and we went home only on Sunday. There were many *tlacololeros* and I went along with them because I didn't know anything. They put me in charge of the *tortillas* and I carried the load with a tumpline around my forehead. There were lots of *tortillas* because we each brought a week's supply. That's what we ate from Monday to Saturday, hard *tortillas*. Sometimes we pulled up wild sweet potatoes and cooked them or even ate them raw. It took me seventeen days to clear a little plot.

When I returned home, my *mamá* was very bad. My stepfather was also ill in bed. Seeing this, I went to work on the *hacienda* to support the household. My aunt Paulina and her daughter and two sons were there and I supported them. My stepfather was ill and couldn't work on the *tlacolol,* so I left it and went to work as a *peón* to get money.

A few days later my mother died. I should have had a premonition about it because of a dream I had had. I dreamt I lost a tooth. It was in the atrium of my *barrio* chapel and I was at a fiesta. As I got halfway across the atrium, I felt a tooth get loose. I pulled it and, *caramba*, how many I got! All my teeth fell out, every one of them!

Then I began to think, "*Caray!* I am still just a boy and now what will I do? What am I going to eat with?" And I began to cry. There was a pile of teeth there, like grains of corn. Then my cousin came over and he says to me, "What did you lose?"

"My teeth."

"Well, what can you do?" he says.

So I say, "I am ashamed to go around without teeth, a young fellow like me." Then suddenly he was gone and I began to gather up my teeth. But what did I want them for? They were lost, now! There was nothing to be done any more.

This dream was telling me that I was going to lose my mother. A little later they came to the *hacienda* to notify me that my mother was dead. When I arrived, she was already laid out. They invited me to eat. There I was, eating, and thinking to myself, "Well, I'm all alone now. I had better leave. I'm going to go to San Vicente." But no. My bride's mother and aunt came. They came to visit the deceased. So my aunts said to me, "Get up. Here comes your mother-in-law."

"What mother-in-law? I have no mother-in-law."

Then I remembered about my bride.

My aunt says to me, "Go on! There's your mother-in-law, man, with the one who is going to be your aunt. Hurry up, go and greet them, for politeness' sake."

Well, I went. The two of them were there alone with my dead mother. Then they spoke to me.

"Well, what about it? What have you thought?"

"Well, nothing. What did you expect me to be thinking about? About burying my mother. Now she's dead. What else!"

"And what about what was left up in the air with the girl? What are we going to do?"

"Whatever you want. I am all alone, now. So I don't think anything."

"Ah, so now you don't think anything?"

"Well, no. I am alone. If you are willing to accept me, if you will allow me to be your son-in-law, but with no mother now to help me, I can stick to the bargain. But I spent money on the sickness and I am going to have to spend money for the burial."

"Of course! Come around a little later. We'll be expecting you."

Well, I went there at the time I said.

We were neighbors; it was just a block away. My brother-in-law, her brother, was standing on the street corner. He saw me go into the house. He was so touchy that he wouldn't let anyone enter his house. But I went in and he saw me. I found only the girl and her mother inside. Being a village girl and very humble, she tried to hide. But how could she, if I was already there?

So then my mother-in-law began to talk. "Yes, that's why we came over. We didn't say as much as we should have because, in the first place, you are in mourning, and there were your aunts. So that's why I am asking you now, 'What have you got to say?' "

"No. Speak to the girl first and let's see what she has to say. If she says yes, I want to hear it from her own mouth. In that case, I will keep my part of the bargain. I certainly will! I want to warn you of only one thing. I am alone and I have no money left. But I will earn more and save. And then after that, we'll see if we can't get married right away. One good thing is that my mother went and bought everything already. She had an idea that you were going to give your consent. She bought a *rebozo* and even shoes. Everything is there already. So actually there isn't very much more that I need."

"Good, we don't want a thing. That's the least of it."

"Well, then, if you really want me, orphan though I am . . . You will be my mother."

And she answered, "When it comes to that, as long as I am alive."

So we buried my mother and then I went to call my aunts and uncles together and we began to arrange things. But seeing my stepfather, who was still sick, and the large family I had to support, I said, "As there is no money left, I am going to earn money for my wedding."

I had a horse and I went to the *hacienda*. But I couldn't work any more. I couldn't work at all on account of the grief I felt for the one who had recently died. I just couldn't. I would work a little and then I would begin to think, about this and that . . . and that's how it was. I couldn't work for mourning. I felt her death deeply. *Újule!* A month went by like that. We were in April.

Well, now what was I to do? The rainy season was about to begin and I was not marrying and not earning. I was barely able to pay for the kitchen expenses.

The worst part of it was that there was no work anywhere. I went to the Hospital Zacuaco *hacienda,* to Atlihuayán, to Oacalco. I passed through San Vicente, Temisco—no work. I traveled as far as San Gaspar before I finally found something, but I earned only two and a half *pesos* a week.

I said to myself, "No, this can't go on. I am in very bad shape. What am I waiting for? When am I going to earn enough for the wedding? To whom can I speak? My stepfather? He says he is sick. My aunts? Would they pay for my wedding? No, no."

And so I went back to the *tlacolol* in Atlihuayán, to continue to clear it. I gathered the brush and burned it and prepared the land for seeding. The custodian called about twenty of us to fix fences for the *hacienda,* but then we went back to our own planting. My stepfather got better and went to work as a plowman in Yautepec. He didn't help me at all with the *tlacolol*. I worked again on the *hacienda* fences and then I did the reseeding. The corn was beginning to grow.

I said to myself, "When I begin the harvest, who is going to serve me? It won't work out, so I'd better get married. I'll sell my horse and get married now."

I went home. My aunt was the same as a mother to me and I said to her, "Look, aunt, I'm back."

"You've come back, son? Why? Is there no work at the *hacienda?*"

"No, it is not possible to earn anything. So what is the use of working? Do you know what? I am going to get married this week, once and for all."

"Then do it, son. Why wait?"

And so I began to get things done. I went to see the man who said he wanted to buy my horse. I went to him and said, "I want to sell the horse now."

He began to laugh and he says, "You are going to trade him in for a mare, aren't you?"

"Yes, that's it exactly."

"All right, then. I'll buy him. How much do you want?"

"Well, just what you sold him to me for."

"All right . . . thirty-two *pesos*."

I took my money and went running. Now there was enough for everything, turkeys and, well, everything! All that was missing were my shoes; they cost three-fifty. Everything was cheap then. A church wedding cost nine *pesos*. Thirty-two *pesos* was a lot of money in those times.

So that evening I went to my bride's house. The time had come.

"I didn't earn any money, but it can't be helped. I am going to get married anyway. Are you still willing?" I asked them.

"Well, yes, of course."

"All right, then. We'll present ourselves tomorrow."

So the next day to the church and *zas!* two weeks later the wedding. It took place right on the first of May, 1910.

After the marriage we went to the house of the godfather who was also a relative of mine, *don* Jesús Román, son-in-law of my uncle Maximiano. He was a shoemaker. My uncle had said, "Why look elsewhere for a *padrino?* Jesús is from the same family and won't demand that you spend much." Of course, that suited me. My godmother was also a relative of mine.

My godparents brought me to their house to give me advice. What for! I had more to tell than they. Nonsense! They didn't tell me a thing. And they locked us up in a room, me and my wife.

"*Caray!* They've locked us in here in the dark. Now we're prisoners. What do you say to that?"

"Now what? What do we do?" she said.

"Well, nothing. What is there to do?"

We had just received communion a little while ago and there we were now just sitting, that's all. And the others kept looking in at us every little while through a small window.

My aunt says, "It looks bad. Things are not going to work out with those two. They are not talking to each other. Each one is sitting in his chair and they don't speak!"

We didn't know they were watching us. Bah! So my aunt says once more, "Well, nothing doing. They don't talk. I don't think they are going to like each other."

I wasn't speaking to my wife because she seemed afraid, because she acted like she didn't know anything. She didn't want to talk. Finally, I said a few words to her, but she would not answer because of the language I was using. I was speaking to her in Spanish. It wasn't until a long time later that she finally says, "You want to talk to me in Spanish and I want to speak in *mexicano*."

Then I changed. Then I spoke to her in *mexicano*. That was why we were shy of each other, distrustful, because of the language.

It was the fiesta of San Pedro. It fell on the thirtieth of April, but as it was a Saturday, it was pushed ahead to Sunday, May 1. My godfather says, "Let's go. These two have no spirit. They don't even talk, they are not celebrating anything. We'd better go to the fiesta. Don't you think so, boys? Let's all go to San Pedrito."

So we went, me with a wife, now. I had a little handkerchief, a silk one with my name on it, which was supposed to be very elegant. I had a wedding handkerchief but no money. All the money I had was a silver fifty-*centavo* piece, tied up in that handkerchief. As we got close to the fiesta, I said to my wife, "Here, spend these *centavitos*." I gave the handkerchief to her, too, out of love, by then. A lovely scene as I remember it, eh?

Everything was so cheap then, she bought all she wanted with fifty *centavos* and still had money left over. Most things cost one *centavo*. She bought a roll, but that cost two *centavos*.

Well, we left early. They said, "Let's walk them home," and they accompanied us to my house, the bride's new residence. And when we went in, my aunts received us. Nobody waited for us with incense; it is the custom in other homes, but we didn't do it. My aunt was the one who made all the arrangements. I had turned over everything to her. Well, then they began giving us advice, my uncle and my godfather of marriage. They began telling us how we ought to live. They told us to live right, about the obligations each of us had to the other. That was all. But I knew all about it. *Qué va!*

And she . . . after a while she began to pick up courage. Pretty soon she went into the kitchen. A little while later, she changed her clothes . . . and that was it. Then we had our supper. There was turkey *mole;* they had made lots and lots of food for our relatives. There were turkeys, about six of them.

Then I showed her where I slept. Well, finally, we retired at about ten o'clock at night. In the kitchen they were washing dishes and talking and talking. My aunt and my stepfather slept in the kitchen.

So there we were, the two of us. She was kind of frightened, uncertain, and I, since I was an old hand, I wasn't afraid. I enjoyed it. She said nothing, she just trembled.

"Why are you afraid? Don't you trust me? Why?"

"Who knows?"

I said to her, "Who knows! You belong to me now. What more do you want? Now you can do nothing about it."

I was talking to her in *mexicano*.

She says, "Well, yes, here I am. There's nothing to be done now."

"That's right. Now let's lie down together and, in the same way, we will get up in the morning."

CHAPTER III

ESPERANZA

Youth and Marriage

I must have been about seventeen when I got married. I can't tell because my mother said that she gave my baptismal certificate to my grandma and they threw it away. So that's why I never really knew when I was born. That's why I never celebrated my birthday or even thought about celebrating it.

My *papá* was a field hand. I was a month and a half old when he left us. My mother was married before to Carlos Zúñiga and had four children with him. Three of them died. The only one who lived was my half-brother Emigdio. It was he who supported us. My *mamá* was a very poor woman and had to live with others—we had no house of our own. The only thing she worked at was gleaning the fields. I was little and she carried me everywhere. She said I nursed for three years. My brother borrowed some land and they gave him permission to put up a little house on it.

My poor little mother, always suffering want. My *mamá* would tell me about what went on in the past. My brother took the place of my father; little as he was, he worked in the fields. He didn't even have a shirt and would go naked with my mother to plant the corn. They left me tied under a tree while they worked.

In the house, my brother scolded me and my mother beat me, and I never talked back. Actually, my mother hit me little because I was the

only child. One time she sent me to the plaza to buy some liver but I took a long time for they did not serve me. When I returned home I explained what had happened but my mother began to beat me right off. I said to my *mamá*, "You hit me so much that I would rather go to my godmother." My *madrina* liked me a lot and gave me many things.

Then my mother hit me more, hard with a rope. I went running out into the street looking for my godmother's house. My mother came after me and threw a stone at me. Possibly she just wanted to frighten me, for it fell to one side. Later my brother came and defended me. "Why do you hit her so much?" he said to my *mamá*.

I had no liberty whatsoever in my house. In truth I never went anywhere. Many times people wanted to hire me to take care of their children, but my brother would never allow it.

Two other boys from the *barrio* of San Martín asked for me before I married Pedro. I couldn't have been more than fourteen at the time. My brother was already married and had children. I had no idea of getting married, but my mother said, "Better get married. Look, your brother is married and if I die you'll be left all alone." It never entered my mind that my mother could die and then I thought that if she did I would go to live with my godmother. When the men asked for me she said, "Get married . . . get married! You won't have to work hard, they have a little money." But I kept telling her I didn't want to get married.

I knew nothing of evil things at that time because I had not gone to school and I never went out to visit others for my brother would not allow it. I had heard girls speak of sweethearts but my brother had advised me not to talk to boys or be alone in isolated places because boys might do bad things to me. I respected my brother very much.

I knew no vice. I saw infants and wondered how they had come into the world. I imagined women had to be split apart to take out the babies. Not until I married did I learn about these things. I began to have my monthly period at about fifteen. Like a fool, as soon as it happened I told my mother about it. She said to me, "That's how it is. Now you must be careful. Don't bathe when you are this way, nor eat 'cold' foods. Also, be careful your brother doesn't see a stain on your dress. He is a man but he knows about these things and it always makes one ashamed." I never kept to a diet when I was a girl. Many times one cannot because of poverty. There may be only tomatoes in the house and one has to eat them even though they are "cold."

Some people say a girl is not a virgin if she has her period. They say if a girl doesn't marry, the period never comes. But that is not true because I got it before I married.

I lived around the corner from Pedro's house. I didn't know it, but he was already asking for me. My *mamá* said, "I'll see what the girl says." My brother was of the same opinion. "Whatever the girl says. Even if I have to go on supporting her . . . even if I like the boy, if she doesn't want to marry him, she doesn't get married!"

Fifteen days went by and Pedro's *mamá* came to find out the answer. As I didn't want to get married, they didn't give her any at all. After that my poor little mother-in-law kept coming back and coming back, hoping to get a definite answer. My brother had a talk with Pedro and said, "I like the boy. He is a hard worker."

As a matter of fact he was. Pedro was always working on the *haciendas*. So they kept telling me, "Get married . . . get married." After Pedro's mother died, they kept insisting even harder.

Then my *mamá* would say to me, "Poor boy, what a pity! All alone . . . nobody to make his *tortillas* for him." She and my brother kept insisting so much, I finally said to them, "If you want me to marry, I will marry."

Pedro never visited me when we were engaged. He only came to the house when my brother sent for him. My brother was very strict and would say, "I don't want that young man here because it may happen that the engagement will be broken and if people see him coming here there will be talk."

I never had any conversation with Pedro before we were married. When he came to the house my mother would talk to him. I would go into the *corral* and wouldn't return until he had gone. Once I was grinding corn when he came and I couldn't go to the *corral*. That time we almost ate together but we didn't talk to each other. What could I have talked about?

After Pedro had asked for my hand I was always afraid of him. Once my *mamá* sent me to sell some eggs and when I went out I saw Pedro standing at the street corner. He saw me also but we did not speak to one another. Because of my fear, I ran all the way to the market place. After I sold the eggs, I came home more afraid than before. First, I tried to hide in a doorway and then I passed by him at a run. I felt cold through and through and had a feeling down my back as if he already had his arms around me. I looked back but there he was, still sitting at the corner.

We were married on the feast day of Saint Peter, in the month of May. Pedro bought me the dress I wore. It was rose color. It was the first dress I had ever worn because I had only worn blouses and skirts. Pedro had on a new shirt and white pants. After the wedding, my godmother took us to the *barrio* fiesta. Pedro gave me fifty *centavos* to buy myself something but I didn't buy anything. What was there to buy?

When we arrived at Pedro's house after the fiesta, my aunt and Pedro's aunt began to make the evening meal. I was inside the house and Pedro was walking around outside. They called to us when the meal was ready but neither he nor I ate much. I wished my mother were at my side.

I remember the night we married, I was very scared. Pedro still bothers me sometimes when he says jokingly, "Why were you so frightened that night?" To tell the truth, I don't really know what was the matter with me. Chills came over me and I began to tremble. I was very afraid for never, never had we spoken to one another.

A few days before the wedding, my mother gave me advice. "Now that you are going to marry, you must change your character. Here you have one character but there you must have the character of your husband. If he scolds you, do not answer. If he beats you, bear it, because if not, your husband is going to ask what kind of upbringing we gave you." And that is the way I have always been. Whenever Pedro hit me I only sat down and cried. He hit me many times.

After we ate, my aunt went away. Pedro's aunt went to bed and so did he. I was standing near the table and didn't want to go to bed. Pedro called to me but I didn't pay attention to him. His aunt also said, "Go on, go to bed," but I didn't want to. The light was on, and we could all see each other. He had gone to bed with his clothes on. He has always done that. I also always go to bed with my clothes on.

The aunt told me that for this I had got married and that I should go to bed. Then they put out the candle and I finally had to go to bed. I was very afraid and ashamed. Pedro covered me with the blanket and then began to embrace me and to touch my breasts. Then he was opening my legs and went on top of me. I didn't know what men did to one and I said to myself, "Maybe it has to be like this." I felt like crying or going to my mother, but I remembered that they were the ones who had married me. Then I said, "If I die, I'll die. I have to go through it even though he kills me." And I closed my eyes and waited.

Pedro knew how these things were done because he already had a daughter with a married woman. I don't remember that I bled, but it hurt a lot. I didn't cry because there were others there and I was ashamed to be heard. Pedro did it three times that night.

The next day when I got up, how ashamed I felt! Two weeks later I was still afraid but, little by little, one picks up confidence. I didn't talk about these things to anyone, not even my *mamá*. I told only Pedro's cousin what my husband was doing to me. I said, "All men do is play with a person! What do they have to get married for?" She said, "That's how men are and you have to let him, otherwise he will roam the streets at night."

After about two months I was feeling pleasure and I began to love my husband.

CHAPTER IV

PEDRO

Becoming Independent

And so we began to live, very quiet, very happy, the two of us. Before I was married, when I was still a boy of fourteen, I dreamed that when I grew up and got married I would be rich because there would be only my wife and myself to support, not like before, supporting my mother and my aunt and her children. The illusions of youth, no? Once I marry, I thought, I will be rich because all the money will be for me. How much can the two of us eat? I will be able to save.

But, no. Right off, I took on the responsibility for everyone in the house. That's the way I was. I had taken charge of my mother's expenses too, for my stepfather was very stupid. After I married he didn't even pay for the kitchen expenses, not even for his own illness! I was the one who knew what was spent for everything. I brought the firewood, the water, everything.

Soon I had to pawn half of my house site to a rich man for ten *pesos*. Money was worth a lot then and I couldn't pay him back. He planted corn on my land for ten years because I couldn't pay him. But he was a very good person and he let me pay little by little, at times six *centavos*, at times nine or twelve *centavos*. And he gave back the title while I still owed him two or three *pesos*. Many times I pawned half of my house site, later my hog-plum trees, for that is what we do here when we need money. In those days, too, I borrowed one hundred *pesos* for five *pesos* a month, not like now when many lend money at ten and twelve *pesos* per hundred.

I worked on my *tlacolol* and became a *tlacololero*. It was harder to plant on the hillside than to work on the *hacienda*. But I liked it very much. The difficult thing about it is that it is dirty work. Your clothes get dirty and your hands get scratched and calloused and split open. You can tell a *tlacololero* by his hands. He works with a hoe and a *machete* but also with his hands. The land is steep and you have to step with care because if you are the least bit careless you can fall and really hurt yourself. It is all volcanic rock and leaf mulch; the soil gets washed away.

And the animals! Aside from poisonous snakes and scorpions, there were badgers and boars, but they didn't do so much damage then. One cannot plant there any more because of other animals, like the squirrels. Whew! Those squirrels don't leave a thing. They begin to eat corn from the time they are born. Then there are the rats, great huge ones, and the ferret, the fox . . . all these eat the corn. Later I moved to another location, closer to the village. There, yes, one could work because only cattle were around and if you took care and put up a good fence, nothing happened.

My *tlacolol* was still far away, two hours walk, and naturally my wife had to get up at four in the morning to have the *tortillas* ready by six. She made me *tacos* with *chile* or whatever she had. I would get up early, too, to bring water for the kitchen. If there was a bit of coffee or lemon-grass tea, I would drink it and go off to work. At that time I worked alone because I had no money for *peones* before the Revolution. I would walk along with some of my neighbors, but once there, each would work on his own plot.

At about eleven o'clock it would begin to get hot. Then the body starts to sweat and one drinks water and more water and more water. We ate at about two. A few neighbors would come together, build a fire and heat the *tortillas*. Because of the work and the sun we kept drinking water. That's just fine when the water is good, but when it rains the water in the streams is practically mud! By four o'clock when we were ready to go home we were all bloated with water. We filled up with water and didn't even feel hungry. We couldn't digest anything any more.

So we walked back for two hours and arrived home tired, without appetite and with all that water swirling about inside us like in a gourd. I would lie down to rest, without even wanting supper. But there was my wife preparing the *ponche* with alcohol and orange leaves and sugar. "Come on, here is a bit of *ponche*." And we would drink it. Then I would feel the water go down and my digestion would begin to work. That is when I began to get hungry. "Now, yes, give me my supper." Then I would feel good again.

My aunt Paulina was living with us, but after a while she and I had a falling out and she went home. She took her children with her. It was on account of my sister that they left. My stepfather also bawled out my aunts, because they divided up among themselves all the clothes my mother left. I didn't say a word. They left just one dress for my wife and the only reason she got that was because I snatched it. Even an uncle, poor thing, may he rest in peace, wasn't ashamed to come and ask, too.

I said, "What is this? What do you want? Did I ask help from you for the burial? For that you didn't help, right? You didn't give even a pin, but now you all want the clothing she left. No, go work, uncle, you're still strong enough."

All he said was, "Thank you very much, son," and he left.

Everybody wants the inheritance. But what inheritance? All my mother left were her clothes! Ah, but the house site? The house site was all mine, not even my stepfather could touch that. It was very much mine. My stepfather said, "Yes, that's true. It does belong to Pedro. It's not mine or his mother's, it's his."

My wife's family was very humble, completely humble. They even went beyond the limits of humility. I tell you, the mother was so meek that she was afraid of her own son. Her own son! As if he were her husband! That's why I judge her to be very humble. Suffice it to say that when I married her daughter she respected me as if I were some important gentlemen.

When she was a young widow, my mother-in-law would visit the house of her sister, who was married to my father's cousin, *don* Ángel Martínez. He was the son of my father's father's brother. Víctor Martínez was *don* Ángel's brother. Víctor's marriage had broken up and he had left his wife and two children in Yautepec. He came to his brother Ángel's house and that is where he saw my mother-in-law. They met and fell in love. They lived together for a time and there was an offspring, the one who is my wife. After that, *señor* Víctor died and my mother-in-law was left alone once again, young and all alone, with her son Emigdio and the baby Esperanza. She did not marry again.

My mother-in-law was so humble she attached herself to her son, even working in the fields with him, because he was still a youngster and could not work very well. Lots and lots of women went into the fields in those days to help their families. The men would send the women into the fields and would even play around with them there.

My grandmother used to say that the people here were more cruel

in the past. For example, the way they treated their mistresses, the loose women who went with many men. According to the old people, these same men would get together and say, "Well, how is it that she is going with me and with you and with him? She is just causing trouble. Why should we fight and kill each other while she has a good time? So, now let's do something to her."

One of them would take her out and then they would all get together and carry her off into the fields. And the things they would do to her! They drove a sharpened stake into the ground and greased it with a lot of lard. Then they all made use of her and had fun with her. They didn't kill her first but stuck her onto the point and there she sat until she died. Then they would undo her braids and put a *sombrero* on her head and a red kerchief around her neck, like a man. They would put a cigar in her mouth and cross her shawl on her chest the way a vagabond does, to show that she tried to revel and make merry like a man. When she was found the next morning, people would say only, "Well, now, who could have killed her? I wonder." They could only guess, but nobody really knew.

That's what the old folks told us they used to do. We would say sometimes, "Why do some people beat their women so much, their wives as well as their mistresses?" The old people would say, "What you see is nothing. It was worse before."

As I said, my mother-in-law was a loyal woman and she loved me very much, even more than her own son, because he was very mean and I wasn't. And I loved her very much, too. Yes, I did. She never forgot her daughter and was always with her, always. What a shame the Revolution had to come just then and we didn't have a chance to show our affection more!

My wife didn't know how to do anything, not even to cut out a piece of clothing. One day I bought a piece of cloth for underdrawers for me. We laid it on the *petate* and between the two of us we tried to cut it out. My mother-in-law came and found us there.

"Well, what are you doing?" she says.

"We're trying to cut out a pair of drawers."

She began to laugh. "Man, you have ruined the cloth because this is the way it is done. Why didn't you tell me?"

"Well, yes . . . teach her. My wife is responsible now and ought to learn. Look, we have ruined this."

"Yes, but I will fix it. Now, daughter, watch so you can learn."

So she taught her. Esperanza could not cook either, or even sweep. My mother had always obliged me to do these things. She was very strict and made me learn. So naturally, when I saw that my wife couldn't sweep, I showed her how. She knew absolutely nothing, my poor wife. They say her mother loved her and didn't make her work. But anyway, very poor people have practically no domestic chores and since Esperanza had her mother and her sister-in-law to do the work, she didn't have to. And another thing, my wife had no mother-in-law to teach her. Perhaps God loved my wife and that is why he took away her mother-in-law!

My wife's mother was not cold toward me, judging from the way she spoke, at least. Naturally, she could never caress me. That would have been impossible! But you could see that she loved me, that she was fond of me, because she would put aside for me, for the two of us, part of every tidbit that she ate. If I was not at home, if I had gone to work, she would go to my wife and say, "Look, daughter, take this little snack and put it aside for my son. But save it for him! And when he comes home, give it to him."

"Yes, *mamá*, yes."

Well, that was her habit. Naturally, as Esperanza was just a girl, she couldn't resist. "I didn't save it," she would say. "I ate it."

My mother-in-law would come back again to wait for me. When I arrived, she would greet me and say, "Are you back, now, son?"

"Yes, I am back, *mamá*."

"Did you see what I brought for you?"

I wouldn't answer.

"Then, you didn't give it to him, daughter?"

"*Mamá*, I ate it."

And she would half scold her, "That's why I gave you some for your share and some for him."

Then, when I saw that, I would say to my mother-in-law, "No, don't say any more to her. She's my wife. It's the same as if I had eaten it. Let her be, let her be. Next time."

"Come tomorrow and I'll give you more. There is still some. I'll save you another piece."

That's how I could tell she was fond of me, that she loved me, and that's why I say that for me she was not cold.

My mother-in-law and my mother were very different. They couldn't be compared! My mother was a very able woman, very expert. At first, she was humble, too. But from the time she went to Yautepec and began to work, she changed very much. My mother was very strong-willed. She had been timid, even about speaking, but after she learned how to talk Spanish, then she was very forceful and very courageous. No, my mother-in-law wasn't half the woman my mother was. She could barely speak a few words of Spanish, not even the prayers, though she was a good Catholic and devoted to the Virgin of Guadalupe. But she had confessed only three times in her life. She was very Indian, though fine in her way, and affectionate.

My mother-in-law was completely meek. I'll give you an example. One time I became very angry with her. As a mother-in-law, she should have answered, "You, what business is it of yours?" Right? But not that poor thing. She began to cry as if she were my wife. And do you know why? It happened when I was living in her house with my wife for a time. One day I came home and, as I am by nature very suspicious, I began to look around. The house was just a little cane hut and I hunted between the cracks of the cane, and, aha! a wad of paper! With something wrapped up in it! My mother-in-law was not at home and my wife was grinding corn. I opened the ball of paper and there was something like a black lump of dirt in it. I said to my wife, "Listen, you, what is this thing?"

"Who knows?"

"What do you mean, 'Who knows?' Nothing doing, this interests me. What is it? You must know!"

Just the two of us were there. "Oh," she says, "you know, I'll tell you what it is."

"Aha, tell me." I was very curious by then. "Tell me, what is it?"

"Well, you know, Dorotea came." Dorotea is my cousin Eutimio's wife. They killed him later there in Yautepec.

"My *mamá* went to her house and told her about my brother Emigdio, about how bad he is and mean-tempered and all that. And Dorotea took it upon herself to tell my *mamá* to give him this medicine to make him change, so he wouldn't be so bad-tempered any more."

I said, "Aha! You don't say! If she does this to her son, how much more would she do to me! This really troubles me. That kind of women I don't like because they are evildoers. They go and sorcerize their own sons. And me, what can I expect? I am going back to my house."

Right off I got angry. A cousin of mine named Clotilde had died because of sorcery. One of these evildoers came to her house regularly, and one time my cousin gave him a plate of fish. She ate it, too. The very next day she began to feel bad. Then she got a little better, suddenly. A few days later, she was sick again and this time she never got up. She died. There was a lot of talk about this man and how he went around doing evil. What was he coming to my cousin's house for? He lived away at the other side of the village but yet he came all that distance to her house. So, there is no doubt that this man made her die.

Another cousin of mine, Lorenzo, the son of my uncle Crescenciano, was also sorcerized. My poor little cousin married into a very bad family. His mother-in-law knew a lot about herbs and mixtures and cures and they say she even knew something to keep people from having children.

Lorenzo was a strong man, and very daring because he could rope and mount bulls, but his wife and mother-in-law gave him something to drink which made him lose his mind. Those women finally killed him.

And now this wad of paper! I was angry with my wife, but after a while I realized she was not to blame for she had told me about it. Then my mother-in-law arrived. Her son was not there so I said to her, "Say, what is this, anyway? This, that I just found?"

I didn't give it back to her but kept it in my pocket. The poor thing didn't want to tell me. She was frightened.

"What is it? I want to know. If you really care about me, you'll tell me, because I assume that it is something bad."

"Well, yes," she said. "Look, I'll tell you plainly. I went to Dorotea's house and I told her about my son's mean character. You know how nasty and foul-tempered he is, almost as bad as his father. Well, I told Dorotea about it and she gave me this medicine."

"And how much did it cost you?"

"Five *cuartillos* of corn."

"So! A fine thing! If you have the heart to do evil to your son, to make him tame as a sheep . . . if you have the heart to do that, then what am I to expect from you? I'm only your son-in-law."

"No, son, no. That's why I haven't given it to him. I've had this here for three months and I didn't give it to him. I was just tempted."

She began to cry. I said, "Look, mother, I love you very much. I respect you, you know that, but I don't approve of this. Do you know what medicine it is? How will you feel if your son suddenly becomes an idiot or goes crazy, as I have seen happen? What will you do then? Will you support him? And his children? If you love him, never see those women again, not Rufelia or Dorotea. They are not even your relatives. What they do is seduce good people; they are harlots of the streets. And you, as humble as you are, you still wanted to do this to your son!"

She continued to cry and said, "No, son, you know what's best. Throw it into the fire."

My mother-in-law was very affectionate with my wife. She was, indeed. And what was more, we loved her. As I was an orphan, without father or mother, when I would see her, I felt such an emotion in my heart, as if she were my wife, as if she were my real mother. I loved her very much and she favored me, too, but completely.

When my wife was ill with child, my mother-in-law took care of her. Then I, too, became ill. I went to my *tlacolol* but I could barely walk or carry my sack. Fever gripped me and I couldn't do even the easiest task. My head hurt, my back and my calves, too. They said it was *chipilez*, the illness of jealousy, and that it happened to newly married men when their wives were expecting a child. My mother-in-law tied a piece of my wife's skirt around my neck and soon I was well again.

When my wife's time came and the baby was born, the Revolution had already begun. My mother-in-law didn't want me to hire a servant at two and a half *pesos* a month; she preferred to serve us herself. She ground the corn, made the *tortillas*, washed—everything. In those days, the wife stayed in bed three months after giving birth, but because the government troops came, my poor wife rested only one month.

Once the soldiers came plundering and took my mother-in-law's *rebozo*. Poor thing! She began to cry, "They took my little *rebozo* and now what do I do? What am I going to tell my son? He will get angry."

My brother-in-law was so mean, he wouldn't even buy her another *rebozo*. I said, "No, *mamá*, it will be a sacrifice, but I'll buy you one. Don't cry. All they cost is seven *pesos*."

Her daughter-in-law, Emigdio's wife, who was also very humble and good-hearted, said to me, "Listen, Pedro, we will both buy *mamá* her *rebozo*."

"Yes, I'll give half and you the other half."

So we went and bought it. I said, "Don't cry any more, *mamá*, here is your *rebozo*." My brother-in-law noticed it when she put it on for the first time.

Then I ventured to say, "Look, *mamá*, if you are not happy with your son because he is so mean, come with us. I'll find a way to support everybody. I will work for you. You two will look after me, and I'll take care of you both. I am an orphan, I have no one. I have even supported my aunts, all the more reason why it should be you. That is my idea."

She said, "*Ay*, I haven't the courage to leave my son. I am not brave enough."

"You are so humble and so attached to your son, and look how he treats you."

"Yes, it is true, but I have to put up with it. What can I do?"

In the end, she only served me a few days because the plague came —typhus—and it was good-bye. That was the end of the story. My mother-in-law died.

My stepfather and I had a big fight. He tried to take away my house, he tried to take away my *tlacolol*, he almost got to where he wanted to take my wife. But, of course, I didn't let him.

As he was sick and in such bad shape, he began looking for a woman, and right off, he married again. So there we were in the same sack.

He went off to Yautepec to be an ox-team driver. He planted for himself, too, but there in Yautepec, with a plow, on rented land. I planted with a hoe in the *tlacolol*. I still kept on working for my step-father in good faith, but I didn't want him to take the whole crop any more. I told him, "Look, the *tlacolol* is ready. I cleared it, prepared it and planted it, and now it's ready to be harvested. Now there will be corn in September and look, I'll give you a share, apart from your own harvest in Yautepec. I won't touch that; that's your work. This is my work, but since I recognize you as my father, I am giving you more than half."

He said, "No, no!"

I was actually giving him the main share because the *milpa* yielded a good crop, sixteen *cargas* of corn. I asked him for five which left him eleven. The rent was one *carga*, so that would leave him ten. But he didn't want it like that.

And there he was selling corn on time. He sold about eight *cargas* so his wife wouldn't lack food. And what about me? It made me mad that he should be selling corn before the harvest. Where was he going to get it from? He was already counting on my *tlacolol*. He wanted to get it away from me. But I didn't let him. Not I! So I brought it up again later. In October, I said to him, "Look, it is about harvest time, now. Give me just five *cargas* of corn and you can have all the rest. I'll deliver them to you and pay for the hauling."

He says, "No! Let's set up house together and there will be enough for the two women."

I say, "No, this woman is not my mother. How do you expect the two of them to be together here? They'll quarrel and neither your wife nor mine will be free to put her hand to things. If my *mamá* were here, she would take charge. But you have a different wife now. So just give me five *cargas*, that's all, and the rest is yours."

He didn't want it that way. He wanted to take charge of every-thing. I didn't say anything but I could guess what was in his mind. I said to myself, "This friend here is after something, but he's not going to make a fool out of me."

Harvest time came. He was going to Yautepec to take in his crop. On the way he stopped and said to me, "Look, why don't you come and give me a hand, and then we'll harvest the *tlacolol*."

I said, "All right. I'll be there. If not tomorrow, the day after, but I'll be there."

Meanwhile, I went to see the judge to get everything straight. I told the judge what it was all about.

He said, "*Újule!* How mean your stepfather is!"

I said, "Since he didn't even work the *tlacolol*, I am giving him the corn out of pity because I want to recognize him as my father. But he wants to take everything for himself. So now I don't agree."

The judge said, "No, no. Go ahead and take in the harvest. Hurry."

"Then give me a claim first."

"Why, sure. Right away."

He gave me the claim and, *zas!* the very next day, with my wife and my brother-in-law Chico, and all the *tlacololeros*, *zas!* we went to take in the harvest. Yes, we had a lovely harvest. It was nice then. We were working on our *tlacolol* when the big comet appeared. The great star came out and the burst reached halfway across the sky. And, yes, it yielded a good little harvest.

That was the first year I was married and the first year I sowed a crop of my own. I was strong then. From all that distance I carried half a *carga* of corn on my back. I also carried hog plums from Azteca to Xochimilco. I hired a fleet of animals to carry the fruit but, in addition, I carried a box, walking all the way, a day's walk.

My uncle Agustín harvested his *milpa* which was not very far from the village. He harvested it but there was no one to carry it for him. After my harvest was in, I went to see him in his *milpa*. There he was, poor thing, sitting and guarding his corn. He says, "What happened? What are you doing here?"

"Man, why not? I came to haul the corn for you right now. I'll even carry it with my tumpline on my forehead. I don't have an animal. Just wait until I have my supper."

And there I go. I made six trips that night, carrying half a *carga* of corn. Seeing that, my uncle got busy and looked for teamsters, though it was dark. My effort gave him courage. He said, "*Ay*, Pedro, the truth is I didn't believe you but you are killing yourself. My son will guard the corn while I look for teamsters. Just look at this man, how he risked himself to haul my corn!" He paid me that time but everything was cheap then. I got fifty *centavos* for each load, three *pesos* for six loads. He said, "*Caray!* you really are tough."

I said, "Sure. I am powerful, I want to haul loads. I worked during the day and now I can work at night, too."

"Come, Pedro, have a drink. You are tired now. Come and eat."

"Yes, uncle, I am tired now. But I am still strong."

I took the drink and it tasted sweet to me.

My stepfather came back to Azteca when he finished his own harvest. He arrived when it was all over. I had gathered everything. He went straight to Yautepec to take out a claim, too. Did he get mad!

Furious! He came back and said, "Why did you do this to me?" and I don't know what else.

I said, "Don't you remember what I offered you? But you didn't want it. Now you get nothing."

"What do you mean, nothing?"

"That's right. Nothing. You didn't work it. How many *peones* did you put to work on the husking? You can't answer. How many *cuartillos* of seed did you put into the planting? No answer. How many *peones* did you put on the clearing? You can't say, either, so the answer is no. There is nothing for you here now. You wanted yours apart, so now we'll have everything apart. You have your own crop. Did I ask you for any of it? I didn't, did I? Because I put no work in there, or you here. I still wanted to go on recognizing you as my stepfather, as a father, that is why I offered you a share. But now I don't want to give you a thing. We can go to court whenever you wish."

This made him mad and two or three days later he went around whining, "You are going to have to appear in Yautepec."

I said, "I am not from Yautepec. I am from Azteca. If we can't settle the affair in Azteca, then it's Cuernavaca. That's where I belong. Tell the lawyer that I don't belong there and, for that matter, he doesn't belong in Azteca. And right here, I also have my claim. Look!"

"How's that? So you went too, did you?"

"Exactly. Knowing my relatives, naturally."

Well and good. He got all my family believing him. He went around crying and they felt sorry for him. All my people began to scold me, all the relatives with whom I went to plant and harvest there. I paid no attention to them.

Well, my stepfather came around once again. He began to cry. Now I began to feel a little sorry for him.

He said, "So, you are not going to give me anything?"

I said, "No, nothing. We are shelling the corn here already."

"*Caray!* How mean you are, man! You are very ungrateful."

"Look, I'm not ungrateful. It was your fault. I'm not mean, either. Go and bring a teamster. I'll give you four *cargas*. Here's the corn."

That did it. He was happy.

I went to Yautepec to pay the rent for the cornfield and *zas!* I had ten *cargas* left and one *carga* of squash. So, every day I sent *cargas* to my mother-in-law's house because my stepfather was living in my house. I thought to myself, "Well, now that he wasn't able to get my harvest, he is going to go after the house. Nothing doing! He won't make a fool of me."

At that time my stepfather had a man by the name of Juan advising him. Juan acted as a lawyer. He didn't know how to read but he was the big adviser of all the villages around here.

One day when I was passing, this "lawyer" stopped me. "Say, Pedro."

"Yes, sir, what can I do for you?"

"Look now, don't play around with me. Don't try to make a fool of me."

"I? Why do you say that? When? What do I owe you?"

"Oh, yes, You sent me four *cargas* of corn. But it was all rotten, awful."

"I sent you? When?"

"The corn you offered your stepfather. And you sent me four *cargas*, but it is rotten."

"I never sent you anything. Nor did I ever come to borrow money from you, either. Don't you know I am married now? He is, too. How can you expect us to live together? Haven't you got a head? Sure, I gave him four *cargas*. But it was a gift, not because I owe him anything. Nor do I owe you anything. I owe nothing."

"Aha! So you think you are smart, but you are making a mistake if you start up with me because I can do with you as I like."

He worked with the *caciques*, of course.

"Go ahead, then, go ahead. You have the idea that you are dealing with the villages where they are all like little donkeys and you make them do as you please. Well, I'm not one of them. Do what you want with me. We'll see how far you get. I don't owe you one *centavo*."

"*Ay, caray!* Get out of here! On your way, then, and stop insulting me."

"People believe in you because they don't know any better. How could I take you seriously when you don't even know how to read?"

"No, no, go on, get out of here. Stop bothering me."

"All right, then, don't be stopping me. What did you block my road for?"

As I was leaving he said to me, "Now you will have to reckon with me. Now it is no longer with your stepfather."

"Sure, sure. Whatever you say, old man."

I was just a youngster and here the Revolution was approaching. Right away I began to check up on the deed to my house, to make sure of my position. I got hold of *don* Ezequiel. He had schooling and was practically a lawyer. He said to me, "Don't worry. Nothing will happen. I made out that paper of yours myself. Even if twenty more Juans come, nothing will happen to you."

After that I went to somebody else. His name was *don* Pancho and for years he was the municipal secretary. I consulted him, too. He looked over the papers and said, "Nothing can happen to you, boy. Nothing. Twenty Juans could beat their foreheads, but with this document there's nothing anybody can ever do to you."

Well, now, all the more reason for us to get busy. *Don* Ezequiel liked to drink. "What you are going to do, Pedrito, is have a drink with me. Come on!"

"All right. Let's have a drink." What could I do? So we began drinking . . . me with the idea of getting his help.

I had my papers there in Cuernavaca and I began to legalize them all and have them recorded. I said to myself, "I'll do everything else necessary and then let's see when he takes it away from me."

But the Revolution put a stop to all our affairs. Good-bye to everything! Toward the end of 1911, one day at about seven in the morning, I passed by old Juan sitting on the street corner. He was all bundled up. He was an old man and felt the cold in the winter. I said to him, "What happened, *don* Juanito? When am I going to see what you will do to me? How about now? I'd like to see right now and get it over with. Didn't you say I had you to reckon with? Well, now's the time."

But he wouldn't say a word. He had thought it over carefully. I was going about with that bandit, who was a colonel by then. He was my friend and I went with him, but I was not armed. I said to myself, "I can count on him. Now let's see what the old man can do to me." My stepfather had given up already. In the meantime, old Juan had taken the sewing machine away from him.

Well, after that there was my *corral*. At that time it didn't have fruit trees and I planted corn. So I began to pick out seed for planting. Then my stepfather came around asking, "Is it still no?"

Now I began to think it over. I am always thinking. I thought to myself, "He is friends with Filiberto Toledo and Mauricio Sánchez, the generals. He has only to give a bad report about me and those canailles will kill me. All because of my house. No, now I better butter him up."

So I said to him, "All right. I'll give you half. Now you can see I am still decent. I'm not low like you. You are a vile person. How many times did you have my mother put in jail? You had that damned lawyer lock her up in Yautepec. I wish he were here right now. You put her in jail twice, didn't you? She wanted to leave you but you held on to her by force, even jailing her. That time you were dealing with my mother, but not now. Now, it's Pedro Martínez. Now try something with me!"

"No, man, look . . . whatever there is will go to you. It goes without saying."

"You should have thought of that before. Now even the sewing machine is in someone else's hands."

"If you want to get it back, it has a hundred *pesos* on it."

"No, what do I need machines for? It's my house I am defending."

I suddenly thought, "I'll give it to him now, but only temporarily." Then he asked me for the deed.

I said, "No, what for? We're in a revolution. Papers now are useless. What do you want it for?"

As he was a bit stupid, he believed me. I never gave him the papers. The troops came and the troops left, and we got out. We separated and after that it was good-bye stepfather. I never did give him the papers. He left, too. He went to Mexico City and then to Puebla, and there he died.

PART TWO

CHAPTER V

PEDRO

The Revolution Begins

In 1910 the Revolution came. What could we do? It began in Morelos on account of Patricio Leyva, the son of General Francisco Leyva. Yes, in 1908, Patricio tried for the governorship. Most of the people were on his side, and I followed along with him, all through his campaign tour. I followed him as far as Cuautla, listening to his speeches. Since that time, since I was a youngster, I have liked politics. He had the majority, against Escandón. All of us were *leyvistas* and nobody was for Escandón, because he wasn't even from the state. Pablo Escandón was a *gachupín*, a Spaniard, landlord of the Atlihuayán *hacienda*.

Well, Escandón won. He won because he was imposed. He became Governor of the State of Morelos. Before the Revolution, every citizen paid a personal tax of twenty *centavos* a month. When Escandón came in he abolished the personal tax. Now we didn't pay it. Then he taxed capital instead; he charged capital a certain percentage. And so, all of us peaceful men who were against him before, changed. "This is good. Now he has abolished the personal tax. No more of that." So we were satisfied.

But others were still against him because he was imposed. And they were not in favor of the re-election of Porfirio Díaz because he had been President for about thirty-five years. Again, he was going to sit in the chair by imposition, only they called it re-election. That is why afterward Madero did not agree with this. He did not agree with it and that was when he began to rise up.

In 1910, the action was in the north. It was still possible to work, then. So, once again, there I go to the *haciendas* looking for work. But the foremen didn't do anything to us any more. They were afraid, now, and besides we didn't take it any more.

Well, there we were one day and it was time for lunch. We were all hunting for wood to make a fire. We had only cold *tortillas* to eat while those who belonged there, the permanent hands of the *hacienda*, had coffee and two pieces of bread. They would swallow it down as fast as they could and get back to work. When the call came to get to work, they were ready, but we were still gathering wood to make the fire to heat the *tortillas*. The foreman shouted, "Come on, up on your feet."

"But we haven't had lunch yet."

"What's that to me? Come on, on your feet. Time is up."

But nothing doing. Everybody said we wouldn't go back to work until we had eaten. There were about sixty of us in a big circle. So the foreman said, "Oh, so you won't, eh?" And he rode his horse into the circle and trampled the *tortillas* we were warming. The horse was about to step on one of the men but he grabbed it by the bridle. The foreman raised his whip to hit him. Then we stood up, all of us. We dropped the *tortillas,* napkins and everything, and each of us picked up a stone. In a single voice we said, "We are going to kill this one. What can they do to us? We are many."

"Are you going to let go?" said the foreman. But the man didn't let go. The foreman started to reach for his pistol, but he saw us all with stones. And we said, "Go ahead, go ahead. Draw your pistol. What are you waiting for?" And we said to the one who had his horse by the bridle, "Don't let go, don't let go!"

The foreman didn't touch his pistol now. Then we let him know that we were on the point of quitting, that we had not sold ourselves to anyone. "We're going now. Get out of here before we cut you to pieces." He left.

Then the whole gang said, "Let's go and leave the tools so we all have a right to our pay." They still owed us for three days. Then everybody said that all they do was take the shirt off our backs. We said, "If they try to do anything to us, we'll make mincemeat out of them all. Don't give in!"

The manager came, wearing boots up to here. He saw us all at the ticket tent. "Fellows! Why aren't you working?"

"Because the foreman did this, that, and the other to us."

"No, look, boys, go on and yoke up and I'll pay you the full day. And as far as that damned foreman is concerned, I'll take care of him."

He went to leave his horse and came back. He didn't even stop to take off his spurs but went right to the tent. The foreman was there, making out the tickets, when he lit into him. He treated him like a dog and fired him.

On the eve of the Revolution, early in 1910, a *peón* rebelled in Temisco and an *hacienda* administrator named Juan Posada killed him. I saw it because I was there. The Spaniard came upon the *peón* standing idle and without warning the administrator beat the man with the very whip he used on his horse. The *peón* got angry and insulted the man: "You wretch, why do you hit me, you son-of-a———" Then he grabbed a stone and wanted to throw it at Posada. That's when Posada took out his gun and *zas!* But the people were determined not to submit any more and Juan Posada was put in jail in Cuernavaca. After that, we worked more contentedly, more freely, and if anyone said anything, the *peón* answered back. Now the foremen knew this; now they didn't say anything to us.

There was justice then! Not like now. This man Posada was rich and was an administrator and yet they did not let him go, not even for money. They kept him in jail and it wasn't until the Revolution came and the rebels opened the jail that he got free.

That's why I say there was justice in those times. It is true that we were almost enslaved, but *don* Porfirio was *don* Porfirio and his was a true government. There were not so many little governments then, no Agrarian Department or Forestry Department or so many courts to fatten themselves. There was only *don* Porfirio and although he favored the rich, laws were obeyed and the poor got justice. Now, if you have money there is justice; without money there is none!

In those days, it was the *caciques* in our own village who oppressed us most. They had money and rode fine horses and were always the officials. They took advantage of poor girls. If they liked a girl, they got her—they always enjoyed fine women just because of the power they had. One of the head *caciques* died at eighty in the arms of a fifteen-year-old girl. Another, José Galindo, had yokes of oxen and hired many peasants. He gave the men *tortillas* and sent them to the fields, then he would go to their homes, just for a little while, to be with the wives. These rich men worked hand-in-hand with the Díaz government and if someone complained he would be punished.

Before my time there had been an effort to overthrow the *caciques*, but it failed. The people were very angry because the titles to the communal land had been sold. The titles were lost when the authorities of Azteca, fearing that a revolution was coming, decided to deposit the documents with the ex-priest of Azteca who was then living in San Agustín Tlalpan. So they went to that village and left the papers there and only the elders knew where they were. Ten years went by and the elders decided to bring back the titles. They went again to San Agustín Tlalpan and learned that the priest had died.

"What about the land titles?" they asked the priest's servant.

"Who knows where he left them?" she said.

Later it was learned that the *hacienda* of San Gaspar had the titles. The *hacendado* set up a cattle ranch on the land and put in several forest guards. Now the Aztecans couldn't go there for firewood any more because they would be killed. They or the forest guards would be found dead in the morning. A lot of blood ran on account of the communal lands. If any outsiders came to Azteca at that time, they were killed before they got out of the village. The Aztecans were angry.

The owner of San Gaspar decided to get rid of the land. "A great deal of blood has flowed because of this. I am going to sell it." The *hacienda* of Temisco agreed to buy it, but first the owner of San Gaspar sent a letter to the president of Azteca telling him that if the land was not redeemed in twenty-four hours it would be sold to Temisco. A courier was sent with a white flag and the letter tied to his gun. Only this way would they let him in. He rode his horse to the Royal House, which is what they called the municipal building in those days, and lots of people followed him. The president read the letter which said the village had to pay eight thousand *pesos* for the land. The president was sad, for where were they going to get such an amount? He rang the church bell to summon all the people. They came and the plaza was full, and the president read the letter to them.

Felipe Galindo and all the rich men were there, but no one offered the eight thousand *pesos*. It was a lot of money then. Felipe Galindo could cover the amount so he called the president aside. "You, come here," he says. "Look, there is money. Tell the people if they like I will redeem the land tomorrow but they will have to pay me back in installments. I will do this on condition that the ranch and all the cattle go to me. They can pay me from what they earn in the forest."

Well, everyone agreed and they accepted it. The next day they organized and marched, with music, to San Gaspar. There, the rich man made a banquet for them and received them well. They said, "We have the money, now let us see the titles." He went to get the documents. They were the very ones that had been given to the priest!

The people were paying off the installments, a little at a time, twelve and a half *centavos*, twenty-five *centavos*, when the uprising came. It began in Guerrero and about twenty Aztecans joined when the leader came to Morelos. One day, the Revolutionaries were riding in the plaza, past Felipe Galindo's house. He had a big house on the corner of the square and he was standing on the balcony, watching them.

He said aloud, "Poor things, there they go. With two *centavos* worth of lard I could fry them." That's what he said . . . because he had money.

Sure enough, a woman heard him and immediately went to tell the Revolutionaries. "We'll see about that!" they said, and sure enough, someone else went to tell Galindo. "Be careful because they are going to kill you." So he was on guard, but instead of killing him the group went to see the leader from Guerrero. They told him they would join him if when they got to Azteca they would all go and kill Felipe Galindo. The leader promised he would do this if they helped him fight. When the Revolutionaries got to Cuernavaca, Felipe Galindo secretly went to see the leader. He brought a big sack full of money and said, "Look, I don't want you to pay attention to the men from my village. They are trying to kill me because they are angry. So don't listen to them."

The leader saw the money and said, "Don't worry, go home because nothing will happen to you." And he held back the men who wanted to go to Azteca. "No," he said. "Now we are going to Mexico City. We are going to take the city first, then we'll go to Azteca and you can do whatever you like."

The Aztecans resented that, but they obeyed. When they were in the forest, they deserted and went back to look for Felipe Galindo. That one, not being worried, had just come home from the fields when he learned they were looking for him. He had time only to run into the *corral* and hide in a haystack. They searched the house and they followed his dog. The dog went straight to the haystack and gave away his master, whom they killed on the spot. That ended the village debt. No one had to pay Felipe now because they had killed him.

Time passed and Felipe was forgotten but later a son of his, José, sued Azteca and won. But it wasn't for eight thousand *pesos* any more. This time it was twelve thousand. That was an enormous sum and the people had to pawn everything, their grinding stones and their earthenware pots. The other villages in the district helped out when they heard that the district seat was in trouble. That's why San Agustín and Santa Catarina have receipts stating that they own part of the forest. Everyone rejoiced because the money was raised and paid and the land titles were not lost. But what good did it do? Soon after that the *caciques* took over and wouldn't let the poor plant any more.

The Revolutionaries entered Azteca for the first time exactly on March 17, 1911. There weren't many of them, only about thirty, led by Lucio Moreno. They wore their *sombreros* on the back of their heads and held their muskets in their hands as they rode in.

I was on the road at the time, almost at the entrance to the village.

With the help of my neighbors, I was carrying my wife to the *temazcal* for a steam bath because she had given birth to our first child. You see, it is the husband's obligation to bring the water, to heat the stones in the bathhouse, and then to slowly, carefully, carry her there on his back with a tumpline. So that's where I was when we heard them coming. Naturally, they took us by surprise.

Moreno and his men had come to kill a few people and I was already resigning myself. I said, "Well, they will kill me because of my wife but I will not leave her." I took her into a yard and crouched down behind the wall. "Now, how will I get out? If I run, the more likely they will kill me. Better let them find me here with my wife."

Well, I stayed there and some of them rode in and didn't say anything to me. They went on riding fast, with their muskets high, running, running, until they reached the first corner of the main street. They shouted, "Long live the Virgin of Guadalupe! Long live Francisco I. Madero!" and rushed to the *palacio* and began to burn it.

I left my wife in the *temazcal* and went to see the *palacio*. I was worried about the land titles that were there. I remembered, eh? I came running. "They must have burned them already," I thought. I began to hunt among the papers. A lot of us from the village gathered there. I asked an old man, "Listen, what about the deeds? What happened? Did they burn them already?"

He said, "No, boy, they haven't been burned. The deeds are in San Agustín Tlalpan. They are stored there. Don't worry. But you are doing right. You use your head."

So then I left, satisfied. I wasn't worried about the papers of my own house because they were safe in Cuernavaca. I was thinking of my village.

Everything continued to burn there because they threw gasoline on it. At that time I didn't even know what gasoline was. After that, Lucio Moreno's men remounted and left for Elotepec. No fight took place. Nothing!

The next day when we went to the *hacienda* to work, the foremen asked us what happened. "Have they entered Azteca? Did they enter already?" they wanted to know.

"Yes, they were there."

"And how many of them were there?"

"Hmm, well, about three thousand or so." That's what we told them!

"*Caramba!* And what did they do?"

"Nothing. That is, not to us. It's the *caciques* they are after. They all ran away, all the *caciques*."

"And are they well armed?"

"*Uuy!* well armed, nothing but shotguns and plenty of ammunition!"

"*Újule!* Then we are really in trouble. Look, if anything happens come and warn us."

"Sure, sure, don't give it another thought. I'll come." Of course, I wasn't going to come! Why should I?

It wasn't until afterward, about ten days later, that Bernabé Labastida came. He, too, was a *maderista*. He, too, began to shout about the same things. "Long live Madero! Long live the Virgin of Guadalupe!" But he had about sixty men. Bernabé Labastida and his brother Ezequiel had been jailed by the *caciques* of Azteca. Demetrio Guzmán was the one who had them sent to prison because they were *leyvistas*. People like that had been jailed all over the state.

Francisco Leyva had ruled in favor of the Labastidas returning. He got them out and sent them to Azteca. They came and began to hunt for the enemies who had sent them to Quintana Roo. They began to search but found no one. All of them had fled! The president had even left without his trousers and took off for the hills in his underdrawers. He was the president of the *municipio* and all the *caciques* who were there had left. They didn't wait for Bernabé Labastida. So, this Labastida went to the Guzmán house but didn't find the person he hated; instead, he found the brother, Palemón. But that was even worse. Palemón didn't run because he hadn't done anything. Well, Labastida took him prisoner, carried him off, and shot him.

Then, after that, Bernabé went out of the village. We were with the auxiliaries in a trench up there at the exit of the village. I had no gun; only the older men were armed. There were about twenty of us, but I was just an onlooker. Then all at once we saw Labastida with a great big *sombrero* on a great big horse. All the armed men jumped into the trench and shouted, "Who goes there?" He began making signs to us with his *sombrero* not to do anything. He came over to where we were and greeted us. He was a very good man, when he was a nobody. But when he became colonel, *újule!* he became a terror. Well, that was where we met Bernabé Labastida.

We had always complained about what was happening to our village forests. We had a special feeling about the forests. The *caciques* had finished them off, swallowed up everything, cut down the forest. It was on account of the forest that they were rich. So, this was what we shouted to Bernabé Labastida: "We'll help you fight, but for the forests! The forests!"

"Don't worry," he answered. "The mountain forests will be preserved."

Then we went to the *barrio* of San Pedro, to take positions at the foot
of the hill called the Hill of Honey.

After a while, *don* Jesús Mora arrived. The soldiers of his own side
brought him in. They went up to the Mountain of the Treasure to get
him. That was where he was hiding. He was a nobody, a hanger-on,
the caretaker of the town square, that's all. Well, they killed him there in
San Pedrito.

Then after that, the soldiers went back up and we came to see if
Palemón was dead yet. There we were, all of us, watching the poor
fellow. He hadn't died yet. So we stood around him and he said, "Take
me away from here." But we didn't dare to because we were afraid of
Colonel Labastida.

Then somebody said, "Let's take him over there to the first little
house. Nobody is living in it. Let him be there and perhaps he won't
die."

There was a man by the name of Cleofas, a forest guard, and this
one Bernabé Labastida did not kill. But as Cleofas had gone around
with the *caciques*, Bernabé took him prisoner. The only punishment he
gave him was to make him an errand boy, a courier. Bernabé said to him,
"All right, now you are going to kill Palemón. He hasn't died yet, has he?"

Cleofas told him the truth—that he was still alive.

He said, "Now, you are going to kill him." He gave Cleofas a pistol,
a great big one. "Go on now, with this you will kill him," he said.

Well, when Cleofas got there, we had already moved Palemón over
to the little house that no one lived in. There we are, all around him,
when this man arrives.

He says, "Well, it can't be helped. I am going to kill him because
Bernabé ordered me to. So, there's nothing that can be done."

So then he comes over close to Palemón, who was lying down, and
says, "Well, what would you have me do, brother? I am going to kill
you because the colonel ordered me to."

"Don't kill me, man! Don't kill me! Wait and see if I recover."

"But he already ordered me to. If I don't, he'll kill me."

Then all of us said, "But, man, you can leave from here and that
will do it. Don't kill him. Better go away from here. What we better
do is bring him back to his house and see if he still has a chance of re-
covering."

Then one of the men who was on the street corner called, "Go on.
Here comes Moreno . . ."

So, as there was nothing else he could do, Cleofas began to shoot.
He was firing with his face turned away. He had no courage, he was
afraid. He turned his back. That's the way he was giving it to him.

Naturally he didn't hit him. Well, finally a few landed. After that he says, "Come on, here he comes now, hurry."

They were already digging in the San José cemetery. It was right close by. Without losing any time, they grabbed hold of Palemón and went to put him in the hole, almost still alive. And they buried him. What else was there to do!

After that came the discord between Lucio Moreno and Labastida. That was when, because of all the things he had against Moreno, Bernabé Labastida went to kill him. They were up in Tlatlacapa there on the rise on the side of the mountain, at the exit. When he arrives, Moreno was there with his troops, but they were dispersed. They hardly expected anything. They were cleaning their guns. When he saw Labastida, Moreno said, "Well, well, the enemy approaches." He began to get the idea that they wanted to kill him. But he trusted him because Labastida called out, "No, comrade, what are you going to do? I just want to talk to you. We are comrades. We can't do anything to each other."

So he trusted him and let him approach. He greeted him without showing his gun. And that was when Labastida stopped short. He turned his carbine on him and put a bullet into him. Just like that! He had him right there in front of him and he shot him. And when this one felt the bullet go in, he wanted to shoot, but he was already keeling over and didn't hit him. The orderly, the one who attended Moreno, screamed. But Moreno fell over dead, immediately.

When Moreno's men saw this, they shot Labastida. They were cavalrymen and he was on foot, so they caught up with him right away and killed him. The others then picked up their arms to start a battle, but Teófilo Méndez spoke up. "What for? Why do you want to kill each other? What could be better than that you all join together, now that the chiefs are dead."

Well, so everybody accepted to join under one colonel. This was when Méndez said, "All right, then, let's go over to the trench and settle everything there."

So they all went down. I was still unarmed. As a civilian, I just followed them about. We came to the trench and everybody from the two groups got together and began to discuss who should be selected. Well, as Méndez knew how to talk and wasn't from around there, they trusted him. They said, "All right, then let Teófilo be the chief of us all, of the whole village."

But the post they gave him went to his head. Now that he was a colonel, he went to the village and began to drink. Then he fell in love with the sister of the Solís brothers. Marino, Rafael and Teodoro Solís had a sister, and he began to make love to her, right off, being a colonel.

He said, "Me, I'm going to get rid of all the Solís. To tell the truth, the men of Azteca aren't worth a thing, in my opinion."

This reached the Solís' ears. So they began to call their gang together. There were the three Solís brothers, Alfredo Herrera, Emilio, and Guadalupe, and some others. And this is what they decided, "Now we are going to kill this man, because it has already gone to his head. He says he is going to get rid of all of Labastida's men. So that it won't happen, we'll kill him first."

So out of this small group, Rafael Solís was named colonel. Then they sent a spy to see where Teófilo was drinking. He was in the little *cantina* on the corner of the *palacio*, drunk, and saying all kinds of things. So they went there and Rafael went in and stepped up to him. "Look, Colonel," he said, "we would like to discuss a small matter with you. Let's go over to the *palacio*."

He had no idea of what was going to happen. When they came to the *palacio*, they didn't go toward the president's office, but turned into the *corral*. When they got there, he began to think, "Oh, so they are going to kill me." He didn't want to walk any more and sat down in the middle of the *corral*. That was when Guadalupe put the bullet into him. Then they picked him up and threw him into the jail. The next day they buried him and that was the end of that.

Now Rafael Solís was colonel. But all the Moreno followers left and went to get a colonel and a general to lead them. Eutimio and José Conde were the men chosen by the Moreno group. But they didn't stay around. They were afraid that they would be attacked. Rafael's followers won out and that's the way it remained.

Things got tighter as time went by. Everybody left, even the chickens! Everything was lost. I was left to the four winds. At the end of 1912, going into 1913, they didn't let us work on the *haciendas* any more. So I went back to doing what I did before, making rope. But the thick rope didn't sell then, only lariats. With that we supported ourselves. I also began to plant in the hills, and that was all. That was my whole life now, planting the *tlacolol*. My wife did the same. "How else?" she said. "You can't work on the *haciendas* now."

It reached the point where martial law was declared. There was no way of getting out now. At the end of 1913, and into 1914, you couldn't even step out of the village because if the government came and found you walking, they killed you.

And the troops dug everywhere, looking for buried coins, because in my village there was a lot of money buried. Think of it, even the very poor were saving then. If a *peso*, one of those great big old silver ones, fell into their hands, they wouldn't change it and spend it but would rather go and pawn it to a rich man, if they needed a little money. Later they would get the *peso* out of hock and bury it. So the soldiers, the *carrancistas*, did a lot of digging.

That was when my second child, Manuel, was born. He died when he was eight months old. I was hiding in the hills when the troops took all the women to Cuernavaca. They came to take out my wife, though she was still in bed. She hadn't yet got back her strength when they made her walk from Azteca to Cuernavaca.

I was young then and we men were angry because they took away our families. About two hundred of us got together and we were thinking of rebelling and attacking the train because they said our families were going to be taken to Mexico City. We had all decided to rebel against the government, but no, we hadn't eaten for two days and we went to look for food in the village. *Uuy!* What destruction we found there. Corn was scattered in the streets . . . the *carrancistas* had destroyed everything.

Somehow we found food. Then we heard the cry, "Here come the women! They freed them in Cuernavaca and now they are returning." Esperanza was with my mother-in-law, carrying the baby. There I go running to meet them. They were unharmed but because she had walked to and from Cuernavaca, my wife had a relapse and became ill.

Then some soldiers entered my uncle Crescenciano's house to take away his daughter Berta. He was blind and mean but he was very brave. He grabbed a stick and hit whomever he could. While he was clubbing them and they were kicking him, my cousin Berta ran away with the neighbors. She wasn't violated but they practically killed my uncle. He went to Cuautla after that and died there. Later, Berta went off with a colonel. What else could she do, now that she had no one?

When my aunt Paulina saw what was happening to the girls, she wanted to marry off her daughter Macedonia. A widower from the opposite side of the village came to ask for the girl and my aunt said yes. But this man was very bad and none of the women in his *barrio* would have him. They said he practically kicked his first wife to death. And while we were making arrangements for the wedding, he carried off Macedonia without waiting to marry her. My aunt called on me because she loved me a lot, and I was the one to have to go and speak to him. Macedonia had three children with him, but one son died. I have always looked out for Macedonia and her children, and for her half-brother too, because they were the children of my aunt Paulina who brought me up.

The first village to be burned was Santa María, in 1913. I was at home when it happened and I went to see it three days later. It was entirely destroyed. The *carrancistas* had burned everything. The dead were hanging from the trees. It was a massacre! Cows, oxen, pigs and dogs had been killed and the people, poor things, went about picking up rotten meat to eat. All the corn and beans were burned. It was a terrible pity.

The people of Santa María began to come to Azteca and that's when the typhus epidemic started there. Two families came to my house and soon my entire *barrio* was sick. In every house there was fever and it spread through the village. My house looked like a hospital; all the sick people came to stay and then, *újule,* I got it and my wife, too. As my mother was dead, we went to my wife's mother so she could take care of us. My brother-in-law was there and he got angry because we brought the sickness. But what else could I do? I left my wife with her mother and went to my sister, who was living in the hills. She would give me a *taco,* for with my wife sick what was I going to eat? There, my other brother-in-law got angry because I carried the sickness to them. But I decided to be comfortable and I said, "Someone must support me until I recover!"

Well, both brothers-in-law and my mother-in-law got sick. She even died. Between the epidemic and the *carrancistas* we were nearly wiped out! Two weeks later, the soldiers came and burned my house. They wanted to kill me but they saw how I was and asked my wife what I had and she said, "The fever." Then they were afraid and left me alone. They took us out and set fire to the house. It was made of cane and they threw on some hay and lighted it and reduced it to nothing. That day they burned the village and threw out people everywhere. Even the municipal building was burned down.

Before we left my house, my wife said, "Let's put out the fire." And I said, "If I am going to die, let it burn up. Let's go." We left it burning and went to the hills, along with all the neighbors whose houses were burned. While we were running away, Carranza was bringing in more soldiers and telling them they could do whatever they pleased in the State of Morelos because it was Zapata's state. They could sack and kill, and all civil guarantees were suspended. He gave the order to destroy us and they killed and hanged everyone, even dogs, pigs and cattle. That's why it makes me angry when they celebrate a fiesta for him now. When I see Carranza's picture it nauseates me. I cannot bear to see it because of the ugly way he mistreated us then.

We lived in the hills for about three months. I built a little shelter for my wife and me and the baby. It was the rainy season and we had a little corn, so we managed until we dared go down to the village again. By then we lived wherever we could.

• • •

The Madero Revolution was almost over, and I still hadn't joined in the fighting. Madero was already President when Emiliano Zapata began to be heard of. It was in 1913 when his name was talked about, but we just criticized. Then you began to hear about Emiliano Zapata everywhere. It was Zapata this and Zapata that. But we said that he was only a peasant, not an intellectual man.

According to history, as it was told to us, he was born in Anene-cuilco. His father was a *ranchero* and the *hacienda* of Tenestepango cut him off from the land. They fenced in everything and he had to look for hay for his horses and cattle. Once the foreman stopped him and took away two loads of hay. The father did not protest. They just unloaded it and that was that. From the time Emiliano was a little boy, the *hacendados* had already invaded the lands around Anenecuilco and all of Morelos. The people had no land at all, everything was taken over by the *hacienda*.

One day the foreman beat his father. So Emiliano said, *"Papá,* why do you let him?"

"Well, my son, just think, they don't leave any land for us any more. Now it all belongs to them, water and all."

"Well, then why don't the people fight?"

"But how, son? Don't you see how strong *don* Porfirio is?"

"Hmmm. When I grow up, you'll see. I am going to fight."

From the time he was little, he was already dreaming. He saw all the injustices of the *haciendas*. The peasants had nowhere to plant except on the rocky hillsides. Not even water did they have! There was plenty of water, but it was for Tenexcapan, for Casasano, and for all around Cuautla, but not for the peasants. But Emiliano had made his plans. "Just wait until I grow up and you'll see!" he would say.

One time he went to fetch hay. Of course, he had to open the gate to get his horses through. The foreman caught him at it, took the hay away from him, and scattered it all over the ground. Emiliano said nothing. He just took his horse and left. The foreman says, "Just look at that damned upstart. I am going to teach him a lesson." *Zas!* He took several shots at him but Emiliano paid no attention and just kept riding.

So then the *mayordomo* said to the foreman, "But, boss, what have you done! Don't you know that the Zapatas of Anenecuilco are dangerous?"

"Hah! That doesn't mean anything to me."

"It's not just him. There are two of them. Eufemio and this one, Emiliano, and they are dangerous. You can't just talk to them any way you please. You'll see what is going to happen."

That was in 1909. When Madero was rising up, he invited Eufemio and Emiliano Zapata and Genovevo de la O to join him. Three of them went to San Luis. Madero had not come out in the open yet and Pino Suárez was with him by then. Pino Suárez was a lawyer.

Well, they sent Pino Suárez a message telling him where they would meet him. When he saw them arriving at a distance in the hills, Pino Suárez said, "But those poor fellows are only peasants. They are not going to be of any help to us."

They waited. They arrived. They greeted each other. Zapata spoke first. "Are you my general?"

"Well, yes, I am about to be. And you, where are you from?"

"I am from the State of Morelos. What are you fighting for?"

And so Madero told him what his plan was. "I am fighting for 'Effective Suffrage, No Re-election,' because *don* Porfirio is re-electing himself right along."

"Well, I have another plan in mind."

"What is it? Let's hear."

"I want guarantees for the peasants. I want the lands taken away from the *hacendados* and given to the poor, to the people. I want the land to be for the people not for the rich. My idea is—'Water, Land, and Justice.'"

Pino Suárez said, "Wonderful, man! That is a good plan. Let the peasants not suffer any more."

"Yes, that is my plan. If you come through for me, I will help you. I'll raise the people. Leave the entire south to me, all the way from Guerrero. All of it! I'll take charge."

"All right, then, it's agreed." And they said good-bye and left.

When they got back to Anenecuilco, he began to get the people together. Now we were strong. We had a plan ready, the Plan of San Luis as it was called, and it was accepted by General Madero. All we had to do now was to wait for the call to arms. Then it came. "Now!"

The people were fed up by then and they joined. Zapata and Genovevo de la O got everybody around there to rise up. Genovevo de la O took all of Ocuila and Chalma, all that sector. He aroused the people, all Indians, the ugly-looking kind from up in the mountains. And he attacked the trains. It didn't take long before he was well armed. He was the very first to have Mausers. Zapata's men had only rifles. Well, they established good communications and *zas!* the attack began.

Zapata was already on the march when Bernabé Labastida and Colonel Lucio Moreno entered Azteca, but his name was not yet widespread. He began in Guerrero in 1910 but it didn't get here until a year later.

I liked Zapata's plan and that's why, when he came to my village, I went to him. I still hadn't joined but I went up in the hills with *tortillas* and water. Instead of going to my *tlacolol* I went to see Zapata in his camp. He was in a little house but they wouldn't let me go in. They were suspicious. There were two guards right in front of the door. I stood at a distance, watching. He was sitting inside with his general staff. And he calls out to me, "What do you have there, friend?"

"Nothing, *señor*. Just my *tortillas*."

"Come in."

So there I go and now the others didn't stop me. He was a tall man, thin, and with a big mustache. And he had a growth on his right eyelid but it was later cut off. He had a thin high voice, like a lady's. He was a *charro* and mounted bulls and lassoed them, but when he spoke his voice was very delicate.

"Let's see your *tortillas*. Take them out."

And I gave them all to him. How he liked my *tortillas!* He and his staff finished them off.

"And what do you have in your gourd? *Pulque?*"

"No, *señor*, water." And he drank it.

What I wanted was to speak with Zapata, to sit with him. I had ideas although I still couldn't read. Well, I hung about for two hours when news arrived that the *zapatistas* had been attacked and that Rafael Solís was dead. The first shot fired by those tramps hit Rafael! Zapata ordered the whole line to move down because a leader had been killed. I went along with him until he said good-bye to me and left to fight. He said, "Tell the people of Azteca to give Rafael a funeral." So I waited to see Rafael and we carried the body back to the village. He was my countryman, even my neighbor, and I knew him well. I said, "Yes, now he is dead, there is no help for it."

Zapata was a *maderista* then. Yes, that lasted until 1913, when you could say that Madero turned. He became President but he didn't know what he was doing. He yielded to all the *porfiristas* who were around him. His very cabinet were all *porfiristas*, and Félix Díaz, the nephew of Porfirio Díaz, was among them. Why did Madero surround himself with the followers of Porfirio? Why did he believe them? General Victoriano Huerta had been going after Zapata but he halted when Madero took over the presidency, so Madero told Zapata to lay down his arms because they had won. Zapata and Pancho Villa went to Mexico City to arrange the peace and Madero told them to stop fighting now.

"It's all over. The Revolution is over. We won!"

Villa said, "But, General, the Revolution is not finished."

"It's not? Of course it is! I promised you we'd win."

"It's not true," Zapata said. "No, General, we must not stay here even for a little while. We can be betrayed. You trust this man Huerta, but I don't. The Revolution is not over."

"Yes, Zapata, I tell you it is. Everything is all taken care of. Huerta has placed himself under my orders. It's over, it's over!"

"No, I'll be going because if I don't they may cut me off here. I didn't even bother to have de la O called because he is more distrustful than I am. Villa can decide if he wants to stay with you or not, but I am leaving."

"Since Zapata says that he is going, I am going, too," says Villa.

They left and Zapata went off on his own. Madero considered him a traitor. But soon Huerta again began to go after Zapata and his men. That was precisely the reason why Zapata felt that he had to draw up his own plan. He called the people together and said, "Now Huerta is giving orders, and they are coming against us. Madero has betrayed us and is asking for peace."

Then Magaña, the famous lawyer who was Zapata's secretary, said, "Well, something has to be done. The people are up in arms and who is going to represent them now? Madero has turned."

This was when Zapata appointed Magaña. They held a meeting there in El Higuerón. He called together all the generals and said, "Now Madero has turned and there is no leader. Who is going to take over? Somebody has to be named and a plan has to be made. We are not going to go along with 'Effective Suffrage, No Re-election' any longer. That is what Madero fought for and that is finished. Now, for our plan."

"What is it called?" everybody asked.

Magaña said, "Let it be called the Plan of Ayala. The question now is to see who is going to take charge."

They began to vote. Magaña was elected but he refused. "No, not I," he said. "I'll help him, I'll stay by him, whoever he is, but I won't be the leader myself."

The same happened with Lorenzo Vázquez and with Montaño. They turned it down. They said, "No, in that case, let us appoint Zapata. That would be very good. He is a general, besides, and our leader." Everybody liked the idea. "Then, he is the one."

Zapata says, "Well, I guess that's it, since you have all voted for me. It means my death, I want you to know, but there is no other way. The responsibility is a great one. You are going to have to see me through."

"We are all with you." There were Montaño, Vázquez, and Soto y Gama, who is still alive.

I learned all of this during the ten years of the Revolution. How could I not have learned? After that I joined Zapata and was with him through 1914, 1915 and 1916. Luckily, I wasn't a *maderista,* I was a *zapatista.* I took up arms to go south with him. I said to myself, "I can't stand this any more. It's better that I go." My wife stayed behind.

Now we knew what we were fighting for—Land, Water, Forests and Justice. That was all in the plan. It was for this reason that I became a Revolutionary. It was for a cause! Many joined just to get rich, to steal whatever they could. Their sons are rich now, because the fathers robbed. When a plaza was captured, they would sack the houses and give half the loot to their officers. But others were true revolutionaries and joined to help Zapata.

In my judgment, what Zapata was fighting for was just. Porfirio's government took everything away from us. Everything went to the rich, the *hacendados,* those with the power were the masters, and we had nothing. We were their servants because we could not plant or make use of any lands that did not belong to the *hacienda.* So they had us subjugated. We were completely enslaved by the *hacendados.* That is what Zapata fought to set right.

I joined the Revolutionary ranks because of the martial law in Morelos, declared by Carranza. If they found you sitting in your house, they would shoot you. If they found you walking, they would shoot you. If they found you working, they would shoot you. That was what they called martial law. There was *no* law! Naturally, when I saw this, I said to myself, "Rather than have them kill me sitting, standing or walking, I'd better get out of here." And so I went to war along with the *zapatistas.*

CHAPTER VI

ESPERANZA

The Revolution

I was not afraid when the Revolution began because I didn't know what it was like. After I saw what it was, I was very much afraid. I saw how the federal troops would catch the men and kill them. They carried off animals, mules, chickens, clothes. The women who came with the soldiers were the ones who took away everything.

The government soldiers, and the rebel soldiers too, violated the young girls and the married women. They came every night and the women would give great shrieks when they were taken away. Afterward, at daybreak, the women would be back in their houses. They wouldn't tell what happened to them and I didn't ask because then people would say, "Why do you want to know? If you want to know, let them take you out tonight!"

For greater safety, we would sleep in the *corral*. Our house was very exposed because the street is one of the main entrances to the village and the soldiers would pass that way. Pedro took us to a relative's house further into the village. There the soldiers never entered. The *zapatistas* were well liked in the village, because although it is true they sometimes carried off young girls, they left the majority of women in peace. And after all, everyone knew what kind of girls they took. The ones who liked that sort of thing!

Sometimes the *zapatistas* would come down to the village and send someone from house to house to ask for *tortillas*. At other times, the government troops did the same thing. We always gave them whatever they asked for. After all, what else could we do? But the government men were the ones who behaved the worst and did us most harm.

One time the government called all the women together in the village plaza. I was in bed. My baby had been born a month before. Sick as I was, they made me get up and go. When they had us all there, they told us to go and grind corn and make *tortillas* for the soldiers and then come to sleep with them that night. We ground the corn and delivered the *tortillas* and went off into the hills. Sleep with the soldiers! Not for anything would we have stayed for that!

My mother remained in the village with my brother because he had corn and beans to guard. Sometimes Pedro would leave me with my mother and he would go back to the hills and come down at night. One day my mother died. She died at three o'clock one afternoon and we buried her at six o'clock because they were saying, "The government is coming." We didn't make a coffin for her, poor thing. We just wrapped her in a *petate,* put a board on either side of her and buried her. Pedro was angry when he came home that night and learned that I had already buried her.

I didn't feel my mother's death, probably on account of it being a time of revolution. Since we were always on the run from the government, I didn't grieve so much over her. After my *mamá* was gone, Pedro took me with him to the hills.

There was no work here any more and Pedro had nothing to do. There was no way to earn money for food. But I didn't want him to go as a *zapatista.* I would say to him, "Even if we don't eat, Pedro." He would answer, "What are we going to live on? If one works, the government grabs him and kills him." That's why when someone cried, "Here comes the government!" Pedro would take his *sarape* and make for the hills.

One day Pedro appeared, carrying his rifle. He told me, "Well, I've done it. I've joined up." He had become a *zapatista* because they offered to give him food. I got very angry but he said at least he would have something to eat and furthermore they would pay him. Then he told me he would have to go to Mexico City with the rebels and he promised to send me money.

He went with the *zapatistas* and left me without a *centavo.* There I was with nothing and I had two children to support, the girl of two years and the boy of two months. Also, I had in my care Pedro's cousin who was about eight years old. I cried in anguish because I didn't know what to do.

My brother was angry with Pedro. He said Pedro was lazy and didn't want to work. Pedro had planted corn seed but he didn't want to go to the hills to take care of it. My brother said, "Just as soon as he returns I'll tell him to take back his children and I will support you."

I would leave Pedro's little cousin to rock the baby and go to my brother's house to grind corn. I made the *tortillas* in my brother's house and then I would go running back to see about the children. My sister-in-law would let me have six or seven *tortillas*. I wouldn't eat until after I had divided it with the children.

That way the time went by, eating only a few *tortillas* a day. I had some china plates and I went to sell them. They would give me a handful of corn for each plate. I sold my grinding stone for three *pesos*, but at that time corn cost one peso and a half a *cuartillo* so the money lasted no time at all.

My brother became angrier with Pedro. "When he comes back give him his children, and you come here." I would say, "How can I leave him? I don't know where he is but he has gone to get money."

At last Pedro sent me sixty *pesos* with Pablo Fuentes. But where to buy corn? No one in the village would sell any. A neighbor woman told me to go to Yautepec where they had corn. We went together early the next morning. I had an infant in my arms and so did she. On the road we met the government troops marching to Azteca, but they didn't harm us.

We reached Yautepec and went to the house of an aunt of mine. She said to us, "Ah, my little ones, what have you come here for? Why did it occur to you there would be corn here? Here there is nothing."

The next day we returned to Azteca without a single grain of corn. I continued living all alone in my house. My neighbor, seeing me alone, began to talk to me of love. He would say things . . . that I should sleep with him and he would help me get food. I told him, "You are old enough for me to respect you as a father and you should stop saying such things to me." Then he asked me not to tell Pedro, but I said I was going to.

I never did tell Pedro, to avoid a fight and also because he might think that maybe out of necessity I had paid attention to that old man. And why start bad feeling with one's neighbors? I did tell my brother, though. He said, "Don't pay any attention to him. He is an old man. I will talk to him. He thinks because we are alone we don't know how to behave ourselves."

It was a dreadful time. We suffered a lot. I no longer had clothing and I wore a soldier's khaki shirt. For Pedro I had to make a shirt of some heavy unbleached muslin.

Then Pedro got sick and I had a very hard time. I had to sell everything I owned, a few little turkey hens and another grinding stone. When we get sick we always have to sell everything.

CHAPTER VII

PEDRO

Fighting with Zapata

I joined up with Colonel Leobardo Galván and traveled as far as Tula
and Toluca with him. I didn't really get into Tula as the lines were already moving toward Mexico City. We went to Coyoacán where we
were stationed for about a month. When they attacked us, they caught
me in what is now Revillagigedo Street. I was just coming in when the
shooting started.

I took off along San Antonio Abad Boulevard, all of us running,
with the *carrancistas* after us. When we got to the outskirts of the city
there were trolley cars coming in from Xochimilco. So I said to one of
the boys, "Let's grab a trolley because if we don't they'll catch up with
us."

And that's how we did it. We ran and ran and I hung on to the
first trolley car that came along. It was going pretty fast but I jumped
and caught it. It's wonderful how light on your feet you are when you
are young! I hung on tight and the other fellow caught me by the hand
and hung on to me. I could see another *compañero* hanging on in the
back and being dragged along. So I pleaded with the conductor, "Slow
down a little! Slow down or my *compañero* will get killed!"

He slowed down and we all managed to get on the trolley. I was
carrying two ammunition belts but had lost quite a few cartridges while
I ran. When we got back to the camp there in Coyoacán, the chief was

waiting to give us hell as we were really not acting under orders, if the truth must be told. But we did get away.

"Come on, now! Take up positions!"

We climbed up on the roofs, but the *carrancistas* never came. That same night, at about nine o'clock, our chief took us out of there. Who knew where they were taking us! Finally, we landed in Contreras. We stayed there a while and at about five in the morning, "Let's go!"—and off we went as far as Toluca. We waited there three days. Then the train arrived and we got aboard. First it took us to Lerma and then to Salazar, where we joined the men of General de la O. And wham! the fight started. They were real battles, day after day. They gave us two *pesos* a day and when we were under fire, they gave us one *peso* more. Daily. Yes, the money was paper, just plain cardboard, but it was pay.

One time, in Milpa Alta, they began to give us *chivo*, that is, our pay. It seems that the other men in the company were envious of us because they were not given anything. Well, we were talking and there was one of those bad characters, the rude ignorant type who curses and who is thoroughly bad. So this one says that tomorrow at this hour who knows which one of us the devil will have taken. I just looked at him and didn't answer. What could I say? And he was a captain, too! Well, the next day they shoved us out into the field at three o'clock in the morning. We had to be quiet. They didn't even let us talk. *Caray!* We crept close to the line and when we were almost upon them we opened fire. There were three detachments and we pushed right into their encampment and set fire to their shelters. Their corn and beans were laid out on blankets to dry in the sun and we even destroyed that. Some of us wanted to take the blankets and the food but no, we left everything strewn about and burning. It hurt us but after all it was a revolution! The *carrancistas* fled from us and we chased them through very rough country. We believed we were winning, but man! it wasn't that way at all! We followed them without knowing where we were going. They stopped on the other side of a hill, at the entrance to San Gregorio, and there a fourth detachment withstood us so we pulled back and joined our forces. There were five thousand of us but we were extended from San Gregorio to Topilejo. Our guides were local peasants and they sent General Chon and his men through the mountains. He was from Guerrero and he didn't know these mountains so they sent him to the worst peaks. His men were stopped but we weren't. We were sent along the side of the highway and General Teodoro's men went on the highway because they were all on horseback. The *carrancistas* had artillery and cannons but the shots passed over us because we laid down in the ditches. We were most afraid of the small bullets but even the machine guns didn't hit us.

But then we entered a place, a little cornfield in a valley, where the fighting was very bad. The *zapatistas* were on one hill and the *carrancistas* were on another and we were in the middle, fighting hand to hand with other *carrancistas*. The two armies got all mixed up, there in San Gregorio. There was a tremendous hail of bullets and the dead piled up like stones in a *milpa*. The man just next to me fell. We were together but the bullet hit him. At five o'clock a bullet got the captain who had been blaspheming the day before. In the dark we didn't know who was a *zapatista* and who was a *carrancista* because even the *carrancistas* didn't have uniforms then; we were all dressed just as we were, like peasants. We didn't even know whom to shoot at. The *zapatistas* on the hill above us shouted, "Don't shoot below because they are our men!" The *carrancistas* on the other hill also yelled, "Don't shoot because they are ours!" They stopped fighting; only the ones in the middle fought each other with the butts of their rifles and with knives. *Caray!* I will always remember that fight.

All I did was try to defend myself. They gave us a password to say. When anyone asked, "Who lives?" the answer was "Azteca!" or "Tlayacapán!" But then the other side also had a password, "Carranza!" If you gave the wrong answer, you were killed right off. The one who didn't answer at all didn't die. So I didn't answer. "Who lives?" I didn't say anything. Even if they put a bullet in me, I didn't answer. That's how I saved myself. We were being chased and I met up with someone. "Who are you?" I said. He answered by yelling to me, "Catch the man next to you! He's a *zapatista!*" So I shot at him instead. I stopped him but who knows if I killed him? In all my fighting, I never saw with my own eyes whether or not I killed anyone.

At first we believed we were winning but after two hours we could see we were being defeated. They drove us out of San Gregorio. Just before dawn I took the path we had come by. Others got lost but I saved them because I remembered the way. We got out and by dawn we could look back and see the battlefield from a distance. But how many dead! Yes, many *zapatistas* and *carrancistas* remained there. We couldn't get them out to bury them. How could we? From where we were we could see *carrancista* cavalry reinforcements coming. They shot at us but we were so far away we paid no attention. By then, many *zapatistas* were making their way back with us.

We got to Milpa Alta at about nine o'clock. We went to see which of our countrymen had been killed or wounded. None of Colonel Galván's men had a scratch, two of General Marino's men were killed, two of another general and five of Teodoro's. My colonel was pleased when he counted us. "Very good, men. We came out of it well. We ran and they chased us, but they didn't get one of us. Fine!"

But of General Chon's men, only the leader was alive. Not one of his men got out. They had come all the way from Guerrero just to die in San Gregorio. When the general left the line, he cried.

Ever since that time, I bear testimony that God saved me from all dangers. Because I was a believer, that's why. Having always been a very pious Catholic, whenever I went into action I would commend myself to God and nothing ever happened to me, not even a scratch. Not then or since. Yes, I came out of the war with a lot of experience. I have been in some very tight spots, at that time and later, too, in politics. All my former political opponents are gone, all gone. And so I am a living testimony that the one who entrusts himself to God will be protected from everything.

I came through another defeat in San Salvador. Again we were trying to reach their lines and each day we pushed forward, then we stopped and put up little straw shelters, with straw on the floor to sleep on. Mmmm, we were very happy and warm there, especially when it rained. We were sleeping one night, when they fell upon us at four in the morning, in a surprise attack. *Caracoles!* There we were nice and warm and *taca, taca, taca,* we jumped up and ran wherever we could. The people of San Salvador were coming out, screaming and screaming. How those women and children screamed! We didn't even shoot back because we were running. All of Galván's men got away, except a colonel who was ill. He couldn't get out and they killed him.

It was very cold and the hailstones were so big they hurt and even cut open the women's skin. One woman was hurrying away on horse-back when the horse caught its foot in a chuck hole and stumbled, throwing her. But the woman got up quickly and kept running on foot. They were civilians and we were armed and we fled together. We rested at dawn in a place called Soltocán. The *carrancistas* came after us again and there were no rocks to hide behind, only pine trees and brush and tall grass. We hid as best we could and waited for them. Man, it was cold! We heard the cavalry coming very close and our hearts were already jumping when the colonel gave us the signal to fire. *Caray!* They retreated because one side was a stream and the other side a steep hill. The horses couldn't run because of the chuck holes. They fell and couldn't stand up again. Then we began to go after the men but not those who escaped across the stream because they had entrenchments on the other side. We killed about 150 before we got away. All the people of Milpa Alta and San Salvador were living up in the hills and they gave us hot coffee and boiled *pulque* to warm us. We asked them for *tortillas* and they gave us many. At about ten o'clock, when the sun had warmed up a bit, we left for Salazar. They took us as far as Toluca where we camped for about two months. Then we went on to Alimaya, at the foot of the volcano, for about a month. After that, I got as far as Guerrero, fighting all the way. It took our detachment a week to get back to Cuernavaca. I finally got to Azteca.

When I arrived, I found my wife dying of hunger. She was still living in my house. We were practically newlyweds then; we had three children but one had died and we were left with only two.

But now I began to give her money and to provide food. I was earning money, with my gun, as a *zapatista* in the army, and we also found food in the abandoned *milpas*. One day I went to the fields to bring squash to eat. I went with another man and we saw something in the sky. What did we know about airplanes then! We hid between the stalks and were afraid. What thing was up there? The plane spotted some rebel lines marching near Yautepec and dropped two big bombs. How we were frightened!

A few days later the government troops entered Azteca and things were very bad. The *carrancistas* finally drove us out. This time I took my wife and children with me.

We still kept fighting. I would leave my wife in a nearby village and would go to join the battle. We had many combats over here near Santa María, and still more over toward Yautepec. Marino Solís, the general from my village, was in charge at that time. It was my colonel, Leobardo Galván, who joined us up with General Marino. Sometimes we were ahead and sometimes the *carrancistas* were. There were heavy losses, men and horses too. Fleeing all the time! Yes, sir, to the south. After they drove us out of Santa María, we went to Tejalpa. After a few days in Tejalpa, we went on to Jiltepec. One week in Jiltepec and then to San Vicente, where we hung around for a month.

The people were tired. They didn't want to fight any more. I remember well when Zapata came to San Vicente. He had been driven out of Cuernavaca and he said to us, "If you don't want to fight any more we'll all go to the devil! What do you mean, you don't want to fight?"

Everyone was quiet. They didn't respond. "Bah!" he said. "Then there's nothing I can do." We were exhausted, sleepy, tired, and the *carrancistas* kept chasing us, almost to Jojutla, near the border of Guerrero. Marino went to the general headquarters in El Higuerón and got together five or ten thousand men. He said, "Who wants to go with me? Let's go and break up their base! Our situation is desperate. We are at the state boundary. Where else can we go? Now let us go back!" Then he opened fire and his men cleared a path all the way back to the *municipio* of Azteca and made camp in the hills of Tlayacapán. There his brother Teodoro, who was in hiding, joined him. Marino was very brave. During the night they met the *carrancistas* and overthrew them all. He killed so many in Yautepec they piled up like stones. Later, he finished off practically all the *carrancistas* of the north because they ate mangoes and got sick and while they were stretched out Marino went in and just had to take aim and *zas, zas,* he finished them. That's why they named him General Mango. At that time, the peasants brought their mangoes to Yautepec. There was nothing to eat so people ate mangoes. A detachment of *carrancistas* was there, and when the peasants entered the city carrying their net sacks the soldiers took away their fruit and ate it. In a few days, *zas,* the entire army was shivering with chills, they were all dying of malaria. All of them! And what doctor was there then? What medicine? The streets were full of corpses and the women who followed their men in the army searched among the bodies to find their dead. But I didn't see any of that because by that time I wasn't in the army any more.

Meanwhile, Zapata followed the lines to Yautepec and went as far as Tizapán. He had cannons and machine guns but he lost them all. That was the last big battle of the war, there in Tizapán, in 1916.

That's where I finally had it. The battle was something awful! The shooting was tremendous! It was a completely bloody battle, three days and three nights. But I took it for only one day and then I left. I quit the army and left for Jojutla, without a *centavo* in my pocket. I said to myself, "It's time now I got back to my wife, to my little children. I'm getting out!"

That's why I left the army, for my wife. How I loved my wife! I didn't leave because I was afraid to fight but because of my wife, who had to find food for herself and the children. I said to myself, "No, my family comes first and they are starving. Now I'm leaving!" I saw that the situation was hopeless and that I would be killed and they would perish. Especially because my colonel hated me and wanted to kill me.

The colonel got angry with me because I said to him, "Give me a voucher to get corn for my family. You told me to bring my family and now I want corn for them. It is being distributed in the mill so give me a voucher."

"Why do you go asking for vouchers? Go into any house with your rifle and take some."

That bothered me. I didn't have the kind of character suited to the Revolution. I was not good at it because I was not base enough. So I say to him, "Look, I didn't leave my village to become a shameless thief. Indeed not!"

"What did you say?"

"Well, I say that I am not a thief to take things by force if there is another way to do it. They are distributing corn so why should I go and loot? I didn't come to rob."

"Shut your mouth because I am going to let you have it!"

Bah! I moved closer to the wall. I had a .30-.30 with me and I said, "Well, go on. Let's see. Just because you are the chief, you don't have the right."

He was getting up, taking hold of his pistol. Marino, the general was there, playing cards. He just saw what was happening and said, "Careful, Leobardo, eh? Don't go mixing with the soldiers, because they also carry guns."

At that time they were attacking us in Yautepec, so the colonel says to me, "We'll settle them first."

Later I spoke to my cousin Domingo, who was a *zapatista,* too. He was the son of my uncle Ángel Martínez. I say, "Well, what do I do now? I put myself in bad with this canaille and here he is my colonel. *Carajo!* Now I must get out of here because he is my enemy. But how?"

He says, "Yes, he can shoot you in combat."

"There you are! I will fall in combat. What is it to me that we are winning in Yautepec if he is going to shoot me? In truth, this is not good. Now I have two enemies. If the *carrancistas* don't kill me, the colonel will. It's all right to have one enemy but not two. Between them, they'll let me have it. So let's go. Even if you stay, I am leaving." Domingo's wife was with my wife so I said, "Man! We are going to die here and what will become of the women? Let's go and get them and we'll leave!"

That's what we did and we took them to Tleltlatenango, where we had to spend the night. The place was swarming with *zapatista* troops. We were now civilians but we hadn't turned in a thing. We had put all our guns in a sack. My cousin and I were very worried that the men might try to take the women away from us at night. A poor little thing of a colonel looked after us. He locked us in a room and slept against the door. At five o'clock the next morning he opened the door and got us started on our way.

We arrived in Jojutla at about seven in the morning. From Jojutla we went as far as El Estudiante, where we stayed for three days because I ran into trouble there. We were nearly killed by a general! I saw the general coming and I said to myself, "Now we're in for it!" Because we were deserters. Not only that, the general had ten men with him and we were only two. But the general and his men went past us on their horses and started across the river to enter Guerrero. A colonel from El Estudiante stopped us and said everyone was supposed to be disarmed; no one could enter the State of Guerrero with guns.

He asked me for my pistol but I gave him one that didn't work, the one I was carrying. My good one was hidden along with our rifles, under the clothing and blankets. I said to myself, "If they take away a gun let it be the worst one." They didn't see the rifles.

We were still standing near the colonel, when I said to my cousin, "Listen, the general just passed through with some soldiers. Let's go. We'll tell him we are going to Santa Fe to leave our families and are coming back to join him right after that."

And so we started to cross the river. The colonel had overheard what I said to my cousin and he began firing over our heads. He and his men were on horseback and we on foot, so naturally they beat us across the river. When we got to the other side, they had already taken away the general's rifle, horses, and all. *Újule!* They had disarmed him.

So this little colonel shouldn't have said anything, but no, he told the general, "Your own soldiers are turning you in. They said that you are a general. You have left the State of Morelos and so you have to give up all the rifles. Here is the order. So everything stays here."

"No, I am a delegate!"

"Doesn't mean a thing. Everything stays here."

So they took everything except a little pistol they let him keep as he kept begging for it. They even took away his horse and left him on foot. That was that, and the colonel took off.

Then the general said to us, "Ah, you scoundrels, you are going to pay for this. Even your lives are not going to be enough to pay me back for what they took away from me."

Caray! So I said to my cousin, "Bah! Let's go back." And we went back to the other side of the river where the women were. But the general and his men did not leave. They wanted to do something to us. On the other side of the river we were in for it! There were only two of us and they were ten, except that they had no arms any more. I said to my cousin, "What do we do now? What about the women? If it was just us, we could take off through here some place and that's all there would be to it. But with these women . . . ?"

He says, *"Caray!* Now we're in a jam. They are going to cross the river during the night and do something to us. We'd better get going."

"Yes, but what if they cross over and catch up with us? Look, you have a gun and I have this pistol and the rifle. We have plenty of ammunition, so why should we worry? We'll shoot at them and finish them off. If the soldiers come and try to surprise us the women will yell and warn us. We'd be right close by."

This is what we decided. So there were our families on the edge of the river and when night fell we moved away, only about fifty meters. We stayed in a cornfield like rabbits, just listening. We didn't sleep. We just listened and listened and said, "Come on, now, and you'll see what you'll get!"

Well, they never crossed the river. They were afraid, too. Fine! The next day they didn't leave. They were waiting for us to cross over. Then later, that little colonel came and spent the day with us, so the general thought that now we were with him. They finally went away on the third day. We didn't leave for Santa Fe until the following day.

We came to Santa Fe where civil rights were already being guaranteed. There was no more martial law and they didn't search us. We had a horse too, so from there we went to Buena Vista.

I worked in Guerrero for three years, as a plowman. They grew tomatoes and *chile* peppers there. I also planted corn for myself on the hillside. Then one of my babies died of a scorpion sting. It was a boy, too, twenty-two months old. We were making rope and had gone to eat when the scorpion stung him. It happened at about ten in the morning and he died at seven that night. We went to Buena Vista to bury him the next day. It was about two hours walk to Buena Vista. After that I joined up with another work gang and stayed with them a year, cultivating *chile* peppers.

Of our three children, now we had only the little girl María left, and she was sick, too. María was our first child and our favorite while she was the only one. My wife loved her as much as I did, and because we were ignorant you might say we were responsible for her death. Like fools, we didn't know how to take care of children so we gave her all she wanted to eat. We gave her bread every little while, bread and meat. I gave her all my meat . . . meat was cheap then. It was always, "Come, this is for my daughter for I love her so much." With that we practically killed her because her stomach went bad. She became sick with *ética*. She lasted a long time, until she was seven, but she never got better. And the Revolution made things worse. After that we had no way to cure her. There were no doctors and she died. They say she died because we loved her too much.

On the same day my little daughter died a battle broke out in Buena Vista between the turncoats and the fleeing *zapatistas*. Zapata came, Saavedra came, de la O came, lots of generals came, and about ten thousand men. They came by way of the hills, through rough places, along the roads, and they attacked Buena Vista because the *zapatistas* there got fed up with the Revolution and became *carrancistas*. We heard the shooting and later the landlord of a place in Buena Vista arrived, without his *sombrero* and with his clothing torn. He was a rich man and he was hungry. "Give me a *tortilla* because I haven't eaten since yesterday. They chased me out. The truth is they let me have it. I had no idea what bullets were until now."

I say, "How many did they kill? They used so much ammunition!"

"The truth is they are devils. Who can guess how many are dead? I didn't know what a volley really was. It is frightful! Are they dogs? If one fell, the others went right over him. We couldn't even take aim without trembling with fear."

The shooting went on for days so when it was time to bury my little girl we couldn't go to the cemetery in Buena Vista. We had to go to Tlaxmalaca and that's where we buried her.

And so we had no one left then. But the following year, in 1917, my daughter Conchita was born. She was like a first child and we favored her a lot. She would throw things and we couldn't do anything with her. That's the way she was, very bad-tempered. When we left Guerrero she was about two years old. We had been there three full years. In all that time I had no other women, absolutely none. I couldn't because I didn't earn enough. But I didn't suffer the hunger people in my village were suffering.

In 1919, we left for Jojutla. After three months there, we went on to Cuernavaca and from there to Azteca.

Ah! I was on the way back from Guerrero when the news of Zapata's death came. Mmmm! It hurt me as much as if my own father had died! I was a *zapatista* down to the marrow of my bones. I had a lot of faith in Zapata's promise, a lot of faith. I did indeed! I was one of the real *zapatistas!* I felt very bad, but there I was on my way back from Guerrero. I believed the news. Yes, I believed it right away. First they killed his brother Eufemio and then they killed him.

They tricked him, that's what they did. They tried so many tricks on him before, but he never fell for them. I guess his time must have come . . . he took the word of a man by the name of Guajardo.

This Guajardo was a colonel in Carranza's army, with a detachment in Oacalco. When General Marino was encamped in the hills of San José, in Tlayacapán, Guajardo sent him a message saying, "Either you come here or I am coming there." He was asking them to fight and, feeling very cocky, Guajardo went there. And, yes, the *zapatistas* lost. About five men of Azteca died there in San José. Later, Marino sent a message, "You beat me for the time being. This one was yours. Now it is my turn. I want you to visit me again."

Now Guajardo felt very *macho*, very brave, and he went. *Újule!* All his men were finished off. Marino began in San José and then took all Tlayacapán, all Cahuamilpa, and even Oacalco. Oacalco was left without a man! Then Guajardo says, "In truth, in all the combat I have seen, this has never happened to me. Now I have no more men!"

It was because of his fury over this that he betrayed Zapata, in 1919. First, Guajardo attacked his own comrades, the *carrancistas*, in Jonacatepec. When Zapata learned of this he sent his congratulations. He said, "Guajardo has turned. Now he is a *zapatista* because he fought *carrancistas* and won." And Guajardo wrote to Zapata and said, "Yes, now I am a *zapatista*. The proof is that I stood up against Carranza."

Yes, Zapata believed him because Guajardo had killed a lot of men in a whole day of battle. Zapata went to see him and congratulate him. Guajardo said, "Yes, my general, you can count on me. Here are my men." Zapata said, "That's fine." In that sense he believed him. Then Guajardo said, "Let us have a little celebration. You say where."

"Well, in San Juan Chinameca," said Zapata.

"Good. I will go there and we'll make a fiesta because I am pleased that we are united."

They agreed to meet in San Juan Chinameca. But what this Guajardo did was set up an ambush. Zapata came down from El Higuerón with all his troops. He went ahead with only four of his men. Zapata's *compadre* arrived first and went in to where Guajardo was. They greeted each other and had a little talk. The clarinets played a welcome in honor of the visitors, but when Zapata stepped into the net, *zas, zas, zas,* they shot him and he died. The three men with him also fell. The *compadre,* who was with Guajardo, said, "What is that shooting I hear?" And the other one said, "You would like to know, wouldn't you? Well, it is this." And, *zas,* he pressed his pistol and killed him. That's the way it happened.

Then Guajardo had the idea of calling together all the people there and asking them if they knew whether the man stretched out was Zapata or not. Many said it wasn't Zapata and he shot those. So the others were forced to say it was Zapata. But later, when Obregón turned *zapatista,* the tables were turned. Obregón was the head of Carranza's entire army but he went to join up with Genovevo de la O, he went to place himself and his army at de la O's services. But de la O had a lot of men and was very brave and he ambushed Obregón. Obregón said, "Look, now I am a *zapatista,* now I am your comrade."

Genovevo de la O was very amusing. He spoke like a little Indian, the way I do. He answered, "Is that so, friend? It won't be for me the way it was for my general, eh? You aren't going to be the same as that traitor Guajardo, will you?"

"No, man! I am now with you."

"The truth is, I don't believe you. Do you know how I will believe? Have Guajardo killed because in betraying my general he has betrayed the nation. He is going to betray you, too. For me to believe in you, first kill him. I will wait for you here. Until I see him dead, I won't trust you."

So Obregón had that Guajardo killed and then Obregón became a *zapatista*.

CHAPTER VIII

ESPERANZA

Three Years in Guerrero

We went to Guerrero because Pedro was a *zapatista*. We could not come back to our village for they would have taken him prisoner and killed him. We went to Guerrero through Jojutla by way of Tlaltizapán. When we crossed the El Estudiante river, he threw away his rifle so the Guerrero authorities wouldn't arrest him. My cousin Domingo was with us. We had a black horse that belonged to him. Who knows where he got it from . . . it was the time of the Revolution. Domingo was a *zapatista*, too.

We crossed the river and then we were in Guerrero. "Now where are we going to stay?" Pedro asked me. I said, "You know best."

We arrived at Santa Fe. There were some women there grinding corn. They said they were from Guanajuato. They asked us to take them to Buena Vista on the horse. Domingo said, "Let's go have a look." So we took the women to Buena Vista and once we were there Pedro and Domingo decided to stay. So we did.

In Buena Vista we went to *señor* Bernardo Cantara. "If you want to work for me," he said, "I won't look any further for *peones*." He asked them whether they wanted to be a plowman or a field hand. Pedro chose plowman.

Later on, when the rainy season was close, Pedro said, "Now we will cut palm leaves to make our house." We were well off in Buena

Vista because the men were paid and in addition were given corn. We had no problems there. They built two huts, one for Domingo and his wife, and one for us and our two children.

We continued working, but Domingo could not stand the work and soon left. We stayed on quite a while . . . three seasons. Then, *don* Bernardo gave Pedro a little plot of land to plant.

I ground corn and later on washed clothes for *don* Bernardo's family. I would take my two children along so they could be at my side in the master's house. We had another boy, Manuel, but he had died of smallpox in Azteca. Then María and Gonzalo also died on me and I was left alone. The girl died of a sickness. She got very thin and as it was the time of the Revolution, there was no doctor to go to and she died without medicine. The boy died of a scorpion sting.

And so I remained all alone. *Don* Bernardo's wife saw me there so sad and crying, and would call to me from her house. She would say that everyone had gone to work and that I should come to be with her. That's how I began to make *tortillas* for them. I always grieved over the death of my children but as there were other people there in the house I had to act as if nothing was wrong.

In the afternoon, the *señora* would take me to the gully to bathe. We would also bring the men their dinner. The death of the children affected Pedro, but it is not the same as with a woman. He cried a little but the grief soon passed. I believe men don't feel, or they feel very little. I feel deeply. Three months went by after their death and I was still crying and crying. I kept remembering how they were. I couldn't get out of my mind the way they walked, the clothing they had . . . I even wanted to sleep in the cemetery and stay there all the time looking at the bit of earth that covered them. And he, when he saw that I was crying, would scold me and that made me angrier and more resentful.

My daughter Conchita was born practically on the Buena Vista hill and was baptized there. *Don* Bernardo was her godfather. A woman took care of me there but I don't know whether she was a midwife or not. Anyway, she lived there and knew how to care for women who were going to give birth. The way she attended me was different from in Azteca. There in Guerrero they don't give massages or medicines for *los aires* during pregnancy, and they don't bathe the mother in the sweathouse after the baby is born. The midwife takes no more interest in her and doesn't even come back.

I got on my feet about two weeks later and bathed in lukewarm water outside the house. And that was all. I received no other treatment.

I was like a new person after I started to have children again. I was no longer so lonely. I really missed those children who had died and

that's why it made me so happy when Conchita was born. We loved her very much and it was as if she had been our first-born. We spoiled her a lot as it was five years before the following child was born.

We spoiled her, but we also beat her when she cried. She was very bad-tempered. She always wanted to be fed first. If she saw that we were going to eat before her, she would throw herself on the ground and thrash around in rage. That is why her father said she should be given her food first. It made us laugh; we didn't hit her for that. Her father would take her out for a walk so that I could eat without her seeing me. If she saw us eating, she would want to be fed also and it could have done her harm to be eating all day long.

Whenever Conchita got angry, she would throw herself on the ground. She was a real crybaby. Later, when she was bigger, she would get mad because we didn't allow her to go everywhere she wanted.

We came back from Guerrero because Pedro did not want to stay there any longer. He said, "We have our own house in Azteca and that is where we belong."

I was sick, too. I think it was from "cold" as they did not bathe me in the *temazcal* after I had Conchita and I didn't always have "hot" food to eat. Pedro would go out to sell the tomatoes he had planted. He would leave me sick and alone. I was often hungry and would look at the tomatoes and feel like eating them. One time I got up out of bed, took two tomatoes, roasted them on the hearth and ground them up in the mortar. Then I ate the tomatoes with *chile* peppers. Later on he arrived with the *tortillas*. "Have you eaten?" he asked me. I said that I hadn't, that I had only prepared a tomato with *chile* pepper for myself and that was all. He said that they were bad for me because they were "cold." "Cold" foods are bad for a "cold" illness.

My trouble was that my abdomen hurt me very much. I was skin and bones and had fevers every day. Pedro had a lot of people look at me, but nobody cured me. He said to me, "As soon as I have the harvest in, we will go to Azteca. They will cure you there." That is the reason we went.

When we got to Azteca, he had a woman look at me. "It's because you are pregnant," she said. "That's why your belly is big." I was here for about five months and nothing changed. So then Pedro said, "The thing is that you are not pregnant at all." And he took me to another curer. This one said that I had "cold" in the belly and she really began to treat me. I was sick and that was the reason I wasn't having children. "It doesn't matter," Pedro said. "The important thing is for you to get cured." She gave me a medicine to take and smeared greases all over my body, oil of camomile, oil of rosemary, and others. There were five different ones that she used. Then, when I was better, my aunt Gloria said to me, "Silly girl, now that you are cured, you are going to have another baby."

"It doesn't matter," I said. Being sick, I couldn't go out anyway. I always had a fever.

I wanted to be cured as I never felt right. But I didn't want any more children. I have always had a horror of having children. The thought of being pregnant would frighten me and sometimes it would make me angry because I was the one who was going to suffer. I cried and cried every time I felt that I was pregnant, especially with the first child because I didn't know what was going to happen. Then I cried even in the daytime and when I was walking in the street.

At night, when my husband took me I became angry because of the danger he put me in. But when I didn't want Pedro to come near me he scolded, saying, "You don't want me because you have some other man." So I had to let him and then I would be pregnant again.

I know that what happens is God's will, so I say, if children come, good, if not, so much the better!

I was glad to be back in Azteca. The village was the same but a lot of people were missing because they had died of hunger. They swelled up and died. Almost none of my people were still living. My brother was alive but he was far away in Puebla. His wife had died and so had his children. I went around asking for my brother and they told me he had gone far away. When he came back later, it was just to die . . . he was very sick by then.

The Revolution was almost over when we came back from Guerrero and Pedro began to work in the fields. He planted the *tlacolol* and hired himself out as a field hand and in the dry season he made rope.

Five and a half years after Conchita's birth, Rufina was born. It didn't matter to us whether the child was a boy or a girl. Pedro said that it was all the same to him. "Whatever the ladle brings." All children mean money, because when they begin to work, they earn.

But we always wanted our children to be born when the moon was full, so they would come out strong. Even a tree should be pruned in the full moon to have it bloom again.

PART THREE

CHAPTER IX

PEDRO

Village Politics

When we arrived in Azteca there was nothing here. The streets were completely deserted. It was like a forest, all the streets were choked up with weeds. That year, in 1919, in January it had rained four days and four nights. What a downpour! We said it was the Deluge. That's why when we came home, everything was covered with weeds and plants. My house was overgrown with flowers and grass but we began to live in it right away. I cleaned it up and pulled out the weeds. Then I went to see my uncle Agustín's house. All I could see was a narrow path because the streets were covered up. *Újule!* What a terrible state his house was in. The *carrancistas* had burned his kitchen and taken away what remained of the roof tiles. Most of the roof was gone. Everything was gone!

The people who had stayed on here, those who didn't take up arms, were the ones who took advantage of the situation. I went off to the Revolution because of an ideal, to follow Zapata. Naturally, there was no gain in it for me. But a number of those who stayed behind, who didn't even leave their houses, took things that didn't belong to them. My neighbors, for example. They remained and took everything others left behind. When we got back, they had cleaned out my house, appropriated everything!

You could say there was peace around here by the time we came back, but for a long time I didn't go out of the house for fear of the *fede-rales.* There was a detachment of *carrancistas* in the village and I had been a *zapatista,* so naturally I was afraid. I didn't go out. There were no more *caciques.* They had all gone to join the Aztecan colony in Mexico City. My neighbors and relatives still hadn't returned to the village. Then, little by little, they began to come back. We had been scattered but now we began to ask for all the families and soon we began to live again.

I wrote to my uncle and told him I had returned and what should I do about his house? He sent back word that he wanted me to take care of it. "See if you can get back the roof tiles. They are in the trenches outside the village. Tell my *compadre,* the president, that I give you permission to take the tiles because they are from my house."

I showed the letter to the president and he said, "Yes, yes, go get them." When I got there, other women from the center had already made two trips to carry away tiles, but I took all the rest. I carried them to my house and kept them there for my uncle. Then I received a letter from him. "Man, I am sending a few *centavos.* Buy the wood and whatever you need to cover up my house."

Very well. I hired two masons and tiled the roof over the main room of the house. The kitchen was completely destroyed. I wrote to him, "There are some tiles left over. They are here."

This goes to show that I am not covetous. If I had been I would have told him there were no more tiles. I did all that without pay because he is my uncle, but I didn't take a single tile for myself. I didn't steal a thing because my honor is worth more than a hundred tiles.

My wife and my little girl were sick when we got back here. I had them treated by herb healers because there weren't any doctors. Conchita was cured right away but my wife was sick because of her ovaries and took longer. That was why I brought her back to Azteca, to be cured. There was no happiness until my wife got well and a baby girl was born. This was my daughter Rufina who died later, when she was already big. Eighteen months after she was born, my son Felipe was born. Now my wife was back to normal. That was what I wanted.

When Felipe was eighteen months, he got the *chipilez,* the illness of jealousy, because his mother was about to give birth to Martín. Jealousy, that's what it was, because the baby keeps on nursing at the breast even though the milk isn't good any more. The breasts are dry by then. That is what does them harm.

Felipe nearly died of *chipilez.* He became skin and bones. He was brought up on nothing but cow's milk after that. He couldn't eat solid food any more. So the doctors recommended nothing but milk. The doctors were medical students who were sent to the village. *Doña*

Juliana and other curers were treating him too. Besides, *don* Nieves, a
homeopath who knew about treating children, was also curing him. He
was very good, too.

And so Felipe kept growing and growing. He drank so much
milk, the milk sellers had a battle there in front of the house. He drank
one liter a day; all he was eating was milk, milk, milk. And so each of the
two milk sellers tried to get the business for herself. One day they met
outside and began to fight, breaking their jars and spilling the milk.

In 1920 the president of the *municipio* was *don* Alberto Bello and
he was not doing much for fear of the Revolution. The people did not
respect him. They stole and committed all kinds of abuses. There was
no money and men couldn't find work.

Then we learned that Obregón became a *zapatista*, and all the poor
and ragged of Azteca began to shout, "Now we are all comrades! Our
General Obregón is a *zapatista*, too. This is it, *compañeros*. The Revolution is over!"

I was happy and I even went to see the people who were shouting.
They said, "Don't be afraid, comrade, now we are all *zapatistas*. The
very government has turned."

Obregón was seated right away because Carranza fled. They killed
him there in the port of Veracruz and then Obregón was the President.

After that, things began to change in Azteca. The state Governor
sent Colonel Jesús Montoya to be our president. Being an energetic
and tactful man, and representing the Governor, naturally, Montoya
tried to win over the people. But as he came in uniform we were all
afraid of him. He began to call us together. As a matter of fact, I did not
go to the first meeting. They told me that this Montoya was giving us a
lot of assurances and saying that there was no reason to be afraid any
more . . . that anyone who tried to kill an Aztecan would die! I could
hardly believe it. "Just politics," I said. "I'm not going."

Finally, he began to get us together. He went on horseback round-
ing up the people to come to the meeting. "There is no reason to be
afraid any more. Come on! Lots of times you were right. You've been
burned. But I'm president now, so don't be afraid. Now whoever is
against the people has to deal with me!"

Fine! Well, little by little he convinced us and finally we went. I
still had my doubts, but Montoya got us together. He encouraged us
and even defended us from a colonel who still wanted to suspend our
civil liberties. He was about to hang a *zapatista* but Montoya came
running out with his pistol and stopped him. The colonel left Azteca
but some men were already waiting for him and he was ambushed and
killed. After that we believed in Montoya and went to work to improve

things. We began to clean the streets and whitewash the chapels. He even organized dances! There wasn't any music, just a mandolin and a small guitar, but he would say, "Come on, dance! There is nothing to be afraid of any more."

But there we were, naked, and we were embarrassed. We had already worn out our old clothes and there were no new ones. So he said to us, "Look, boys, aren't you ashamed to be going around like that, almost naked? The forest is yours. Go on and make charcoal . . . get to work. Enough is enough! Forget the Revolution. What's done is done! Whoever is dead, is dead. Those that are left, are left! So, go on, get to work. Make charcoal and go and sell it. And if you can't sell it, I will buy it myself. I have axes, saws, and everything here. I will give them to you so you can get to work. And get some clothes! Just look at yourselves!"

Fine, but not I. I was afraid of the *federales*. I did not go, and as a matter of fact I didn't know how to burn charcoal. I held back but my relatives asked me to come along. "Come on, man, come on! What's wrong with you, boy? You have to learn how to burn charcoal."

I had an old ax, an awful one that didn't even cut any more. I said, "What, me with my old ax? But I won't beg for another one."

Well, I filed my old ax and went along with them. That's necessity for you! My relatives helped me set up and fire my first kiln. As I didn't know how to take care of it, the wood burned up. The second one came out all right.

And so we got to work in earnest. Once we were there we forgot all about selling the charcoal to Colonel Montoya. We sold it to whomever we pleased. There were a lot of us. The whole village became charcoal burners. We practically cut down the forests at that time. We piled up our charcoal and then we carried it ourselves for there were no animals. So it was up onto our backs and over the mountain to the railroad station.

The charcoal sold for twenty-five *centavos* a sackful. In four trips I made a *peso*. I felt I was earning a lot of money. And while I made the trips, I had my own little kiln in the forest burning more charcoal. We got no less than fifty or sixty *pesos* a week from one kiln. Whew! I felt I was rich. And there were no taxes then; there was only a provisional government, not a constitutional one like now.

We were able to dress ourselves and we finally began to eat decently. Now we began to come back to life. After that, the next most important thing was to get drunk once more! I said to myself, "Now I'm back on my feet. Now I've straightened myself out. Good-bye, Guerrero! I'm never going back. This is the place. The forest has brought me my freedom!"

And so I kept on prospering more and more. I realized that I my-self was destroying my forest but everyone was doing it and, well, man! I wanted to eat a bit, too!

In those days gold was in use. They paid us with it like any other money. It circulated among us but the merchants did not want to change it for us. They wanted a discount even though it was gold, pure gold. And there were no stores like now, only little tents in the market.

Well, about eighteen months went by when those damned Aztecans who lived like drones wanted to get rid of Montoya. Even the *caciques* in Mexico City interfered. They said, "Why should an outsider be ordering Aztecans around? We have had enough! He has exploited the place and gotten fat and now it's enough!"

Then they showed their claws. Whew! The things they didn't blame him for! And as always, the humble people of Azteca remained meek and silent, even though they had reason to speak up. But nobody said a word. Poor Montoya said, "Aztecans! Say something! What harm have I done you? Speak up! Say it to my face."

But who was going to answer? We were barely beginning to get over our timidity, but not to the point where we would demand proof. Not that! Bah! Anyway, they put up *don* Hesiquio Olivares for presi-dent. *Don* Hesiquio went around ragged, with the seat of his pants out, peddling chewing gum, but by the end of the year he had built a house, and a fine one too.

It all came out of the forest. At that time, a carload of charcoal paid the *municipio* ninety *pesos*. Well, there was a lot of money coming in! Three or four and sometimes five and even six carloads a week went out. There you have it! He built his house and fixed himself up. Now it is an *hacienda*. He got rich. Yes, sir! I kept my eye on him. He was president for two years and that was enough for him. It was a free *muni-cipio* in those days and that was why he was able to pocket all that money.

In those days, *don* Luis and Alfredo Núñez were contractors, but they brought in outside people, from Toluca. They began to cut down trees, little thin ones, starting from the railroad station on down. Natu-rally, they soon ran into me. I was in the way and they went right over me and my kiln as if I were nobody.

I said, "All right, now, why are you covering over my wood?"

"We'll get ours out of the way very soon because by tomorrow it will be charcoal."

Mine was just beginning to be ready because we cut down big trees. They cut little ones and it was charcoal the very next day.

I said to them angrily, "Look, who brought you people here?"

"*Don* Luis. He brought us from Toluca."

"Well, something has to be done. You'll see!"

Well, about two weeks later Azteca rose up to reclaim the forest and the foreigners were all put in jail.

We Aztecans still burned charcoal, but neither *don* Luis nor Alfredo was in the village any more. They ran away. They got rich from the forests and took off for the capital. Yes, they were the ones who wanted to exploit the forest, the sons of the *caciques* who had fled to Mexico City.

After *don* Luis and Alfredo left, the other contractors didn't bring in workers from outside. They used only us Aztecans. I and others, like Nacilifrando, Refugio Gutiérrez, the Herrera brothers, were against the cutting down of the forests. But we just looked on as we couldn't say a word. The people weren't awakened yet.

In 1920, I was *mayordomo* of San José and I organized many co-operative work parties to improve the *barrio*. The first co-operative was to fix the streets. My street was a rough, rocky hill and I began to talk to the neighbors about paving it. I got the idea because I had gone to a meeting called by Víctor Conde, the schoolteacher, to set up an improvement committee. Six people from the center had arranged the meeting and when I arrived they sat me way in the back, as though I wasn't even a citizen. "Very well, so I am not a citizen here," I said to myself. They elected a teacher to be the president of Material Improvements and they claimed they were going to fix the streets and do a lot for the village. Fine, but I thought to myself, "This is all a lie. These people are teachers. They're not going to bother themselves about the streets. For that you need a peasant."

They were fooling themselves and I told them so but the six of them were all in agreement and they didn't pay attention to me.

So after that I began to get my neighbors together to pave our street. Margarito, Mauricio and I were the leaders and we organized the work. I myself collected money from passers-by to provide drinks for the men who worked. At first the municipal council wouldn't help me but later they contributed the barbecue. What else could they do? We worked only on Sundays, starting off with fireworks and ending up by eating and drinking together. And we worked only between planting seasons so it took five years to finish one street, from corner to corner.

Some of my neighbors even hated me because I made them work. One woman was very angry and she ran to sue us because we were digging in front of her house. Just think of it! Such ignorance!

The president summoned us and told me the *señora* was complaining. I said, "Come and see what I am doing and if it is bad, put me in jail." He and the *síndico* were my political enemies, but privately we were friends. So when the secretary jumped on me and accused me, they defended me. I said, "But, *señor* secretary, at the meeting of the Improvement Committee I heard them say they wanted to fix the streets and the terraces and now you are against it. Who am I going to listen to, you or the Committee? The Committee didn't do very much, did they? Right off, I thought that the good teachers were not going to bother with the streets. Let them see that the children don't grow up as ignorant as I am and let them leave the streets to us. They didn't pay attention to me at the meeting and now look at my work."

Yes, ever since that committee treated me like dirt I wanted to show them that we peasants had the drive to do it. Maybe we were not good in things of the spirit but in material things, yes. We fulfilled our duty and they didn't!

The president and the other officials went to see what we were doing and they saw that it was something good. After that, the neighbors didn't say anything. On the contrary, they even backed us up and worked with us. One man who had complained that we had knocked a stone from his wall even provided us with *ponche*.

When we finished paving one street, I wanted to begin another, and then build a water fountain, so that the people would be grateful. The fountain cost Mauricio and me a lot of work, we went all the way to the Governor in order to get the water pipes. We finished it and we have it to this day. And everyone admits it was because of me. Most of the people were not interested and didn't want to work, though I would argue, "But it is good for the public, isn't it?" Even my wife was angry with me because I was doing so much for the public and I wasn't giving her expense money. But how could I? I was always thinking of what to do for my village and he who has ideals doesn't eat or sleep.

In those days I didn't know a thing about politics. I still didn't know anything about elections but in 1920 they appointed me president of a voting booth. Elections were legal then, not like now when the candidates are picked beforehand. Not in those days! Well, we electors set up our tables and that was all there was to it. Then, it was the duty of the presidents of the voting booths to go to the electoral college, which was in the school. A week later we went there to elect a new president for the electoral college. It was his job to count the votes and mark them on the blackboard. The watchers had a right to see the votes and count along with him.

Víctor Conde, an honest candidate for the presidency, was ahead of the other candidate, Serafín Zúñiga. Conde was leading the whole village when Serafín Zúñiga came in drunk. He had money; he was the son of a *cacique*. Well, he came in, looked at the blackboard, and said, "To me that doesn't count at all. Zúñiga is going to be president anyway."

We just looked at him. What did we know about such things? Then I said, "How can you be president? Víctor Conde is ahead."

"It doesn't matter if Víctor Conde wins or not. I am going to be president anyway."

Then a man by the name of Manuel got into the discussion. He was young and strong in those days. "What did you come here for, anyway? You are drunk, so get out. No drunks are allowed in here. What do you mean by saying you are going to be president? Have you bought up the votes?"

"Who cares about that? I, Zúñiga, am going to be president."

Well, we were fools, you know! The count of the votes from Azteca, the municipal seat, was finished and Víctor Conde was ahead. Then came the surrounding villages of the *municipio*. The votes from Santa María arrived. They were just tied up, not in a ballot box or anything, just a package. So the president asked, "What do you say? Does this pass or not? The way they delivered it is illegal."

We should have said no, that they weren't valid, but all of us fools said, "Yes, let it pass."

Well, all of Santa María was for Zúñiga. Whew! Now it began to make more sense that he said he was going to be president, because with that village he beat out Víctor Conde. And then there was *don* Pancho, the secretary, who campaigned in San Sebastián. When Santa María was finished, San Sebastián came up. Nothing but votes for *don* Pancho! So then he said, "But don't take me into consideration. I am secretary and as an employee here I can't be president. So don't figure on me. It is going to be Zúñiga, that's certain."

I was the only one who was still half against the whole thing. I had already consulted with *don* Gumersindo, who knew about elections, and we had agreed to block Zúñiga. But as Gumersindo was old and gluttonous (the town council provided meals then), *don* Pancho said, "Gumersindo, you go over to the town hall and bring the food." And Gumersindo went and brought back a basket of bread, sardines, cheese and *chile* peppers. He no longer cared about what we had agreed on. He even forgot about it. So I stood alone.

Don Pancho took me outside. We were still *compadres* then; he was the godfather of my daughter Rufina. He says to me, "Listen, why don't you want it to be Serafín?"

I said, "It is not that I don't want him. It is that it is unfair that he went and bought votes. I can't speak for the others. I don't agree but don't pay any attention to me as I am not a majority all by myself. In spite of our agreement, *don* Gumersindo is not backing me up. So don't worry about me."

Don Pancho said, "Then it's Zúñiga. Yes, Zúñiga is already president."

So he won. He won because of the villages of Santa María and San Sebastián. That's why I said it was half-crooked. There were six councilmen in those days and they were all the sons of *caciques*—Prudencio Barra, Valentín Quiroz, Serafín Zúñiga, Emiliano Orfila, Nacilifrando Muñoz, and one other.

Nacilifrando was the son of a *cacique* but he was with us. He, too, wanted to save the forests for the villagers. Then we heard that two Aztecans in the colony in Mexico City were also demanding the preservation of the communal forests. They were Carlos Omega and Tranquilino Herrera. Carlos was a member of the Typographical Union and of the CROM, the *Confederación Regional de Obreros Mexicanos.* Later he and Tranquilino even came to Azteca to help us.

The day finally came when the people began to do something about putting a stop to the uncontrolled cutting down of the trees. When they saw that the municipal forests were being ruined, some of them stopped making charcoal. I fired my last charcoal oven at that time. We all got together and really showed our claws. We tried to close down the forest. Our opponents, the *centrales,* called us the *bolcheviques* because of our stand in defense of our communal forests. That's when "bolshevism" appeared in our village, because of the forests.

At first, we thought the word *bolchevique* was a dirty word but then we were told that we should not resent it because it meant "union." And when we asked why the CROM flag was black and red they told us what happened in Chicago. Man! They told us that in Chicago there was a rich *hacendado* and there was a lot of slavery because they worked more than twelve hours a day. And so the peasants organized against the rich to demand only eight hours of work. They asked the government to support them but, instead, the government came and killed them, almost all of them. It was a big massacre. So they lost because all their leaders were finished off, but after a time they grew again and then they won. The peasants prevailed and eight hours of work was established and then they became workers. The flag is black and red, to mourn the blood that flowed at that time. That's what they told us.

People said that the members of the CROM were socialists. It is true that the CROM leaders taught us that we, too, were going to work only eight hours a day; that there was going to be a fight for justice, or against injustice; that there should be equality, so that a man of high standing and a *huarache*-wearer would be equals.

And then, they told us, those who had wealth were going to share it with those who did not. At that time, a certain man who was director of a school in Cuernavaca would preach to us and give us pamphlets.

He said, "We are going to reach a point where money will go out of use. So there will be justice, and injustices will not be committed. Then you peasants are going to plant and that will be only the beginning. It will be the same with the worker; he will make the clothes and all the other things that workers make. The workers and the peasants will be the most important men. Then it will be, 'You give me your seeds, and I will give you clothing. You give me this and I'll give you that in exchange.'

"A time will come when everything will be stored. All the churches will be turned into warehouses. Everything the peasant produces will be brought there and an inspector will come, or maybe two or three inspectors, to inspect and to say how the fields are. This will happen in every area where there are peasants. The inspectors come and write down how much you spend each day and how much you earn. That's how they get their statistics and check up on you.

"We all have to eat the same. Whether you are intelligent or rich or poor, you eat the same and dress the same. That is the slogan of Russia. So we are going to be like that. They give you everything there. The government is also going to make the houses. Everything the same! The landowners who are rich now will have their lands taken away from them and they will be given to the poor to work. The rich will work also and everything will be stored up."

That is what they told me in 1921, in the CROM. Well, we believed it. "All right. It sounds fine to us that way." But the rich people interpreted it badly and that's why they didn't like us.

They said, "What do you mean, give them half of what we have? That is impossible!" They got angry because this version began to go around.

Some said, "But how can I take anything away from others? Wouldn't I be ashamed to eat what doesn't belong to me?" or, "Pssht! Who knows how long it will take for this to come about, if ever!"

The thing we all said was that we wanted justice. We were promised by all of them, the CROM, the Governor, and all the men over there in the capital, the ones they call intellectuals, the ones who understand everything or who are supposed to. They promised to defend us in every way. But they asked us not to do anything violent. That is what they preached to us, that if there were an injustice or wrong accusation against a person, they would stand up and defend us.

What those fellows were telling us was all a lie! Or who knows? Who knows how things are in Russia? I don't, and that's a fact! But it did not happen like that in Mexico. Of course not! Nothing happened! Here it is a matter of money and that's the end of justice. Money talks. Every time! But in those days we believed all the promises.

Because the councilmen were all sons of *caciques*, they began to say, "No, look here, *señores*, think of all the cattle our fathers lost. They persecuted our fathers and even killed some of them. It's not right! Why should we let the *huarache*-wearers come out on top? Look here, we must fight them. They are poor beggars and thieves. What reason do we have to say 'Viva Zapata'? We want our cattle back!"

That was what they went around saying. Valentín Quiroz was the top *cacique* before the Revolution and he tyrannized over us all, even the peasants with a little land, because he didn't like them. Now again, he and the ex-*caciques* were trying to prevent the people from planting on the communal land. I was one of the representatives who went and defended the peasants, I defended the poor and that is why the *caciques* hated me. But I said to them, "No! You still remember the times of *don* Porfirio when they tied the dogs with sausage instead of letting the people eat. Those days are over now. That's why the Revolution came, to give us a kick and wake us up. That's why Zapata rose up, to awaken the humble people. Times have changed and we do not permit these things any more. The truth is, the more the peasant gives in, the more he is trampled upon."

We continued to fight for our rights. The *caciques* were quiet but after a while Valentín began to work with the government. He wanted to get rid of the Herrera brothers, the Tyrants, as they were called, who were the leaders of the ex-*zapatistas*. Valentín kept saying, "Let's go after the Tyrants."

The so-called Tyrants were Revolutionaries and they were still armed. They had fought with Zapata. When I came back to Azteca in 1919, I heard that the Herrera brothers were bandits and went around stealing and collecting *tortillas* and food for the Revolutionaries. That was why they were called the Tyrants. I had known the four of them since we were kids. Pascual, the eldest, was my age, but we had not been close friends.

Before the Revolution, I was a customer of theirs. The father, José Herrera, was an old-time maguey-fiber worker and the sons followed his trade. They gathered maguey fiber, cut and prepared it, and sold it. I bought it from them to make rope. I earned more than they did, poor fellows. A pound of maguey fiber was worth twelve *centavos*. How much could they have made?

There was still no talk of the Revolution in those days. When Madero rose up, the brothers were still my cutters. They weren't even *ma-*

deristas. It was not until much later that they went with Zapata and became revolutionaries.

Well, when the Herrera brothers found out what the councilmen were up to, they drew up a petition to have the council removed and they collected signatures for this purpose. I was making rope outside my house when they brought the petition to me to sign.

Pascual said, "Valentín is seeking revenge and we are going to accuse him. He is saying we are scoundrels and thieves and that they will finish us off. Why? The Revolution is over, according to Montoya. Nothing doing! This can't go on."

Because I had been a *zapatista* myself, the council might do the same thing to me. So I gave Pascual my signature. Then Refugio Gutiérrez made another petition to stop the uncontrolled cutting down of the forests. I signed that too. Later, Pascual and Refugio joined together and we all traveled up to the railroad station to meet Carlos Omega, who came to give us advice. He listened to us and then he said, "What you want is easy! Why don't you ask me to join up with you? We belong to the CROM, which is strong, and we'll get that town council out for you right away and we'll stop the exploitation of the forest at once."

That was more like it! The villagers got down to work and we joined together, about two hundred of us . . . no, ninety-five was all at that time. We began in one of the small *barrios,* then we moved to the center. We had an office there. We sent a committee to the municipal *palacio* to demand that Valentín be removed but the committee came running out to call us—it was just a short distance—because the council was threatening to arrest them.

"Let's all go then!" So we went, about two hundred of us by then, carrying our flag, the red and black flag of the CROM. We were two hundred men when we started but when it became a question of prison they began dropping out until there were only seventeen of us left. Pascual was one of them. His brother Alejandro, who was a colonel, wanted to leave too, but Pascual would not let him. He grabbed him and held on and just wouldn't let him go. Well, the seventeen of us went, led by Pascual.

It is hard to describe the pride we felt. We were still carrying the memory of the Revolution with us. We had influence then, with Obregón. We had strength and we went and bought cigars, which I didn't even know how to smoke. Everyone had his instructions. Flag and all, we went into the president's office, smoking our cigars.

Don Pancho was there. He was the secretary. He said, "What is this all about?"

"Well, we are fighting for . . . this . . . about the work."

"What about the work?"

"Well, we want to be free . . . to . . ."

"Well? And why are you coming around here acting so fierce? What have we done to you?"

"Nothing. But we will see about that later on. We are just letting you know with all sincerity. Well, that's that . . ."

"Who is your lawyer?"

"Well, no one."

"All right. Then this is how it is . . ."

Well, a colonel came, the little captain who used to be with the *carrancista* detachment, and wham! before we knew it the seventeen of us were in jail! Pascual was with us and he tangled with the colonel. He said, "Go ahead, kill me! You know it is a crime to kill a man in prison. We'll have to have it out in the field. Don't think I am a peaceful man. We are going to have it out!"

Then they had a terrible argument later because Pascual's mother came to give us food and they pushed her around and wouldn't let her in. So this *señora*, who was also very brave, went after them with her fists and they ripped her shawl. But she brought in the food!

So Pascual got very mad and said, "It's just too bad I am locked in here! But it won't be long. That little captain is going to see what will happen to him."

The colonel tried to reason with Pascual. "Look, *compañero*, those are my orders . . ."

"That doesn't make any difference to me. You just better be ready. Pushing my mother around! We'll see about that! We'll find out who is more of a man, you or me."

Well, they had a terrible argument. We stayed in jail only seventy-two hours. At seven o'clock they took us to Cuernavaca. This same little captain took us. This was in 1922. We marched in ranks to Cuernavaca. There were ten of them and seventeen of us. But the captain said, "I am not tying them up. Let's go, man! Let's behave."

"Yes, we'll go. We haven't done anything but we are going. Why? For what? Bah!"

We left Azteca behind. There we were out in the country, but still we did nothing. "Don't worry, Captain. We won't run away. What for? We haven't done anything."

We even fooled around as we walked along the road. When we got near Cuernavaca, we all stopped. We said, "Look, Captain, won't you let us have our flag? The flag is arrested, too, so lend it to us. We'll form ranks with the flag in the middle. That's how we'll enter. You be at the sides and us in between."

We marched into Cuernavaca with the flag flying. We were shouting in unison as we went. "Long live the CROM! Up with the *huarache-* wearers! Down with the *caciques!* Down with the aristocrats!"

Whew! Were the people excited! They came out on the streets and said, "It's the rebels again! It's the rebels coming with the flag! Here they come!"

A whole lot of people followed us. We kept shouting and Nacili- frando even leaped up and down. Well, they did not let us in at the president's office in the town hall and they sent us to the Cortés Palace where our colonel turned us in. The captain there said, "Let me have the flag, please."

Well, we turned it over to him and wham! to jail. We were locked up for twenty-two days. Delegates came from the CROM but they wouldn't let them in because we had not designated them to rep- resent us. We could get nothing now. The offices were all closed to the CROM delegates. There was nothing to be done. So the delegates left. Whew! There we were, practically abandoned.

Then the officials threatened Pascual, Nacilifrando and Refugio with exile for having used the red and black flag in the town hall and for "sedition." The rest of us were to get five years in prison. There was nothing we could do. Well, five years pass quickly! ·

A fellow from our village stayed around, trying to console us. "Don't worry. Don't worry. Everything is being fixed up in Mexico City."

Then the jailkeeper came in with the newspaper. Whew! It said that if the seventeen peasants in jail were not set free in twenty-four hours, then the judges of Cuernavaca would go in under the same charges. Signed, Obregón! Even the jailkeeper jumped. He said, "Man! You've got influence! Just look at that, even signed by the President of the Republic!"

Whew! That was that! The next day came and at twelve o'clock they still hadn't turned us loose. What was up? It was anybody's guess. But they didn't let us out. My wife brought us food that time. She certainly did! She was always loyal. I could depend on her. In jail they gave us thirty-five *centavos* a day for food. Everything was cheap then.

Well, time passed and I thought they were never going to let us out, when all of a sudden, at seven-thirty one night, there was a shout, "All right! The seventeen peasants from Azteca . . . outside!"

José G. Parrés was Governor then. He was also playing politics be- cause some people wanted to get him out of the governorship. At that time it was only a provisional post. They wanted to get him out and he came around trying to fix it up.

So, they took us to see him. When we came out of jail, the delegates were there already . . . Carlos Omega, Tranquilino Herrera, and some others. All those who worked for us were there.

Carlos said, "This is more like it. This is a victory for us. Don't go and do anything rash. I know you are very angry right now."

I certainly was for one. I was ready for anything. I was good and mad now. More than ever before. I said to Pascual, "Look, let's go right now. Let's finish them off, beginning with the councilmen. We can do it in one night. Come on!"

"Calm down, calm down . . ."

"I've made up my mind! What sort of a thing is that? What do they mean by locking me up when I committed no crime! I've had enough. My mind is made up."

"Calm down, now, calm down."

There were older men around now, people who knew what it was all about. They took us there to Governor Parrés. He saw that we were all furious and said, "Look here, boys, those scoundrels took advantage of you because I wasn't around. I am a member of the CROM, too, so don't you worry. This is a great victory. But don't go around causing any sudden deaths because then we'll lose everything. None of that, eh! All that sort of thing is finished. Everybody observes the law, now."

Hmmm! Where did that leave us? I was very mad. Then we spoke. "Well, all right, but let us have a demonstration at least!"

"Do it, but make it an ordinary one."

So then we said to him, "But, man! We came to have the town council changed. We don't want them to continue in office. Also, we want the uncontrolled cutting down of the woods to stop. The forests should be closed now."

Nacilifrando decided to stop walking a tightrope and he announced his resignation from the council. He explained his reasons to the Governor. "In view of all the irregularities I have seen committed by the town council of which I am third *regidor*, I must resign. I go along with my people because I am not interested in revenge. It is true that my father was a *cacique* and died, but that is now a thing of the past. So, I resign my position and take my place with the people."

All this pleased the Governor. He said, "Well, fine. As far as the forests are concerned, they will be closed immediately! Now, in regard to the town council, the truth is that it is a difficult matter as Azteca is now constitutional. Look, why don't you give me three months? I will call for elections."

But Carlos and Tranquilino, as delegates of the CROM, did not want to accept this, nor did we. "No, nothing doing! Out with them, right now! It is the people themselves who are here asking. If not, we will drag them out."

Well, the Governor saw that he had a problem. "No, men! Don't insist. Don't go beyond the law! What can I do? The law does not act in that way."

And so that was when I learned this saying: "When the people rise up, there is no law." The people put them in and the people can take them out.

"No, sir! We make no concession, not even one month."

"All right, give me a week."

"Well, all right, eight days, then!"

The Governor got more courage! Genovevo de la O was Chief of Operations in Cuernavaca at that time and he was on the side of the Tyrants because they were his soldiers. They already had a plan, but Genovevo said, "Go and see the Governor. If he doesn't get them out, I will. I will get that town council out if I have to use force."

So, they said, "Well, señor Governor, you don't want to, so we will be going. Good-bye."

The Governor suspected that now we would be going to see the Chief of Operations. Well, the final arrangement was that we would give him five days to have the municipal president resign. Now we left satisfied. And that is the way it turned out; five days later Zúñiga resigned.

Well, so they set us free and we started back. But, first we bought a piece of red and black cloth and made another flag.

And off we went, the whole bunch of us. The people of the village were all waiting at the foot of Treasure Hill. They were a big crowd. The mother of the Herreras was there with a whole lot of horses. Plenty of cavalry. We stopped there and fixed up the flag and then entered Azteca once more.

We went as far as the plaza shouting, "Long live the CROM! Death to the Aztecan *caciques!* Long live the *huarache*-wearers!"

Man! And *doña* Prisciliana, the mother of the Herreras, was on horseback with her great big *sombrero* and her hair flying. What a woman! Whew! *Don* Nieves was there. He was connected with the *caciques* too, except he was kind of weak. He was standing all hunched up in the doorway of his house when Prisciliana rode her horse at him, making it rear up. *Don* Nieves just shrunk back as he could barely walk any more.

"Now what, you old fool, you old this and old that! Didn't you say that you were going to have my sons thrown out? Go on, why don't you do it?"

He did not answer. And everybody closed their doors. Wherever we passed, the people closed the doors. That was how we went as far as the plaza, where we turned around, still shouting. Then we rested. Now we felt a lot better. We had finally won out. We met every day to talk things over, to exchange opinions, and we always had the idea that we weren't going to kill anybody.

Well, now, this was it. Now the Union was formed, the Union of Aztecan Peasants, affiliated with the CROM. Now they had respect for us. The Union had won and we held even more demonstrations against the others, going through the streets shouting, "This is it! Look, the Union is on top!"

We threw out two town councils during that time, in 1923, and our people went in. Jesús Herrera, representing the Union, became president. Every first of May we put a red and black flag on the peak of the highest hill. When dawn broke, there was the flag of the CROM, on top of the peak! And three times we had a demonstration here. As a matter of fact, one of us even died on that account. His name was Remigio Herrera. A counterdemonstration was waiting for us with bombs and bullets, there in front of the town hall, and Remigio fell. After that we had no more demonstrations, but the Union of Aztecan Peasants continued to be strong.

In 1923, when Huerta went against Obregón, Carlos Omega and Tranquilino Herrera came to organize Azteca against Huerta. That was when the Herrera brothers again joined General de la O. The general gave them fifty rifles for the members of our union and we were very strong in the village government.

Pascual and his brothers were the leaders of the Civil Defense. In 1926, the churches closed down to protest against the government. That's when the *cristeros* began the business of attacking the Revolutionaries who, they said, were persecuting them for their religion, or who knows what. The *cristeros*, the ones who call Christ "King," came into Azteca but the Civil Defense fought them. There were only five *cristeros* and the Tyrants killed one of them. They never came back. What would they come back for? They knew the village was now armed.

So the government gave the Tyrants credit for it and kept them supplied with arms to continue the Civil Defense. They said, "Keep it up. Keep it up. You are loyal." Even I was given a rifle then. They thought that now we would defend the government and the state.

In 1925, the Union was still in. The term was over and the same town council went in again, Nacilifrando as president, *don* Prosperino, *don* Miguel and *don* José Ayala. That year they even made me *regidor*.

I didn't know about it at the time because I was practically in hiding. I was still angry at having been unjustly imprisoned and I was the enemy of the ex-president. From that time on I didn't present myself for guard duty and I kept away from the *palacio*. I didn't obey the law and yet they sent me my credentials as *regidor!* I went to the town hall and the president said, "Come in, *señor regidor.*"

"What do you mean, *regidor?* I am a criminal right now! I violated the law." But no, they respected me now because I was a candidate. I was the only one who accepted because the others were afraid, that is, they had named some *caciques,* too, but they were afraid of the *bolcheviques.* The *caciques* didn't open their mouths any more. Not a word did they say. We were on top now. So we set up an advisory council of three *regidores,* all of the union. I went home happy because my transgression of the law was forgotten.

Now I was a councilman but I was illiterate. I knew a little spelling and reading but beyond that, nothing. I had responsibilities and how was I going to carry them out if I didn't know anything? The secretary at the time was a man of schooling, the brother of a priest. Once I went to him and said, "Listen, I have been commissioned to make out receipts for guard duty because I am the Chief of the Guards. Make out the receipts for me."

"I won't make them out. I won't do it."

I felt rather bad at that because I was giving the orders. And he refused!

Then he said, "Now, look, don't be surprised. You order me and I am your servant. But at the same time I am your teacher. He who wishes to learn can come to me because I am a teacher. I am ready to teach you."

I liked that and I said, "In that case, I will be your first pupil." I really wanted to learn. That was my ambition. I attached myself to him and stuck it out and he taught me everything. He even taught me how to drink because he was a first-class drinker. A real drunkard! But I stayed with him in order to learn. We would close up the office and go to his house. I was always asking him to show me this and teach me that. I wouldn't leave his house until midnight.

I studied with him for six months. Then I began to answer the president. I said, "Now I know my work. Now I can function." By that time my eyes were opened.

Pascual Herrera was one of the very ardent *bolcheviques* at the time. He went as far as Ciudad Juárez to attend a political convention. It was on account of this that Pascual wanted to impress me and that was when I told him so many things that it nearly cost me my life.

He was coming out of the court one day because he was acting as a lawyer in a case, and I was sitting outside with Marciano, the magistrate. Pascual stopped to talk to me. He began to tell how much money he had spent in Ciudad Juárez and how he had made sacrifices for the village. He told me a whole lot. And then I plunged in.

I said, "Listen, do you want me to answer?"

"Yes, yes, of course."

But I was careful. "Now don't get angry, but I am going to tell the truth. I did not see you when I got back from Guerrero. People just told me, so don't go and get upset."

"Speak up, speak up. Why should I get angry? Not at all."

"Look, do you remember when you used to sell me maguey fiber? You were maguey cutters, the four of you, and your father. How is it that in that time you never went to Ciudad Juárez? Because you couldn't, right? How could you have gone to Ciudad Juárez on the money you were earning? But later you were more or less on the government payroll, they were paying you for being a Revolutionary, so to speak. A little from them and a little from the people helped you along.

"When harvest time came, we were the ones who went and harvested your *milpa* and brought it in to you without it costing you a *centavo* for *peones* or transportation. Then, when I came back from Guerrero you were buying a soap so fine that not even Mexico City could have produced it. You've got mud on you and it is coming off on the people. The people are with you, aren't they? How was I to know anything about your behavior when I returned from Guerrero? But people told me that the Tyrants were collecting *tortillas*, that they went from house to house robbing in order to eat, and that now they are considered thieves. That's why the people from the center don't like you. They don't say anything to us poor people, but we have mud on us, too, on account of you. And you can never get that stain off you. And so that is why I warned you not to get angry because I tell the truth.

"I was a Revolutionary, too, for a while, but there is not a soul who can point his finger at me and say that I stole a cow or that I stole anything at all. That no! When the begging for food began on account of the starvation, I was in Guerrero."

That's what I told him and more. "You went to Ciudad Juárez, but on the government's money, not your own. Sure, anybody can be a man on that basis!"

The magistrate was sitting there and Pascual said to him, "What do you say, Marciano? *Don* Pedro is telling me I am a beggar and a thief. How do you like that!" He even slammed his hat down.

I said, "Now, don't get angry."

"No, I'm not angry."

From appearances, he did not get mad, but he was really just holding it back. At a fiesta a few days later he wanted to kill me. I had finished my work in the court and was on my way home to dinner. The fiesta was going on and he was already drunk when he saw me. He saw me turning the corner and without my knowing it, he drew his pistol and said, "Here comes that so-and-so and now he is going to pay for it."

With him was another fellow by the name of Ambrosio, a relative of mine on my wife's side. Ambrosio grabbed his gun and said, "No, man! What are you trying to do? He has a bunch of little children. Cut it out!"

Ambrosio defended me. I passed by without going in and never even knew what was happening. I didn't find out about it until later. He was drunk, that's all, for after that he always spoke to me.

Well, I was *regidor* and once I had to bring the village guard to the *comandante*, there in Elotepec during the fair. The *comandante* was *don* Enrique, the uncle of my sister's children. I saw my nephew José there, already quite drunk. So I say to the *comandante*, "Listen, *compadre*, take care of the boy José, because the Herrera brothers are around here and they will abuse him." The Herrera brothers had a band of about thirty men, all armed and really dangerous. "They will hit him with their rifle butts, so please take good care of him for me."

He says, "Don't worry, I will."

I had my wife with me and later I say to her, "Just look at how this José is behaving! Something is going to happen to him so you go home and I will defend the field here a little while longer."

Then along comes the *comandante* and says, "Look, *compadre*, look at what he is doing. And he doesn't obey me."

I say to him, "Lend me two guards and I will put him in prison. That will be best. I will take him to the jail."

So we took him. He gave in easily, as though it were nothing. When we came to the bridge I say to the guards, "I will take him. He is going along nicely. You can go back to the *comandante*."

But when my nephew saw that they had gone he began to resist. He tried to beat me and no longer wanted to go along. At that moment Pascualina, the aunt of the Herrera brothers, passed by. She went and told the Herrera men that someone was beating up the *regidor*, so they all came, the whole Herrera band, with arms.

When my nephew saw this he headed for an alleyway which led to his *barrio*, but they cut off his retreat. They caught him at the crossing, on the road to Santo Domingo, and I came running up, shouting, "Don't hurt him! Pascual, just don't hurt him! Take him even if you have to carry him, but don't go hurting him on me."

"No, no, now I know he is your sister's son."

"Yes, take him to the jail. Tomorrow he will do public work, so don't do anything to him."

As there were many of them, they practically carried him off to the *palacio* and threw him in jail. On the following day, very early, my brother-in-law Chico, the boy's father, arrived. As he had no manners and was completely crude and didn't know what was right, he came running into the presidency and right up to the president's table, with his hat still on his head. Without waiting, the president said to my brother-in-law, "Who are you? Why do you come in this way? *Señor comandante*, take him to jail! Go on, go on, this is not the woods! Take him away and let him learn to behave properly."

And so they locked him up. Nor did Chico say anything, for what was he going to say? He had come to make a complaint, but with his hat on. Think of it! So they put him away. I said, "*Caramba!* now my whole family is in trouble." I didn't know what to do. My brother-in-law became very angry with me so I went and said to the president, "Oh, this is bad. It looks very bad for all my family to be in jail."

"But it's only for a little while," says the president.

I say, "Well, you are right. What does he mean by coming here with his hat on? *Caramba!* One shouldn't even enter a private house with a hat on, and more so here!"

In a little while my sister arrived. *Újule!* She really blew up against *don* Enrique, the uncle. He came running to me, saying, "Come on, *compadre*, your sister is here and *újule!*"

I say to him, "Make her stop! The president will surely put her in jail, too, because she doesn't have good manners either."

Then the secretary says to me, "Say, is she your sister?"

I say, "Yes, she's my sister. I do not deny blood that is mine."

"But, man! She doesn't resemble you in character or in anything. Just look at the way she is behaving before the president and *don* Enrique."

I say, "I am even ashamed to say she is my sister but she is, except that she is completely without breeding. All her family, too! Look at the way she is talking! Now how in the devil am I going to forgive this? But she is my relative, what can I do?"

Well, the president didn't lock her up, he only threw her out. By then my sister wasn't speaking to me. She was ready to hit the ceiling when she left. After that, I didn't give up until I saw my relatives out of there. We went to eat and when we came back in the afternoon, I said to the president, "Listen, shall I let out my brother-in-law?"

Yes, the president let him out and began to scold him. Well, my brother-in-law admitted his fault and was ashamed and asked to be excused. He left without speaking to me.

Later, I got out the other one, the son, who was in my charge. I say to him, "Do you realize what you have done?"

"Yes, uncle, but I was drunk."

"But restrain yourself, man. I have loved you all like my sons, I have clothed you, you are almost my own children. But you aren't grateful, nor your father, nor your mother. Instead you all have mouths that are completely ill-bred, without control. It wouldn't cost me any work to keep you here fifteen days, but no, it hurts me because you are my own blood. Get going, but correct yourself. And don't be hard on your father, because he is more than you. Also your mother, and one cannot say anything to them because they are old. No matter how much you pull the reins on an old one, the snout is already too stiff."

"Very well, uncle, yes, don't worry." And he left, also a little ashamed.

Then the president comes and says, "*Carambas!* What a race you come from!"

"Thank you, *señor,* they are my race, but what would you have me do?"

They began to laugh among themselves. I thought, "*Caray!* they are laughing at my race, but what can I do because it is true."

Well, that passed. About two weeks later, again I met my same nephew drunk. I said, "So you are going to start again? Here you are drunk." But no, he came and begged my pardon.

"Uncle, forgive me. I offended you, it is true, but forgive me."

I say to him, "Don't worry, you are forgiven, but don't continue with this, eh? I am your uncle and I love you like my sons, but if you go on with this inconsiderateness you will lose everything."

This nephew never gave me trouble again, but later, after their father died, I had a quarrel with Rodrigo, another of my sister's sons. This one also wanted to fight me, over a debt he owed me. But no, I preferred not to be paid than to fight with him. It happened this way. I had a little corn but it was only enough for planting and since it was already May, I was saving it for that. One day my nephew says to me, "Listen, uncle, lend me a *carga* of corn."

I say to him, "But it is the only *carga* I have and it is what I will begin planting with. It doesn't make sense for me to give it to you. No, no!"

He says, "Well, then just half of a *carga.* In eight days I'll return the corn."

Well, I gave it, sack and all. But it wasn't eight days! I waited fifteen days and nothing. I waited twenty days and nothing. Then I went to see him. I say, "Man! all I had was that half a *carga* you left me with and I've already finished it off. Now I want my corn."

He says, "Yes, uncle, yes, yes. Don't worry, this very week I am going to receive eighty *pesos* so I'll give you half, either in cash or in corn."

"Very well."

I went to him three times, and nothing. A month later I went again and he wasn't there. "Ah, the man is getting wise," I thought.

In a week I went back. This time Rodrigo was there and acting very brave. He still didn't want to pay me. He said that I spoke against his father, that who knows what . . . "My mother will hear about this!" he says.

I say, "What's bothering you? If you don't want to pay me, just say so. Why do you pay me with this coin? Don't think I am going to demand it or sue you. No. I am a man who knows how to lose."

"No," says he, "I'm going to give it to you, right in the snout. Just come here."

"And you are going to hit me, son?"

He was shorter than I and thinner, so I dragged him into the street, like a dog, like a dead dog. "Come out here, right in the street, if this is the way you are going to repay me. Come on, I'll show you how to be a man and how to be without shame. You faker, you've eaten it up and now you say no! Is that the way you pay?"

I stood up to him but he didn't want to fight. "No," he says, "I am in my own house, this is my home, why do you treat me this way?"

Well, we quarreled, but to this day I didn't try to make him pay me. Later, my sister got sick and they sent for me to bring the four hundred *pesos* I owed her. So I brought the money. "Look, sister, here is your money. You sent for it and it took work for me to get it, but here it is."

Then she says, "Look, brother, I know you had some trouble with my son. Take from this the forty *pesos* he owes you."

"No, sister, now I don't remember exactly what happened. I was drunk when I told him he could have it and after that he never paid me. No, I have given it to him as a gift and what goes out of my mouth doesn't go back in. That is a matter between him and me. As for you, here is your money."

She took it all and Rodrigo was there listening. Since then I haven't heard a spark from him. He never paid me and I never demanded it, though he is still here in Azteca. My sister finally threw him out of the house because of his wife and her two sons. It was that woman who was the bad one! She even tried to hit my sister and that's why she threw them out. It hurt my sister's heart. All her children came and drove out Rodrigo.

Then my sister sold the house and divided it among her children as their inheritance. She didn't give anything to Rodrigo. She gave most of it to José because he was the eldest. She sold the house for five thousand and gave three thousand to José and five hundred to each of the other children. My sister was left with only one thousand for herself. She bought her daughters a sewing machine and I asked to borrow the rest.

I told her, "You won't lose it. Lend it to me and I will keep it for you. But I want this money not to go to your other children. I want this money for Rodrigo. It is true he has hurt my heart too, but he is still our blood. If you don't want it to go to him because of his wife then give it to his daughter, your granddaughter. You have brought her up so let the money be for her."

Rodrigo had this daughter but his wife hit her so much that my sister took the child. This is why my sister didn't like her daughter-in-law.

My sister says, "Brother, what you say is good. Hold the money for me and when I die, if it is not used up, let what remains be for my granddaughter."

I say, "And now I'll tell you a story. Look, there was a father who was poor but who managed to make a living. This father was foolish because when he felt old he says, 'I am going to die. Now I will divide what I have among my three sons.' And so he gave each son his inheritance.

"The father was left with nothing, believing his sons would support him. But they no longer paid attention to him. Now they could get along, now they had their inheritance, now they didn't need him. The man was old and poor and he couldn't work. So he took his sack and went out to beg. He met a faithful old friend who knew him when he had money and he told him what he had done.

" 'Oh, how foolish you were!' said the friend.

" 'There you are. I am so old and now I don't have a thing.'

" 'I cannot help you for I am poor but I can give you some advice. Look, here is some money. Go buy a good thick chest. Then go to a junk yard and fill the chest with pieces of iron and glass and anything else there. But fill it full so it is heavy. Put a lock on it and keep the key. Put the chest at the head of your bed and never leave it without locking your little room. Soon one of your sons or daughters-in-law will come to visit you. They will ask, "What is this box?" And you must say, "Ah, my daughter, this is what I am saving for one of my sons. I don't want to spend any of this money. This chest is for the son who loves me best. It is full of money." And then let them look at it and shake it so they can hear it. You do this and you will see how they all come around again.'

"And that is what the old father did. He locked the chest in his room and went out to beg. When he returned he sat next to the chest and never left it. That is where he ate and everything.

"One day, his daughter-in-law comes in. '*Papá,* what are you do-ing?' She didn't bring him anything to eat. 'Are you tired?'

" 'Yes, daughter. I walk the streets to earn my food. But what can I do? Yes, I have my money here, but I am saving it for the son who loves me most. Look, it is all in this chest. It's full. Here, shake it. Do you hear? I am saving this for my best son.'

" 'Aaaah! How nice,' says the daughter-in-law. She left and that evening she told her husband about the chest of money. He says, 'Ah, *caramba!* And we didn't pay any attention to him! Don't say anything to my brothers and bring him something to eat. Tell him not to go and beg any more.'

"The next day, there she was bringing the old man his breakfast.

" '*Ay,* my little daughter! God bless you. You have pity on me. You are going to enjoy this money, eh?'

"For several days the daughter-in-law attended him well. The other couples noticed it and said, 'Well, why is she waiting on him now? It must be that he has something.'

"So another daughter-in-law went to see the old man. Then the three sons began to look after him. Now he had more than enough to eat and to wear. After many years, the old man was about to die. Each of his sons outdid each other in bringing tidbits to their father. Just before he died, the father said, 'My children, please do not open the chest until I am buried. The money is for all three of you. Divide it without quar-reling. Don't misspend it or give it to the government. It is all for you, but open it after you have buried me.'

"The sons did what he said. They buried him well and built a tomb. They had a wake with lots of ceremony and prayers and rosaries and then they opened the box."

I went on studying with the secretary but I didn't last out the year because what would my family do for food? I stuck it out through the dry season but in May I went to struggle, to earn something, for my family. I had little children and there in the town hall one did not earn much. I received ten *pesos* a month. That was not earning! So I went to plant my corn on the hillside. I also worked as a plowman for others.

I was very poor at that time, as though I had just returned from the war. My cousin Margarito was also poor but he had a *burro* to count on. I had nothing, not even a *burro*. So my cousin and I rented a piece of land in Yautepec to plant more corn for our families. It was not very big, only twenty *cuartillos* for the two of us. But for lack of money we couldn't go on and Margarito backed out. "I won't plant any more. I'd better turn over the plot to you."

Hmmm, now what do I do? *Caray!* And here it was already time to pay the rent with cash and I didn't have any. Margarito advised me, "Better get rid of it. I have no money."

I told a man, Francisco, that I was going to give up the plot, and as he knew the piece of land, he says to me, "Ah, *caray!* And why didn't you let us know?" He was working with his nephew Heraclio and he had his little team of oxen. "Let us plant it. You will also have a share. We will plant corn."

He encouraged me. By then I didn't want to plant because I was too poor. I had nothing.

"We have a team of oxen and a plow," says Francisco, "that way all you have to do is help us with your work, like a *peón,* and you get a share of the harvest."

"Hmmmm," I say to him. "All right, go ahead."

I went with him and I saw that he and his nephew were very good. Just the three of us went. At that time there was a shortage of rain. We planted and nothing grew. But we didn't get discouraged. We waited until the day of Santiago, the twenty-fifth of July. On the very day we planted again, the first rain fell, and the corn we had planted before was already growing.

I kept on working without knowing whether I would get anything out of it or not. Francisco didn't pay me, I worked as a *peón.* They were very good, they were friends and this Diódora was his wife. Diódora was just a girl, another one who wanted to get entangled with me, poor little thing, and because of that I became her *compadre,* so as not to be tempted into doing something bad to her. That was my thought when Diódora became godmother to one of my sons. But that was later.

Well, we produced a nice little harvest. Even though we planted at a bad time, the *milpa* produced. Each one of us gathered his share of corn and then we continued as friends. Francisco and I became very, very friendly, almost like brothers, even closer than his nephew, who later went off on his own. Francisco also got into politics and we went around together. Where he went, I went. He visited me, I visited him. We never left each other, we were always like brothers.

Later, when I was *mayordomo* of my *barrio,* I asked him to be godfather to the Holy Child and that is why we called each other *compadre,* but we were not really *compadres.*

I noticed that Diódora took an interest in me but I gave no thought to that. I paid no attention. I always went in and out of Francisco's house as though it were mine, but very honorably. At their fiesta time, I would say, "I will be at your house without fail." And that's the way it was for a long time.

Then he died. Refugio Gutiérrez was president at the time and he had tried hard to improve the village. He called together a *cuatequitl*, a volunteer work party, to build public washbasins and pave some streets. Then he fixed up the market place and the bandstand and a lot of sand was left over. The president had called upon the citizens to contribute one or two loads of sand and my *compadre* began to co-operate. He was very patriotic, too, a man of ideas.

I was making rope in the street in front of my house because it was not yet the rainy season then. So Francisco says to me, "Well, I already brought one load of sand for the presidency, now I am going to make another trip to get some for my house. I am going to whitewash my house."

"That's fine," I say, "but be very careful because that cave is no good any more."

Says he, "Don't worry, *compadre*, don't worry. I will do it quickly."

And he and his young son and two other men went. The Church bells rang at twelve and they didn't come back. Three o'clock and nothing. They didn't arrive. At four, Diódora came and said to me, "Well, what happened to your *compadre*? He isn't back."

That's when we began to run. "Let's go and look for them because the four men didn't come back. Four of them and not one returned!"

Yes, they were already crushed in that cave. They all died. The sand fell in on them. That night we didn't sleep. We went to get them out. Even the municipal president went and said he would get them out that night even if he died, too.

The next day I went to see Refugio. I had thought about it. An idea had come to me. I said to the president, to the *síndico,* to the treasurer, to the five of them there, "Look, *señor* president, the people are taking this badly because, in truth, they are saying that it is your fault for calling so many men to bring so much sand and you forced them to bring it and now this misfortune happened and now they are blaming you. And now what are we going to do for them?"

At that time cement mausoleums were not yet in use, people were simply buried in the ground. I say, "Look, wouldn't it be good if you would help me? I am going to collect money and we will bury the four of them in a mausoleum, but at our own expense. How much are you going to help me with as municipal president?"

He says, "That is a very good idea. I am going to give twenty *pesos.*"

We were still *bolcheviques* then. I covered the whole organization, beginning with the Herrera brothers. They say, "Who started this? This is very good." And they gave ten *pesos*. I made a list of all those who co-operated.

"Now let's go back to the town council, because they promised me money but so far they haven't given it."

We got there and the president says, "*Caray,* the truth is, there is no money in the treasury. Treasurer, let's see how much there is!"

And the treasurer says, "*Uuy!* there's not enough! There are only fifteen *pesos* here."

"*Ay, qué caray!* Then here are fifteen for you."

"Hmmmm. But I was promised twenty."

"Yes, but I don't have it. The treasury is poor."

"Hand over the fifteen." But I had an idea and I said, "All right, this is from the administration, now how much will you personally contribute?"

Then Celia, who was the treasurer and who had once been my secretary when I was *regidor,* gets up, takes out five *pesos* and says, "Here is my quota."

The secretary says, "Now the *señora* has done us in! Now we have to yield! Let's see what we can pull out of the treasury. See if it can lend me five *pesos.*"

Don Prosperino says, "Now there is no way out. A scourge on the treasury! This woman has compromised us. There goes five *pesos* from each of us."

I collected a pile of money, a little more than one hundred *pesos!* And everything was cheap then! I went and said to my *comadre* Diódora, "Look, you have nothing to worry about. They are going to be buried in a mausoleum. We are going now to see about the masons and the material."

Well, so now my friend was dead. After that, I never had another friend so close, so intimate, so much like a brother.

The Agrarian Reform began in 1925. That was another revolution! I call it the social revolution because that's when they began to distribute land. The *Agraria* wanted to establish itself so that the lands of some of the *haciendas* would fall to Azteca. I liked the idea of extending our *ejido* lands, for then parcels could be distributed to the landless peasants, but Pascual Herrera and the Union of Aztecan Peasants belonged to the CROM and the CROM opposed the Agrarians. They said that where the *Agraria* takes root, the CROM falls apart. They were afraid the strong Union would break up.

The government had sent two boys, one as fiscal agent and the other as treasurer, to set up the Agrarian Reform for the *municipio.* These two boys thought a lot of me and came to my house to get me to attend the meeting. I wasn't a member of the town council any more; I had withdrawn by that time. I refused to go to the *Agraria* meeting because the truth of the matter was that we were all afraid of the Herrera brothers. But they got me to go anyway. The fiscal agent and the treasurer took me by surprise by seating me in the middle, right in the center of things.

"What is going on?" I said. "I am here only as a distant observer."

"No, we want you to be the general secretary of the Agrarian Reform," he said. "Look, this is something that will help the peasant. You belong to the CROM but that is for workers not for peasants. The Agrarian Reform will benefit you."

Well, they took me by surprise and so I said, "All right, I accept under one condition, that you give me a piece of land from the neighboring *hacienda* . . . for Azteca."

"That is exactly why we are here. Half of the land of the *hacienda* is for Azteca and half for Yautepec. That is what we came for."

And so I went into it with pleasure. Parcels of land in Amitingo, which had been returned to Azteca from the *hacienda*, were given as *ejidos* to about two hundred peasants. One hectare fell to me and I began to plant part of it. As general secretary of the Agrarian Reform, I applied for other *hacienda* land for Azteca and was carrying on correspondence with Cuernavaca about it. Then something happened and I could not go on with it.

The two boys, the Agrarians, went to see this rent collector who had two daughters and because the boys spoke to the girls, this was used as a pretext to kill them. It was given out that the boy friends of the two girls killed the Agrarians because of jealousy, but that was not true. They were killed because they set up the Agrarian Reform and the Tyrants were the ones who killed them. When the deed was done, the Tyrants came to me and said, "Well, now those two are dead. Next comes *don* Pedro and his Agrarian Reform." But they didn't do anything to me. Later, they even made me *regidor* again.

After this, when I went to Cuernavaca to see the officials about the granting of the land, they were angry and said, "Murderers! Azteca doesn't deserve even water, let alone land. Just leave the papers and forget about them. Now you'll get nothing."

And that is why we have stayed where we are. The Herrera brothers were to blame. What did we get out of their bolshevism? Nothing! We joined them to defend the forests. For ten years we took care of the forests but it was in vain because later the Forestry Department began to give permission to cut down the trees. We had struggled for nothing.

Then *don* Valentín Quiroz became secretary again. But before that he had his say. "Why should the *huarache*-wearers win out? For what reason? Who is this Pedro Martínez who is going to be *regidor?* I don't know him but I would like to make his acquaintance. What school did he go to? Where did he study? No, gentlemen! Just because his parents were what they were, why should we now give him special consideration? No, not that. Never!"

Well, when they told me about it, that was the ruination of that man. If it hadn't been for him, nothing would have happened. He and his men were going around agitating to kill the Tyrants, the Herreras, that is, and all the *bolcheviques* who were following them. But Valentín did not succeed. There were more than two hundred of us in the society and we said, "No, we will never be a party to it." This time I was with them again.

But the *caciques* were after Pascual in earnest. Valentín began to hold meetings in his house to plan how they were going to catch him. Of course, someone went and told the top chief, that is, Pascual.

One night, two Herrera brothers got in under the fence in back of Valentín's house and listened to what the sons of the *caciques* were planning.

Well, now this Pascual really didn't want any more fighting and he had gone to Mexico City to arrange to serve as a kind of mounted guard. He was acquainted with all the leaders in the capital. So Pascual told me, "Look, I went to arrange for us to go to Mexico. I am working on it now. You are going to be appointed Chief of the Civil Defense."

I said, "But it is not up to me. What will the people say, and the Union? If they want me, well, there is nothing I can do, but really, I cannot accept just like that. All right, but only if our comrades say so."

On the third of January, 1927, Pascual's brother Alejo went to get Valentín. We were all at the fiesta in one of the *barrios*. We were eating when the messenger came. "Hurry up, your brother Alejo has Valentín and is taking him over toward Elotepec!"

Pascual got very mad. He even cried! *"Carambas,* that Alejo! I had it all arranged to go to Mexico City and now he has to go and ruin everything." He got awfully mad and didn't even finish his dinner.

So then I went to the president's office. The president, Refugio Gutiérrez, became very worried. "Now we are out of luck," he said. The five of us members of the town council met and arranged to make a report to the government in Cuernavaca the next day. As our hands were clean, we were going to explain what happened. Valentín had already been killed.

That night all the Herrera brothers left, even David, the one who never went around with them. But that time he got out.

Others ran, too. I was loyal to the president and stayed. The only others who stayed were the secretary and *don* Prosperino. The next morning *don* Prosperino and the president went to Cuernavaca.

The secretary was getting ready to run to Mexico City with his wife. He wasn't going to show up either, but I was so legalistic I insisted that he come with me to Cuernavaca. I said, "Let's go! Let's go and see our comrades."

We went to the railroad station to catch the train. There was no passenger train, so we got on a freight car. The stationmaster was an enemy of mine because I had been a forest inspector and had accused him of shipping charcoal without paying the *municipio*. It was worth ninety *pesos* a carload, so, of course, he didn't like me. That's why he immediately got in touch with Cuernavaca to arrest us.

When we got into the Cuernavaca station, there was the car and the police waiting for us. I was with the secretary and his wife, and the rent collector, who came along with us. They put us in the car and took us to the police station. A short time later *don* Prosperino and Refugio came in—prisoners, too. They got us all together there. We began to laugh. "*Carambas,*" we said. "What is this all about? We haven't done anything."

"Don't get scared. This is just a report they are going to make. You'll be leaving in a little while."

But what happened? The later it got the more incommunicado they had us. And at night they stuck us in the cells, real prisoners, now. Then, the chief of operations came in and got to work on Refugio, the president. This chief favored the *centrales* and had armed Valentín and his men. Now the *centrales* had their own Civil Defense under Sereno Hidalgo. That's why Alejo Herrera struck down Valentín when he did.

The chief of operations began to argue with Refugio.

"Well, so I finally get to know you. You keep completely out of the way, don't you? How many times have you paid a call on the main office or the state government? Never, isn't that right? You are one of them, you are an accomplice of the group that rose up. The thing is you are a rebel."

Well, they had a big argument. We listened in. Now they are going to roast us, but what could we do about it!

Day after day they tried to get us stirred up, but we asked for counsel and so a certain lawyer was able to get us out. I don't remember what his name was, but he was very brave. They wouldn't let him in. He pushed past them saying, "I am a civilian and I am going to enter because these prisoners in there are civilians. They are not military personnel."

The next day he got us out of there and had us transferred to the civil prison. The day after that he had us free. They were really going to kill us that time as this chief was a killer.

Here in Azteca, the *caciques* came and went freely. Sereno Hidalgo was the Chief of the Civil Defense, not Pascual any more. The ones from the center formed their own and were now the authorities. There were about twenty of them who took up arms. We had to resign. *Don* Prosperino and Refugio went to Mexico City immediately. And me? Like a fool, I remained for a time. I stayed in my house but I was good and scared.

I went to Yautepec to work. I was running away from the Civil Defense and Sereno Hidalgo. The Herreras had gone and Hidalgo's men were looking for them. So I left my wife, for no more than a week, and went down to my cousin Eutimio's house in Yautepec. I had no money for my *tortillas* so I went to work for him. Eutimio was also in politics and they had already taken him to prison in Cuernavaca where they wanted to kill him. He had a lawyer and went free, but anyway they killed him! Even though he had been hurt in prison, even though they cracked his head open there, they still had to kill him. They got him because of politics and I was in hiding because of the rebellion of the Herrera brothers.

It was on a Tuesday when my cousin disappeared. I was weeding his field and he didn't come to bring my food. I waited and waited. I didn't eat at all that day but I kept on working. I thought, "Well, what happened to my cousin?" In the afternoon, at about five, I went to Eutimio's house and suddenly on the corner I passed Sereno Hidalgo and his men. I didn't speak to him and he didn't speak to me. He saw me go into my cousin's house.

Eutimio's wife, Dorotea, gave me the news. "Eutimio is in jail! His friend Nabor, too."

"So that's why he didn't come to see me!" I said. "In that case, I won't continue to work."

"No," she said. "Not now, because who knows how things will go with us. What hope is there that he will ever plant again!"

Then I said, "I won't go back to Azteca until I know how things go for him."

So I lay down to sleep. At about ten o'clock at night, we heard a woman calling, "*Comadrita, comadrita.*" It was Dorotea's *comadre*. She said Eutimio was incommunicado. Then she said, "Is a cousin of his staying here? If he is, get him out because they are coming for him. The chief of Azteca is here and they are going to kill him."

"*Ay, caray!*" I said. "It is Sereno Hidalgo! Where will I go now that it is dark?"

Dorotea took me at that hour to her son's house near the station, where they hid me in a sack of corn. There I stayed quietly like an old mouse! "*Caray,* things are going very badly for me," I thought.

At about eight in the morning, Dorotea came and said, "Eutimio is nowhere to be seen. Nabor's wife and I went to the jail and they are not there, so we are going to look for them. Who knows where they were taken! So if you want to leave, go ahead."

"Well, then I am going."

I set out for Azteca, keeping to the hills until I reached home. After that I began to sleep in the *corrals,* for fear of being caught by Hidalgo. I was waiting to hear what had happened to my cousin. The news came three days later. They had killed the two of them! I said, "Then what can I hope for? Then there is no way out for me."

I didn't leave the house for eight days. I stuck it out until the Herrera brothers came back and the massacre occurred. It was in February during the Carnival that the Herreras entered the village in costume, to kill off their enemies in the Civil Defense. They came dressed as dancers, with their guns under their robes. First, they sent in a spy, also in costume and mask, and he told them how things stood. Then the others entered and surrounded the plaza. It was all done face to face, during the day. They started to fire at Hidalgo's men but they killed many bystanders . . . men, women, and children . . . twenty-two in all and even more wounded.

Then I knew I could not stay any longer because, having been a member of the Union, I would be killed. I said, "Now, yes, I will not wait. Now with this, who knows? There will be much revenge taken."

My relatives sent for me to go and pray for Eutimio but I said, "No, I would be a fool to pray now. I am leaving."

I left Azteca with an aunt of mine. My sister's son José and his new bride also went with us. They had just gotten married and there had been a murder at the wedding. A certain rich man's store had been robbed by the lover of Pascualina Herrera, the aunt of the Herrera brothers. This lover was a relative of my brother-in-law and so, feeling safe there and not at all ashamed of what he had done, he went to the wedding and got drunk. I didn't go because I knew that my sister and her husband were angry with me. Besides they didn't invite me. Well, the rich man found the thief there and killed him. When the Herrera brothers came back to Azteca and the massacre occurred in the plaza, my nephew was afraid they would take revenge on him, too, because of the murder of Pascualina's lover which took place in his house. So when I was leaving, he came and said, "Let's go, uncle. I am going to Mexico City, too. Take me!"

Before we went, I told my wife I would send for her as soon as I found work; that meantime she should sell the corn and everything else, to be ready to leave. Then we took to the hills and went to Mexico City.

CHAPTER X

ESPERANZA

On Politics

When Pedro went into politics and people told me he was going to be in the government, I was happy because I thought that now we would lack nothing and that he would earn lots of *pesos.* I also liked to have people know that we amounted to something and that they should look up to us. But when I saw that instead of improving, we were worse off, I didn't like it any more. In addition, politics brings danger and enemies and threats to Pedro.

During an election campaign, Pedro doesn't live at home. He stays in the presidential candidate's house with the group of leaders and there, between one drink of *ponche* and another, smoking cigars, they direct the campaign. He doesn't come home until after the elections. Then he seems to wake up from a dream. If they won, he is happy and if they lost he is full of anger and is insupportable, he scolds and scolds us for any little thing. I don't like it when he is in the government for then he becomes a real despot.

Sometimes I tell Pedro I don't like politics. It just serves to bring together a band of thieves who steal everything. Then he says, "We need a radical change, even though we go to the devil. We are fed up with promises."

I tell him not to mix into it because politics serves only to grind us into dust. But he says, "Are we then supposed to be like women? A man has to get into these things. I don't want to be like your cousin Margarito who knows nothing and says yes to everything."

Because of politics, Pedro has gone to jail three times. When they took him the first time, I had two babies, Conchita and the little girl that died. My brother had recently died. I cried every day, very much, over my brother's death for he was like a father to me. It happened like this: Pedro went from meeting to meeting. Every week he had a meeting. They would come to pick him up. They left early and would not return until after dark, sometimes drunk. My brother stayed with us and was very ill. He would vomit blood and seemed almost dead after it.

Pedro once went to a meeting while my brother was sick. We had no doctor to take care of him as it was during the Revolution. Pedro left, telling me, "Today you take care of him."

I said, "What can I do? I don't know what to do?" But, as always, he left. I stayed, caring for my brother and crying all the while, afraid that he would die. In the evening I told him, "Take this to eat, *papá*."

He says to me, "Don't cry, *mamá,* don't worry, I feel better now. I'm not vomiting any more. I'm not going to eat, I don't want anything. I am still nauseated." Later, about two in the morning, my brother cried to me, "I am going to throw up again."

I went out running, calling for my cousin Cecilia to help lift up my brother so that he would not choke on his own blood. All the neighbors came out and we went back to my brother. By the time we entered the house he was dead. Still I tried to raise him. "Lift up my brother!" I said to them. And they told me he was already dead and I screamed and screamed. The entire bed was covered with large clots of blood.

The neighbors asked me, "Where is Pedro?" I said he had gone to the plaza, thinking that if he had been here, perhaps my brother would not have died. Twice before Pedro had lifted him up and revived him; but my poor brother choked on his own blood as there was no one to help him.

Then I went to look for Pedro. There were many men in the meeting and he was inside with the Tyrants. They told him I was there and he came out. When he learned about my brother's death, he said, "Go home and mourn for him while I get some money for the wake."

About eight days after the death of my brother, Pedro went again to a meeting. I waited and waited for him until finally someone came to tell me they had all been put in jail. I brought his supper to jail but I was not allowed in. They were going to take him to Cuernavaca.

Pedro in jail, my brother dead, and I alone with the children! I cried and cried. I kept wondering, "Now what shall I do?"

I went around asking others what to do. I said to myself, "I will sell my chickens and go to Cuernavaca to see him." I asked the secretary's wife if she would accompany me to Cuernavaca but she did not want to. I was afraid to go alone because at that time there was no road and one had to go through the forest. That night Esteban, a friend of Pedro's, came to see me and asked, "What's happening with *don* Pedro? People say they have killed two of them, the one with the little beard, *don* Refugio Gutiérrez, and another one with a mustache."

I wept the whole night. I wanted to leave that same night as I was very worried. But Esteban had told me, "Why walk through the forest and arrive in Cuernavaca at night when the authorities only see one in the daytime?"

The secretary's wife came to say she would go with me, and we decided to leave very early. She would come to pick me up. I spent the night sleepless, just thinking and crying. At about two in the morning I got up. There was no one in the street. All I could see was a teamster carrying corn to Cuernavaca. I went to leave my daughter Conchita at a friend's house, after which I prepared *tortillas* for the trip, took my baby in my arms and went to the corner to wait to be picked up. But no one came. All I could see were the teamsters carrying corn to Cuernavaca. They were the only passers-by.

The woman did not come to pick me up as she had promised. I was in a state of anguish, thinking that by now they would already have shot Pedro and that I would never see him again. I knew how to go to Cuernavaca but I didn't know who would take me. Then I saw a man approaching with two horses. I decided to ask him if he was going to Cuernavaca. He said yes.

"Who are you?" I shouted, as I did not know him.

He answered, "I am Juan Pérez," but I still don't know him. He asks me, "Do you want to go to Cuernavaca?" and I answered, "Yes!"

And so I went with him, following behind as he went, shouting to his beasts. He was on horseback and I, despite the moonlight, was not able to walk easily. The good man waited for me. "Be careful," he says. "Don't fall with the baby."

I told him I was going to Cuernavaca and it happened that he was a village councilman, so he told me why they had all been jailed. While we were in the forest, two women caught up with us, *doña* Eustaquia and *doña* Tomasa, who were also going to Cuernavaca. When the man saw that I had company, he went on ahead. I never noticed when he left so I did not even have the chance to thank him for his company.

Once in Cuernavaca the women who were with me went on to sell their produce. I went to ask if Pedro was still in jail. There they told me he was not. Again anguish possessed me and I sat down in the plaza, not knowing what to do.

Then I saw the woman who was supposed to come by for me and she said to me, "I have just come, we were late. They have your husband Pedro in the barracks, but don't go to see him, for you will incriminate him more!"

She was returning to Azteca and invited me to go with her, but I replied, "I am not leaving until I find him."

Later on I found *doña* Tomasa and told her what I had learned. She took me with her to the lawyer Álvaro, with whom she was to arrange some business. The lawyer asked if he could help me and I told him why I had come. He said to me, "You are the wife of Pedro Martínez?" and went on to tell me that Pedro was being held incommunicado, but that through a soldier's wife he sent out a letter from the prisoners to the lawyer. That's how Álvaro had learned about it. "They were going to be shot," he told me, "but as they have asked for mercy, they are going to be let out. Don't worry, nothing will happen to them. They have already asked for mercy."

After this, I went to the barracks. There were many soldiers. Not knowing what to do, I finally approached the corporal and told him, "I want to see my prisoner." He asked, "What is his name?" I told him and he said, "Now let's see how we can do it."

Then they went in to find out. They took a long time to come back with an answer, but they finally allowed me in. I entered, after they searched me to see if I was carrying anything. They put their hands all over me and I felt a great shame because some of them were feeling me. Even my little girl was searched under her shirt. They even searched the *tortillas* I was carrying. Then they took me way inside the barracks and I was becoming uneasy since I did not know where they were taking me. But the prisoners were really there. Pedro became a little happy on seeing me and said he would immediately write another letter to see if I could take it out. The letter was soliciting his freedom. I managed to take it out and gave it to the lawyer.

I had to remain in Cuernavaca to continue helping Pedro and I would go to see him as much as three times a day. I slept in the house of a countryman who was married to an aunt of my brother's wife. I went back to Azteca to sell my chickens and to look for someone who would lend me money for food but I returned to Cuernavaca and stayed until Pedro was freed. I did not walk back with them because they had to go in a roundabout way through the forest in case someone was planning to attack them.

Another time Pedro was jailed was when they killed Valentín Quiroz. Pedro went to the courthouse that day, returned at noon, went

to bed and told me to call him at two o'clock. I shouted to wake him up at about three. He went back to the courthouse, not knowing what had happened there. He sees everyone running about and asks them what is happening but they pay no attention to him. Then he sees them sending a message to Cuernavaca and so he knows they have taken Valentín.

Then Pedro said to the president, "Let no one say we handed him over. We have to go to Cuernavaca, for we are all officials."

In this way, Refugio Gutiérrez, Pedro, and all the ones from the village council took the train to Cuernavaca to testify. In the station at Cuernavaca there was a car waiting for them. They said to themselves, "As we are from the council, they have come to await us." The man in charge of the car even embraced them when he learned they were the authorities from Azteca. He tells them to get in the car, which they did, and drives off. The car takes them directly to the barracks. There each one was put in a separate cell so they would not discuss their testimony with one another. By nightfall the soldiers had taken them out one by one. They thought they were going to be killed, but they were only asked to give testimony. All said the same thing. So it went for two nights; after that they were held imprisoned there. Twelve days later they got them all together and put them out on the street. Again the prisoners thought they would be killed, but nothing was done to them.

This time also, I went to Cuernavaca. By then Felipe was born. I had to sell corn or borrow money until Pedro came back.

The third time they jailed Pedro I don't remember what the reason was. I only remember that by then my sons were grown up. On that occasion people gave me sugar, *chilitos, tortillas*. Sometimes they came here to my house to leave me things, all out of pity which they felt for my children.

The people would say to me, "Why does he keep mixing in politics? Now the children are alone, poor innocent ones, with nothing to eat. Tell your husband he has nothing to win by it, only jail sentences and his family's ruin. He might even get killed. They are being used as instruments; the politicians make promises and they foolishly follow. The politicians enter it because they have enough to eat, but the others have nothing; they are poor and are ruined. In the jail the prisoners are fed, but here, what do you have to eat?"

I would tell all of this to Pedro and he would answer, "I won't mix in politics any more. If you see me doing it, scold me." I always scold him when he gets involved in political things and he always goes back to it and pays no attention to me.

This last time, he was in jail in Cuernavaca about thirty days.

When he was set free, he was so enraged by his imprisonment that he refused to do village guard duty. Since then he has never done guard duty. This time when he was imprisoned, I didn't stay in Cuernavaca because I had many children to care for. I would just go there and come back. I don't remember why Pedro was jailed, only that it was because of politics.

Later, when Pedro was a judge, the economic condition of the house improved a little. People came to ask him to arrange something about the land, or to settle married couples who didn't like each other any more, or to talk about an abduction. Then, when the matter was settled, they gave him one or two *pesos*. He wouldn't accept it but finally he did, when they said it made them happy.

Pedro was also paid when he was a judge but after two months he never brought me his complete pay. I keep all the money of the house. He hands me a certain amount and when it's gone, I say, "We don't have any more money, we have to get some." I tell him there isn't any money for corn, or for clothes, or for whatever we need. Then I would sell something to get a little money. Meanwhile, I see how I can get through the day. If there is corn, I make *tortillas* and I exchange them in the market for peppers, cinnamon, tomatoes, or anything to eat. If there is no corn at home, I try to get it on credit or I must go to the neighbors to ask for a loan for the day.

Pedro was in the streets every day and didn't do anything. Later, he sent the boys to work in the *tlacolol* but he spent the whole day in conversation with his friends. He was not careful with money. He gave away a lot of it. For example, he paid ten *pesos* to rent a piece of land from a woman and he didn't even plant on it. And once he loaned ten *pesos* to his friend who didn't have money to celebrate his Saint's Day.

Pedro is always sought after and everyone tells him he is a real politician. Others attack him and say he is just out to get something for himself. I think it is better to be far removed from politics since that way no one is mortified. I tell him, "When someone comes to the court-house, you don't even know where to hide. You already have many enemies." People get angry because they think an injustice has been done them, but Pedro says, "Justice is justice, and the one who owes must pay."

In 1928 we went to live in Mexico City. It was the time of the Carnival in Azteca. On Sunday we did not go to see the festivities so the next day I said to Pedro, "Let's go to the celebration." I wanted us to take the little girls, but he told me to take them myself. I was very angry and did not want to go because when I go out alone and come back late he scolds so much. Conchita thought the same thing. "Let's not go alone," she said to me. "If we return late, my *papá* will scold us."

Pedro sat down by the side of the house and began reading the Bible. Suddenly we heard what sounded like a clap of thunder, and then began a succession of the same thunder-like noises. Pedro said, "What's happening? They must have gotten into a fight over there!"

As I was already angry, I told him, "That's what you like, right? Now see if you don't go running to the fiesta." Sure enough, he ran out toward Darío Barragán's house while we saw a great many people running by. One old man in costume had his gown rolled up and was running as fast as the others. We heard them saying, "They have already killed a lot of people! People are lying in the square like slaughtered cattle. We stepped on some of them because we were in such a hurry we didn't see them."

I had five children at that time; Conchita, Rufina, Felipe, Martín and Macrina, who was very young. "Now you see," Pedro said to me, "you wanted to go and get killed!" And I was thinking that it was exactly what they would have done to my little children. The Tyrants—Alejo, Pascual, and some others—came in costume and did the killing in the plaza.

Pedro went to his uncle Agustín's house to get advice. His uncle told him, "It is better that you leave here. Go to Mexico City, otherwise they are going to seek you out." And so it was. That night the Tyrants came looking for him because they knew he was on the council.

Later on Pedro came and said to me, "Tomorrow my aunt Chucha will take me to Mexico City so I am leaving. You take care of the corn, store it, shell it and sell it, then you can also leave. I will write, telling you when to come so that I can meet you at Tacubaya."

I followed his instructions, sold the corn, and waited for his letter, but it never came. His nephew, who lived with me, would tell me, "We had better go to Mexico City, aunt." And I would answer, "How can you tell me to go if neither you nor I know the city?"

My aunt advised me not to go because I would get lost. But finally the boy convinced me and we left with the children. I rented a horse to take us to the railroad station. We put some boxes on the horse and sat the children in them, all except Felipe, who did not want to. He cried a lot. I had to carry him in my arms all the way to the station, and Pedro's nephew carried Macrina.

CHAPTER XI

PEDRO

In Mexico City

In the capital, my nephew José and I went to the house of my relatives who had a shoe shop in the Colonia Moctezuma. There we stayed. I didn't know anything about Mexico City, not a thing, but I went around looking for work.

There in Mexico City were all my old friends, *don* Prosperino, Refugio Gutiérrez, all the members of the town council of Azteca! I found a job with the help of my friends. The brother of one of them got me into a soda factory. I earned one *peso* and fifty *centavos* a day and the hours were steady. They put me to washing bottles and loading the truck. The only thing I didn't like was that I had to stand in water almost all day. I said, "This will do me harm; I'll get rheumatism! I won't stay."

I lasted only seven days and in that time I was plenty scared because I didn't know the streets. Colonia Moctezuma was still in the country then. It was not built up yet. I was always saying, "Well, now, which way do I go? How? And where am I going now?"

Just think how little I knew! Once I went out at night to earn a few extra *centavos*. I went out and said to myself, "Now how do I get back?" I was going to take a bus, but which one? I didn't even know the difference between a bus and a taxi. So I went to stand on a corner, in the dark. I would stand on any corner, waiting for a bus. Along came a car and the driver told me to get in. I gave him the address.

"Which direction is it in?" he asked.

"Well, I don't know."

"What street is it near?"

"Well, I don't know."

"*Ay, caray!*"

He let me off near my street and I gave him ten *centavos*.

"No! This is not a bus. This is a taxi. It costs fifty *centavos*."

"But I don't have any more than ten *centavos*, because that is what the bus costs."

"Well, give it here and get going. Run! And watch out for yourself!"

I told my uncle and all my relatives, my uncle's brother-in-law and his wife, his sister and her daughter, all of them living there—I told them what happened and they all laughed at me.

On a Saturday I learned that my wife was in Mexico City. *Ay, caramba!* how that pleased me! She came with the five children. She brought them in a box, like chickens, and my eldest daughter, Conchita, helped her. She was with her *compadre, don* Basilio, near the market of Tacubaya, so that was where I went.

I went to work for some masons, but they didn't pay us. Those bricklayers were great drunkards and very selfish. They wanted me to spend everything I earned to give them *pulque*. And that didn't suit me at all. But if I didn't give them *pulque* they wouldn't pay me, so every week I had to bring a policeman to make them give me my pay. They were supposed to give me one *peso*, fifty *centavos*, but they gave us whatever they wanted to. I finally got fed up. "No, this is not the way to do business." And I quit.

I became an orange vendor. I sold on the streets but I didn't earn much. I bought the oranges at the Merced market and sold it in the Plaza Juárez. I earned just enough to pay the rent. I was paying rent by then. We had a large room over there in Tacubaya. It was the first house I had with electric lights. We paid twelve *pesos* a month rent, including the lights. My nephew and his wife lived with us and paid half the rent.

I began to look around for another job and I ran into trouble with an employment agency, the kind that finds jobs for workers. One of the Herrera brothers told me about the agency. He was the youngest brother, the peaceful one who never carried arms. He was selling charcoal and passed by my orange stand and said, "Are you looking for work? There is a blackboard over there saying they are looking for workers and will pay sixty *pesos* a month."

In those days, sixty *pesos* was a lot and everything was cheap. My nephew and I wanted to work, so we went to look right away. Why not!

"Just look at that blackboard! It says it very clearly!"

We went in to the agency. The man there attended us very politely, very nicely, with sweet words. We told him what we wanted and *zas!* he gave us a little paper with two addresses on it. That was all.

"One *peso* each, please."

Well, one *peso* didn't seem a lot to us, so we each gave it to him and went to look for the first address. We didn't know the streets, but we asked along the way and arrived. We greeted the man there, the owner of the trucks, and spoke to him. He almost didn't want to speak to us because we were wearing our white *calzones* and it was plain we were from a village.

"No, I don't need any workers." That was all he said to us. So we left, very angry. We walked all the way to Santa María la Redonda, to the next address. There we go, the two of us. With difficulty, we found the place in an alleyway. The manager came out and we told him what we came for.

"Ah, what bandits they are! Don't believe them, they are just thieves. Where are you from? How did you find the agency? How long have you been in the capital?"

We told him and he said, "*Caray!* No wonder they took advantage of you! They robbed you vilely. How much did you give them? They see our announcement in the newspaper and they put it on their blackboard, just to rob humanity. I know that kind! I'm going to call them up and insult their mothers, because they cheat and exploit people."

He went to the telephone and we heard him talking but who knows what they told him. There we were, just standing, but very, very angry. I said to my nephew, "You see? You insisted that you wanted a job. Now they have cheated us. The only *peso* we earned today, they took from us."

We were furious! We went back to the Plaza Juárez where the women were looking after the orange stand. We were so angry, we didn't even want to speak. They robbed us, a *peso* each! The *peso* didn't bother me as much as being tricked. And since I don't know how to let things be, I said, "Well, now how can I get even? How can I get rid of my anger?"

At about five o'clock in the afternoon, we went to leave our sacks of oranges at the *tortilla* stand of a fellow villager, Porfirio Hernández. When he learned how we had been robbed, he said, "If I were you, I

would not accept this. Let's go to the agency and get back the two *pesos!*"

He took me there. The agency was only a block away. But what was I going to say? I had already stopped by to complain. Porfirio spoke for me. "I want you to return the two *pesos* you took from my countrymen."

"No. Money cannot be returned. Money put into the cash box cannot be taken out. The only thing I can promise is to give them the first job that comes in. I've already told them that."

I said, "I don't need work. What I want are my two *pesos.*"

"No. Money cannot be returned."

"Very well, but be prepared for the consequences," said Hernández.

Then we left. I said, "Listen, can't we sue this canaille?"

"Of course! But I would have to take you there and I have no time."

"No. Just show me where. Take me there this minute and tomorrow I will find the way. I will not let him get away with this!"

He took me to the Eighth Delegation, to the Commissariat on the second floor. I was questioned by the Commissioner, and I explained everything.

He said, "Ah, what a friend you are! The Chief of the Markets is cleaning up all the thieves now and this man will be sent to his grave, to the Islas Marías, the worst prison in the country. Nothing will save him! But all you have told me must not be changed."

"No, sir! I can repeat it twenty times and I wouldn't forget even one word."

"Good! Take this summons and give it to the policeman on duty near the agency. But see that he gives it to your man because there are police who will sell it."

Well, I saw the policeman present the summons. I was hidden so the man in the agency didn't see me. The next day, I went to the Delegation but he did not answer the summons. I got another summons and it was presented to him again. He didn't come until three summonses were sent. From the start I gave myself over to this. I worked at the orange stand for a short while and then I went after the agency. I was beginning to know the streets by then. Porfirio thought they were not paying attention to my case and so one day he sent his wife to go with me. Porfirio was my friend but he was so stingy that even the diapers his son wore were too small. The boy went barefoot and his pants were all torn. His wife didn't have decent clothes either and was very sloppy.

After the third summons I arrived at the Delegation with Porfirio's wife and son. The man from the agency was there and when he saw us he ran out to speak to me.

"Are you the one who sued me?"

"Yes, sir."

"Is this your wife?"

"Yes, sir."

Then he took out two *pesos* and said, "Here are the two *pesos* you are fighting for."

"Listen, sir, things are different now. Now you will put them on the Commissioner's table."

The Commissioner called us in and we stood behind the railing.

"Is your name Delfino del Monte?"

"Yes, sir."

Oh, *caray!* Then the Commissioner began to threaten him. Delfino del Monte put the two *pesos* on the table, but the Commissioner would not receive them.

"No, not that. We are still going to investigate your agency. Keep your two *pesos* and we'll see what my chief has to say. Now go with the guard downstairs to the doctor."

We went too, and Porfirio's little boy was frightened because we walked between two guards. The boy grabbed me and began to cry and they had all the more reason to believe he was my son. I was impressed by the kind of justice they had in Mexico City. The doctor began to examine us. Whew! How frightening! I didn't tremble but the other one shook so much you could see his pants move. And the doctor hadn't even touched him yet!

Then we went back to the Commissioner. From the beginning, the Commissioner had given me so much advice that I even lost my fear. Once more he said to the man I was suing, "Do you accept everything? Declare yourself and sign this!"

Delfino del Monte declared and signed. Then the Commissioner called the guards and said, "Take him to his destination!"

Uuy! The prisoner was frightened. *Qué caray!* He looked terrified. He said, "Sir, one favor, please."

Then because he considered me so beneath him, so humble, he began to whisper in the Commissioner's ear. I think he offered him money. The Commissioner said, "No! I can't do that. I can't."

Again the prisoner whispered something. And a third time. I think he must have raised his bribe. But the Commissioner said, "I told you. I can't because General Ibarra is over us. So, get going. Take him away to the jail."

Ay, ay, now I got him! My two *pesos* tripped him up! The Commissioner said, "You see? We've got him now. Now you go upstairs to the superior office, but don't change your story."

I went upstairs alone and showed them the order. They sent for the prisoner. The Commissioner had warned me, "Don't let him jump over the railing because it is three floors up and he will be killed and that is no punishment! That's the way thieves are. They prefer to kill themselves so as not to be punished. And death is no punishment because in any case we have to die. No, man! Don't let him. Grab his feet!"

Caray! I am looking at the railing and thinking I had better not be weak because he might pull me with him!

Delfino del Monte came in looking very scared. They said he had to leave for Islas Marías the next day. "Please, sir, have the kindness to . . . I would rather settle the matter here."

"Are you prepared to pay the fine? And all the expenses and damages to this man?"

"Yes, sir. I will pay everything, but I want to settle it here."

The officer took the telephone and called the general. Then he said to the prisoner, "My friend, tomorrow the car leaves for Islas Marías and it is not full, so you have to go. There is no help for it."

The prisoner got even more frightened. They called in a man, a lawyer or a doctor, I thought, but no, he had a stick. He gave the prisoner a blow and knocked him down! With a kick, he made Delfino get up. "You want to be thieves and scoundrels but you are not man enough to bear up. Go on and sign!" Then he gave him a punch in the jaw and knocked him down again. Man! Delfino was big and the other one was short, but still he knocked him down!

I was watching and I thought, "With this I don't mind losing the two *pesos*. Now he got what I wanted to give him! Now I am satisfied." I signed the document and they took away the prisoner. I went back to the Commissioner.

"You see, Morelos? You have ruined that man! Now, tomorrow take this note to the Sixth Delegation and then go to see General Ibarra near the *Caballito de Troya*."

"Very well, sir." I didn't even know where the statue of the Trojan horse was at that time! The next day Porfirio's wife took me there. Poor thing, she didn't even have time for breakfast because they said we had to be there at seven o'clock in the morning. There was a long line of women waiting there, the wives of the prisoners. There was the wife of Delfino del Monte, too!

Very respectable, she looked! Even her hat, with its plumes . . . she looked very decent. How could they be thieves? "That's the way

thieves dress here," said Porfirio's wife. "*Caray!* And she is here because of you!"

They gave us another paper and sent us to the general's headquarters. So there we were, walking again. We didn't take the bus
often in those days. At headquarters, an officer said I would get back
my two *pesos* and my expenses for the five days, twelve *pesos* in all,
but I had to wait to see the general until Monday, at six in the evening.

Porfirio wanted to go with me on Monday. "*Carambas!*" he said,
"I never thought you would get so far with this man."

"You didn't believe it, but I really wanted to do this! Even if they
don't pay me, it doesn't matter because I saw him punished. I am satisfied just with the punch they gave him. That's worth more than two
pesos!"

"Yes, of course. That is justice, legal justice. Now you have seen it."

On Monday they let in only me to see the Chief. Porfirio had to
wait outside. *Uuy!* The Chief was fat and had a huge belly. He was
sitting alone. I asked him for my twelve *pesos*.

"No, be satisfied that you have put him in jail! Just think, he has
three lawyers working for him and who knows how much he has already spent."

"Yes, sir, I am satisfied. Only I want to say that you should get rid
of these agencies because it is a center for bandits. And they rob and
cheat all the newcomers who come from the villages. It is us they exploit."

The Chief smiled. "*Ay*, my boy, have you thought all that? The
government will resolve it, not you. Don't worry about it, the government will take care of it. Now go on, run along."

After that, I quit selling oranges and went to work at the Concordia
ice-cream factory, as a vendor. There I began to earn more. I had to
wear a white uniform, even white shoes and a white cap! *Don* Prosperino signed a bond for one hundred *pesos* for me and they gave me
my cart and after that I was better off. The least I earned was two
pesos a day; at times on a Saturday or a Sunday I earned triple that,
even as much as ten or fifteen *pesos*. And then I really got to know
the streets. I got a better job at another ice-cream company. I was so
honest they made me a foreman.

One day, on the trolley car, I met one of the *caciques* from Azteca.
I wasn't afraid any more, so I sat down beside him and said, "*Señor*
Campos, how are things going with you?"

"Very well, *señor*."

"Don't you recognize me? I am Pedro Martínez."

"No! But man, how different you look!"

"And how are things in our homeland?"

"Well, things are quiet now. And where do you work?"

"Nearby." I didn't tell him where. I'd be a fool to, because he was my enemy. I said good-bye and got off at the wrong stop.

I liked city life. My wife, poor little thing, worked as a washer-woman when I sold oranges, and once she worked in a *tortilla* shop. But when I was an ice-cream vendor, I didn't let her work any more. I said, "No, take care of your children. Leave things to me. After all, I am now earning well."

She went back to Azteca in '29, in August, because of the wife of my good friend Francisco. Diódora loved us a lot because of all the favors I had done them. She didn't stop writing to us to tell us to come back. She even sent money for the fare. So when my wife was ill with child, with our son Ricardo, I urged her to go back to Azteca.

"Look, go back because the rent here is a burden." My nephew had left and we were living alone. "Look, you go and I will stay an-other month or two."

"In that case, I will go," she said.

I had been intending to get another woman at that time, but still had not done it. Being alone, I was thinking of a girl I had already deceived, a girl of fifteen, whom I was going to marry. This is the way it happened.

First, there was the married one. I was selling ice cream when I first spoke to the married woman. She joked with me and came out with the fact that she liked me. She said, "Look, I like you a lot. You appeal to me." Because I was young then. I didn't have gray hairs or such whiskers.

"But no," she said. "Don't get any ideas. Do you know why? Be-cause my husband is very faithful. He gives me everything he earns. He buys me whatever I want. He takes me wherever I want to go. What do I lack? That is why I say no to you. I like you a lot, but I can't."

Then she said to me, "Do you know what we'll do, vendor? I will get you a girl. But you are a bachelor, aren't you?"

"Yes, I am a bachelor."

"Good, then I will get you this girl. She is an orphan but my mother-in-law brought her up. Her father is living but he is a drunk-ard."

And sure enough, that very week, I made a conquest. It was easy since I went there every day and gave her ice cream. And while we were talking, I flattered her and she gave in. There you have it! She told me to ask the *señora* for her hand, and then her father. And I did.

Qué caray! We got together and made all the arrangements for the wedding. But when it was about to happen, a letter from my wife came, saying, "My time has arrived. Come back!"

Újule! That night I didn't sleep, thinking of the girl, thinking of my wife and my children. Whew! I had two hearts! I said, "Now what will I do?" The girl was already asking me to bring my laundry for her to wash. I had no money because I had paid the rent. All I had was twenty-five *pesos*. Should I go, with my money, or without my money, or what? I thought and thought about it.

That Saturday I went to see the girl, but I didn't say anything; my heart was numb, and my mind, too. The girl really was attached to me. She even asked for my laundry and told me to move into her house. What should I do? What should I do?

That Sunday I earned twenty *pesos* and I thought, "With this money I will leave." So I went to the girl's house and I told a big lie.

"Look, I am going to my homeland in Jojutla. They let me know that they want to sell my house because I owe money on it. So I have to go but I will come back. In four days I will be here. Here is my address."

I just made it up. The poor girl began to cry. I left and I never went back!

CHAPTER XII

ESPERANZA

In Mexico City

We took the train to Mexico City and went as far as Tacubaya. In Tacubaya there were many of our countrymen and they came over to talk to me when they saw us arrive. "Where's Pedro?" they asked.

"He is with my aunt Chucha," I answered. They asked if I wanted them to take me to Pedro or to leave me with my *compadre* Basilio, who was living right there in Tacubaya. I stayed with my *compadre* and the next day Pedro arrived.

"Now you have come," he said, and then added, "We better stay here with my *compadre* because my aunt Chucha lives in a little room and so many of us cannot fit."

My *comadre* would get very angry with the children, and, for that matter, so would I. She had some of her own and they fought with mine, and shrieked and yelled. When she was angry, she wouldn't let my children go to the toilet. I would say nothing to my *comadre*, thinking to myself, "Let her get angry if she wants to. Let her get angry!"

In view of all the arguments, Pedro said, "It will be better for us to move. We will rent a little room."

I liked Mexico City very much, with its cars and trams; what I did not like was that it all cost money.

Here we had to pay rent for the house and it was too high. We paid thirty *pesos* a month and no sooner did we finish paying one month when the next month was due. In Azteca, everything is different. Sometimes we don't even know what month it is, we don't take notice since we have no rent to pay.

Without money we could do nothing, not even light a fire. Here in Azteca things also cost money, but not firewood; there in Mexico City, one has to use charcoal. Sometimes we had no charcoal, and there was no one to go to for help. I couldn't borrow a *peso* or a *cuartillo* of corn. Life is very hard in the city.

In the beginning I was afraid to go out through the streets because I didn't know my way. Once, Pedro took me to the church in the Villa. He knew the city well because he went everywhere selling his ice cream. We went to the Villa, starting out early and coming back late. When we were near the house, they left me on my own to get corn dough. They told me, "The house is just nearby here, you won't get lost." But I just stood there, not knowing which way to go, until Pedro came back for me.

My children were content in Mexico City and were not afraid. Conchita was going to school, and I took her back and forth. We were very much afraid the cars would run over her. Boys and girls were together in the school, but I didn't complain because Conchita was just a child.

We went only once to the movies. It was a picture about a girl and her sweetheart, and there was a death in it. They spoke in Spanish. Only the grownups went, Pedro and I, his nephew and wife. We did not take the little ones.

We also went to a fair once and took all the children along. I don't even remember what sort of things we saw, but the children liked it very much. "Let's go again," they said, but we never did.

There were some people from Azteca where we lived in Mexico City. Sometimes the women and I would go together to the market, but we didn't get to know anyone from the city. We had no friends.

For a while I was hired to do washing in Tacubaya. I would go one day to soap the clothing and the following day I would go back to wash. But I never made friends among the people I washed for. When we saw each other on the street or in the market, we wouldn't stop to speak. At other times I went to make *tortillas* in a *tortillería*. Pedro did not want me to go because of the baby girl, so I would sneak out. Conchita would bring the baby to the *tortillería* to be nursed.

For doing the wash, at times they gave me one *peso*, seventy-five *centavos* or one *peso* and a half, according to the amount of clothing, but I didn't know how much to charge. My aunt Chucha would say to me, "Don't be a fool, for the sheets you charge separately. Besides, they have to give you soap. You should not have to bring it."

In the *tortillería* they paid me ten to fifteen *centavos* a *bola* and

sometimes I would make four or five *bolas* a day. In addition to the pay, at noon they would give me dinner.

The people for whom I worked would ask me how long I had been in Mexico City, and like a fool, I would say I had just come. That's why they were able to exploit me.

Selling ice cream, Pedro earned about ten *pesos* on Saturdays and Sundays, and during the week about four or four fifty. By dawn he had already left, and would not come back until nighttime.

Pedro became very ill in the stomach—he had a bad dysentery. One morning he was not feeling well but went to work anyway and came home the worse for it. I went to see the doctor. He gave me a medicine and a purgative for Pedro, but it did not cure him. Then we went to see *doña* Prisciliana Herrera, who was also from Azteca. After she massaged him he soon recovered.

Pedro and his nephew, when they were selling ice cream, would sometimes return at eleven or twelve at night. A few times they came home drunk. Once he told me he had been in a *pulquería* and a woman came in and began to embrace him and kiss him. "And then," says Pedro, "she asked me if I had a woman. I told her no, and she stuck to me, hanging on to me, and I didn't know how to get rid of her. I told her where my house was, as I was drunk, and since then she seeks me out and when she sees me she always hangs on to me."

I think this is one of Pedro's jests, because women are not allowed in the *pulquerías*.

As I became pregnant again, I went back to Azteca. In the first place, the midwives in Mexico City get paid much more than here. My *comadre* Diódora had written letters to us from Azteca. She loved us very much and was always asking that we return. Pedro answered that we would, as soon as we had the money to get back. My *comadre* wrote again sending the money we needed, as a loan.

With that money Pedro sent me back here. He sent me with my cousin Margarito and I had to stay in his house. I had said to Pedro, "And now, Pedro, who is going to take care of you?" But he insisted he was not leaving yet because he had paid for the room for fifteen days more and was going to stay it out.

My cousin yelled at the children; if they sang or shouted, he and his wife would be very annoyed. So I told my *comadre* Diódora that I had better go to my own little house, because Margarito got angry with the children. My *comadre* told me it would be all right, that I should go, and since I had no furniture or household goods she said to me, "Take this mat, take this pot, this grinding stone," and many other things she gave me. "I will come to see you daily, to see what you need."

And thus I moved here, where I was all alone. Two weeks later Pedro came, and as he is always jesting, he told me, "I have a girl in Mexico City. I told her I was a bachelor. She was taking care of my clothing, then she introduced me to her parents and I asked for her hand. Now she is my *novia* and I am going to marry her."

Once back from Mexico City we returned to country life. Pedro looked for work; he hired himself out to work for other people. We had come back in August and the time to plant had passed.

PART FOUR

CHAPTER XIII

PEDRO

Conversion to Protestantism

I was very poor when I arrived in Azteca from Mexico City. I didn't even ask for my *ejido* land because they had already given it to someone else. The new Commissariat didn't like us ex-*bolcheviques* and so, because of cursed politics, I lost my right. I was very humble because the Civil Defenders were still there and I thought they wanted to kill me, so naturally I didn't make any inquiries. That's why I was left behind and didn't get any land. Those who weren't mixed up in politics were the ones who benefited. Many years later, when my friend Ángel was the *Ejido* Commissariat, the only land left was sterile and I didn't want it.

In Azteca, the CROM was finished. The Herrera brothers had fled and one by one they were found and killed. Their few followers who were left joined a new party called the *fraternales,* and they began to go against the people from the center once more, though most of the leaders of the *centrales* had been finished off by the Herreras in the massacre. The majority of the *fraternales* lived in the upper part of the village and their opponents lived in the lower part, so they were known as "those above" and "those below." This division began back in 1920, when we were fighting to save the forests.

But I was through with politics. No more of that for me! I went my way as an ordinary citizen.

So when I returned in 1929, I planted my corn on communal land and when the hog plums were ripe, I borrowed some old crates from a *señora* and I became a fruit dealer. I borrowed about thirty very old crates that I had to keep mending and I bought more old ones for fifteen or twenty *centavos* as I needed them. I knew two or three fruit contractors in Mexico City who loaned me crates which I filled with plums and sent back to them. I borrowed money at 10 percent a month and bought the crops of plum trees and hired fruit pickers and teamsters to carry the crates to the railroad station. There was no highway then. Every third or fourth day I sent off twenty to forty loads and in that way I made a few *centavos*. In 1930, a crate of 1,500 plums cost me one *peso* and I sold it for five or six *pesos*. I paid fifty *centavos* a crate to the pickers, fifty *centavos* to haul it to the train and even after I paid the freight, I still made money. But some of the contractors were shameless thieves and that is how they got rich. One of them cheated me of forty *pesos* but I beat him out in court. Those contractors were always cheating me and I began to do business with two women who sold fruit in the market. They were both legal and honest but very stingy. I stuck to them and began to earn more. There was another woman who bought my fruit and after a few days she became my mistress. I visited her whenever I went to Mexico City.

One day, in the village, there I was with my sack of fruit, buying up plums, when Sereno Hidalgo spoke to me. "Look, *don* Pedro," he says. "Come with us. We are going to nominate our future president. It would be well to forget the past. What happened, happened. Now let us unite as sons of the village, like brothers."

I say to him, "Fine! You are doing the right thing. Unity is much better and let's forget all the other things."

There was a meeting and we nominated someone, I forget who. I kept quiet. All I did was give my vote, nothing more. Then came the elections and after that the Forestry Co-operative appeared, with Sereno Hidalgo as its chief. The Co-operative had been organized first in 1926 by the village of San Pablo because they were making a lot of charcoal and sending it to Mexico City. San Pablo was near the railroad and as they didn't have much farm land, they began to exploit the communal forests excessively.

The *fraternales* protested because they said the forests were being ruined. The municipal authorities in Azteca also protested but only because they and Sereno Hidalgo wanted to take the Co-operative away from San Pablo and locate it in Azteca, the seat of the *municipio*. The people of San Pablo brought the case to the national government because now all the forests, even our communal forests, were under the jurisdiction of the Forestry Department. Sereno won out and in 1930 the new Forestry Co-operative was formed in Azteca.

I didn't get involved in the Co-operative or with the *fraternales*. I just minded my own business and went on planting my *tlacolol*. Sereno Hidalgo and I were enemies in politics but privately we were friends because he was an understanding man, even though he was young. He respected me and spoke nicely to me. He sought me out and we became close friends.

Later, when Sereno became the president, he said to me, "Now that I am president of the *municipio,* how are you going to help me?"

"In whatever you say, in whatever you command."

"Well, can't you bring a few loads of sand to repair the public buildings?"

I had two horses and on the very next day I went to get the sand. At that time trucks could not get in and everything had to be done with animals. I made two trips to the hills to get the sand, then later, two more trips.

I co-operated, even with *pulque.* At that time, I gathered maguey and made my own *pulque.* The president would come to my house and say, "Come on, Pedro, I need some *pulque* for the workers," and I would sell it to them.

Sereno said to me, "Good. It gives me great pleasure. I like to get co-operation. If only all the villagers were so understanding."

While he was in office, Sereno repaired the *palacio* because the hall of the building was practically crumbling, and he built the first public toilets. The little schoolhouse, where the present kindergarten is, had a roof which was falling in, but Sereno began to repair it. He fixed the village clock, which also wasn't working, and he repaired the bandstand and a number of streets. All this pleased me because he used the money from the Forestry Co-operative to improve the village.

From that time on I said, "Well, finally I have seen a president who really looks out for his village. Before the Revolution, the *caciques* managed to build themselves good houses and fill their pockets with money, but they oppressed the peasants. We had an independent *municipio* and the forest belonged to the people, but we never got a thing out of it. Not now any more. What I am now seeing is really a model. This one is really a president. I believe that we never had one like him before and we will never have another like him again."

The Forestry Co-operative was collecting money in the treasury and Sereno had a lot of influence with the Governor. Sereno also had money from the Co-operative and I suppose he also took some from the government. But he had many enemies and they finally killed him. It

was unjust and I criticized it very much because that man behaved well
and did a lot for the village.

He was killed by a man named Faustino. This Faustino had stolen
a typewriter from the president's office and Sereno found out and got it
back. Then Faustino got together with a man from San Pablo who had
had a fight with Sereno over the Co-operative and *zas!* they killed him.
People say that the *mamá* of the Herrera brothers and some rich men
who were against Sereno paid Faustino to kill him. This was when
Sereno was no longer president. Faustino and about thirty men, followers of the *cristeros,* whom Faustino was using as a cover, went to the
town hall and shot it up. They knew that Sereno was there, drunk, because it was his Saint's Day, and they carried him off to kill him.

But Sereno's wife followed them and Sereno was so much of a man
that when they were about to kill him, he begged, "You are going to kill
me and there is nothing I can do about it, but I beg you not to do anything to my wife. Please, it is dark now, I ask you to let her go. If I
owe you something, I will pay, but don't touch her. Go, woman, leave
me now!"

"Don't worry," they said. "No one will put a hand on her." Then
they stood him up and shot him.

But later Faustino was killed, too. At first, twelve Aztecans were
put in jail for Sereno's murder, but they weren't the guilty ones. The
next president caught Faustino carrying a gun and shot him on suspicion. Faustino didn't die right away. He confessed and told them the
name of his partner. Then Sereno's relatives finished off Faustino. They
went to the village of San Pablo and got the partner, too. He was more of
a man because when they asked, "Who were your companions?" he answered, "No one, only Faustino and myself. The twelve you put in prison
don't owe you a thing. They are not guilty so let them free. It is an injustice to keep them there. I am going to die but I am guilty."

Well, they killed him and let the prisoners go.

I kept out of all this. I left politics and took hold of the Gospel. I
first heard that a missionary had come to Azteca from Yautepec in 1927.
There was nothing of this here then, nothing. He came during Holy
Week to teach us. He gave me some pamphlets, but at first I just
laughed at him.

I was very Catholic! My *mamá* was religious, of course, and a believer and she taught me a lot. She showed me the path. We were strict
observers. She told me to go to church; she taught me to confess and
took me to everything that went on in church. I confessed and went to
communion once a year. I went to Mass often. I respected the saints
very much; they were gods to me.

Yes, I was very Catholic but I hadn't studied much. They taught me to pray in a private school in Yautepec. They taught the Our Father and the Credo and they hit me a lot there. Here in the village I went to religious school only once a week and they hit me many times. On the *haciendas* where I worked they taught us hymns. And when the priest gave a sermon I stayed near the pulpit and followed his discourse attentively. I liked to hear the sermons so much I even memorized some of them. When the Catholic missionaries who travel from village to village came, I practically lived over there with them. I was in church every day. Every day! That was the kind of faith I had, just praying and praying.

But Catholicism has never really existed here in Azteca. The people think they have only to make a fiesta with fireworks and bullfights to be a Catholic. Some are fanatics and they do lots of things, but that isn't Catholicism. A true Catholic is different—he fears God.

There are many here who know nothing of religion. My neighbor is forty years old and doesn't even know how to make the sign of the cross. She says that is why she and her husband never married. They are afraid to confess because the priest asks about the catechism and they are unable to answer. Before, people were not required to confess; now the priest is beginning to insist that they do. But they still confess very little and go little to Mass.

Before I changed my religion, I had much respect for the gods. I respected them so much, I even knew something about them. I was a prayer leader, and on Holy Week my uncle Crescenciano, who was a real prayer leader, would sing hymns at the church and the chapels and at wakes. He taught me to raise *la sombra,* the soul of the dead, to help the soul leave the body. That is the custom here. We had to go to the place where the person died and at times they even paid us for it. Once when someone was struck by lightning, we had to go to the hills to pray for him. First, we made a cross of lime or sand, and we prayed the *rosario* and the Litany. Then we swept up the cross with the broom, put the lime and sand in a cloth, and took it to the cemetery where the person was buried.

I was in the middle of it all! My devotion was deep and I prayed a lot. That is why when I went to Guerrero I was outstanding there, too in praying and singing the hymns. I was also a prayer leader there. They told me, "You know even more than we do ourselves." I said to them, "Well, I've been taught all that." They thought a lot of me there and in Azteca, too. I was distinguished for it. They would come by for me and say, "Come on, Pedro, let's go to the fiesta together."

I was the principal man in my *barrio.* Twice I was *mayordomo* and in charge of everything. After the Revolution, nothing was left in the *barrio* chapel, not even a piece of wax for a candle. At the meeting I said, "Men, we have nothing! The fiesta is coming and now what are we going to do? Because there isn't a thing, not even a candlestick!" Then I said, "What do you think of this? Let us put a quota of three *pesos* each for the Mass and expenses. And each one will give one pound of wax."

That was what we did and the four old candlesticks appeared! They had been hidden away by the former *mayordomo*. But we still needed eight more to make twelve. I said, "We'll ask for a loan." We began to borrow for everything. We went to the priest and said, "Come, give us a Mass for twenty *pesos*."

Then we went to work and planted the saint's *milpa*. This land was put in my stepfather's name, but it belonged to the little saint of the *barrio*. My stepfather got it from the *barrio;* they entrusted it to him because the saints were no longer allowed to own land. Later, it was passed on to my name and I paid the tax. Now they have sold it, but it was really the saint's.

From 1919 on, I planted the saint's *milpa* to buy whatever the chapel needed. The others in the *barrio* co-operated. Those with money bought the cloths, others cleaned the cemetery or worked on the *milpa,* or decorated the chapel and the cemetery at festival time, all laboring for the saint. And I went along with the others. I respected my religion and I observed it. I was completely devoted to Catholicism.

In past times the *Posadas* were celebrated with more ceremony than now. *Újule!* There were big rich men who came to bring things on credit. They had big stores in Yautepec and in Cuernavaca and they gave things on trust. Everything was sold on credit. They even distributed things, "Go on, take bread or whatever you want." Then everyone carried big baskets well filled with bread, chocolate, sugar, and cakes of wax for candles.

After the *Posadas,* on the first of January, we did almost nothing for the Divine Providence; we only paid our contribution and that was all. We did pray for the Virgin of Guadalupe on her fiesta, but my wife and I never went on a pilgrimage for her, not in our entire life.

And on the Day of the Dead, it was prayers and prayers and then offerings. As Catholics, we would put out bread and chicken for the dead. The souls of the dead children come on the first day and for them we put out rice and milk, bread, also *tamales* and pork with green *chile* sauce (*mole verde*). Even for the children! The priest said the souls of the dead began to arrive at three in the afternoon. That is when the candles are lit. At night, the food is put out.

The souls come and are given the offering, but the food remains there. The next morning, in the cemetery, the candles are lit. That is the belief our ancestors gave us.

But now the priest says it is not necessary to place offerings, that one has only to pray. He says the souls do not come and they do not eat. And how the old women cried and shouted to the souls! But the priest realized that the dead don't want anything. When one sleeps, what is one in need of? Nothing!

On Ash Wednesday we went only to Mass and only to get myself marked, because according to the Catholic religion, all Christians must be marked so that God will receive them at that time. That is what the priest taught us, but many people in the village thought the cross was a protection against the bad spirits of the air, against sorcery, against witchcraft. I never believed that. Never!

Twice I have gone to Jiutepec on the first Friday of Lent. I had great faith in that procession. I went to pray and to fulfill my devotion. I never asked the saints for anything; I just went to venerate them, to adore them. Each year on the third Friday of Lent, I went to Tepalcingo. Yes, every year I went, with devotion to Catholicism, and we almost had to push our way in to hear Mass at three o'clock in the morning. That was important. And there I gave my contribution, my candle, and things like that. Now I still go, but only to sell rope in the plaza. I don't enter the church any more.

To the fiesta of Tlayacapán, I never go. There they have the *Virgen del Tránsito*, when the Virgin was stretched out, when she died. This Virgin once belonged to Azteca. They say that the people of Azteca went to Tlayacapán for the fiesta, carrying the Virgin with them. But when they took her home she held back. She didn't want to go. The men could no longer bear up under her because she didn't want them to carry her any more. They couldn't get her away from there and then the men said, "Well, then let her be here. Let her remain." And there she stayed and there they built her little house.

Holy Friday begins Holy Week but first comes Palm Sunday, which for us is a very solemn thing. All those who want to, go to church. On Palm Sunday we went with our olive branches, or laurel or palm, to be blessed there by the priest. We had much faith, much fear. No one worked then and on Holy Monday and Tuesday we ate fish. On Wednesday we fasted. We observed Holy Week very carefully. That was when we lived in Yautepec when I was a boy. Every day we went to church. It was nothing but church, day after day. My mother took me to confess and she would even confess herself, at times. But not my step-father. He didn't want to because he was ignorant and didn't know anything. But they took me by force. "Come on to confession! Then we'll have communion and they will give us a good breakfast there."

Even after I was married, I spent Holy Friday in church, all day and all night, praying and singing. And the next morning on Saturday there we were, still in church. Then the priest recited the *Gloria in Excelsis Deo* and there was no dancing that day. No, indeed! And the bells began to ring. From the time of the Resurrection which now they say is at ten o'clock, the bells ring and the door is opened, and it is over. There is sometimes a carnival afterward.

On Easter Sunday some people were accustomed to eating meat *tamales,* but I didn't make any. I never did, perhaps because of poverty, a question of economics.

But we did celebrate my *barrio* fiesta. That, yes! For that fiesta we began to prepare eight days ahead of time, to make *mole* sauce, to buy alcohol, and to prepare the whole fiesta according to custom. First, we went to give our contribution to pay for the priest, who gives the Mass, and then a contribution for the fireworks, for the *castillo* and the *torito,* and for the candles. Everyone gives for this.

The fireworks on the *castillo* are burned, and at night we see the *torito,* the little bull with the man inside, who runs here and there startling the crowds, with its pinwheels going and its firecrackers popping. And during the day, in one's home there is chicken in red *chile* sauce, or green *chile* sauce, alcohol with sugar, and all things that go to make *ponche* and then *zas!* to give it to one's friends. That is the custom in our *barrio* and in all the others. "Now I am going to visit my friend because today is his *barrio* fiesta." A man already knows that he will be given a bit of *mole* and a bit of alcohol. We like the taste and that is why we dance and leap until the end of the fiesta.

How miraculous is San José, the little saint of our *barrio!* I know one miracle they told me about because it happened before I was alive. Once there was a cholera plague that nearly wiped out the *barrio.* So they commended themselves to the saint. They had a Mass and he sent away the sickness. That was one reason. Another is that it might have been because of suggestion. We had such faith!

Once, during the fiesta of San José, we were keeping vigil in the chapel, and the *huehuechiques,* as we called the old prayer leaders, were praying. We were kneeling when we began to see many scorpions climbing up the walls, hundreds of them. We saw the walls becoming black with them. We just looked and the *mayordomo* said, "Don't kill any, don't kill them, or you will get bitten." So we just moved over to one side. We didn't kill them and they all went up over the walls. No one was bitten. The ceremony was over and we went outside and began to talk of the miracle. I said the saint was angry because of our lack of faith. Why else would he put scorpions there?

Another time there was a man who played the *chirimía,* the flute we used for ceremonies. Well, this man held back and didn't want to play. We begged him but he got angry and didn't want to. We all said, "Go on, man, play!" But he wouldn't. "Well, then, go away," we said, and he began to go.

This was in the cemetery and when he was almost as far as the fountain he came back and said, "All right. I'll play, but only if you can pay me so much."

"Yes, man, we'll pay you, only you must play on the roof of the chapel." Can you imagine, when he climbed to the top of the chapel he fell dead! He had an attack. *Újule!* We were frightened and we explained it by his lack of faith, that is, his reluctance to play. He was punished because he almost had to be forced to play.

And the miracle was this: we lifted him up and tried to bring him back to life. And yes, in about two hours he revived but from that day to this he's been a halfwit. He even went blind later.

I have always prayed to San José; I prayed to him for everything I needed.

As a prayer leader, I went to pray at the fiestas of all the *barrios*. I would stay in the chapels all night. After I was married, I sometimes brought my wife. I would eat at the homes of the friends who invited me. All good friends! The best I ever had, like *don* Justino, now dead, *don* Jesús, now dead, or *don* Maximiano, still living. I had many friends like that, who would invite me.

I went to pray, right? But then a cousin of mine, the one who knew how to sing and play the guitar, came and we would go out to the street corner to sing songs. We would sing a little, then pray a little. Those were the two things I did even after I was married. I also went to pray at the fiestas of different villages, Santiago, San Salvador, Elotepec, and others.

Yes, I was a Roman Catholic and I liked to go out and celebrate by getting drunk almost every day, and by going with women. But I was a good Catholic because I confessed often.

I had great faith but later I began to lose my belief because I saw the way the priests behaved. There was a priest called Aníbal Ruz, who lived in Mexico City but who came here frequently because he was born here. This priest had a woman, except that he said she was his servant. She had a child called José Ruz, who must have been the son of the priest because he inherited all the fortune when the priest died.

This same priest had a brother, David Ruz, who was on the town council at the same time I was. He was the secretary who taught me when I was *regidor*. We were friends and we would get drunk together and then he would tell me all about his brother, the priest. One day I went to see the priest and the sister came out. She told me to go get her brother David, who was very drunk and was stretched out among the pigs. I found him in a mud hole and when I asked why he did this he said he wanted to die because his sister didn't let him get together with his woman.

It was David who told me that the new young parish priest had a sweetheart and got together with her regularly. Another of our priests had his mother in Mexico City and that was why he was always going there. I have heard that this priest went to bad women there and ordered special prostitutes, the kind you pay twenty *pesos* for. His parents were rich and were *caciques* here.

Way back in 1908, there came a priest who stayed here a long time. They say he was effeminate. There have been many men like that in this village. Our present priest is not thought to be bad but everyone says he owns property in Mexico City. He has made a lot of money. Even a disciple of his told me this.

Once this priest got the idea of having a raffle to raise funds. He had tickets printed and sold them at one *peso* each. Later he held a type of lottery. The one who bought the winning ticket would get a free Mass said for his dead ones. I made up a joke about this, saying that now even the dead gamble in the church. Perhaps the priest heard about it because he didn't do it any more.

From the start, I liked religion very much, but what I liked most of all were the sermons during Holy Week. I would sit right below the pulpit to hear what the priest said. How I would have liked to be able to speak like that! I said to myself, "Well, now where does this man get so many fine words to talk about God? Where, where?"

Sacred books pleased me because they had pictures and I spent a lot of time looking at them. Once there fell into my hands a Sacred History and a Catechism and I said, "Here is where the priests get all their things!"

But I saw that there were other more profound things in the sermons and I tried to learn where to find them. I began to buy books, cheap little books, and at first it seemed that this was it. But then it all sounded different in church. Well, for all the books I read, I never found anything in them.

I already had the Bible, but I had not studied it. I didn't buy it; it was given to me. In 1927, the missionary from Yautepec came and showed us some pamphlets. Later he sold my *compadre* Francisco a Bible for five *pesos*. I didn't pay any attention to this, but when my *compadre* died his wife Diódora was left with the Bible. She gave it to me because she believed it was a sin for her to keep it.

"You'd better take it," she said. "I don't want to read it because it is not a Catholic Bible and the priest has forbidden us to."

So I took it. That was when I began to learn. I said, "Ooooh, this is it! This is what the priest says." This was the real thing, of course. I read all about the Passion. I saw it all, all! Because this was it! Now I had found it! And I treasured the book like a saint. I still have it to this day.

At that time, there were no Protestants in Azteca, except the evangelist who came from Yautepec. He tried hard to convince me. I paid no attention to him because I liked my pleasures too much, but I did begin to read some of his pamphlets.

But man does not stand still. In 1928, I left for Mexico City because of the massacre, and there I stayed. In the city in those days, the evangelists sold little books on every street corner and I began to buy them. They were cheap, only ten *centavos* each. I looked them over carelessly, because I didn't know what they were about. But by then I liked what they said. Well, I spent eighteen months in the city and then I went back to Azteca. The same missionary who had sold my *compadre* the Bible came back to the village and again I heard him talk. I began to like it.

One day I had an encounter with my uncle Agustín, in his house. It was one year since the death of his son, and my uncle came to invite me to the celebration. They had prepared a lot of *ponche, tamales,* and coffee and bread. We said two prayers and everything was in order, but because we had drunk a lot of *ponche* and because my uncle liked very much to argue, we began a discussion.

First, my uncle began to criticize the Revolutionaries who, he said, were against the Catholics. I set myself to defend them. Then we passed on to discuss the evangelists. I hadn't studied yet but I talked against the Catholic religion. We got all heated up and my uncle was roaring mad. He said, "What can you teach me? I went to school and you didn't. You are mistaken."

Well, the discussion continued and all the people went away. We talked until seven o'clock the next morning. We really grappled with each other, he and I. We were very tense and forgot all about praying. Instead, I began to tell him about the Gospel without knowing anything. I told him that everything the priest says is a lie! For example, the Bible doesn't say anything about the Virgin of Guadalupe, about her being God, or anything.

In that same Bible it didn't say anything about it and that is exactly why I think there is nothing to it. After all my experience and all my studies, I still think the Virgin of Guadalupe was *la India Bonita* of Cuernavaca. I've thought about it and studied it and that is what I believe.

Even the church brothers began to study it and they say that the Viceroy fell in love with that woman, *la India*, and he promised that if she gave him her love he would make her the mother of Mexico. Of course she was ignorant, just a little Indian girl, and he was the Viceroy, naturally he was a Spaniard . . . I think it was Maximilian, no? . . . and that is why he did it. He got what he wanted and, yes, he left her portrait, because he had her portrait painted so that all Mexico would respect her to this day. They painted her like a saint and took it to that hill. The Viceroy picked the most stupid one, Juan Diego, to hear the picture speak. The Viceroy himself spoke and the fool heard and went to the Bishop to report the apparition. It was pure deceit! That's why the Vatican didn't want to recognize her until later on.

That's what I told my uncle Agustín. It was five o'clock in the morning, and there were three of us, my uncle, I and *don* Prosperino, he as a friend and I as a relative. They resisted me and I contradicted them, and they argued in return. My uncle said to me, "But if you are ignorant where did you get this from? Why do you contradict me? There is nothing like the Catholic religion!"

I responded, saying I was still a Catholic but nevertheless I disagreed with him. I didn't give in. We became more and more heated and as he got angry, I did too. So I said, "Look, uncle, wait for me one year and I'll answer everything you ask me."

And he answered, "Whenever you like. What can you teach me? You didn't go to school. When you want to I am ready to combat you. I'm not afraid of you."

I said to him, "Yes, uncle, you are right. I have no schooling but I will answer you and in terms you will understand. Wait until the end of one year."

I went away saying to myself, "Now this son-of-a-bitch uncle of mine has gotten me into it! Now what am I going to do? I must study, cost what it will."

That was when I began to look for a place to study. I left politics and began to study religion. I went to sell *zapote* fruit in Santiago. A man there who bought my fruit always spoke to me about religious questions. His name was Juan and he was a Protestant. I said to him, "*Don* Juan, listen, where do you people study? Take me there right now. Yes, I want to. I have a Bible."

And there we go on Saturday to Yautepec. He took me to the house of Maclovio, who was a great believer in the Bible. *Újule!* Once there, Maclovio didn't even let me sleep! He began to indoctrinate me and devoted himself completely to me. The next day he even gave me a tiny New Testament, for the pocket, they say.

The real truth is that I had so much faith that even at night I studied and forged ahead. And when I went to work in the fields I sat down to study a bit. All I did was study, study, study, because what my uncle said to me had influenced me quite a lot. It was almost because of him that I was studying and studying. I met with the evangelists more and more and went around with them. I would say, "Come and explain this to me. I want to know. I don't want to be ignorant."

Finally the year ended and I went to my uncle. At that time the priest sold the four Gospels in little books for one *peso*. I bought several but asked that they give me stamps with the church seal on them so I would know the books were authentic. This helped me combat the errors and changes made in the Gospels by the priests.

"With his own books I am going to fight my uncle. Today the year is up and now I am going." I took the Bible and the four Catholic Gospels, and I said, "Uncle, now I have come. I have the answers."

He looked as though he didn't believe me, and I say, "Yes, uncle, now let's go. I have here a lot of material to chew on."

Said he, my uncle, "I don't see what you are talking about."

"Well, is this book good or not?" I said, to see what he would answer.

"No, not that. That is Protestantism."

"Well," I said, "look at the seal. It is the priest's."

"Man, that's true! I also saw this book but I didn't read it."

"There you have it! You are lax. Why didn't you read it? Read this and we will see. Look, we'll start with the index. Let's see if the dead really return. Why do people talk about the dead this and the dead that? What dead? Which dead? Here it doesn't say a thing except to warn about the pitfalls. But that is for the living, not for the dead. How can this serve them if they are already dead? What hope can the dead have? Nothing!"

But he said, "No, I am not going to read. I have no time. You have time but I don't." And he got angry again.

"All right," I said, "then we will talk as always."

For a long time I had wanted to tell him about the lies, the ten lies. I really gave it to him good. I showed him all the lies. The first is the Virgin of Guadalupe. There's nothing to it! And then the dead. Nothing! And then Sunday; it is not the day of rest because Sunday is Saturday! And then baptism. It is not like that because baptism is done by immersion. And then comes confession. That is a very useful thing, but not with another human being like myself. Not that. That's another lie. Communion is indispensable but that's another lie.

Then Purgatory, Hell . . . all that is a lie. I don't believe either in Purgatory or in Hell. No! It isn't the way they say, that those who have sinned go to Purgatory and then leave it and go to Hell, or, if not, more Purgatory, until they leave and pass on to Heaven. It is not like that.

I believe, according to the Bible, as Isaiah says, that the dead are asleep until that day when they will be resurrected. But all the other things are just lies.

And there are lies about the saints too, these pictures before which they cross themselves. All that is a lie. And what about the deeds of the priests? Why don't they get married? They know they have a need for women but they do it hypocritically and then say they do nothing. That is hypocrisy and I am not going to believe it. I saw all that for myself. And as far as being charitable, they aren't that either. They don't take pity on the poor. Those of us who aren't anything at all have more pity. All this was the reason for my change.

Don Prosperino was there again and he stopped our discussion by telling us a story about a rich man who left home to seek perfect happiness. He met a lion who said he was happy because he did not have to work. He just waited for animals and then ate them. The man didn't think this was happiness because the lion had to take the life of another and was not always certain of a meal.

The man then came to a tree that thought it had great happiness because it was unmolested. But if the tree didn't get water, it would die, and the man said, "This is not the happiness I am looking for."

Finally, he came to the ruins of an *hacienda* where an old man was singing. When the old man learned the other man wanted to live happily he said, "Sell what you have and think no more but give yourself up to God, for that is true happiness."

The man returned to his land very contented and sold or gave away all that he had and attained true happiness.

After the story I said to my uncle, "This is a biblical story and I like it very much because it is something concrete and not like the things you invent. The lion and the tree are symbols of man's temptations. The things you tell me are only for simpletons."

And so again we grappled with each other and spent the whole night in discussion. When my uncle saw that he could not get the better of me, he said, "You are already lost. You don't believe in God because you are a Protestant."

So then I said, "How strange that now when I am old you want to give me advice on how to behave. Why didn't you advise me when my poor wife came to complain to you that I was behaving badly because I had given myself over to vice? You didn't say anything to me then, but now that I have given up vice and that I follow the path that seems more correct to me, now you come to advise me to return to my bad ways."

And that was the way the discussion ended. I was so hard on my poor uncle I even made him cry! Since then I have never returned for another talk with him. From time to time he came to visit me and when he got drunk he said, "You are lost because you are a Seventh Day Adventist. You are a Jew."

I paid no attention to him because I respected him as my uncle. But I continued my religious studies.

It was evolution that led me to change my religion, for man should not stand still. I returned from Yautepec with malaria and found my wife very sick. There she was, her whole body stretched out, half paralyzed, and the little girl, Rufina, nearly dying. And me without money! All we had were twenty-one *pesos* saved from our earnings. That was all. We didn't even have corn. Conchita and the boys were well, but there were the other two stretched out. How was I to cure them? With what medicine? What doctor? There was no money. And no one to prepare my food . . . who? There I was, all alone. My faith was completely uprooted.

The day I got back to Azteca my chills stopped . . . the malaria was gone but it left me awfully thin. Then I began to see what I could do for my wife. I began to treat her, although blindly. I collected herbs and more herbs and I did get her on her feet. My dedication was what cured her.

The neighbor women stopped coming to visit because they said my house was burning hot . . . because now it was inhabited by devils. That was when I made up my mind. I said to my wife, "All right, once and for all, let this be a test God is putting me to. I am going to die sometime, so if I die now, I'll be dead, and if you die, you'll be dead, and that's the end of it. Let's get it over with."

I took down the pictures of the saints and put them all in a pile. I had a lot of pictures there. And I said, "No more of these for me! I am through praying to them! They are . . . nothing!" Yes, that's how it was. I became stubborn and it was no, and no, and no! Well, I got my wife on her feet. She was all right in about twenty days. But my little daughter died. Yes, she did die.

One time my *compadre don* Pancho came to the house. He had been talking about me because I was a Protestant. He went around saying all kinds of things about me. So I put a lot of questions to him.

I said, "You told people I undress my daughter Conchita and pray to her like to a saint, didn't you?"

"No, that's not true."

"Oh, yes, you did! They come and tell me the things you say. And they go and tell you whatever I say. Now, is it or is it not true? And to prove it to you, stay around for a service and you will see how I strip my daughter."

"No, it's not true, *compadre*."

"All right, and you also said that I burned the saints."

"Oh, well, of course! Why should you have them around if you don't believe in them any more? That's why I said it."

"Do you think we are living in the days of Autenaco or Constantine, or what? They are the ones who burned the saints, not I."

"Ah, that was the time of the persecution. But that is not what I was referring to. I meant the pictures."

"Oh, the pictures, is it?" I said, "Let's begin with them."

I had twenty-four pictures of saints and I began to question him about them, one by one. He couldn't tell me anything. Like all the Catholics in my village, he didn't know much about the saints. I, too, though I was a prayer leader and very Catholic, didn't know much about them.

"Finally we have come to the point," I said to him. "Now I'd like you to tell me what it is that you sing at Mass. After all, you are choirmaster."

He couldn't answer this. All he said was, "*Ay, compadre*, sure, I will tell you, our religion . . ."

"See, it's true!" I said, "You don't know anything. First, you know nothing concerning the saints, and now it turns out you don't even know what you are singing at Mass."

All he could say was, "Well, they just taught me to sing and that was all. I don't know the meaning of the words in Latin."

"There you are, *compadre*. Are you a Catholic or aren't you? That's how it was with me. But I am not satisfied to be ignorant and I am going to study."

Well, he was no longer my *compadre*. Now I stood alone.

As I said, when I was a Catholic I knew nothing about the saints. I knew only a little something about Saint Sebastian and that was all. After I had the Bible I learned more. Now, yes, I can tell you about the saints.

The story of Saint Michael is not a legend, it is written down. Saint Michael was Christ himself. They are the leading angels . . . Lucifer and Saint Michael and especially Gabriel, who is likewise an angel. Saint Michael was an angel whom God loved very much. He was the son of God, who later came to the earth. He was incarnated in the Virgin to save men.

Now, about Saint Peter. Well, there are many Peters. The Peter who is the village saint is not one of the apostles. The apostle was the other Saint Peter, who was the main leader of the apostles after Christ.

He went around curing and even revived the dead, preaching the Gospel.

Our Saint Peter hasn't performed any miracles here in the village. Nothing! Because no one believes in that any more, not even the Catholics. They don't take that seriously any more. All they are concerned with are the fiestas and the drinking.

Saint Paul was an apostle also, for the gentiles. He was a big general in the army of the heretics and so he was a persecutor of Christians. He was the one who went around burning and killing all the Christians. Then one day he set out to Damascus with his army to go and kill the Christians who were there keeping the Sabbath.

While they were on the road (Christ was not alive by then) his horse threw him. He fell to the ground and the dust blinded him. And while he was blind he heard a voice say, "Saul" (as his name was Saul), "Saul, why do you persecute me?"

He began to look around, but he couldn't see because he was blind. And he said, "Whose voice do I hear?"

And the voice said, "I am He whom you persecute. Why do you persecute me?"

So Saul says, "Tell me what you wish me to do for you, Lord."

And the voice says, "Look, go to Damascus and I will send you a messenger who will tell you what to do."

So he gave in completely because he had lost his sight and he says, "Yes, Lord, I am going right now."

Now blind, he arrived there and went to an inn where the apostles were locked in a room for fear of the Jews. An apostle comes who is going to open Saul's eyes so he can go to preach to the gentiles, because he was dedicated to them. Peter was to go to Judea . . . and Saint Paul to the gentiles.

Then Matthew comes and says to him, "Saul, what are you doing?"

"Nothing. Here I am," he says.

"What do you think about what He said to you?"

"Nothing, *señor*. I am prepared to do whatever He commands."

"Your eyes will be opened."

And Matthew smeared saliva on Saul's eyes. He awakened and his eyes opened. Matthew says to him, "Now go, go to the gentiles to preach the Gospel until such time as He tells you where you may go." So Saint Paul left.

Thereafter he was called Paul, with which name he was baptized. Now he was Paul and not Saul any more. He began to preach in Samaria and passed through all the villages of the ancients, preaching until he came to Rome, where they took him prisoner. They put him in prison, but he kept on and on and on. Even while he was a prisoner he continued by what we now call correspondence . . . by sending letters to the villages. He said, "Do not submit, continue to follow the doctrine of Christ." And that is what he kept doing until they killed him. He preached for three and a half years.

According to legend, Saint Isidore . . . this is not mentioned in the Bible . . . was a farmer, a very devout man, very fearful of the Lord, even when he went to work. He was always a believer and that is why he was a great farmer. They loved him like a saint. The fiesta of Saint Isidore is in May but I don't know what day. Well, but the only saint I really know something about is Saint Sebastian.

Saint Sebastian lived before Christ. His chief was a Pharoah. I learned this in a sermon. I always liked the priests' sermons on Saint Sebastian. There was a man! A soldier, and young, but yet a captain. He had his command, but was not a general like Paul.

So they arrested the Christians. They persecuted the Christians. Then came the King Pharaoh's decree that the Christians should be starved to death in the prison. The King Pharaoh ordered Sebastian to guard the place so they could not escape. He went to stand guard but then he felt compassion because the divine revelation had already come to him. And instead of starving them, he went among the neighbors to ask for food and water though he realized he would have to die for it because the Pharaoh was very strict.

He said to the prisoners, "I will protect you. I will not let you starve to death as long as I remain alive. But, look here, keep in mind that I am going to die before you, so you will have to keep on believing in God. And you'll see, you will win a crown of laurel in the presence of Our Lord.

"Our body is only a shell, our body is nothing more than a vessel. Treasure the spirit which God, the Father, has given us. He who is with Him will have a new life. That is what you must treasure. The body doesn't matter, even though they divide it into little pieces, or eat it, if that is possible. It does not matter. So don't swerve. I have already told you I am the first who will die, here in front of your prison, to prove to you that I am now a Christian, that I am no longer a heretic."

And so he admonished them day after day. Two weeks went by and they did not starve to death. Why not? Because he was looking after them.

Well, after a while the neighbors got tired of giving them food. So a woman goes and says to the Pharaoh, "Lord King, you want those people to die in the prison, but how are they going to die if Sebastian is taking care of them? You put him there as a guard because you trust him and he is feeding them and as for us we are sick and tired of him. He comes around every day asking us for food and water."

"How is that possible?"

"Well, it is. Just have him spied on and you'll see."

So he put a soldier to spy on him in disguise. And the disguised spy went to watch him and sure enough they caught him. They arrested him immediately and still he said to the others in the prison, "You see, I am the first who is going to die with you."

And they took him before the Pharaoh, and the Pharaoh says, "Well, what are you thinking of, Sebastian? You used to be such a faithful soldier. What made you change? Why haven't the prisoners died?"

Saint Sebastian did not deny anything and he says, "Yes, *señor*, I will now confess to you. Of course they have not died because they are my brothers and have the same flesh as I have. And having the same flesh they should move you, too, to pity . . . just as I would feel pain for you if you were suffering. Well, they are also my fellow men and I do not want to see them suffer. They are children of God just like you."

The Pharaoh says, "I do not know who God is."

So Sebastian says, "All right, maybe you do not know him, but you are a son of God yourself . . . yes, you are. So, the thing is, I am willing to die."

And the Pharaoh answers, "No, don't do it, Sebastian, man! I'll give you so many hours of grace. Think it over carefully."

So Sebastian says to the Pharaoh, "All right, but I've already told you. Whether you give me any grace or you don't, it's all the same. I've told you. My decision is final and I can't do anything about it."

"All right, then," said the Pharaoh, "I'll leave you alone for a few minutes."

So he left and then he had him called again and Sebastian said, "The answer is no, as I said. I told you I couldn't change it any more. I am a son of God just like my brothers and like you, too."

"Then are you ready to be a martyr?" asked the Pharaoh.

"Sure I am. But there is one thing I would like to ask of you. When you take my life, let it be done before the prison where I was on guard. That is where I want to die, to give up my life."

And the Pharaoh said, "Don't give it another thought. That's no problem. I will see that there is where you die."

"Yes, master," said Sebastian, "I am ready."

So they tortured him to see if he would change his mind. After the torture they brought him to the Pharaoh again. And the Pharaoh again asked, "And now, Sebastian, what do you think?"

And Sebastian answered, "Well, I think the same . . . the same as I said to you. Even though I have now been tortured, I still say no. I cannot change my mind. I have already made the decision and I will deliver up my soul to my Father, as there is no other like Him. There is no one else in the universe like Him."

So the Pharaoh said, "All right then, more torture!"

And they burned his feet and, well, they put him through a lot of torture. Then they took him to the prison again but he didn't waver and in the same voice said, "No, I told you. Take my life once and for all here in front of the prison. I cannot walk now, I cannot stand any more . . . enough torture . . . that's enough!"

So the Pharaoh said, "That's just it. Think it over so we may still grant you life."

Sebastian said, "No, *señor,* I have thought it over. Let them slice my body into pieces, into strips, tiny particles . . . my body is a shell, my body is nothing, my flesh is nothing. What I preserve is my spirit which is my Father."

"So is that your word?" asked the Pharaoh.

"Sure. I'm ready right now," said Sebastian. And so now the Pharaoh sent soldiers to take him to the prison to be killed.

Then Sebastian asked them to let him talk there a little bit. "Sure, go ahead," they said. "Why not? You are going to die anyway, so talk as much and as long as you want."

In front of the prison, Sebastian says, "Look, what did I tell you? That I was going to die before you did. Look, my body is a shell. If these men want to eat it, let them eat it! What I preserve is the spirit God gave me. You are my fellow men and I told you I was going to die before you did and to prove it to you . . . just watch, I am going to die right here. So do not change. Die, but keep your belief."

Well, so they killed him with arrows. Saint Sebastian was a great martyr and a great hero.

He was almost like Zapata. Except that Zapata was an ignorant man and did not have the spirit. Well, he had spirit, but only of this world . . . and it was just an ideal. But Zapata too, was very religious, yes, indeed, he was very Catholic.

Well, now, I know something about the other saints, too. Who was Saint Joseph? The thing is, there are two Saint Josephs: the husband of Mary, and Joseph of the Revelations who lived before Christ and was the father of Israel. He was the son of Jacob. The one I am referring to now is Saint Joseph, Mary's husband. This Joseph was not famous for anything, except that I know there were forty-two generations of David. They kept purifying the flesh of each generation for Christ to be born.

When this lineage was born, when Christ was born, his lineage was good and pure . . . completely pure. It was holy even to the blood.

Saint Joseph was Mary's husband, and regarding the birth of

Jesus I believe what it says in the Holy Mass, that Saint Joseph was not his father. No, and Mary was not his mother. They were just instruments, because as I was just saying, they were pure, only a vessel, the flesh and the blood of Mary and Joseph were purified. Joseph was a righteous man and that is why he did not defame the Virgin, see? He was married to Mary but he didn't touch her.

Mary had already had a vision of Gabriel and he announced that she was going to conceive a son. She went out into the yard when she heard a voice calling her, "Mary, Mary!"

She raised her eyes and said, "What salutation is that?"

Archangel Saint Gabriel says, "I, Mary, I, the angel Gabriel, who comes only to announce to you that you are going to conceive a son and you will name him Emmanuel because he is going to save his people."

Mary says, "And how can this be, if I have not known a man?"

So he says to Mary, "Do not fear, the spirit of God will cast a shadow over you and you are going to conceive a son."

And then she said, "Here is the slave of the Lord who carries out thy will."

Then, a few days later, Joseph, her husband, noticed it. As I see it, this was when Joseph got jealous and then he wanted to leave. Little by little, he drew away. Joseph's mother, Mary's mother-in-law, did not say anything.

And Joseph says, "All right, on account of what I see, I had better leave. Even my mother, because she indulges her . . ."

And then he had a revelation again. I mean he saw a vision and it said to him, "Joseph, why are you doing this? Take back your wife, because what you see in her is the Holy Spirit's and she is going to conceive a son and give birth to a child and she will name him Emmanuel or Jesus because he is going to save his people, and he will be King."

So this was when Joseph changed his mind and he went back to her, but not to touch her, not that, not until the nine months were up. After that, all right.

But Joseph kept on seeing revelations. It was the custom then to go to Jerusalem at Easter, like the pilgrimages nowadays and all that. And like the rest of the Jews, Joseph and Mary went to Jerusalem to spend the Easter fiesta, see? And with the Virgin, now in a family way, they arrived in Bethlehem, as has been written by the prophet Isaiah. They could not go on any further so they stopped there and the prophecy was fulfilled.

Well, when they arrived they began to ask for lodging because the time was getting very close . . . but there was nothing because the houses were filled up with visitors coming from all over. There was no room, not in the inns, not anywhere. But nothing at all! Joseph, who was desperate by this time, said, "Now what? Where can I take her? Where? It is coming surely at any moment now, and what am I going to do?"

Finally, in the last house, after a lot of pleading, even there they told him there was no room. "We are filled up. The place is full of people," they said to him. Until at last one of the owners of the house said, "All right, in that case, if your wife is unwell"—naturally, they did not know who she was— "come in, you can rest in the stable. Let the animals be taken out and you can stay there because there is no room in the house any more."

So they sent the groom and he took out the horses and all that remained was the hay and the manure. The groom, who slept there too, took everything out and the whole family moved in, that is the two of them, and within a little while the Virgin gave birth.

This was when the shepherds outside of town saw everything in revelation. They were warming themselves because it was very cold. They were in a circle warming themselves when they saw a light which shone like day. And they began to look. What was it? What was all lit up?

They didn't see anything and then finally they heard a voice. It was the same voice, of Gabriel himself, which was saying, "Go to Bethlehem to worship the King of the Jews who has been born."

So off they went, all of them carrying their little lambs with them for fear of the coyotes. Then, after forty days, the Wise Men of the East looked at their stars and after that it was said that the King of the Jews had been born. Before that they did not want this King of the Jews as they were important men and how could he be King of the Jews! They thought he would come from the sky. That is what they believed, but then they learned he was the son of Joseph, the carpenter, whose father was . . . I don't remember his name.

Everybody discussed it, "But, man, how are we going to believe that he is the son of God? King of Heaven! What kind of stuff is that!"

Well, that was how they all felt, especially King Herod. But forty days later, the Wise Men arrived, following the star which guided them. They entered the city and the star disappeared. They came to King Herod and asked him, "Where was the King of the Jews born?"

And Herod answers, "Well, man, I don't know a thing, but wait a moment." So he called the priests who were reading the Bible and he asked them, "Where is the King of the Jews going to be born?"

So the priests said, "Ah, well, according to the Holy Scriptures, in Bethlehem. According to the prophet Isaiah, it is going to be in Bethlehem."

So, after that, he said to them, "Go, then, the King of the Jews will be born in Bethlehem. Go and see what is happening."

Then they said to him, "We are going to visit him, to worship him."

So he said to them, "Go and then come here again and let me know if he is there. I will go to worship him, too."

But that business about Herod wanting to worship him was not so. What he wanted was to kill him!

So those people left and the star came out again and it kept moving, moving, until it came to Bethlehem, and when everybody arrived there, the star came down. They looked around but there wasn't anything. So, they kept on looking and looking. They went there but nothing happened until after forty days. Then they found the Virgin and Joseph and all of them, and they began to worship Him and bring Him treasures. Everyone worshiped Him.

At night in a dream, the same Gabriel notified Joseph and Mary. He said, "Tomorrow, or whenever it is that you leave, do not go to see Herod, as you did before, because he wants to kill the child. Take another road."

In fact, that is what they did. They took another road and did not go through the city again. When Herod saw that, he believed he had been made a fool of and that was when he gave an order to kill all boys two years old and younger in Bethlehem, so that he would catch Christ.

This was written by Joel, I think it was . . . I don't remember which prophet. So that was what he said and they killed them all.

But that same night the angel Gabriel came to Joseph once more and said to him, "Take the child and his mother and go to Egypt so that what the prophet said will be fulfilled. Go there as far as I tell you, because Herod is trying to kill the child."

So he picked himself up and left for Egypt where he stayed a long time, until King Herod died. Then from there he went to Nazareth, but on orders from Gabriel, who came to see him once more. So, what happened was that the child finished growing up in Nazareth so that what the prophet said would be fulfilled, "that he will be called Jesus, the Nazarene."

But there was a blood brother of Christ, whose name was also Judas, but not Judas Thaddeus. Yes, Mary was his mother, also, and his father was Saint Joseph. The first-born was Christ.

The truth of the matter is that not even my own religion believes in that, but because I have studied, I learned that Jesus did have brothers. I found it out from the Bible. There where Saint Matthew says, "And Joseph did not know Mary until he knew her first-born son."

Now, what does that mean? It gives you to understand that afterward he did have a hand in things, like any ordinary person, right? But this did not stop them from being righteous people until they died. She did not die a virgin. But all the religious people believe that when she died she was still a virgin, truly belonging to God. I have studied and it is not true, because Christ himself never called her mother. Never! The people and all the Jews said she was his mother. But not he, never! Not even John understood this when Christ was crucified. John the Revealer knew that John the Evangelist was Christ's brother because when he was on the cross he called to John and when he was going to die, he said, "John, here is your mother Mary." He did not call her mother. Instead he says, "Mary, here is your son."

Why did he say that? This was why! And because of this I realize that Mary was only an instrument, no more, because she came from a pure lineage, as did Joseph. I say pure, in that there was not the slightest bit of sin in the flesh or the blood. It is not a sin to have a husband or a wife. No, they were righteous in that they never committed adultery or a robbery or had some evil thought—things like that. They were pure in every way.

The blood is purified the way a strainer purifies. Isn't that about how it is? The strainer strains and the bad remains above and the good below. And it is even better after forty generations. The good and the bad . . . well, nowadays in the world we are in, who knows who is righteous, who is holy, and who is bad? We do not know, but God knows.

I learned this story in the Scriptures . . . mm . . . and I don't think that here in Azteca they know all this. And I say this because my *compadre,* who was a Catholic and a choirmaster besides, couldn't tell me anything about these things.

Of the Johns, to me only John the Baptist is important. Saint John the Baptist was the one who, according to the apostles, was the prophet Elijah. He died and was born again. That happens occasionally; a person dies and his spirit goes to another person. That is believed in other religions, particularly spiritualism, but sometimes I believe in it myself because it is written that Elijah was incarnated again in Zachary and Sarah. I think that the people of Azteca do not believe in this reincarnation. They don't believe in anything! All they believe in is the bottle, and besides they know nothing about these things.

My neighbors began to laugh and to make fun of me. They took the pictures and then went around even more, spreading the word that I was with the devil and who knows what else. The neighbors never said anything to me directly and did not speak to me now or come to the house any more, because I was damned, they said. They even wanted to beat me up at that time, but they never did because they could find no pretext.

Afterward, my faith deepened. The Gospel was sacred to me. And it was something to see! My character changed. According to the Bible, he who becomes modernized takes on more fear and better manners. In Roman Catholicism you learn nothing. With them there are only sermons, but no fear. There is nothing. Yes, the priest inculcates a little something but because there are so many Catholics, naturally, he doesn't fulfill his obligation. He does nothing! That is why it was a change for us; because he who follows Adventism completely, must give up all bad habits.

I wanted to purify myself, to ask God from the bottom of my heart to forgive me for the errors I committed in my ignorance. Fasting converts a man and that is why I did it, asking for divine inspiration to understand the full meaning of His word. I fasted four times because in the beginning I thought I was, well, a sinner. All my four penitences were for adultery. That was the only sin I committed because I do not like to steal or fight or anything like that. Nor was I evil-minded, but I could never resist the women. My religion pulled me out of the swamp of sin.

I gave up vice. I did not go out at night any more with my friends. No, no more. They didn't even want me now. For twelve years I didn't touch alcohol. The thing is, a person doesn't change his way of living unless it is through religion. Then fear enters, and it makes you want to change in every way toward your family as well as toward the neighbors. The family becomes more correct, more obedient, and there is more respect in the home. The deeper my faith became, the more I changed. Before I gave up my bad habits I would shout at my wife, but when I knew the Gospel I began to think differently and stopped scolding her. The more time passed, the more love there was. I have admitted my past errors and have repented. I even felt more love toward my relatives. But unfortunately they were afraid of me because of my religion. They said it was the devil's religion.

I was the first one in my family to know the Gospel. My wife was an ignorant little thing and because she didn't know how to read, she couldn't understand. She knew absolutely nothing. Her mother and her brother were completely ignorant and had taught her nothing. She just grew up, without ever having an idea, without ever thinking. She didn't even believe in Roman Catholicism because of certain things she saw among the priests. The only thing she believed in were *los aires,* the spirits of the air. Many times she came to the *milpas* and put crosses of *pericón* at each corner so that *los aires* and the wind wouldn't come to blow down the crop. But she wasn't the only one; everyone did. She thought the rainbow was bad because it brought *los aires.* She didn't want me to get fertilizer from ant hills because *los aires* that were there could make me ill. It did make some people ill, but not because of *los aires.* My idea is that the pimples and swelling are caused by the smell or the vapors from the ant hill, because the ant manure is "hot." It never bothered me because I am not sensitive to it. I have even carried it in a sack to put on my plants.

So when I came to know the Gospel, my wife didn't want to learn about it. She became angry and rebellious but, of course, I explained it to her and also told her about this fear. Apart from that, we went to services and to the Adventist school. Because of me she did believe a little. My wife didn't know a thing but she died in the faith. Being the person I am, naturally I converted her.

My children were little when I got to know the Gospel and so I taught them, too. All of them! That is why they are not ignorant. I plunged in all the way, and they did, too. And how well they understood the verses of the Scriptures or the Bible! They were the ones who stuck to it faithfully because they were little and I guided them, and my wife too. When they were older, I bought another Bible. When they learned to read I bought more. Felipe had his, Conchita hers, and Martín, too. Each one had his own and in this way I began inculcating this religion. All my children were completely addicted to it, more so than my wife and I.

Once a week and at night when we were not too tired we all studied, because I needed it just as much as they did. I saw to it that they fulfilled their obligations, that they studied and kept the Sabbath and loved their fellow man, and that they observed the Commandments. I told them that they should not do any wrong, that they should respect the authorities and the teachers as well, because they are the superiors. I not only advised my children but I showed them that in the proverbs there is a lot of good counsel which applies to children and even to myself. I didn't tell them stories or legends but, as examples, I told them all about my own experiences so that they wouldn't be like I was before. But mostly we studied the Bible.

I enjoyed these studies very much. Everything that has to do with spiritual education gives me a great deal of pleasure, especially the book *Seeking the Path,* and the Bible. I also read the Holy Scriptures, *The Conflict of the Centuries, The Road to Christ, The Finger of Destiny, The Future Deciphered,* and a lot more. I have them all in my house. The *Sentinel* comes every week. It is sacred reading but it also carries news about religion from all over the world.

I was the first in Azteca to be converted to Protestantism. After me, the second one was my cousin Margarito. I converted him. I converted them all, but he was first, as I lived practically next door. That is why. Then came Guillermo Cruz, Fulgencio, and my son-in-law Juan, Heraclio, David Fuentes, and after him, Celerina Vázquez. Ángel came much later. These were the first ones I got to join up. Margarito was converted through the sermons. It took two or three years because he does not know how to read. But he didn't resist.

It was easy to convert them! Yes, naturally! Because it was for selfish motives that they came in and nothing else, understand? The thing was that even though I had a lot of children in the house at that time, we always managed to get by . . . to eat, that is. And so, every Saturday the converts would come to my house and I would feed them. At twelve o'clock I fed them. All of them! It was an obligation I assumed.

I also contributed to my new church. I earned little so I gave little, and only at harvest time. For twelve years I gave my contribution. Apart from that, I gave an offering every week.

Then we were baptized, my wife and I. I have photos of the baptism in Yautepec. My wife was baptized in about the year '32 or '35 . . . not right away. My wife and I went with all the brethren who were going to take part in the ceremony. It was on a Saturday, in a place where there was water . . . a big pond. They took us there and put us in the water. It was baptism by immersion.

The pastor examined us carefully to see whether we were really Christians or not. He explained to us that baptism signifies a burial and a rebirth. Then I made a protest, saying that if we were going to leave this world, were we going to come back and continue in the same condition we were in? He said if we had any quarrel with one of the brothers, we should become reconciled first. We were going to bury our sins there and be reborn again. Then he prayed to God, the Holy Spirit, and baptized us. I prayed, too, and I felt a great emotion, almost as though I was speaking to God.

Whew! After that how the neighbors persecuted me! My *compadre don* Pancho was the one who would call them together in his house. He explained to them his ideas on the Roman Catholic religion and he told them not to believe in me. He was angry with me and worked against me.

They persecuted me from the beginning. Even before I was baptized they wanted to stone me. They threatened me, especially the people from the *barrio* of Santa Cruz, who are not my neighbors but who are more fanatic. They set about doing me harm a number of times. The children of neighbors also came to stone my house.

There came a time when the members thought we should set up a temple or a meeting house. So we began to use a house no one lived in. We got together there and considered it our church. From that time on I stopped feeding the congregation. We would meet there and not in my house any more. When they saw that I was no longer feeding them, they began leaving little by little. Finally, only the most devoted remained.

Celerina, David and Heraclio left. But Heraclio left because he had come in for selfish reasons anyway. *Don* Maclovio had a stepdaughter and Heraclio made love to her. The girl was young, fourteen years old. So, after he made love to her, that evil man threatened her because he realized she was not a virgin.

Well! He began forcing her to talk, the poor little girl. He scared her and she told him that her stepfather had abused her first. Was it a lie or was it true? Then this friend got angry and says to her, "Now you are going to have to prove if it is true or not, but in my presence and his."

As he had frightened the poor girl, even threatening to hang her, there was no way out and she said that Maclovio did it. That's what she said, but we do not know whether it was true or not. I won't commit myself, this is only what Heraclio got out of her.

Heraclio was from the center of the village. Well, he planned to go to our temple at night (because no one was living there) to tear up our papers. He invited others along and they went in and tore up everything there. We said the devil got into him to do such a thing.

Well, from that time on everyone began to be demoralized. This was in '38 or thereabouts. I had been a member for quite a while by then . . . for years. Then this Heraclio decided he was going to attack Maclovio. He wanted to kill him in a fight, because of what he had done to his stepdaughter. It was precisely for that reason that the demoralization came. *Don* Maclovio had to go to the hospital because Heraclio tried to kill him. He cut him up with a razor. He wasn't even drunk or anything like that. He wanted to cut off Maclovio's head, but he just got him in the cheek. *Don* Maclovio went to the hospital and all the members withdrew.

Meanwhile, we began to investigate Heraclio's motive. You know, I believed there was some truth in all that. Do you know why? Because when Maclovio converted me, he would come to the house to see if he could stay overnight. And my daughter Conchita was not such a little girl. She was already fourteen.

We slept in the same room here on the floor. And my daughter over a little further, see? And *señor* Maclovio over here. Well, one night, he surprised the girl by moving over close to her and she did not tell us right away. She just said that who knows what it was squeezing up against her. That is what she told us during the night. Well, it happened three times, and he made believe he was sound asleep.

I didn't think the least little bit about it. It was the furthest thing from my mind as I had so much faith and trust in him, understand? Until finally, the third time it happened, I said, "Look, daughter, better lie down over here with us." Not until then did he stop bothering her.

The next morning, *don* Maclovio got up at dawn and said, "Good-bye, I have to leave early for this and that." He gave some reason or other. All right. And he left. I thought it was because of something unexpected or because of fear of something . . . because we were accustomed to pray every morning. I got up right after that and so did my wife.

I began to haul water. Then my wife and I noticed that he had left his shirt. "Well, now, what is this? He went out of here as if he were scared. Why? He even left his shirt behind."

Maclovio came back later and said, "I left my shirt." After that we began to wonder. But the girl kept silent. She didn't tell us anything. Until finally, a week later, she said, "I didn't want to tell you because I don't want you to do anything to the *señor,* but he wanted to . . . I felt that it was he!"

"What! What's this? And why didn't you tell us right then?"

"No, because I was afraid you would do something. But I am sure that he was the one because he spoke to me."

"There you have it! What did he say to you?"

"Well, he told me not to yell."

He had a wife as well as the stepdaughter. So when that business came up with Heraclio, I was inclined to believe it because he wanted to do the same in my house. Well, when it was all over, I found out it was true. As a result, I was left wondering about my religion. That was when my decline began. From that I realized the truth, that no one lives up to his obligations. Later, as I had this daughter of mine, another man from Yautepec who also had a wife and was old besides, wanted to make love to her. I chased him out of here, too. He was an Adventist, but he did not take advantage of her . . . he just wanted to make love to her.

That is why I cooled off. I tell you, when that happened, everything fell apart . . . the whole congregation. Gone were all the new members who had joined. Everything went to pieces and they left. We were alone again, Margarito, *don* Federico and I. Federico was the very first to indoctrinate me in 1927. He was the one who brought the message from Yautepec to Azteca.

But my faith in God and in Jesus continued. Based on my experience, and as I was once a Catholic, I had a lot of faith. Very much! I believe that Jesus was true and that he came to live on earth. I have testimonials of the good He has done for me. Yes, the Lord has done me many favors. But I also have experienced His punishments.

CHAPTER XIV

ESPERANZA

Conversion

Pedro was converted to Adventism in the year 1930. He came back from Yautepec ill with malaria. I was in bed with my leg paralyzed from *los aires,* because I had gone to wash clothes when I had a fever. And my little daughter Rufina was sick with vomiting and diarrhea.

The girl was big already when she died, seven years old. I do not know what she died of. She was just sickly. She was already sick when we brought her to Mexico from Azteca.

I don't know what it is that happened to her. She kept getting skinnier and skinnier. She would get better and then before we knew it, she would be sick again with diarrhea. As some people said she was *ética* and that she had worms, we gave her the flesh of a woodchuck. This animal is given in a special *chile* sauce. In order to prepare the dish it is necessary to go from house to house asking for squash seeds, old *tortillas,* that is, anything eaten by mice. The animal is cooked and the meat given to the patient together with the other things. They say that this cures *éticos,* but it did not cure my daughter.

So next we gave her the "little blanket" cure. This consists in the godmother of the sick child bringing him bread and a little blanket, which is put on him. The godmother is then served pork with green *chile* sauce and *tamales.* I have given this cure to five of my children. But, in spite of all the cures we tried, the little girl died.

She was the goddaughter of *don* Pancho. My daughter loved her godmother very much and kept asking to go to her house all the time. Pedro went to notify my *compadre* Pancho of the wake and to see how much he would charge to make her coffin. *Don* Pancho refused to make the coffin because he said Pedro had burned the saints. He didn't even come to see his godchild. We bought the coffin in Cuernavaca.

Because there were so many calamities in the house, Pedro said that God had put him to the test. But people said that all the sickness was a punishment because he did not believe in God any more.

Pedro got angry and said, "Because people are talking so much, I am going to become a Protestant so they can be speaking the truth. I am going to take down all our religious pictures and, once and for all, either we die or we will be saved."

Afterward, the neighbors, *doña* Gloria and other ladies, came to visit us, and when they saw the saints weren't there they asked about them. Pedro said he had taken them down for good and was going to burn them in the *corral*. So they said he should not do such a thing, that he better let them have the saints. And they took them all away.

The Adventists came to visit us, to see how we were getting along, but they did not help Pedro economically. I cured myself with herbs and nothing more, with *teloloache* and lard. Afterward, Pedro was cured too, and went back to work.

Pedro's sister scolded me because he changed his religion. She was angry because the Adventists met in our house on Saturday. She said, "It's awful, what he has done, to remove the saints and have those devils meeting in my mother's house."

I did not answer. All I said was, "What can I do? He's the boss. Besides, they come here and don't do anything bad. They just study."

But my sister-in-law got even angrier and advised me to abandon him . . . to leave him and his children. "And then you'll see," she said, "how quickly he will leave the Adventists."

Later on, Pedro said it was not nice that only he should be an Adventist, that I, too, should convert, and that if I didn't want to, at least my children and I should stop going to the church, and the Carnival, and to the *barrio* fiestas. I answered that it would be no trouble at all as I went to very few fiestas anyway. Besides, when I went to the church I would hear the women saying in *mexicano*, "That woman's husband is an Adventist, so what is she coming here for?"

Then I said, "All right, let them be saying the truth, once and for all." And I became converted also.

As a matter of fact I went to church very little before becoming converted. I was never very religious. I remember one time I burned a cross they had made for the saint's plot of land. My husband was

mayordomo of the *barrio* at the time and he brought home the cross and set it up in the *corral* to protect the house. One day Pedro went to cut wood and told me to have his *tortillas* ready when he got back. But I had no firewood to heat the *comal*, so I burned up the cross and made the *tortillas*. When Pedro returned he asked about the cross and I told him I had burned it. "You burned it!" he said. "You really are a Protestant!"

The difference between the Catholic religion and the Adventist is only a matter of the day that is observed. Instead of Sunday being the Sabbath, it is Saturday. Then, too, the Adventists do not make fiestas like the Catholics.

My relatives told me that it was not a good thing to leave the religion of our parents. "Protestantism has just come out. It is something new. Besides, Protestants don't believe in God," they said.

I explained to them, "The Protestants always believe in God, we always have faith. The Catholics go and confess but then they come out of the church and go right on sinning, they go on talking about people, they quarrel. It is always the same thing. Everything they say in church is only lip service."

All the saints perform miracles, so long as you have faith in your heart. But everything happens through acts of God. One time after I was converted, I was so in despair that I went to the chapel of San José to pray to God to give me peace in my home because Pedro was unbearable. And he really did calm down after that.

Another time, my son Felipe got sick a lot and after a while was nothing but skin and bones. I didn't know what to do for him. I took him to Elotepec to see if they could cure him for me there. I took him everywhere, but it was no use. Finally, I brought him to Saint Peter. I invited my cousin to come along. "What are you going to do?" she asked.

"I am going to buy flowers and a candle and offer the boy to Saint Peter to see if he will cure him," I answered. I cried an awful lot in the chapel and said to the *señor* Saint Peter that he should cure my child and that afterward he would dance for him.

From Saint Peter I brought the boy to *señora* Juliana, the curer, and he got better right away. Felipe is a man now but he never went to dance for Saint Peter because his father was against it.

F E L I P E

Childhood

We were very poor and we suffered a great deal as little children. Later, when we began to work, my *papá* was able to plant more corn. But at this time we still didn't have corn and my *mamá* went through many difficulties to get it for us. She was very much concerned that we should eat.

When we had nothing to eat my *mamá* would get up very early to see where she could buy corn, if she had money, or if she didn't, to see where she might borrow corn. If she came back without corn because no one would lend her any, she said, "Well, I will go somewhere else." By then it was almost eleven o'clock and we still had no breakfast, not even coffee or a piece of bread, and my poor little mother came back, almost crying, if she was unable to get either money or corn.

She would go again to try, until finally she would come back with two or three *cuartillos* of corn. Then she would put it to soak and cook until one or two in the afternoon and though the mixture was still hot she would begin to grind it and make *tortillas*. Sometimes she had to use poor quality corn that was partially putrified and rotten but she would come home and prepare it so we could eat. It no longer had the flavor of *tortillas;* it tasted like earth because the corn was rotten. But that's how we ate it because there was nothing else. She would count the *tortillas* and would give each of us two so there would be enough for all. She would save some for my *papá* to eat when he came home from the fields. Sometimes my *mamá* didn't even eat because there wasn't enough to go around.

When there was no corn, my *mamá* went to buy a little rice and she would make *atole* of rice with boiled water. She would give us two plates each and that was our breakfast, and when she had absolutely no money to buy anything she would go to her *comadre* whose husband was a butcher and they would give her some leftover meat that was already green and rotten, decomposed and full of worms, large worms. When she came home she would say, "I am back, my children," and she prepared her pot to cook the meat. They had given her about four kilos and when she cooked it, the worms dropped to the bottom of the pot and looked almost like rice. She gave us the meat and sent us out to the *corral* to eat because my *papá* would scold her if he learned that she gave us this meat. My *papá* didn't like it. It nauseated him and that is why she made us finish it out there, so that he would not see it. "Now you're not going to tell him," she said, "because he will scold me." Sometimes she would have to hide her cooking pot under the bed so he would not see it when he arrived from the fields.

I still remember when they took me from my village to Mexico City. They put me and my brother Martín in a box on one side of the horse and my sister Conchita in a box on the other side. But she was bigger than we and didn't cry. We cried all the way up the mountain to the railroad station. My *papá* had hired a teamster to take us to the station with all our things. He and my *mamá* walked ahead of us, and when we lost sight of them we cried and screamed all the more. I remember that we were sweating from crying so much in the strong sun. Then they covered the two of us with a shawl to shade us.

I was just a little boy of five when we were in Mexico City. My brother Martín was four. My sister Conchita would go to buy water when we needed it and I went along with her to keep her company. She got half a can of water for a *centavo*. In those days my brother and I wore short pants and went barefoot; sometimes we went around without any pants at all.

My *mamá* worked in a *tortillería*. Sometimes she did washing for others because my *papá* had no work. He started peddling oranges but didn't earn enough and, instead, he went around selling ice cream in the streets. Then my *mamá* did not have to suffer by going out to work any more.

When my *mamá* went to the market, she brought me back little toys, a ball or a little car, and my *papá* would bring us marbles when he came home from work. I remember I used to play with a girl named Feliz. Once she bit me on the nipple and I began to cry. She did a lot of things to me, even pinched me, but I was so small and she was about twelve years old. Every day she would come to my house to get me to play, and would give me toys and some of her *taco*. My uncle Margarito visited daily, bringing squash and gourds in a sack. *Doña* Diódora, my *mamá's comadre*, also came. She would tell my *papá* to go back to Azteca, that there was no danger now.

Finally, we returned to Azteca and went to my uncle Margarito's house. But he and my aunt were angry with us all the time because we played too much. One day my *mamá* said, "Let's go home, children." When we got to our house, it was in a terrible state. The yard was covered with weeds so thick we couldn't even get in. The gateway was closed up with big rocks. We could see that horses had been kept inside the house. There were even fleas and *mamá* began to sprinkle hot water on the earth floor to kill them. We saw big holes dug out where pigs had been sleeping. My *mamá* and Conchita swept it up and there we stayed.

A few days later my *papá* arrived and he cleared the entrance to the street. He took away all the stones, cut some branches to make a gate, and then my brother Ricardo was born. Diódora's sister Mercedes came to help with the housework and she scolded us because we ate. When my *mamá* was able to get up again, she began doing the chores herself. My sister Conchita was about twelve years old and she couldn't do all the work.

When someone from the family came to visit, my *papá* and *mamá* would tell us, "He is your uncle, greet him," and in this way all the people in our family were made known to us while we were growing up. Sometimes my *mamá* took us to visit our godfather Basilio. She would tell us that our godparents were like our father and mother, and that whenever we met them we should kiss their hand. Then our *padrino* would give us twenty *centavos* apiece and some bread, because he was a baker. When we said good-bye, we kissed his hand again.

When my mother ground corn she would give me the water that was used to soak the dough, saying, "Go ahead, drink this dough water so that you'll be able to speak well." Once she took me along with her to leave incense at the *barrio* chapel of San José and she carried a key to open the door of the chapel. When we arrived there she took out the key and said to me, "Open your mouth." I opened my mouth and she put the key into it and said, "This is so you will speak well," and she turned the key twice in my mouth.

When I was little I played with my brothers and sisters. Sometimes other boys and girls, neighbors, would come to play with us. My godmother taught us to play the enchanted ones and the onion and stealing a soul, in which we all held hands. We boys would play bullfighting

and horses and marbles and tops. Sometimes we would play one was the butcher and the other was the storekeeper and I was the miller and my sister goes and buys. We also played at sweethearts with the girls. Then we formed couples, but we changed them often. I had to play sweethearts with Elida, or Susana or Lucinda, and we embraced as sweethearts do, but innocently, because it was a game and we did it in front of everybody.

My sister Conchita was very playful. We would run around the *corral* chasing butterflies or we would take a rope and make a swing. We would swing together and sometimes the rope would break and we would fall. At times we would chase each other into the *corral* with corn dough and water and smear the corn dough on each other's faces or throw water at each other. Then my *mamá* arrived from the market and would scold my sister and say to her, "What have you been doing? You haven't been doing the chores." But my sister defended herself; she would tell some lie in order to avoid a scolding and sometimes she told my *mamá* that we would not let her work and my *mamá* would tell her not to give in to us, that there was always a rope or a stick to hit us with. My sister was silent and that was all. Sometimes my *mamá* would hit her and sometimes she would only scold her.

Conchita would teach me how to read. She taught me the first few letters and how to count on my fingers, but for the most part we just played together. Then my mother gave her the baby to take care of and we would go to the *corral* to eat berries from a tree there. And sometimes when my *mamá* went to the plaza, my sister would toast a *chile* in the fire and she'd grind it on the grinding stone and mix it with a little water and salt and we would eat the sauce with a spoon. When there were no *chiles* she would toast seeds and we would sit down together to eat them. Sometimes Conchita would go out into the *corral* to look for birds' nests with little eggs in them and she would bring them down and fry them on the griddle with lard and we would eat them with a little bit of corn dough. When there was a chicken egg or a turkey egg we would also eat it. She would give each of us a little bit and tell us not to say anything about it to *mamá*. She would wash the griddle carefully, so that my *mamá* would not notice it when she returned. My *mamá* would come and say, "Where is the egg I left?"

My sister said, "I don't know," and would make signs to us not to say anything. My *mamá* would always scold Conchita because she was the eldest.

Sometimes we would go to steal guavas in some other *corral*. We would steal oranges and when the owner saw us we would run. And sometimes I would knock down a little chicken and it would break its leg and when my *mamá* saw it she would ask my brothers who had done it and they said they didn't know. Then she would ask me, "Felipe, didn't you see who threw something at the chicken?"

I would say, "No, I didn't see anything."

When the neighbor's chickens came in, I would drive them out with stones. Sometimes I would hit them in the legs and would break them as they went running off. And if I ever hit them in the head, they would fall down for a minute and then slowly get up. That is the way we always did our little mischief.

In those days we slept on the dirt floor. We children all slept together on a straw mat and we covered ourselves with a single blanket. We would wake up, one on one side, the other on the other, and the blanket somewhere else. We would urinate on the mat at night and we got up with our white *calzones* full of mud. Even our shirts and heads were full of dirt and we would get up and go out into the sun to warm up and get dry. Then we would begin to play and my mother would send Martín and me to the mill. We would always go together. This is why people would call us "the twins." When the two of us went to the fields or hauled water, we always went together. And if someone wanted to hit us we would defend each other.

When I was about eight, my *mamá* would leave me at a neighbor's house so that the lady of the house might teach me to read. She was my *mamá's comadre* and my *papá* paid her a *peso* a month. I went there every day and Conchita would come to take me home. I kept this up for a year.

There were three girls there and one of them was my first sweetheart. She was big and already knew about bad things. She was the one who began it. It happened that the lady who was teaching us left us alone sometimes to go to the market to buy things. Once, the girl and I were alone and she said, "Do you like girls?"

I say, "Why?"

"I'm just asking you. How many girl friends do you have?"

"None."

Then she got up and went to a dark corner and called me. I thought we were going to play hide-and-seek, but she took off her pants and I said, "And what does that mean? Are you going to urinate here?"

But then she said, "Come here," and I leaned against her. "Give me your hand," and she took my hand and put it between her legs and I took the opportunity to put in my finger. We embraced each other and from then on she said we were sweethearts.

I also did some bad things with Elida, the daughter of my aunt Gloria. She was the one who provoked me. She sat on my knees and said, "Hug me," and I would hug her. She would grab my hand and put it where she wanted me to touch her. We went to hide in dark places where no one could see us and there I stuck my finger in her. When Elida stayed in the house to sleep because it was late, I went to sleep with her and we embraced a lot. But I didn't know how to do the sexual act so I didn't do it.

Then my *papá* took me to the primary school. I was a little afraid to go to school because I didn't know how to behave. But I never cried. My sister Conchita took me to school and brought me home every day. I only got to the second grade because I was absent a lot. At times I missed two months or one month or a week, depending on the work at home. Sometimes we stayed out of school because we didn't have any clothing, sometimes because we didn't have any school supplies. My *papá* had a hard time of it when we were in school.

Wherever my sister went, I followed her. I went along when she brought water from the fountain. She would leave me near the water tap with her water can and would go to see her sweetheart. Later, when she returned, she told me not to tell my *mamá*. She said, "If you do, I will not like you."

But once she was late and I left and went back alone to the house. When my sister arrived, my mother scolded her and even hit her and then my sister was angry with me because she said I had told on her. She scolded me, but I followed her about a great deal. Whenever she went on some errand, there I was behind her. And when we walked through the street, some boys would say to me, "Now, brother-in-law, where are you going?" or, "Take good care of her for me." Then I would pick up stones to throw at them. But they only laughed and called me "brother-in-law" again.

And so we grew up. Conchita was getting older and my cousin Talinda began to visit her. They would talk about their sweethearts. My mother would go to the market, leaving chores for Conchita, but my cousin would come just to make my sister waste time. The two of them would talk secretly, writing letters which they did not want us to see, and getting angry if we did.

Later on, another cousin named Miranda began to come by, and the same thing would happen when my *mamá* wasn't around. Miranda would come to talk with my sister and waste her time. Once, one of them stole a pair of scissors which my *mamá* used for cutting cloth and my sister said Talinda had taken them. My *mamá* scolded and hit my sister, and went to tell my aunt Ágata that her daughter had stolen the scissors. My aunt said it wasn't so; my mother got angry, but they didn't give her the scissors. After that, Talinda didn't come to visit any more, only Miranda, when my *mamá* was not at home.

When my *mamá* found Miranda there, my cousin would quickly

say, "My mother sent me to see if you could let her have a lemon." Sometimes she asked for a bit of onion or a clove of garlic. In this way she would save herself from a scolding. If she didn't, my mother would chase her out, saying, "Go home, go on, your mother needs you. I don't want you here because then my things are stolen."

When Conchita was in the fourth grade she would sometimes see her sweetheart, Juan, on the street corner and give him a letter, or he would hide behind a tree or a stone wall and give her a note. He would do it so that people would not see what was happening. But later my aunt Adelaida would give them each other's letters.

My mother realized there was something bad going on near my aunt Adelaida's house and she spied on us. When we turned the corner and had barely walked a few meters, we heard my *mamá* yelling to my sister, "Conchita, come here!"

And my sister said, "What for, *mamá?*"

"Come here, Conchita!"

"But I'm late for school, *mamá.*"

"It doesn't matter. Now you are not going to school. We are going right back to the house." And when we were home, my *mamá* began to question her about what things she had given to her aunt, about what kind of little papers had she given her. And Conchita said it wasn't true.

My mother said, "Now you tell me, or you will see." But Conchita told her nothing. And my mother began to beat her, she beat her real hard. She even beat me because she wanted me to tell her. And I said that I didn't see anything. And my mother said, "If you don't tell me now, when your father comes I will accuse both of you, Felipe because he is not telling me, and you because you are boy crazy."

When my *papá* came she told him and he began to scold my sister and he hit her hard. From that time on he began to hit her daily. Every time he remembered, he hit her. My sister was eating and my *papá* remembered and he gave her a slap so that her *tortilla* flew out of her hands. And then my *mamá* went every day to take my sister to school and to wait for her at the door after school so that my sister and her *novio* could no longer send letters.

Well, Conchita tried to find a way to send letters. When we were on the way to school she would leave a letter at the corner in a little space between the rocks because they had arranged this beforehand. And each of them would find letters waiting for them there.

My *papá* liked to go out a lot at night. He would get drunk and come home late in the evening while my *mamá* waited for him. She would wait up until he came back. I remember that sometimes by twelve at night my *papá* still had not arrived and *mamá* would stand in the doorway, waiting. She would peep out the door to see if he was coming, then go back in, and then go to the door again.

My *papá* would come at about one or two in the morning, drunk, and my *mamá* had to give him his supper. He would get angry. "Why are the *tortillas* cold? Why aren't they hot?" he asked.

My *mamá* heated them but he wouldn't accept them. "I'm not in the fields to have to eat cold *tortillas!*" And he ordered her to make fresh *tortillas* in spite of the hour. If there was no dough ready, he made her grind the corn on the grinding stone and she made hot *tortillas* for him.

When my *mamá* was sleepy and went to bed without waiting for him, my *papá* would get her up and scold her. "Why did you go to bed? Aren't you going to give me supper? Get up and give me something to eat in a hurry." And my *mamá* got up to feed him.

If there was any little thing that displeased him, he hit her. When he went to pray at a wake, he stayed out all night without telling *mamá* about it, so she waited up for him. Sometimes she went to bed at dawn, about four or five in the morning, but only for a little while. Sometimes he didn't come home until noon the next day. My *mamá* would go to look for him, even in distant *barrios*. Then when he arrived home and she hadn't come back yet, he would get angry, "And your *mamá?* Where did she go?" he asked my sister Conchita.

"Well, she went to look for you because you didn't come home last night," she answered.

"Go and get her, tell her to come back." Then my sister went to look for *mamá*. Shortly afterward, my mother arrived and he yelled at her and hit her.

"Where did you go? I've been waiting for you," he asked her.

"I went to look for you because you hadn't come home," she said.

"That's not true, I came from there and I didn't see you. You went elsewhere. You are not going to make a fool of me. You better tell me where you went or you'll see what I'll do to you!" he said. And then he would begin to beat her with a rope.

During Easter it was worse. He would leave and not return all night and all the next day. He would go to church to pray or to a wake or to the *novenario* for some dead person, returning the following day. On the Day of the Dead it was the same. He would go and drink the whole night and day. My *mamá* suffered a lot because he mistreated her.

Once, in the month of January, some gentlemen arrived at the house. It was during our *barrio* fiesta. They came in and sat down to talk with my *papá*. They talked a long time, then my *papá* gave them dinner. They continued to visit him often. Afterward some men from Yautepec and some from Cuernavaca visited him, and then my *papá* stopped drinking and mistreating *mamá*. They gave him a Bible and my *papá* began to study it by himself. My sister Conchita already knew how to read but my *papá* taught her to read from the Bible, and we all sat around him while he taught us to pray the Our Father. While we sat with him, he taught us everything the Bible said, God's laws, the Ten Commandments, and he didn't allow us to eat pork. He warned us of many things and filled us with fear. The men told us we must obey them and we must pray when we get up and when we go to bed.

My *papá* did not go to the village church any more, nor did he give a contribution. Then he told my mother not to do any work on Saturday, to prepare everything on Friday, the *tortillas* and the food, and to just reheat them on Saturday. Nor was she to buy or sell and we were not to work. On Friday we were to rest from six o'clock in the afternoon because that's when the Sabbath begins. We did nothing on Saturday and neither did my *mamá*.

We studied and my *papá* even bought us notebooks and lessons. He taught us and, really, it was nice. He didn't go around in the streets any more but stayed at home and taught us every day.

Then he gave away the saints to the neighbors, but they felt sorry for the poor saints and got very angry with my father. They said my *papá* didn't believe in God any more but in the devil, and they thought that *papá's* house was going to burn. But my *papá* just smiled. "Poor people, they don't know what they say. God forgives them," he would say.

My aunt Julia, my father's sister, said my *papá* was not a Protestant, but an animal who no longer believed in the saints. She said he could never be pardoned, that he would be burned; she said a lot of things to him. And then my *papá* said, "If my sister is angry, let her be angry. I don't go to her for food, so let her get angry. If there were twenty sisters, they could get angry but I will not fight with them. If she doesn't want to visit me, then let her not visit. All the better for me."

Each time my aunt came, she told my *mamá* to leave my *papá*. She said so many dirty words! She told my *mamá* to go alone to church, to leave candles and flowers and to pray that my *papá* repents. She said, "You are still young and we will help you. If you want to bring your children, bring only the smallest ones. Leave the rest!"

But my *mamá* also liked evangelism and wanted to study. When we had time, she would say to us, "Study, boys. Even though I want to study, I cannot for I don't know how to read. You study and teach me. I want to learn more."

And the people and the neighbors were angry and called us "Protestants, Protestants!" Even in school, where my brother and I went, they called us "*sabadistas!* Protestants!" But we answered them. We said,

"You don't know what you are saying. You say Protestant only because you hear your parents say it. But you should ask them, 'What is a Protestant?' What would they answer? Do you want me to tell you what a Protestant is? This word means that they are protesting against worldly things, like smoking, like all the vices. That's what Protestant means. You say we don't adore the gods, but Protestants worship their God. You have another God. That's fine. You say we don't go to church, but how are you going to force us to go to a Catholic church? Our house is our church."

That's the way it was. Even the schoolteacher helped defend us, little by little. When my *papá* first began to study, they threw stones at our house. When I was about thirteen, they once threw stones on the roof during our services and broke a roof tile. No one went out because we knew why they were doing it.

My *mamá* once sent my brother and me to buy corn from *don* Pancho. We went inside and there were the *señor* and the *señora*. We asked if they would sell us some corn and they said, "Yes, but unless you kneel before the saint, we will not give you any corn." We kept insisting that no, we didn't want to. But they said, "Go ahead," and we said, "No," until they finally gave us corn.

When we arrived home, my *mamá* scolded us for taking so long and we told her why. My *papá* became very angry and went to protest to them and asked them why they had done this to us because we were just little children, and that if they would ever do this again they would have to account to him. After that *don* Pancho and his wife never said anything like that to us again.

Every Saturday some men from a little town called Salvador came by. There were about six of them and they came to study with my *papá*. We also sat with them and he taught us. They arrived at about eight in the morning and began to study at nine. At noon they rested and we all ate. They began to study again at two in the afternoon and finished at five. Then they would go home. My *papá* studied every day from a notebook they had given him.

An old man named *don* Federico was coming to the house every day. Sometimes he brought gifts which he gave to my *mamá*. My sister was about sixteen years old. My *papá* went to work and took *don* Federico along, but he was one of those who came to our house to study. And when they returned at night, *don* Federico would bring an armload of dry firewood. Sometimes he stayed a week, sometimes two, then he'd go home for awhile, a week or so, and he would return bringing little gifts to my sister Conchita. Later, he also began hauling water for us. And when he and my father left early for work, he would cover my sister with his blanket. But I was sleeping with her. I always slept with my sister.

Then *don* Federico told her he wanted to marry her, but my sister didn't want to. She paid no attention to him, saying she wasn't thinking of getting married. She was still young and was in school. And this man was a widower and had grown children. He kept on staying with us. He was a good person and a hard worker. He stayed with us a long time but my sister didn't want to marry him. Then he went to Yautepec and would walk from there to our house, a three-and-a-half-hour walk. He always walked with his sack full of many things. And he always dressed like a peasant, in rough white *calzones* and *huaraches,* a large *sombrero* and a white shirt. He was dark and had a long beard and mustache and had two teeth missing in front.

Then my sister went to Huaxtepec to study in the normal school there. And when she left, *don* Federico even cried because he wanted to marry her. My *mamá* also missed her and cried a lot. I, too, missed my sister because I had always been with her. After she left I felt all alone. When I went to school, it was alone. But when she came home during vacations, she would take me to bed with her, because I always slept in her bed. And when she left for school again, she left me her bed and her blanket.

My *papá* took her to Huaxtepec by horse. They would get up early in the morning, at about three o'clock. My *papá* prepared the animals, my sister prepared herself, and said good-bye to my *mamá.* Then they were off. My *mamá* cried and sometimes she would go to visit my sister and would take me along. I would miss school so that I could go to see my sister. And my *papá* went every eight days or every fifteen days.

My *mamá* never failed to send something with him; at times she sent meat *tamales* or *tamales* filled with beans or corn, or peanuts. My *mamá* went to bed very late at night because she was making tamales until two o'clock in the morning. I stayed up with her even at that hour. My *papá* would get up early and feed the horse and saddle it and at about six o'clock in the morning he left, taking the *tamales* with him.

At that time my father had a mean horse. Once my *papá* and Conchita left early and on the road the horse threw her against a barbed-wire fence. She was bruised and scratched and she began to cry. My father went to lift her up and he wiped away the blood. He took out his extra shirt and bound her arm with it and then he lifted her on the horse and returned to our house. When they arrived, my *papá* immediately put her to bed. My *mamá* began to cry and cured the wounds with lemon and my sister was screaming a lot because of the pain. She stayed in bed until she recovered. Then, again, my *papá* went to take her to Huaxtepec.

I suffered when Conchita went away to study and left my *mamá* ill. I was a little older and my *mamá* was in bed and could not get up so I did everything. I went to the market and to the mill and I washed the dishes, I swept and then I made the *tortillas*, any way I could. I did this every day and didn't even go to school because I had to do the chores. I didn't go back to school until my *mamá* could stand up and do her work, little by little.

Everything was cheap at that time. When my mother sent me to the plaza I would buy a big piece of liver for three *centavos*, tripe for one *centavo* and lung for two *centavos*. There were pieces of bread that cost only one *centavo*. Even field hands earned only one *peso*, fifty *centavos* a day and corn cost only seven *centavos* a *cuartillo*. My mother sent me to sell corn to the women of Santa María who came to Azteca on market days and sometimes they would give eight *centavos* for a *cuartillo*.

I remember the time the road was under construction and it had barely reached the village. In September, when the hog plums were ripe, my *mamá* sent Martín and me to sell them to the men who were working on the road. We would take a whole crate full of plums which were bruised or damaged and sometimes we would sell them all and sometimes not. Then my mother would send me to the plaza to sell *tortillas* to the pilgrims who came by from Puebla on their way to Chalma. We would also take along acacia pods to sell. My *mamá* would tie them into little bundles and we sold them for five *centavos* a bundle. Sometimes she cooked *chayotes* or squash and we sold that. My *mamá* was strong and fat then. She didn't get really sick until much later.

My *papá* was very strong and worked alone in the field. Sometimes he worked as a plowman with a yoke of oxen and he had to stay with the oxen in the open country through rain and cold and storms. At times he worked all season as a *peón* to earn enough for food. My *papá* suffered when we were little and could not help him.

When my *papá* cleared a field in the hills, he sometimes took me with him. I went only to guard his things while he cut and burned the brush. I would stay under a tree in the shade, and when I wanted water he would give me some from his squash gourd. He also took me along when he planted and when he weeded but I would go only to sit in a nearby cave. I helped him very little because I still couldn't do much. And later, when the corn grew, the badgers would eat it. Then my *papá* would go there at night and sometimes he would take me along. When we came to the field he would leave me in the little cave under the rocks and he would walk around the field banging on an old tin can to make noise. He also exploded some firecrackers in the middle of the *milpa* to frighten the badgers and ferrets because they ate a lot of corn and then the corn would rot and be ruined. So he guarded the *milpa* day and night until the ears of corn were full.

Later, my brother and I would go to guard it daily. We would go early and my *mamá* would bring our breakfast. She was barefoot, as always, and brought large *tortillas* called *memelotas*. The three of us would sit down in the shade at the foot of the hill to have our meal and we would sit there all day until about five or six o'clock in the afternoon when we would husk ears of corn to take home. And then all three of us would carry our sacks of corn. At that time my *papá* was working somewhere else in order to earn money for expenses and so we were the ones who had to harvest the crop.

Once Martín and I went to work with *don* Refugio, to pick corn and to gather fodder. My brother could not stand the work and had to sit down. I did, too. I wanted to cry, I was so tired. But we had no corn to eat, so we managed. We bore it and we worked for a number of days. Then we went to work with *don* Maximiano, who is a relative of my *mamá*. This time, too, we harvested corn. And again we got very tired. But the *señor* hurried us. He said, "Hurry, boys," until we couldn't any longer. We just sat down . . . our backs hurt. That is how we learned to work, by working for others.

The following year we went to the cornfield to help our *papá* from time to time. Sometimes we would stay at home to water the plants in the *corral*. We would carry tins of water and as the *corral* is large we finished at about noon. When we planted corn we would also water it and my *papá* told us to hill the young corn, that is, to heap earth around each stalk. Then he would take away the tools from us because there was only one digging stick and one hoe. For example, I used the hoe and he used the stick, then he wants to take the hoe from me because it is more useful and it takes less energy to work with. It is harder to work with the stick and he would get tired. Later, my *papá* bought two hoes and so each of us had one.

My brother and I would hurry and race each other and the one who lost would have to pay the winner with some of his meat or he would ask my *papá* for a *centavo* to pay. Later we played at tops and at marbles and my brother would get angry because I would win his marbles. He said that I was too good. Sometimes he and Ricardo didn't want to play with me any more and would give me the worst marbles. They would say, "No, because you are always winning. You are too good."

Once, in the month of September, my *papá* was picking hog plums and he asked us if we wanted to go to play in the hills. "Go play with your kites," he said, "and come home soon. And be careful! I don't want you to fall." And so we went, Martín and I, taking our kites. We began to play when a boy came and wanted to hit us. He told us to lend him one of our kites but we didn't want to and he threw a stone at my brother's kite. So we grabbed him and we slapped him and beat him. Finally the boy said, "*Ay, mamacita,* leave me alone." So we let him go and he began to run. We would never let anyone get the better of us.

My brother Martín and I fought a great deal, too. He is the one who gets most angry. Once my mother had gone marketing and we stayed home to play among ourselves. While playing, Martín saw that I was winning and we had a quarrel and began to fight. He went to get a *machete* to hit me with and I grabbed a stone. We confronted each other, face to face, and we were no longer playing. Some neighbors were nearby making rope and one came running to take away the *machete* from my brother.

In a little while, my mother comes and they tell her. My *mamá* scolded us and when my *papá* came, they all accused us, that is, they told him about it. Then my *papá* scolded us and even hit us. He told us that we should never fight and he ordered us to embrace each other and to beg each other's pardon. My brother didn't want to and my father forced him to do it.

Martín has a different character and a little more fury than the rest of us. Once my *papá* wanted to scold him and I don't know how my brother felt but he seemed to get something like attacks. He felt that he was getting numb and finally they went to see a doctor and he said it was just his bile. And the doctor said, "This boy gets attacks because you scold him. He is very sensitive." After that my *papá* didn't say anything to my brother, who would begin to cry. It was better for my *papá* to bear the anger. It is true that I, too, became angry when my *papá* scolded me but it passed and that was all. And when Ricardo was scolded, he got rid of it when he played. Ricardo and Moisés had the best characters because they hardly ever got angry. Each one had a very different mind and a different spirit.

I once had a big fight with my brother Martín when we were a little older. It was at night and we were going to bed and I threw off all the things that were on my mat. Martín took his mat and shook it on mine.

I said, "Don't put it here. Can't you see that I already cleared off mine? Dust yours somewhere else."

He says, "And who are you?"

I say, "I am who I am."

Then he put his mat on mine again.

"Take it off! Can't you see that I am going to lie down?" and I took it off and he put it on again.

He says, "Who are you to order me around?" That was when I gave him a slap, with a closed fist. No, I never gave in. I hit him on the mouth. He gave one scream and fell down and my sister Macrina was there and she began to yell and cry and went into the kitchen and my *mamá* also and another woman, my aunt Filomena, began to scream.

My *papá* said, "What is happening?"

"Felipe hit Martín and he fell and is just lying there with his face down." They spoke to him but he didn't answer. He was unconscious. They covered him with a sheet.

I said, "But I didn't hit him hard."

My *papá* said, "No, you are always like that. You are always hitting your brothers and those who are not your brothers."

"Well, let them not get me angry."

My *papá* grabbed me, took off his *huarache* and began to hit me on the head, and when he saw that I didn't cry he threw away his sandal and took a rope and beat me and beat me but I wouldn't cry. I just held back. He grabbed a stick and began to hit me on the head. When he saw that I wouldn't cry he began to hit me with his hand. He wanted to see me cry, but I wouldn't cry. Again he grabbed his *huarache* and began to hit me on the head.

And then my aunt Filomena came and said, "Let him alone. You hit him a lot. Something will happen and then you will have more trouble."

My *papá* said, "That is what gets me so angry. This one always hits his brother and is rebellious in everything with me."

And she says, "Well, let him alone if he is that way. How are you going to change it? It is impossible."

I have never hit my brother Moisés because he was the youngest. Martín was the one I hit most. They got my brother up and gave him sugar water. Then my *papá* said to me, "If you are so strong, tomorrow I want you to lift a load of ten crates of hog plums onto the animal." I said, "Yes," and I did it.

Then he said, "And I want you to beg your brother's pardon."

I say, "Who is the elder, am I or is he? If I beg his pardon, it means that I am less than he. I won't do it!" And then my *papá* became angrier with me.

My *papá* took us along with him to the *milpa* and we planted thirteen *cuartillos* of corn. Then we began to clear the brush and the trees in the hills, to plant a little more. We were already helping my *papá* and he was taking us there daily. Martín carried the water in the water gourd or in the pigskin and I carried the *tortillas*. My *papá* carried his shotgun and his blanket.

Each of us was assigned one *cuartillo* of land and we hurried to see who could finish planting first. I hurried to try and beat them. I finished first, at about three o'clock in the afternoon. Then I would help them finish their work. When the planting was over, we would go to replant the seeds which the badgers and other animals had taken out. And when the corn plants sprouted about twenty days later, we would come again to do the weeding.

Many ticks would get into our body, little red ticks. It is difficult to see them but they itch a lot and you scratch yourself. And when you scratch, it's even worse. And these little things, *tlalsaguates*, get into the armpits and practically everywhere. They don't let us sleep because we scratch so much we get scabs. We can't stop scratching. The only way we can get rid of them is to kill them by bathing ourselves with lime water. And when we got rid of them, in my house we would make green *chile* sauce with *tamales* and we would drink *ponche* and we celebrated it with firecrackers because this is a custom in my village. It was customary also to put a cross in the middle of the *milpa* when we finished the third cultivation. This is what we call the *acabada*. After that we just waited for the harvest.

When there was no work in the fields, from December to April, my *papá* taught us to make rope. My father sold the rope at that time for about fifteen *pesos* each. A pound of *ixtle* cost fifty *centavos* and we would wet and beat the *ixtle* and straighten it out and separate it and dye it. Then we would lift it off the ground and wrap it in a fiber net and pull out the threads to twist them into rope. That's what we did every day until the time came to go to work in the fields because by that time the rope wouldn't turn out well any more on account of the rain.

And so we'd go to the field to clear the stubble and prepare the ground for planting. We were planting a little piece of *tlacolol* which my uncle Rufino let us have. It was a plot of about six *cuartillos* in a place called Mimituapa. We sowed it and weeded it. After that, we dedicated ourselves to guarding it. We went there daily but it was still only a game to us. My father would send us to watch the cornfield but we delayed along the way to throw stones at the birds. At times we took so long killing birds, we never got to the *milpa*. We would kill six or seven birds and it would be late and we would go home. If my *mamá* had told us to bring home squash we would get four or five from other people's fields.

I remember once, toward the end of September, we were carrying ears of corn in our sacks and we went into someone's *milpa* to eat guavas. We were just about getting to the guava tree when we heard someone whistle. We stopped to see who it was and he whistled again, closer to us. We kept looking everywhere and we didn't see anything. Finally, the whistle came a third time, very close to us and we saw nothing. We began to run and even when we were far away the whistle kept coming and there was no one. When we arrived home we told them what happened to us and they said it was the ghost of a man who had been killed in the Revolution and who was always frightening people there. We never returned to that spot.

Another time we went to look at our *milpa* and we were carrying home beans, when it began to rain. The sun was out and we looked back and there in the distance behind the hills, was a rainbow. So I said to my brother, "Let us run before we are caught in more rain." We were halfway home. We looked back again and we saw that the rainbow was closer to us. I said to my brother, "Look, the rainbow is closer, let us run before it reaches us." And we began to run harder. Each time we looked back the rainbow was much closer. We were already very tired of running, and when we came to Elotepec the rainbow had almost caught up with us. We couldn't run any more. We were just going along very slowly, and when we came to the bridge the rainbow had already passed us and was in the hills. After that we went very slowly and the rainbow no longer followed us.

We were afraid of the rainbow because they had told us that when it is over a person, it does him harm. It makes the stomach swell because it fills the stomach with water and it causes a lot of wind to blow. That is why we were so afraid of it. They say that once the rainbow touched a man and his stomach grew and they tried to cure him but they couldn't. As much as they did for him he didn't get well and he died. They also say the rainbow follows a person who wears a red shirt or a green shirt, or something which has the color of the rainbow.

It was in school that I learned about bad things. I figured it out alone. Among friends, you talk a lot about these things and then you begin to think about it and you learn a lot.

Once I was with my classmates and some of them were older boys. A pregnant girl passed by and the older boys began to joke with each other. One said, "So, you have already made one, haven't you?" Another answered, "It looks that way." They even included me in the joke, saying the child was mine.

"But I don't know anything about this," I answered. Later, I began to think about it and then I realized where women get their babies and how they make them.

Elida was my sweetheart then but I looked for another one in school. I was in the plaza with two boys, watching the girls pass by. One of the boys said, "Here comes a girl. Let's follow her and see which one gets her."

"No," I said. "I didn't come for that. I won't go with just anyone, only the one I like."

I waited for another one and along came the daughter of Baldomero Reyes. She had a fair skin and I said, "I'll go with this one." I waited until she left the market and I followed her and began to speak to her. But she didn't say anything to me. I talked and talked as we walked along and all she did was look at me. She said nothing. I said, "Why don't you answer me? Why don't you speak? Are you afraid to answer me? Or ashamed?" She didn't say a word. So I grabbed her by the hand and said, "Now, answer me, yes or no!"

Then she said, "Look, I don't know what to say. I never had a sweetheart before."

"Well, that's easy. I am speaking seriously with you and all you have to do is say yes. It won't cost you anything."

"Well, then, yes, except that now my *papá* is over there and I cannot talk."

She said it would be better not to speak to each other for fear of her father or brothers, but that I should write to her instead. On the following day I wrote a letter and handed it to her. I asked when she would answer it and she said on Saturday. I waited but she didn't bring me anything and I asked her why, was it because she was ashamed or because she didn't know how to write? She said it wasn't because of those things but because she didn't know what to put in a letter. Then I said that if she wanted, I would write the answer and she could copy it and give it to me. She said yes, and that is what we did.

Once I wrote a letter to her and I didn't have time to finish it, so I put it in an envelope and left it with some papers and books on the table in the room where we all slept. I thought no one would see it but my *papá* found it, tore open the envelope and after reading the letter, tore it up, too. He asked Martín whose letter it was and my brother said it was Felipe's. "That's good," my *papá* says. "I thought it was Conchita's."

Later, I remembered my letter and went to look for it. I found it in pieces and I became very angry, thinking that in this house one cannot keep a thing. But Martín told me what had happened and my anger passed because I thought it was my own fault for having left it where it could be found.

. . .

Then I had pretty bad luck. I lost the sight of an eye. It was in 1934, when the new *peso* bills appeared. I was eleven years old. It happened one day when I returned from school. I left school at five in the afternoon, and when I passed by the market I met my *mamá*, who had gone to the mill.

And she says to me, "Have you already left school, son?"

"Yes, *mamá*," and I took her hand and kissed it, the way we always did.

"Then wait for me. I am going to buy what I need and we will go home together."

So I waited and we went home together, talking on the way. I helped her by carrying the pail of corn dough. It was the month of May and it began to rain. When we got to the house we saw a dust storm coming from the hills.

My *mamá* said, "Now the wind is coming and I have not yet made the *tortillas*. Hurry and get me a few sticks of wood to heat the griddle before the storm comes, because with all that dust I cannot make the *tortillas*."

Quickly, I put my notebooks on the table and ran out to gather the wood. There were some dry branches in the yard and I began to break them up. I picked up one and stood on it to hold it with my foot while I pulled it upward with my hands. As it was dry, it broke suddenly and hit me in the eye. I screamed and threw myself down on my face.

My *mamá* came running out and lifted me up and asked me what happened. She looked at the eye and said she didn't see anything but an ordinary scratch on the eyelid. Inside the eye, to one side of the pupil, something like a little piece of skin was raised up, but it barely could be seen. And my *mamá* told me that a little bit of blood came out, but very little, and it was washed away by my tears.

Then my *mamá* took my hand and brought me into the house and didn't let me gather wood any more. She went out for the wood and came back and began to make the *tortillas*. By then it was night and I still didn't feel anything. My *papá* came back from work and we all sat down to eat. But my *mamá* didn't tell my *papá* anything, because what had happened to me was just an ordinary thing. We finished supper and were sitting for a while and then we lay down and went to sleep.

The next day, we got up early. My *papá* went to work and my brother Martín took the two water cans and the shoulder yoke and began to haul water for the plants. At about eight o'clock, I told my *mamá* I was going to school. The eye didn't hurt me at all, but everything looked different to me. The ground looked wavy, as though it was furrowed.

My *mamá* said, "No, son, don't go to school because there you will be looking at white paper and it will do you harm."

"But yesterday they chose us to run a race on the road."

"All the more reason to stay home, for the sun will do you harm."

So I didn't attempt to go to school. I just walked around the yard without a care. But at about ten o'clock, I felt a little bothered by my eye. At about eleven o'clock, my eye began to swell and I couldn't look at the light at all. I got into a dark corner because I couldn't see and my head and my eye hurt me a lot. I screamed because I couldn't stand the pains. It didn't give me any rest, not even for one moment. By then my eye was completely shut because of the swelling. And I was like that all day.

In the evening, my *papá* arrived and he asked my *mamá* what happened to me. She told him but he didn't believe her, or he didn't take it seriously. He came over to me and asked, "What's wrong, son? What happened to you?"

But with the pain I had, I could barely speak. "My eye hurts and I can't see anything."

He kept speaking to me but I couldn't answer him any more. I kept screaming. I felt that my head was splitting and that my eye was going to burst. Then my brothers and sisters came to look at me and they asked me how I felt. I told them. "Don't speak to me because I cannot answer. I can't even move my mouth now because my head hurts so much."

And I felt so angry, I couldn't bear it. I didn't know where this anger came from. It came upon me all of a sudden and it was so strong I felt like tearing myself apart. And that's the way I was all night. I didn't even sleep; my *papá* and my *mamá* and my brothers and sisters sleeping, and I screaming with pain. Finally the dawn came but I was the same. My parents got up and my *papá* went to work. My brother Martín went to school and I, as before, stayed in a corner, in the dark, where not a bit of light could reach me.

Well, that's the way I was for about fifteen days, in the same corner. And my *mamá* began to cure me, to take down the swelling of my eye. It was so swollen, I couldn't open it. Little by little, the swelling went down and when it opened, my eye was already clouded over.

Then my *mamá* says, "Your eye is clouded but we are going to cure you."

I couldn't see with that eye but I thought I was going to get better soon, that it would be easy. Every day, every moment, my *mamá* went on trying to cure me. When she heard of something that was good for the eyes, she would put it in. She was so anxious to cure me she would use it two or three times, until she heard of another good medicine.

Meanwhile the eye was getting worse and worse. But my *mamá* didn't stop curing me.

By that time I felt very sad and I began to think, "Will I get better or not? And what will become of me later on?"

Once, some doctors from the Cultural Mission came to the school and my *mamá* took me there to be cured. And they said it would be necessary to operate for me to get well, that if not, I was going to lose the other eye.

My *mamá* didn't want them to operate on me. She said I would lose the other eye if they operated, that I was better off the way I was, that she would go on struggling to cure me. And she went on using the home remedies people told her of. She used so many medicines but I didn't get better! I was very tired of it but my eye didn't hurt so much any more, only at times. Later, they put a little black cloth tied with a string over my eye, so that the wind wouldn't hit it and the sun wouldn't harm me. But I believe a wind did hit my eye because again I had bad pains in my head and my eye swelled. So much that I rolled around in the bed, so much that it made me cry. Every eight days, every two weeks, the pain came back again. And that's the way I suffered for a long time; my eye would not leave me in peace. For about five years I was suffering.

And my *mamá* went to a lot of trouble for me. She felt very grieved to see the way I was. And my uncle Margarito took a lot of pity on me. When I was very ill, he brought me a jar of milk and two pieces of bread in the morning. And, then, at noon, he sent my dinner. And that was every day!

Later, little by little, the pain began leaving me. But I felt the cloud in my eye growing and I felt as though something inside was throbbing. I couldn't get used to the bad eye, for I couldn't see anything with it. Only with one, and I felt very different for lack of the other. And because of this I stopped going to school for a long time. But I cried because I didn't go to school. I would dream that I was going but I couldn't go. I didn't even have hopes of going. And I saw my brother going to school and I felt bad and I became sad. I wanted very much to study. I had been ahead in my studies when I went. I was always number one in the group.

But because of what happened to me, I fell behind. I forgot everything I had learned, because my brain hurt so much. I felt that now I didn't have the same intelligence. Although I returned to school later, it wasn't the same. Now my brother Martín was way ahead of me. But I didn't go much longer because then my *papá* said that we had better help him work because now he didn't have enough to support all of us.

Then we began to work in the fields, to plant and to help my *papá*.

I still tried to go to school, at least for a few days, but my *mamá* began to get sick. Then with more reason did we have to stay at home. When she was in bed we couldn't go because my *papá* was working or because we didn't have clean clothes. I still tried to go. Once I said to my brother, "Let's go to school today."

We began to haul water for the plants and we hurried to do our chores. Then we washed ourselves and ate breakfast and went to school.

But I was ashamed to go out into the street because of my eye. It looked so ugly. I got red in the face because I was so ashamed. The boys just looked at me and some asked me what had happened. And when I arrived at school, everyone just looked at me and I felt very embarrassed.

That day we went for just half a day. That whole year, we went to school only that one half-day. And even then, when my *papá* came home from work and we told him we went to school, he became very serious because he didn't like it. He told us not to go any more, that it was better for him to teach us to work in the fields, that what we knew was enough. Because my sister Conchita was studying in Huaxtepec, that's why, and my *papá* didn't have enough for all. That's why he took us out of school.

Well, so we helped him. When my sister began to work as a teacher she bought me a pair of green eyeglasses which cost her thirty-five *pesos*. That's the way I went to work for a long time, for about ten years. But I got tired of them because when I worked I would sweat a lot and they would be covered with perspiration and every moment I would be cleaning them. And if I was caught in the rain and they got wet, I couldn't see through them. That's why I took them off and went without them. But many people tell me I ought to have glasses because of my bad eye and for protection from the wind.

When my brother Martín was angry with me, he would say, "Blind one, one-eyed!" I wouldn't say anything, I would just look at him. Then he told my brother Ricardo to say it to me also. The two of them would say it to me. And when my *mamá* heard them, she scolded them, at times she even hit them, and she told them not to say that. Sometimes they would just form the words with their lips, so that my *mamá* wouldn't hear.

And from the time my eye went bad, my *mamá* began to love me most. She pitied me a lot and favored me over all my brothers and sisters. And I was the one who loved her the most. When the tenth of May, Mother's Day, came, I always gave her a little gift. I embraced her and gave her a kiss and handed my offering to her and she was very pleased with me. And when my *papá* scolded me, my *mamá* told him not to because I had a bad eye. He would get angrier because she was always defending me. He said I was her favorite. My brothers were also envious and said she loved me more than them.

PART FIVE

CHAPTER XVI

PEDRO

On Conchita

I did my best to educate my children. It wasn't like in the days of Díaz when only those who had money studied. Then there was one little school and two teachers and the great majority of children did not go to school. But after the Revolution, progress began. The government made an effort to raise up the Indian and in 1923 and '24 they even went from house to house, inviting the youth to go to study. They practically took them by force and offered scholarships to the normal school. To me, that is progress!

I wanted at least one child of mine to finish school. Conchita was the first. I wanted to have a learned daughter! God willing, she might become a teacher. Naturally, until the others grew up, that was all I could do. I thought, "I will send this one to school so that later she can help me send the others."

I had a quarrel with my wife about my daughter's education because Esperanza had little desire to send the children to school. She wanted Conchita to stay at home to do the household chores. But when my daughter finished the four years of primary school and wanted to go on studying, I looked around to find a way for her to do it. It cost me a lot of trouble because by then it was more difficult to get a scholarship. Finally, a preacher who came to the village encouraged me. He spoke to the schoolteacher, Víctor Conde. "Is *don* Pedro really a poor man?

Because we want to help his daughter get an education with the Adventists. We do not want her to go to Huaxtepec because it is a socialist school."

So Conde answered, "Man, that's fine! I, too, feel sorry for him because he is completely poor and I would like to help him with a scholarship. But, if you intend to help him, then let her go to your school."

There was an Adventist school in Tacubaya, in Mexico City. The preacher says, "Tuition is five *pesos* a month."

Víctor says, "All right, I will pay six-months' tuition if Pedro takes her there and supports her. I will pay six months, while he gets her settled. And how do you propose to help?"

"Well, I am going to help in this sense. Let her go and stay with my wife. It will not cost her anything for food or lodging. She will help my wife and all she will have to pay is the tuition."

So far, so good. Then Víctor Conde called me in and told me how things stood. "That is much better, man!" he said. "I like that very much. The Adventists! So it is best that your daughter go there, but at once . . . write there immediately."

I wrote but the preacher never came back. I never heard a peep out of him again, even though he was in Cuernavaca. Twenty days went by and the scholarships in Huaxtepec were almost exhausted. So Conde said to me, "All right, now look . . . I am going to get the scholarship. If there is still a chance with the Adventists we will forget about the scholarship. If not, she had better go to Huaxtepec or she will lose time."

Indeed, he did arrange it, but then the preacher wrote, telling me not to worry and that Conchita could come to Tacubaya. Well, like a fool, there I go to Mexico City with my daughter and a pack containing her dresses and her blanket. I had forty-five *pesos* with me, which was real money in those days. We arrived in Tacubaya and I spoke to the preacher, who was a good man. He said, "Well, Brother Pico is looking for a little servant girl. She can go to school in the afternoons, because now there is an afternoon shift. During the day she will help her mistress."

My daughter Conchita had malaria at the time. But she was so enthusiastic about studying that she wanted to go, sickness and all. So I brought her. It was a two-story house, a glorious sight, like heaven! I only saw it from a distance, like Moses when he went to . . . just from a distance. Yes, the house was pretty, but I didn't get past the kitchen. This pastor was a director, the main Adventist leader, but that so-and-so treated me like dirt. I thought they were refined people, but it was only skin-deep. Just varnish!

My poor daughter started right in helping his wife, even though she was very sick. I said to her, "Come on, let's go. I don't like this man's character. I can tell he is very harsh and his two children are even worse. No, this doesn't suit me. They are completely bourgeois, even though they are only Indians from Tlaxcala. You are shaking with malaria and still you have to do the chores. They will make you wash the clothes and you can't. So, let's go."

She answered, "I am not leaving even if I die here."

Hmmm, what could I do? The pastor invited us to the evening services and said I could sleep there that night. They gave me a cup of coffee and when it was time to go to bed they took Conchita upstairs to sleep on a dirty carpet in their daughter's room.

Then friend Pico told me to make myself comfortable in the kitchen. But how could I make myself comfortable? They didn't give me anything, not even an old rug did they throw at me. The floor was made of cement and was still wet from being washed. It was very cold. I thought, *"Caray!* Are these people Christians?" That's how I began to lose faith.

So I said to myself, "This isn't right, but what can I do? I'll stay this once. After all, it means her future." Well, I suffered through it. I didn't sleep all night long. I just sat down on my pack and leaned against the edge of the charcoal burner. As bad luck would have it I had to go to the toilet, but couldn't find a place to go. There was a great big dog outside the kitchen door in the patio and as soon as I opened the door a bit he would start to growl, grrr! He was an enormous dog and angry. I shut the door in a hurry. Now things were worse! Now I was a prisoner! The animals there were just as bad as their master. God was punishing me.

I said, *"Ay,* I'm in a fix. What wretches these people are. And now here is their sentinel! How can I get out?"

I sat down and there I was, controlling myself. Finally, what do you think I did? There was a screen on the window and a flower box outside. So I go get a saucepan and relieve myself in it. Then I dumped it out through the screen. I won after all! Well, I felt better, but I didn't get any sleep.

At about four-thirty in the morning the mother came down stairs to sweep the sidewalk. She was so much of an Indian that her children treated her like a servant. Just imagine! The children and the husband sleeping and the poor mother out in the street, sprinkling and sweeping. She didn't speak to me. She just passed by with her broom as I was sitting there. And these people are Christians! The son came into the kitchen at night and he, too, didn't speak to me. Just walked past me. *Qué caray!* What kind of upbringing do these people have?

At five o'clock my daughter came down. She saw me sitting there and said, *"Papá,* let's go. I have decided. There is no need to tell them. They are animals, so we will be too. Let's go."

The *señora* was still sweeping the sidewalk. I said, "My daughter isn't staying after all. Good-bye and many thanks for the hospitality."

"Good-bye." That was all she said to me.

We had hot coffee and rolls at the corner and then we went to the home of my countryman Porfirio. Yes, there we were well treated. Poor little Porfirio even ran out to greet us. They gave us *tacos.* We all ate together. And at night they put three straw mats down for us and covered it with a blanket. And they gave us a pillow.

So I say to my daughter, "Look at this! The others who were Christians didn't treat us like this. And here, these Catholic unbelievers, who don't know anything . . . just look! Here we are in heaven! Those other people aren't even human!"

My daughter understood better than I did. She said to me, "Yes, they are bourgeois, the kind that don't work."

That was the way those Christians treated me. It entered like a big thorn and hurt a lot. It went to my very bones! To the marrow! It hurts to this day. That man a Christian? A lie! That man a brother? A lie! I hated him. May God forgive me, but I still hate him. I wrote him a strong letter saying, "You are not a Christian, you are a drone who doesn't work. You are nourished by the health of the faithful. You are even worse than the priests."

After that, there wasn't much hope. We returned to Azteca, my daughter shaking with chills. I said, "Now I am not going to take you anywhere else."

I began to make rope again and Conchita helped me. Later I said, "Look, daughter, I will just finish making these ropes and then we will go to live in Mexico City. I know whom to turn to for help there. I will support you." I encouraged her. "I will have to pay five *pesos* a month, or whatever it is. But we should be there so you can study. We won't have anything to do with those other wretches. Don't worry, we will go."

I went to see Víctor Conde and told him what had happened in Tacubaya. He said, "No, no! One shouldn't depend on others. Better to Huaxtepec! There is no other way."

Conchita was in Huaxtepec for a little over two years. She had to leave for several reasons. As a matter of fact, she got into trouble because of a boy. He was a believer, too, from Yautepec. He is an Adventist to this day. Well, it was his idea to visit her because she was a fellow evangelist, but then he took advantage of the situation. He kept right after her, understand? He wanted to take her out for a good time so he took her and one of her girl friends to Cuautla.

The school principal got angry because they looked for Conchita one day and she wasn't around. So he expelled both girls. Well, naturally the principal sent for me right away. When I came, he said, "Better marry off your daughter. She cannot continue here."

What was there to do? Of course, I got angry because of her misbehavior. She came home and I said, "Now what? Where will you study? You lost this chance, now there will be no more."

Conchita has caused us many headaches with her boy friends. My wife has always gotten sick because of the bad times that girl has given us. Before she went to Huaxtepec we found letters from her boy friend, Juan. The letters fell into our hands unexpectedly, just before she had to leave, and we couldn't find out whether she was having secret meetings with him. Anyway, Juan had to leave her alone after that because we sent her off to Huaxtepec.

Then this boy from Yautepec came to ask for her hand and she said yes, right off. Afterward, he changed his mind and that was a calamity, another headache for us. That's when Conchita became very upset. She wanted to die. In fact, she poisoned herself by eating a whole box of matches. She did it out of anger because she was expelled from school and because her *novio* didn't want to marry her any more. At that time there was a doctor here in the village, an interne, so without knowing what she had taken, I went to get this doctor. As he was still a student he told me the truth. He said, "Whew! who knows what she's got?" But he gave her a purge and when he saw what was in the chamberpot, he says, "*Újule!* She poisoned herself. She ate matches. See what it looks like? It is smoking! *Caray!* What a woman! But this I can cure. She won't die."

Just then the boy from Yautepec arrived with his mother, to ask for Conchita's hand. But my daughter was in a serious condition. The doctor was there and he was injecting her . . . giving her serum. I was holding up the serum bottle so it could go into her vein slowly through the tube.

I said to the boy, "Look, there isn't anything we can discuss right now. How? It is not a question of talking marriage at this moment, it is a question of seeing to the patient. Look at the condition she is in!"

"All right," he says, "then we'll talk later on."

The boy offered to help by holding up the bottle of serum but when I took a look at him he was shaking strangely, as if he was going to have an attack. Weak-minded, he got scared. Then his mother came over and said, "Give it to me. This is bad for you." *Caray!* There was the boy rolling on the floor kicking and screaming. Who knows what happened to him? He was holding the bottle of serum when he began to act like he was going to faint and then this attack came. His mother got angry and said, "This is no place for my son." And who can remember what else she said?

"Who sent for you?" I asked. "Why are you getting angry? Who went to call you? You came on your own, didn't you? So, you have nothing to say."

"But here you serve bad food, so that a person gets poisoned."

"What business is that of yours? Let him not come, then he won't have to eat our meals. Certainly I am poor and we eat common food. You are rich and can eat fancy dinners. Why do you let your son come to my house then? You go give him good meals!"

The doctor was trying to do something to help the boy, sticking him and sticking him with a needle, and finally we had to tie him up so he could be injected. But the boy kicked the poor doctor in the stomach. Naturally, the doctor got angry. "Look, let him die. He kicked me!" But with hard work, the doctor revived the boy.

Then my daughter got worse and my wife had another nervous attack. Once more we had to carry her to bed because she thought her daughter was dying. *Újule!* Then the boy's mother, who was holding up the bottle, suddenly said, "Take it, take it, take it. I am going home!" Her son was just standing there swaying as if he were going to have a fainting spell. I said, "All right. But you take care of my wife!" So I took the serum bottle and held it up. It didn't bother me to do it. What people! . . . getting faint just from holding this bottle! And my wife, too, with an attack because she thought her daughter was dying. I said to myself, "*Caray!* What a scene is going on here!" After a while, the boy began to feel better and left.

I said to his mother, "Go on, go on, take him away. Give him something good to eat, there is no decent food here."

They left. Now they were gone. That night my daughter had recuperated after receiving the serum. We were there with her, and my wife said, "*Carambas!* It was just like a movie, what went on here this afternoon. The *novio* over there rolling on the floor, my daughter dying, and me in bed, the *señora* holding the bottle of serum and yelling. The whole thing was like a movie!"

I said, "*Carambas!*"

My daughter was well now and she began to laugh. "*Caray!*" she said, "the things I saw here. It was a real comedy." Well, it was over and we laughed. Some comedy!

Afterward, the doctor takes me into his office and tells me, "Look, I am just going to give your daughter something to calm her down, but

even if she gets better she will not be cured. Let her quit her studies and get married, because that is what she needs." Then he showed me the human skeleton and explained about our bodies, how we live, and where the bad part of the woman is and of men. "And so," he said, "I am just going to calm her down, but in order to cure her she has to get married."

Naturally, after that I understood what he was saying . . . that she had a very passionate nature. We are not all alike in that.

Later, we had a lot of trouble because Conchita insisted on studying again. She kept saying, "No, *papá*, I want to study. I want to study."

"But, man! You were well off in Huaxtepec! Why do you do these things? Now how? Where do I go?"

Well, I am a father, right? I had an obligation and I had no money. Then I began to work on the Governor. The Governor himself! He was once a peasant, and he was very nice to me. He said, "I don't have anything for your daughter, but I will do what I can. I will send word with Víctor Conde."

Three times I went to see the Governor and that is what he always told me. Mmmm. So I say to Conchita, "Look, daughter, we had better go to Mexico City. I will support you there. Because here . . . well, we can't be sure." I was impatient because a whole year had passed and nothing had happened.

Finally, the Governor himself gave the news to Víctor Conde. But by then Víctor and I had had a falling out because of cursed politics and we weren't speaking to each other, although we really liked each other. When it was a matter of politics, we hated each other, otherwise we were friends. So at that time he wouldn't speak to me. Instead, he sent for my daughter and said, "Hurry! The Governor wants to see you. You have to take an examination because you are going to Coyoacán. So get going! Immediately!"

My daughter came home jumping for joy, "We've made it, *papá!* I am going to take the test in Cuernavaca and then I'll go to school in Coyoacán."

"You see? My efforts have counted! So go on. Be quick! Let's see how you make out."

I went with her and, yes, she did well. She went to secondary school in Coyoacán. There she lasted another two years. She lived at the school and all I had to buy were her uniforms, shoes, books, pencils, and things like that. It was the same in Huaxtepec, except there I spent money on a bed, sheets, and once in a while on extra food . . . little things like that.

It wasn't much, but, yes, we suffered while Conchita was in school.

Those were difficult times for us. I took my daughter all the way to the capital! And, of course, while I went off with her, my wife and little ones suffered here. Even I suffered . . . I didn't have clothing. And why? Because I sacrificed myself for my daughter!

I had to work harder now because I had a lot of children. A bunch of them! And I was responsible for everyone. I had my two horses and I worked as a teamster, carrying things, anything at all. Occasionally, I went as far as Yautepec to sell firewood. But you know the setbacks that come! I could not go on as I had no corn. I had to sell the horses and go to work as a *peón*. I worked three seasons for my day's pay, so my daughter could study.

But I still had my cornfield in the hills and I said to myself, "Let's see if I can get a little ahead." So for the first time I took my two sons, Felipe and Martín, to the field to work. One son was about seven and the other eight and it was over a two-hour walk. Very far! I brought them there to see if they could learn to weed while I earned our bread working for someone else.

By that time the weeds were very high and had to be pulled up so the corn would grow. It was too difficult for them. They began to play with the insects and that was all their work amounted to. Even though I had planted very little, the boys just fooled about. Naturally, a father is going to scold. Of course! But I said to myself, "What is this, now? I am only bothering my sons and nothing gets done. I can't be here watching them, and they do nothing. Better not bring them at all!" I didn't take them there again and I got along as best I could.

My wife was no help to me at all. She was a good person, and docile, but she was not progressive, not industrious. At first she was even afraid to kill a chicken! I had to do it for her. When the first corn mill came here, in 1925, I told her to use it but she didn't want to go, not even once. She said, "No, I'm not armless. I can grind the corn myself. We can use the five *centavos* here instead of giving it to them."

But she wasn't the only one. Most of the women said the same thing. And the men were against the mill because they said the *tortillas* were tastier when the women ground the corn at home. The mill owner didn't even earn enough for beans and he had to leave the village. When the next mill opened, more women went and so my wife began to use it, too, but only once in a while.

My wife didn't know how to make use of her time, anyway, and I could not depend on her to earn anything. She was not smart. Besides, it is not the custom in Azteca for women to work because there is talk about her husband. If a woman works, she doesn't respect her husband any more. She says, "My husband? What do I need him for? I can support myself." That's why we do not allow it. I would rather ruin myself working to give food to my woman so that I have the right to speak up. In Santa María the men take their women to the fields to sow and reap and cultivate, and in Elotepec when a girl gets married the relatives give her a basket to carry *tortillas* to Cuernavaca to sell. They say the women earn more than the men and that's why those people are so well off. But that's being too materialistic! In Azteca, we men do not take advantage of the women and that is why I was poor and at times my family even suffered hunger. Yes, I do not deny it. There were weeks when we ate only *tortillas* and salt.

Once I was on the way to Cuautla with a friend when we came across a dead cow. Here was good meat! Some people were cutting it up and they gave us big chunks. We were going to Cuautla to get sweet potatoes to sell and we put the meat in our crates. Naturally, with all that sun and heat, it went bad. I did not realize it and when I got home at about five o'clock in the afternoon, I said to myself, "All kinds of dogs are following me. I wonder why?"

I didn't know the meat I was carrying was stinking. When I got to the house, I said to my wife, "Look, here is some meat and here are the sweet potatoes." Then I noticed that the meat had gone bad and so I said, "Give it to the dogs," and I left. When I got back the family had eaten it! "Man! Why did you go and feed it to the children? It was no good."

"Is that so? And I liked it! What did you bring it for, then? Of course we ate it!"

Well, what could I do? I should have fed it to the dogs myself. But no, my wife really liked rotten meat! *Caray!*

CHAPTER XVII

PEDRO

Back to Politics

My religion forbade getting involved in politics but I couldn't resist trying to improve the village, to straighten out things. That was my idea and again I became involved in village affairs. The first thing we needed was water. There simply wasn't enough. Azteca needed electricity because it was like a forest at night. There was no light, there were only fireflies. We also needed more schools and a better market place. The market here is still fit only for horses! And above all we needed a road.

Our local government officials never do anything much here because the *municipio* has very little income. This holds them back and they don't accomplish anything. The officials aren't active and don't use good tactics. They are like stones, and if one happens to be intelligent, he is usually lazy!

The only thing I got out of all the meetings I attended was that I crossed the threshold of the president's office and I served in the government. I was never the president but I was a councilman three times, and later even a judge. Although I was illiterate I figured there! Yes, I was illiterate, of course, since I had no schooling. I didn't have a good head but the people realized I was dependable in everything. That is why they trusted me and I have the documents to prove it. I was always serving my village, as president of the committee on national fiestas, as inspector of the parks, as inspector of charcoal production, as president of the commission to get drinking water for the village; and, of course, I always volunteered for the *cuatequitl,* the collective work-party.

Then I became the leader of the *tlacololeros.* At first I was only an ordinary *tlacololero,* planting corn on the communal hillside, but then the Forestry Department began to interfere and wouldn't let us work. They said the forest land was a national park and we couldn't make clearings just anywhere. Now we had to have a permit to do what our ancestors did!

I thought to myself, "And how are we going to support ourselves now? Are we not also sons of the nation?"

So I began to organize my neighbors to petition for a permit to stay on the land. I got together about twelve or fifteen men and we took our petition to the forestry officer in Cuernavaca. But he wouldn't give us permission. I said to him, "Why don't you give it to us? The woods are being ruined by the wood cutters and the charcoal burners. They cut the pine and the oak but we cut only the worthless scrub. Why do you let them and not us *tlacololeros?* Isn't it because they give you money and we don't? Isn't that why we don't get permission and we don't eat?"

I explained my reasons clearly and finally he said, "All right. We will send in an agronomist and you show him the place and he will survey it."

Fine. The agronomist came and we showed him where we wanted to make our clearings and he turned in the report. Well, they let us enter and clear the land. Seeing this, more people went with us the following year, about three hundred, and they planted everywhere. I began to be the leader, because they followed me. Each year we had to make another petition to make more clearings. Once we had about two hundred signatures and ten of us went as a committee to the Forestry Department in Cuernavaca. The officer there was a lame man and he was very hostile when he saw our petition. That cripple was really angry! He said, "No more! From today on no more cutting, not even one stick of wood. You insist on cutting the forests and that's why there is no water. You people are a problem. You really are a problem to us."

That's how he began to talk. So then I took my place as spokesman and I said, "Yes, isn't it a problem though! We are poor and have no land and nothing to eat. And now, sir, out of courtesy and obedience we have come to our government to beg permission, but if you don't give it to us, with or without it tomorrow we will go and make our clearings. It is hunger that makes us do this, for we are hungry."

"No!" he says. "Then the federal troops will come!"

"Let the troops come. Let's see what articles of law punish us.

Let's see the article that says poor peasants should not eat!" I had my two sons with me and I said, "Look at these boys. I am not teaching them to be bandits or to steal, but to work. If they can't go to school, at least let them work. We are begging for permission to work ourselves to death, so why should you stop us?"

After that, he didn't say anything. Then he decided to send Guevara, the agronomist, to make a survey. We went home content. I said to my men, "Look, boys, tomorrow we will take Guevara to the worst part of the *texcal*, where no one ever goes, where it is all rocky, with no soil or plants." The men agreed with me, and then I said, "So now let us chip in and bring him some lunch and a bottle of *tequila*."

The next morning we met at the *palacio* and, yes, Guevara came. We had a horse for him and a big sack of food. We took him to the worst parts and soon he was saying, "This is terrible! Is this where you plant? Is it all like this? No, I am not going any farther." He took out his tape and measured a few trees and wrote it down and then he wanted to go back.

"Let's go in the shade, *señor* Guevara," I say, "to have a bit of lunch." We all sat down and began to take out the food—sardines, bread, cheese, even a cooked chicken someone brought, and the *tequila*. He was impressed. "Man! You really went to a lot of trouble. A whole chicken!" We began to eat and we gave him the bottle of *tequila*. "Come on, boys, how can I finish all this alone? Drink up! Keep me company. And don't worry about your land. All will go well. That cripple favors me because I am always giving him bribes."

We brought Guevara back to Azteca on horseback and there we gave him about five beers. Then, in the name of the others, I asked him, "Well, *señor* Guevara, now are you going to report in favor of us?"

"Yes, of course. Now I realize that the land you want to clear is worthless. Yes, you can go in there to plant."

"Fine! Here are twenty-five *pesos* from the boys. They want to give it to you so that at least you didn't come here to lose time."

"Well, boys, thanks. And don't pay attention to that little cripple. Come to my office tomorrow and I will give you the permit."

And that is what we had to do, year after year, to make new clearings. Afterward, the Forestry Department got suspicious of Guevara and didn't believe him, so much so that the cripple himself had us take him to see our *tlacololes*. What happened then was very interesting. Only about ten of us went with him. We brought our own food but we didn't take any along for him, not a thing. Why should we? That man made us so angry. He was awful! We took him a long way, to where the land is very rough. I am a peasant and can jump and climb very well, but he? And what a sun! It was blazing, and as he annoyed us by wanting to see everything, we avoided the paths and took him through the thickets, where his clothing was torn and where he could barely walk. And he kept saying, "But see? These trees are valuable. I don't want these cut down. Now let us take a look at the next hill." And so it want all day.

At about three o'clock we sat down in the sun to eat. Each of us heated our *gordas*. All we gave him was a stale *tortilla*. "Go on, eat it with *chile*," we said. We gave him the strongest *chile* and after that all he could do was shake his head. He couldn't speak! Sure, let him eat what we peasants eat!

On the way back, again we walked where there were no paths, climbing over rocks and stone walls. The man was a wreck when we arrived, but after all, he was the one who insisted on sticking to the letter of the law. And would you believe it? That poor fellow died just because of this outing! I found out when I went to get his decision, to see whether he would let us or not. But that so-and-so was dying and he didn't even give his report. He had to go and get sunstroke! They wouldn't give us a permit until they sent out someone else. But I gave *señor* Guevara another ten *pesos* and we continued to make clearings wherever we wanted.

Then we had trouble with the municipal president. He comes to me and says, "What is going on here? You are still making your clearings? I am in charge of the forests here and these clearings are not allowed."

"But here is my permit, from the Forestry Department, it cost me two *pesos*," I say. I was still collecting two *pesos* from each *tlacololero* because that's what Guevara wanted us to give the forester for the permits. There were two hundred men and the amount would come to four hundred *pesos*.

"And the money?" said the president.

"Ah, I'll give it to the forester."

"No, look, don't give it to him. Better put it here, give it to the president. After all, it's the communal land."

"But the permit comes from the forester, not from you. They take care of it in the office in Cuernavaca so I don't have anything to do with you, nor you with me. And much less with the Commissariat of the *ejido*." Because the Commissariat was there, too.

They said, "Well, that's bad. It is too bad that you are not giving us anything."

"But the forester did not say I should. He told me he was going to give you this money to repair the plaza or something. Take it up with him."

The president and the Commissariat were angry and one day the president sent the guards to the hills to take the *tlacololeros* prisoners. I don't know how many they brought back but *zas!* they put the men in jail.

I was at home making rope when some of my men came and told me. "Well! And now what do we do? Those men have still not paid for their permits!" I ran quickly and got together twenty *tlacololeros* who were willing to pay for the men's permits and there I was making out receipts for each one. Then we go to tell the forester what the president and the Commissariat had done.

He says, "*Ay*, what fools! But what nerve those officials have. This is a matter for the Forestry Department."

And we all went to see the president. The forester scolded him and said what right did he have? And he said the Commissariat was in charge only of the level land, not the forests. And so the prisoners were set free. The forester said to them, "Go back to work. Only when Martínez here tells you to stop, should you stop. Don't stop for anyone else."

Later, I told the forester that the president was complaining about not getting any money for the repairs, and he says, "Now I won't give him a *centavo*. Why does he do these things? I don't have to give him anything."

"Well, I'm just telling you. You know what you are doing. Otherwise how can you support two women?" Because he had two women. "It's no business of mine. The thing I want is that they let us work."

"Yes, yes, Martínez. Go on and work. Don't pay attention to them."

That's the way it was every year, a real war, a tremendous fight. I fought like that a lot and that's why the people followed me. I had a great many people, all *tlacololeros,* and when election time came around, *don* Pancho himself came and said, "Listen, *compadre,* you have a lot of followers. Why don't we do something, like run a candidate for president. Let's nominate someone, or even you."

I say to him, "No. I do not aspire to that. All I want is to work." But he talked me into it. I didn't enter the race but we put up someone else. There was a meeting at *don* Ángel's house and lots of people came, even the yard was crowded. *Don* Pancho brought his little typewriter and began to write up the platform. We called ourselves the Union and we even had a seal.

Well, we didn't win because my *compadre don* Pancho was stupid about it. He was no good at politics. I said to him, "In politics one must go all out. I had followers but what good did it do? I didn't dedicate myself to this."

The truth is, it embarrassed me to go running about asking people to vote.

Little by little, the people began to talk seriously of the necessity of opening a road to Cuernavaca. Being a man of ideas, I, too, wanted the road, to improve my village. So when my people, my race, that is, those of us who lived "above," spoke to me about working with them to carry out this plan, I accepted and co-operated with them. They named me spokesman of the pro-road committee. At the same time, "those below," who were mostly sons of *caciques,* also asked me to help them on the road. I worked with both sides. My ex-*compadre don* Pancho was serving as secretary with the *fraternales* at the time the work was begun. It amounted to a general movement of the entire village. Even the Aztecan students came from Mexico City and Cuernavaca to help build the road.

The *fraternales* chose to work from the Cuernavaca side and the opposing group began to work from Azteca. That way we worked toward each other. The road was to be unified at the point where we met. The students couldn't reach the others because the cars couldn't get in and so they worked with us, the *fraternales.* They came every week and people from the village brought them a lot to eat and a lot to drink. But we peasants were there every day.

All through the Lenten season I didn't earn a *centavo* for my family because I helped build the road. It made no difference to me that my wife and children might starve. It couldn't be helped because I was working for my village, which counted for more. What I aspired to was the improvement of my village! *Don* Prosperino also worked, and Nacilifrando, Refugio, Juan Rojas, well, there were lots of us. We were about thirty. We arrived in the morning and then others came and so we kept changing shifts. We even slept out there at times. We worked until the dry season was over.

There was a time when I fought with the people of the pro-road committee because they did not even provide us with water after we had worked under the hot sun for several hours. I told them the Constitution prohibited forced labor and that we had the right to at least a meal. The president of the committee said I was right but that I should not open the eyes of the workers. But I said to my companions, "Let us leave, boys, because here they don't even want to give us water." And I showed them their constitutional rights.

Finally the two opposing work groups met, but all we succeeded in doing was to open a clearing for the highway. Then the people from Mexico came again and there was lots of food and drink. Even the local government provided some. *Újule!* We began to get drunk. Lots of people, practically the entire village, came out. And then the Aztecans from Mexico City began saying, "Man, why don't you unite to end this division in the village?"

And so they spoke to us about unity, but it was impossible. No! We never united.

Shortly after the clearing was finished, we were in the center of town, near where the saloon now is, sitting and talking, when this fellow comes by and says, "The President of the Republic is coming!"

"What would he be coming here for? Where is he coming?"

"He is coming through here."

"You're crazy. There are no signs of preparations. We haven't received any official notice. It's not true. That old man is *loco*," we said.

Well, a few minutes later, Chico comes rushing by like crazy. "Hurry, hurry, the President of the Republic is coming!" And there he went, running and running. Now, Chico is no fool, he has a good head. By that time I was running too. Where was the President? He had to come through the dirt road on horseback. Well, we saw a mob of people there and it was really he, it was President Lázaro Cárdenas, and we came running up.

But what a shame! no preparations, no nothing! Rodolfo was our president at the time and he rushed someone out to buy at least a dozen rockets to shoot off. But President Cárdenas was already there and while he was speaking they shot off the rockets. Then he went to the *palacio* and all the people crowded around there. Afterward, automobiles arrived and some motorcyclists. They came through the road we had cut. Then Cárdenas said, "This is fine but it is only a clearing. We could pass through, yes, but it is not a highway. Do you have any buses here?"

"Just one. We bought only one. It is a co-operative bus."

"Well," he says, "I am going to give you another bus, so you will have a pair."

Fine, we hoped he would. But this Chico put his foot into it by saying, "No, no. They will kill each other over the buses. No, better not send it."

So then Cárdenas gave other things . . . not to me, though. He gave a huge pedigreed bull, and a great big pure-bred pig, and a little light-colored *burro* that was still nursing. Everything went to the cattle raisers and that was all. He gave Víctor Conde a pair of beautiful tall horses. No one else got a thing. They got the gifts because they were the flatterers who knew how to talk. They got next to him so they could soft-soap him.

Then President Cárdenas said that the next week or the following

one, the highway would be started. "Don't worry," he said, "I am going to build the highway for you." And immediately everyone drank to that. Well, the municipal president didn't know what to give him. What was he going to give him when he was taken by surprise like that? So he sent for some rolls, filled them with sausage meat, and offered them to the visitors. "Go ahead, Mr. President," he said. "This is all we could improvise."

"It doesn't matter. This is fine," Cárdenas said. "I am a peasant myself." And he picked up one of the rolls with sausage and ate it. But he ate only one.

Then, after that, I don't know why they took him to the church-yard. While we were keeping him busy, the teachers prepared a dinner for him there. They fixed it right out in the open air near the fence of the atrium. They served him dinner there under the trees. The teachers organized everything and then they collected from all of us.

That was the only time Lázaro Cárdenas came to the village.

In 1939, they appointed me judge and with that I was able to catch my breath again. They paid me seventy-five *centavos* a day and I got along a little better. Now that I was earning some cash for the daily expenses I was free to plant more corn. I no longer planted five *cuartillos,* or even eight, but *nine.* And in addition I planted another *tlacolol* that a cousin of mine had offered me. He said, "Pay me for the work I did on it because I am not going to use it any more."

I bought it for four *pesos* and it already had three *cuartillos* of corn planted on it.

The corn was fairly high by then, so I brought my boys there once again. I showed them how to work. We began with weeding. Well, I harvested a few ears of corn out of the patch and managed to get by. The bean crop was better than the corn. I got sick of picking beans after a while. I picked about three *cargas* of red beans and my boys were there in the stony field, helping me pick. Then, like real men, they carried a full sack as far as Azteca. I got no less than ten *cuartillos* into a sack, pods and all. But beans were cheap in those days. I sold three *cargas* of clean beans in Cuernavaca at eight *centavos* a *cuartillo,* that is, eight *pesos* a *carga.*

The following year I went to another spot called Barrera, which I cultivate to this day. My sons were a lot bigger by then. Now it was different, and they really worked. I began to show them how to plant. We were three men now. Although they didn't work very hard, still they were a help to me. I didn't have to hustle so much any more. I had my little supply of corn; now we were eating. I harvested about eighteen *cargas* of corn that year.

The year after that I planted thirty *cuartillos* of *tlacolol* and then I really had corn. That little house of mine was full of ears of corn. But I had to sell corn every year "on time," that is, before the harvest. Every year, in July and through August and September I did this. There are people who buy up corn this way, almost at half price. Because, look, if I start planting, with what am I going to clear the land? And with what am I going to pay the *peones?* So, I sell in advance. Then, I have something to work with and I can hire *peones* to help me.

Being a judge was an education for me. The village courthouse was my school. There I learned what justice was supposed to be. Justice means to be just and that every man gets what he deserves. Justice should be done in accord with each man's rights. That is why I like the saying, "Blessed be he who hungers and thirsts for justice."

But he who seeks justice is hated because that isn't what the world wants. People came expecting favors; I began to lose my friends. Always, everybody prefers injustice. Even the government itself never takes the legal road. It only makes a show of justice, but it is false. There is no justice! If that is how it is with governments, what can be expected of us!

I studied the Constitution so that I would know the law. I wanted to know what our rights were. *Don* Pancho was the secretary then and he said, "Yes, but do not tell the young people because then they do not behave."

One day, my neighbor Clemente came to see me. He was trying to get his son out of jail and *don* Pancho kept saying no and no and no. Víctor Conde and several lawyers went to *don* Pancho, but they couldn't get the boy out of jail. So Clemente said to me, "Look, brother, what shall I do? Here it is time for the Carnival and I cannot get my son out, all because this *don* Pancho is so stubborn."

Then I said to him, "You may be big but what good does it do if you're stupid? You believe in Víctor Conde because he is a teacher but he doesn't know what is written, the poor thing. He doesn't have a copy of the Constitution. Now, I will tell you how to get out your son right away. Go to *don* Pancho and say, 'According to the Constitution, Article Twenty, my son can get out on bail.' Get yourself a bondsman to sign for him. *Don* Pancho is going to get angry but it can't be helped. You are so humble, you will get frightened, but with the law in your hand you can be firm."

Clemente took my book on the Constitution and showed it to *don* Pancho. "I came in accordance with Article Twenty of the Constitution. Here it is."

And *don* Pancho gets angry and says, "You're so big and old and yet you go asking others for advice. Who told you to do this? Don't be stupid. Don't you see that this is why there is no respect any more? This is why boys are so badly behaved. Right off they say, 'The Constitution, the Constitution!' *Caramba!* What kind of a man are you?"

"I am just trying to get my son out of jail, but you do not understand and so this is the only way."

And then *don* Pancho says, "Go bring me the prisoner! The Constitution forces me, so bring him." And he gives Clemente this advice. "Don't go listening to people. This is exactly why the youth do not believe anything any more and do not respect anyone. They have been corrupted because of the Constitution."

The next day Clemente came to bring back my book. He began to laugh. "*Caray! Don* Pancho bawled me out, but my boy got out. He saw the Carnival."

"Man! Didn't I tell you? You even paid others and they didn't help you! And *don* Pancho argued against it, didn't he? He told you not to believe what people tell you, didn't he?"

"Yes, that's just what he told me."

"Yes, I knew what he was going to say. He is one of the old-time *caciques*. They still want things to be like in times of *don* Porfirio. They want you to be blind-folded and not know anything, so they can dominate you. No, don't allow it. Go and buy a book on the laws like I did. Why should I be the only one? This is why we had the Revolution, so that not only the *caciques* but everyone can have a copy of the laws and the Constitution!"

A few months later, Clemente, Timoteo, Crescenciano, a man named the Rattlesnake, and four or five others were charged with violating a woman during the Carnival. The woman was from another village and had come to sell *enchiladas* at the fiesta. She was sleeping alone in the market arcade and that's where it happened. They grabbed her and took advantage of her while everyone else was at home asleep.

The next day, her husband came to the *palacio* to complain. "Man! but do you know who they were?" we asked.

"Yes, we know who one of them was. He had a big *sombrero* and he was tall and had a long black mustache."

So Benito, who was my secretary at the time, says, "Oh, then it must be the Rattlesnake."

"Shut your mouth," I whisper to him. "If it's true, keep quiet." Then I say to the husband, "We don't know who it is. You will have to point him out to the *comandante* if we are to arrest him." And that's what he did, and ever since then the Rattlesnake was my enemy. He had seventy-two hours to learn his fate, then we would have to send him to Cuernavaca. The Rattlesnake appointed Baldomero as his lawyer.

This Baldomero was illiterate and he was a lawyer like I was a lawyer. He called the other men together, without accusing them, and they all went to Cuernavaca to get counsel.

My secretary, Benito, went and told the Rattlesnake he would not be sent to Cuernavaca so the lawyer, Baldomero, gave Benito seventy *pesos* which he was to give to me and my assistant. But Benito never gave it to us. He stole it and didn't even tell us about it. Benito himself made out the order which sent the Rattlesnake to Cuernavaca.

The first thing the Rattlesnake did when he was set free was to ambush Benito near his house and cut up his face with a broken bottle. When they took Benito to the hospital, Clemente told me about the seventy *pesos* and everything. Now I didn't know if they were my enemies, too, and if they would come to ambush me! One day I came home late from my office and Gloria's son was there, talking to a neighbor. "Oh, uncle," he says, "you were almost killed because the Rattlesnake was here with about ten men, waiting for you."

"How nice that you tell me now! *Caramba!* Why didn't you come to my office to tell me? They would have killed me by this time and you would have just been entertained by it all. Hurry, let's go to look for them."

I took the two of them to the *palacio* to get rifles. I was full of anger, and I told the others not to be afraid to shoot if we saw them. Suppose they had killed me! Bah!

The lawyer, Baldomero, was drinking in the *cantina* with a lot of people and there were only three of us. No one spoke when they saw us with guns. The Rattlesnake and his men were not there. We looked through the streets and around corners but the gunmen were not to be found.

That night I waited in my *corral*, with my gun and my long *machete*, to see if my enemies came looking for me. I sat in the doorway, listening, and I heard some men singing. I even heard one of them mention my name. I saw someone enter the *corral*. I saw him jump over the gate and I said, "This is it. Now I am going to get him." I stood up and took aim. "Who's there?" I said.

"It's I, *don* Pedrito, I." It was Dímas, my neighbor, crossing the yard to get to his house.

"*Caramba!* What a start you gave me, man! What are you doing here so late?"

"I'm drunk."

"What do you mean, drunk? Man! why do you go around at night? Something might happen to you. I thought you were someone else. *Caray!* I almost gave it to you. Now get going."

Then he saw that I was well armed and he went running.

Some time later, Froilán, the brother of the Rattlesnake, came to my house at night. I wasn't going out then. I never went out at night any more. My sons answered his call and I told them to let him in. He entered carrying a big sack, but he wasn't armed. He greeted me and told me not to be suspicious. "I have come because you are my brother now. Yes, we are brothers in Christ. I have converted to evangelism and I have to come to reconciliate myself with you. You were my enemy but now you are my brother. Don't be afraid of me or of the Rattlesnake."

"By my life, I don't know whether we are enemies or not," I say.

"We were angry because we had to sell our house to get my brother out of jail. We had this in our heart and we had evil intentions toward you. Now, I want you to pardon me."

He sat there and cried. "Yes," he says, "the missionary said that to enter the church we must reconciliate with our enemies and that is why I came. Forgive me."

"Well, I don't know whether we are brothers or not, or enemies. I know we are fellow countrymen and that is all I know."

"Yes, we are brothers in Christ."

We talked all that night and I was very pleased because now he was my friend. He stretched out on the floor and went to sleep. In his sack he carried mangoes, great big yellow mangoes, as a gift for us.

Later the Rattlesnake killed a *comandante*, who also happened to be an enemy of mine because of a legal case involving his wife. I heard that this *comandante* was going around saying I had falsified his signature and that he was going to pay me back. He passed by my house with a *machete* and I prepared myself. But then he fell in love with a woman who was the Rattlesnake's sweetheart. She said she would accept him if only he would kill the Rattlesnake, because she was fed up with him. But the Rattlesnake was already suspicious and killed the *comandante* first, although he didn't want to. The Rattlesnake ran away but when he came back they put him in prison. I saw him there because it was my custom to visit the prisoners and give them cigarettes. His brother Froilán was visiting him, too.

"Come in, come in, *don* Pedrito." He invited me into his cell. "Here I am suffering and Froilán comes only to scold me."

"No, Froilán, why do you want to do that? A person in prison is like a person ill in bed. Whatever your brother does, he is your race, your seed. What happened when Cain and Abel were brothers? One belonged to the devil and the other belonged to God. And what about Jacob and Esau?"

We spoke for a long time and the Rattlesnake enjoyed my visit. They asked me to look for a lawyer who could get him out of jail. I spoke to my friend Moreno, and as he was a judge and distributed bribes to all in charge, the Rattlesnake was finally set free. His brother Froilán had to sell his team of oxen because Moreno couldn't manage it for less than 1,500 *pesos*. The Rattlesnake had to go into hiding for a long time and that is how I got rid of another enemy.

As a judge, I learned a lot about the nature of men and women from all the cases I heard. There was one case of a married couple who had separated but their godfather of marriage was trying to bring them together. He brought them to me several times but they didn't want to have anything to do with each other any more.

One day, I closed my office and left to cultivate my cornfield, as one doesn't earn much in the courthouse. I was already on my way when I met the godfather bringing the couple to discuss the case once more. I said, "No, I am not going to open today. I am going to work."

He said, "But, *señor*, I would like you to do us this favor so that we will not have come in vain."

"I can't do it. I have no *peón* to do my work for me."

He said, "We will talk just a little while, all right?"

I said, "I am going to lose time but let us sit down here."

We began to talk and I explained a few things to him. I told him it was impossible to unite this couple. "The trouble with your godchildren is something secret. They cannot go telling it to their parents or their godfather or the judge because the thing is, they are not good in bed. Do you know why?"

"No, why?"

"You don't understand. You don't have a head for this. You are old, but I am older still."

He said, "I am the one who is old. I saw you grow up and my hair is already gray and that's how I know I have many years behind me."

"Yes, but I have observed more and I will prove it to you. Look, there are many kinds of people in this life. Some are very high in temperament and some are very low. When the man is by nature passionate and the woman isn't, they do not harmonize. And if one is harsh and cold and the other is very affectionate, they won't be able to bear each other. That's how the world is and how can you expect me to bring them together if their own nature doesn't?"

And I told him more. There is the bed itself. Some want it every month and some want it every week or every night and that is when they don't agree. They fight right there in bed and at dawn how are they going to tell their parents or their godfather? Lots of times when the man is weak in sex and the wife bothers him because she wants him to embrace her, to caress her, he gets annoyed and ends up with, "Get away! Stop bothering me!" But the wife needs it and she gets annoyed, too, and that is why what happens happens.

A widow once said to me, "Well, who knows all the things that go on in this world! My neighbor here is well off, her husband gives her everything and still, she ran away with another man. Yes, and her husband loved her, except that when he went to bed or went out on a spree, he paid no attention to her. He would sleep alone and wouldn't 'cover' her. The wife didn't care for that at all and pretty soon she went off with someone else, even though now she doesn't have enough to eat."

Caray, the lengths nature goes to! Other men are very mean with their wives, and very strict. They go too far. They are bad-tempered and naturally the wives don't like to be made slaves of. A lot of times the husband won't take the wife out anywhere and won't even let her go to the door. Of course, the wife gets fed up. You must remember that we are equals, and we have the same rights and why should we go making slaves of our wives?

But everything depends on us men. The man is the main axis of the home. If he doesn't give money to the wife, and he still expects to be fed, how is the wife going to end up? The woman gets desperate and one fine day decides to commit adultery. And why? Because of the husband!

Some men are jealous because it is convenient for them, others because of inheritance, and lots of times they just turn out that way. It depends on a person's character. There is an example right here in Azteca. I know a rich fellow who is really jealous. *Újule!* The man had his mistresses and he made them suffer so much he practically killed them. There is another rich one here who carries around a lot of money but yet his wife goes barefoot, bruised, asking for food on credit. Other men seem to be very free, squandering their money, but they don't let their wives have any little luxury. It is in ways like this that a person shows his character.

If I like a saddle horse, a well-trained one, and I don't know how to handle it, I will ruin it or it will kill me. That is what happens between men and women. Many men don't know how to manage and some women are smarter than their husbands. If the man gives in and isn't free even to get drunk, that's bad. If the man lets his wife raise a hand to him, that's bad. When a man gives in, the woman expands like a leafy green plant. One must know the ways of the women of my village. I understood and I always knew how to manage.

In the twelve years that I practiced Adventism most faithfully, I did not touch a drop of alcohol. That is how I got sick. I couldn't eat chicken or eggs or fish or sardines . . . nothing at all. But after two years duty in the courthouse as judge, there I was back at it again, a champion drinker. And good-bye sickness . . . all my troubles left me. You might say that I was almost a Catholic again.

I was still an Adventist, though I was withdrawing little by little. By then, I was saying that the Adventists were Catholics. They are like Protestants in that they are evangelists protesting against Roman Catholicism, because there is much to protest. I liked everything about Catholicism except the hypocrisy. I don't like it when they try to fool me. I don't mind fooling myself but I don't like anyone else doing it.

I had three Bibles, the Modern, the Galea and the Catholic, and I still studied all three of them daily. That is why I say having been an Adventist hasn't done me any harm. It hasn't brought me much material good, but spiritually, yes, it has helped me.

When I first entered office, I kept trying to resist drinking but the politicians would say, "Come on, won't you have a drop of anise? A bit of *tequila?*" Until finally one day the *comandante* himself betrayed me. It happened that I had the grippe but I was so faithful to my job that I went to work though I was sick. Well, this *comandante* went to the barmaid in the *cantina* and worked out a plan to trick me into drinking. So he comes and gets me to leave the court with some fake story. And off I went with him to the *cantina*, like a fool, to look into the case he had told me about. I said to the barmaid, "Are you the interested party, *señorita?*"

She said, "Just a minute, she'll be right here." Meanwhile the barmaid picks up a bottle of *tequila* and a big tumbler which she fills half full. "Come on," says she, "You are good and sick, give yourself a treatment while you wait. This will cure you. Put in lots of lemon and salt."

I said, "No." Then the *comandante* said, "But you can't refuse a lady." And the barmaid picks up a great big glass, fills it and says, "I am going to drink with you both, just to show you." And wham! she tosses it down. That's where I said to myself, "Well, I guess I'm licked."

The *comandante* said, "See, even the *señorita* took a drink. Now, you can't back out." Then I realized it was all a put-up job. But there was nothing I could do about it. I drank my drink and *zas!* That was it! From that time on they came at me from all sides . . . even lawyers . . . to make me drink. It was: "Say, *señor* Judge . . ." and little by little I began getting into stride once again.

Naturally, I learned a lot as a judge. When my term was over, people who knew me came asking for advice. Well, I would put them on the right track and I am doing it to this day. As I had lots of lawyer friends in Cuernavaca, the peasants would ask, "Don't you know a lawyer for me?"

"Sure. If you like, I'll recommend one to you." I almost always recommended the lawyer Moreno, who had helped me the most. I would take the peasant to him and say, "I brought you this case, but it is a tough one. I would like you to defend this client for me."

I would let Moreno know if the peasant had money and it would be so much the worse for him if he did. Moreno would ask me to work along with him on the case and he would get more money that way. Naturally he taught me a lot. We would go to the courthouse and he would show me the records and would teach me the law. That is the way I learned. When the case was over, Moreno would ask me what the client paid me.

"They just gave me my bus fare and my meals. That is all." I didn't tell him that they paid me for the day. That I never told him. Then Moreno would say, "Such people! Why don't you ask for more?"

"No, why should I? They are my compatriots. I don't have the nerve to."

Moreno would ask the client for more money and would give me a share, two or three hundred *pesos,* sometimes even more.

I'll tell you about the most interesting cases. I know countless cases, but there are two in particular.

There was the case of *don* Santos, from the little neighboring village of San Pedro. *Don* Santos was a sorcerer who had made an awful lot of money. He was rich to begin with. I took him to Moreno, even though the case already had been lost in Cuernavaca. *Don* Santos had been telling me about it ever since the time I was judge. For ten years he had been fighting the case without being able to win. Finally, the judge told him, "You've lost the case, old man! Now you are dismissed. Stop making a nuisance of yourself here because you are through."

So *don* Santos came running to my house and said, "Listen, I've lost. The judge himself threw me out. That woman won. But I won't accept it. How can I accept being beaten by a woman?"

The woman was from his village. The two of them got into a dispute over this piece of land which they both claimed. She said it belonged to her and he said it was his. Naturally it was in litigation.

I say to him, "A bad business! How many times have you harvested it?"

"Twice, already. And another harvest is ready but they notified me that I lost. Listen, take me to a lawyer, I'll buy your bus ticket and your food there and pay for your day besides."

"Fine. Let's get going."

Well, as I was telling you, this man was a sorcerer. He goes to Puebla or to Toluca and brings back at least two thousand *pesos* in a week. He really gathered it in, that witch doctor! Well, when we arrived at Moreno's, I said, "Here I brought you this gentleman. He is your client now and I want you to take care of him for me, eh?" And there I am giving him our signal to squeeze him for money.

"Well, let us see, now. Have a seat. What is the case about?" So we explained it. Then he says, "Let's go to the record office. I will ask for the file and look it over." But the case was ten years old by then and it was a big fat file. "Whew!" says Moreno, "what am I supposed to do with this?" and he begins to leaf through it. "When am I going to have time for this? The national holidays are coming soon and I am preparing my speech. I was selected by the Governor. Well, anyway . . . I'll leaf through." Just the "leafing through" cost *don* Santos three hundred *pesos!*

"Fine," says Moreno. "Then I'll start working as of now. I will tell the Governor I am sick. I won't deliver my speech."

Three days later we went to Moreno. He said to us, "*Don* Santos, I have had the judge's action thrown out already. The case is in my hands, now. Your lawyer lost it completely. He's no good. I got rid of him. Now I am going to commit myself to winning this case. Except that you have to loosen up."

"How much, *señor?*"

"Two thousand *pesos.*"

"*Újule!* No, *señor*, where am I going to get that kind of money?"

So I say, "Look, *licenciado*, the piece of land is not worth more than seven hundred *pesos.*"

"That's all right. If he doesn't want to, he doesn't have to. Let him lose it. It is true that the lot isn't worth the money. But the whim is, eh? The whim is what is worth the money. But, if you both think it is expensive, then he had better drop it. He lost it already, so forget about it."

Then I say, "See, *don* Santos, you didn't want the woman to beat you, and now you let these two thousand *pesos* scare you off."

"No, it is a lot of money."

"Who can say? Whims cost money."

"Well, I am willing to give another five hundred *pesos.*"

"What are you talking about? Five hundred *pesos!* I don't work for that." Well, after a lot of discussion a thousand *pesos* were squeezed out.

Caray! A week later *don* Santos showed up with a sack full of money . . . nothing but old coins, pure silver. Whew! Old ones that I guess would be worth double today. That is what he brought and we went to the bank to change them. *Caray!* it was a mountain of money and me there just looking on in envy. What could I expect out of it? He was just going to give me a miserable sum. What would it amount to? Well, we went to give the lawyer the thousand *pesos*. We had emptied the bag of coins and brought him paper bills.

Moreno counted the money and said, "Look, *don* Santos, go to such and such a place and buy me this. Let *don* Pedro stay here." And off went the old man.

"Well, I guess we did it, eh? Here are two hundred *pesos* for you."

"You don't say? That's fine!" That was more like it!

Then *don* Santos returned from the errand. He brought back a package of paper and that was all. Moreno had sent him out just so he could give me the money.

"Now, come back on such and such a day." We did. "Now you are in. You won. I had everything thrown out. Now it is all going to be-gin with a new slate. Go to the court clerk now and have him sign."

We went to the clerk, who knew me, too, and he says, "Hello there, *don* Pedro, still around, aren't you?"

"Yes, I always am."

"Well, well, I imagine you must be a lawyer by now, eh?"

"No! A lawyer! of all things!"

So Santos signed and that was that. Then Moreno said, "Now just wait. Come back in two weeks. If they haven't taken out a stay at the end of that time, I will close the case."

Two weeks later he says, "Whew! The other lawyer put in a stay, so now it goes to the Supreme Court in Mexico City. Look for a good lawyer to push things for you there."

"But what about you? Can't you do it?"

"How can I? I am nobody there. Here I am a magistrate, but there I am a nobody."

"But I want you to go."

"All right, but . . . you know, *don* Pedro is going to come along too. That will be two thousand *pesos*."

"But *señor!* It cost me thirteen hundred already and now, more. No!"

"Well, then you better find another lawyer. I don't work for less. You have a sure thing and that is what you are paying for. We are going to have to stay over there, pay for hotel, meals, and everything. The two thousand *pesos* won't even cover it."

"I'll give you another thousand *pesos*, and that is all."

"Well, all right, then. Listen, *don* Santos, I'll leave on Monday.

Your case will be finished." The old man was glad now. "And I am going to take *don* Pedro here along with me. But give him money for his ticket, his hotel and meals, eh?"

"Yes, sure, how much?"

"Give him a hundred *pesos,* and call it a day. Who knows it if will be enough."

"All right. I will have it for him on Sunday morning so you can go on Monday."

Sure enough, early that same Sunday he gave me my hundred *pesos.* "Ah, *chihuahua!*" I said to myself. "This is all mine, because he told me so." And at seven o'clock on Monday I was in Moreno's office.

"Hello. Did the old man give you your money?"

"Yes."

"See? We finally got it out of that old buzzard. He doesn't want to pay, he is very stingy. What you got is for yourself, eh?"

"Now, what? Are we going to the Supreme Court?"

"No, of course not. What for? No, we are going to Jojutla." He had a car and we drove to Jojutla. When we arrived he said, "Now to the court." Whew! He introduced me. Now, suddenly, I became a lawyer. What a rascal, that man! He says, "Look, Your Honor, I have my lieutenant here. Take good care of him for me when I can't come around myself, as I am a magistrate. I will send this man in my place and whatever he says, you do for me . . . you will be good enough to take care of it."

"Don't worry about it, *señor licenciado,* we will take care of him."

So, now I was a lieutenant. It made me feel very important. Whew! Now I was a lieutenant lawyer!

"Well, that's that," he says. "Tomorrow I am going to the Supreme Court, but just me alone. I'll be there for a little while and then I'll be back. Bah! We are going to get more money out of our friend. What does he mean, he doesn't want to pay?"

Sure, Moreno got a lot of money from *don* Santos—all lawyers do that—but, in the end, it didn't cost the witch doctor at all because he won back the land after having lost it.

Then there was this other case . . . a nephew of mine, the son of my cousin Macedonia. It was a criminal case. Rape! *Úuujule!* That meant the penitentiary and it carried the death penalty. They caught the boy and put him in jail.

His mother, Macedonia, says to me, "Look, man, what do we do, now?"

I said to her, "Well, this needs money because he is in jail already. If he were out it would be a different matter. I'll hurry to Cuernavaca to look for a lawyer, because this is serious. But let us wait until the plaintiffs arrive at ten o'clock and see what kind of a statement they make."

Well, they piled the assault charge on my nephew because he was dragging this girl along the road from Huacatlán to Azteca, out in the country. She was from Azteca and he beat up her parents, their faces were all black and blue. And it was an American who caught him, a man who lives there. That was what did it! This American came out with a rifle, took my nephew prisoner and called the militia. That's how he got caught.

Well, there I am in the court waiting, waiting for whatever might come up. *Caray!* I am making plans, because the president is a bit stupid. Well, ten o'clock passed and nothing happened. Eleven and twelve, and still nothing. So then I said, "Look, *señor presidente,* the Constitution and the law say, 'When the plaintiff does not appear, there is no crime.' He has to be here at the time he is called. If he does not come, then there is no crime."

"We will just wait until one o'clock."

"All right." And there I am praying that they don't appear. Finally, it got to be two o'clock and I said, "See, they did not appear. So there is no crime to prosecute."

"All right. Let him pay twenty-five *pesos* and he can go." I said to my cousin, "Come on, come on, let's have the twenty-five *pesos.*"

"Sure thing! Here."

"All right. Let's have the receipt."

Wham! the receipt and let's go. When we were on the way, I said to my nephew, "Now go and hide because the police car will be here any minute. Go hide, get to the hills, because they will be here looking for you. They are on the way from Cuernavaca now. I put one over on the fools here. If it had been anybody else, they wouldn't have let you out. But as the president is stupid, I tricked him, so now get out of here. I will go to Cuernavaca tomorrow."

Then I said to the mother, my cousin, "I need five hundred *pesos* right away. This is a serious business."

"Sure, of course. I'll go get the five hundred *pesos.*"

"Come with me. I will pay the lawyer right in front of you."

"But how can I go? I can't."

"All right, then I will go myself. But see that he hides. Don't let them catch him. Because once they do, there is no way out."

I went to Cuernavaca and told Moreno what had happened.

"Man, what a good job you did! Very well done! But now let us go over to the Inspector's office and see what kind of statement the old people made."

Mmm! But what went on there! The Inspector took me aside and said, "What is this boy to you?"

"My nephew, *señor*."

"Well, turn him in. Because, if you don't . . . he has to die. It is a case of assault in an unprotected area. Last night they went with the patrol car to pick him up and they couldn't find him. Where is he?" Then the Inspector threatened me.

So I said, "But he doesn't live with me. He doesn't live in my house. How can I turn him over?"

Then Moreno said, "Don't worry about it, *señor* Inspector. Listen, I'd like to take up this matter with you."

"Very well, come on, step over here." He got us into a corner. He got us in there, and began with this and that and the other.

So Moreno says, "Here are a hundred *pesos*."

"Ah, don't worry about it, *licenciado*. Even though they give me the order to go and arrest him, I'll act like I am going but I won't go. Don't worry about it. Count on me."

"Fine, then we'll leave it at that."

We went over to the Public Ministry where Moreno said, "*Señor*, we would like to look over the record to see the statement of the plaintiffs."

"No, you are not allowed here. Go to the District Attorney's office."

"Oh, come on, man. I know it is here, show it to me." And a paper bill was passed. *Zas!* a hundred *pesos*.

"Well, all right." And he showed it to us. The *licenciado* began to read it and then he called me over and said, "Come over here. Look at this. Assault, nothing! They are fools. Look at the old folks' statement. This is going to be a big help to us. The plaintiffs themselves say that they left Huacatlán on foot and this drunk on horseback caught up with them and went along talking with them . . . the three of them and the girl. They walked along talking with him on horseback. When they left the forest, the drunk got down and continued on foot, leading the horse and talking with them. An assaulter doesn't converse! The assaulter does what he wants when you least expect it. This is not assault."

Then I suggested something. I said, "Now, suppose you write that the girl is his sweetheart . . . that there was something between them and that is why he pulled her away. That's how it ought to go."

"Don't worry about it, we'll get him free." Then he says, "All right, here is the file. Here you are, but please send it right over to the District Attorney."

"Yes, right away, *licenciado*. I'll send it now." But here he had already gotten a hundred *pesos*! We went to the District Attorney's office. Now Moreno says to him, "Whew! this looks nasty. They are charging him with assault but there was no assault. So it might be rape because he dragged off the girl. But that was all. Her parents were right there. Not only that, she is his sweetheart."

"You don't say? We'll see when the file gets here. I don't know what's in it yet."

A telephone call . . . and there goes another hundred *pesos*. That made three hundred, altogether.

Moreno says, "Now, look here, let us . . ." Wham! another hundred *pesos*. "You see, *don* Pedro, this money isn't for me, it is all going for bribes."

"Yes, I can see that."

"But you know we are going to win, don't you? They can't get the better of me, right?"

But we had trouble with the court clerk. They really had a battle, Moreno and the clerk. The clerk also knew the law. He was steeped in it.

"No, *señor*. Look at the way it stands. Let's read the whole thing out loud. Pay close attention." Finally Moreno comes to this part and he says, "What does it say here? That they were conversing. Does an assaulter walk along speaking? A rapist talking?"

"Man, that's true! I believe you are right."

"Of course, I am right. Right and to spare. Naturally, after walking a while, the boy took hold of her because there was something between them. The parents couldn't let that go by and jumped on him. They beat him, and as he was drunk he hit them with his fists."

"Well, well . . . all right. This can be arranged."

"Here are a hundred *pesos* . . . go on."

"Ah, *licenciado*, don't worry about it now." *Zas!* that was the end of the five hundred *pesos*. "Well," he says, "just now we closed the door. Now the case is ours. But keep him hidden."

My nephew was up in the hills for a month and a half while we went through all the transactions here. Two thousand five hundred *pesos* were spent. But he did not go to jail.

After Moreno won, he said, "Look, you have put in a lot of work with me. It is only fair . . . here, take this." And he gave me a present of three hundred *pesos*. "It's only right that you get your share."

Well, as I was saying, I know lots of cases. An infinite number! I know the law and I know the right people.

PEDRO

The PRI and Village Politics

The PRI [Institutional Revolutionary Party] is in bad shape and is poorly organized but it controls the whole country anyway, eh? It imposes itself everywhere. In the PRI it is no longer the people who count, except, as they say, "to pull the wool over their eyes." The national elections are used just as a cover-up, to fulfill the law. The elections are a sham, not the real thing. Those who know the Constitution believe that the people are going to choose, but it is all arranged there in Mexico City or by the government here. It is really the PRI that rules.

It wasn't like that in the past. Before, elections were legal. When I began in politics in 1925, there was still no PRI. Then it was really the people who nominated the candidates; the will of the people was carried out. Not like now when they don't count for much. The PRI didn't even exist, only the voice of the people.

Just think, here in Azteca in the year '25, I was opposing the administration and nevertheless I was elected. When I came home from work my wife showed me the credentials. They had nominated me and I knew nothing about it. I was *regidor* without knowing it! When I was in politics in 1940 and 1945, the PRI worked well because it proclaimed itself revolutionary and was still run by us.

Now, of course, there is no more politics here. There is practically no opposition, no division in the village, any more. Now everything is imposed from the outside. We accept it and that is that. The one who is put in by the government wins and that is all there is to it. The one who has money becomes the municipal president. One goes to the PRI and is told, "You should know that the one who brings a thousand or fifteen hundred *pesos* gets it. He who brings the most is the one who will win. If you bring us two thousand *pesos* you will be it." The PRI takes it all and accepts money from everyone who brings it. That's why it is called politics, because they never announce the candidates until later. It is no more than a business deal and it ought not to be like that.

In the past, no one paid anything, except what was spent on propaganda. First, whoever wanted to be president made propaganda to get the people's votes. Then they made promises.

Right off they would promise the village of San Agustín tile for the school roof, or they'd promise Santa María help in getting water, and so on. And the villages would promise to help the candidate. That's the way they did it here. The candidates also went to talk to the PRI and to all of their friends in the party. Their true friends would say, "I am going to work to help you win. I will tell the president of the PRI to support you."

After that more propaganda was needed. Placards had to be bought and put up on the street corners. The candidate and his backers themselves wrote up the announcements and paid for the paper. Then there were the expenses of providing drinks and even barbecues to get the people's votes. The candidates would give thirty or forty *pesos* to their men to supply drinks in all the villages of the *municipio*. If there were three candidates they would spend about four hundred *pesos* among them in this way. They didn't give anything to the PRI and the PRI barely took part in it.

Now the PRI works differently because they pay no attention to the people any more. The leading members of the PRI here first call a meeting of about ten or fifteen men and they get together in a private house or in the *palacio*. The ones who are going to run come to the meeting and the slates are agreed upon. They say, "Well, choose to see which ones you want to run." But it is only a gesture because they have already been named by the PRI. All the little local politicians already know, but one says, "Well, don't you agree that we should put forward so-and-so?"

"But won't there be an opposing candidate?"

"Yes, but that is why we will put up so-and-so and back him to the hilt, with cloak and dagger. We'll work for him in the offices of the PRI, if possible we'll go all the way to the capital. But we'll have to work with him, without getting a *centavo*, eh?"

And we all agreed. If there was an opposing candidate, there would be another convention. Lots of people came to these conventions just to look on but there were the photographers who kept taking pictures and claimed that all these people were supporters of the candidate. This is the way the people become involved and even cast a vote in the primaries, although the slates were already made. This is the truth about the voting and this is what they call an election. I began to realize that all this was done just to make it look right.

Then each group of politicians goes to the PRI and to the state government. "Well, here we bring our candidates. He represents the people and has lots of signatures." They go to register him with the PRI and there the PRI chooses and the one who brings the most money is the one they choose. The president of the PRI and the Chamber of Deputies both examine him and ask questions and meet among themselves to decide who it will be. That's why they call together the entire state so that all the *municipios* can register their slates. That is when we run to the PRI, to see if they will register us and to see if we come out ahead.

One must identify oneself to the PRI and show one's membership card. I had to do that when Abraham Fuentes was a candidate. I presented myself and they asked, "But are you in the party?"

"Yes, sir. I have been in the PRI many years and I haven't left yet. Here is my credential."

"Oh, very well, you are all right."

When we went with Abraham, we all identified ourselves. There were about eight of us, apart from those who came later. Abraham kept going and going, sometimes to the PRI, sometimes to the state government, and we accompanied him. We went as a group, that is, all those who were his followers. The candidate had to go often and he wanted us to go with him. He brought us and it was his money we spent. Twice Abraham even took us to Mexico City to the president of the PRI of all Mexico. As he was the real head, like the President of the Republic or a general, he gave the orders. "Go back home and work it out there." The second time Abraham went, the president again said, "No, this is a state matter, you must fix it up there."

They sent us back to see the president of the PRI in Morelos, who spoke plainly to Abraham. "Fine, now look, you are going to be the one but bring me five hundred *pesos* right away."

And the very next day, *zas, zas,* Abraham gave the money and bought himself the post. The members of the other party in Azteca, the Revolutionary Party, were the ones who always acted as a counterforce. They had another slate and wanted to run but Abraham had it all sewed up and those poor peasants couldn't do a thing. In addition, they were ignorant and didn't bring money. But they were told, "Yes, don't worry, don't worry. Just keep working." They were told that the PRI didn't know who it was going to be and the poor fools believed that everything would be legal and that they would win. And the one whose money was accepted also believed he would win. But neither side knew exactly and that is why it is called politics. But the PRI knew very well who was going to win, though they kept saying, yes, yes, to everyone.

As Abraham progressed, the president of the PRI said to him, "We will need this and we will need that, so bring us more money."

"How much?"

"Well, give me at least two hundred *pesos*."

"Very well."

Then Abraham told us, "Now everything is going fine. Now I have it sewed up."

The PRI did it with the help of the Governor and the Chamber, eh? There were three other parties in this, the Popular Party, the *Sinarquista* Party and the PAN. But no one paid attention to them since we knew they never won. The PRI kept encouraging the other candidate and didn't tell him that Abraham was the lucky one because the other candidate had backers, too, even though now the people don't count. So the other fellow couldn't do a thing, not a thing, especially because he didn't know how to speak, he couldn't find the right words. In this work one also needs a good head and plenty of words, eh?

Abraham made no promises to the people. He only spoke to his men, for example, he said to me, "Look, *don* Pedro, I will promise nothing nor am I going to make predictions. The only thing I am going to do is fix the plaza and the *palacio*, that is all. And when I do that I am leaving, I am getting out. That's why I want the assistant to be one of us."

Then the Chamber and all the representatives of the government of the PRI came together and there they decided. They said, "Abraham Fuentes is going to be the candidate." *Uuy!* Abraham had a lot of schoolteachers among his followers, and they were all allowed to enter the room where the matter was being discussed. The followers of the other candidate were only peasants and about four of them got in, but what of it? They were the kind that couldn't speak. What would those poor things have to say? Almost all the peasants were left outside whereas most of Abraham's men were allowed to enter. All of our men were sharp and knew how to talk. I, too, could put in a word and I wanted to get in but they left us there in the street. What could I say outside?

So we all exclaimed, "*Caray*, what nerve! They give preference to the teachers and not to us. What good can we do out here?" Some of the others went home but we decided to remain, complaining and consoling ourselves by saying, "But more of our men got in and the teachers will defend Abraham. Only four of theirs entered and what can those poor little things have to say? So we are doing well."

We sat down and waited until Abraham came out. Well, yes, they finally came out and we followed Abraham home.

"What happened?" He told us what the final slate was. He had had opposition and so they had mixed up the people and formed another slate, putting in some from the other party. The opposition were even winning because they had put up a fight. Some men from Cuernavaca had ganged up on Abraham. But as I was saying, what did it matter if they had more supporters when it is not a question of people. They had plenty of backers but what good did it do them? None!

Abraham came out ahead. He said, "But they mixed the slate so that there are two of us and one of them. And all the assistants are theirs. That's how the PRI consoled them."

Then I said, "Well then, you realize that you should not resign because if you do, the peasants will take over. Even if it kills you, you must stick through the three years."

Says he, "Now they have me trapped, because if I resign they get in. And what good will those poor peasants be? Now it can't be helped. That's the way the slate is, so what can I do?"

And the slates were announced and everyone knew who was going to win. That is why I say that the public is controlled by the PRI. One can almost say that the votes are not valid, they are only a legal requirement, because it is not the people who decide. Even against their own will the people say, "Why should I vote for so-and-so if he is not going to win? The other one will win so we will all vote for him."

Everyone wants to be on the winning side. If I vote for the other one I am left out. I am nothing. Even though he has a lot of supporters and lots of votes and it is according to the law and our conscience, it will do no good. No, no, no! Even if he had a majority, the PRI would come along and say, "Mmm, no, not this one." And what the PRI says goes and that is all there is to it. There have been independents who have not registered but they count even less. So it was better before because the people were given some weight then.

When Crispín Conde ran for president and I for *síndico* we won. We were with the PRI and we won but Víctor Conde was against us and he made fools of us. He got them to disregard our votes. There were three slates, ours, Víctor Conde's and another. Víctor was Crispín's uncle but nevertheless he worked against us.

The name of the party we established was the "Party of Emiliano Zapata." In our propaganda we said a vote for our party was a vote for Zapata. We went out to all the villages several times a week and at election time we gave the voters alcohol, *ponche, tequila* and *tacos* of

barbecue or sardines. We had lots of supporters. The voting took place in the plaza and we won but because of our many enemies they said it wasn't legal. Víctor Conde had a lot of weight in the PRI and they backed him.

After the election, the PRI withdrew because they only function up to that time. Once the results are announced, the PRI no longer takes a part. That was when we went to work. We went straight to the Governor.

"*Señor* Governor, we won with two hundred or so votes so why were we pushed aside? The other got only one hundred twenty votes and the third only eighty-five, so what happened?"

Then the Governor said, "Look, I am going to tell you something. On your slate was a minister of the evangelist cult."

So that was it! Víctor Conde was going after me.

Then I said, "Look, *señor* Governor, I am the one they credit with being a minister. Tell the one who came to denounce me to give me a license to be a minister so that I won't have need of the government any more. Ministers are trained so what do they need the government for? But tell this to the one who spoke to you. I already know who it is."

He says, "Ah, so you are the one he was talking about."

"Yes, the very one."

So the Governor turns to Crispín and says, "Well, this man will be all right but get rid of the other one, Ángel. Get rid of him because I cannot back him at all. You know how the people are. They don't want him because he isn't from Azteca. It's true he has been there a long time and married there and has the right to run but . . . get rid of him and put another in his place."

"Very well, that can be arranged."

"But," I said, "*señor* Governor, we will play again and I'll make a wager that we will win. If the last election is invalid we will have to do it over again."

The Governor said, "Listen, Crispín, I swear to you that now it is I who will back you, not the PRI, because the PRI has already gone. Run once more and if you beat them by one vote you will rise to power. What this man here says is right."

"And I will back up my words."

"If you win with only one vote, you can get in. But change that man who is not an Aztecan."

That's why we changed Ángel for another man from Santa María. Then we had another election and we lost in Azteca. We took a crushing loss and I said, "Crispín, man! We have lost here, so why go on? It was carried out properly, all legal, so what do you want now?"

He said, "No, now let's go to Santa María."

We went and there we won! The people of San Agustín also went there to vote and they voted in favor of us. In the first election they were against us and in the second they switched because Crispín promised to pay for a new roof for their school, so it increased our votes. We won by only three votes, but we won! As soon as we knew, we went to take over the presidency of the *municipio.* It was already March of that same year, 1941. Before that there had been an interim president appointed by the Governor.

So Crispín was my companion in office. He was not an ignorant man, he had a good head, but when he took office he believed he had entered a place where money just piled up. That's what he thought, but it wasn't that way. Besides, he was a bad administrator and he didn't have the right tactics to raise money.

Crispín and I were the only ones in the administration who did any work. The *regidor,* who was from Santa María, might just as well not have been alive. Once in a while he came to the treasury. As Crispín didn't know anything, being new and not fit for the presidency, I was the one who took care of it all.

When they came to collect the money for the roof tiles for the school in San Agustín, there was no money in the treasury to pay for it. There wasn't enough to pay our salaries! "*Caray!* Where will I get the money? Here they are, charging me for the tile."

"Now you see? Why do you go offering things you don't have?" I say. "How will you pay now?"

"Well, I guess from my salary. Whatever pay I get, I will give them."

As president, he earned more than I did. I don't remember how much, but it wasn't ever enough. And here he was giving it all to the tile maker. He was left in rags. He was the municipal president but he wore patched trousers! And that man wasn't an ordinary person. He had gone through school!

To make matters worse, he had recently married and was having a hard time because of that, too. We believe here that newlyweds always suffer a lot. It is inevitable, because when one marries there are many things to buy and poverty strikes. There are many superstitions about this. That's what happened to Crispín and he looked poor, really poor.

"Man, what happened to you?" I say.

"I am going to the devil. It is getting embarrassing to beg my brother for clothes. He gave me this old shirt. Now I don't even have money to give my wife for the baby's diapers!"

Uuy! He complained a lot because the money they gave him for being president wasn't enough. My wage was enough for me because I had plenty of corn at that time. I had my sons and together we were planting thirty *cuartillos*. I rented a team of oxen and we had plenty to eat. I wasn't in need then.

One day Crispín went to Mexico City, as he often did, to see about getting electricity for Azteca. He went complaining and lamenting that he had nothing and was very poor. At that time we opened the municipal office in the *palacio* twice a day, in the morning and in the afternoon. We left at dinnertime and I was going up the hill toward my house when I met a fellow who said to me, "Hurry, come, they have set fire to the forest and are going to burn it."

"But who?"

"Those . . . what do you call them? . . . those movie people are filming in the hills and they made a forest fire!"

So there I go running to the hills. All the other municipal officials had gone away, and the president, Crispín, was in Mexico City. Sure enough, they had set fire to the forest for their movie. And *újule!* they had a lot of workers with them, village people who were there as extras. I asked who was in charge and a man stood up and said he was.

"Why, *señor*, why are you burning the forest?" And I scolded him, the way I do. I said, "Now, put out the fire for me because if you don't I will report you to the Forestry Department."

They were eating but as soon as I gave the order, about forty men got up to put out the fire. Then I said, "Now, let's go to the president's office." They had a car and two of the men took me to the *palacio* in the car. I sent for *don* Chico, the *comandante*, and said, "Please take these two gentlemen to jail."

"But why? This is not a question of imprisonment!"

"And why not? Why did you come here to do evil? You have no right to scorch our land and burn our trees. How many of our trees will dry up? Every tree is a life and that is why you people will have to go to the Forestry Department. You cannot get out of it."

And one of the men said, "Who are you?"

And I answered, "I am the *síndico procurador* of this *municipio*. Come, I will unlock the office." I took out the key and then they believed me. Also, because I gave orders to the *comandante*. I said, "You will throw these two into jail for me." How they stared! They thought I was a nobody at first.

One of them says, "Well, we will pay."

"Pay five hundred *pesos* and you can leave. If you don't pay I will send you to the Forestry Department and there they will pry loose thousands of *pesos* from you because I will tell them what you came to do. You come because you like the scenery, right? You come here to film the landscape, the cliffs, the peaks, don't you? But what you did was make trouble. It is bad because the young trees will dry up and expire. You have taken their lives!"

"Look, please, we will pay. But don't ask for so much, because we are Mexicans."

"That makes no difference to me. Because you are Mexicans you come here to cause trouble? The foreigners, the Americans, behave better. They ask permission. No, it is the jail for you!"

"Please, sir, look, do us a little favor, we beg you. We will pay but the company is poor."

"What business is it of mine? I didn't send for you, did I? The forest is still burning and the more it burns the more I will demand."

"We'll pay two hundred and fifty *pesos*."

"Well, hand it over."

I was hungry by then and I couldn't give them a receipt because the treasury was closed. They said it didn't matter and so I gave them a provisional receipt and they left me the 250 *pesos*.

Now, if I had been an ambitious man, that money would have been for me, don't you think so? That money was mine, something I made on the side. But the next day Crispín came back. He was the president and I saw how patched and tattered he was, so I said, "Let's go to Cuernavaca."

"*Carambas,* how can I go if I don't have money?"

"Let's go. I invite you. I will pay the fare. Let's go."

"No, how? *Carambas,* I'm not going," he says.

"Come, I know what I am talking about. Don't worry, I will pay. Let us do it like this at least one day in the year."

"Well then, let's go." He went almost in disgust because he had no money. But I was carrying the 250 *pesos* and when we arrived I led him to where they were selling clothing. I said, "Go on, buy yourself these pants. It is a shame the way you go about."

He says, "What in hell can I do about it? I have no money so how can I buy pants?"

"Go ahead, try on the pants. Get at least two pair. I will pay for them."

"What? Are you my father that you are going to buy me pants?"

"Go on. I'll explain later. Meanwhile, buy it."

It embarrassed him but finally Crispín chose two pair of pants, ordinary ones which were cheap at that time. "How is it you have money?" he asked. So then I told him what had happened the day before. I said, "I remembered that you were hard up and so I didn't put the money into the treasury. It would be better to use it to clothe you.

Why should you be ruined? You are a learned man and look at the way you go about! Better buy yourself a shirt and stop complaining so much. After all, I have two hundred and fifty *pesos!*"

Crispín laughed. "Man, that's fine! What luck!" And he bought two shirts, good ones, and all the other things he needed. He even asked me to buy a few diapers! It was with satisfaction that I did it, because I had the money. Crispín told me to buy something for myself but I didn't need anything. I told him I have my sons, I have my corn, I have enough to eat, that I needed nothing more. But he insisted and so I bought myself a little *sombrero* and I was satisfied with that.

I said, "Look, there is money left over. Let us go and finish it off with our friends." We went to get the secretary of the *procuraduría* and my friend, the lawyer Moreno, and *zas*, we went to the *cantina* to drink. We were drunk when we got back to Azteca at about ten o'clock that night.

It is true that I did not save the extra money I earned. When I was a councilman I made money but because I had so many lawyer friends I spent it all. I kept going to Cuernavaca and there I have many friends, all of whom like refreshment. They would say, "Let's go for a little drink," and we would go. I would warm up to it and begin to order. I have spent as much as sixty *pesos* at a time, but never more than that. They were all lawyers and I would treat them!

One day, a person by the name of Bonifacio wanted to exploit the forest and he came around to see the new president, to give us a bribe of five thousand *pesos*. So Crispín said to me, "Bonifacio says he is going to give five thousand *pesos* for us and ten thousand for the market. What do you say? Shall we take it or not? But he wants the right to use the dead wood in the forest."

So I said to him, "Look, accept it if you want to. Not I. I'm leaving. I don't want to soil my name. The last president got rich off the forest because he took advantage. Are we going to do the same? When will the village ever progress? It is true that the rule of law is losing out, but you see what condition the people are in. So why should I dirty myself? You accept the money if you want to, but I am going home. I won't do such things, and that is precisely why I accepted this job. I never take anything, even though they say I am a fool, which I am, because I don't get a thing out of the administration. Why? Because I don't like to stretch out my hand. That's not for me. So, if you want to accept the five thousand *pesos*, accept them, but me . . . I'll be leaving."

Crispín did not accept the money. He wanted to all right, but I pulled on the reins. That's one thing I won't tolerate.

I was also very strict about the water supply and I had a lot of enemies when I was in charge of it. The trouble was that people had been getting permission from the authorities to set up pipes and bring water into their own homes and as a result the public fountains were not filling up, especially in the dry season. Before the Revolution, only the *caciques* and the president had a private water supply and that's why the corner fountains were always full. When the president went out of office, the people themselves went to his house to disconnect and take away the water pipes. They were strict about it then.

To improve the distribution of water, Crispín and I called in an engineer (he was from Azteca but he lived in Mexico City) to make a survey of our water supply. He said we would have enough water for the entire village if we set up a big tank in one of the upper *barrios* and distributed it to the street fountains through water pipes. So we collected money to set up the tank and we got the President of the Republic himself to contribute the six-inch water pipes. But our term was over before we could finish the job. Later, when the Department of Resources came to Azteca, the situation got worse. They gave permission for private piping to whoever paid and then the lower part of the village had no water at all for two months of the year. Later, the municipal officials collected twenty *pesos* from each house in the lower part, promising to put in a water tank there and remove the one in the upper *barrio*. But they never did this because those above, about two thousand of them, became aroused and stopped the president when he tried to destroy the tank. There has always been a lot of conflict over the water supply.

When I was in office, a woman tried to put a spell on me once, because of the water. She was a very bad woman! Now she is a known witch. I do not believe in witchcraft but, according to the Holy Scriptures, there are sorcerers and there are also completely ignorant people who do evil. They are not witches or sorcerers, just evildoers. The thing is, there are lots of poisonous plants and with them such people have all they need to do evil.

So this woman fell upon me and let me know she was going to bewitch me. It was all on account of the water. I went to cut off her water because she was using too much and the village insisted on it. She went after me but it was not I alone. It was a whole bunch of people, though I was in charge. That is why she got so angry and yelled and swore at me every time I passed by. She would even curse my mother! I asked a sorcerer about it and he told me that I couldn't be sorcerized because I didn't have the blood for it. "They can never put a spell on you," he said.

Well, I paid no attention to her and I saw no sign of anything. On the contrary, because she threatened me so much, nothing happened to me but now she is lame. One day when she was scolding me, her grandson was there and he said, "Stop it now! Why do you say things like that to *don* Pedro, *mamá?* What if he really gets sick one of these days? Then he'll put the blame on you."

That is what he said to her and it made her so mad she went after him with a *machete*. Being a man, he just grabbed the *machete* and held it. She pulled and it slipped out of her hand and she fell down hard on the stones. She cracked something up here in her hip and it left her lame. She can't walk to this day. So, instead of doing me harm, she harmed herself.

When *don* Rafael, the *mezcal* manufacturer, came from Puebla to Azteca, Crispín gave him a spot in the village to make the beverage. *Don* Rafael wanted the free use of village water, but I opposed it. He dug a large number of holes where they were going to put up a factory and then wanted to make a connection in the big pipe which is the general water supply for the plaza, that is, for the population as a whole. He even sent us five hundred *pesos*. This time, too, Crispín said to me, "Say, *don* Rafael sent over five hundred *pesos*. So, we'll go fifty-fifty, all right?"

"Oh, yes? And what is it for?"

"Well, a bribe, what else?"

"You get bribed, not I. I am poor and need money, but the answer is no." I was getting along fine with my children at the time. I had enough corn . . . I had my animals. So, what did I need? Ambition? One can never satisfy that. I will not accept those two hundred and fifty *pesos*. What good are they to me? My honor is worth more than two hundred and fifty *pesos*.

"Then you won't accept it?"

"No, I won't. Do you know why? Because I am against *don* Rafael and I warned the people in the central *barrio* that they were going to need that water. So I am going to take that water away from the *mezcaleros*. I already warned *don* Rafael that he could not count on me. If you gave them water you did so arbitrarily under your own responsibility, without my consent. The only reason I left it that way was because I did not want to break with you."

"But they are friends!"

"I wouldn't care if he was my father. Nothing doing! Here it is the law that counts, not *compadres* or friends . . . that is for private life."

He hadn't even charged them the tax, but I went and said to the treasurer, "All right, have them called in immediately. They are going to pay now."

Crispín was in Mexico City at the time and when he got back it was all over. The next day he said to me, "Say, why did you go and charge *don* Rafael the tax? Don't you see that they are our friends?"

"That doesn't mean a thing to me. Why should they have privileges? They are doing harm to the village and they don't even pay the tax! Nothing doing!"

"Well, all right, I guess you've won."

In almost every administration, at the end of the term, when it was time to turn it over to the next one, the outgoing officers would make off with whatever they could. In 1925, when there was nothing to take, the president put all the fines into his own pocket. I was in office then and I didn't like that at all. I said, "No, this is going to soil me, the very thing I have tried to avoid." So I resigned and left.

Later, when the presidential officer finally managed to borrow a typewriter and buy some chairs, those were the things that were taken. It wasn't much but when we went to look for them, well, they weren't there. In 1927, when I was in with my friend Refugio, again I couldn't bear to see what was going on. I grappled with him and we quarreled and I left. I went to work in my cornfield instead. Sure enough, at the end of his term, he made a clean sweep of it. He even took the paper!

The next administration bought a clock, a typewriter and other little things. Fine. The end of the term arrives and let's take a look. Now there is no typewriter, no clock, no chairs. There is only an old rifle they overlooked. There you are! And these are people? They are cynics because they have no shame. They take everything. *Caray!* Sure, and because we are all of the same village, who is going to make a complaint? They say that the things taken are not worth the trouble. It's because no one is interested. Suppose I go to see, what can I do alone? We begin to talk about it, to lament, but we don't go any further. One says, "Well, what are we fighting for, eh? Not for myself, because it wasn't mine. Not for you, because it wasn't yours. So? Besides, they have taken it away already. It's all gone."

That's the way it is with all the administrations, to say nothing of the commissary. The same thing! There is an inventory but at the end of the term no one pays attention to it. There was a president who even took the wood and the roof tiles that were stored in the yard, to pay off his drinking debts.

The only president who didn't get away with anything was Crispín, because I didn't let him. He wanted to but I said, "No, not I." Why should I steal? I wasn't born for that. That's why I am poor and they call me a fool, because I was in office four times and I got nothing out of it. I may not even have a *petate* to sleep on, but it is better that way with honor. I go in and out of the presidential offices and the courts and no one has anything to say about me.

Now the officials get rich on bribes. Before, there were no bribes because they dealt only with people of the village who knew them well and didn't pay attention to them. But now it is a question of dealing with outsiders, with people who want to build here, or buy land or use the forests. They pay big bribes to keep the officials from giving them trouble. And the cattle thieves! They are the most worthless and shameless ones of all and the ones I don't like. They gave bribes, too, but the last time I was *regidor* I annoyed the butchers because I tied their hands. When my term of office was over they blessed God that I was leaving. Naturally! Because they were accustomed to slaughtering the cattle at night. By dawn, the boxes were full of meat, ready to be sold. When I took office, I immediately prohibited this, and slaughtering could not be done before seven o'clock in the morning. They went as high as the Governor to complain about me! I didn't give in even though they had once killed a *regidor* there in the slaughterhouse. The Governor sent for me and reproached me for not opening my office until ten o'clock. They had told him a lie and I showed him a circular I had made, announcing that to avoid the slaughter of stolen cattle, anyone who had lost cattle could come to inspect them before they were butchered at seven o'clock. After reading the circular, the Governor had nothing more to say. To this day, the rule holds, and I was the one who made it.

For a long time there had been a quarrel over boundaries between village Azteca and village Jalalpa. We *tlacololeros* had formed an organization because they were not permitting us to clear our hillside cornfields. I was the representative and the leader of all of them, even of some who were not *tlacololeros*. I got together a lot of people and brought them to the palace of the Governor of the State of Morelos. There were about two hundred of us. That was when I went and claimed my rights. It was a matter of defending myself so I dared speak up. At village meetings I spoke very little, almost not at all, but when it came to defending Azteca I have even spoken in the Supreme Court of Justice.

This time I spoke to the Governor. I said, "*Señor* Governor, village Azteca has fought in the Revolution; the bullets have whizzed past our ears, too; nevertheless, we have not been paid with a piece of land with which to support our families. Since they gave us nothing, let them not touch what belongs to Azteca. Our land is mostly hills and we have no water here, except the rain. To the south in Yautepec it is a paradise! There they get two or three crops a year; here we get only one. Our land is inferior but we don't want them to take away what we have."

Újule! He really let me have it. What a sharp tongue the Governor had! Very sharp! I felt as though he had boxed my ears. I couldn't find words to answer him but someone behind me defended me. And how I liked these kinds of battles. I loved them!

The Governor said, "You are the ones who are guilty, those of you who took up arms. That is why they created the Agrarian Law . . . for the landowners."

And I couldn't say a thing. No sooner did I want to answer him when he broke in. He wouldn't let me speak. But the young man behind me responded. He interrupted the Governor's words and in the meantime I recovered and joined in. I said, "*Señor* Governor, allow me to answer what you said to me."

"Yes, speak, my son. Let's see, tell me, what is it?"

"Look here, *señor*. You tell me that those of us who have taken up arms are guilty of bringing on the Agrarian Law. But all laws are good. All! The Agrarian Law is very good, if only they would carry it out. Do you know who are the ones who twist it around? They are the big government leaders. They are the ones who distort things. They are the ones who make a spiral out of it. And the people are innocent. How can we be guilty if we don't even know how to read? What fault is it of those who have taken up arms? It is the present leaders who are guilty. They put the law to one side and they do with the people as they like. They are the ones who are guilty, not we. Now I have expressed my opinion." That was my answer to him. I felt resentful. Of course, who is the leader? It is he! As the Governor, he is the leader of the government, isn't he? I felt that I had gotten the better of him.

That was when he began to give us advice and he said to us, "Look here, boys, as Governor, I do not want the people of Azteca and Jalalpa to fight. Wouldn't it be better for you to come to some agreement so that you could avoid bloodshed? This dispute over the boundaries has been going on for two hundred years and neither side has ever won. Wouldn't it be better to mediate it? It would be a good idea to stop this killing. Later we will draw up the documents and make a boundary line and the fight will be over."

And then again I stood up and responded, because I was quite a talker, eh? I said to him, "Look here, *señor* Governor, your idea is very good, very healthy, but I wish it depended only upon us who are here. We here would agree right away but when we go back to Azteca, the people will fall upon us. They will say we have sold out. You know how the villagers are."

He says, "You are right, old man. Now that they see I am the Governor they are already saying I am a millionaire." Then he said to me, "Please return to Azteca and on such and such a day I will come.

But you must help me lead the people. Let us see if we can convince the villagers to enter into this agreement."

I answered, "Very well, we will wait for you there, *señor* Governor. We will wait for you and see if the village will agree. And if it doesn't there is nothing we can do."

And he really came. But what good did it do? No one accepted. So I said to him, "Now you see, *señor* Governor? How can we alone come to an agreement? Yes, I like your idea, but unfortunately, one person cannot decide. One person is nothing."

He says, "No, there's nothing we can do. Go on killing each other."

Well, yes, that's what happened. Then when Crispín Conde was the municipal president, he was called upon by those from Jalalpa and from the government to settle the boundary question. That was when Crispín gave away a large strip of municipal land. It was precisely to prevent this that I got involved in the struggle with the Governor. I aroused a lot of the villagers to fight for this piece of land.

Well, so Crispín sold out . . . at least they say he did. The villagers claim this even though it isn't true. I don't really believe it. Why? Because I know the administration and I know the character of each of them. They are good people, yes, all the Condes are good, too good . . . except for Víctor Conde. That is why I believe that Crispín didn't really sell out, except that he is very understanding and easygoing about everything and they got him to sign. They confused him with drinks and they confused him with a banquet and then they made him sign over the land to Jalalpa. But it turned out that only *he* had signed this document. No one else had signed. I saw it myself in the Supreme Court of Justice. Of course the *síndico* protested immediately and sent the agreement to the Supreme Court and then Crispín Conde repented. That is why I say he is a fool and it is easy to deceive him. He signed another statement saying that he did not agree with the document he had already signed, that he didn't know what he was doing at the time, that he now wants to withdraw the statement. But the Minister of the government paid no attention to this.

At that time I said to Crispín, "Why did you give away this piece of land?"

And he says, "And why in hell do we want it? What do you need it for?"

And I say to him, "You who own land may not need it. Why would you want inferior *texcal* land? But we landless ones do. It is practically all pure rock but we hillside farmers need it."

"Well, you will have to see what you can do about it yourselves because I'm leaving." And then Crispín went to the United States to work as a farm hand.

We began to fight the case and took it to the Supreme Court, claiming that the president of the *municipio* had signed away the land he had no right to, since it was a matter for the *Ejido* Commissioner. Moreover, no other members of the town council had signed and so we were not in agreement and we protested. That was in 1947.

There were just three of us representing Azteca, the lawyer Rocias, Frudencio Barra and I. The lawyer was next to me and he admired the way I spoke to the Minister Carreño. I told him what was bothering us and I ended with these words: "Now, if you do not give us justice we will take it ourselves. The village is ready."

"No, don't go and do that," Carreño says, "because that way we cannot work out anything. If the people rise up, even less so. On the contrary, you will lose more."

"I understand this. That is why we are here asking for justice. If it were not for us the people in the village of San Agustín would be taking it with bullets. We are holding them back but if our government doesn't give it to us then we are going to take it ourselves. How else? That is why I ask you very frankly, very sincerely, to see to my people."

Then the Minister says, "I am worried by what you say. Don't go and do this. I am here, you can count on me. The case is in my hands."

That was the first interview. We said good-bye and waited outside while the lawyer Rocias spoke to the Minister. Later, we asked him what happened.

"Well, think of it! Carreño asked me who you were and I said, 'A peasant from Azteca.' And he said, 'Well, he may be a peasant but his words are those of a politician. He is no ordinary peasant. He spoke well. Tell him not to do anything. Tell him he can count on me.'"

"Very well," I said. "And so he was impressed by me?"

Rocias said, "Yes, he was impressed."

Fine, at least he noticed me. And, think of it! He called me a politician.

Well, after that, six men from the Colonia Azteca of Mexico City came to the village because our president had called on them to help with the boundary dispute. Before the meeting began, Rocias, the lawyer, introduced me to one of them, Pedro González, a sharp talker. González said, "Yes, yes, I know *don* Pedro. We were from the same *barrio.*"

"Yes," said Rocias, "but you don't know what he has been doing. If there were only ten like *don* Pedro Martínez in the village, Azteca would be different!"

There were about sixty of us who had come together and we had a meeting right there, around the table in the president's office.

The speeches began. *Újule!* all six of them spoke, one after the other. Then this González spoke. What a beak! *Caracoles*, what a speaker! But what he said hurt me. It pierced me to the cockscomb! Because he said that all the village councils of the past had been absolutely inept and good-for-nothing. I said to myself, "This one is really giving it to me! Now I am going to beat them down." When he was through, I said, "Listen, *señor* González, will you allow me to speak?"

I began to speak. "Look, gentlemen, excuse my words because they are completely crude, but we are all Aztecans here. What pretty words you have spoken! What nice speeches! I am glorying because I am in the midst of all this light, but what a pity that this light is going back to some corner in Mexico City. What a pity it is that as soon as someone learns to spell, he goes to the capital to attend the banquets of Mexico, and leaves us dumbbells and fools here.

"What you say is true, that all the officials here are fools. I am one of them. But what could I accomplish? I am an illiterate man. We don't have personnel to form a good municipal council. What can we do if you aren't willing to sacrifice yourselves and come to your village and eat *chile* and acacia pods with us and be our representatives? I liked the way your lips spoke. I wish those lips could speak before Governor Castillo López. What good does your fine talk do us? Those big words do not amuse me. I want action. You have light in your head so why don't you come and help us with our problems? When have you come for that? All you do is criticize!

"Let's see which one of you can tell me about the negotiations between Azteca and Jalalpa. Let someone speak. Which one? Only the lawyer Rocias came out with us. He is a true Aztecan, not like you. I am a dumbbell, an ignorant fool, the least in my village, nevertheless I know all about the subject. Yes, I am illiterate, I am just trash, nothing at all, but it hurts me when you step on me, when you walk over me."

González shook his head, but I was right. We don't owe anything to the Colonia Azteca. All they do is bring gifts and candy to the children on the Day of the Kings. They started that business after the Revolution. That's fine, but what help is it? I said, "Each year you come to give this to our children. What can I do with five *centavos* worth of candy? That doesn't interest me. What interests me is that you grapple with the problems of our village. Then we would be grateful. Now you will choose a committee but I am sure it will only be like the burning of a straw mat, a flash fire. You won't come back for another twenty years. Now, excuse me, I am through speaking."

Yes, I gave it to them. I beat them down.

"*Chócala!* Congratulations! Now, you have given it to us," said Vicente.

"You have hit us on the head!" said Isidro. "It hurts but we deserve it."

Then the brother of the director said, "You have pulled our ears. What you said is very good. You have let us have it but it was good."

Even *señor* González said, "Congratulations!" but with bad grace.

Well, they named a committee of five: González, Isidro, the two lawyers and then my neighbor, Juan Villamar. They were to go to the National Archives in Mexico City to look for the land titles. I say, "Well, I haven't been chosen but I will also go. I want to see how far my countrymen get."

So we went to the capital and spoke to the Director of the Archives. He says, "Yes, I have gone through the papers of Azteca and the main things are here. Azteca is the only *municipio* in the entire country to have good documents. Now, I want you to name one of you to come here for one week to look for the document you need." González told me to stay but I said, "No, I am illiterate. Why doesn't *don* Villamar stay? He knows something."

Villamar said, "No, how can I? I have to earn money for my family."

I say, "Right away he thinks of his family! What's this! To be a true hero and patriot you must never think of home."

"Well, yes," he says. "Maybe you, but not I."

Then the lawyer says, "*Caray,* Pedro! There's no holding you back from speaking. You hit *don* Villamar right where it hurts. Well, we will pay him. We'll give him ten *pesos* a day, at least for his beans."

When Villamar came back to Azteca there was a meeting and he showed us where we bordered with the other *municipios*. There were four *municipios* who disputed our borders and wanted to cut wood on our land. I spoke to the *síndico* and told him to get moving on the matter of Aztecan jurisdiction. I said, "Go on, man, get this subject moving. The document from the Archives is almost the same as the title here, so move yourself. You're the *síndico* so you have to do it."

But no, he didn't move. He moved, but only at night, in bed! After that we began to organize, to activate the villagers. Ángel and I were at the head of the movement, together with Ermilo, the local president. I had all the *tlacololeros* at my command. I was very aggressive at that time. Yes, sir! I told the engineers from the Agrarian Department that if they didn't give me justice I would let the people raise an outcry. I said, "And it is going to work because the people of Jalalpa are just a bunch of kittens. Right now they don't measure up to us one bit."

Now we were going to cut a clearing at the boundary line by

force because, the truth is, the government doesn't understand us or even listen to us. Those from Jalalpa were already opening up a clearing on our side of the boundary. They went too far! In anger, Ángel, Ermilo and I gathered together eight hundred men from our village and went after the men from Jalalpa and burned their wood to stop them. Then we cut a clearing through the forest along the line which had been established by the Presidential Decree of 1927.

CHAPTER XIX

FELIPE

Youth and Courtship

The good thing about my father is that from the time we were small he taught us how to behave, and to know things, especially religion. And he gave all of us schooling, even though it was little, and he showed us how to work. There are fathers who say that because they love their children they do not show them how to work, but my father made us work and he showed us many things that benefited us. In a way, I say he *should* have been good. I have even told him so at times when he scolded us unjustly. I told him, "Look, you who know everything, who studied the laws, you study for others but not for us here at home. Us you want to order about at will. You speak to us as though we were servants, you shout at us, so I don't know how you can serve the public."

Well, he began to get angry. "What business is it of yours? I know what I am doing."

Knowing the word of God, he even served as teacher when we all got together in Cuernavaca. But that was a long time ago. He gave up all that, he gave up studying when he became a judge and began to drink again. Then he came and beat my *mamá* and threw the plate of food on the floor or in her face. I don't know why but he didn't give her expense money then and my poor little mother had to hustle to get us food. We had no corn or money to buy any.

One day, when I was about thirteen, my *papá* was preparing fiber to make rope. It was in the month of March, and my *mamá* says to him, "There is no corn to make the dough for today. I am going to take a little turkey and sell it."

"Go ahead," says my *papá*, "and see where you can buy corn cheap."

"I will take Felipe to help me shell the corn."

"Take him then," says my *papá*. I liked to go with my *mamá* when she went on an errand. We went all over the village and could not sell the animal. On the way home, we passed my mother's cousin's house and my *mamá* says, "I am going in to see if I can help Ágata so she will lend me some corn."

When we entered, my aunt knew right away what we wanted. She gave us some ears of corn and a sack to shell them into but we had to hide because her husband scolded her when she sold corn. We hurried because we were very much afraid he would come and scold us too. My *mamá* was also afraid that my *papá* was going to yell at her because it was so late. We took long to shell the corn for it was quite rotten. It cost us a lot of work, and then my *mamá* had to help my aunt make some *tortillas* for the men working in the field. We left at about two o'clock with six *cuartillos* of corn. I helped carry it. We walked quickly and my *mamá* was very scared. She said, "Now he is going to scold."

When we arrived home my *mamá* said, "Here we are." My *papá* answered, "What were you doing that kept you until now?" But he didn't want to listen to what my *mamá* was saying. He was furious and grabbed a rope and began to beat her. "Why do you go to that relative of yours? What do you want there? That woman is bad and I told you not to mix with people like that. I don't want you talking with bad women. She has made a fool of her husband and that's what she will advise you to do to me."

My *mamá* was leaning against the wall and my *papá* beat her with a heavy rope. The rope was doubled and he beat her hard and left marks all over her back. There was a gourd on the wall behind her and when the rope hit it, the gourd flew off and broke in two. Well, my *mamá* suffered a lot that time.

My *papá* never let her go to her cousin's house again. Someone told my aunt Ágata what happened and she got very angry with my *papá*. "The poor thing!" she said. "If that little fellow were really brave he would come and put himself in my hands!" When my *mamá* met Ágata in the street they would talk to each other. My *mamá* told her, "What he believes is not true but I think that I will never go to your

house again because he won't let me. Even if I die there, I must remain at home. Where else can I go? I have no one to help me. I must
suffer at home, no matter what happens."

My *papá* thought ill of my aunt Ágata because he believed she
would give my *mamá* some medicine to use against him, medicine
which would make him stop scolding her even if she went walking in
the streets or did something disorderly. Because my aunt Ágata was
one of the experts in doing evil. I, too, knew that Ágata had evil
thoughts because once she was going to sorcerize someone and she prepared some food with medicine. She put it aside on a shelf and went
to do an errand. Her daughter found the food and not knowing what
her mother had put in it, she ate it all. When my aunt came home she
didn't say anything but in a few days the girl felt ill and stayed in bed a
long time. Little by little she improved, but when she got out of bed
she was paralyzed and couldn't walk or talk. She lasted that way for
twelve years and then she died.

That was why my *papá* was upset and imagined bad things.
But my *mamá* could see no advantage in sorcery and besides she was
very humble and didn't even think of such things because many times I
heard her tell others that she was not capable of doing that to my *papá*.

When my *papá* was mean to us or to my *mamá*, we would get together with my sister and talk among ourselves about why he was like
that. Before, he was very nice to us. When he came home he spoke to
us with pleasure and he sat and talked contentedly with my *mamá*.
Then he would say, "Let us eat," and they sat together to eat while we
played. When he became a judge and later a councilman naturally I
felt very proud. Because he was an official, my brothers and I didn't
have to do guard service for the village. They had sent us a notice to do
service but my *papá* went and told them that he had helped the village
many times and that ought to be enough. He said they were even indebted to him and if they would pay him for all the service he had done
for the village then he would let his sons be guards. Well, they never
called us after that.

In a way, it is nice to be in politics because it opens your eyes and
you can defend yourself. My *papá* has always liked politics and in a
way it has helped him. But I don't like it any more because he lost a lot
of time at it. And after he became a judge, he changed a lot. Very
much! Without us knowing why, he would hit us. He once said to my
mamá, "You love your children, but I don't love them. I don't know
why but I don't love them." My *mamá* told me this before she got sick.
And for any little thing, he hit us. He even bought a whip, the kind to
beat animals with. Once I was crying, I don't know why, and my *papá*
took down the whip and gave me five lashes on my back and lower

down on my legs. Naturally it hurt. My *mamá* was sitting near the grinding stone and she grabbed me and said to my *papá*, "Leave him alone. Don't hit him any more."

"Get away," he says, but then he left and my *mamá* pulled down my pants and there were welts where he had hit me. My flesh had turned purple. That's the way my *papá* hit all of us when we were boys. He treated us all alike then. It was later that he began to hit me more than the others.

He scolded me more than the others because he said I was rebellious about everything, especially with him and with my brothers. I didn't let them order me about, not even my *papá*, unless he was right. I was big now and I knew what I was doing. But even though he yelled at me, I didn't talk back because what good would it do me to answer my father badly? Yes, I could answer him, I could say more than he said, but what for? It would serve no purpose, so I kept quiet. My *mamá* told me not to talk back to him so even if I was angry, I couldn't answer. Sometimes I didn't speak to him for days. My brother Martín talked back but didn't stop speaking to him and that is why my *papá* said he could count more on Martín.

We continued studying the Bible at home with my father. Sometimes he took us as far as Yautepec and every Saturday my father and I, my brother Martín, and another fellow named *don* Ángel, went to Salvador.

Later, we didn't want to go there any more because they began to complain when my *papá* became a judge and he went with us only once in a while. That's why they were angry. Then he became an assistant to the attorney and again they were very angry because they said my *papá* was mixing into politics. The wife of *don* Maclovio was the one who became most angry; she said we didn't fulfill our obligations, that only she did. She dreamed that she spoke to God, that she saw the angels, that she was already in Heaven because she had fulfilled her obligations, that she no longer thought of worldly things.

Then when we began planting a lot she got angry again, saying we planted too much, that this was ambition, that it is not good to have wealth, that wealth is worldly and not for us. And from then on my *papá* withdrew little by little. But we continued as usual, going as far as Yautepec once a week for a year. Then we didn't want to any more because we suffered a lot on the road. When it rained, the mud was so deep we could barely walk. There was no bus to Yautepec then and it was far away. Afterward it was better for us to go to Cuernavaca because there was a bus. Martín and I went once a week for a long time.

One Saturday there was a big disagreement in the congregation in

Cuernavaca. Many people were there, almost one hundred fifty. Some had even come from Mexico City and they began to argue. A man stood up in front to speak, saying that the women should wear plain dresses that covered their knees. And those who don't have long hair should cover their heads with a scarf or shawl and those who have long hair should wear it braided and not hanging loose. And women should not wear rings, earrings or combs, or fancy ribbons or high-heeled shoes or necklaces or bracelets. And the younger women were to cut their finger-nails and not use makeup or wear tight skirts. And the men who had mustaches or beards were to cut them and if they didn't have hair they were to cover their heads with a beret.

Then someone else stood up in front of the first man and began to contradict him. Then the first one steps in front of the other and they both began to talk and would not let the other speak. Others stood up to speak and everyone was arguing. No one understood anybody else. Each grabbed someone to argue with. They argued for about five hours.

My brother and I did nothing more than watch all that was going on. We left when everything was over. We told my *papá* what happened. He didn't say anything. The next week we returned but the meeting place was closed. We went home and told my *papá* that now there was no congregation in Cuernavaca.

Now we had no place to go. We studied at home and once in a while we went to Salvador. I went to the Methodist group to study and also to the Pentecostal group. But I didn't like their meetings because some of them would cry and others would bend down to kiss the ground. They were obliged to do this and I did not like it. I also saw that their studies were not advanced but were simple and unimportant.

Little by little we stopped going, and my *papá* paid no more attention to Bible study. He began to drink again, though not as much as before, and then he made us work on Saturdays.

The first year we opened a large clearing it was in a place called Barrera. We planted about thirty *cuartillos* and there was a good harvest of corn and squash and beans. We were picking corn and beans for about two weeks and we didn't finish because it had rained a lot. It was in November and it rained night and day. We had harvested everything except the beans and we continued to work in the rain. We walked around wet, soaked, and no matter how much we hurried, even if we went without eating, we would still leave the field as late as six or seven o'clock.

Once my brother and I left at half past seven at night and we each had to carry a sack full of beans which were very heavy because they were so wet. We had to walk about twenty kilometers in the rain. We walked with much difficulty because it was dark and the road was rocky and full of mud. The rain didn't stop and our burden became heavier and heavier.

We walked without resting, and when we arrived at Elotepec I could no longer carry my burden. We kept falling down with our sacks and we would stand up full of mud. Our *huaraches* were so worn we were almost barefoot. I was very tired and we still had to walk much more. My brother went ahead; he was waiting for me. I began to cry because my sack was very heavy and I couldn't walk any longer. Martín said, "Be quiet, don't cry, we are almost home."

Then a little farther ahead we met my *papá* and *mamá*, who were coming to look for us. My *papá* took the heavy sack from me and he carried it. We kept falling all along the road and finally, at about ten o'clock at night, we arrived at home. We took off our wet clothes and they gave us dry ones and they asked us why we came so late. The very next day we went back because we wanted to finish the rest of the harvest. But it continued to rain and there were already a good number of cattle in the *milpa*. Finally we gave up and left the remainder unharvested.

The following year we planted in the same plot. At harvest time, in November, the cows entered and we had to drive them out. There were about fifty head of cattle and it took us about three hours, but we finally drove out all except one cow. She was very stubborn and continued to come into the *milpa,* breaking the brush fence we had built. She would come in at night when we weren't there, and when we arrived the next day, she was gone. Finally my *papá* stayed to watch for her. He didn't sleep and had to wait there many days and nights until once the cow broke the fence and got into the field. My *papá* had a shotgun and shot at her. She went running and never entered our field again.

Well, we stopped planting for two or three years, and then we began to plant again, but not so much. This time we planted only about ten *cuartillos* of *tlacolol* and another few *cuartillos* with a hired team of oxen on a piece of rented land. My father left the *tlacolol* in my charge and I would go daily to look at it.

At that time we had a little *burro* and I would take it each day to the cornfield. This little *burro* was very stubborn and wouldn't let itself be tied. One day I arrived at my plot of land and I tied the *burro* to a stick. I was looking around when I saw some cows inside the *milpa*. I thought there were only three or five but when I got closer I saw that there were many of them. There were almost two hundred cows in the cornfield! I looked at the fences and could not find the place where they had entered. I began to bring the cows together so I could drive them out. Little by little I was beginning to drive them out but some would get in again at one side or the other and it cost me a lot of work to get them together again. I was battling with them all day. Finally I found where the cows were getting in and I got rid of all of them.

By then it was about seven o'clock at night. I still had to cut some hay for my *burro* and I was terribly afraid because there were a lot of snakes there. I cut the hay very, very carefully, just feeling my way along, because I couldn't see anything any more. Then when I wanted to put the hay on the *burro*, he wouldn't come. No matter what I did, he wouldn't come. I didn't know what to do. I wanted to cry. It was already late and I still had to go and examine about two thousand meters of fence. But finally the *burro* let me load the hay onto him and I mounted and went to check the fence. I didn't leave until about eight-thirty at night.

When I arrived at the outskirts of my village I met my father and mother and my uncle Maximiano and my uncles Federico and Asunción and my mother's cousin Margarito with their shotguns and *machetes* and clubs. I asked them where they were going and they said they were going to look for me because it was very late at night and I had not arrived. "What happened to you? Why did you come back so late?" And I told them what happened. I felt happy when I arrived home. It was eleven-thirty at night.

The next day my brother and I went to the *milpa* and we carefully put back the fence where the cows had broken through. I kept going back daily, because it was my responsibility until the harvest was over. But the harvest was very small, only two large sacks of corn.

We began to buy animals. First we bought a little horse, then a donkey and later on a mule to work with. It was necessary to find pasture for the animals and we went out looking near Yautepec and even as far as San Carlos. Sometimes we couldn't find any pasture until about three in the afternoon, so we wouldn't get back home until almost nine in the evening. From then on, we began to suffer hardships because of the animals, trying to get food for them or make them work.

In the rainy season I had to chop cornstalks for feed. I would go in the rain to do this or to tie up the animals in the fields so that they could eat, and in the afternoon or even at night, I'd have to go to bring them back, or sometimes I slept in the fields with them. During the dry season I slept outdoors, under the avocado tree, to be able to feed and water them during the night. I would get up at about two or three in the morning to get enough water because later on the neighbors got up and would finish it all. So I hurried to water the animals and the orchard before dawn. I would make about thirty or thirty-five trips to the fountain and that would go on day after day until the rains came.

Sometimes I lay down at about eleven o'clock in the evening but would not go to sleep. I was watchful, because people say that a dead man cries out at about twelve or one in the morning. I would not go to sleep before that hour, just to see if I would hear something. But I never did, nor did I see anything either, while I was staying outdoors. Once, at about midnight, I was lying down when I began to feel my body slowly shrinking. I shivered and felt my body go numb. I made myself strong to resist it. I sensed that something was there in the *corral*, a breeze, a sound, something like an apparition coming closer and closer to me. I felt a gentle wind and heard noises in my ears, and I was becoming more and more petrified. I couldn't bear it any longer, but by then I couldn't move or even scream. My hands were glued to my body. My whole body was shrunken. I was numb.

I heard the gentle breeze moving quietly through the *corral*. It went away from me, very slowly. When I sensed that it was gone, I tried hard and began to get up slowly. I sat up, covered with my blanket, and remained that way for a long time, my body still petrified. In my heart I was saying, "Who are you? If you are the devil, speak to me and tell me what you want. Don't just scare me. Tell me what's the matter. Come here, talk to me, but don't touch me. I want to find out what you want. If you come from the other world and just want to frighten me, go away, because you will get nothing from me. If you are Satan, don't harm me. Go away and let me be. Stop bothering me. There is a God superior to you, and as long as I am with Him you cannot tempt me. If you couldn't tempt Christ, you won't tempt me. I am of this world and yours is the underworld. God will not let you possess me. The angels said the right thing when you were expelled from Heaven. They said the Earth will belong to those who live on it, not to you. The day will come when not even ashes will remain of you. You will be ended forever."

I thought all of this as I was sitting there, waiting for him to return. But I heard nothing and I lay down, still watching, until sleep possessed me.

At about six in the morning I got up to water the orchard. When my brothers and my *papá* and my *mamá* woke up I didn't tell them anything. Later, I told my brother Martín and he said, "They were dwarfs, that's why you felt that way." I thought that dwarfs must be disciples of the devil because they had his powers.

I continued sleeping outside under the avocado tree all through the dry season. At the beginning of the rainy season, in May, I went back to the house to sleep.

Then my *papá* bought a little pig and built a little shack for him to sleep in during the rainy season. The pig grew and was sold, and the little shack was left. When the rainy season came again, my *papá* said to me, "It would be better if you slept in the shack since the pig is not there any more, and you could watch the animals without getting wet." So I put my cot in the little hut, and there I stayed, guarding the animals during the night.

Once, I remember, I heard a noise under my bed, like a chicken scratching in the soil. Then she would stop and begin to dig with her beak, and I could hear the soil being tossed aside. It sounded as though there were papers under the bed. I kept quiet, thinking it was just a chicken which they had forgotten to put into a box or which perhaps was left there on purpose in order to bother me and not let me sleep. I was angry at heart because it would not let me sleep, digging all the time and making noises. I began to hush it with my hand under the bed. It would keep quiet and stop digging but soon it would begin all over again. Then I took my hat and began to hush her with it under the bed, until I got tired.

At dawn I peeked down under the bed to see if it was tied up there but I saw nothing, no signs of digging, no papers, nothing, not even a mark! Later I asked my *mamá* if they had left a chicken out or had tied one under my bed in the hut and forgotten about it. She said, "But we have no chickens. We have only turkeys." I told her everything I had heard during the night and she said, "Then it's the devil who comes to tempt you and to take you away."

"But I wasn't frightened. I didn't even think of fear," I answered.

"If you had been afraid he would have taken you." And then she added, "It's because when you go to bed you don't even remember God. You go to bed any which way. That's why things happen. When you go to bed think of God, ask him to care for you night and day and to see that nothing happens to you."

I continued to sleep outside. The only thing that disturbed me sometimes was people going by at midnight. The drunks would yell, dogs would bark, and boys would sing on the street corners.

To make extra money my brother and I would go to Yautepec to sell firewood. Sometimes by noon hour we still hadn't sold any, and neither we nor the animals carrying the load had eaten. But we had to bring home money in order to buy corn so we sold the firewood very cheaply. When we got home, my *papá* would scold us for returning so late. After that, we didn't go any more. We sold wood to a sugar *hacienda* because we planted nearby. We were paid eight *reales* a load. There we even found regular customers, so that sometimes we made two trips a day until we finished the planting. We made about four hundred *pesos* selling the wood there.

My *papá* left two animals in my care and I used them for carrying the firewood. It was in April, and I was stocking dry firewood for the rainy season. On the way back I was climbing a very steep hill when I noticed that the first animal was lying on the ground and the other was falling behind, unable to carry the load. When I saw the one on the ground I rushed to take off the wood so he could stand up, and then I began to reload him, quickly and haphazardly, because the other animal was also having troubles. It also lay down, even before I finished loading the first one. I let him go and rushed to the other horse to unload him. When he got up I loaded him again quickly because the first one had gone on alone along the road, leaving me far behind. I ran to catch up with him because I was afraid he would fall again or get hit by a truck. But no matter how fast I went I never did catch him. When I got home he was already there, and my *papá* asked why I had let him return alone.

I continued working with the animals. When there was no firewood in the house I went to the woods to get more. During harvest time I used the animals to carry corn and when this was finished the two animals hauled corn stalks twice every day. I would get up at two or three in the morning, feed the animals, saddle them, and then leave for work.

Then my *papá* bought a very big mule which he let me work with. At the beginning, when she was still a bit wild, it was hard for Martín and me to train her. In order to load her, we had to blindfold her, holding her all the while with a rope. My brother Martín was a muleteer. In those days, while the mule was only semitame, we had three animals. We would load them at about four o'clock in the morning and Martín would leave with them. Sometimes he took my brother Ricardo along to help him in case one of the animals fell down. Otherwise, Ricardo and I would go to the *milpa*.

We had a lot of trouble taming her. Afterward she was the most gentle of all our animals. She walked quickly so we did not have to hit her. We just commanded her in a loud voice and she would go on all by herself. When I loaded her, people would laugh because I was so short and the mule was so big. But I paid no attention because I like big, strong mules.

The mule didn't know how to pull logs, but I taught her. She let my *papá* and me load her willingly enough because she was tame, but when she started walking she felt the pulling and began to kick and run, and even broke the saddle. Then we took off the logs and left them in the woods. The next day I took the mule back to the woods, along with another animal, and cut two long, thick logs, as heavy as I was able to lift. I loaded her carefully, and then pulled her along with a rope. She felt the weight but didn't balk, and was able to walk. When I arrived home my *papá* came out and helped me unload because the mule could not carry it much longer. Then he said, "Why do you load it like this? This is so heavy and long!" I said I always loaded heavily when I saw the animal was able to stand it. When I went to the *hacienda* to get sugar-cane leaves, I would load the mule with a lot of them and when I returned home my father would help me unload her.

"You put too heavy a load on her. How can you put such a high load on?" he asked me.

"I just put it on my shoulders and heave it up," I told him.

And thus I worked with the animals, sometimes as a muleteer, other times as a field hand. Once my brother Martín and I each had a mule-drawn plow and we went to work for a *señor* who had a yoke of oxen. One day, as we began to do our chores, the owner told me, "You go over there to plow with the mules. Your brother and I are going to plant." I yoked up the mules, attached the plow, and began to work. He said, "If you can't finish today you can do so tomorrow." Then he explained that once the field was plowed, I had to plow it again cross-wise. We went to work, he in his place and I in mine. I began to plow very rapidly, working the animals without respite, back and forth, and I finished at about two in the afternoon, in an incredibly short time. The owner had given me two days for the job and I had finished it in almost half a day!

Then I went to him and asked, "What do you want me to do now?"

"Have you already finished?" he says. "But how can that be possible? Let's go see how it looks."

He went to look at it and said, "It's all right, but how did you do it?"

"Well, I rushed to finish it," I explained, and he said, "Now just let the animals eat and rest, then help us to plant."

The three of us, Martín, Ricardo and I, kept on working. I would stay in the *milpa* to guard the tomato plants, or one of my brothers would do it. Once my *patrón* said to me, "Tomorrow we will go to San Juan to get beams."

"What time are we leaving?"

"Early, at about two in the morning."

The next day I got up before two, fed my horse, saddled up, and left without even drinking coffee. I didn't take along anything to eat, not even *tortillas*, thinking to myself, "I'll eat when I get back."

I went to pick up my boss and we left. We went through the woods, which were very cold, and I figured that by nine in the morning, at the latest, we would be back. But then we went to pick up other men, five of them, so I asked, "Where are we going?"

"Just nearby, we are almost there," he said.

Then all of us, with our beasts, continued through the woods and over the hills, enduring a great deal of cold. I even felt like crying because it was so cold. I could not move my feet or hands. By eight o'clock in the morning I was already hungry and the end was not in sight. Finally, at about ten o'clock, we got to where the beams were. They were thick and about twelve meters long. We began to gather them up to load the animals, but they were very heavy. Four people would lift a beam and load it on an animal. I tried to lift one but couldn't raise it five centimeters. I applied so much strength I saw stars, but it wouldn't budge. When all the animals were loaded we began walking. My horse had not gone more than ten meters when the saddle broke in two, but everyone was still around and they tied it up with a rope. I began walking again, but after about fifty meters the rope broke. About two hundred meters further, one of the beams fell off. There was another man with me so he quickly helped me load it on again. Then he went ahead and left me behind.

The rest of the men were far ahead, I couldn't even hear them any more. When I was about midway back, they had already arrived in town. Then the rope broke again, and I didn't know what to do because I was all by myself. Alone, there wasn't much I could do and I was trying to decide whether or not to leave the beams. "But if I leave them they will get lost and the *patrón* is going to get angry."

I began to struggle, trying to lift one. I couldn't even move it. I tried again and managed to lift it about twenty centimeters, but was completely weakened by the effort and couldn't continue. Finally, I found a way to hoist up the beam using the rope, with much pushing and pulling on my part. My hands were badly scratched during the struggle, which lasted about one hour. By the time I had finished loading it I was so weak I was seeing little stars and everything became dark around me. Only by exhausting all my energy was I able to load the horse. When I arrived at my *patrón*'s house the other muleteers were there, already rested. They asked me why I had fallen behind and then they helped me to unload.

"How did you manage to load it alone if it took four of us to lift one of the beams?"

"Well, I looked for a way to do it. It took me one hour, but I finally loaded it!"

It was about three in the afternoon and they served something to eat. We were very tired then and the men began to drink *ponches*. I did not want to drink. I only wanted to round up my horse, say good-bye, and leave for home. At home, I went directly to sleep. That is how I taught myself to work with animals.

My sister Conchita gave me the little cot she had bought and when she came home from school, she would sleep with me. Once, at about one o'clock in the morning, I was sleeping alone on my cot and my eye was hurting, when I felt the bed squeaking. I felt that someone was lifting my bed up about one-half a meter and then down, with me on it. I just kept quiet and didn't move. I said to myself that one of my brothers must want to frighten me. Little by little, I turned my head and saw them and my *papá* and *mamá* fast asleep on the floor. It wasn't one of them. My bed kept going up and down and I finally fell asleep. I didn't tell anyone about it until much later.

Once again I was lying in my little cot. This time the bed was near the door. It was about one o'clock and I was not asleep yet. It was in November and there was a pretty moon. I heard someone kick at the door, a strong kick from the outside, and I kept looking through a crack but could see nothing. And the kicking against the door continued strongly until the door seemed to lift up. I just watched it until I got tired. But I couldn't sleep. On the following day, I didn't say anything. It was much later that I told them. Then they said, "Why don't you tell us when you hear something? Wake us up so that you will not get frightened. If you hear some noise, get up slowly and let us know so we can go out and see what it is."

Sometimes I heard something like a horse running past the house, meowing like a cat. It went down the street and toward the fields where no one lived. This happened every night until I knew the very hour it passed, at one o'clock in the morning. I told my family about this a year later. And again they said to me, "Why didn't you tell us?"

But I said to them, "What for? I know that it is a ghost and is just trying to frighten people. He doesn't get tired of it but comes back every night. He tries to tempt me and I won't let him." That's why I pay no attention when I hear a noise or see something of that sort. I just look at it and at first I'm afraid but later I realize that it can't tempt me and my fear leaves me and I pay no attention to it.

Once I was gathering wood with my brother Martín, when he says, "Look!" When I turned I saw a man with his dappled horse. He looked like a cowboy with his *sombrero* and shoulder blanket. He was going by an old path where no one ever walked. It was about midday and we watched him, until little by little he disappeared. Later, when we went home they said it was a devil.

Martín and I once went on an errand to the store in Juan's house. On our way back we were running past a little street where no one lived, when we heard someone yelling to us. There was another cry, almost like a whistle and I stopped. I saw someone like a person leaning against a plum tree. He was sticking out his tongue and his face was half disfigured. His body could not be seen very well because he was behind the tree trunk. I called to my brother and said, "Look at what's there!" But Martín couldn't see anyone and I said, "You do not see him? Then let's go!"

We began to run and he kept on yelling to us. When we got home we told my *mamá* what we saw. She asked me how and exactly where and what he was doing. Then she said it was a ghost and that it always came out at midday to frighten people. My *papá* went to look for him but saw nothing. I always had the luck of seeing and hearing things like that as I grew older. But it never frightened me at all.

My *papá* often went to Mexico City to sell hog plums and when I was fifteen years old he took me with him for the first time. We stayed in the house of Deolandra, a woman from Azteca. It was the first time I was there and I didn't know a thing. My eyes were closed. I knew nothing at all. But there was a girl there, Celerina, and I saw that she was nice and I liked her a lot, and well, I fell in love with her. I talked to her, but not about love, and three days later we left for home.

She attracted me very much. There wasn't a moment that . . . well, I thought a lot about her after we got back home. My heart was always with her, there were times when it almost seemed to burst. I was restless, nervous, and for a week, I couldn't sleep. I was very much in love with the girl, and I thought, "Well, I want her."

So I say to my *papá*, "Do you know, I like the girl Celerina, the one who lives with Deolandra in Mexico City, and I want you to go and ask for her."

Then my *papá* says, "So you like her?"

"Yes," I say.

"Well, then, if you like her there is no way out. But you know you are very young and not yet ready and she is older. She is big and you are still very little. It isn't right but if that's what you think, very well. As a father, I am obliged to see you all married. But I must also make you look ahead."

And so he made me see all the things that didn't look right to him or that wouldn't suit the girl because she was from the capital and I was from a village. "Consider it well. We don't know what she's like. She might even be a street woman for all we know." But I was so much in love that I said yes, I wanted her. He discouraged me and said no.

But I said yes. "Is it still yes?" he asked. Every day he asked me and I said, "Well, yes."

He argued against everything I said and I stubbornly kept saying yes, I loved the girl. Then he said, "Well, if you want to go, I will take you. I will leave you there with the girl and you will speak to her to see what she says. If she says yes, then there is no way out. But you know this doesn't please me because you are a peasant and she is not going to want to come here. She has other customs. She is not going to want to get up early to grind corn. I suppose you are going to wake her up at three o'clock in the morning! She is going to want to get up at eight, and is that the hour you will leave for work? Is it still yes?"

"Well . . . yes."

Every day he asked me if I still wanted to get married, but now as if he were joking. Everyone laughed when he asked me. He joked and even made my mother laugh at me. And every day he scolded me, saying that I am still little and don't help him at all. He tells me I won't work but I know that I work and that I get up at two or three in the morning to go to the cornfield and that I left school when I was twelve in order to work. I got very angry and stopped speaking to him.

So one Sunday when he said, "Let's go to Mexico City," I didn't want to go with him. By that time I felt discouraged. He went and I stayed behind. But on that very day, the girl came to my house with her uncle. They came to visit us but I paid little attention to her. I thought, "My *papá* doesn't want me to marry her, so I better not." Suddenly I thought he was right.

Celerina was the very first girl I fell in love with. I didn't love again from the heart until I was older, about twenty-two. It lasted about eleven years . . . I really loved Zenaida. She lives on the same street, below our house. I spoke to her about love when she was still little, about thirteen. I was big already and my *papá* told me, "Why don't you speak to the daughter of Dímas. I like her. The little girl is pretty and she is fair and of a poor family. Speak to her and then I'll go and ask for her so that when she grows up you will have her. Now that she is young it is easy for you to control her. By the time her eyes are opened, she will already be with you."

I liked Zenaida a lot, and because my *papá* wanted me to marry her, one day I waited for a chance to speak to her. I was picking plums and I thought, "So he won't say I just look at her, I'll speak to her any way I can."

She was playing in her *corral* with other little girls and I spoke to her. I told her what I was thinking and that I had good intentions toward her and that I know she is still young but that I love her with all my heart. She just looked at me and laughed and didn't say anything.

I say, "Well, is it yes?"

She said yes, then no, then yes . . . she was just playing. Well, she was still little. Finally, she said she would tell me later. A few days passed, until one day I was twisting rope in the yard and she was playing in her *corral*. I made a sign with my hand, to ask whether it was yes or no. With her head, she said yes. That night I sent her a note and told her we were sweethearts. I spoke to her about three days later and she said, "Yes, but only if you stop studying what you're studying, then I'll marry you, because I don't want you to continue with your religion. I want you to marry me in church and you won't want to."

I say to her, "Well, I have already stopped studying for some time, and as for me, I am ready to marry you the way you wish. I don't intend to play around with you. I mean to treat you honorably, the way I should. I don't want to fool you. It would be easy to but I won't. I want to honor you as God commands. There are other girls to fool around with but I don't want to with you."

She says, "Well, if you've stopped studying, that's fine."

Then we were sweethearts and we talked together every night in the *corral*, behind the wall where no one could see us. Her mother was very strict and watched her carefully because Zenaida was the only daughter and still young. I didn't tell my father she was my *novia* until several years later.

When Zenaida was twenty-three, we were still going together. She told me to ask for her and so I sent my parents to speak to her mother and father. Her *papá* said, "For whom is it, for Martín or Ricardo? Or Moisés?"

"No," said my *mamá*, "for Felipe."

"Ah! Felipe. Why, are they already sweethearts?"

"Yes, the two of them are in agreement. We have come only to see whether you consent to it."

That's when her *mamá* said no. She said, "No, because I believe she is already given to another. They have already asked for her hand and if we say yes to you, we will have them upon us. Rather than tell you to come back in a week, it would be better to say no now."

When they returned to the house, I asked, "What did they say?" They told me it was no, because she was already given to another. The girl said yes and the father said yes, but the mother said no.

I felt upset, I felt bad, as though I were ill, and I began to cry. My *mamá* says, "Why are you crying?"

I say, "Because I cannot bear it."

She says, "But you haven't even eaten. Eat something."

I say, "I don't want anything."

"Eat. Think of it, we went to ask for her and they didn't want to, and now what? By force? Now you arrange it with her."

"But how?"

I couldn't hold back. I cried very much. Later my *mamá* said, "Why do you cry? When I die, cry for me. Don't cry for this woman. Look for another. Forget her and look for another quickly."

"I can't. It is impossible. To forget her I need to leave here."

"Not that! It is not enough to make you leave your home. Just don't look at her. When she passes by, go inside. Don't pay attention to her. Eat and don't think about it because it will do you harm."

"No. I am not hungry. It's because I like her a lot and I cannot bear it."

"Well, if you want her, take her away, far away, without telling her where you're going. When she finds out, at least she will have been with you a few days. Then if she wants to go back to her house or if they want to take her from you, at least you will have made use of her, you will have known her."

But when Zenaida's mother found out that the girl wanted to marry me, she hit her in the mouth and made it bleed. They said that if she spoke to me again they would put her in jail. So the girl was afraid and didn't speak to me. I spoke to her but she wouldn't answer. She paid no attention to me. I said to myself, "If she is angry, let her be angry. I fulfilled my obligation to her. I asked for her as she wanted me to, so she cannot go and say it is my fault. If she doesn't want to now, it is up to her."

So I looked for another girl until Zenaida herself came and spoke to me and asked me why I was angry and why didn't I speak to her and did I have someone else.

I say, "If you care more for your parents then stay with them. I will look for someone else. You said you would go away with me, so jump over the wall and I'll marry you."

She says, "How can I do that? I love you but I also love my parents."

"If you go with me that doesn't mean you will never go home again. We will return and make it up with your parents. They cannot be angry forever and they won't kill you."

"I don't know how I can leave them. Let us just go on the way we were."

So I stayed and we continued talking, talking. But I was angry with Zenaida's mother. Once she tried to hit me in the street. I was with my nephew Aurelio, my half-sister's son. We were going around buying plums . . . it was in September. Zenaida's mother was fat and tall and she tried to grab me unawares but I saw her coming toward me. She had stopped me in the street but I saw that her hand was raised and that she wanted to hit me in the face. I took three leaps and by the time she was ready to hit, I was ten meters away. Her plan didn't work out and she got mad. She said that only she gives orders in her house and no one can make a fool of her, no one can step on the honor of her house, that she takes good care of her daughter and that what she says, goes. She stood there, screaming at me until I got tired of it. Zenaida was on the wall, making signs for me to leave. My nephew Aurelio said, "Speak up to her, too. Don't give in. Tell her to go to hell."

I told him, "If I talk back then I'll be just like her, a scandalous woman. If she were a man, we'd have it out."

The mother got mad and I did, too, and we never understood each other. I trampled on the honor of her house and she never knew it. I did what I wanted with her daughter and with her daughter-in-law, too.

I spoke to Juana, the wife of Zenaida's brother, who lived in the same house. I spoke to Juana and right off she said yes, so there was no way out. Right off, I made use of her. We did it very secretly. Her husband was an intimate friend of mine but she wanted to so there was nothing I could do about it.

So, after that, I went with both women. When one wasn't there, I saw the other. Later I left them both, first one, then the other. But before that I asked for Zenaida's hand a second time. My godparents had come to ask but Zenaida's mother and father took her to Cuernavaca to hide her. While my godparents were waiting in my house, the sister-in-law sent for me because no one was at home. I met her in back of the *corral* and that's where her husband saw me embracing her. It was drizzling and he came home early. We heard a whistle in the street but paid no attention. At the third whistle, he came around the kitchen into the yard and saw us. I jumped and ran through the *corral* and over the wall. I heard him ask, "Who is that?" and I heard him give her a slap. I went running home. My godparents were talking to my *mamá* and *papá* in the house. My *mamá* was not well then and there was a girl in the house working as a servant. Her name was Chole.

She says, "What happened to you."

"Just think, Andrés surprised me with his wife. He saw me clearly and even hit her."

"Now you see what you have been doing!"

"Look, tell my *mamá* that if Andrés comes to ask for me, she should tell him I am not here. But hurry, before he comes."

I didn't have time to tell her myself because, right off, Andrés arrived. I wasn't there so he asked to speak to my *papá*.

"Come in, Andrés, what can I do for you?" says my *papá*.

"No, *don* Pedro, I want to speak to you right here, although it is painful, it is shameful, to have to say what I am going to say. But a man says what he feels."

"Yes, what happened to you?"

"Well, you know, I went out to the corner, feeling confident that my house was safe. I went out but I know how to take care of things so I didn't stay long, and then when I returned I saw Felipe with my wife. He was hugging her and well, why should I do anything about it? If he wants her, if they like each other, let him take her. I give her to him, but she must take the baby and I will take the older child. I agree to it. Why should I get angry? It wouldn't cost me anything to get angry and to fight but we all saw each other there and I don't want to know any more. So if he wants to, let her and the baby go with him. That is what I wanted to tell him. Speak to him and see what he says."

"*Ay*, what a boy! I don't know what they do when they go out. But don't worry. I will tell him when he comes."

And there I was listening. When Andrés left, my *papá* came in and said to me, "What have you been doing?"

"Nothing."

"Then why does Andrés say you can have his wife? He knew you were going with his wife but not until now did he come to tell me. You should have been careful. Do you have so much self-confidence that you go to his house?"

"But we weren't in his house, we were in the *corral* . . . just talking."

"No, he said you were hugging his wife."

"I was only asking about her sister-in-law. Then she asked me for a lemon and I gave it to her. It is not true, what he says."

"Good! So it was only gossip?"

"Yes, just gossip."

Andrés didn't speak to me for a few weeks but I wasn't angry. After all, why should I be angry?

I continued being Zenaida's sweetheart for a while. We quarreled sometimes and stopped speaking to each other for a few days. Then we'd begin again. We went on that way until once we quarreled, this time forever.

It was in October and I was buying plums. I'd get up early, at six in the morning, and go to the storeroom my father had rented in the plaza, to store the plums before sending them to Mexico City. Because she didn't see me all day, Zenaida got mad and said I had another girl. When I went home for breakfast at about ten o'clock in the morning, her niece was there and I asked her, "And where is your aunt?"

"In the *corral*, picking plums."

"I am going to speak to her. I hope you don't tell."

I went to the *corral* and I saw her up in the small plum tree. I was ashamed to stand below and be looking up at her so I went no closer than five meters and I said, "Zenaida, are you picking?"

She didn't answer me. I spoke again and she didn't answer. In all, I spoke six times and she didn't answer. "Zenaida, is it that you don't hear? I'm speaking to you!"

Then she says, "What do you want? I don't want you to bother me any more. I've wanted you to stop for a long time."

"But why are you mad? I know I haven't done anything to you."

"I don't want you to come near me any more. You've been talking about me. You've been saying that I'm going to marry you. You've been talking a lot about me."

I say to her, "I gain nothing by going around talking. It's your aunt who is talking about you. She says things that are not true."

She says, "And I don't want you to speak to me any more. Don't come near me, stay away."

"Yes, I'll stay away. Don't think I'm going to be with you forever, nor try to take you by force. Don't think I am going to stick with you or depend on you. No, you even do me a favor to let me go because you won't marry me or let me marry someone else. I'm grateful to you because you let me free from this day on. From this moment, I am nothing to you, nor you to me. I leave you forever. But remember the many years we have been sweethearts. I loved you and I still love you and I did my duty in all you asked of me. Even now I want to kneel before you so that you may know I love you with all my heart. I never treated you badly. Never did I say a vulgar word to you. I behaved the best I could and now I don't know how to care more for you. I would like to give you my heart but you don't understand me and you believe gossip. You'll be sorry but then it will be too late. Time is a good friend and will make each of us pay by our destiny. You are a woman and I am a man and we are here in the world as teamsters. We'll meet on the road and look into each other's face to see who has the stronger gaze."

She says, "Ah, if someday I feel something, I know it will be for you."

And there we ended everything.

PART SIX

P E D R O

Conchita and Family Problems

I am proud of my sons because they helped me. It is useful for boys to go to school, but it is also good to teach them how to work in the fields. My experience shows me that when an office worker gets fired he has no place to turn. But a farmer—who is going to fire him? They can't! I know a mason who is just standing on street corners looking for work. One day I said to him, "Why don't you get to work?"

"I am a mason," he said. "I am not trained for farm work." That is a disgrace! Why even when I was judge, I would leave my office and join my sons in the fields.

I say, men to the fields and women in the kitchen! I taught my sons to work according to their ability, to get up at five o'clock in the morning, to fetch water for the house and for the plants. I would say to them, "This site was nothing but an empty lot before and now there are plums, oranges, coffee and peaches. It is the man's obligation to take care of the trees and plants, and to bring wood, so that the woman doesn't have to, and after that, off to the fields."

My two older boys were working like men. I took Ricardo out to the fields in the rainy season, in June and July, and I was teaching the younger one, Moisés, to run errands and to twist rope. I also took him to the fields to weed. But this child was born kind of weak and he was no good in the fields. He had trouble with his feet ever since he was little. They said he had been bewitched, that he had the evil eye. I called in a man with a black heart and he cleansed Moisés with a handkerchief and an egg. He even gave Moisés his mustache to keep as an amulet but the boy continued ailing. It looked like Moisés was going to be very intelligent, and I thought with a little fertilizer he would yet grow up to be a man.

Felipe and Ricardo did poorly in school one year. I think it was because they are backward. I think that besides being absent a lot because of the chores, it might also be heredity. Because of their mother they have no memory. Nothing enters her head and her memory is completely stopped up.

I like my sons to be wide-awake but the first thing I tried to take out of them is aggressiveness and talkativeness. All my boys are modest, humble, obedient and hard-working. Martín is more affectionate and even more intelligent than his older brother. He now knows everything I know. He is the best of my older sons. But all my children are very reserved. I said to them, "Look at the neighbor's boys. They are all more Indian and more thick-headed than we and yet all of them are very affectionate toward their parents. They go over to their father and say to him, 'Papacito lindo, I love you so much.' And they do the same to their mamá. That is how a family should act toward each other. You are supposed to be more intelligent yet you don't behave like that."

Well, what can you do? What I wish for my children is that they have a good life. The main thing is that they be humble and honest in everything. I tell them that a man who behaves well is always trusted. You can see that from the sacred writings . . . one must be good to be rewarded by God.

My wife was very affectionate with her children. But she was very strict, too. Even though they may be only a little bit disobedient she would get angry right away and punish them with a rope. I was just as affectionate, and strict, too. You can see how they are always working. But I love them very much.

I insisted that my children work, for they must be taught. The neighbors say, and they have said it to my face, that I walk along behind my sons like a boss with his three workers. I answer my critics like this, "Who raised them? You? I suppose I began to exploit them ever since they were babies? Sure, I started when they were still nursing! You people talk just to hear yourself talk." That is how I spoke to them.

"Now," I said, "you do not exploit your children. And what are they like? Just let's see, let's compare them with my children. None of my sons is illiterate. I have done all I could for them. I have given them schooling, even though none of them is especially apt. But your children

are dunces, idiots, who can't even sign their names. Where have you spent your money? What about the first daughter I educated? Did the children help me then? No, I was the one who made her a teacher. Which of you has a teacher among your children? Who, let me hear? They cannot even read! What kind of parents are you who don't live up to your obligations? You are the ones who exploit your children because you do not send them to school. You send them right off to work. Not I! I set them an example and anybody can see that my children are not ignorant."

Oh, sure, I was well aware of that gossip about how domineering I was, that I was very demanding, that I gave them no leeway and practically exploited my own children. I insisted that they work. They have to work for me. That is why I have sons. They have to compensate for our sacrifices. Now I work if I feel like it, and if not, I don't. As long as they are in my house, as long as they are not of age, my children have to obey me, to submit, and they may not question their parents' actions. Naturally, we should set our children a good example. We must give them self-confidence but not allow them to lack respect. They must respect their *mamá* because she gave them life and their *papá* because he gives the orders.

One time my two boys, Felipe and Martín, ran away because they were very angry. That was practically the first time they gave any signs of rebelliousness. They were still young, still minors. Well, I knew this woman, she was married but her husband left her, the poor thing, he abandoned her. Well, the poor woman supported herself. She had no man at all, she struggled on her own. And as I know how to make rope, this poor thing says to me, "Say, why don't you make me a few dozen ropes?"

"Yes, sure. Why not?"

But it was completely aboveboard. There was nothing like love making, either on her part or mine . . . everything was honorable. I did this for her every year. But this time my sons were more grown up and could help me clean the fiber and twist the ropes. I can't remember what caused the disturbance. Oh, yes, I went to work and left word that they should clean the fiber as the fiesta of Tepalcingo was coming. When I got back they had done nothing. Naturally, I got mad and beat them. Hadn't I left word that they should do that work? Do I work for myself alone? Yes, sure I beat them. That I did.

The next day they were nowhere to be seen. They had gone. Hmmm. Well, I began to make the rope. I was more powerful then and could finish them in two days as there were only a dozen ropes. The next day my wife was crying. Well, she had always loved her children. As they were still young, she wanted to look for them.

We went to a spiritualist's house in Cuernavaca. She told us, "Your children will come back, don't worry. Don't let it upset you. They are in your nephew's house. So they will be back." And that is the way it was.

Meanwhile I sent word to the poor woman that I had cleaned the fiber but had not twisted the rope because I couldn't now that I was looking for my boys and that she should get somebody else to finish them. Who knows where the poor woman took them, but as they were hers she carried them off. I charged her almost nothing for my work because I was angry. And just because I didn't charge her, people said there was something between us.

If I never told my wife about the women with whom I really had something to do, why would I tell her about this poor woman with whom I never had anything to do? I didn't know her well enough to say whether she was a man or a woman! We were friendly, yes. I would go to talk with her once in a while in the evenings, but nothing ever happened. But people, the neighbors, heated up my wife's blood and my sons'. Mainly it was my cousin Margarito and the widow Gloria. I was Gloria's lover for a time, but she never mentions that.

My affair with Gloria lasted about two years. Her husband, my cousin Julio, had died in 1928, just before I went to live in Mexico City. When I came back to Azteca, Gloria was living with Juan, who later became my son-in-law. Gloria already had one child with him and in the next three years she had two more, but they say the third one was not his. Juan left her and went to live with his half-sister in his father's house. He opened a little store there, and as I was a teamster at the time, he hired me to bring him supplies—alcohol, sugar, soap—from Yautepec. I worked for him about a year and then he began coming to my house to convert, not because he had convictions but because of my daughter Conchita.

Gloria had always been very mischievous and she began to joke with me and play with me, so there was no way out of it. I spoke to her and, yes, she accepted right off. I was already a judge by then. I would meet her in the *corral* and take her to the cornfield. I don't know if my *señora* ever found out about it. Gloria never asked me for money but I gave her two or three *pesos* now and then, as well as corn when my *señora* was away from the house.

One year before my term of office was over, and while I was still seeing Gloria, I took up with another woman, the widow Rutila. Rutila had been living with a man called Gabriel and she had a daughter with him. But then she threw him out and he left, taking the *burro* and the team of oxen with him. The animals were in his name but he had bought them with the money her husband had left her and so there was a dispute over it.

Gabriel found another woman and one day he came to my office to ask me to marry them. I agreed but I didn't know then that Rutila was going to send a summons to prevent the wedding. She claimed there was an impediment to the marriage because of the daughter. She wanted a settlement made for the child and she said that if I didn't do her justice she would sue me in Cuernavaca. "I am in trouble," I said to myself. "Here I have already spoken for Gabriel and now this woman comes with her summons."

But not being a fool, I sent an official note to the president, telling him of the impediment but saying that it was up to him to decide whether or not the marriage could take place. Now it was out of my hands. Poor little Crispín was president then, and instead of marrying them the fool told Gabriel that I said they couldn't be married until there was a settlement. Now I was in trouble with Gabriel, a hot-tempered man. He believed I was turning against him but I was only following the law. Crispín should have married them but he didn't, and here I had to defend Rutila. Crispín called us all together to settle the case.

Rutila says, "I don't mind if they get married. My protest is because of the child. This man took my *burro* and my oxen and now he must pay for my daughter's schooling."

And I say to Gabriel, "See? She is not against your marrying, but why did you take her *burro*, which wasn't even worth the trouble? And the oxen? You bought them in your name but it was because of her husband. He was no fool and he left her what he left her and now, man, you are taking advantage."

And that's why Gabriel was angry with me and became my enemy. But the woman, Rutila, came every day to speak to me, as my office was in a separate room. I think she already had intentions about me. When I said, "Here I am, do you want to?" right off, she answered, "Yes, of course."

Fine! That is how it began. I said, "Now you have nothing to worry about. I will help you." Gabriel didn't know about us until much later, although she came to my office every day. Naturally, people began to gossip about her. She came and waited until I left work in the evening and then we would go into the fields. I didn't want my *señora* to know about it so I began to take Rutila to Cuernavaca. Every four or five days we met there and I paid the bus fare and two *pesos* for a hotel room. *Újule!* That woman was hot! Even more than Gloria, and I liked her better. I gave Rutila money every day, at times five *pesos*, at times three or ten, but it was every day and I earned little.

Every day, every day, until it frightened me. I said, "This woman is too much for me but how can I get rid of her?"

One day I made the mistake of asking Gloria to meet me in my office after all the officials had gone home. I was sitting there waiting for her when the other one came. Rutila beat her to it and I thought, "What shall I do? Gloria will come and see us."

So I say to Rutila, "Let's go to Cuernavaca right now."

And she says, "Yes, but . . ."

"No, no, let's go right now."

Just as we were leaving, Gloria came. *Újule!* Rutila was Gloria's *comadre* and the two of them sat down together and began to talk. Then Gloria says, "I'm going now. I am in a hurry," and she leaves.

"Well, what do we do now?" I say. "She caught us and now she is going to talk. I don't want my *señora* to know, so you better go home. Gloria is going to spread gossip about us now."

After that, Gloria was angry with me and didn't want to any more. Just because of Rutila she got angry and left me. I continued with Rutila until my term was up. When I cleared out of the office, Rutila even cried. I said to her, "Look, now do me a favor. Have patience for fifteen days because I cannot leave the house on account of my enemies. I am going to lay low to see what happens." At that time, I carried my old rifle with me everywhere.

After fifteen days I saw that there was nothing to be afraid of. Holy Week was coming and so I brought Rutila a kilo of dried codfish. But she didn't take it. I said, "Let's go to Cuernavaca," but I could see that she answered me coldly. Then I understood. I realized that fifteen days was too long for her. But then she agreed to go to Cuernavaca. "Let's meet where we always meet," I said.

She kept her promise and met me there at the hotel. On the way out I said, "When will I see you?"

She said, "Now I will tell you. I came to tell you it is all over."

I say, "Well, then, many thanks."

"No," she says, "that's why I came. I won't bother you any more and don't you bother me."

And that's when everything ended. Yes, but I was grateful to her. I liked the fact that she told me because there are some women who fool a man and compromise him.

"Very well," I said, and I took out twenty *pesos* to give her, but she didn't take them. She left them lying there and ran out of the hotel. That was our good-bye.

So I didn't have either Gloria or Rutila, but after that I had lots of other women. I even had one in Mexico City, the merchant to whom I sent hog plums.

•   •   •

Conchita arrived at the house unexpectedly one day. I believe she failed in her studies and left the school. "Now I am going to look for work, *papá*," she said. She was grown up by then, about twenty-three years old. She had gotten tired of going to school. My daughter was advanced for that time because people with no more than primary education were given jobs as teachers. That is why there are quite a number of teachers in Azteca who have no teaching certificates. Some of them are still studying to become certified teachers. But not my daughter! She had two years in the normal school and two years there in the high school in Coyoacán. So she was quite well off.

"All right," I said. "Go ahead. Let's try to find you work."

So, I began to help her again. As I was younger then and had more energy, *zas, zas, zas,* I tried until I got it for her. Except that she had to work as a temporary teacher and for three months she received no pay. After that she got a regular appointment . . . state, not federal.

They assigned her to an isolated little village. I brought her there myself and left her. But that evil professor there, the principal of the school, saw that she was a *señorita* and not so young any more, and he took advantage of her. The two of them got together. He told her he was going to leave his wife. She believed him but there was nothing to it. He was married and still is to this day. Anyway, they did it, the two of them, and when I least expected it, there she was pregnant.

Conchita came home bringing two teacher friends with her, so that I shouldn't say anything to her. I saw that something was up, but what was it? It still didn't show in her eyes or her face. I said to myself, "Something is not right here. But what?" I had to control myself as she had the two teachers with her. When they left, I went along part of the way with them, but her friends didn't leave her alone for a moment. They took her back with them and that was when I finally realized. *Caray!* I didn't know what to do with that woman.

I didn't say a word to her, but her mother had plenty to say. She really began to scold me. My wife really was angry with me, but she was right. She blamed me for letting Conchita get an education, that being a woman she had no business in school, and so on. I didn't say a word. The neighbors also said I was a fool for sending my daughter away from home like that . . . after this happened. Well, I didn't say a word. As a matter of fact, there was nothing I could say since it happened because of my ambition to have my daughter learn. But it turned out this way and she was ruined.

She came back a week later and this time I said to her, "What happened to you?" And I scolded her. She didn't answer. There was nothing to be done any more . . . it had already happened. My wife kept yelling and scolding me. She said, "Now do you see? Where is your schooling now?" I didn't say anything because it was my fault. I took into consideration that my daughter was, well, a chip off the old block. "After all," I said to myself, "that's how I am, that's how my family is, what can I do? She is of age, and competent, and now particularly after what the doctor told me about her being of a strong nature, what is there to do? The doctor said, 'She'll die if she doesn't do it.' I cannot attack her, nor can I give her what she wants, so there is no help for it."

Much later I asked my daughter, "All right, now why did you go and do this?"

"Ay, papá," she said and began to laugh, "if you could only understand! I even prayed to God to give me a baby. I concentrated on it, papá. What more is there for me to tell you?"

Well, that's how it stood and I accepted it. I did not talk to the principal. How could I accuse him of anything if she did it because she wanted to? I understood. But not my wife! She kept nagging me.

Conchita continued to teach until her time came. My son Ricardo went back to school with her and came to notify us that his sister was about to give birth. He was just a little boy then and I don't know how she could have sent him, but she took the chance. He walked all the way to Azteca, not even taking the bus.

I said to my wife, "Look, what do you want her to do now? She is your daughter. Better go and take care of her."

"All right," she said, "only because you send me. I don't want to go, but I will." When she arrived she found another novio there, not the father of the child, but another one by the name of Vicente. The man who "did her the favor" had retired from the scene. Well, what a laying-out my wife gave friend Vicente, and she chased him away.

He said, "But look, señora, I know I am doing the best for your daughter. There is nobody to take care of her. I have taken charge of her now with the understanding that she agreed to marry me. I undertook the obligation of helping her and of getting her back on her feet. But now you come and chase me away. Well, then, I will leave. But I will still be around . . . no one can take away my love." He was still a boy and, more than that, he had money. He was a businessman who made a good living. But my wife would not let him stay, she preferred to run him out.

After two weeks she came back home, my poor wife, all skin and bones . . . she hadn't been eating. That village nauseated her and made her angry. She went after me and rightly so. "Nice things your daughter is doing. What have you got to say about it?"

I said, "Look, I have been here suffering, too. Don't think you are the only one."

"Well, it makes me furious. You better go and fetch her then. You want to have your daughter here, so go fetch her."

Twenty days later I went to get her. She came with her little son Germán, to get back her strength here in the house. She requested a leave; they gave it for three months. After that she went back to work again, in a different village. She took Germán with her, but now Macrina went along to be his nursemaid. Ricardo and Macrina kept following after Conchita. That is why they hardly learned anything. I would say, "Teach them. You are a teacher. Teach them." But she never bothered about them. She used them only to do the chores.

And that Vicente began to pursue her. I said to my daughter, "Man, you have already half-promised him. This fellow is acting in good faith. He wants to marry you. And he is willing to be responsible. Furthermore, he proved his love because he helped you when you were unwell. He was taking care of you; what more do you expect? So, I think it would be advisable for you to accept."

At first she said yes and then it was no and no and no. He came all the way to the house to ask for her hand. He came three times and each time she said no. I said to her, "You did a very bad thing. Why did you encourage him, then?"

"Just to have some fun."

"Have some fun! He isn't a toy. He is a man, and an upright one. Why are you fooling him?" Well, I half-scolded her, but that is as far as it went. So I notified him, "No, Vicente, she doesn't want to. So, you better not come back any more."

And the man turned on me. "All right, but only because you are chasing me away. Nobody can control my love. I love your daughter and I will marry her." Conchita moved to another village because he was pursuing her. But he even followed her there. But my daughter had by then taken up with Juan once more and soon they were married. Still, this Vicente continued after her and kept coming to the house.

"Listen," he says, "it doesn't matter. I'll take her to my village. It doesn't matter if she has a husband. I am not going to leave her."

Conchita continued teaching and one day she came from her work to see me. She said, "*Papá*, that man keeps bothering me; what can we do? I am married but he doesn't stop. He will be waiting for me in Cuernavaca when I go back to school."

"Then I'll go with you. I'll take you back."

When we arrived in Cuernavaca, sure enough, there was Vicente near the buses. What to do now? I called a policeman and had the fellow put in jail. He gave a bribe, who knows how much, and he got out. But that was good-bye. He never came back again. I had gotten rid of him.

When Conchita got married, I took her son from her. Germán was fourteen months old at the time. She wanted to take him along with her, but I put my foot down. I said, "No, not that. Juan is a stepfather and is going to mistreat the boy. Germán has already cost me something so now I'll bring him up." And my wife and I brought him up. Macrina was really his mother because she looked after him until he grew up. I put him in school and he is going to this day.

My son-in-law and I liked each other for the first few days. But I soon saw what kind of a character he had and from then on we began to part. He was a completely ambitious person and wanted to exploit us. He wanted me to be like his son, to wait on him, to work for him and all for nothing! Being older and responsible, that was not for me! Once we went to harvest for him, my sons and I, the three of us, and what do you think? He doesn't pay us! After we had gathered some corn, I said to my daughter, "But, man! Just pay my sons, that is all I ask. I am the father and it is my duty to help you, but not my sons. We can't all work for nothing. What will their mother eat?"

That was what the quarrel was about . . . because I had charged him. He paid us reluctantly. My daughter gave us the money, practically secretly. Later my son-in-law said to me, "Don't worry. We will plant more and we will all have plenty to eat here." He spoke as though he was taking care of everyone. He was ordering my sons about, even sending them to his cornfield at night to bring back corn. He wanted to use them as slaves—and me too.

I had to laugh. "Look," I said, "what is going on here? Am I supposed to be a son of the family or what? How can I be a son if I am the father? No, no, no . . . I have been a *regidor*, I have been a judge, and he comes along and tries to boss me! No, that is not for me!" The bad feeling between us became worse.

Then his half-sister came to live with them. As soon as that happened Juan began to drink heavily. It became a daily thing and he beat his wife a lot. That's why I think there was something between him and his half-sister, because he gave her whatever she wanted, shoes, a shawl, everything. How strange, because he didn't give my daughter anything. He had another sister and he never gave her anything either. Then when Conchita was expecting his first child and was helpless in bed, his half-sister went to Mexico and Juan went off to Cuernavaca to drink, leaving my daughter alone. The midwife came to get us and my wife and I stayed there with her. I paid for everything and that night she gave birth.

My wife went back to the house to look after the boys but I stayed on with Conchita. I was sitting there when Juan arrived at about two in the morning, dead drunk. That made me very angry. He was so drunk he didn't care about anything and began to throw himself on top of her. When he heard the baby, he pushed it away. And there I was defending them.

"What has gotten into you?" I said. "Can't you see she is sick? What are you doing?" Well, I gave him a good laying-out, but he was so drunk he didn't understand a word. I pushed him. He fell and there he lay without moving. "You can stay there all night," I said.

I didn't get any sleep. I just sat up on the bench beside my daughter, guarding her from him. I was afraid he might get up and hurt her or kill the baby. I had no blanket and it was really cold. Bah! That night I suffered.

The next day I said to Juan, "Man, why did you go to Cuernavaca and leave my daughter? You're not even a man, to do such a thing."

He says, "Yes, but I was counting on your being here."

"Well and good, but if we had not been with her, you would have injured her and killed the baby. So, the only reason the child is alive is because of us."

He had nothing to say. But then I got a bit angry. "*Carambas!*" I said to myself. "That's no man for my daughter. And after giving her an education . . . letting her study so she could support herself." Then it really began to hurt me.

And Juan kept on getting drunk. I sent my daughter Macrina to be their servant. And did he pay the servant? And did he pay the midwife? Nothing! His sister went all the way to Mexico City so she wouldn't have to look after Conchita. She ran! Well, my wife and I were the ones who paid. There we were and we made Macrina stay and serve them until Conchita was well.

And Juan had no sense of obligation! Naturally, as we had corn to eat, we gave them some. He had corn, too, but kept it locked up, waiting to see what would happen. Well, what could I do? We suffer all our life long! Then the other child was born. It was the same thing all over again; Juan took no responsibility. That is when I tried to take Conchita away from him. But this is what my daughter would do: when she was angry with her husband she would come to me and denounce him. When the anger passed, she would go back to her husband and tell him what I had told her. And that way she would cause us to fight.

The trouble with Juan continued. I took Conchita away from him three times. I tried to get her away for good but couldn't. The last time he even brought suit against me. But I had him thrown into jail. Yes, because what he had done to me was not fair, I had him put in jail. He brought a lawyer, but I paid no attention and got into a fight with him, too.

In 1947, the last time Conchita was in my house, another little girl was born. But the midwife did not do the job right and practically killed the baby. She was born all right, but the midwife left the navel too small, and it got inflamed. It began to burn and it killed her. My daughter wasn't right after the birth either. She developed a fever and the pain would not go away. This went on for four or five days. Then, I said to myself, "No, this is not right." And I went to call the little doctor, the pharmacist. He came to see her. "Hmm, *caray!* This is very bad. It didn't turn out right. But I can't touch her . . . I am a man. Let's call Juliana and I will tell her what has to be done. Have them call her."

So I ran to get Juliana. She did the things he told her, and, yes, they cured my daughter. But the little girl died after fifteen days. We had a wake with just bread and coffee but a lot of people came. All my friends! They gave me this support and I thought to myself, "Now I feel more closely joined to them. We are all one and never again will we be separated in the political struggle."

The death of the little girl made me very angry. I said to myself, "Now I am not going to pay the midwife. Now I am going to bring suit."

Her price was twenty *pesos,* but as my daughter and her husband were separated, the midwife went to collect from him. She made up a lot of things against us and so this man Juan brought suit against us. We sued him, too, the three of us, I along with my wife and daughter. Conchita had been in bed for only twenty days and was still delicate but I took her in the bus, all the way to Cuernavaca.

I was no fool, see? Before I did anything else, before I took my daughter away from her husband, I had gone to the lower court and said to the clerk, "I would like you to draw up an affidavit for me." So they entered a request for separation in which there appeared the reasons why I was taking back my daughter. I put everything into it and even applied the criminal code. Naturally, I kept a copy of it. We went to appear in Cuernavaca and there was this little lawyer, a real fool, and also the District Attorney's clerk, who was my friend and still is to this day. My daughter was the first to be called.

"Now, *señora,* you are accused here by your husband of abandonment of the home. Well, why did you abandon him? What is it you left?"

"Nothing. The bed."

"What do you mean, 'the bed'? What about him?"

"Well, I left him, too, but in the street because he was out drinking. He was always out. He is irresponsible and my father came to get me because my father has always looked out for me ever since my first child was born." So then the clerk stood up and asked for the affidavit I had filed. After reading it, he said, "Look here, man, this document says . . . *újule!* Here they applied the law . . . even with annotations. Now, who is it who is guilty of abandonment of the home, you or your wife?"

"She is," says my son-in-law.

"Is it true that you did not see her through any of her deliveries?"

"No, because my father-in-law did me the favor of looking after her."

"But who is the husband, your father-in-law or you? Your father-in-law even carried her to the sweatbath. And how much did you pay the servant?"

"Nothing, because she is my sister-in-law."

"And how much did you give the midwife?"

"Nothing. My father-in-law took care of her."

"So, now, who is the one who abandoned the home, you or your wife?"

"Well, I believe she is."

"No. Look here, you have confessed that everything was true. Here it is. You are the one who is responsible, not your father-in-law. And now you are the one who is going to jail."

They called my wife, who made the same statement. I declared the same things again. I said, "Look *señor* clerk, where does a husband show his love and affection? I want you to do me the favor of telling me that."

"Well, in the home."

"Yes, certainly, but most of all in bed." The stenographers misinterpreted what I meant and began to laugh. So I said, "No I don't mean what you think. I say this because love and affection are proven in the bed, when a person is prostrate with illness . . . on a sickbed."

"Man! How true that is!" Then the clerks and the secretaries also said, "Yes, that is true."

"Now, don't get a wrong idea. I am married and have been for a long time. Let my wife here say how many times I have abandoned her. I never abandoned her; the slightest little illness and I am at her bedside. That is what love and affection means . . . when one is helpless in bed. When I am in good health she doesn't even have to pay any attention to me, but when I am sick that is when I need my wife's help. But it is the other way around with this man. When he sees that she is really sick, he goes out and gets drunk. What kind of a man is he? An irresponsible man!"

So then the clerk says to my daughter, "What do you want done with your husband? Jail, right?"

My daughter says, "I don't want anything."

"And you, *señora*, what do you want done with your son-in-law?"

"Nothing. I just want him to stop bothering us. I have the other child here with me. Look, he is sick."

So the women said, "*Caray!* What decent people! He should be put in jail. Why are they feeling sorry for him?"

Then the secretary called me aside and said, "And what do you say, *compadre?*"

"I won't ask for anything. I am not a tyrant or a vengeful person. I am not like him, nor am I as ignorant as he is. All I ask is that he doesn't bear us a grudge and that he leave us alone."

Then the clerk says to Juan, "How do you like that! What a fine family you found. You are lucky . . . drunk and worthless and on top of it nonsupport and abandonment of the home . . . and still they don't want to bring a charge. You deserve to be in jail, but they aren't asking for any punishment. Well, this is as far as it goes, then. They are pardoning you."

"Yes, we pardon you for everything. We don't want anything."

But not many days passed before Conchita and Juan were at it again . . . secretly . . . like sweethearts. She couldn't stand being without a husband . . . she was jumping out of her skin already to get together with the man. It was the last fiesta of Tlaltenango which falls on September 8, and I went. I was passing by in a bus when I saw them walking along together. That really hurt me! When I got back home, I said to my wife, "Look at your daughter! She leaves the baby here and there they go, the two of them."

My wife got angry and said, "Who knows if she will even return today?"

Conchita didn't get back until the following day. I didn't say anything to her, but then my wife and I came to a decision. My wife said, "Chase her out. The truth is, we can't put up with this any more. Let her go."

And that's the way it was. The next day I said, "Listen, little daughter . . . I want you to do me a favor."

"Yes, of course, *papá*."

"Get your rags together and leave . . . get out . . . beat it. Go run to your husband."

"Oh! All right, I'll go. He is my husband. I am better off with him than with my father."

"Go on, then. But I am warning you that from this day on do not stand in my doorway and I won't stand in yours. Never again. Just act as if you already buried me, and I will do the same. What you have done to us is no small thing, and that's the truth. But I am not going to scold you now. So just leave . . . go on."

"I'll go right away."

And she went. About two weeks after they had gotten together, I happened to pass by their house. She came to the gate and said, "*Papá*, he beat me last night."

"Praise the Lord! How is it he didn't kill you? And why do you tell me about it? I am nothing to you. Didn't we say that everything was finished with us now? Why come complaining to me? Didn't you say that you are better off with your husband? I don't care any more. Let him kill you if he wants. You don't understand, you are a jackass, but now it doesn't matter to me any more. If he kills you, he kills you."

I don't know what she felt, but she began to cry, and I left. All my children, Felipe, Martín, Ricardo, Macrina, Moisés . . . they are all my children and I love them . . . but not that one, not her. Conchita wounded me to the heart. The thing is, when Conchita married she lost her love for her father. She went around talking against me. She is ungrateful. She is no longer my daughter. We want nothing to do with her any more. I should say not!

Yes, we loved her very much, her mother and I. The proof is that I sacrificed myself to give her an education. She became a teacher. I went around to the places where she worked, bringing her things. Yes, indeed! I did all that and yet now she says that I did not help her, that I didn't put her through school . . . that her husband Juan helped her more. How could she have the heart to say that? They have no learning! The truth is these little schoolteachers do not know anything as they do not get a complete education. All it is is a mixture and they don't come out well. Anyone who behaves like that is not educated. That is why I say a woman whom you just half educate like that is ruined. She just does what she feels like and forgets everything she learned.

Her husband continued to beat her. He said, "Now you are going to pay for what they did to me." Well, let her pay! But afterward he changed. He took to the Scriptures and changed. She did too. Juan then turned against his sister and took away the house and plot for himself. When he began quarreling with his sister, he began to love his wife.

To this day, Juan doesn't drink any more, because of his religion. It was also because he got hold of money. That means a lot, too. Before, they had nothing and then overnight, all of a sudden, he lifted himself up. He built a house, opened a new little store and bought some cattle. People say that he found the money buried in the woods. Juan was gathering maguey fiber when he saw a man digging in the ground at the foot of a hill. The man dug up a sack and opened it. He took out money and spread it in the sun, to warm it and look at it, then he buried it again. Juan stopped working to watch, and as soon as the man left, Juan went down the hill and dug up the money and took it home. That's what they say, but who knows?

My wife began to get sick because of those two daughters of mine! It began with Conchita and then Macrina finished the job. Macrina practically killed my wife when she went off with that fellow from San Martín without telling us. That's what my wife finally died of—anger! Like a fool, I too would get angry with Conchita, but not now any more. That is all over with.

The worst part of it was that my wife took it to heart. She loved her children very much. She even loved me. She loved me a lot! But she didn't love other people's children, not even her grandchildren. She didn't care much for Germán. What I think is that she got jealous at the time I took in that child and the jealousy remained with her, because she was very angry when he was born, so angry it practically caused her death.

The day Macrina ran away I was in Mexico City selling fruit. I came home and found my wife thrashing around and crying. I said, "What is the matter. Did you have some kind of attack?"

"No! Your daughter is gone."

"What do you mean, gone?"

"Yes, it's all over. And who knows who carried her off?"

So, to comfort her, I said, "Is that all that is worrying you?"

"Yes, of course. I thought you would get mad."

"Why should I get mad? Stop worrying. Come on! Let us eat something. Don't think of your daughter. She needed a man . . . what would you want her to do? Leave her alone. She won't be killed. It would be different if she were a boy, because that would mean danger. But she is a woman! Well, so her sweetheart carried her off. So what! Let her be. She is enjoying herself and here you are crying. That's not right! That is the way she had to end up."

"But I didn't do it that way. I got married."

"Well, that was you. Also, I wanted to do you the honor . . . I asked for your hand. And I was even an orphan. I did not want to do you wrong for I thought you were going to be mine. That is why I didn't deceive you like I did the others. I wanted to behave right with you. But there aren't very many who do that."

"Yes, but your daughters . . . look what they have done to me!"

"Well, sure! What do you want now? That's how the world is. What can you do?"

After our last baby died, my wife had trouble with her womb and I took her to Cuernavaca. There they know all about superstitions and spiritists and spiritualists and all that. So I took her there. My wife had a lot of faith in them. We entered the office with flowers and candles. The spiritualist told me that it was the ovaries or a hernia or something like that and they would operate on her spiritually. When it was time, she cleansed my wife with herbs and prepared her very well beforehand, just like any doctor. Then she said to me, "Now we are going to operate. Go home and, here, apply this to her." Then the spiritualist gave me the instructions.

She said to me, "You are husband and wife, so shut yourselves in a room and have the children sleep elsewhere." I put all the boys in the kitchen and my wife and I were in the room, with me taking care of her. I did everything just as I was told. I had to put four white flowers in the form of a cross in a dish of water and a lighted candle at the head of the patient's bed.

The spiritualist had said to me, "What is in must come out. It will be expelled and you must throw whatever comes out into the middle of the yard. And if you see or feel something, do not be frightened. Do not get scared, for it is the spirit who will come to cure her."

Well, it turned out to be true! I did as she said. I sat there, drowsing, but sitting up. At about one o'clock in the morning she really expelled it. Whew! What came out of my wife was something frightful. *Caracoles!* Like big clots, like liver, huge pieces, and it stank awfully. I said to myself, "Well, now my wife is going to die. How is this possible?"

Me get frightened of spirits? Ridiculous! What frightened me was the illness! As the spiritualist said my wife should not move or turn, I held on to her, and said, "Now, don't turn over because who knows what will happen to you." I was scared now. I went out carrying the chamberpot to empty it in the middle of the yard. It was dark. We had no flashlights then. All at once I felt something brush past me. *Ay, carambolas!* I stopped still and began to look around everywhere. What was it? Pssht! After all, the woman told me not to get frightened, so I didn't. About half an hour later I felt it again, but only slightly.

My wife began to speak. "Now I feel better," she said. "Yes, I am going to get well. Nothing hurts any more."

As the spiritualist had told me to notify her, I went the next day. She began to laugh. "How did it go?" she asked.

"Fine, but an ugly, ugly thing came out."

"And didn't you see anything? Or feel anything?"

"Well, I went out into the yard and then I felt something that was like a breeze that brushed past me."

"That was the spirit who went to see what your wife expelled. Now take care of her, because she has had spiritual surgery. She was operated on without being touched."

"Hmm, well . . . yes, of course."

My wife had a lot of faith in her but not I. Of course I didn't! But, yes, she got well. It must have cost me about a hundred and fifty *pesos*, more or less, as the spiritualists don't charge so much.

That same year I got sick. The trouble was with my penis. I had never had any sickness like it and I thought it would go away.

At this time I had a dream which had an important meaning for me. I was walking across a narrow bridge, over a canyon, and when I got to the middle of it I saw a snake. It was about ten feet long and fairly big around. I ran after it; I wanted to kill it, but it moved very fast. Further on there was a cave and inside it I could see a fire. The snake went in and I thought, "*Ay, carambas*, now I will be able to kill it."

I stopped and watched the fire burning. I saw something like water in front of the cave but it was liquid fire, throwing flames. Then I saw little doves, pigeons, and they began to come out of the cave and walk through the fire without being burned up or even getting scorched. They did not stay there or die or anything. The snake was inside the cave and I couldn't see it any more. Then I felt that I was going down, further below, it was downhill, and there in a clearing I stopped to watch the little animals that were in the fire. They were like doves and they walked around easily in and out of the fire. I thought to myself, "There are fire animals, just as there are water animals and land animals." Then I saw a kind of circle being drawn on the ground, like a game we played as children.

This dream meant something bad for me, that a calamity was going to befall me, or that my family was going to get sick. The fire meant poverty, that I was going to be left down and out. The snake represented sickness, and the doves health, meaning I was going to recuperate. So I knew what was in store for me.

This happened when my wife and I were sick. She felt better by then and I said, "Well, now it is my turn. Let me see what the spiritualist says." So I went to her office and showed it to her. I was scared because pus was coming out now and there were scabs and it was getting worse.

"Hmmm, you are in bad shape," she said. "But I am not going to treat you."

"Why not?"

"No, you do not have faith. The spirit tells me that you do not believe in us. You are a Bible-reader."

"Yes, that is so."

"So, I will not treat you spiritually. You had better do it the material way, with a doctor. I recommend you to Dr. Toledo. He is a good friend of mine and he will operate on you."

This woman knew what she was talking about as she was a nurse, apart from being a spiritualist. She herself brought me to the doctor's house. He was a real doctor; in him I did have faith.

"This is a contagious disease," the doctor said.

"It can't be," I said. "I know I haven't done anything with anybody else. That is for sure. I know what I did!"

"All right," he says. "The thing is I am going to give you a shot of penicillin." He put fifteen hundred units of penicillin into me and with that I felt well. Nothing hurt any more and the pus even stopped coming out. So I said to the doctor, "Say, I'm better now . . . why operate?"

"This is just preparatory," he said. "You are not going to get well just with that. Come on, I'm going to cut off your member."

That really scared me. "Better kill me!" I said. How could I know he was joking?

"Come on," he said, "I'm only going to give it a treatment."

Whew! What pain! They did it on the raw. They scraped it with a razor. I thought I wouldn't be able to stand it, but the nurse gave me some pills and the pain left.

Five days later it was time to operate. To the military hospital! I borrowed three hundred *pesos* from *don* Prosperino to pay for a place there. It was the first time I had ever been in a hospital. Well, I began to feel very sorry for myself. "What did I come here for?" I thought. Now there was nothing to be done. They had already readied me and I did want to get well. Whew! They operated on three of us. One died, the other didn't, and I also didn't. But I had a higher fever than the others. The doctor said, "Well, well, old fellow, you are scared, aren't you? That's why you are having such a high fever."

The nurses were keeping me on a strict diet. They prescribed only chicken. Not so bad! My wife stayed with me. The nurse told me that it was a circumcision they did on me, because my member was all clogged up, with the disease on top of it.

I think that what I had was a scratch which got infected from having made use of my wife. My blood became poisoned because I did it so much. I know that the women I had were clean; they were all women of the village. Besides, I am certain it was not something I caught because it was over a month since I had done anything with other women. I had just left my job as judge and that is why I wasn't going out, not even to walk in the street, because I was afraid. I said to myself, "Someone must have it in for me for something. I won't go out until things cool off a little." And I didn't go out. That is how I know my illness wasn't contagious.

CHAPTER XXI

ESPERANZA

Family Problems

Pedro has always had a bad temper. He scolds for everything and rarely says an affectionate word, not even to his children. When they were little he would hug them and say nice things to them, but not now any more. He hardly speaks to them, except to scold or tell them to do this or that. He loads them with work and doesn't like to see them rest. He takes care of them, yes, the way he takes care of his mule, so they can keep on working.

The boys sometimes get angry and tell me, "He hardly ever works. Only we work and he does nothing." They are right, too. Pedro almost never goes to the fields any more. All he does is arrange cases in Cuernavaca. He goes with someone who is suing or being sued, to see a judge or a lawyer or even the Governor.

The other day, Felipe woke up angry and didn't say good morning to his *papá* because he remembered the scolding Pedro gave him the night before. It was about the mule. Felipe took the mule to work and when they returned, the animal lay down on the ground. This mule is very tricky and refuses to eat or drink when he is tired. Pedro thought the animal was sick so he asked Felipe what the mule had eaten and if anything had happened.

But Felipe was on strike and wasn't speaking to his *papá*. He was still angry because of a quarrel they had had and he didn't answer.

Right off, Pedro got angry and began to scold. He even hit Felipe because that one wouldn't say one word. The boy is made of stone! Even if he were dying, he wouldn't speak.

The next day the mule was fine and Pedro told Felipe to take the animal to work again. Felipe didn't want to and Pedro began to get angry. My poor little son! With all that Pedro said to him the night before, how would he want to take the mule again?

But I said, "Come on, son, saddle the mule. Don't be angry with your *papá* any more. You know how he is." And I myself began to saddle it. With my tears and little pushes, Felipe finally went off with the mule.

When Conchita went away, she left her dog here. The dog always goes out with Pedro and even accompanies him to the field. One night Pedro came home very angry. It was late and he said, "I have had my supper. Just feed the dog."

"Very well," I said, and I got up to warm the dog's supper. In a little while, Pedro says, "Have you fed the dog yet?"

"I am still warming it."

Then he got angry and began to say mean things to me. "You're a bad one. You don't want to feed my dog. I am the only one in this house who loves him and you want to kill him by starvation. If I weren't so tired I would get up and make you suffer for what you are doing."

That's the way he is, always getting angry.

Ever since we were married, Pedro has demanded that I wait up for him at night, with the candle burning. If he finds me asleep he scolds me, saying, "Lazy one, it is not so late that you must sleep." If I put out the light and lie down, he gets angry. "Now you don't care whether I come home or not!" If I protest about his coming so late because I must get up at four o'clock in the morning to grind the corn and make the *tortillas*, he says, "Why don't you lie down? Why do you have to wait up until I arrive?"

He must always be scolding. I say, "With you, I don't know what I am supposed to do! You get angry at everything, either because I do something or because I don't do it."

When the children were little, they would wait for their *papá* to come home and when they saw him coming, they would begin to shout, "*Mamá, mamá,* here comes *papá!*" Then they would run to meet him and hug him. But Pedro would push them aside. "Get away, you are blocking my path," he would say.

By the time he entered the house, he was already angry. "So you are spying on me with the children! You send them out so they can shout and let you know when I am coming. What is it you want to hide? With the children outside and you here inside, who knows what you are doing!"

Once in a while, if Pedro has money, he buys us clothing when he is in Cuernavaca. He says to me, "Here, I brought you this shawl; do you like it?"

I have to say I like it even though it is not so. One time I said, "I don't like what you brought me," and he got angry and said, "If you don't like it, throw it away. I won't buy you anything again, ungrateful one." That's why I have to say I like whatever he brings. The only thing I can do is not put it on. But then, at times he will say, "Why don't you use that shawl I brought you? Go on, get it." And I have to to put it on.

Sometimes he takes me to Cuernavaca to buy me a dress. He says, "Go on, tell me which one you like most." I tell him but he says, "No, that is very ugly. This one is better." He shows me the one he likes and that is the one he buys.

Pedro has always fooled around with women. I say that I'm not very jealous, but it does make me angry to see him do that. My cousin Gloria is angry because she says that I am too jealous and that I seem rich just because I have a husband. She says she even prays to God that my husband dies, because I act badly toward people.

Once Pedro went to Xochimilco to sell some peppers and tomatoes he had bought in Oacalco. People said to me, "He's got so and so," a woman from a *barrio* in the center. I told them, "It doesn't make any difference to me. Just so he supports me he can do what he pleases." But inwardly I was very angry.

That woman even came to the house to get him, and he told me, "Give her something to eat." I was nursing the baby so I said, "I can't move now. I can't stop. Why don't you get it for her?" Then he gave her some food and she went away, but she realized that I was very displeased. Then I told Pedro, "I don't want this woman to enter my house. Although I'm poor, I won't consent to having your mistresses come here."

He said, "Do you think I told her to come here? She came to look for a basket I had to leave at her brother-in-law's house."

"So you're even carrying her baskets for her now," I said. I was very angry and even became ill. He promised that the woman would never again enter the house. And so it was. She never came back.

He had another woman whom he was going to marry when he was a boy. But she married another man. After I married Pedro, she would scold me every time I passed by her house. Later I saw the letters she wrote him. He had left them out, believing that since I don't know how to read I wouldn't notice. I hid them. Later he asked, "Didn't you see some papers I left here? You took them, didn't you?"

I answered, "I don't even know how to read. What would I be doing with your love letters?"

Later his cousin came and I asked her to read me the letters and they really were from that woman. In one letter she asked him when they were going to go to Yautepec to live together. It seems he told her they would go sometime. Once she went to wait for him in a certain town. From there she wrote, saying, "I am waiting for you. Come soon." But he didn't want to go and he used the pretext that he had to finish a job.

That woman also scolded my children when they passed by her house. When they told their *papá* about it, he said, "I am going to talk to her husband and if he doesn't call her to order, I know another means of silencing her mouth."

Sometimes Pedro and I have quarrels and he hits me and I get angry. When I am very angry, I become ill. Then I don't know what to do. I want to shout as though I were drunk and soon my stomach hurts me. When I am that angry with Pedro, I don't speak to him for a week or so. My left arm trembles and becomes paralyzed. When Pedro tells me I am an Indian, or a *burra* and that he shouldn't have married me because I can't earn money like intelligent women, like Gloria or Eulalia, then my arm trembles more. Then I feel something like a bird flying in my breast. I feel the wings beating and hitting me inside my breast.

We always sleep together but when I am angry I don't let him touch me. He says, "My anger soon leaves me but you keep yours a long time. I go to the field and everything is forgotten and I have nothing against you any more. But you keep it all in; you are very Indian!" Then he begins to threaten me by saying he will look for another woman and leave me.

I don't answer him because I am still angry.

Once, Pedro beat me very hard and that time I resented it because he almost drove me out of the house. He wanted to give some rope to the widow Eulalia, a neighbor, saying that he and other neighbors were going to make rope for her because she was very poor and didn't have anyone to help her. However, I knew that Eulalia and he were lovers and this matter of helping her was only a pretext. Pedro had a sister in Cuernavaca who was very poor and whose sons had abandoned her. Pedro never thought of helping her, not even with one *cuartillo* of corn!

Pedro would see Eulalia every day. He went from the court to her house. He said to me, "Tomorrow I am going to make the rope for *doña* Eulalia." I answered, "Better make it right now." But immediately we quarreled over her. He understood that I was angry and then he said to me, "I am a man and I can do what I like. You have to watch yourself because you are a woman." And he began to scold me. Soon he hit me, very angrily, then he left.

In a little while he came back. I began to grind corn and without saying anything I served him his meal. Then he said to me, "Who asked you for a meal? Do you think I don't have a place to go to eat." He grabbed the plate and threw it at me, beans and all, and he scattered the *tortillas* on the floor. Then he came over to me and said, "Aren't you going to pick up the beans and eat them? Now I suppose you are really angry. Well, as soon as you don't like it you can go somewhere else, because here I am the boss. I can do whatever I wish. If I want I can bring the other woman here and you would have to attend us both. Go on, get out!"

He left, but after a long while he came back and said to me, "I've thought of a better way. I am the one who will leave. I know where I am going and with whom and it's none of your business. You are in your home, you are rooted here, you have your sons here. You remain and I will leave and it's none of your business what I do."

When we quarrel, my sons do not say anything, poor little things. When they want to defend me, he says to them, "Don't you mix in this! I am the father and you don't know what we are quarreling about." My sons, poor little things, don't answer. When he scolds them, I don't interfere either because he gets angry. He says, "Don't you interfere because I am the one who bosses and if you mix in, I'll give you a clip."

When the boys ran away from home and went to Cuernavaca, this is the way things stood: I had asked Pedro to take us to the fair of Tepalcingo, but he said he had no money, that he had already borrowed money from *señor* Prosperino and if he took me he would have to borrow more. But then he said he was going to take Eulalia and that made me very angry.

Later, Eulalia came to the house and said I had not received her well but that's a lie. I was washing. Pedro was in the yard. Eulalia said she came to find out if Pedro was going to take her to Tepalcingo after all and furthermore she wanted to see if he was going to pay the interest on the 166 *pesos* she had loaned him. I told her Pedro was in the yard and that he had already told us he was going to take her to the fair. Then she went to see Pedro and told him I had received her badly.

Pedro scolded me right away, saying I had been ill-mannered. I said to him, "I didn't do anything to her, I am not going to hug and kiss her. We talked for a while and I told her to sit down and after that she went to see you. I don't know why she says I received her badly."

After that Felipe and Martín started to work, making rope. Martín said to his father, "Are you going after all to Tepalcingo? Why don't you take my mother? And if you aren't going to take my mother, take Macrina."

Pedro got angry and said, "I know when I should take them. Stop asking because it makes me mad. If they want to go alone, let them go. They probably have an appointment with someone. Some man must be waiting for them."

Then Pedro went away, leaving the boys working.

Then Martín asked me, "How many ropes are ours?"

"I don't know, little father. That is your *papá's* affair."

My sons were disgruntled because they had to work Eulalia's ropes without earning a *centavo*. I said to them, "Little fathers, come to breakfast." By that time they had already sprinkled two ropes.

When Pedro came back, he found them not working. He scolded them. "Sluggards who don't wish to work," he said. "Go amuse yourselves. I can do it all alone."

Martín began to unwind the hemp but Pedro took it away from him and wouldn't let them work. Martín took it back from his father about five times but Pedro wouldn't allow him to remove the fibers. "Go and amuse yourselves," he told them. "I can do everything myself. Don't say that I can't do anything. Run along, dress yourselves. It looks like I have young ladies here who aren't fit to work."

He made them change their clothes to go out and amuse themselves. Martín came home and sat down to read the Bible. Felipe, too, took a book to read. Meanwhile Pedro went to work in the yard.

After that Martín wanted to go to bathe in the gulley. I said, "No, *papacito*, it might harm you because you've been working." But he went anyway. Felipe remained reading for a while and then he said to me, "I'm going for a shave." They both left and did not return.

By four o'clock we were running here and there looking for them. Pedro was scolding me. "Why did you let them go? You are very stupid. You're worthless." He had to look for someone to help him twist the ropes but no doubt the boys had told the neighbors something because no one wanted to help him.

I, for my part, was very worried, thinking that something had happened to the boys when they went to bathe. I spent the whole night crying and screaming.

The following day, Eulalia came to rebuke Pedro and to urge him to go to the fair. I had already said to Pedro, "Would you dare go and leave the boys lost?" So he told Eulalia he couldn't because he had to look for the boys. He tried to convince her it was better for them to go to the fair of Matamoros because there he was sure he had a customer who would buy the rope. But Eulalia told him that *don* Enrique was inviting her to go with him to Tepalcingo and that probably she would go with him. Pedro said to her, "Well, you know best, but I am telling you that Matamoros is the better fair."

After that we found the boys. They said they had returned for my sake, because they knew I was suffering.

Pedro decided to go to Tepalcingo to look for Eulalia. Who knows what happened there but he came back from the fair terribly angry. He asked me for some *tacos* and I fixed him some *tortillas* with little *chiles*, onions and other bits. He began to eat, then he said angrily, "You give me fire to eat. No one can eat this stuff. You eat them!"

When Pedro is angry and tells one to do a thing, it is better to do it or he gets worse. I started to eat some *tortillas* and he said, "I'd like to tear you to pieces because you serve me grudgingly."

Then he left and I began to cry and cry. I had a big knot in my throat. When I get like that I have a great desire to scream in despair. But I controlled myself. Instead of screaming it's better to drink water and begin to get calm.

With the departure of the boys for Cuernavaca and the quarrels with Pedro, I got very sick with fever and bad pains in the abdomen. I didn't want to say anything to Pedro for fear of angering him, but he saw that I was very sick. He got angry and said, "When one is ruined everything has to happen to one." After that he took me to the doctor, but all along the road he scolded me. I didn't answer him.

CHAPTER XXII

FELIPE

Problems at Home

My mother began to drink because of the death of a baby daughter
whom she loved very much. When the little girl died (she was about
six months and her name was Sara) my *mamá* cried very much. She
said she missed her baby and she cried day and night. After that she
began to drink, only very little at first and not daily. But then my
father taught her how. When my *papá* would come home from the
fields very tired, he said to my *mamá*, "Prepare a little water and make
me some *ponche* because I am very tired." My mother prepared the
water and made his *ponche* with alcohol and lemon and sugar and she
gave it to him. Then he would say to her, "Don't you want a little?
Take some, if you like."

He would set some apart for her in a little clay jug and the two
of them would drink. But my *mamá* was still strong and stout then, and
no part of her body hurt. My *papá* treated us very well at that time
and meanwhile my *mamá* began to get the habit of drinking. Sometimes even when she didn't want to drink, my *papá* would give it to
her, saying, "I have set some aside for you. Have a drink if you like, but
only here at home. When you drink, close yourself up here in your
house and don't go out."

So my *mamá* began to get the habit of drinking. At first she drank
honey mixed with a little alcohol. Later, my *mamá* began to drink with

more confidence because my *papá* allowed her to; when he saw her half dazed he said nothing to her. Nor would we say anything at the time because she still wasn't drinking very much. But later she began to drink more and more and bought alcohol just for herself.

We didn't say much until we saw that she was spending a lot of money. My *papá* wasn't aware of it because when he came home at night my *mamá* would give him only a little *ponche*, explaining that she had bought little because she had no money. When my *mamá* had no money to buy alcohol, she would sell corn. Then we really got angry because she was no longer taking it as a medicine; it had become a vice and she was spending a lot.

So then we began to tell her to stop drinking because it was very ugly and she said, "But I drink only here in my own house. I don't go walking in the street like other women." And with this she excused herself.

Later the neighbors took my *mamá* for a drunkard. She discredited herself very much. A visitor would come to the house and there was my mother, drinking. She couldn't even talk sometimes and this made us terribly ashamed, because she couldn't pronounce the words clearly and you could smell the alcohol from her mouth. Then I said to her, "Don't drink like this because it's bad for you. Instead of buying alcohol, buy yourself something that will be good for you. Buy yourself some eggs, some milk, some meat. Or buy yourself a little bottle of sherry wine because that won't do you any harm and it will improve your health. But when you buy alcohol and get drunk, you don't even want to eat and this is bad for you, *mamá*. Then you get sick and go to bed and nothing matters to you. Then we are upset and have to spend money to cure you. And all this because of your desire."

But she paid no attention. When my *papá* went out he would come home drunk and my *mamá* would be drunk also. We just watched them. When my *papá* was drunk he didn't look bad because he was a man, but my *mamá* looked awful. It was much worse because she was a woman. It made me very angry but it didn't bother my father. I tried to find a way to stop my *mamá* from drinking. Finally, I told my *papá* that she drank a lot when he was not there and he should tell her to stop. My *papá* said it was a lie. He said, "It's a lie. I never see her drink."

This made me even angrier, but I controlled myself. There was nothing left for me to do but hide the bottle of alcohol. My *mamá* looked for it and sometimes my brothers would tell her I hid it and she asked me for it. Sometimes I would give it to her because I pitied her. But when she asked me for it in anger, I would not give it to her until my *papá* arrived. Then he says, "Why do you hide the bottle?"

"Because my *mamá* drinks so much and to prevent her from drinking, I hide it." He said nothing to me at first and I continued to do this. When my father came home my *mamá* would accuse us of having hid the bottle and would scold my brothers.

Then my *papá* came over and scolded me. He told me, "Look here, Felipe, you are the one who always hides it. Am I not asking you for it? Get going! Give it to me. If you don't, you will see what will happen."

I say to him, "I am not giving it to you."

He says, "Give it to me. Don't think you are talking to your *mamá*."

I tell him, "I already said no. When I say no, it's no."

Then he begins to scold me but I pay no attention. Sometimes I would give the bottle to them after three days or when I saw that they had no money to buy his *ponche*.

Once I remember it was a fiesta day and we bought alcohol to make *ponche* for the guests. After the fiesta there was a little bit left but I didn't know it. Every day I saw my *mamá* drunk early in the morning. Then my brothers told me that a liter of alcohol had been left over. I grabbed the bottle and smashed it against the rocks. Later my *mamá* asked my brothers where the alcohol was. My mother scolded me. She said, "If you don't give me the bottle, I am going to tell your *papá* as soon as he comes home."

I was standing in the street in the gateway to our house, when my father arrived. He went into the kitchen but I didn't follow him. Then he asked for his alcohol and *mamá* told him I had hidden the bottle.

Then my *papá* comes out to me and says, "Felipe, give me the bottle."

"What for?"

"I want it. You are always doing these things with us!" And he began to scold me. Then he said to me, "Don't you understand that you shouldn't be doing this? Don't you know that alcohol costs money? That is why I save."

"*Papá*, it would have been much better to buy other things which are useful. What benefit does the alcohol bring you? Nothing! Why don't you buy something with your money that will be useful. Something that you can eat?"

So he says to me, "Then you're not giving it to me?"

"No!" I say. "And another thing. I am doing something good for you."

Then he says, "So you are going to continue like this?"

I say, "Well, if you continue like this, I believe I will, too."

So he says, "If you don't like it, to the street with you! I have had enough! Don't you know who gives the orders? Is it the son or the father?"

So I say, "Of course, you give the orders. But what I am doing is in your interest. I have told you many times about my *mamá* and you don't believe me."

He says, "I have already told you, if you don't like it here, to the street with you!"

"Very well, then." I couldn't fix things any more. Now he had run me out. I didn't answer. I left. I didn't say good-bye. I just took my little blanket and I left. I went to my sister's house and stayed there about a month. But my father didn't know. I would go to the cornfield to work but I returned to my sister's house where I ate.

My sister said to me, "What can we do? You have to take it. If you were married you could live separately with your wife. But at least quit working for him. After all, he has driven you out. Work on your own. Why don't you work for yourself?"

I say to her, "No, the poor little *milpa*. It is so full of weeds. There is still much to do. When the *milpa* is pretty, one can see the corn grow with a will." I say to her, "How can I leave it? Poor little *milpa*. It makes me sad."

At that time I was weeding the *tlacolol*. The corn was still very young. I worked all alone. I would stand in the middle of the cornfield and look at the weeds and the corn. I was only half through weeding. There was still a lot to do. Well, I became sad. "Is it possible," I thought, "that I can finish this large plot?" It was about fifteen *cuartillos*. Yes, I was sad. My brother was working elsewhere with a team of oxen. I didn't know where my *papá* was working.

My sister said, "Oh, let my *papá* take care of the field. Here you are helping him and he drives you out! He scolds you. You are doing a good deed for them, but they don't understand."

"Well, what can I do? I have to bear it."

"It would be better to work somewhere else. But no matter what happens, I will continue to grind corn for you and to feed you. My husband does not object. He agrees."

So I say to her, "Very well, but it is bad for me to be here this way. I am going to finish the *tlacolol* and then I am going to see what my father thinks. If he really no longer wants me to go back to the house, then I will leave. I will look elsewhere. I will stop working with him. I see that he is tired of having me in the house."

Well, I continued to go to the *milpa*. Then Martín came to work with me. He told me, "*Papá* is going to come. He says he is going to bring *peones* to help with the work."

I say, "Let him come, but don't tell him where I live." He agreed. "Hasn't he asked you where I am?"

"Yes, he asked whether you come to work and I told him yes, and when he asks where you are living, I'll tell him I don't know. I just tell him I see you arrive in the *tlacolol* and I see you go when we leave the fields together."

One day when I came to the field, my brother says to me again, "*Papá* is going to come soon with *peones*."

"Let him come," I said. "I am not afraid. If he wants to scold me, so what. Let him. If he doesn't want me to continue working with him, I will leave."

And my brother says, "Here he comes." Then he arrived. Later in the afternoon, we warmed our *tortillas* together in the fire, and my *papá* says to me, "Eat. Here are some *tortillas*."

And I say, "No. I am carrying my own."

He says, "Where are you staying?"

I say, "Oh, I am around."

"But where are you? At your sister's house, or where? Why don't you come home?"

I say, "No." But as the *peones* were there he said nothing more to me. When we finished working, he said to me, "Come on, let's go home." We left the *milpa* together and walked together on the path. But later on I began to separate myself from them and little by little I remained farther behind while my brother and father walked ahead with the *peones*. Then I took another road so that he shouldn't think I was at my sister's house. I waited until it became dark before going to her house.

I didn't go to see my mother during this whole month, but I did ask my brother Martín and my sister Macrina about her. Macrina would secretly give me *tortillas*. She would bring them to Conchita's house. She would bring my coffee, too. Sometimes Macrina would say to me, "Come home to eat, but hurry before he comes. He went to Cuernavaca."

And so I would go running home to eat. Once Macrina came at night and said, "*Papá* is not at home now. He went to the plaza with *mamá*. Come on and have supper."

"Good. I will come soon."

I entered my house. It was already late, eight o'clock at night. I sat down and she gave me supper. Then I put my nephew Germán outside as a guard. I said to him, "Stay there in the gateway and when

you see them coming, let me know, so that I can run out through the *corral*." The boy would play outside in the yard and every once in a while I would say to him, "Are they coming?"

"No," he would say, "they are not coming."

And there I was having my supper. I had finished eating, and was talking with Macrina and my brother Moisés. And then about an hour later I heard my *papá* speaking outside. He had already entered the patio so I ran out of the small door which led to the other side of the *corral*. I got out just as they entered the kitchen. They must have heard my footsteps.

"Who was here?" says my *papá*.

"No one."

"Wasn't it Felipe?" said my father. "Why is he hiding? Why does he run out? I am going to scold him. Tell him to come in."

"But it wasn't Felipe. It was Moisés."

"Well," said my father, "in that case there is nothing we can do. Don't you know where Felipe is?"

She says, "No, I haven't seen him. I don't know where he is."

He says, "Ah, well, I wonder where he can be."

Meanwhile I was listening to all this hidden out there among the banana trees. And when I heard him go out, I ran through the orchard, jumped over the stone wall and went on to my sister's house.

My sister says, "*Papá* told me he is going to come to look for you. He is spying on you to see if you are hidden here."

But I put myself on the alert. And, yes, he came to look for me. When I saw him walking up the street I hid myself behind the wall of the house in the patio, and as he went into the house without looking behind it I had time to run away. He looked all through the house.

"Isn't Felipe here?"

"No, not here," my sister answers. "Why?"

"Well, it has been a long time since he has been home. It is almost twenty days. I was told that he has been around here but I don't see him. Why doesn't he come home? Why does he hide? Is he afraid that I will scold him? It is over now. My anger has passed. After all they are my sons. I have to forgive them."

My sister says, "Why did you scold him?"

"Oh, for something or other. Because he hid the bottle of alcohol and when I asked him for it he wouldn't give it to me, so I ran him out. After all, you know how your brother Felipe is."

My sister says, "Ah! You ran him out."

"Yes, I said it, but I really didn't think he would go away."

So she says, "Well, I don't see him."

He says, "But if he comes, tell him to come back to the house. I don't want him to stay here."

My *mamá* had also come to look for me, and my brothers said she cried a lot for me. Once she came to my sister's house and I wasn't there. As she was leaving, I arrived and we met at the door. She says, "Ah, my little son! Where have you been? I haven't seen you for a long time and I have been looking for you everywhere."

And she took me by the hand and said, "Well, now we are going home."

I said to her, "No!"

She says, "Let us go. Let us go." And she held my hand more firmly now. She says, "Now I won't let you go. We must go back to the house." She was dragging me.

I say, "But what do you want me to do? My *papá* has run me out. If I come home now, my *papá* will say that I have given in. I will only yield if it is worth while. For a good reason, yes. If I submit it will just make him more bossy with me. Then he will scold me for any little thing."

She says, "But, son, you know how your *papá* is. Forgive him. I was also drunk at the time. Why, I even scold myself sometimes because I drink. I don't know why, but I drink. But now, for your sake, I will make a special effort not to drink. I admit that it is my fault." She began to berate herself and said, "How stupid I am. But let us go to the house. Your *papá* won't scold you any more."

There she was dragging me home and I no longer resisted. So we went home together and she fed me. She says, "Eat. Haven't you eaten?"

I say, "Yes, I have eaten."

She says, "But where were you? I was looking for you everywhere. Were you at your sister's house?"

I say, "Yes, I was there."

I am grateful to my sister Conchita because when my *papá* threw me out, or if anything happened, I would go to her house and she accepted me without saying anything. She would hide me from my *papá*. She gave me food and never said she didn't want me there. She protected us and always respected our rights. Her husband, Juan, also treated me well. I have nothing against them, they were always nice to me.

When I was wrong about something, I would recognize my error even if my *papá* didn't say anything. I knew what to do before he said anything and I would try to correct myself, working harder, hauling water, going to the woods for firewood, hurrying all the while. Upon returning, I would get busy with something else. The fact is, even if my *papá* didn't scold me I punished myself. I was angry with myself and would take it out in work.

Once I went to take a walk through the center of town and met up with a friend. It was about five in the afternoon, and we got together with my cousin Pablo who plays the guitar. We were invited to the house of one of his friends and once there they began to sing and drink, though I would not drink. Then another cousin of mine, Víctor, came and we were invited elsewhere. I didn't want to go because they were going to drink and it was already about ten in the evening. But my cousin said to me, "Let's go for a short time. Come with us even if you don't drink."

"Well, I'll keep you company for a while, but then I'm leaving."

When we got there they sang *"Las mañanitas"* on the doorstep, then we went inside. They served *ponche* but I wouldn't take any. By midnight I was very sleepy. At about a quarter to one we left, and once in the street one of them said, "Now we are going someplace else, nearby."

"Well," I said, "if you want to go, I'll leave you here. I'm not going to stay up until dawn while you get drunk. I have far to walk and I'm leaving now."

They went to a house in another *barrio* and I went home. When I got to the corner of the plaza, I stopped to hear the hour toll. It was one o'clock. In those days there was a guard detachment at the municipal building. People were free to go about in the streets until midnight, but after that they would call to anyone passing by the *palacio* and if he didn't answer they would shoot at him. I was afraid, and to avoid going near the *palacio* I went in a roundabout way through another *barrio* and past the public washing place. It is said that ghosts and *nahuals* frighten people around there, but I saw nothing. The devil is also said to come out on the bridge, disguised as a bull or a *charro*. He gets in your way and doesn't let you pass. I went past all these bad places but only dogs followed me. My *mamá* and my *papá* were waiting up for me and they scolded when I got home. I said nothing because I knew they were right.

Another time, I stayed out all night. It was the Day of the Dead and I went for a stroll at about five o'clock in the afternoon. I got together with some boys and they invited me to the house of the boy whom my sister Macrina was marrying. Later we walked through the streets of all the center *barrios*. We spent the whole night walking. By the time I got home it was six in the morning. I hadn't slept at all and I had to work the next day. My *mamá* was already grinding corn for the *tortillas* I would take to work. My father was angry. "You didn't come home last night. Aren't you going to work?" I didn't reply. I just kept quiet.

Then my *mamá* said, "Why didn't you come home, son? I was awake, waiting for you the whole night, but you didn't come." I just kept quiet. "You are not going to work today!" she said, but I told her I was.

She began to wrap my *tortillas* while my *papá* scolded me. "Where were you? Where did you go? And why didn't you come home all night? What time is this to go to work?" But I said nothing, because I recognized my mistake and my guilt. My *mamá* gave me coffee and *tortillas*. I took my shoulder bag and went to gather hay in my uncle Remigio's *milpa*. Thus, without having slept, I managed to work the whole day. At times, I fell asleep without realizing it. I vaguely remember working, not completely aware of what I was doing. When I got home in the evening my *papá* didn't say anything else to me because he wasn't angry any more.

By then I didn't like my father to scold or hit me. He wouldn't hit me any more; he just yelled at me or ran me out of the house even if I hadn't done anything wrong. Then I would get angry, because he scolded me just for the sake of scolding. Sometimes when I was feeling happy, he would suddenly come in and begin yelling at me and I didn't know why.

The scoldings went on daily. I tried to work as hard as I possibly could, just to keep him pleased with me, but he kept scolding me over any little thing. I felt like working day and night to please him. That's why I was almost never at home. I went to work in Cuernavaca or at times in a little town called Ixtepec, where I stayed. I went home every third day or at the end of every week. That way I was better off. I ate in peace. When I eat at home and my *papá* begins to upbraid me, I lose my appetite. Sometimes I ate secretly so that my *papá* didn't know about it or see me.

My *mamá* would say to me, "Go ahead and eat, son, while your father is not here. Eat quickly before he comes, because once he is here he won't even let you eat, yelling so much!" If my *papá* arrived while I was eating I wanted to stop, but my *mamá* would say to me, "Don't stop, son, keep on eating. Don't be afraid." I remained seated but stopped eating, even if I was hungry. Then I would get up when he wasn't looking and leave quietly.

When my *papá* ate with my brothers, I would go to the *corral* or out to the street and think of all the suffering I had to go through. The tears would begin to roll down. Sometimes I felt like a stranger living in that house.

Once I even told my *papá* how I felt. I said, "It seems to me that you treat me like a stranger. I feel like I don't belong here. I am even sorry to be in your house, that's why when I go to work in the fields I don't want to return. You scold me so much, and I don't even know the reason why. Sometimes I come home happy, not thinking about anything, but you get here and begin to yell at me. Sometimes you make me think bad things, things I shouldn't think. You force me to answer back but I don't. Even if you beat me, I don't talk back to you! My brother Martín talks back to you when you scold him, and yet you say nothing to him. But I, who never say anything, you scold more, and if I do reply, you say I'm ill-behaved.

"Clothing I never ask you for, nor *huaraches*. Never! Nor for haircuts, or a *sombrero*. You never give me money for a fiesta, nor do I ask. When I have no money for a haircut, I get one on credit because I feel bad asking you for it. If I were a drunk, or lazy, and did nothing but bum around in the streets, you would be right. When I haven't got clothing or *huaraches* or anything that I need, I go to work to buy it, but when my brother Martín asks you for money, you give it to him. When you scold me rightfully, I say nothing and am even happy. I don't get angry because you have the right even to beat me."

Once, in the month of October, I left early with the horse to bring fodder from the *milpa*. I hurried in order to get back home early. When I got to the *milpa*, I began to cut the corn fodder very fast and finished quickly. I gathered a few ears of corn for us to eat at home, then got on my horse and there I go. I arrived home early, about four in the afternoon, very pleased.

My *papá* was waiting for me at the door. "I'm home already," I said, but he didn't answer me. He came over to me while I was still on the horse, and right off, began to yell at me. I got down to unload the horse and then I tied it up. My *papá* followed, all the while yelling at me. "If you want to work then stay, if not, say so. If not, you know what you can do. I have told you many times, but you don't understand. You always do what you fancy but not with me!"

I just looked at him and said, "But what is it? Tell me, because I don't know why. I came home happy, I didn't say anything to you or think anything, and I know I have done nothing to be scolded for."

"It doesn't matter," he said. "If you want to stay here, you can, otherwise, get out. I wasn't born with sons, I was born alone. You can stay here if you want to, but now you will have to pay ten *pesos* a day for what you eat, or at least five. From now on you pay for what you eat, if not, there are no meals. I'm going to tell your *mamá* not to give you anything to eat unless you pay ten *pesos* daily. I'm tired of paying the kitchen expenses. You never ask if we need money here."

"But I have nothing! What can I give you if I have nothing?" I said.

"Well, then, into the street! There's no food here. Go and look elsewhere to eat."

My half-sister María, who was in the house, heard everything and told *mamá* later, "Poor little Felipe, his father is scolding him terribly. He treats him as if he weren't his son. Poor Felipe! And the boy doesn't say anything, just keeps quiet. He was right when he told me his father scolds him a lot, but I didn't believe it until now. I see it's true. Doesn't he feel bad about treating his son that way?" My *mamá* was making *tortillas* and María said to her, "Why don't you defend him?"

"I can't mix in because his *papá* will only get angry. That's why I never intervene when he scolds them. Then he says I am the children's *alcahuete*. If I answer back, it's worse."

Then María says, "In my home, the father of my children also scolds but he never talks about charging them for food! *Don* Pedro doesn't realize his children are grown-up and they are hurt by what he says. Some day they will get fed up and leave him. Then he is going to be all alone. The boys are already grown and yet they endure the way their *papá* treats them. They are good boys, they aren't run-arounds or drunks, they have no vices, and still *don* Pedro is not pleased."

"But he mostly scolds my son Felipe," said my *mamá*. "When I die, who knows what's going to happen here or where my poor little son will go!"

And my sister María said, "It would be better if he got married and went away. That way he will avoid suffering. It's good that he is a hard worker; that way he won't have trouble with his wife."

I stood in the doorway, not even sitting down to rest. I just stood there, thinking of what my father had said to me. I wondered where I could go. Now my *papá* is charging me for food and I have no money. I was hungry but my father had just denied me food. I felt like a stranger there, displaced, powerless, the only one with no rights. In these moments, while standing there, everything began to make sense to me. I thought, "Am I a son here or not? Why does he treat me this way? Why is he most mean to me. Only he knows whether I am his son or not."

I couldn't bear the strong grief I felt and I wanted to cry but tried to control myself. I felt the tears rolling down my face but held them back, not to cry in front of my father. But I felt as if I weren't on this earth. I thought a great many things in those moments. I thought about leaving, but I said nothing of this. Instead, I told my *mamá,* "I'll be back right away. I'm just going to the corner."

"Yes, but first eat something, then go," she said.

"No, I'll be back soon," I said to her.

"You won't come before nightfall. Better eat now and then go," she told me.

"I won't take long; I'll be right back."

I took my blanket and left. Within my heart I said good-bye to my home. "I'm leaving, I don't know if it will be forever or only for a few days." Then I went to visit all my aunts. I began with the nearest *barrio* and then went to the others. There they fed me. I went to my sister Conchita's house and slept there. I hung around about three days, then I went to Ixtepec to work for a man named Donato Gómez.

I arrived there by nightfall, and went in and said hello to the *señora*. "Good evening, *doña* Valentina."

"What a miracle that you came, Felipe," she said.

"Well, I just came to visit."

"Good, come in."

I entered and she offered me a chair to sit down. Then we began talking, but I felt a sorrow in my heart, a hurt feeling, because although I had a father and mother I had to ask for shelter in another's house and look at other faces. But I didn't say what my heart felt, and she asked if I could help them with the work.

"Don't you have time to help us, Felipe?" she said.

"Of course. I'll do whatever you say."

"Well, you can clean and shell the corn, then you can work in the fields," was her answer.

I began right then to help them shell corn. We finished at about eight in the evening, and afterward we ate supper.

Señor Gómez said to me, "Do you want to stay and work for us? Because we have a lot of work."

"If you want me to, I'll stay," I said.

"You can help us until we finish harvesting." I agreed, and there I stayed, but I never told them that I had been thrown out of my house. Well, I continued helping them until we finished, and they paid me six *pesos* a day plus room and board.

Once I got ill and they took care of me so that I was able to keep on working. When the harvesting was over, we cleared the fields for planting and we carried firewood on horseback. On Sundays I would go to Azteca to walk in the plaza and from the plaza I would walk back. But I never went home. And so I continued for about three months, only asking neighbors of my village how everything was at home. Some of them would tell me my *mamá* cried a lot because she did not know where I was. She asked for me but no one told her anything. I thought about this, and went to my sister Conchita's house to tell her I was at Ixtepec working, but that she shouldn't tell my *papá*, just my *mamá*, so that she wouldn't keep on crying. Then I went back to where I was staying and remained there until all the work was finished.

Then *señora* Gómez said to me, "Look, Felipe, we have finished now. You have helped us and I'm very grateful because you have worked honestly, not like others who do well in the beginning, then start with their tricks and stealing. You have stayed here a long time and we haven't missed anything."

"One doesn't gain anything by stealing," I said to her.

"Well, Felipe, many thanks, and don't forget to come and visit us, because you have been good with us," she said.

"Yes, I'll come back often to visit you. Many thanks, and good-bye." Then I left for home.

I arrived there at about eight in the evening and when I entered, my *mamá* was seated by the hearth, keeping warm near the fire. My brothers were there, too. My sister Macrina was making *tortillas* for supper. My *papá* wasn't in. When my *mamá* saw me she got up quickly, embraced me and kissed me on the cheeks. She started to cry. "*Ay*, my little son, you have come! I said you would never come again because you stayed away so long. Where were you that you never came? Where did you eat, who fed you? I waited for you every day. I would say, 'See if my son is coming.' I waited day and night, saying to myself, 'If he doesn't come during the day, he'll come at night.' Every day I thought and asked about you. Then I lost hope. But I blame your father because he always behaves like a crazy man, scolding you for no reason at all. But you know how he is by now. He gets angry, but it passes right away and he speaks nicely to us again. You shouldn't have paid attention to him, you shouldn't have gone."

I answered, "Now I feel more at ease in someone else's house than here. There, if they say anything mean to me, at least I know it's not my home. But here in my own home, even though I work hard, my father scolds me, charges me for the food, and throws me out! Naturally I feel bad, worse than if I were a stranger. I feel like an outsider here, as if this were not my home."

Then my *papá* came, and I was very much afraid when I saw him enter, thinking he would beat me out of the house. But he didn't, and instead he said, "My son has come! You finally came, son!"

I said, "Yes," and then I embraced him and kissed him on the face.

"I thought you wouldn't come back. Where were you, why didn't you return?" he said.

"Well, I am working in order to buy clothing, because I had none. Now that I have bought some, I came to find out whether you still think the same about what you told me. If you do, I'll leave right away. I just came to find out. Don't worry about me. If you tell me to go, I'll leave right away. And don't think I'll take anything, not even a blanket. You can sell it or burn it. You know what you are doing. If you tell me to take off the clothing I have on, I'll do so and leave without even my *huaraches*, so you won't say I took anything from here. I have no rights to anything here. You are the only one who has rights here since this is your house. You paid for it. And don't think that I'll be angry if you cast me out. No, I can't be angry with you because you are my father. I can have no rancor toward you."

"Well, forgive me for what I said. I had been drinking a little too much. I had one drink and it went to my head. You know when one is angry one doesn't know what one says."

"You don't have the courage to tell me when you are sober, but you get brave when you are drunk. How nice! When you are sober, you should back up what you say when you are drunk. I can take it. Just tell me to go and I'll go immediately," I said.

"But where can you go and what will you do?" he asked. "Stay, and forgive me if I said anything to you. You know me by now. I get angry but soon I'm all right again. It passes."

"Look," I answered, "I see you get angry because I won't allow my brothers to order me around. You gave my brother Martín the right to dictate to us all, but how can you expect me to do what he says when I'm the oldest? It's impossible that he should boss me! Let him boss my brothers who are younger than he. He has a right to tell them what to do, but not me. You yourself have said my name was not on your list, that I was no more than a *peón*, that you can't depend on me for anything. When you have business to arrange, you and my brother Martín do it together. I am not even told about it. When I ask about it, you just make fun of me. When you go to rent land for planting, you two attend to it. You won't even tell me what you are arranging. All I do is look on. Well, if you want to do all the business by yourselves, do all the work also. I'm going to work elsewhere. Am I good only to work the land? Why do you want to treat me like a child, you doing all the business and I just working!"

It was toward the end of April in 1953 when I again had a little trouble with my father. In those days I was desperate. I had no money at all and no clothes. I didn't like being without money. I always liked to have at least five or ten *pesos* in my pocket. So when one of our neighbors asked me to help him bring hay to the *hacienda*, I wanted to go. I told my *papá* that night but he said no. "You are not going. Better help your brother put up the new kitchen because the rains will begin soon."

"Very well, *papá*, I won't haul the hay."

The next morning we ate breakfast and I say to my brother, "Which do you want to do, make the mud or the trench for the mortar?"

"It's all the same to me. You make the mud and I will prepare for the mortar."

Fine. I grabbed the shovel and the pickax to scrape the earth and I hauled water to mix it with. Then I beat the mud with my feet. Meanwhile my brother made a trench where the wall was to be built.

"Do you want the mud now?" I asked him.

"No, not yet. I am going to lay the stones in the trench while you go on making the mud. I will let you know when I am ready."

I went on making the mud and every once in a while I asked my brother if he needed it and he said not yet. I was busy with the mud when my cousin Tomás came by. He saw me and stopped to talk for a while but I kept on treading the mud with my feet. My *papá* was lying down reading a paper and my *mamá* was not at home. She had gone to my sister's house to borrow a few *centavos*. My cousin asked me to go out with him, to visit his brother, but I said I couldn't. We kept talking for a while and I think that's what made my *papá* get angry.

"Hurry and give your brother the mud!" he said.

"But he doesn't want it yet," I told him.

He said it again and I answered him again. Then I saw him jump up and come toward me. "I told you to give your brother mud because he hasn't any." I just kept looking at him. My pants were rolled up and my feet were covered with mud up to my knees and I kept looking at him. That made him mad.

"Now why do you keep looking at me?"

"So I am not free to look at you?"

He stood in front of me, with the shovel in his hand. I thought he was going to knock me down with it but no, he pushed my face with his hand. I didn't flinch. I just waited for him. I felt the palm of his hand on my cheek and I fell face down but I didn't know yet that my eye had burst. I felt something hot and when I stood up I felt something like warm water on my face and in my mouth. It was blood. My whole face was running with blood and I saw something like the white of egg going down my cheek. At that moment I became very angry and I said, "Look, *papá*, since you don't want me to look at you any more why don't you kill me once and for all? You don't want to see me nor do you want me to look at you, so kill me!"

"And why do you say that to me?"

"I know why I am saying it, but do it right now, right now. If you don't do it I will do it myself!"

I washed my feet quickly in the pail of water and ran into the house, with the blood running down my face. I knew there was a knife in the chest at the head of the bed. I wanted a weapon to get rid of my anger on myself. I pushed open the chest and grabbed the knife but my *papá* came and pulled me from behind.

"What are you going to do?"

"Let go of me. Leave me alone. Nothing will happen to you. Let go!"

He held me fast and I shook him loose and jumped up on the chest, still holding the knife. I didn't hit him, I didn't do anything except try to see that he didn't touch me. When he saw that he couldn't hold me, he called my brother Martín to help him. So the two of them grabbed my arms and tried to get the knife. But I shook them off and threw them aside. When I was free I tried to take advantage of my opportunity but someone ran up to me and didn't let me. They called Moisés to help them and I kept yelling, "Let me go, let me go. I know what I am going to do. Nothing will happen to you. Don't be afraid. Let me go."

They couldn't hold me and my aunt Gloria came in and she too grabbed hold of me. All four of them couldn't hold me. I threw them all off. I was so angry I couldn't bear it. Just then my *mamá* came and she began to cry and to embrace me. I thought, "She is my mother and I respect her." She was not well and I didn't want her to strain herself. When she tried to hold me back I didn't do anything any more. They put me to bed and then I felt the pain of my eye. In a little while they went to call the doctor. He brought me an injection and pills. I don't know what medicine he gave me to calm me.

Later Conchita came to see me. "What happened?"

"You already know what my life here is. My *papá* cannot look at me. Now he hit me with his hand and burst my eye."

"While you stay here you will always suffer. Resign yourself."

I stayed in bed and didn't say anything after that. I heard my *mamá* making the *tortillas* in the kitchen. She was scolding my *papá*. He was talking to Martín and saying, "It's a pity there is no revolution now so I could go and join it. Because the truth is I am desperate. That's why I hit your brother. He gets angry with me and when I hit him he is worse. With what happened here, he is going to be still worse."

"Now he will treat me like an enemy," I thought. "If he does, well, he'll see. But in any case, I am going to consider him as an enemy."

I slept that night because they gave me a pill. The next day my *papá* told Martín to get a doctor to treat me but my brother paid no attention and went out for the day. I had a strong pain in my head and my eye. It hurt me very much. My uncle Margarito came and cried when he saw me. I told him all that had happened, the how and the why of it.

He says, "Well, as he is your father, there is nothing you can do. Whatever he does is good and you should never tell him anything.

While you are here you must bear it. But aren't they going to cure your eye now?"

"Who knows? I am waiting for the doctor to come again but no one went to call him."

"Well, what can we do? If I help you, your *papá* will get angry. He will say that I am giving you bad advice. I had better not. Let's see how it goes with you."

He left but in a little while he sent me a cup of milk and two pieces of bread. That night I was the same. The doctor didn't come. My head hurt so much I couldn't eat. I couldn't move my mouth because my teeth hurt. Later, without telling anyone, I left quietly and went to Conchita's house. I told her they were not curing me and she said, "If they don't cure you it will get worse. You will get a *cáncer* in the head and there is no cure for that. Look, I will help you but we mustn't tell anyone. Juan will take you to the hospital very early tomorrow, without anyone knowing."

I was afraid that in the hospital they would operate on me, but in order to get better, I agreed. My brother-in-law couldn't go with me because he had to work, so he brought me to my uncle Margarito's house and at five o'clock in the morning my uncle and I took the bus to Cuernavaca. In the hospital they put my eye back into the socket and sewed it up. They forced me to tell how it happened. I told them everything and I said I wanted justice. Then my parents came, my *papá* scolding me and my *mamá* crying and embracing me. My *papá* wanted to take me home but the doctor said he couldn't because I was still in the hands of the Public Court of Justice. An accusation had been made against my *papá* and he tried to defend himself but he couldn't. The doctor told him to keep quiet, that it would go badly for him, that it wasn't just a little thing he had done. I kept yelling, "I want justice! I want justice!" They were going to put my *papá* in jail but he hid and only my *mamá* came to visit me about four times that week.

I stayed in the hospital for seven days but I wasn't getting enough attention, so I asked permission to leave and I went home. The next day I went to a doctor who cured me. He fixed up my eye and it was even better than before and since then my *papá* has changed a lot because the Minister of Justice has reprimanded him.

Once my brother Ricardo and I went to work on the sugar *hacienda* cutting sugar cane, because we needed money. I noticed that Ricardo was upset because he had no spending money. It was in the month of February, and I said to him, "If you want to, we can go to the *hacienda* for the cutting season."

"Yes, but I haven't got a *machete* to cut cane with," he said.

"If you want, I'll hurry over to Cuernavaca to buy one and a file to sharpen it." I went and when I returned, I said, "Here's your *machete*." He took it, cleaned it well and sharpened it. Next we went to ask one of my *papá*'s friends, Heraclio Herrera, if he wanted to come with us to cut sugar cane and he said he would go.

When all was settled, I told my *mamá*, "Tomorrow Ricardo and I are going to cut sugar cane. We are leaving at about four in the morning."

"Then I'll get up early to grind corn," she said.

We were up at about three to get ready. We took along our blankets, stopped by for the other man, and we walked to the *hacienda*. It was about eight in the morning when we got there. We went to see the foreman who assigns the work. We told him we wanted work and he apportioned us eight furrows each. My brother and I had never worked at this and we couldn't do it. Heraclio had done this before, but not us. We began working, but no matter how much we rushed we didn't make any headway because we couldn't do it right. We got blisters on our hands but we kept on. Slowly, we caught on to the way of doing it and we began to make big piles of cut cane to load onto the truck. We didn't stop until about two in the morning of the second day, when the first truck arrived and we began to load our cane. By dawn, we had loaded four trucks. When we finished we sat down to eat. Then we began to cut more cane. On the third day we stopped again at about one in the morning to load up. Sleepy and cold, we loaded one truck after another. By dawn, we had loaded six trucks but we were bathed in sweat. We rested a bit and then gathered firewood to heat our *tortillas*. When there was a moon, we would begin to cut at about five in the morning, and we stopped at about eight or ten at night. Then we would make a fire to heat up our *tortillas* for supper and at about twelve at night we would go to bed. Every third day we loaded the trucks with the cane we had cut.

We worked like this for about three weeks, but we didn't continue because they paid too little, two *pesos* per ton of cane. The two of us were making sixty *pesos* a week, sometimes eighty or ninety. But they wouldn't pay for the whole week outright, only for three days at a time. The other three days they withheld for the following week, at which time they paid it, but kept back another three days for the next week. That's why we didn't want to work any more. We went home because it wasn't worth while. Instead, we began to haul firewood because the rainy season was near.

Up to this time, I had worked only in the fields but because my *mamá* was ill I looked for a way to earn more so she wouldn't lack

money, and also to buy myself something. First I was working on tomato cultivation but I saw that I could not earn much there, so one day
I decided to look for work. Without knowing where to go, I told my
mamá, "Tomorrow I want to look for work."

She said, "But why?"

I said, "Well, here I don't earn much and I need to buy things for
you. They told me there is work in Cuernavaca. Over there one earns a
little more. So I will leave on the first bus tomorrow morning."

She says, "Then I will grind early."

She made my *tortillas* early in the morning and then I got up and
went to the terminal and waited for my bus. It was very early and still
dark. A relative of mine was there but we didn't recognize each other
because it was still dark.

He says to me, "Felipe!"

"That is my name," I say. "Who are you?"

"I am Pablo."

"Ah, of course," I say. "I am going to look for work."

He says, "Come to where I am working on the highway, because
they need many *peones.*"

"Do you think they will take me?"

"Yes," he says. "I will speak to the overseer. I will ask him to take
you on."

I say, "How much is the fare?"

He says, "Twenty-five *centavos* a day."

I say, "Fine." Then we went. There were some other people from
the village who were working there and they spoke to him for me. The
boss came and I greeted him.

"Good day, boss. Do you have a little job for me?"

He says, "Of course. Give this boy some work. Give him his
tools."

I began to work. I didn't know how to but I watched the others.
They sent me to work on a hill. It was very dangerous because of the
landslides. I earned ninety *pesos* every two weeks. We began at eight
in the morning and stopped at five o'clock. We worked six days a week,
not Sunday. We stopped at three o'clock on Saturday. When they
finished the stretch my boss was working on, we all said good-bye to
him. Then I passed on to another boss and continued working there.
They finished that stretch and then I went to another place called the
Pear, where the road curves. There one couldn't even move because it
was very dangerous. There were many deaths in these passes. Some
were crushed by landslides or falling rocks, others because the machines
overturned. We had to be careful. We were halfway through the pass
and the sides were one hundred meters high and we were in the mid-

dle. There was a huge rock and the *peones* couldn't push it. The boss was hurrying them and he said, "Get away. Let's see. You can't do it!" he yelled at them.

Then he went up and the *peones* made way for him. He went up on the rock and began to move it, then suddenly the rock rolled over and went down with him. When the *peones* saw the man going, they threw him a rope, but he didn't have time and he went down with the rock. When they got to him he was almost dead. He was all smashed. He just took two breaths and that was all. He was from the village of Santa María. His family came and was given something, I think five thousand *pesos*.

We were very much afraid of this operation because there was machinery above and machinery below and we were between and suddenly a rock or a machine could fall on us. But we continued working. Once my cousins Tomás and Pablo and myself were shoveling earth, a lot of it. I was excavating inside and one of the boys was shoveling the earth over the edge. I was excavating and excavating but they didn't shovel away the earth quickly enough to make room. Then the overseer says to me, "Let one of the boys help you so that the machinery can come closer to work."

So, I say to Pablo, "Help me. I am tired of excavating. I have been excavating for two hours and you can't shovel away the dirt. I have done all I can and now the overseer is pushing us and I can't any more."

And he says, "Let's see. Let me do it."

He came opposite me and I said, "No, don't stand there on the edge because the dirt will go on top of you and will knock you over."

He says, "No. I have plenty of room."

So he digs and digs with his pick and I dig too, but about two meters away. Well, all the dirt fell on him and knocked him over the edge and I yelled, "But I told you not to do it!"

It all went down on him, the rocks, the stones, and the earth and carried him to the bottom. It was about fifty meters high. I thought, "If he gets to the bottom and doesn't stand up, it is because he is dead."

I was watching from above. I saw him get up and run but his head was already split open. I, too, almost went over, but I grabbed my head a little this way and lifted myself upward. I took two steps down because it was very steep, when the rest of the boys yelled, "Be careful. There goes a rock."

I saw a rock come my way, a huge one, and I thought, "I don't have time to get away, neither this side nor that side," but I took another step down. I knew that the falling rocks were going to hit me. When they were close I turned to one side and put my hand up to my face to protect myself. I was scratched when I fell on the rocks but it wasn't much. It tore my ear and it opened up my eyebrow. I felt the earth moving and I wanted to get up and run away but instead I threw myself to one side. Someone said to me, "Stand up," but I couldn't. I felt something swell on my forehead. My hand was full of blood, and my face and my ear.

They took both of us to the hospital in Cuernavaca. I left my tools buried there. When the nurse saw my cousin she said, "You come here first. But wash your hands because they are full of dirt and blood." He washed his hands and face and they treated him. They told me to wash my hands too. I yelled with pain when the water entered the wounds. They began to wash it with peroxide. They cured all my wounds. I screamed. I even cried. They opened the wound on my forehead and used tweezers to get out the dirt. I didn't want them to touch my ear but they grabbed it and opened it, and then I asked for the medical certificate because otherwise they wouldn't pay us.

At the end of the week we went for our pay. We continued to work there until the highway was finished. It was about eight miles. I gave my money to my *mamá*. I always gave it to her. I told her, "Buy whatever you want."

When the work was almost over, an engineer says to me, "Look, I know you. I know how you work. I know what you are like. I want you to come to Poza Rica. You can pick out whatever work you want. If you want, you can be the storekeeper, or the operator's assistant or the checker. You are going to earn more, about thirty *pesos* a day."

I say, "Fine. When are you going to leave?"

"In the middle of the week. If you wish, you can come with us. It doesn't matter how much you spend, the company will pay. If it takes us two or three days to get there, you will be earning without working."

I didn't go because my *mamá* was very ill. Instead, I went to Cuernavaca to look for work. I found it in Chinepa on the same highway. This highway took a long time to make and there I had another accident but they paid me one hundred *pesos* for the week I didn't work.

When my *mamá* was very ill, I went to see my cousin Rodrigo. I went to ask him about a girl. He was a spiritualist, or something like that. He cured sick people and also boys would go there and ask him to do them a favor of getting a certain girl by means of witchcraft. Boys would come, women would come, girls would come. I saw what he did there. He would sit down and put a glass of water on a dish. He covered his head and he covered the dish and would remain that way. His wife would sit at one side and then both of them would begin to pray. He would begin to speak to the saints, to the Virgin, to the apostles. He waited a while, about ten minutes, then he would say, "Come down, Saint Peter, come down, Lord Santiago."

His wife would note the names of the saints that came down. Then he would tell the people who came what they were supposed to do to get what they wanted. So I went once to ask him about this girl.

He said, "Well, let's see. That will have to be private. It will cost three *pesos*."

I say, "Yes."

Then he began. "What is the girl's name?" He wrote it down, Cristina. Then he shouted to a saint, I don't know which one, and told him to come down and tell him what I had to do. There he was talking to the spirit and his wife was writing in a little book. She wrote everything the saint said and when the spirit left, he told her, "*Adiós, adiós,*" and took his leave. About five minutes later, when his head and eyes had cooled off a bit, my cousin uncovered himself and looked at the note-book. "What things did he say?" he asked his wife.

"Well, he said that Felipe should bring flowers and a candle at midnight and at eight in the morning and at noon. He has to pray an Our Father three times and bring a candle. If he can't do it every day, then every third day, but he must bring a candle."

Well, I came no more than once and then I didn't continue. I say, "After all, if Cristina wants to, she will, so why do I have to continue doing this?"

Once my cousin says to me, "Why don't you continue?"

I say, "Because I don't have time."

"Ah, or is it that you don't have faith?"

"If I didn't have faith, I wouldn't have come."

Then he says, "I am going to call to see whether you have faith or not. Even if you don't pay for it."

I say, "Well, go ahead." Then he began again with his glass of water. He began to shout to the saint. And his woman was there writing everything down because he didn't know what the spirit was saying. My cousin only repeated what the spirits told him while his eyes were closed, and he didn't remember anything afterward.

I was listening and his wife was writing. My cousin repeated everything three times. If he didn't hear, he would say, "Excuse me, Saint so-and-so, is this what you said?" and the spirit told him again.

"He is saying that your *mamá* is going to suffer a bad illness," his wife tells me. "Your *mamá* is going to be sick, she is going to die of this. She is going to continue drinking. The vice is going to take hold more strongly and no matter how much you cure her, she will not get better unless she comes here to see me. Then, yes, I will cure her and she will get better. But only if she repents and does everything I tell her. If not, no."

I say, "Well, what does she have to do?"

My cousin says, "She must go to church to confess. She must do everything the church says. If she continues to drink, she will never be cured. Your *papá* should cure her, but because he has big sons who can support him, he depends upon them. So you had better cure her."

Then I kept quiet. I thought, "He is not saying this because the spirit is telling him." I was suspicious because people had told me he had bewitched my *mamá* to make her drink. An aunt of mine, Ágata, told me, it was because he hated my *papá*. She told me everything that Rodrigo had against us, and that he was going to make orphans of us. She said he had done this to my *mamá* fourteen years before, but that it worked little by little, not all at once. Slowly, steadily, the vice took hold of her.

My aunt says to me, "Your *mamá* got this vice because of witch-craft. Your cousin Rodrigo did it to her and that is why he can cure people. He was going to do it to your *papá*, but your *papá* is very strong and it didn't work. Instead it passed to your *mamá*."

I say, "Yes?"

She says, "Yes. I tell you this because we are of the same family but don't go saying I told you. He did it in front of me. Everything! He said in so many years your mother will die. They made a little doll of rags and put it in alcohol and stuck a pin in it on the side of the heart."

"So that is what he is doing!"

She says, "Yes. But don't go saying I told you, because then he will do something to me. Do you swear that you are not going to tell him?"

I say, "Yes."

And she says, "What will you do to prove to me that you are not going to tell him?"

I say, "No. Do you think you are speaking to a stone? I will keep in my heart all you have told me. I am not going around telling others."

She says, "Really? Will you swear?"

I say, "Yes. With me it will go no further."

Then I began to tell my aunt how my mother was feeling, "My *mamá* feels this way. Her heart hurts, then her legs hurt. Then, at times, she gets something like attacks."

"Yes," she says. "Now you know why."

I was about twenty years old when she told me. I didn't get frightened. What I did was get angry and I thought bad things about my cousin. My *mamá* was just beginning to get sick. She was still not very sick. I thought, "If anything bad happens to my *mamá*, he will have to deal with me. Wherever I meet him, I will get him. If I meet him on the street I will say, 'Would you like to have a little beer or some refreshment?' Then I will take him out and get even with him. It doesn't matter if I have to leave the village."

Because my *mamá* was ill, my *papá* got a neighbor's daughter, Eustolia, to work in our house as a servant. I knew her family ever since I was little. They lived over there near my uncle Margarito's house and we played together. Much later we began to love each other and I took advantage of her. The first time I had her, I had just finished bathing and washing my hair when she passed by the yard and saw me rubbing my head with a towel.

"What are you doing?" she says.

"Just standing here, that's all."

"And where is your *mamá?*"

"She's not here. She went to the market."

"Isn't anyone at home?"

"No, they all went out."

"Then, can I come in?"

"If you want to, but hurry, before they come back." I went on drying my hair and she came in.

She says, "Well, hurry, come on, otherwise they'll come back and see us and run me out."

So, right there, we did it for the first time. She already had a son with another man but she had nothing to do with him any more. After this, she gave herself completely to me. She came to the house every day and later she began to work for us and slept in a corner. And then she says to me, "You know what? Why don't you come and lie next to me at night?"

"But how can you want me to sleep with you, knowing that my sister and the rest are there?" My *papá* slept next to the wall, Macrina slept with her little girl in the back, and Martín somewhere else in the room. My *mamá* and Germán slept in the kitchen. "For me it is all right, but you will lose your job if they find out. How can we do it?"

She says, "Look, when your *papá* is asleep, come quietly to where I am. I will lie near the door. But don't make any noise."

That's what we did but then my sister Macrina found out and told my *mamá*. All my *mamá* said to me was, "Do you get next to Eustolia at night? Macrina saw you."

I didn't say yes or no, so she said, "After all, you are a man so what does it matter? You have nothing to lose."

Later, Eustolia's mother died and she went back home because her brothers were alone. Her *papá* was already dead and they were orphans. She continued to work for us during the day. She came to our house at about eight o'clock in the morning and went home at about ten at night.

I say to her, "Well, now we can't any more."

She says, "Yes, we can. You can say you are going out and we can meet under the banana trees in the *corral.*"

Well, we got together in the *corral* every day. I know I made a lot of use of her. Then one day she says to me, "Now I am not well. I am with child. What do you have to say about it?"

"Who knows? You tell me this but how do I know what you do."

"I have only been with you. I don't have anyone else."

The days went by and my *mamá* and *papá* must have noticed something about her, some defect in her. They did not know yet that she was ill with child, but one day, when I came home from Cuerna-vaca—I was still working on the highway at the time—she says to me, "Do you know what? They chased me out of your house. What do you say? Do I go or do I stay?"

"Well, right now I cannot tell you. I cannot decide for you. I am working but I have no money. I have already told you that I am going to set up a house for you but I have no money now."

Then she tells me what happened. "Your *mamá* and *papá* are going to tell you gossip about me, that I am going around with someone else, that it is a habit of mine. Your sister Macrina told them so many lies that they want me to leave. Macrina doesn't want you to go with me. She said I went after you, that you don't want me any more, that you ought to love your sister more."

"My sister? Then is she jealous of you or what?"

"That's what I think. I believe she wants you to lie with her."

"So my sister wants me to lie with her! But how am I going to do a thing like that? Impossible!"

"That's why she doesn't let you go with me. When she sees you cover me when I am cold she says why don't you cover her? Why do you cover only me? That's why she is angry. So lie with her, if only to get her to stop!"

Then I say, "Don't pay attention to her."

"But, think! Now they have run me out."

That day, when I came home, she was in the corner of the kitchen with her son, and they were scolding her and telling her to go. I just looked at her and went into the other room. I didn't give myself away. Later, she came out and told me what they said.

I say to her, "Look, be patient, because right now I have no money. You don't have a job here any more but stay and work. Even though you won't earn anything, do the chores well. I will give you your expense money, I will give you food. See if you can please them, see if that way they will tell you to stay."

They let her stay on, but twenty days later she says, "Well, I think I will leave. They are chasing me out again. What do you say?"

"Be patient. I say stay here even though they scold you. Don't say anything to them. I will see what I can do. I give you money so don't go."

"I am willing even though you give me only five *pesos* a day. But I need a dress. I don't mind working all day without pay, but they ought to give me clothing."

One day, when I returned from work, I asked, "Where is she?" Well, she was gone, they didn't know where. I went looking for her but I didn't know where she was, until about a month later she sent word to me that she was at her *comadre's*. She went there to give birth. My *papá* and *mamá* didn't know the child was mine, except by hearsay. My *mamá* says to me, "That woman Eustolia is saying that the baby girl she has is yours."

I say, "Well, who knows?" How could I say yes to my *mamá?* I am the only one who really knows the child is mine. Eustolia wanted me to marry her at the time she was in my house, but later I didn't want to because my *papá* told me she had another man, that my *mamá* had seen her with him, and well, there was no lack of gossip for them to tell me.

It was the plum season and I was working in my father's little store-room. One day, I saw her there. She says, "You know that I already gave birth. Now I want to know what name you choose for the child and if it should be baptized or not."

I say, "Well, on what Saint's Day was it born? Give it the saint's name. It is up to you. If you were living with me, then I would decide."

"Well, as the father, tell me what name you like and what we should do about the baptism. That's why I came to see you."

"I cannot tell you. You are living apart."

We were talking that way for a while. She sat down beside me and I put my arm around her. I was kissing her when my *papá* came in. She had said, "Give me something to buy myself what I need." I was giving her five *pesos* when my *papá* saw us.

He says, "What are you doing?"

"Nothing."

"What a surprise that you came," he says to her. "Have you already given birth?" After that he didn't say any more. She left in a little while, saying, "I am going now, *don* Pedro."

"Very well. When are you coming again?"

"I will see."

When she left, my *papá* says, "You know? I don't like that woman. Look for another one who is still a girl."

I don't know where she is living now. When I see her in the street I greet her and ask about the child. I never give her money nor has she asked for any.

PART SEVEN

CHAPTER XXIII

PEDRO

Esperanza's Death

Every now and again, I would dream the same dream about my wife. I dreamt we were traveling somewhere far away in a bus and I kept losing my *huaraches,* or sometimes it would be my hat. That made me think something was going to happen to my family . . . that someone was going to pass away. Sure enough, it turned out to be my wife.

I had another dream about her, while she was still here, well and strong. We were walking, my wife and I, on a great plain and we came to a big bridge. The train was coming and I said to her, "Look, wait, here comes the train. Let's get on so we can get there faster." The train stopped at the station and we got on. After a while we arrived at another station where we got off to change trains. My wife was in the waiting room and I went out to see if the other train had come yet. It was pulling in, whistling, and then all at once a woman friend of mine appeared there. I left my bundle with her, saying, "Take care of my bundle," and I went running in to get my wife to put her on the train. I ran very very fast into the waiting room but I did not see my wife. She was lost. I went about looking and looking. Where could she have gone? Here the train was going to leave and my wife was gone. I came running out. Now my bundle was missing and so was the woman who was keeping an eye on it. She even took my *huaraches!* Whew! Here I was all alone and without even *huaraches!* Now what do I do? The train was gone and the woman had gotten on it together with my bundle. That was the way I was left standing there, without my wife, without the woman, without my bundle and without my *huaraches*. How was I going to be able to work now?

I felt that I was going down a straight street to the center of town when I woke up. This made me wonder. Who knows what was going to become of me with that business of losing my wife and my bundle and my *huaraches*. It must mean something!

I also kept dreaming that I went naked to a fiesta. Without shame, I walked in the street wearing no pants! I wore only a shirt. All this worried me. Why did I dream this? It certainly meant a loss . . . of my wife.

Esperanza, my wife, was in bed for two years before she died and I spent a lot of money. She was sick, sick, for about ten years but in bed for two, and yet I did not even feel annoyed. I took care of her until she died in the year 1956. I kept spending money for medicines and the doctor. The doctor wanted to bring her to the capital to operate on her but she was very much afraid of that. I did not want it either. I told her, "If they are going to kill you there in the hospital, you had better die here," and we refused to go.

My sister and her daughter lived with us, to help with the household chores. I paid my niece sixty *pesos* a month but my sister received only her food, which meant I was supporting her. Later I also had to support my daughter Macrina and her two little girls, Ana and Ester, because Macrina didn't get along with her husband and came home to live. I had a mule and a horse and I sold the mule for 1,050 *pesos* to pay for the treatments, the household expenses and then the wake and burial. That is why I didn't get ahead in those years.

My sister and Macrina were taking care of my wife and they would get angry with her because she was becoming as helpless as a child. Well, one day I was away and when I came back my wife was in her last agony. I said, "You see? The hour has come and you were getting angry. Now go out and leave her with me, for after all, I am her husband."

We had my wife on the floor but I put her on the bed and my children gathered around. Moisés and I began reading the Psalms. Felipe was crying and holding his mother in his arms. She was in agony a long time and could not die. The neighbors got word of what was happening and they came. Gloria was there and she told us to go away, especially Felipe, because he was not letting his mother die. Gloria took his place and my wife died in her arms. That's the way she ended, in Gloria's arms.

Gloria and my aunts changed her into clean garments and put her

rebozo around her. Then we put her on a table with a candle at each corner and we prayed. Many people came that night, bringing candles for the wake. What could I do with so many candles? Later I gave them to the *barrio* chapel. I sent my son Martín with some money to see about the grave. He got bricks and lime and took them to the cemetery, just as I told him. The next day we buried her and that was all. I let my uncles "lay the cross" of lime and sand and set out flowers and votive lamps. Every day people prayed in front of it and on the ninth day the prayer leader "raised the cross," calling out my wife's name. I did not say anything but let my Catholic relatives and neighbors do whatever they wished because they believed in it. My uncles even set out a food offering a year later for my wife's spirit and I did not interfere.

I felt the separation from my wife deeply. For almost half a year I did not eat and people said I was going to die. I missed my wife and with good reason. She helped me a lot. Very much! She worked hard. At times she even helped me carry firewood. I remember how she followed me about, how faithful she was to me. She had twelve children and raised six. My wife was a real woman!

I loved her, you can't imagine how much! And she loved me. Yes, we loved each other an awful lot, but an awful lot! I always thought, "The poor thing. She doesn't know anything and needs me."

The only thing was, as I always said and still say, she was very cold by nature and I wasn't. That's how I won her, because I was very affectionate and she wasn't. And she was worse when she got angry. She would never never make up to me. Not that, ever! She wasn't like some women who try to content the man, who pet him so he'll feel better. No, she was too virtuous.

We lived together many years, but that made no difference. If I was in a temper, she would never try to soothe me. Not with words, that is. That was something she couldn't do. She wouldn't speak. As soon as she saw I was in a temper she stopped talking to me. Sometimes she wouldn't say a word to me for two days.

Of course, I take into consideration the fact that I would say to her, "Look, when I come home angry, don't answer me. You can tell the way I am when I arrive. Sometimes unexpectedly my friends in the street make me angry, or an animal, or anything that might come up. Try to find some way to keep me from staying mad, try to find a way."

Occasionally, I would come home that way and scold her, unjustly sometimes, like any man can do. Then I regret those things of the moment and I try to console her, but I do it with words. I say to her, "Look, daughter, forgive me. Really, it's not in your nature to ask me why. You know how it is, how a man can be going along and something enters his heart or his spirit and makes him feel violent, on account of poverty or because of one of his friends, or maybe it's a debt . . . well, you know . . . the main mortifications of this life of ours. The thing is, don't you realize, I don't want you to get angry."

I would embrace her and kiss her and say, "Come on, don't be mad." Then she would feel happier. I would do it with my words, but not she. She couldn't! She didn't know how to show her love except by her deeds. That way, yes!

Do you know what she would do? Instead of speaking to me with her lips, at night when we went to bed, she would embrace me and put her legs around me. That was the consolation she offered me, but I never knew words from her. Naturally, when I saw that, I thought to myself, "Poor thing, she doesn't know how to explain herself. This is the only way she knows of consoling me."

Throughout my whole life I never knew her to do evil. In forty-five years I never saw her do anything to deceive me. That's why I say one must not teach one's wife to enjoy sex because she becomes addicted to it. Then her husband cannot satisfy her and she must look for other men. A man should not make a whore of his own wife! I never did and my wife remained virtuous.

Once, when she was recently married, or it seems to me that we already had one child, a neighbor of ours passed through the *corral* and bothered her. To tell the truth, I had a violent nature and was not afraid to kill or be killed . . . when I was young. Now my energy is gone, but at that time my wife saw what I was, so she didn't say anything to me but went and told her brother.

What her brother did was call the man to accounts and give him a bawling out. He said these words, "No, my sister is not a woman of the streets. If she were one of those, I wouldn't butt in, but I am glad she trusted me enough to tell me so that I could call you to accounts. My brother-in-law looks like a little fellow. He's still not a grown man but his spirit is full-size, bigger than you, and if he finds out, God help you! We are in the middle of a revolution and when he finds out, poor you! He will kill you. Better drop it. I am giving you advice, like a friend. My sister did enough in not telling her husband anything."

So he said, "Don't worry. I made a mistake but I won't say anything to her again."

But my wife never told me. Years passed before my brother-in-law told me.

After I had children, another incident came up.

This time Esperanza says to me, "Listen, so-and-so said this and this to me."

I smiled. "Is this true, really true, or are you just trying to test me?"

"No, really, that's what he said."

"And you don't owe him anything? You are sure you don't owe him anything?"

"I don't owe him a thing."

"All right, then. Look, if he says it to you again, tell him to come ahead, that I am not home."

"*Ay, papacito,* but then you'll kill him!"

"No, no, I won't do anything to him. Tell him to come at such and such a time. I will put on your dress and wait for him. Let's see what he does."

"No, better not. I know what you are thinking. As long as I don't give in to him, let that be enough. I told you confidentially because I don't want to make a fool of you, I don't want to cheat on you. But I don't want you to do anything. There will be violence and you might get into trouble."

Frankly, it made me laugh, but I just said, "No, daughter." She was almost crying. "Don't worry. The best thing is for you not to have anything to do with him. For the love I have for you, I thank you for telling me, but only if you really are not hiding something. I get around, you know, and can spy on you."

"Go ahead and do what you wish." She said, "You'll see that I won't give him a chance."

That's why I say she loved me truly.

It is true that I was quite a rascal because I was very fond of the ladies. But one thing I must say, I never exposed my wife to a single one of them, never. Not once! I always gave her due respect. She was my wife and she was the one who made the home and if through some careless slip she got to know of one of my affairs, I would break it off to show her there was nothing to it. But even though she really was not jealous, sometimes she did get angry. Then I would convince her the gossip was not true and she would believe what I said because I never allowed her to know the truth. I am not like those men who brag and even parade another woman before the wife's eyes. Not I! Nor before my children either!

And I didn't forget that I was married. I always took care of the household expenses and would never go off on sprees. If four days passed without my worrying about the expenses, it was because I had already left her enough to eat, or if not, when I got home I would ask how much she owed and I would take care of it all.

There were times when I beat my wife, it's true. When I recognized my error, I asked her to pardon me. I would beg her forgiveness. Aztecan men do get drunk sometimes and they do beat their wives, but not very much any more. Before, it was done in every house. If my grandmother wasn't beaten, she wouldn't eat. She even liked it! It is a matter of village custom and the ways of the women. Here, if a man is easy on his wife and then hits her later, she will raise her hand to him. That's why one must premeditate about these things.

But I did not make a slave of my wife. I was a poor man, I know, and it's clear that I didn't give her enough to enjoy life, to go out or to . . . not those things, but I gave her equal rights, except that I did not have the kind of character to let her dominate me. The rights I gave her were: not to be treated badly, not to be beaten, to be given what she deserved.

Whether I was drunk or sober, I would always say to my wife, "Just don't answer back! When you see that I am angry, don't answer back. That will be enough. Just by doing that you'll be able to control me. You'll see, I'll give in even if you did something wrong. I'll let you order me around. You can even send me on an errand! It wouldn't matter."

I gave in in that sense but not in matters of moral principle. Not that! My wife never grumbled and never went against me. She respected me. That's why we lived together very peacfully for all the forty-five years we were married. She was more mother to me than my own mother because she was with me longer. I still miss her and with good reason. She was everything . . . she helped me in everything and naturally I remember that.

Caray! Since my wife died, things have gone badly for me. The harvest was not very poor but it had been better in other years. My son Felipe fell ill and I was feeling the pinch because I owed money everywhere. I had borrowed three hundred *pesos* at interest after the funeral and they were asking for it. They also loaned me five hundred *pesos* to buy some plum trees. I got this money cheap, at only 5 percent interest a month; every other year they gave me loans at 10 percent. So I had to pay out a lot of money, but I got something out of it, enough for my beans, at least.

I was supporting a lot of people and after a while my sister left because Macrina was there to serve us. When my daughter's divorce came up, it was no problem because it was only a civil marriage.

The trouble between them was the fault of my son-in-law. He was one of those foolish men who went with other women and then told his wife about it. He even showed my daughter a photo of his sweetheart! Naturally, Macrina was going to get jealous.

I told my son-in-law on various occasions when I met up with him, "Look, my boy, if you don't like my daughter, leave her, man! There's nothing compulsory about it and its nothing to quarrel over and get mad about. If you buy a horse that is no good to you, sell it! The same thing with my daughter. If she is of no use to you, change her. Leave her and look for someone else. Why get angry?"

Well, he wanted to fight over it. "No," he said, "I'll take her back but let her change her character."

"And how am I going to change her if she was born like that? It is all a question of how you look at things. That's how she is and if it's all right with you, take her, if not, leave her. I make no demands on you."

Well, that is how it stood between us, but I did not lose my temper. My son-in-law came around to see us every now and then. But it was all calculated because once he came and after greeting me very respectfully, he said, "Look, this is what I came for. I want to ask Macrina once and for all whether she is coming with me or not."

But here we knew that he already had another woman, although he hadn't yet taken her to live in his house. So my daughter said, "What do you want me for? Haven't you got the other one any more?"

"No, who told you that?"

"Sure, we all know it."

"It's not so. No."

He came three times but Macrina didn't want to. It looked like he was begging her to go with him but actually it was just a sham because at the same time he was begging her not to, saying that if she changed he would take her and if she didn't, he wouldn't.

I said to him, "Why are you being so stubborn, man? She isn't going to change. On the contrary, the difference between you is going to get deeper. Why have a bad mate? Better be rid of her. You've separated as a matter of fact, anyway."

The last time, he said, "All right, now I came for one thing. If she doesn't want me to take her, I want her to sign a divorce."

"That is up to her. See what she says."

Well, my daughter didn't want to. The neighbors were even worse. "No, no!" they said, "don't sign it, don't sign it!" Just ignorance!

I said to her, "Go on, sign it. Don't be foolish. You will be free. You will be able to go with anyone you want. Let him get married and you can find a nice fellow for yourself, and that is all there is to it. Why not? This way you are tied up, neither one of you can make a move. Let's face reality. Don't be foolish, sign it."

This seemed to leave her thoughtful. It even reached the point where he promised to give her a fine cow. But I said to him, "You know how it is. I make no demands on you . . . no demands. My daughter has a place here with me. She will not want for anything. We will not be rich but neither will she lack food. And your children are well off here with me. So what have we got to worry about?"

"Well, yes, but I promised I was going to give her a cow. The only thing is she has to agree to sign and I'll bring her a cow." But my daughter did not want to.

"Sign it, man!" I said to her. "I'll take you to the civil court in Cuernavaca. That way you will be free and so will he. And *zas*, off you can go to look for someone else."

"Well, all right, then."

As a matter of fact, he kept his bargain. He himself brought the cow . . . an ordinary cow. Well, it wasn't bad and we began to milk it. She signed the divorce and I went along with them. He bought dolls for the little girls. He even took us to eat in a restaurant.

But after that he came to take away Ana, the older daughter. He came and stole her but I said to my daughter, "Look, man, he has a right. After all, it is her father who is taking her. Let him take her. Don't make a fight over it."

"No, but I miss my daughter!"

"Don't worry about it. You have the other one."

Well, he was happy now that Macrina signed and he got married to the other woman right away.

I said to my daughter, "See? Now it is over and you have no right to say a word. Tomorrow or the next day if he comes looking for you, he has no right to you either. So it's all over with, but there is just one thing . . . about the cow . . . better sell it, as I am not going to be wasting my time taking care of a cow out in the fields. And another thing, if it should die unexpectedly you will lose everything. So better sell it and buy yourself a sewing machine. You will not lose that investment. It is as safe as if it were buried. You can be here taking care of it, all by yourself. It won't be any bother to me or to your brothers. The machine will be all yours."

"All right then," she said.

And we sold the cow for a thousand *pesos*. Then we went to get the machine, but by then she had used a little of the money. "Look," I said, "now you have the chance, so buy the machine because you are beginning to spend the money."

"Yes, but I had to, for my little girl. Where was I to get money for her shoes?"

"That's just what I mean. You start taking off money and the next thing you know it is all gone. No, let us buy the machine right away. I will make up the difference."

So I did, and we bought the machine.

Sure enough, the cow we sold died. I said, "See? Now the cow is gone, but meanwhile here you are looking at your machine. That man lost out."

"*Caray,* what bad luck . . ."

"Yes, he had bad luck, poor fellow."

"Well, I hope they don't kill us!"

Meanwhile, Conchita and Juan had been inviting Macrina to live with them. They were inviting her on account of the sewing machine. And that foolish girl believed them. But I was against it and said, "I hear you are going to go with Conchita, isn't that right? Well, you can go, but the machine stays. The machine doesn't leave here, because it does not belong to you. It is the little girl's . . . Ester's. And not only that, I have a right to it, too, as I made up the difference for you. It was my money, too, because I was selling fruit at the time. I know just what your brother-in-law is thinking. He has an idea he is going to get his hands on the machine, but one thing is sure . . . with me around he won't be able to."

Well, she did not go. Juan was a big opportunist. Just think, at one time Conchita got hold of all the money Macrina's husband gave her and Conchita never paid it back. Macrina's husband had gone to the United States to work and had sent her money. Conchita kept borrowing from Macrina and never paid it back. It amounted to two hundred *pesos* or more. Conchita would visit her sister regularly and Macrina was very much under her influence. We had a little corn and Conchita would take it. One time she was in the *corral* when Martín surprised her carrying corn. He bawled out Macrina. "Why are you giving her corn! And look how much! It's spilling over. What are you doing it for?"

Well, we scolded her a lot. Macrina said that she owed Conchita money. She was always owing her. "And what do you owe it to her for? It is not true!" Conchita got angry and did not set foot in the house again. Now that the two sisters had fallen out, Macrina made a confession. "I did it because I felt sorry for her. But look, she is not sorry for me. She owes me money and now she doesn't pay me."

So I said, "No wonder she came. Funny that your sister began to come around after she had stopped visiting her *mamá* and me. She kept appearing on account of you, especially when we were not at home. The neighbor tells me that you have been handing out corn to her every day. What is the meaning of this? You are being a traitor to us!"

But I finally stopped telling Macrina to demand her money back. I said, "Let her have it. After all, you don't lack for anything here with us."

CHAPTER XXIV

FELIPE

Leaves for Mexico City

When my *mamá* was ill I felt very sad. I couldn't work peacefully because I had I-don't-know-what on my heart. What would become of
me within a month, within a week? I knew her illness was much worse.
She couldn't stand up alone any more. She would say to me, "Get me
up, take me to the kitchen, take me to the yard." I got her out of bed,
and when I was not there my father did, or one of my brothers or sisters.
Yes, my mother's life was very sad when she couldn't get up alone any
more.

I was working in Cuernavaca at that time, on the new highway. I
earned ten *pesos* a day and I went all the way home every night to
sleep. I was very upset about my mother. I did not know if she would
live or die. What would become of me? One day when I came home
Macrina told me that my *mamá* had fainted. But when I arrived she
was herself again and was able to speak. I said, "I have come."

"You've come?" she says.

I say, "Do you feel anything?"

She says, "Nothing."

"Then I can go to work? Can I leave you?"

"Yes, you can go. I don't need anything."

I went to work the next day. When I got home that evening my
sister said my *mamá* had fainted again. Then I was more upset. I

thought, "I don't know if she'll die. I'd better not go to work." My *papá* was there taking care of her, sitting at her bedside. I asked him, "How does it look?"

"Bad," he says. "Who knows how it will go tonight. She may suddenly get away from us."

Then I felt very sad. I said, "What do I do?" I felt a great grief. I wanted to help but I had no money. My mother was asleep. I went to talk to her. "*Mamá,* how do you feel?"

"I don't feel anything right now."

"Tell me how you feel so I can know whether to go to work or to stay here with you."

She says, "Right now I do not feel anything."

"I'd better not go to work. I want to watch you."

I sat down to take care of my mother. I saw that she was in the last stages and I wanted to be with her when she died. So I sat there, sleeping, my head nodding, but I didn't want to lie down.

My *papá* said, "Lie down. You are very sleepy."

I said, "If I lie down and something happens during the night, she might call for me and I won't be here."

My *papá* sat there, too. At dawn, my *mamá* awoke very agitated. She was almost in her last agony. I saw that nothing could save her and I began to cry. I didn't leave her side, nothing could make me leave. I hugged her and kissed her for the last time and then I kneeled and asked her forgiveness. I said, "Pardon me if I did anything to you in your lifetime or if I offended you. In these last moments, forgive me, don't count my bad behavior to you." And my tears rolled down.

My father felt sad, too, and cried; my brothers and sisters also. I was hugging her and she was already in agony but she couldn't die. I cried hard and I shouted into her ears to see if that way she could answer me. She made signs only with her head. I called her by name but she only nodded. She couldn't speak any more. My father told me, "She is going to leave us now, now it is over."

I said, "What is going to become of me from tomorrow on? What will become of me?"

Knowing I had a mother, I came home. Even though she was ill, even though she was in bed, I knew she was still alive. But tomorrow or the next day, when I come home the bed will be empty, she will not be there. I always went to talk to her, to tell her I was home. And she always answered, "Now you've come, little son?" To whom will I talk now? What will become of me? There's no other way, I'll have to marry soon, out of necessity. My sister is here to serve me but it's not the same. She is a married woman now and is her own boss.

My mother died at about six o'clock in the evening. When she was dying, I called my sister Macrina. I said, "Ask my *mamá* to forgive you now in her last moment with us. Beg her pardon for your bad behavior to her, for what you have done to her."

"What for? She's going to die. Do you think that just because I ask her to forgive me she'll get well? No, if she's going to die now, why should I?"

They went to call Conchita. My *papá* says, "Beg your mother's pardon while she is still here."

She says, "What for?" When it was over, Conchita said, "Well, it's over, what can we do? She has gone and left us. From now on, I'll come for the sake of my brothers and sisters."

Then my *papá* told my sister Conchita to go tell *don* Ángel to bring the Adventists to sing hymns at the wake. He said Catholics should also come and they could pray on one side while the Adventists sang on the other side. My sister didn't say anything but she went and told Ángel that she didn't think it would be good. "It would be like making fun of God to have the Adventists and the Catholics together. My father has many friends, even among the priests, and they will all come." Ángel said, "I don't like it either. In that case, let him receive only Catholics. Tell him to bring all the Catholics he wants."

When they told my *papá*, he said, "Well, what can I do? The Adventists don't want to accompany us. That isn't what I call Christianity!" So he went to hire an old man who was a Catholic prayer leader and everyone began to pray. Many people came . . . my father's friends and my aunts and uncles and cousins. Someone told my aunt Ágata, the one whom my *papá* had not allowed in the house, and she came, too. She brought flowers and asked my *papá*, "Where is Esperanza?" and he said, "Inside on the table."

She entered and cried and begged my mother's pardon in case she had ever offended her. My aunt said good-bye to my mother and left a candle and a votive lamp. Then she reminded my *papá*. "Do you remember when you hit Esperanza that time when she did not deserve it? She never thought what you imagined, she never asked me about anything bad. Why don't you hit poor Esperanza now? You are very sorry because you have lost her but she is better off. She no longer has to suffer so much."

My aunt told the whole story there and my *papá* couldn't bear it and began to cry. But he was angry and when my aunt left he said, "Instead of coming to console me she came to tell me things. If I were not in mourning I would have run her out of here!"

We were up all night, singing hymns and praying and crying. My sister Conchita didn't stay long because she had just had a baby. She cried very little. Martín, too, cried very little. Germán was there, but not Ricardo. He was away and didn't know when my *mamá* died. Of my brothers and sisters, I am the one who missed her most, the one who cried the most. I couldn't bear it. At times when I went to eat, I remembered her, how she spoke to me. Even when she was ill, she spoke to me: "Come, son, come to eat." She begged me to eat. When I saw that she was no longer there I started to cry, like men do. I couldn't bear it. Her death ended the love she had for me.

My father said, "Don't cry, it will harm you." But I didn't feel that way. So what if it harmed me! I cried and cried and cried. Ten months later, when I went to Mexico City, I still cried at times. But then I resigned myself for it must have been my destiny.

When it was time to bury my mother, my *papá* said, "How shall we do it? Shall we take her to the Catholic church, or how?"

I said, "It's up to you."

He says, "Well, as a courtesy to the people, so that they will not talk, we'll take her to the church." And so we yielded to the people. But the priest was not there. We waited for him but he did not come. We do not believe in the Catholic religion but, as my father said, it was to please the people. For us it didn't mean a thing.

Well, so I had to look for a woman. A few days after my mother's death I brought home this girl, this poor wretch, Pánfila. She was from Santa María. I had first met her the year before, during the plum season, when my *papá* was buying up plum orchards, that is, crops, to sell. We were picking plums in the *barrio* of San Miguel and there was a woman called Fulgencia who was a healer. This girl was at her house for a cure and I, without knowing the girl, not even knowing where she was from, well, I liked her, just to fool around, nothing more. And so I was in the *corral* and I began to talk to her, making signs from a distance and she began to answer me, with her hand. It was just a passing affair for me and I didn't even propose anything to her. Absolutely nothing went on between us. I left and I still didn't know where the girl was from.

It wasn't until almost a year later that I saw her again. I was in my father's storeroom in the center of town, adding up the accounts. I was sitting at the window, on the balcony which faced the street. A little boy said to me, "Someone wants to talk to you." I paid no attention. After all, he was only a little boy and I continued with my figuring. But again he says, "A girl there wants to talk to you."

So I jumped over the railing and went to the corner and she says to me, "What are you doing?"

"I am counting plums. Where are you going?"

She says, "I am just going to do an errand."

"Then, shall I go with you?"

"Yes, let's go."

And there we go, talking. Then I began to speak to her about love.

She says, "I don't know if you are married. Suppose you are married and will leave me? You may have a wife."

I say to her, "No, I have no one right now. So you tell me if you want to get together with me and I will marry you. Of course, I cannot promise that I will marry you right away but little by little."

I accompanied her to the house of the man who was curing her because she was ill, and then we didn't see each other again for about a month. What we had together was what you might call one of those street romances, nothing more.

Well, once I was carrying water from the fountain to our house to water the plants. It was about ten in the morning when a woman arrives at our house and says, "Good morning." My sister came out and the woman says to her, "Does a young man by the name of Felipe Martínez live here?"

I came out and asked what I could do for her and invited her in. The *señora* said, "That girl sent me, the one you already know about."

"What girl?"

"That girl from Santa María. She sent me to see what you think and to bring her a message from you."

I said, "Right now I have no message because I didn't know anyone was going to come. You caught me by surprise and now I have no message to send her."

She says, "Well, I don't know, but she sent me to get a message. If not, I will take you to speak to her. The girl is alone. So if you like, you can come to speak with her because her father won't return until the evening."

I asked the woman to wait for me in the plaza while I went for water one time more. I hurried and then I went to meet her and we left by bus for the village of Santa María. When we arrived she said, "Wait here a minute. I'll go to see if she is alone, and I will signal to you to come."

When I saw that the girl was alone, I went in and we began to talk. The girl says to me, "Ask for my hand. I will marry you." And I say, "No. Better just run off with me, because now I have no money to marry you. Moreover, your *papá* will not let you marry me. He does not know me."

So she says, "It is better that you ask my *papá* for me. I would like to leave my house in a respectable way. It doesn't matter if we have only a civil marriage at first; later we can get married in church."

I say, "No," and that was all.

I was working in Cuernavaca then and I would stop off to see her in passing almost every afternoon. We kept talking this way but I was in a hurry because my mother was dead and I needed someone to serve me. Again she told me to ask for her hand and I said, "Look, your *papá* will not agree, and he will put all kinds of obstacles in the way. If I ask him, he will say to wait for a year or perhaps two years. I want to marry because of necessity, not for pleasure. Leave with me. Don't think that I am just trying to fool around with you. I am speaking to you honorably."

She says, "Yes, but I'll think about it and let you know."

And I say, "Oh no, tell me now, yes or no."

And she says, "Well, it is yes but not until four months. In the meantime my father and my brothers can finish the harvest. How can I leave them alone? They have no one in the house. My *mamá* is no longer alive. My sister-in-law lives apart. I am alone. I grind the corn for them. I take care of the kitchen, and if I leave, who will cook? If I leave now and my *papá* comes home he will come to look for me."

So I say to her, "Well, they won't die of hunger. When your sister-in-law sees that you aren't here she'll come and help them. If you keep thinking this way about your father, you will never get out of here, you will never marry."

She says, "Wait another few months. At least two months."

And I say, "No, the most I could wait is only one month, about twenty or fifteen days, then you must tell me yes or no, so I will know whether to wait for you or get myself another woman."

She says, "All right. Wait for me the twenty days."

"No," I say. "Fifteen days. I am ready to take you today or tomorrow."

"But how can I leave without telling my *papá?*"

"And what will you gain by telling him? Do you think that girls who run off with their sweethearts first advise their fathers? When I take you to my house, of course I will tell my *papá* that I plan to marry you, but I won't tell him when."

"Very well. Wait for me fifteen days."

At that time I had five sweethearts. One was Elida from my *barrio.* Another was Cristina. And then there was this one from Santa María. Another, Ambrosia, was from a center *barrio.* And finally, there was another in the *barrio* next to mine. When I was with one of my sweethearts, we would talk and sometimes we would embrace and sometimes we would kiss. I had all these at the same time, and I said I would marry the first one who goes away with me. I hurried each one of them. I was working at the time but I kept thinking of the girls. In my head I lined up all five of them to decide which one was best for me. A boy named Fernando was working in the cornfield with me and I asked him to help me choose. And he says, "Take the one who suits you best. I can't tell you which to choose."

Well, on that day I got home late at night. My *papá* and brother were already there. My cousin, the daughter of my father's sister, was also there. I arrived as usual with my little fiber bag over my shoulder at about seven o'clock at night and said, "I have come." My cousin was making *tortillas,* and as it was dark inside, I could not see very much.

Then I see the girl from Santa María and I say, "Ah, you are here. That's fine."

Later I sat down to have supper and I say to her, "Come here and eat. Later we will talk about why you came."

She says, "I came because you told me to," and she sat beside me.

Then my *papá* says to her, "Go ahead and eat. My daughter-in-law has come! That's good." Then he turned to me, "She says you told her to come."

"Yes, I told her to come but I didn't tell her when. Now that she is here I have to speak to her about it."

Later, after supper, I talked to her alone. I say, "Why did you come? Did your *papá* run you out of the house?"

She says, "Yes, he ran me out. I told you how he is with me. He is very mean when he gets drunk and he hits me a lot and chases my brothers and since you told me I could come, I didn't want to suffer any more at home."

So I say to her, "Well, now what do you think?"

She says, "Well, I am here. Now you tell me. Will you marry me or not?"

So I say to her, "Look, I want to know how your father does things. I must find the right way of speaking to him so I can calm him. It is my duty to go see him and tell him what I am thinking of doing with you."

So she says, "Well, my *papá* is mean. But he won't get angry, and if you want to, I will tell you what day you can see him. He is home on Sundays. Other days he works from early morning until eight or nine at night. Sometimes he stays in the cornfield and only my brothers come home."

I say, "Well, then I will go to see him on Sunday. But you are sure he won't get angry with me?"

And she says, "No. Go and calm him. Tell him I am here and that you will marry me."

So I say, "But suppose he comes to look for you and wants to take you away by force, will you go with him?"

"No, I will not go with him. Now that I have come here, I will stay with you. I want to be with you. You told me that you would marry me, and even though you don't marry me right away, I want to be here."

So I say to her, "But who knows how your *papá* will treat me? In your village they waylay people and use sorcery and all sorts of things. But I'll go on Sunday to see your *papá*, and I'll take my aunt with me because I can't go alone. I don't know how he will behave."

Well, my aunt and the girl and I went to see him the next Sunday and my aunt began to speak to him. "We have come to see you about your daughter, to see what you think."

He responded, "No, I do not want to talk now. I have no time."

So then the girl says to me, "You talk to him, Felipe. Calm him, because he is angry."

So I say to *don* Placido, "Look, I came to speak to you in a nice way. Pay attention. I come to ask you how we should arrange for us to marry. I come as a friend." I was pleading with him and he went back and forth in his house, doing whatever he had to do. He kept saying, "I don't want any friend. A father is not worth anything any more. Nowadays only the children arrange things. So go on arranging things yourselves. I won't mix into it. You can do it alone."

And I say to him, "Yes, we have talked together but now, as the father, it is up to you to tell us what you think."

"No, just arrange it with her."

So I left her there in her house and said, "Well, he doesn't want to. I have done everything possible to please him. So if you want to come, come. Think it over and I'll wait."

After three days she was at my house again. This time I slept with her and I liked her because she was very humble, very docile, but what I didn't like was that she was too timid. She hardly knew how to speak Spanish because at her house they spoke only *mexicano*. I could speak a little *mexicano* but I told her, "Don't speak to me in *mexicano*. I am not used to it."

She said, "But I am."

"In your village, yes, but here, no. Speak to me in Spanish, the way I speak to you."

Now that she was at my house, I began to work harder because now I had responsibilities. Then my father said to me, "Well, what do you think about the girl? Are you going to marry her or not?"

And I say to him, "Well, no."

"Why? Why won't you marry her?"

And I say, "No."

My father says, "Well, if you know that you don't like her, you ought not have deceived her."

And I say, "Well, after all, when a man talks to a girl he makes promises and tells her things which are not even true. Don't tell me when you were a young man and spoke to some woman that you told her what you were really thinking? Naturally, one makes promises. I told her in jest, 'I will marry you,' and this one believed me, but I don't want to marry her."

My father says, "Oh, no. Now you are going to get married. I won't let this girl leave the house. No, this girl doesn't leave!"

But I didn't want to marry her. I saw that she was useless to me. Her hands were crooked and the bones of her feet too. Well, I could see she wasn't useful to me. Being a peasant, I work hard. She couldn't get up very early in the morning and she was not competent. I thought, one day she will get sick instead of being a help to me, and I wouldn't get ahead. For a peasant the important thing is to have a wife who can help, who is intelligent and can take care of household things, but I saw that this one couldn't. Also, I didn't want to give her the daily expense money. I still gave it to my *papá*. I didn't even give it to my sister. Whatever I earned a week I gave to him. Then my *papá* said to me, "Give it to your woman, now that you have responsibilities. Give it to her, not to me." No, I didn't even give her five *centavos* and she never complained.

At that time I was working in the gladiola fields. They paid very little, only seven *pesos* a day. Then it was my bad luck to get sick. That day when I went to work I felt bad, I don't know why. I limped a little. On the way home with the boys (there were eight of us), we ran in order to get back early. You know how boys are! We went jumping over the furrows in the cornfields and then I stepped on a little stone and turned my right foot. It only turned a little but immediately I felt something hot inside, near my groin, as if something had burst. I paid no attention to it, and kept running. The next day I had chills and fever. I said, "It must be the grippe." I went on working but the next day it got worse and pretty soon I was getting pains in the back of my head. I had to work because I had my *señora*. I thought, "After all, if I die in the cornfield, they will come to get me. I won't stay in bed!"

But the more I worked, the worse I felt. Four days later I couldn't go on. I got as far as Elotepec but I couldn't walk any more. I wanted to lie down right there. I couldn't take it any longer. My head hurt a lot, my whole body hurt, I couldn't move. The fever felt as if it were burning my face. Well, on this Thursday, when I got home I couldn't even speak. I went straight to bed. I didn't have supper, or anything, nothing at all. I just lay down. I couldn't even move. I hurt all over— my head, my eyes, even my fingers. My cousin says, "See? I told you not to go to work, but you insisted that you had to."

"But I have no money . . ."

"It doesn't matter. You shouldn't have gone, you'll get worse. Tomorrow you are not going."

I tell her, "Look, at least let me finish the week. I have only two days to go."

She says, "If you go, I won't grind the corn for you. I don't want you to go." My cousin was grinding the corn for me because that woman I had wasn't able to.

Then Pánfila says, "What hurts you?" I say, "My head hurts," but I could hardly answer. I told her, "Please rub me."

"Where?"

"All my body hurts, but mainly my head." So she massaged me, but it didn't help. Then they gave me pills, *mejorales*, and aspirins, but nothing helped.

The next day I couldn't even get out of bed. I couldn't do a thing. And I got worse as days went by. I stood up but I couldn't walk. I had a swelling, something like a round lump, here in the groin and it hurt terribly. I couldn't even sit down, I had to sit sideways, I was in such bad shape. At first my father didn't really believe that I was so sick. Finally he says, "Is it a hernia?"

I didn't know but I explained in detail how it happened and where it hurt. He says, "Then you're ruptured, you have a hernia." He told me that when you have a hernia the whole body goes completely out of order. He says, "Why didn't you tell me this before, then you would be cured already. Now let your aunt cure you, she knows how. She has cured her husband."

So he called her. "Cure this boy," he says. I was ashamed to tell where it hurt, so he told her.

She says, "Take off your pants, take off your underwear. Lie down." I lay down, I lost my shame, for I wanted to get well! Then she started rubbing me with medicines. Who knows where she got them. She hung me by my feet and she slapped me on the soles. She rubbed me all over and treated me for three days, but it was no use. She says, "How are you now?"

"About the same."

She says, "*Uuy!* Who knows what you have! It would be better if another *señora* took care of you." So she called another woman, who treated me for two weeks. But nothing! This woman used the same treatment; she hung me by my feet, she shook me, she massaged me up and down all over . . . Then another woman came, my father's *comadre*. He says, "Treat this boy, I don't know what he has. Many have treated him, but he doesn't improve. Let's see if you can cure him."

She grabbed me and started to rub, but this time I cried like a woman. I cried because she rubbed me with all her strength, and all over! I couldn't take it and I cried. She treated me for two months and I began to feel a little better. I still owe her money. Yes, this curer helped me, but only a little. I still couldn't go out into the street. I went into the yard and lay down under the little avocado tree. I felt ashamed because my *papá* was going to say that I didn't want to work, that I'm lazy. Well, I was ashamed, but what could I do?

Then my father says, "Are you going to help us? We're going to work, will you help?"

I say, "Well, I don't know."

"Aren't you better yet?"

I say, "I don't know." I'd get well for one or two days, then again I'd go to bed for about two weeks or a month. I'd begin to feel better and then again back to bed. Even when I was lying down, the little lump that had come out hurt me. I couldn't stand. I couldn't walk. So I took a big ear of corn and pushed the lump inside, and this relieved my pain a little. But when I fell asleep it would come out again and hurt me. Only when I pushed it back in did I feel better.

All this time Pánfila was taking care of me. Then one evening she says, "I have no shoes. What shall I do? I have no clothing."

I say to her, "Well, what do you want me to do? Can't you see that I can hardly stand up? You see what condition I am in now. I am still so weak. What can I do for you? Corn we still have, but it is my *papá's*. How can I ask him to buy you shoes, to buy you clothing? No, I can't. I don't know when I will get better. This might last for another ten months." Then I say to her, "Look, wouldn't it be better for you to go back to your house? Don't think that I am driving you out. Don't think that I am scolding you. Nor do I beat you. You have seen that I have behaved well to you. I have always loved you, but now you see my condition. Go home and when I recover I will go for you, but don't say that I ran you out."

And she says, "Well, in that case, I am going. I realize you are ill. But I will come back to see how you are getting along every eight or fifteen days."

So I say to her, "Very well. Where will you go?"

"I don't want to go home because my *papá* will beat me. He will scold me."

So I say to her, "What can you do about it? Of course he isn't going to be pleased to receive you back and he'll have to beat you and scold you, but he won't kill you. So bear it. It is a father's right. Stick it out, and just as soon as I get well I'll come for you."

She says, "Yes, I'll go home, but if he beats me and chases me out I'll go to Cuernavaca to stay with a woman I know there."

While I watched her, she gathered her few things into a little bundle, picked up her *rebozo* and said good-bye to me. She left and after about twenty days a boy brought a letter from her. She wrote saying she was in Cuernavaca with a woman who was curing her. Then one day when I was almost better, she arrives at about seven o'clock in the morning. My sister Macrina had gone to the market and I was alone. I heard, "Good morning," and she came in.

She says, "Well, how are things coming with you?"

"Well, I am about the same. I don't get better and I don't get worse. The way I feel now, I don't know if I will ever be entirely well."

She sat down and we continued to talk. She asked, "Is there any coffee?"

"There is some in the kitchen."

She went to get herself some coffee. Then she said to me, "Well, what about us?"

"What do you expect me to say? Right now I can't walk, I can't get up, I can't do anything."

She left but continued to visit me every fifteen days, and little by little I got better.

But then I suffered another illness. My throat swelled up one day, without any warning, all of a sudden. I went to sleep feeling fine, just fine, then I woke up at about three o'clock in the morning and I felt I was choking. My throat was dry and I couldn't speak. It hurt a lot. I couldn't even swallow, I could barely breathe. It was in November and my *papá* was harvesting. He was bringing in hay, corn, and all that. My father said, "Well? Are you going to help us? Are you better?"

"I don't know."

"What do you mean, you don't know?"

"I could say yes and then in three days I'll get sick again."

"Well then, stay home, unless you want to help us." He finished the harvest with the help of Martín and Moisés.

My throat remained swollen. One day my *papá* came and said, "Do you want some breakfast?" I could not answer. I felt something inside of me tightening, so I signaled to him.

He says, "Shall I give you corn *atole* or a piece of bread?"

"No, no," was all I said.

He says, "What is it?"

Through signs I told him where it hurt. I felt my throat closing more and more, and I could no longer bear it. I couldn't swallow, I couldn't drink milk or take *atole,* nothing.

My *papá* says, "I am going to buy your milk."

I just answered with signs. I kept getting worse. One day I called my brother Moisés and my brother Martín. My brother Ricardo was there, too. I said farewell to them because I thought I was dying. I couldn't breathe or swallow. I had to turn on my stomach so the saliva could run out onto a piece of cloth. I spoke to my brothers. "I think I won't last. My advice to you is to behave well to my *papá.* When he scolds you, do not answer, do not talk back. Follow my example." To my sister Macrina, I say, "Take care of my *papá* for the rest of his days. Don't abandon him when he gets sick. I think this is the end. Let my *papá* know."

"Why? How do you feel?" says my sister.

"I feel bad." I could barely make signs and I was sweating.

So they decided to call my father. Martín went for him. I say, "No, it is going to upset him. I don't want to bother him."

My father came back at about four o'clock. He says, "What's the matter?"

I could not answer. I just made signs. Then he had the idea of calling the doctor, the medical doctor who lived in the center. Dr. Manfredo came to examine me. He gave me some pills which looked like little stones. I could barely swallow them even after they were crushed. Finally I swallowed them, and I felt my throat relax a little. Meanwhile my *papá* told me he was going to Cuernavaca to have the prescription filled. He went quickly and returned right away. He brought the medicines, some vials, some pills and something to be taken by spoonfuls and the next day I felt better. The doctor did not say what I had. My body felt better but I still couldn't walk. The soles of my feet felt as though there were thorns or ants on them. I was weak but little by little I got better.

Then, when I was feeling a little better, I was lying on my stomach and suddenly in the middle of the night, it was exactly midnight, I had to go to the toilet. It was exactly twelve o'clock, the hour for death and the devil, people say, but I lost my fear and went out to the *corral* and did not care. I wrapped myself in my blanket and went. As soon as I got back, I felt that urge again. I had to go back and forth, about ten times at least. I was wondering what it could be. During the day, every other moment I felt that urge. I could not rest. By then my whole body ached, but I did not tell my *papá* until later.

I was ashamed because it was so long since I had worked. I was not working and yet I was eating. My *papá* might say I wanted him to support me. I was ashamed of even going to the table to eat. Then

I got the idea that I wasn't my father's child any more, for I saw that he was annoyed because I was not working. He thought I was well and asked me to help him pile the corn husks. I really couldn't but I forced myself, even though it would harm me. I worked for a few minutes, and then again I felt the urge to go. So I went out to the *corral*. Then I came back and sat down to help him. In another three minutes, again I had to go. I came back and three minutes later, I went again. My *papá* noticed it right away. He didn't say anything to me but he asked Macrina, "Is Felipe ill? He keeps going to the *corral*. Is it diarrhea?"

"I don't know."

"Is he not eating?"

"No."

"Since when?"

"About four days ago."

"Why didn't he tell me? Doesn't he trust me?"

"Who knows? Maybe he is ashamed or embarrassed."

Then he asked me, "Are you ill? Is it diarrhea?"

"Yes, but I have had diarrhea before and this is different. Something like blood is coming out, and something very ugly that is black, white, green. It looks like mud. I don't know what is wrong with me. Maybe something in my stomach is rotting."

"But this is bad," he says. "This illness is dangerous. It is not the kind that can be cured any old way. Why didn't you speak up? What if you get worse?"

By that time I was so weak I was seeing stars, yellow stars, like the sun, and I saw something ugly, like dark wood. The next day I was worse. I couldn't get out of bed and my whole stomach hurt and I had fever.

"Only a doctor can cure this illness," my *papá* said, and what he did was send for the doctor. Dr. Manfredo came and said, "Well, let's see." He looked in my mouth and then he shook his head. He looked in the chamberpot and shook his head. I don't know whether what he saw was serious or not. He just kept looking at it and shaking his head. Then he wrote a prescription.

My *papá* said to me, "I am going to Cuernavaca to get the medicine because he is in a hurry to cure you. This illness is dangerous and it might get the better of you. But I don't have money. I have only twenty-five *pesos,* so now what do we do?"

Well, I had these hundred *pesos* that my brother Ricardo had sent me from the north, to help me while I was sick. I had kept them in my pocket all this time. I didn't let go of them. I kept them so that when I couldn't go on any more, at the very end, on my last day, I would take them out and give them to my *papá* to spend on anything he wanted. But meanwhile I was holding on to them, in case they would be useful to me in time.

So when this illness came up, I took out the money. What else could I do? I say to my *papá*, "Look, I have one hundred *pesos* here. If you want to spend them, let us see how much is left over."

"Why didn't you give them to me before?" My *papá* was angry but I thought, "No, if I had given them to him before, he would have spent them." I told him, "Now is when we need them. Take the hundred *pesos* and buy the medicine."

So he took the money with pleasure and went running to Cuernavaca. He returned quickly, bringing the medicine, and said, "Tell the doctor to come and see if these are the right ones."

The doctor came again and said, "Yes, these are the ones," and he gave me an injection. The medicines cost eighty-five *pesos* but with them I felt better the very next day, though I still felt weak and was bothered by the lump in my groin. I thought I was going to remain a cripple and would not be able to work any more. I couldn't even lift my blanket or a jug of water. I could walk slowly but I couldn't haul water or run or pick up heavy things.

When my *papá* asked me if I felt better, many times I said yes, just to be brave, but I didn't have much hope. I didn't go out into the street, only from my bed to the yard, from the yard to my bed. I would read a book, then lie down to sleep. I felt ashamed because my *papá* was working, my brothers were working, and I was lying down.

My cousin Filemón, who was living in Mexico City, came once in a while. He is my cousin on my mother's side. He comes and says to me, "Let's go to Mexico City. It will be better than to suffer here."

"But how can I go? I can't even walk."

"You will be better away from here," he says. Every time he came he found me lying down or sitting in the yard. He came about five times, and wanted to take me away with him. "You can work in the garage where I work, washing cars, or selling juice at the juice stand. The least you will earn there is fifteen or twenty *pesos* a day."

"Let me wait a little longer. I am not sure I can work yet, but yes, I think I'll drag myself there. Wait a little longer."

It was in February that he came again, at ten or eleven o'clock in the morning. I was sitting in the doorway near the little garden. I wasn't even wearing decent clothes any more.

"Are you better yet?" he says.

"Well, a little, yes."

"Then now let's go. I'll take you."

"But I don't have money! If you lend me some for the bus fare . . ."

"I don't have any but I'll try my best to get some."

I was feeling a little better, I had a little more strength, so I started to think, "What am I doing here? I am suffering. Macrina is angry with me because I see how she is carrying on with that man *don* Ángel. I complain about her to my *papá* and instead of speaking to her he tells me if I don't like it I know what I can do. And now my sister doesn't give me food."

Macrina would go out at about nine o'clock in the morning and come back at two or three in the afternoon. I would wait and wait and wait. I knew what she was doing and I couldn't stand it, but I bore it silently. What could I do? I was sick. Should I get angry or hit her? No, it's not good for me. My *papá* was in the cornfield all day and was not aware that she was seeing *don* Ángel. And when I told him he didn't believe me.

Then I recalled the things my sister did when my *mamá* was ill. When my mother was in bed and could no longer go out, she became very thin. She needed good food, strong food, to strengthen her body. My *papá*, poor thing, knew this. Now that I remember, I feel sorry for him. He suffered a lot for her. He found the way to buy her milk. He went out and who knows where he got meat, chocolate, lots of milk, many things. Well, he gave these things to Macrina, saying, "I brought this for your *mamá*. Give it to her." She said, "All right." Then my father would leave and my brother would leave and Macrina would give all these things, not to my mother, but to her own child. So I said to her, "No! My *papá* brought all these things for my *mamá* to eat. Give them to her!"

"No, not to my *mamá* any more. It's a waste. It won't do her any good. My daughter needs it. Now she can benefit from it." My sister gave my *mamá* just a little bit, but most of it she gave to her daughter. I just had to bear it for what was I going to do?

Once I hit her. It was when I was very ill. *Don* Ángel had been to the house early in the morning, I don't know what for. After he left she got ready to go to the mill and she said, "I'm going to the market. I'll be back soon."

So she went. Well, when she arrived at three o'clock, I was very hungry. Germán was still little and he was hungry too. I was angry. I thought this whole thing was no good. If she were alone, if she were by herself, she could do as she pleased, she could fool around, but not while she lived in my father's house.

"Where did you go?"

"Well, the mill wasn't working . . ."

"Where are you coming from?"

"From Conchita's house."

Then I asked her, "What did *don* Ángel want when he came this morning?"

"Nothing."

"Then why were you laughing? Why did you leave immediately after he left? Where were you?"

Then she got angry. "After all, it's none of your business."

"So, it's none of my business . . ." I took off my belt. I was sick and it wasn't going to do me any good, but I was going to give her a few lashings. So I gave her two.

"Who are you to hit me? Are you my husband? Are you my father?"

"Shut up!"

"Get out of here! I'm not going to give you anything to eat."

"Don't, but I'm going to tell my *papá* when he comes."

"Go right ahead, tell him."

Then she started to cry. When my *papá* got home in the evening she told him that I had hit her, that I had threatened her. Who knows what else! I was outside when my father called me.

"Felipe, come here! Sit down!"

I knew what was coming. Almost daily my father scolded me. So I thought, "What can I do? Macrina has told him lies again."

"Is it true that you hit your sister?"

"Yes, I hit her, but ask her why. Do you think that I hit her for nothing, without a motive? So let her tell you first why I hit her."

"You have no right to hit her. I am her father and even I don't have that right any more. So who are you to hit her or to scold her? You have no rights here. And if you don't like it, you know what to do."

I understood what he was saying. He was practically telling me that if I didn't like it I could leave. I understood, but I had to bear it for I was sick. I could not get out or go to work, so I endured it. After that my sister no longer fed me. She gave me food, but unwillingly. She threw a few *tortillas* to me. I cried, as men do at times, for all my sufferings. I wondered why I was there, suffering so.

So when Filemón wanted me to go away with him, I thought, "After all, this is the only way I can get out. I must make up my mind. Oh, God"—I remembered God—"the only way I can be well is to be away from home. Then I will be working and I'll see what luck I'll have." So I say to my cousin, "What time will you come by for me?"

"I'll be here at twelve, so wash and get ready."

"But I don't have any clothes."

"We'll go just as you are."

Well, then I washed my head and I washed my feet. My brother Martín came at about eleven and he says, "Do you feel better?"

"Yes, but you know what? At last I'm going to Mexico City."

"When?"

"Well, right now."

"With whom?"

"I'm going with Filemón. Can you lend me fifty *pesos?*"

"I don't have any money but I can borrow some for you. Are you really going? Have you told my *papá* at least?"

"When he comes I'll tell him. I'm not going to go out looking for him. So when he comes I'll tell him."

My *papá* arrived a little later. I didn't say anything right away because he would get angry. But I thought, "No matter what happens I must tell him I am going to Mexico City. Whether he gets angry or not, I am leaving." He was going in and out of the house, in and out, from the yard to the house. Then I made up my mind. "You know, *papá*, I'm going to Mexico City."

"You're going? I wish you success," he said mockingly. He did not take me seriously. He kept coming and going.

I thought, "So he doesn't believe me. I'll show him." I got my blanket and made a pack. "I am going now." Three times I told him I was leaving and he did not believe me.

Finally he said, "Well, what can I do? Now that you've decided, what do you expect me to do? You are big now." Then he looked thoughtful and said, "All this is already written. When your *mamá* was alive, all of you were here together. No sooner did she die when each one went his way. Ricardo left. Your brother Moisés went off to teach, and now you are leaving. In a few days, Martín will also go. What can I do? That is life. Well, when are you leaving? Tomorrow? In a week?" He was still making fun of me.

"No, I'm going now."

"What time? In the evening?"

"No, I'm going right now."

"Yes? In a little while?"

"No, right now, right this minute, I'm leaving. See my pack?"

"But how? Why didn't you tell me? When are you coming back?"

"I can't tell you when. I don't know. It depends on the job I find."

My father went inside. He went to his bed and started to cry. My aunt Julia, my father's sister, was there with her daughter, and she came and told me, "Your father is crying. Cheer him up but do not mind his crying. Even though he cries, go right ahead and leave. Come to visit him every month or every two months."

I said, "I can't tell you now for sure, but I'll be coming every two months, every three months."

"Yes, don't abandon him completely. Visit him once in a while. You can see he's old. But don't pay attention to his tears. When you were here he chased you out, so now that you are leaving, don't consider him. And behave well over there."

For the last time I went to say good-bye to my father and he says, "What can I do? I would like to keep all of you together here at home, but I can't any more. You are grown up now. What I ask of you is to behave well there. And behave well on the job."

"Yes, do not worry, I already plan to do that." So I said farewell and I left for the city.

My cousin introduced me to the man in charge of the parking lot where he worked. The man knew my cousin very well. He said, "If he's like you, all right, but if he starts doing things wrong, if he makes trouble, no."

"No, I know him. He's my cousin."

"Well, if he's your cousin and you know him, all right. He can begin tomorrow morning."

My cousin told me what to do. I started washing cars, and at first I earned only two, three, ten little *pesos*. I worked from eight in the morning to six at night. But I was not feeling very well, and even after two months I wanted to go back. I was living in the city with Saturnino, a fellow from Azteca. My cousin was staying with him and that's how I got there. I did not pay rent, but gave them fifteen *pesos* a week for meals and laundry. I liked the job, but sometimes I didn't earn enough. Sometimes I made nothing at all, or only two or five *pesos,* but when I worked hard on good days I earned about thirty *pesos.* I stayed on the job about four months.

One day as I was leaving the parking lot, the man in charge asked me whether I wanted to take a job as night watchman in the place across the street. I asked what was required and he explained that it was an easy job. I had to sell the fruit juices and do the cleaning, from seven-thirty in the evening until we closed the stand at about one or two in the morning. And I could go to bed right there if I wanted to.

I didn't know the tricks of the business, so the next day when I turned in the account I didn't know if all the money was for the owner or for me. The man who was second-in-charge came and he began to measure with a ruler the amount of juice left in the pitchers.

He figured how much I had sold and how much was left. I handed him the money and he said everything was all right. Slowly I caught on to the whole thing. I worked seven days a week, without a day's rest. I did not have a single day off with pay in all the five years I worked there. I went there daily. I was not sick any more so I worked every day. I did not belong to a union. When I went home to Azteca I just asked permission from the owner and got one or two days off without pay. I liked the job. I was very happy. I was both watchman and juice vendor.

I lived with the family from Azteca for one year. I moved out when I got married. But before I met my wife, while I was still working in the parking lot, I was going around with this other woman, Prisca. I got to know her about two months after I arrived in Mexico City. She came one day to borrow money from the man in charge of the parking lot. She came often, but I paid little attention to her. She would come once every week, or sometimes every three days. One day she came . . . it was Sunday morning . . . and that was when I made a proposal to her. She said to me, "Look, you like me and feel affection for me and you have thought about me, but until now I have had no feeling for you. Perhaps later I will have it, so let me think it over and I will tell you later."

Well, she began to have confidence in me and once she came at ten o'clock in the morning and stayed with me until after midnight. Then she says to me, "I'm tired and I have no place to sleep. Take me to a hotel." And so I took her.

The next day we got up at about ten o'clock in the morning and went to have breakfast. Then we went to the public baths and then I took her to her home. We continued together as sweethearts, and when I changed my job to work at the juice stand she would come to help me.

She was my sweetheart and I loved her very much. I think she loved me, too. Sometimes, when I didn't have money to give her or if she knew I had no money for food, she would give me ten or fifteen *pesos*. I wanted to marry her but no, she never wanted to. I asked her if I could count on her and she told me to look for someone else, that I couldn't count on her, that we could be sweethearts but nothing more.

She says, "There are so many women in the street. Why don't you speak to one of them?"

And so I say to her, "Sure, there are many girls but I don't like any of them. Many of them come to the stand to offer themselves to me, but I don't like them the way I like you. Had I wanted to, I could have had many, but I don't have the same feeling for them."

She says, "Perhaps one day I will marry, but right now I don't want to. Let me think about it."

And I say, "I have already let you think. It is not the first time that I am asking you to marry. It is not only yesterday that we met. I have already talked to you many times. I have tried to show you what's good for your future. I want to help you. My intentions toward you are good. Don't think that I am just playing around with you. Let's get married, if only by civil law and perhaps later, we can marry in church."

She says to me, "Well, I might marry you, but your *papá* won't want it because he doesn't know me."

So I say to her, "You are going to marry *me*, not my *papá*, so if he doesn't like it, what about it? We don't live together anyway. The day my *papá* comes, if he tells me it isn't good for me, well, my father can't really interfere in our affairs. Perhaps in other affairs, yes, but not in this matter."

Then she says to me, "Now look, I have another man and perhaps I love him more. Until now I can't tell whether I love you more or whether I love him more, and that is why I don't want to marry you now. Look for someone who is more like you are."

I say to her, "Well, if you don't want to marry me, I will marry someone else. Do you give me permission?"

"Yes."

"You won't be sorry now?"

And she says to me, "Get married. I give you permission."

So I say, "Now you know that I have spoken to you like a man. I have shown you things as they are. I have offered to marry you and now I will have to marry someone else."

That was when I fell in love with Mago, my wife, the one I married. We were sweethearts only two weeks and I tried to make a decision. Again I asked Prisca, my first sweetheart, to marry me and again she said, "Why don't you look for someone who is better for you?"

Well, Prisca left me for a few days and I heard that the police had picked her up. They said she was a streetwalker and put her in jail. She was still in jail when I married Mago. When Prisca got out she came to see me. But meanwhile the neighbors had told her that I had been married for some time.

And so she says to me, "Did you get married yet?"

I say to her, "No."

So she says, "Now, don't deny it. I know that you are married so what's the point of my saying any more about it?"

"Yes, I am married."

"Do you love your wife?"

"For better or for worse, she is my wife."

I really don't know how I got involved with the other woman, my wife. She was a servant in a small restaurant and sometimes came to deliver my lunch. I didn't pay much attention to her because I loved the other woman I had.

When Mago brought my lunch or came to the stand for a *taco* or to drink juice, at first I didn't notice her but little by little I started speaking to her and a friendship began. I saw that she was meek and docile and I got to like her. I thought, "This one suits me."

One day, without too much thought, I took her home to Azteca. I invited her just as a friend, nothing else. We took a taxi to the bus terminal. When we got to my house I introduced her as a fellow worker. They received her well.

We went to see my sister Conchita. My sister asked, "Are you going together? Have you been together long?"

We answered, "No."

She said, "Well, you ought to get married. My brother is alone. Do you have a mother, girl?"

"No, I don't."

"Well, there you are! My brother is a nice fellow. Get together and later you can get married." Then Conchita served us some food, saying, "Now, eat together, so you will love each other more."

Mago only laughed. We ate together and then I said we had to leave because I had to work at seven-thirty. On the bus I began to tell her what I was thinking. "You know, I have good intentions. Get together with me, set up house with me. I'm not playing around. I want to have a proper home, in an honorable way."

"If you stop seeing the woman who goes around with you, if you leave her, all right."

"I've already left her," I said. "Now you have to decide. It's very simple, yes or no, and that's that. If you say yes, fine; if you say no, nothing's lost. But I want to marry you soon, at least by civil law. We'll get married in a few days when I get some money and we'll look for a room. We will pay some rent and you will quit being a servant."

She says, "Well . . . all right."

"Then it's a deal."

"My clothes are with this woman *doña* Paula. I can't get them now. I'll go tomorrow."

She went with me the next day to get her box of things. It was a heavy box and was difficult to carry. She had lots of dresses and about 125 *pesos*. She bought a shawl and more dresses and shoes. I bought her other things, for I was earning well. She came to live with me in the juice stand. For a whole month we were wandering the streets, looking for a place to live. Meanwhile we slept in the juice stand. When I wasn't working we would go to Chapultepec, to La Villa, Xochimilco, Contreras, Cuernavaca, we always had places to go to. Sometimes we had money, sometimes we had none. Little by little I got to know all the streets of Mexico City. When I had first arrived I didn't go even one block away. Then I went one block, two blocks, three. Now I can go all over the city.

I was still going with Prisca and every day I gave her about ten *pesos*, sometimes fifteen *pesos*. Little by little she began to give herself to me again and I liked to visit her. Mago and I were living together too, but we were not married by law yet. I took Mago to Azteca several times to see my *papá,* but every time we went he was not around.

One day, I think it was during the Carnival, we went and he was there, and my aunts and uncles, too. Then my *papá* said, "Well, why don't you introduce me to your wife?" So they finally met.

"Well, now," my father said, "when are you getting married? I'm glad to know you and I'll expect you to get married."

I did not want to get married yet. I just wanted to be together. She did not want to get married yet, either. I didn't want to because of the other woman. I liked both women and I was earning enough for both of them. I gave both their daily expense money, about ten or fifteen *pesos* each. I slept with Prisca whenever she came to see me, every three days, daily sometimes, sometimes every week. My wife stayed at home, in the room we rented. I was at the juice stand alone, so Prisca came there to be with me.

Then my *papá* came to Mexico City to arrange the wedding. He did not want us to just live together, he wanted a legal marriage. "I want you to marry. I feel responsible because you are not married yet. After you marry, I'll be happy. When I die, I can go in peace."

I asked Mago, "What do you say?"

"Whatever you say. If you want, we'll get married, but as for me, I don't want marriage yet."

I said to my father, "We don't have money for the wedding."

"That's nothing," he said. "It will be about fifty *pesos* in Azteca, but I'll speak to the president. He's a good friend of mine and it won't cost you a *centavo.* Just something to drink for the witnesses, and so that you don't spend a lot of money, let's have it on my Saint's Day. What do you say?"

We did not want to. For my part, I had two hearts, for I did not want to leave either of them. "We will tell you later. We will think about it."

"But I thought that since you were living together, you had already thought about it. So, get married."

We went to Contreras, walking and talking, the three of us. My *papá* stubbornly asking us to get married, get married, get married. I began to worry: "Do I get married, or don't I? What am I waiting for? I'd better marry this woman. Then I'll be able to save."

So I asked my *señora,* "What do you say?"

"It's up to you."

"No, it's up to you. We have yet to see if you love me or not. And to get married one needs money. I need money to buy you shoes and clothes and to buy myself clothes. For that and the other expenses we will need at least four hundred *pesos,* even marrying in the poor man's way."

Yes, I decided to marry her after all. I was thirty-six and she was twenty-two. We agreed with my father to get married on his Saint's Day, to avoid having separate expenses for two different celebrations. So I started saving and buying clothes. I had about five or six hundred *pesos.* We needed to buy things for the wedding, things to drink, things to eat, and we began buying them in the city.

On my father's Saint's Day we went to Azteca. We arrived there at about one or two in the afternoon. When we got there my *papá* said, "Well, so you came! We thought you were not coming after all. Now that you're here I'm going to call the officials to get this over with."

So my *papá* went to get the president and everybody. They made the contract and we signed it. My *señora* was not pregnant yet. Many people were there, Conchita, Martín, Moisés, Germán, Macrina, all the family, my uncles and everyone. Ricardo was not there. My aunt Gloria was there, and all the neighbors, except *don* Ángel. It was my father's Saint's Day and no one knew it was going to be my wedding also. So they began to ask, "Why is there so much to eat and so much to drink?" The ones who knew answered, "Felipe is getting married."

"Where is the bride?"

"She's in the kitchen."

"How did he manage?"

"Going to Mexico City, that's how."

At that time I dressed better than I had before and they were also commenting on the fact that I knew how to write and how to add a little, and how those who didn't were stuck in Azteca while I had got ahead and now I was married. Later, I figured it all out and it seems I spent about five hundred *pesos,* besides what my father spent.

Then we went back to Mexico City and I continued with my work.

My wife didn't know I was still having relations with Prisca, and for a while both women came to help me at the juice stand. But then someone told my wife a big lie and she believed it. And so the two of them were there and they really went after each other. Neither one could put up with the other. They slapped and pulled each other's hair and were kicking until I separated them. They even lost their earrings.

Prisca stopped coming to the stand for a while. Later she came when my wife wasn't there and we were very happy. When I left work she was waiting for me, and we would walk together and have a good time. Yes, we were very happy. She said to me, "Buy me a pair of shoes," and I bought her everything she wanted and I took her wherever she wanted to go. Then in the afternoon I would take her to her house and I would go to my house. At night she would come again to the stand to help me serve the customers and wash the glasses.

Once she said to me, "You know, I am pregnant. Now what do you say? I want to marry you but I can't now because you are already married. Why did you have to have a civil marriage? It is your fault that we can't marry. If you knew you loved me, why did you get married? I have more right because you knew me first, and anyway, you promised you would marry me and now you have betrayed me."

I say to her, "Now, look, it is not my fault. You know I had good intentions toward you and that I wanted you."

After Prisca had the baby, I went to see her every two days in the General Hospital where she gave birth. She said it was my son. When she was ready to leave the hospital, I gave my blood so that she could leave, because I had no money to pay the bill. She lived at her father's place in San Ángel. I still went to see her there every day and I gave her fifteen *pesos* for her daily expenses. Then she moved to her aunt's house in Portales. Little by little she became rebellious toward me and began to make trouble over any little gossip she heard. One day she said to me, "Lend me your radio"—because I had a little radio my brother had given me—"I am here all alone in the house. My father goes away to work and I am very sad. You, too, go away and only come once in a while. I would like you to be here all day."

So I say to her, "But look here, you know I have my wife so how can I be here with you all day? I leave my job at eleven o'clock and I come right here to you by twelve. I stay for two or three hours and then I go to Mago—to my house—for a few hours. Don't think that I go anywhere else."

So she says, "Well, I want you to be here with me every day and I want you to sleep here. What you do is almost like a doctor's visit. You come for an hour or two. No, this doesn't mean that I have a man."

So I say to her, "But I give you your daily expense money. You lack nothing. When you ask me for something, I buy it for you. When you have no shoes I buy them. I buy clothes for the child."

I kept coming to the house and was quite happy. And then she began with her pretexts that I shouldn't come at a certain hour because her father was there. Later I learned from some neighbors that they saw her with another man. Once I tried to spy on her. The neighbors told me that a man came to visit her at five o'clock in the afternoon so I came at this time to spy. Yes, I saw the two of them talking, there on the corner. When she saw me, she tried to pull herself away, but the man wouldn't let her and slapped her. Then he hugged her and she pushed away but he went after her and they began to talk again. Well, by this time I was very angry. She had gone back to her house and I sent a little girl to call her.

When she came out, I said, "I want to talk to you and don't think that I am going to get angry. No. I want to talk quietly with you."

She says, "No, I am nervous now and I don't want to talk. It is better if you come tomorrow."

I returned to my house and came back the next day. I say to her, "What a nice thing you did yesterday, eh? No, don't deny it. The neighbors told me earlier that you had a man, but I never believed it until I saw you myself doing these piggish things."

So she says, "So, now what?"

I say, "Nothing, except this is where we part."

On the following days I continued to pass by her house without paying any attention to her. I could see her in the doorway, and when she saw me she would shut the door. I thought to myself, "Very well, the day will come when she will need me." Then one day a little girl came to tell me Prisca wanted to talk to me. So I went. I said to her, "What is it? What do you want?"

She said, "Why, I wanted to talk to you to see if you are still angry."

So I said, "Why should I be angry? I can't force you to do anything you don't want to. We can put an end to it here and that's that."

And she said, "Didn't you see that I slapped him? That I didn't want to have anything to do with him? It is the neighbors that are making trouble by filling you with gossip. Just to prove to you that there is nothing between that man and myself, let us walk together one day in front of him, arm in arm, and you will see that he means nothing to me."

And we did exactly that. One day we passed by him while she was holding my arm and we were talking. He just watched us but no one said anything. Then she said, "Now will you believe that he means nothing to me? If he were really my man, he would have grabbed me and said something to you."

And so we continued as before.

But one day I spied on her again. I arrived at about twelve o'clock. She told me she was going out for a while near the Obregón Monument. She would always go out at this hour, and when she didn't come back at the usual time I went to look for her and I saw her again with this same man. She was near his house and I was spying on them from behind a wall. When she saw me she turned around and began to run. She was filling her tin container with water at the fountain and this man helped her to her house.

The radio she had borrowed from me was in her house and I say to myself, "Well, I won't talk to them now, I won't say a thing." I was very angry. The man left her at the door of her house and went away so I went in. I could see that she was very nervous, even her mouth was trembling.

She said, "Felipe, why have you come?"

So I said, "You know, give me the radio. I have come to take it." I had great anger stored up in me which I could hardly bear, but I didn't show it. I said to myself, "Why should I fight with her?"

And she said, "No, I can't give you the radio now." She told me to leave because the neighbors would gossip if I stayed on. But I tried to get the radio. I said I wouldn't go unless I got the radio.

And she said, "Now you are very angry. You are so angry you can hardly stand it, right?"

"How do you know?"

"I can see."

"Well, whose fault is it, yours or mine?"

"Yours," she says, "because you come to butt into my business."

And then I say to her, "This is the last time I'll come to bother you. What I want now is the radio and then everything is ended for us. I will never come back to set foot in your house, and if I ever do, I want you to drive me out with stones."

Then the little boy, who was just beginning to walk, came over and began to stroke me and climb on me. I picked him up and hugged him, because he took me for his father. And so I say to the little boy, "You have known me as your father, and you still love me. You know I buy you so many things. I buy your clothing and your shoes. Whatever your *mamá* told me to buy, I have bought you. I recognize you as my son, but I believe this will be the last time I will embrace you, because now I must take leave of you forever. I will never see you again."

And then I turned to her and said, "I ask you to take good care of the little boy because it is the last time I will see him with these eyes." I began to kiss the child and she said, "Leave him alone."

"Don't worry. I won't take him. I am taking leave of you and the child forever."

Then she says, "Why, don't you want to come back?"

And I say, "No, this is it. I no longer have any reason to come here, so it is good-bye forever." But then I thought, "How can I get that radio? It is a good radio. Perhaps I can get it from her by trickery."

So I did come back but it was no longer for her, it was to get the radio. I continued to sleep with her, and I also left her daily expense money about every third or fourth day. Finally she said to me, "Look, I think we had better part. I want to go to Guadalajara with my aunt. Don't think I am going off with anyone else. It is just to go to work."

Well, I became very sad. She went off for a few days, and from what I heard, she went to another part of the city and not to Guadalajara. I came to look for her after a week and found her in her house again. But then one day—I don't know what bit of gossip someone had told her father—but anyway, he came and locked her out of the house and she went off to Contreras. I went to look for her every week and she was not there. I even went to look for her in Portales at her aunt's house but I could not find her. I went to look for her at San Ángel, and the woman with whom she had been living said, "No, don't look for her any more. She is with another man."

Yes, I really loved that woman but we separated and I never knew where she was after that. I was working downtown near the center when a shoe-shine boy told me that Prisca had come to look for me and that she was very ill. Well, the next day she came to see me and she was really sick, completely sick. She could hardly walk or talk. She was very thin.

And I said to her, "What's the trouble? What do you have?"

She said, "I am very sick. I don't know what it is I have."

"If you want, let's go to the doctor," I said to her, and I gave her thirty *pesos*. I said, "You see? Even though you left me, I still love you."

She took the money and went off and I never saw her again.

Meanwhile, I lived peacefully with my wife. I was buying more things, a clock, blankets, a regular bed, cooking utensils, as we needed them.

Then they robbed me. Everything I had at home was stolen. I had gone to Azteca to take some things to prepare the celebration of my father's Saint's Day. We had one child by then and my wife decided to

take the baby and wait for me at the juice stand. She could do my
work if she went there and I could go to Azteca. I returned in the
evening and we spent the night there in the stand.

The next day we got up early, cleaned the place and Mago left
for the house at eight in the morning. I got home at about one in the
afternoon and found my wife crying. My sister-in-law and another
woman were there.

"What's the matter?"

"They broke in and stole everything."

The thing that worried me most were the deposit slips from the
bank, but they were there. I had a lot of money in the bank before
but then I withdrew some and so I had about a thousand *pesos* left.
The robbers had left the receipts but they took everything else. We
had gone to the market to get food for the week and even that they
took, even the *chiles!* I had a blanket that cost me ninety *pesos*, a
bedspread eighty-five *pesos*, a clock ninety-five *pesos*, my wife's
dresses. She had two big boxes full of them, about thirty dresses which
she had bought when she was a servant. Then the baby's clothes!
Well, they took everything they found. I kept thinking, "What am I
going to do now? It was all I had." My wife started crying again.
Naturally, I felt bad. I was angry, then I felt sad, a kind of desperation,
but what could I do? If I knew who it was, I could accuse him and
send him to jail, but I didn't know. It had happened at about one o'clock
in the morning.

Well, I thought about it some more and I told my wife, "There is
nothing we can do now so be resigned to it. Pray to God that I be
well, that I don't get sick, so I can start all over. After all, money comes
and goes, but you still have me."

I suspected a man who lived in the same *vecindad*. He had no
job. There he was without work, coming and going, coming and going,
in and out. I lived right at the entrance and he kept passing by. And
then about eight days after the robbery he moved out of the *vecindad*.

When we went to Azteca on my father's Saint's Day, I told him
about the robbery.

"Didn't you file a suit?"

"But how, if I don't know against whom? If I had seen them, of
course I'd take them to jail, but not knowing . . ."

"At least you should have informed the police."

"What for?"

Then we started figuring out the amount they had taken. We
figured everything . . . tomatoes, *chiles*, beans, rice, oranges, bananas,
clothes, well, everything. It came to about 1,200 *pesos*.

You see, I was able to save all that because I alone was in charge of the sales at the fruit-juice stand. I did all the selling and there was always some extra money after I did the account. Before we closed, I counted the money and I noticed that I usually had more money than I should have had. At times there were forty *pesos* too much, sometimes even fifty. They had a little ruler to measure how many liters there were left in each thirty-five-liter jug and when I began work at seven-thirty in the evening they measured what had been sold during the day. That account was separate. I don't know why, but there was always an excess of money by the time I closed up. I would leave fifteen or twenty *pesos* of the extra money and I would take the rest. The manager always told me when the account was short but when there was an excess he never said anything. On good days we would take in one hundred or one hundred and fifty *pesos*, on very bad days about thirty, forty or sixty. It was a nice job because the extra money I got was apart from my wages.

Since the robbery, things have not been the same. I haven't been able to replace everything. I started to buy little things again but then I lost my job. It was on the last day of February. I turned my account in at about nine in the morning. This time I worked in a stand near a movie house, because they transferred me there. The stand was a new one and the sales were not very good. The first day I sold twelve *pesos* worth, then fifteen, then thirty or forty, something like that. The day I was fired, I sold sixty-three *pesos* worth. When I turned over the money to the *señorita* in charge, I was waiting to hear her say that some money was missing, but she added it up and said nothing. Then I went to the other stand and five minutes later they called me. It was the *señorita* again.

"I'm going to give you a few days' vacation."

I was quiet. I didn't say a thing.

"I'm going to give you a few days' rest. It's fair that you have some rest. In the meantime keep on washing the cars. I'll let you know when your rest is over."

I thought this was some sort of punishment and that it was going to last a week or two. That was nothing, I could get by. Naturally, I felt angry, but did not say a word. I left and paid no attention to what she told me. This happened on a Wednesday. I did not go back the following days, but on Monday I reported to the girl in charge. I greeted her and asked, "Am I going to work, now?"

"I'll let you know. I don't need you now, but I'll let you know."

"Well, shall I take out my belongings?"

"I think so." She handed me my things.

I went to the office to see the owner. "I came to see you because the *señorita* punished me and I don't know why."

"Who are you and where do you work?"

"I'm the watchman at the juice stand."

"Well, if the *señorita* punished you she must have had a reason."

"No. In that case she should have told me. I know I have behaved well. I get there on time."

"You did something, I'm sure, that's why she punished you. Maybe it's because you like to gamble?"

"No, I have never gambled. I don't know how to play cards."

"What about taking money?"

"Money? Do you think that in all this time I've worked I've been taking money? And if I've been taking money do you think I would be dressed like this? There have been times when I haven't even had money for my bus fare."

"I don't know. Go talk to Ruperto, downstairs. He can discuss this thing with his sister and later I'll talk to them."

I told Ruperto all about this thing but he kept staring at me angrily. I told my story but he kept saying that the girl must have had a reason.

Naturally, that made me mad and I say to myself, "Here I am begging them, going to them in a nice way. If they don't want to, let's see if they will pay attention to some other way." So I went to the Department of Conciliation and Arbitration at the Labor Secretariat. I knew about this place and it was my own idea to go there. I went and the lawyer in charge came out to the courtyard and asked me why I was there, did I come about work or about justice? I said I came about my job. He asked me to go into his office and to sit down.

"Where do you work?"

I told him.

"How much were you earning?"

"Eleven *pesos*."

"How long had you been working there?"

"I started in nineteen fifty-six."

"Did you get a vacation?"

"Not a single day. No week's rest, no holidays, no Christmas bonus, nothing, and when I asked for a day off I did not earn my pay."

"Were you working overtime?"

"Yes. I began at seven-thirty at night and stayed there overnight. The next morning I got up at six and started cleaning. When the girl in charge got there everything was clean and then I rendered my accounts. I helped to make the juice, to carry the jugs, everything, and I left at about noon."

"For eleven *pesos*? That's atrocious! But don't worry. Just be sure to come back in three days."

On the third day I went and he gave me a copy of the summons.

He said he was going to send another copy to the place where I was employed and he warned me of the things that might happen. The owners would come to look for me and either threaten me or offer me money, but I should not pay attention to them or accept the money, and I should tell this lawyer what had happened.

On the fourth day my cousin Filemón came to see me. I was having breakfast when he knocked on the window.

"Felipe . . ."

"What is it? Come in, come in . . ."

"No, I want to talk to you. Come outside." I thought it was strange, so I went out.

"What's the matter?"

"What have you done over there on the job?"

"Nothing."

"If you did nothing, why is Ruperto bothering me? He says that you stole money, you stole the jugs and six gasoline lamps."

"So that's it! He can come here and see for himself whether I stole these things. He has my address. Why is he sending you? Why is he causing you trouble? This has nothing to do with you."

"No. But he says that he's going to send me to jail, and you too. Me, because I got you the job."

"Oh yes? This has nothing to do with you. Tell him to stop bothering you. Tell him to come to me. After all, they never said a word to me about stealing. The girl saw me, the man in charge saw me, the owner saw me, why didn't they tell me then?"

"Well, they told me to bring you to settle this thing."

"I won't have anything to do with them. They don't even have a written communication, an official order. I'll settle with the Labor Secretariat, not with this man."

I went to see the lawyer at the Labor Secretariat and told him what happened. He said not to pay attention to them but to wait for the hearings. I could even sue them for defamation! It seems that the license for the place was not in the owner's name but in the girl's name. Everything on our side was in order and they realized that they were about to lose. After six hearings, this girl offered me fifty *pesos,* then five hundred. They did not have any evidence against me, that's why they were offering me money. The lawyer said he was going to ask for three thousand *pesos,* if it was all right with me, because he was going to do it according to the law. He was going to ask for three months' wages, for the days of rest that I didn't get, the overtime that they didn't pay, the holidays I worked, the vacations I did not get, all that. I agreed to this and to split the money with the lawyer.

They refused to give three thousand but were willing to give two thousand. After a lot of discussion they did not have the cash with them, so they gave me a check which we cashed at a bank. I gave the lawyer one thousand and I got one thousand. By that time I owed a lot of money here and there, and I owed rent. I had borrowed two hundred *pesos* at the Banco Internacional and I owed the interest. With the thousand *pesos* they gave me, I paid all my debts.

But after that I couldn't find another steady job. I got tired of walking around the city looking for work. I went to the CTM union, to the section for hotel and restaurant workers, and all that. I went to the Department of Public Works. I went to the Aviation Center, to the Department of Transportation and . . . nothing. They just say, "Come back tomorrow." I go and they say, "Well, think of it, there is no work!" I went to the Department of Sanitation. There they asked me for three hundred *pesos* to get me in right away. At the Hotel Union they had also asked me for one hundred fifty *pesos* to get in. If I had money would I be going around asking for a job? If I had three hundred *pesos* I would rather be a vendor of something. And then they have so many requirements! They ask for letters of recommendation, for a primary-school certificate, for a Military Service Card, for police clearance. They ask for all that and a person doesn't have it. The Military Card alone costs about 150 *pesos!*

When my second child was born it was worse. The boy got sick and I thought he was going to die on me. I had to hustle and get some money to take him to a doctor. I keep borrowing, and the little money I earn is not enough to pay for everything. Now my *papá* comes and says he wants me to live in Azteca because he is alone. He even half-scolded me because I didn't want to go so I reminded him what my motive was for coming to Mexico City. It was not my fault that I left home. I had to find a way out for myself because my *papá* showed more charity for my sister Macrina than for me. Naturally, he is still my father and I respect him and love him because he is the sole author of my life. If he wants me to live in Azteca I will go, but not for more than two or three weeks. My children cannot remain in Azteca because they would grow up without culture, without civilization. I want them to grow up in Mexico City so that they can have civilization and culture.

CHAPTER XXV

PEDRO

Old Age

My life has been very different since my wife died, very different. My daughter was here to serve me so I really had nothing to complain about, but even now at night I remember my wife and the tears roll down. Everything was so much better when she was alive!

In the first place, I know my children are disinterested . . . there is no family solidarity any more. My oldest child, Conchita, manages to get by all right, but as far as she is concerned, I am not deserving of a crust of bread or an old pin. If I come when she is eating then she will give me a *taco;* if not, I get nothing. When her mother died, it was an obligation on her part to help, was it not? As daughter, and as son-in-law, right? Would you like to know what the help was that she gave? She brought the gasoline lamp! There was still no electric light here then. That was all the help I got from her, and who knows where she borrowed it?

My other son-in-law, Macrina's husband, also brought a gasoline lamp. That was the extent of his help too. Two sons-in-law, two gasoline lamps! Well, at least they came and shed a little light! As far as Macrina's husband is concerned, he was right, as he wasn't living with my daughter any more. But not Conchita's husband . . . instead of helping out with some money or something like that, it was just the lamp. Luckily, I had a few *centavos* put aside for expenses as I had sold my mule.

Now my sons have practically left me and are scattered. When they saw that everything was over, they began to go off. The only one who stayed with me was Germán, because he was still in school. First, Ricardo went up north. He says he intends to come back, but not to be a peasant any more, I don't think. He says yes, but my feeling is that he won't because he already has his woman there, a woman who won't be any good to him. In the first place she is not his kind; she is from the city. The worst of it is that the woman is very old and has bad habits and is sickly . . . doctors every little while . . . right now they threw away about six hundred *pesos* on doctors! But all I wish is that they live well and take care of themselves and leave me alone.

Martín wanted to learn to be a baker and that is what he became. But he was restless and kept saying over and over, "I am going up north, I am going up north." That was when you could still earn good money there. So I say to him, "Man, what do you want to do that for, when there is plenty of work around here? And besides, here you have no expenses."

"No, but I want to see what it is like there."

"Well, go ahead, then." So I sold the horse, for three hundred *pesos,* which I gave him. We went around scraping together some more so he could have seven hundred *pesos* for his trip. But first they wouldn't let him through to the United States, then they weren't hiring, and little by little he began using up the money.

Even when his money was gone, he said, "I am leaving, but I owe three hundred *pesos.*"

"What about the three hundred *pesos* from my horse?"

"The man who was going to get us across has it. Now I owe three hundred more."

"So that means you spent it all! What did you do with all that money?"

"Say! You are going back a long way. That was over a year ago and I kept drawing on it and it's gone. Now I am in debt."

"Well, pay it, then." I was cleaned out! Good-bye animals; everything was gone. I was accustomed to having animals but my son says, "What for? I am not a mule driver any more, I am a baker."

"It has nothing to do with you. I need an animal to ride out to the fields to work. I am about used up now and I can't bear the long walk any more. I am going to get myself an animal even if it is a donkey."

"A donkey? After you've owned a mule? No, I don't care for donkeys."

"No, you are a master baker, you don't need one. But what about me? If I sit myself down here in the shade and say to all of you 'All right, now support me,' you can't do it. Where are my *tortillitas* and my little snacks going to come from? You are not able to support me. No, I always have to keep up the struggle."

They had no answer. And that is how it has been. After that Martín, the master baker, went off to Mexico City for two years but he came back here again. I don't even know how much he earns. He says he doesn't make anything but that's because he would rather spend his money for other things. When the Carnival comes he spends hundreds of *pesos* and that's that.

I never liked that trade because bakers don't earn much. A peasant earns more! To this day, I say to Martín, "Man! Better leave the bakery. Raise tomatoes or even gladiolas because it is a good business." But he doesn't want to cultivate any more. He hasn't helped me out since his mother died. When I want to send him off to work in the cornfield, he says, "Sure, sure, I am not a slave."

And I have said to him, "What kind of a son are you? You belong to a family, don't you? You don't lay out anything but you want your meals every day. You live off my money but you won't take anything out of your own pocket. Man, if you want to be part of the family you have to give me your pay."

I told him to get married, but he just let me talk. And he had a sweetheart too, but I don't know what they do with themselves nowadays. He kept telling me that she was going to move in on a certain day, but she never arrived. I was beginning to give up. I said to Macrina, "Now about that woman . . . if your brother had already done some foolishness with her, she would be insisting by now. I would like her to be with us. We need her here."

Why was she holding back? The thing is that that man hadn't done anything to her. He was very stupid about everything. He is very spiritless by nature; he can't even court a woman. Not a single one of my sons has inherited my character! All Martín did was go to work, dress himself up, comb his hair, and go out into the street. That's all. As I have said to him, "You have changed a lot. Since your mother died you have changed for the worse. It is going to be five years and you have helped me very little with the harvests. Get married, at least, and bring her here. If you like, I will go and ask for her."

"Later, later," he says, and I waited.

They kept quarreling and separating and getting together. He even took her out to Cuernavaca but nothing happened. I say, "What happened, man? Do it now, man. Look, your mother is dead. I am here alone. Your sister is going to marry and leave."

"Right away," he says, "but not with her any more."

"What do you mean, not with her any more?"

"Now it will be with another one."

"Hmm. After all, she is not going to be for me so do what you like. You are old now. How can I treat you like a little boy? Let's see what happens."

Moisés, the other one, is a rural schoolteacher and the salary they pay him is a triviality because he had only six months of preparatory school. And naturally, with food so expensive, he can support only himself. But when he comes home on vacation he helps me with the harvest and I take care of him. He is still keeping up his studies and is going to get his diploma . . . that is why I don't make any demands on him. Every once in a while I say to him, "Can't you help me out a little, man?" But he always answers, "I haven't been paid this month!" or, "I can't spare it, I earn so little." Then sometimes he asks me, "Don't you have at least five *pesos* for my fare?" And what can I do? I am a father, so there go five *pesos*.

Then Moisés needed a hundred *pesos* because he had not been paid. Where was I going to get it from? I went around trying to raise it but I couldn't, so I decided to go to Mexico City. Let him solve his own problem, because I was in a bad situation. I owed five hundred *pesos* and he had told me, "Look, pawn the house and I'll get it out of hock for you later." But after I pawned it, he forgot about it. Now my sister has half the property and I pay her 8 percent interest. My sons no longer seem to care about the house.

I say, "Man! Look at the rent. It is due and if I don't pay the five hundred *pesos* they will attach the house. We will have to get out of here, all because of you. You ought to realize it is time you took the responsibility, because I have done my share. I took care of you, I brought you up, now you should be looking after me, not me after you. The least you could do is to get me free of this debt."

Well, they paid Moisés two months' salary and he did give me the five hundred *pesos*. But as he had been borrowing for two months, that was all the money he could give. So then I sold the pig for 350 *pesos*. Well, the boys just notice that I have some money and they stop contributing to the kitchen expenses. They don't want to know how I manage to pay the team driver for hauling the corn or the *peones* for harvesting it. When my sons help me with the daily expenses they don't help with the debt. Of course not! They don't even answer me any more.

I said, "It looks like I'm not going to buy myself anything. I wanted at least a donkey so I won't have to go walking, or carrying firewood, but *caray!* these boys are going to finish me off. They have already finished me!"

It is true that now I don't support everybody. My sons work, but it is worse, I say, because I cannot ask them for a *centavo* any more. If they feel like giving me something, they do, and if they don't, I get nothing.

Nowadays I can't get along on what I earn . . . living is too dear. That is why I say the government only seems to be helping us, but it actually doesn't. Every day I spend no less than ten or twelve *pesos* for the house, sometimes even more. I can't get on my feet so I can't pay my debts and that is why I am behind. We weren't rich in *don* Porfirio Díaz' times but at least we got by. Now I find myself under more pressure.

My neighbors sometimes tell me that I am poor because I don't know how to manage, because I didn't take advantage of my opportunities. One man made me angry because he said, "Look, you have lived so long and you have nothing. Why?"

I say to him, "And you? What have you bought with your own labor? You have two houses and two plots of land and cattle but, tell me, how much did that plot at Tepala cost you? Didn't you take it away from your wife's brother? Your fool of a brother-in-law signed whatever you said and you became the owner.

"And how much did that other lot cost you? One glass of *ponche*, right? Because poor little Andrés liked to drink, all you had to do was give him one *ponche* and the land was yours.

"Yes, you were sharp and sold part of it to buy oxen and cows. Was that because of your work? When did you go south to bring back cattle? Never, of course! You only went around stealing. So don't speak to me of this because I can tell you lots of things. And don't be hurting me with your mouth because no one can say I owe him anything. I go in and out of the municipal offices with my *sombrero* lifted because I don't even owe them a needle."

And then another one, my nephew, comes and also says to me, "Uncle, you are old now and you have nothing. You have less than I."

I say to him, "Yes, it's true, but the house you have is inherited. My house cost me money. You call your children and I'll call mine and let's see who is more ignorant, my sons or yours."

"Oh, well, yes, yours know more because you sent them to school."

"Well, why weren't you man enough to support one of your sons through school? Your sons are illiterate while none of mine are. Your sons help you and you can buy things but you will see that what you have is nothing. You'll see how your sons will end up. They cannot speak on any subject of importance, they can't even defend themselves."

And with that I shut his mouth. They can't tell me anything. No, I tell them. I said, "You have something but you work like Indians for it."

The truth is, my sons are not peasants any more. They don't even know where my cornfield is now! But I love the country! I say to Macrina, "Man, when I go into the fields it even gives me an appetite. But here I just walk around and I don't get hungry." Here, it's diarrhea all the time and my belly constantly hurting me . . . but not out in the fields. That's where I feel happy. Naturally, I love the country. I am a peasant! Mental work such as I used to do in the court is not for me any more. My body doesn't want mental work, it wants physical labor.

But people still come to me for legal advice. As I get about and have a lot of status, I have many friends. I don't go with just anybody. Here in Azteca they don't understand me but in Cuernavaca I am well known. In Cuernavaca you'll find me with lawyers or other persons, and I have a lot of friends . . . politicians, advocates, and there it is a matter of drinking. I have friends in Azteca also, from the center and even in the presidential office, and the judge. Well, we get together to have a drink and then we have another and another and so it goes.

Well, these friends help me out a great deal, with loans, with little jobs. And that is why I say that although God punishes me, he also protects me because of my faith.

When I get sick, I sometimes go and talk to my daughter Conchita about my faith. She has left the Adventists and has joined the Reformers. The Reformers do not use doctors . . . it is forbidden. They are doctors themselves and give themselves treatments. First, they begin with mud, then with cold water, with diet, and so on. They wanted to give me one of those treatments. One time Juan said, "We will cure you, if you wish, but according to our Book."

Nothing doing! I had no faith in that. They were liable to kill me! Conchita says that we Adventists do not fulfill our obligations. She says our religion is false. We argue with each other. I keep telling her that she fulfills nothing because there is no love. "You have no good works to show, daughter," I say to her. "It is true you have faith, but you know what the Holy Scriptures say. 'He who has faith and no good works, is nothing. He who has good works and no faith, is nothing.' So the two things have to go together. As the Lord said, 'Why do you call me Father when you do not love your brother?' The only good works I see you do is to be a vegetarian. Apart from that, you do not see to your neighbor, to your brother, or especially to your father. It is all the same to you whether your father eats or doesn't eat. I ask you for nothing now because God is keeping me strong and vigorous so I can support myself. I am just trying to make you see that you have no good works. How many times have you gone to visit the prisoners as the Scriptures require us to do?"

"How am I going to go there?" she says. "They are nothing but criminals who do not believe in anything."

"And where does it say that? Listen, do you consider yourself qualified to be a judge? The Scriptures also say, 'Hypocrite, why do you see the mote in your brother's eye, when you do not see the life you lead in your own eye.' We have one Judge and He will judge us."

Conchita wants me to go along with her, to follow her lead. I have no obligation to her. She has obligations, but I do not. She has obligations toward her son Germán, too, but she gives him no help at all. A neighbor comes to her and says, "Man, you don't give your son a thing. What is the idea?"

Conchita says, "Oh, who told them to educate him? My *papá* is doing a bad thing in educating my son because the boy will forget God. All men who know things forget God. And why should I have to help when I have so many children here? I can't even help my own father."

Germán has little to do with his *mamá*. I have told him, "You should go to see your *mamá*. It is true that she did not bring you up and you owe her nothing, but she did bring you into the world and you should always visit her." Well, he does go to see her every once in a while, but he doesn't call her *"mamá,"* just "Conchita." As he is very quiet, I have no idea whether he feels affection for her or not. How can he show his affection? If he were working he could always give her a little money, but he hasn't gone to work yet, so he doesn't give her anything.

When my grandson finished high school, I went all by myself to look up Germán's *papá*. But first I said to the boy, "Look, now that you are thinking of becoming a teacher, one fine day you may come up against your father and you don't even know him. You may even be disrespectful to him, so at least you should know who he is. After all, he is your father."

Germán said, "Well, you know best. If you wish, go and see him."

I went to Puebla to look for him and found him there in a school. He knew me perfectly well as I had brought my daughter to him. I said to him, "Look, I came for this reason. Until now you have not mixed into this but I want you to know that your son is living."

"Yes, the coffee merchants who go to Azteca have told me. I have heard his name is Germán but I do not know him."

I said, "Yes, that is the reason I came. It seems certain that he is going to belong to the teaching profession and some day there may be an argument in a meeting and you might show a lack of respect to each other, especially he, as he is young. So for that reason I want you to know him. He has now finished high school and is thinking of going on with his studies. Who knows whether he will get into the normal school in Cuernavaca? Now what do you have to say?"

"Well, I would like him to go to school at Iguala."

"Fine, but that is a matter of making an application and following it up. I don't know anything about those things and it requires influence. I would have to go there and lose time and it is so far away. I don't have money to get around so it will have to be the nearest place I can find. We are preparing to go to Cuernavaca."

"Well," he says, "don't let it worry you. I will take care of the application."

But it turned out to be just a promise and so we sent Germán to the normal school in Cuernavaca. It wasn't very easy for him there, or for us, as it cost money. Right off, it was 150 *pesos*, just to enter. After that, you have to keep paying. It was very hard for us. But then another opportunity came up. The principal of his high school sent word to him that he had gotten a scholarship of 250 *pesos* for him at the normal school in Tenería. Germán came home very excited. I said to him, "I am not willing to let you go to a place so far away for I will not be able to see you often. But, if you want to go . . ."

"Yes, I want to go because here it is a great burden. At least I won't be spending so much."

"All right. If you want to go, what can I do? Go ahead, if you feel up to it."

So Germán went to see his *papá*. But the father had already come to the house once before when I was not at home. He came just so they would know each other. He refused to enter the house but he gave Germán one hundred *pesos* and left. A few days after that, Moisés said to Germán, "If you like, I'll take you to see him." And the two of them went. His *papá* gave him another hundred *pesos*, which he said he had trouble scraping together as he had no money. So now Germán is studying in Tenería.

In spite of everything, the boy has had luck. Because all my children, that is to say, his uncles, were grown, he benefited. All the uncles helped him and they all care about him. He is a good boy, very docile, very obedient, and I can see that he has respect for me. But who knows? Right now it is to his interest and you can't tell yet. Let us see what happens when he gets into harness, when he starts working. That will be the time to tell whether he really has affection for me, the way I have for him now.

I have said to Germán, "Look son, I am giving you a bit of education, just a smattering, but it will be a stepping stone for you. Your children, those of them who are smart, will step up a little higher on the ladder. And your grandchildren, my great-great-grand-children, will get still higher. They may even rise to become the President of the Republic. Yes, it could be. My race can reach as far as that."

That was my idea since I was young, not just to make money and to leave material goods to my children, so that tomorrow or the next day they will be fighting and killing over it. No, I want them to have their inheritance in their heads, not in their pockets.

Sometimes I thought of getting married again because there was no one to look after me, no one to serve me, as there ought to be. My sister couldn't any more; she was old. Of course Macrina was living with me, but, then, I was making her lose time . . . she was young and could still look to her future for her companion. She said she didn't want to look for a husband on account of me and I said I was not remarrying because of her.

But I kept thinking about it. I was looking for my own protection, for someone who would wait on me and take care of me. Now that I was working as a farmer again, I couldn't just order my daughter around and shout at her to get up early . . . it was enough that she did a lot of work. She was humble and obedient but I found myself holding back in this sense. However she served me, I made the best of it. It was not like when my wife was living. Then I would say, "Look, get up because I am leaving early." Now I could not do that. That was why I sometimes thought of marrying a hard-working affectionate woman. I didn't want a rich one because right off she would be treating me like her servant. And if she were still strong while I was no longer able, she would find another man and I would just be looking on . . . watching the two of them.

Then Macrina had a falling-out with Felipe. Macrina got angry because Felipe knew she was pregnant again and he kept scolding her and scolding her. Finally, one day he beat her. We didn't know what it was all about. My sister was living with us at the time and he even hit her. Now, that made me angry. "And what are you hitting your aunt for?" I asked.

I still didn't know what was going on until he came out with it. And Macrina said that no, it wasn't true. But Martín and I did not believe what Macrina told us about Felipe being jealous and wanting to get next to her. Rather than give in to him, she went with *don* Ángel. That is how she defended herself, and the result was . . . this. Later, Macrina said she was leaving.

I said, "Go ahead. So what? But where will you go? Not with your sister, as she knows you only too well. They'll agree to take you in because of your sewing machine. But I am going to take care of your machine. When Ester grows up she can come and get it. Go on, go to your sister."

What could I do? I am a father. Lots of times parents become the cause of the daughter's downfall. If I kicked her out, I would only pity her, especially on account of the little one, Ester. Where would my poor little daughter be roaming, and my little granddaughter? No, it didn't seem right.

"Martín, what do you say?" I asked. "Shall we throw them out?"

"Well, in a way, yes, because she deserves it for what she has done."

"Yes, that is true, it would be justifiable. But look at the little one. Where will she go? Now Germán is still a youngster and is still studying. He needs someone to serve him. If you boys get married, your wives are not going to want to wait on all of us either. We really have a problem here. I can get by some way or other but what about the youngsters?"

"Yes, it is a difficult question."

"There you have it!"

So Moisés said, "Well, now we'll just have to bear it. What else can we do?"

And so we had to put up with Macrina.

Felipe got sick and couldn't work for months. He was real sick, that boy, and I had to spend money on him but he repaid me badly. That wife he got himself from a nearby village was no good to him for anything. She had a big lump on one hand and her feet were crooked. She didn't know anything about keeping house or cooking, or even washing clothes. She was useless. We couldn't depend on her.

I said to my son, "Now, why did you get yourself a woman like that? If you want her, go ahead and marry her, but you will not prosper with her, for she is useless." Yes, I did tell him to marry her because it was my duty as a father. She was in my hands and I was in charge so I had to obligate him to marry her. I said, "She is ugly and lame but, after all, she is not for me, so if you want to, go ahead."

But when she saw my son sick, she left him. I said, "That's better. Now my son will get well." I say a wife who is with you only when you are well, is no good. You are better off without her. He did get better and he paid no more attention to her.

He went to live in Mexico City and, right off, he met another woman and even married her. I don't know why Felipe turned out this way but he had a lot of sweethearts and he wanted to marry each one of them. I think he took after me in that. I don't think much of his wife but what can I do about it? She is not the kind who can help a man. She just waits and prepares the meals and spends money, that's all. If she doesn't help her husband, they are not going to live well together, but they already have three children so how can they separate? Felipe wants to leave her when he gets together enough money. He is already looking for another woman but because he isn't working now he is settling for the woman he has.

After all these years, Martín finally got married, but it made me sad because both he and Ricardo married older women who can no longer have children. The thought has impressed me that everything will die out with them. I am sad, too, because Martín gave himself away to his wife's family, which is a bit richer than mine. Instead of bringing home his bride, he went to live in her house. Now they order him about and he goes running, like an errand boy. That's why I pity him. If I, who am so small and insignificant, never allowed a woman to rule me, why should he? I was an orphan and alone when I married but I wouldn't stand for any slight to me, especially in my own home.

And the wedding itself . . . that is another thing that weighs upon me. Martín and the girl were sweethearts for two years and nothing happened. "Will it be the way it was with the other one?" I said. "Why don't you get married?"

"Well, I don't know. Soon, soon."

"But, man, I want her to come here to live. Your sister has left and I am alone." Because after Macrina had her other child, she went off to live with her lover, leaving me alone. At that time I was preparing my own breakfasts, buying my *tortillas* in the plaza, and eating my dinners in a little *fonda*. It was all right while I was well, but what would I do the day I fell ill?

A few months before the wedding Martín stopped giving me expense money. I could guess what he was doing. He must have been saving his money to get married. He told me he was going to borrow five hundred *pesos* to buy what he needed but that was a lie, because he was saving. They went to Cuernavaca to buy her veil and dress and all of a sudden I heard that the wedding would take place the very next morning. "Well, I am not going because I wasn't invited," I said.

But the priest sent them to get me because they needed the father to sign. I went out of courtesy and as the priest knew I was not a believer in those things, he just looked me up and down. *Zas,* I signed and said, "Well, good-bye."

The godfather of marriage stopped me and told me to wait. "Why should I wait? I have a lot to do at home."

"Come to my house. We are going there to drink coffee."

Very well, I went. I saw her brother drive up in an automobile. All the relatives of the woman were there, but I was the only relative of the bridegroom. How sad I felt. I thought, *"Caray,* this is shameful for my son!" The girl's family had money and this was the result. "What am I doing here? I am not talking to anyone so I better leave."

My son and daughter-in-law came over, saying, "Are you leaving already? Shall we expect you at the house for the dinner?"

"Yes, yes, I'll come, but now I have to see to my horse."

I went home and I didn't go back. At three o'clock a message came inviting me to eat, but it didn't mention the rest of the family. So I said to the messenger, "Look, tell my children that I thank them but that there are many of us and if we all came it would cause them a lot of expense. Tell them that what they prepared wouldn't be enough for us because we eat a trainload."

After that, there were no messages. What can I say? Three days later they came at night. "Listen, *papá,* this is what happened. The whole thing was improvised. My mother-in-law had a fight with my sister-in-law and they called off the wedding. That's why nothing was prepared. But when the time came all the relatives from the *barrio* of Santo Domingo arrived so her brother bought some cartons of beer and we killed two chickens and made chicken soup."

"How nice! She married with a veil and all that pomp and the only thing you could serve at your wedding was chicken soup. Ha, ha! You should have saved me some soup."

"*Ay, papá.* But you didn't come."

"Well, just for chicken soup? One chicken wouldn't have been enough, for there are many of us."

That's the way it was. No one in the family was invited but me. Later I made an offer to my son. I said, "Look, son, it is my duty to help you, so if you like I will plant for you." And I went to work. I even brought my grandson Germán to help. Then they gave me ten *pesos* for each of us. They put it in my pocket. I didn't want it because that meant that I went as their worker. "But if I am the father and I have this duty, I don't want to earn money," I said.

"No, no. Spend it," they said.

Well, what could I do? We went again to plow and again they gave me twenty *pesos* and I didn't want to take it. "Why are you paying me? I didn't come to earn money."

"No, no, go and spend it." And again they put it in my pocket.

The same thing happened once more and I say, "Now I understand. Now I will not help any more because you pay me. You can hire any *peón* so why should I go? Look for someone to help you. I only want to fulfill my duty but you do not recognize that."

I studied the matter and that's what I told them.

It was different when Felipe got married. He was married in my house, on my Saint's Day, and we were all there in harmony. Yes, Felipe turned out better and that's why I love him more. He doesn't even baptize a son until I say so. Felipe always comes and asks me, but not Martín.

I would like to reunite my children so at least they will be here to see me when I die. When Macrina went off and left me alone, I wrote a letter to my son Ricardo and told him to come home. I said, "You didn't see your mother die and now you will not see me die because you are far away." He answered me and invited me to come there to live. But I'm not crazy. If he's crazy, should I be, too? No, I don't go traveling. Why should I be there looking at strange faces? I'd rather die here alone.

I also sent Felipe a letter, a threatening letter. I said, "If you don't come, I will never step through your door again. I see that you don't care for me." Who knows if he will answer? I'm sure he is going to say he didn't receive my letter. I will write again. I am not interested in having him be independent. I want him here to claim what is his father's, although his share is little. I can't take it with me when I go to the cemetery. As the prophet Job said, Job wasn't born with sons, he wasn't born with a woman, he was born without anything and that's the way he will leave. I came into the world naked and I will leave naked, and that is the truth.

PEDRO

Epilogue

At one time, I believed in a lot of things . . . now I believe in nothing. I wanted to see my village improve but with the passage of time I am convinced that it can't be done and no matter how saintly a public official may be when he takes office, he will accomplish nothing. Now I realize that in my village no one understands. We are blindfolded! All of us! Partly because of lack of culture, partly because of lack of unity and partly because of poverty. Perhaps there are some who have a bit of wisdom, but so what! What is the good of my having ideas if I am a poor man? I cannot do a thing!

Now they say that Jalalpa sent a protest to the Supreme Court of Justice and has won the boundary dispute. I am sure that if I were to try, I could arouse the whole village again and we would go against Jalalpa. We wouldn't submit. But now I don't want to. Now I am old. I might lose my life over it! No indeed!

The new generation in my village has opened its eyes to other things but not to politics. When one talks about what is good for the *municipio* or for them, the young people don't come around to listen. Only the old ones do. Nowadays we even shout through a microphone to the young people, but they pay no attention to it. Even the co-operative work parties are falling into disuse.

The other day I spoke with our town council about this. I said to them, "Man! Why don't you get the village guard started again? There is no need for federal troops to come here to take care of us when we can handle it ourselves. The people are willing to help if only you use the right tactics to unite them. The apathy is in the town council, not in the people."

So then the authorities say to me, "Very well, can you organize them? Come and be the head of the police force here."

I say to him, "Become head of the police force? Certainly not! Why should I become chief of police when I was once an important official? I was the *síndico,* I was the *regidor,* and now you expect me to move down to the position of police chief? I would rather die of hunger at home! A police chief here is no better than an errand boy. Why, they even serve as go-betweens for lovers! No, thank you very much."

"Then what do you want?"

"No, I can't be police chief now. I was already up on top! Bah! I suppose you think I am very ambitious to earn *centavos?* No, even though I die of hunger, no! Anyway, I am old and will soon die, so what do I need this for? What I once was, I was. That's all over now."

"Well, suppose they told you to be the president?"

"Ah, that's a very different matter. That, yes, even if I were eighty I would be willing to serve. Then I'd be going up, not going down."

The trouble is, there is no lawfulness here. Even the lawyers agree. I was talking to a lawyer one day and he said to me, "No, Pedro, don't put any faith in the law. It is all a lie . . . law, nothing!" The Governor said the same thing one time. He told me, "Yes, the real law is money. If you have money, the law is yours. If you haven't any, there is no law, so don't you go believing in it."

In a republic like ours, we cannot progress. We are remaining behind. We are ambitious but we cannot do a thing because we are not organized. That's why we Mexicans are not worth much. The peasants are ignorant and more than a little stupid. And if one gets to know something, right off he tries to exploit the poor, the ones who are at the bottom. And then, too, here they kill off those who know a bit more than others. If I had studied, I think I would be dead by now!

In the United States it must be different. I think there the people are more educated and have a conscience. And where there is education, there is money. They have lots of companies and societies that get together capital and because they know how to behave, it doesn't go to their heads. On the contrary, they progress. There is co-operation there because everyone understands, everyone knows, everyone can speak. There are lots of good heads there and naturally things go well. But not here in Mexico. Here everyone is for himself and takes advantage.

I don't even believe in the Revolution any more. So far as I am concerned, the Revolution was a failure because the more peace there is, the more hunger there is. In *don* Porfirio's time you could fill your basket with six *centavos*. Now you cannot even with fifty *pesos!* Since the Revolution, we have more freedom but life is more difficult.

Nobody won in the Revolution; even Zapata lost. When they talk about the Revolution, they mean Carranza's Revolution, not Zapata's. And when ambitious men mention the Revolution, it is only to rise to power. They are all *carrancistas!*

The success of the Revolution was no great advance. It only seemed to be because at that time we got rid of the big plantation owners and the government of *don* Porfirio, who were the exploiters. But now there have appeared even worse exploiters. Now it is the bankers. So it is the bunch that govern who are doing the exploiting . . . the opportunists . . . and the people get nothing. There is more wealth, but I say the rich always try to exploit the people. It is that way all the time. The more money they have and the more they know, the more they try to get out of the people. And as the public is ignorant, they permit everything. Now, with so much knowledge, it is easy to deceive the poor man.

This is just what is happening right now in my village. People are selling their little houses to the wealthy and going up into the hills to live where there is no water or electricity or anything. And why do they do it? Out of need, and because they are offered a bit higher price. And those who don't sell are still dying of thirst because the few springs we have here don't give enough water. The outsiders who are well off come here to build houses for themselves and put up swimming pools and tanks and the poor villagers suffer. As I said, it is heavenly for those who have money. The rest of the people can die of hunger and thirst.

I notice that the more science there is, the more calamities and scarcity we have. Scarcity for the poor, that is, not for the well off. The proof is that everything the poor man and the farmer produce is cheap and everything the worker or science turns out is very dear. That is why I can see that we are headed for bankruptcy. The people don't count for anything any more.

We are going from bad to worse. We have had high prices, scarcity and hunger before, but nowadays in the city and right here, too, a lot of people have no food at all. There are some people in my *barrio* who are not eating. So the more peace there is, the more starvation.

Today we have a lot of freedom, but of what use is it? If you ask for justice, they do not give it to you, and what good would it do us anyway if we are not free to eat well? The monopolists have cornered everything, even sugar and all the essential things. What we need is a government which values its villagers and gives them what they need. It is strictly forbidden for us to go into the forests to cut lumber or firewood, but those who have money are free to exploit the biggest forests.

The government should attack the high prices and give the peasants some benefit from the fruits of the land. They should stop the bankers from monopolizing everything and permit freedom to each to sell his seeds in accordance with his sowing and to whomever he pleases.

I believe that all the revolutions and everything that we see on this earth, come to us already destined from up above and we are only instruments. The next revolution is already written and who knows how much time will go by until it takes place, but yet, that which is written must be fulfilled. Who knows what is happening in Cuba? Since Zapata, many have tried but nothing happens. Everything is crushed because God has not given the word yet. Then suddenly we'll see the revolution of the poor against the rich in Mexico. Not now, I don't think, but it will come. I can't say who will be the leader, but it must be someone.

I have no faith any more, not even in my own beliefs; I almost do not believe in any religion now. But I don't know enough not to believe in anything so I believe only in the prophets.

We are in the last stages. I should think so! First, the World War and after that, the seven plagues. And then, earthquakes all over. It has already begun in Chile. The world is going from bad to worse. The great men should be arranging for peace, but they are not. Here we are negotiating for peace and there we are preparing for war. That is the way it has been predicted in the Holy Scriptures. It says so very clearly in the prophecies of Daniel and John. Christ himself said so when he appeared. He said, "First, science has to increase on a large scale. There will be great wars, people will fight against people, nation against nation, and there will be great famines, earthquakes, signals in the heavens, in the winds and on the earth. When you see that, prepare yourselves, because the hour has struck."

That is why I say that the war is being prepared and is going to take place. We call it the war of Armageddon. Everything, everything, everything is going to be lost, Mexico and all the advanced peoples. This is also written. In the final days, there will be much building. Many will construct great edifices but the people will not survive. After a thousand years, Christ will come again with all his followers.

Well, life is coming to a close. I am an old man now. I have come a long way and death is all that awaits me. What a pity that I am going to leave my beautiful hills! But I am resigned to it. My race is over, the mission God has given me is fulfilled. I have folded the page. Good or bad, I was what I was. Now I want nothing more, except perhaps another wife, just to bury me.

I am thankful to God that I have lived. I have raised my children and taught them the little I know. My responsibility is over. I am not going to give them their inheritance yet. If I give them the house and the lot now, I will have nothing, not even the right to touch a piece of fruit in the garden. No, if they are fools and quarrel over it later, well, that will be after I am dead.

I can no longer think of trying to improve myself, of studying or learning something new, especially now that my sight is beginning to fail. I guess there is good reason why I tire. I do just as much as I can and that is all. But, of course, I will always go on being upright. An old man has no energy left for other things.

APPENDIX

APPENDIX

I

Division of Labor and Family Budget

The division of labor in the Martínez family followed the tradition of "the men to the fields and the women to the kitchen," as Pedro put it. Everyone in the family was expected to work, although only light chores were given to the two younger boys. The men's work was highly seasonal and can best be discussed month by month.

In January, the middle of the dry season, the first task of the day was to carry water from the street fountain to the house and garden. This was done in turns by the three elder sons, who hauled the water in gasoline tins attached by rope to either end of a long pole balanced on the shoulders. It took from six to eight trips to the fountain, about a hundred yards away, to supply water for use in the house. At this time of the year, the garden was watered every third day. This required twenty-five trips to the fountain.

After breakfast, the older boys, and sometimes Moisés, would begin to twist maguey fiber into rope. Pedro no longer made rope except in emergencies, but he would get orders and deliver them. Occasionally he met with the other rope makers, most of whom lived in his *barrio*, to fix prices and discuss trade matters.

If there was no money in the house, Felipe or Martín or both would be sent to the hills with the mule to get a load of wood to sell. They would go three times a week or every day, if necessary, while Ricardo,

Moisés and sometimes Pedro continued to make rope. It was time-consuming to sell wood, for the boys had to go up and down the village streets to find a customer, or even to journey to Yautepec. The wood was sold at three *pesos,* fifty *centavos* a load. Esperanza sometimes suspected the boys of getting a higher price and pocketing the difference, but they always denied this.

In the early days of January, the corn was still being harvested and had to be transported down from the hills. Several days would be spent in shelling the corn. At night the boys prepared the maguey fiber for the following day, keeping the family up until midnight. The next morning, they arose at six or six-thirty.

In February and March, the women would rise at four o'clock to make breakfast and prepare many *tortillas* for the men's lunch in the field. At five o'clock, one or two of the older boys would get up to haul water, for it was still the dry season. By six, Pedro and his three sons were on their way to the *tlacolol,* to do the laborious work of clearing their plot of thirty-five *cuartillos.* It took them two full months to cut down the trees with axes and to clear the brush with *machetes.*

February, when the corn was sold, was the month of greatest income. The next three months were the leanest, and in March the boys devoted as much time as possible to gathering and selling firewood and filling orders for rope. Esperanza had to sell some of her turkeys or chickens at this time to avoid feeding them corn and to raise money for household expenses. This was a time of scarcity and hard work for everyone. They were generally in bed by nine-thirty.

April was still the dry season. The work of clearing the field was over, and the boys gathered and sold about two loads of wood a day. Occasionally, if the need for money was not acute, the wood was piled up in the yard to be sold during the rainy season at five *pesos* per load.

The rains began in the latter part of May and the plants no longer needed to be watered. Water cans were set outside to catch the rain water for washing clothes. Water for use in the kitchen was now carried in smaller cans or pails by the women and the two younger boys. In the early part of the month, the men went to the field to burn the piles of dry brush and to fence in the plot with logs and rocks. On dry days the boys went for wood; on wet days they made rope at home. At the end of May, the planting began and the men again rose at five in the morning, the women at four.

In June, the boys were allowed to rest a few days after the planting. At this time, the peasants who owned land in the valley needed assistance in clearing their fields and the Martínez boys had the opportunity to earn a daily wage by working as farm hands. Pedro hired them out to his friends, relatives or *compadres* but he no longer worked as a *peón* himself. For three or four days he went to his *tlacolol* alone or with Ricardo to do the reseeding. When the boys were not working at anything else, Pedro sent them for wood.

In July and August, the two older boys continued to work as *peones*, and Pedro and Ricardo spent much of the time pulling the weeds which grew rapidly in the fertile *tlacolol* soil. For the next three months the only task in the *tlacolol* was to inspect the field now and then and to guard the corn from thieves and animals.

In September, the hog plums were ripe for picking, and Pedro became active as a plum merchant. Before the season began, Pedro made several trips to the markets in Mexico City to get orders from old and new customers. If he was able to persuade a customer to pay in advance, he would buy up plum trees or extra crates of plums in Azteca. More usually, he had to borrow money at interest to do this. In 1947, he bought the fruit for five to eight *pesos* per crate and sold it at fifteen or eighteen *pesos*. After paying for transportation by train or bus, Pedro made a profit of about eight *pesos* per crate. His earnings depended upon how much time and money he devoted to the work. For a time, Martín was his assistant, contracting for trees in Azteca while his father was in Mexico City.

All through September, Pedro and his sons picked plums, packed them in crates, and carted them by mule to the bus terminal in the plaza or up the mountain to the railroad station. Felipe and Martín also worked as *peones*, picking plums for others whenever they could, or transporting plums at two *pesos* a trip. When they were not thus occupied, the boys went for wood. During the plum season, the women did not work so hard and went to bed at nine-thirty or ten and rose at six.

In October, work on the plums continued for the first week or so. The men went to the *tlacolol* to cut fodder and bring it down on mule back. It was stored inside the front room and kept for the mule to eat during the dry season; otherwise Moisés would have to look for pasture for the mule. If any fodder was left by May, it would be sold. The boys also cut fodder for others. The squash was brought down from the *tlacolol* and the women removed and dried the seeds for *mole* sauce. From the time the men began to work in the fields, the women would once more get up at four in the morning.

In November, the boys worked as *peones*, harvesting beans and the early corn and transporting them from the valley fields to the peasants' homes. In late November, the ground was once again dry and the boys resumed hauling water for the garden and gathering firewood.

December was well into the dry season and water had to be hauled in large quantities. The boys continued to work as *peones* and to gather wood until their own corn was ripe in the *tlacolol*. Ropemaking was begun once again and the rope and wood were quickly sold for much needed cash. If the crop was good, extra teamsters were hired to help carry down the corn. The teamsters worked day and night, and the women of the house had to be ready to serve them a hot meal whenever they arrived with a load. For ten days during the harvest, Esperanza and Macrina snatched their sleep sitting on benches, waiting for the teamsters. If the crop was small and teamsters were not needed, the women went to bed at nine o'clock and rose at two or three in the morning.

The income of the Martínez family was difficult to estimate, for they did not keep track of money spent or earned. In 1947-48 we kept a record of the Martínez' income and of their expenditures for twenty-six consecutive days, and with the help of the parents and the older children, we reconstructed a reasonably accurate annual budget. It was a bad year for the Martínez family. Both Pedro and Esperanza were ill, the former with an infection which required surgery and hospitalization, the latter with a painful incapacitating ovarian disturbance which lasted for about eight months. Conchita, who was estranged from her husband and living with her parents, gave birth to a child who died. The modest funeral and Conchita's subsequent illness were an additional financial drain.

To help meet these expenses, Pedro borrowed three hundred *pesos* early in the year. The widow who made the loan reduced the rate of interest to 5 percent a month in exchange for his services as legal adviser. However, she took so much of Pedro's time that he pawned half his house site for the same amount and repaid her in full. In pawning his house, Pedro gave the lender the right to the produce of his plum trees for one year in lieu of interest.

While in the hospital, Pedro sent Esperanza to *don* Prosperino, a wealthy peasant and a *político*, to borrow 150 *pesos* to pay for the medical bill. Prosperino, who usually charged 12 percent interest per month, surprised Esperanza by lending her the money at no interest. "The important thing is to cure *don* Pedro," he said. Prosperino's gesture moved Pedro deeply, and he vowed to repay this debt before the others. In addition to the payments on the house site, Pedro was repaying a two hundred *peso* loan made the preceding year at 8 percent. In 1948, he sold one of his two mules. The mule was an important source of income, and its sale was a further blow to the family economy.

Prices had risen sharply in 1947-48, compounding the family's difficulties. Corn rose from twenty *centavos* per *cuartillo* in 1943 to as high as seventy *centavos* in 1947. For lack of rain, the harvest was small; Pedro planted twenty *cuartillos* but harvested only seven *cargas*, five of which he sold immediately at the lowest market price. The family consumed two *cargas* and then had to buy corn at a high price for the remainder of the year. Some of the beans consumed came from Pedro's field, and all of the firewood used at home was gathered by the sons. But rarely did this family produce more than 17 percent of what it consumed.

Below, is a summary of the estimated income of the Martínez family in 1947-48:

Source of Income	Amount (*pesos*)
Wages earned by the two elder sons (working as farm hands or teamsters)	640.00
Firewood	622.00
Plums	300.00
Rope	231.00
Corn	210.00
Small sales by Esperanza	60.00
Legal consultations by Pedro	60.00
Beans	32.00
Fodder	30.00
Mule	300.00
Total Income	2,485.00*

* In dollars this was $284.00 at the 1948 rate of exchange of 8.75 *pesos* to the dollar.

This list reveals the heavy dependence of the family upon the work of the elder sons. Because of Pedro's illness that year, they were almost the sole supporters of the family, but even when he was active they earned from 70 to 80 percent of the income. Over half the income in 1947-48 came from the boys working as farm hands or teamsters and from the selling of firewood. Another 30 percent came from plums, ropemaking and corn, all of which depended in large part upon the boys' labor. The small amount of income from Esperanza's sales and Pedro's legal consultations was disproportionate to the many hours they devoted to these activities. Nevertheless, Esperanza's daily efforts to raise money were indispensable and were sorely missed when she was unable to carry on. Pedro's work gave him much personal satisfaction and had certain political overtones since it widened his circle of friends and was a source of prestige. His earnings were greater than he reported, but much of his activity was unremunerated or, often as not, was paid in the form of *copitas* of tequila.

If Pedro and his three sons had hired themselves out as day laborers during the approximately three hundred man-days of work they spent planting their *tlacolol*, they could have earned more than the full crop was worth. And if they had worked for others throughout the year at the prevailing wage of four *pesos* a day, they could have more then doubled their income. However, there was very little year-round work available in or near the village; even on the *hacienda* where laborers were employed, the work was highly seasonal. But more important than the lack of jobs was Pedro's strong drive to be an independent peasant and to have at least his elder sons follow in his footsteps. This was what he had fought for in the Revolution, and though he planted only on communal land, it was for him an important source of self-respect and even of status.

As it was, however, in 1947-48, Felipe and Martín each worked as laborers for only eighty days, from June to December, giving the family a wage income during this period. The sale of firewood stands out as next in importance as a source of income for nine months in the year. In March and April it was almost the only source of income. For three months of the year, January, February and September, the monthly income was over two hundred *pesos;* in March and April, it dropped to a low of 115 *pesos.*

In 1947-48, the expenditures of the Martínez family exceeded their income by 402.35 *pesos.** A deficit of approximately the same amount occurred almost every year, even when the harvest was good and when Pedro was working. This year the deficit would have been higher but for the sale of the mule. Generally, deficiencies were made up by making more loans, but these were usually consumed in repaying previous debts. As Pedro said, "The debt remains, only the creditors change."

If a deficit was not caused by illness or misfortune, it would be caused by some extraordinary purchase—a tool, an animal, extra clothing or household furnishings. When there was money on hand, even substantial sums, it would be spent promptly as a matter of family custom. After the harvest, for example, Pedro and Esperanza always went to Cuernavaca to buy clothing, everyone getting something even though it was not absolutely necessary. Money would also be spent on little luxuries such as extra cups, sweets or a ribbon; Esperanza would buy meat, cheese and bread while the money lasted. There was no setting aside sums for future use or even simple budgeting a few days in ad-

* $45.98.

vance. When the money was gone, the family would eat less as a matter of course, and Esperanza would resume her daily efforts to raise enough money for the most urgent immediate necessities.

We have estimated the family expenditures in 1947-48 as follows:

Item	Cash Expenditure (*pesos*)
Basic food (including two fiesta meals)	1,666.40
Health (extraordinary expense)	470.00
Clothing	207.80
Household necessities	203.00
Barber	95.00
Diversion	50.00
Religion	36.00
Infant's funeral	30.00
Education	10.00
House tax	1.15
Repayment of debts and interest	Undetermined
Total Expenditure	2,769.35 *

* This was $316.50 in 1948.

Food, the largest single item of expense, was 60 percent of the total In other years when there were no abnormal expenses, it was proportionately higher. The special meals referred to were served at the *barrio* fiesta and on Pedro's Saint's Day.

In years when there were only normal illnesses, expenditures for health rarely exceeded .8 percent. Esperanza cured illnesses with alcohol rubs, herbal mixtures and other home remedies; infections were treated with lemon and alcohol. Aztecan families did not generally go to a doctor to be cured; Pedro's willingness to enter a hospital and undergo surgery was quite unusual.

Clothing purchases took 7.5 percent of the total and provided only a minimal amount per person, usually one set of clothing to change into while the other was being laundered. The family spending pattern for clothing followed traditional Aztecan lines: the men received more than the women, the older sons more than the younger. Almost twice as much was spent on clothing for the father as for anyone else. The least was spent on the younger daughter. This pattern is no longer followed by better-to-do families, particularly those with children in school. It is to be noted that in the Martínez family the men wore *huaraches,* not shoes, and the women and younger boys generally went barefoot.

Household necessities (7 percent) include soap, firewood, charcoal, kerosene, matches, and use of the corn mill. Charcoal was used to heat the iron for ironing clothing. The use of a kerosene lamp instead of candles was a recent added convenience for the family. Esperanza exercised great thrift in the use of all household necessities, keeping the embers of the fire aglow all night, for example, in order not to use a match the next morning.

The cost of alcohol refers to that bought by Esperanza for home consumption. A daily drink either in the morning or at night, a regular practice of both Esperanza and Pedro, was viewed by most Aztecan peasants as necessary for good health.

The cost of the barber was comparatively high. Many peasants went for a haircut and a shave three or four times a month, but Pedro and his sons went less often. Very few families in the village invested in razors or barber's scissors for home shaves and haircuts. The amount given for diversion was probably an underestimate. It included only the spending money Pedro gave to his older sons. No one else in the family admitted to spending money for diversion.

The money spent for religious activities included dues and taxes to the Adventist church, purchases of church literature, and the traditional contribution to the *barrio* fiesta and the village Carnival, both Catholic celebrations. The infant's funeral expenses were kept at a minimum; only alcohol, sweetened black coffee, rolls and *chile* peppers, were served at the wake and, because it was an Adventist funeral, no music was played.

The item on education covered the cost of Moisés' books and school supplies. When Conchita and the other children were in school, the proportion spent on education was considerably higher. The remaining item, the house tax, is noteworthy for its very small size. This was the average tax for a house and site in Azteca.

The detailed record kept for twenty-six days helped us to understand the eating habits of the family. The record was kept from July 20 to August 14, 1948, when there was a lull in work on *tlacolol*. The sons were working as farm hands at the time, giving the family a steady, if not a high cash income. Food prices, however, were particularly high in July and August, and the family diet was not much better than usual.

In this period of almost a month, food comprised an average of 89 percent of the total expenditures. Withal, the diet was monotonous and sparse. Corn, in the form of *tortillas*, made up most (72 percent) of it; protein foods, such as, meat, milk, cheese and eggs, were eaten in low amounts. At times during the year, weeks and even months would pass without the family tasting these. Beans, though a staple food in the village, were not eaten as frequently as the family would have liked.

They ate fruit only when it could be picked from their own few trees. Coffee was taken when there was enough money; otherwise, the family drank tea made from lemon-grass picked in the garden, or orange leaves or cinnamon. Bread was still a luxury for the Martínez and was served on birthdays and special occasions. Other items regularly purchased in small quantities by Esperanza were *chile*, salt, sugar, rice, lard, tomatoes and onions. Wild greens, gathered in the countryside, were commonly eaten by the very poor. The Martínez family ate a wide variety of these greens, especially when there was a shortage of money in the house. Despite the deprecatory attitude of the family toward this food, it was an important supplement to their diet.

The family spent more on the corn mill than on any other household necessity, except food. In fact, more was spent on the mill than on either meat or rice, bread, milk or coffee. This was due to the fact that the family had four grown men, each of whom ate an enormous number of *tortillas* at every meal. The task of grinding approximately five *cuartillos* of corn a day was an onerous one and Esperanza's failing health threw the major burden upon Macrina. Had it not been for the mill, Esperanza would have long before insisted that Felipe, the eldest son, marry and bring home a daughter-in-law to help.

More on Pedro's Children

In their subservience to the parents, the Martínez children were carrying out the Aztecan ideal, at least as it was conceived by the older generation. Conchita, the eldest daughter, was the single exception; while still young she broke with tradition by studying for a career. Born after the first three children had died, and for five years an only child, Conchita received more attention and affection from her parents than did any of her brothers and sisters. Until the others were born, Pedro and Esperanza babied her, played with her and enjoyed her to a degree unusual in Aztecan parents. No doubt, this attention gave her the strength to be independent later. However, it also made it difficult for her to accept the restrictions placed upon her as the eldest daughter. Conchita's childhood memories were not as pleasant as those of the younger members of the family.

"I was always sad because I couldn't do anything I wanted. I was kept at home to do the chores and there was no distraction for me of any kind. My *mamá* and my *papá* never let me play with other children or go into the street. And I had no clothes, never more than two little dresses, and they never gave me money to buy sweets or toys . . . nothing like that ever. And I was always hungry as a girl. That's when one begins to have a big appetite, isn't it? But almost always we ate only *tortillas* and beans and lots of *chile*. My *mamá* gave us so much *chile* that I believe I am ill to this day because of it. I always had stomach trouble.

"When I went to school I was better off because I could play during recess. But my *papá* converted when I was about ten years old * and after that I had no friends in school. I wasn't happy because, as I said, my *mamá* left me to bring up the children. She had a lot of work and helped my *papá* buy fruit and he sent her to collect it. She would hurry there with the crates and it took a lot of her time and she couldn't take care of the house. She left me alone with all the children and I had to grind the corn and make the *tortillas*. When I saw that they bought me my own grinding stone, I said to myself, no, I am not staying here to do all the work. I thought I would have a better life if I went away to school and when I told my *papá* about it he agreed. He said if I were a teacher I could help him and that is why I was sent to normal school. I did it out of necessity, to help him.

"There in school in Huaxtepec I had friends and a happy atmosphere but I always thought of my parents. There I had good food, meat every day, and I remembered that at home they were suffering. I said, 'Here I am enjoying myself and eating well,' and I would begin to cry. My parents showed me a lot of consideration when I was away at school because they felt my absence at home. I saw that my *mamá* reacted to it because she managed to send me *tamales* with my *papá*. She was able to show her affection for me then and so I felt that I loved them too."

The entire family was affected by Conchita's schooling. Pedro was criticized by his neighbors and relatives for aiming too high and for exposing his daughter to unknown dangers. But he had faith in Conchita and in the promise of education and he dared to hope that through her he could raise the level of the entire family. For three years Pedro gave up planting for himself and worked as a farm hand to earn cash for her expenses. The rest of the family had to work harder and pull in their belts to a painful degree during this period, and the education of all but the youngest son was severely curtailed so that Conchita could continue hers.

But at seventeen Conchita was expelled from school for leaving the grounds without permission, and her father was furious with her when he was summoned to take her home. Later, when a boy appeared at the house to ask for her hand, Pedro suspected them of having had an affair. He beat his daughter in the young man's presence and then ordered her out of the house at one o'clock in the morning. In desperation she drank a large dose of the medicine she was taking for malaria. When that did not work, she ate the tops of phosphorous matches and

---

* Actually, Conchita was about thirteen years old.

was deathly ill for several weeks. Her suicide attempt caused her father to repent and he sent her on scholarship to a secondary school in Mexico City. She remained there for two years, suffering great privations because her father provided her with very little money for food, clothing and supplies.

Conchita's first position was as an apprentice teacher without pay, in a small distant village. So that she would not be alone, Pedro sent first Ricardo, then Macrina, to live with her, taking them out of school to do so. Pedro supported all of them until Conchita began to earn money, but almost immediately she had an affair with a married schoolteacher and became pregnant. This was a severe blow to Pedro and to the family but they forgave her and continued to help her. After a brief leave of absence to give birth, Conchita returned to work, again taking Macrina with her, this time to look after the child. Conchita nursed her son Germán for about a year and a half and kept him with her until she married Juan, her former sweetheart and her father's friend and convert. Juan was about ten years older than Conchita and had several children by different women in the village. One of these was Conchita's aunt Gloria, with whom Juan had lived in free union for several years. When he took Conchita as his lawful wife, it caused a temporary rift between Gloria and the Martínez family.

Conchita's marriage did not go well. She had continued to teach until the birth of another son. When she stopped teaching, she could not adapt herself to being the wife of a poor peasant who drank, beat her and barely supported her. She no longer used cosmetics or wore good dresses or shoes and stockings or had her hair cut and waved. Instead, she wore her hair in a long braid, went barefoot and, when her sweater wore out, reverted to using a shawl. In less than a year she looked no different from her mother or from other poor women in the village.

Pedro wanted his daughter to live with him permanently, and at first she agreed, suggesting that she return to teach school in order to support her children. Actually, she was not happy in her parents' home. Although she was continually ill, Pedro made her work and sometimes struck her in the presence of her children. Nor was she receiving the food and care she needed, although both parents complained bitterly about the expense she was causing them. Conchita finally contacted her husband, who consented to take her back provided she would never again speak to her family. Pedro was enraged when she left and forbade the rest of the family to see her again. For several years he did not speak to her, but Esperanza, Macrina and the boys, including Conchita's son Germán, visited her secretly.

Conchita's marital situation improved when her husband renewed his interest in Adventism. Juan had fallen seriously ill with pneumonia while working on a road-construction job. Fearing he was going to die, he sent a message to his boss and drinking companion, asking him for money for a doctor. His former friend not only refused his request but also held back his wages and fired him. Disillusioned and hurt, Juan took Conchita's advice and sought help from his Adventist brothers, from whom he was able to borrow money. When he regained his health, Juan stopped drinking, began to study the Bible, and made an effort to live up to his religious precepts. To improve his economic situation, he went twice to the United States as a *bracero* and was able to pay off all his debts. With the help of an Adventist brother, Juan reclaimed the house he had inherited but which had been taken from him by his half-sister. It was a good house with several rooms and far superior to the one-room house he and Conchita and their six children had been forced to live in.

Juan and Conchita joined a more fanatic Adventist group which rejected many modern practices, particularly in education, science and medicine. This group emphasized daily Bible reading and practiced vegetarianism and the treatment of disease through diet, water cures and mud packs. Once so proud of her own education, Conchita now opposed sending her children to school beyond the sixth grade. Her religious outlook also made her more critical of her father and widened the breach between them. She tried without success to interest her brothers and sisters in her group. They preferred to follow their father's lead, albeit with little enthusiasm.

The other Martínez children were less independent and outspoken than Conchita, although they too had grievances against their father.

The second son, Martín, showed many of the same traits as Felipe, but on the whole Martín was somewhat more carefree and independent and better socialized. In telling his life story, he complained more openly about being put to work as a *peón* at the age of twelve and of being taken out of school after the third grade so that his sister Conchita could be educated. "My *papá* protected her a lot and she had all the advantages . . . The main ones to suffer were Felipe and I, as we were older. Ricardo suffered too, but not as much. We suffered because when my *papá* was the only one working there was very little to eat and my *mamá* gave it mostly to him. Many times when she prepared a meal it was just for him, especially as we weren't working yet. She said we could wait but he was working in the field and had to eat more than we did. We would get two *tortillas* each . . . at that age we had a big appetite. We were always hungry, always, always, until Felipe and I began to work."

In spite of his father's disapproval, Martín became a master baker after several years of apprenticeship which he managed between plant-ing seasons. During the time he worked in the bakery without pay, Martín took on the additional job of selling bread from house to house, working at least twelve hours a day to placate his father by earning a few *pesos*. When he was twenty-one, Martín found fifteen *pesos* in the street, and this bit of luck enabled him to go secretly to Mexico City to look for a job. His father agreed to let him stay there, and Martín worked happily in the capital for eight months. Then his mother be-came ill and asked him to come home. For seven years Martín gave up baking and worked in Azteca as a farm laborer at four *pesos* a day. Like his brothers, he turned over his wages to his father but, later, given more responsibility by his employer and a two-*peso* raise, Martín decided to save some of his pay. His employer helped him by withhold-ing a portion of it to make time payments on a mule which Martín bought for six hundred *pesos*. He acquired a horse in the same way.

"My motto was to save, and from the time I began to buy animals my *papá* was annoyed with me because he saw that I was becoming independent little by little. But he didn't say anything for he was afraid I would get fed up and leave . . . The animals were in my name but actually they were my father's because he was using them. Felipe and Ricardo were working with my *papá* then but I wanted to get my brothers together, to unite the three of us. We were not content work-ing under him. We were men already but always under his yoke. I saw that we were not getting anywhere because he was so capricious. He had begun to go into politics again and once in that atmosphere he would take the money and drink with his friends and we would not get a thing out of our work. My *mamá* was useless by that time and Ma-crina had left home, so we didn't have anyone to serve us. We were abandoned like orphans. My *papá* didn't work in the fields, but he earned money at the courthouse and was not concerned. He ate in a little restaurant in the plaza and had a good life but we had no one to attend us. So I wanted to influence my brothers but then my *papá* began tell-ing them that what I wanted was not good, that we should all unite under him. I defended them but my brothers didn't back me up. They couldn't stand up to my *papá*."

All of Martín's attempts to become independent were fought by his father. When his mother took a turn for the worse, the horse and mule were sold to pay for the extra expenses. After her death, Martín tried without success to go to the United States as a *bracero*. Finally he settled down in Azteca as a master baker. He stayed on in his father's house, helping with household expenses and occasionally in the fields. He also helped support his sister Macrina and her children. He kept resisting his father's efforts to dominate him and was secretive about his financial affairs. He spent six hundred *pesos* on a Carnival costume without consulting anyone at home and he used his leisure time to go about with friends who were mostly artisans or bus-line employees.

Like Felipe, Martín had a series of affairs with women and fathered one child whom he did not openly recognize as his and whom he did not support. At age thirty-six, seeing that he was not getting ahead and offended when his father accused him of stealing some money, Martín decided to marry his employer's daughter. He now hopes to farm for two or three seasons in order to get together enough capital to set up himself and his wife as fruit merchants in Mexico City. If he cannot do this, he will continue as a master baker in the hope of buying a baker's oven of his own some day. He and his wife continue to visit his father several times a month and help him occasionally with money or a gift.

Macrina, the younger daughter, bore the burden of the housework because of her mother's illness and her elder sister's absence from home. In 1943, Macrina was still attending school irregularly and she did manage to complete the fifth grade before she was taken out by her parents. She liked school and wanted to become a dressmaker, but she gave up her dream without a struggle and devoted herself to serving her parents and brothers at home. At sixteen, she was doing all the washing, ironing, grinding, and most of the cooking. She was not allowed to have friends or to go any distance unchaperoned. Her diversions were attending religious services with her father or other members of the family and going to an occasional fiesta or village fair.

"My life has always been very sad. When I was seven I liked to play with my doll. I made her a dress and with my friends we laid her out and put flowers around her and had a funeral. But then my *mamá* didn't let me play with friends and I didn't like to play alone. When my *papá* told me I was going to school I was glad but I remembered that I had no clothes for school and we were poor. I had one dress and on Sunday my *mamá* took it off me and washed it for Monday. I helped my *mamá* in the kitchen and if I didn't hurry she scolded me and every day I went to school without my breakfast. Later, when my sister went away to teach I went with her to study but she didn't teach me. We came back because my sister was sick [pregnant] and that made me feel so bad I didn't want to go with her again.

"But now that I was bigger, they scolded me at home if I woke up late, because among us peasants a woman had to get up at three in the morning, that's why. Then when they took me out of school I felt very sad. I had a great desire to study but later I didn't think about it. I wanted to go out to work and learn something useful so that I would have the things I needed. I wanted to know different places but they never let me go out. When Germán was born I was glad to go with my sister to help her with the child. But I was very jealous of my sister. When I saw her with a sweetheart it made me so jealous I cried and I went home. She left Germán with me when he was fourteen months and I loved him very much, like my own son, and he called me *mamá*. I always got along best with my sister and had more confidence in her than in my brothers. My sister always liked me because I helped her with her work."

Macrina had her first secret sweetheart at fifteen, her second at twenty. When she learned that he was seeing another woman, Macrina ran off with another man, whom she later married in a civil ceremony. He treated her well until the birth of their first child.

"Then began difficulties with another woman. I was resigned to it but what made me angry was that he passed by with her so that I and his mother could see. Later he gave me gifts to keep for her. He spent money daily on her and he was always angry with me, even because I ate. He had brought me cloth for dresses from the north but when l went to look for it, it was gone. I had six silver *pesos* and he gave it all to her. I was so angry my stomach hurt and I had to go to bed. Then his mistress died and he said I had done something to kill her and that I was planning to hire someone to kill him too. I finally went home to be cured because he didn't want to buy medicine for me."

After leaving her husband, Macrina lived on at her father's house. She was afraid to remarry because a second husband might not treat her children well. She wanted to work in the corn mill, but her mother was bedridden and the family needed help. For the next five years, and after her mother's death, Macrina worked at home. She had an affair with a widower who abandoned her when she became pregnant. Her father and brothers were harsh with her as a result, and she went to her sister's house to give birth, returning afterward to serve the family. However, she was not happy at home.

"At times I didn't know where to turn because of all the things I lacked and because of my brothers. That's why I sometimes felt desperate and I didn't know what to do. Felipe was the one with whom I had many arguments. We never agreed and we scolded each other and at times he told me to leave because, he said, he gives me expense money and I don't buy anything for him with it. The thing that made me sad was that sometimes Martín also said this. There were many of us at home, and if one didn't work or if he worked for himself and didn't earn anything he wouldn't give any money, and my *papá* didn't either because he said we were all grown and I was married and it was not his obligation any more. That's why I was the one most upset, because they gave me money only once in a while and they still said

I used the money only for myself or for my children. When my mother was still living and they didn't give me money, at times I took some corn to sell and I bought food only for her but the neighbors told my *papá* I was taking out a lot of corn and whenever he was angry he would tell me he didn't trust me because instead of taking care of his things I was stealing from him. I don't deny that when I had no money I had to sell corn but when they gave me money I didn't sell anything. When my *papá* or one of my brothers said this to me I resented it and felt sad."

Macrina remarried in 1961, this time to a man who worked for the bus line. The couple lived in her father's house for a short while, then moved into a house in a neighboring *barrio*.

The younger sons, Ricardo and Moisés, escaped the full force of their father's personality and the hardships experienced by the family in earlier years. Unlike their elder brothers, they do not express feelings of resentment. Ricardo, the third son, having spent three years away from home with his sister Conchita, was the only child who escaped the constricting influence of the mother. After a delay, Ricardo attended school in Azteca for three years. At fifteen, when he was about to enter the fourth grade, his father decided to put him to work full time. Ricardo was pleased because he felt like a man and wanted to be a peasant. He dreamed of owning a plot of land and a team of oxen some day. He worked under the strong hand of his father for eight years, but he resented the fact that his two older brothers were given authority over him and the right to whip him if necessary. Ricardo resisted but didn't want to fight with them because "Martín was too sensitive and Felipe was too short and half blind." Instead, Ricardo decided to leave home.

With some money given to him by Martín, Ricardo ran away from home when he was twenty-three. He cut sugar cane in Orizaba but was homesick and "weak in spirit" and had to return home after a few days. His father scolded him, but only mildly. The following year, Ricardo went to Acapulco for a brief time; in 1955, he entered a naval school in Mazatlán. He left home with feelings of guilt because his mother was ill and his father was angry with him for leaving. His family did not notify him of his mother's death because they thought he might become upset enough to take to drink. Six months later he learned of her death from a friend. "I did not drink because I was not accustomed to doing that but, with a lump in my throat, I said farewell to my *mamá* from a distance."

In the navy, Ricardo worked in the kitchen and in the tailor's shop. He learned to use a sewing machine and hoped to become a tailor. After two years he was sent out on a frigate. He liked the sea but hated the strict discipline. "It was worse than at home because it was military discipline by complete strangers." Although he was promoted to gunner, Ricardo asked for a discharge and left the service. He had saved five hundred *pesos*. Later he joined a cousin in a northern city, where he worked as a kitchen helper. Eventually he married a woman much his senior. Under her influence, he became a devout member of the Jehovah Witnesses. He later decided to go to the United States as a *bracero* and succeeded in obtaining a contract to pick oranges in California. He sent money to his wife, who saved over one thousand *pesos*. The money was promptly stolen by her nephew, who went to jail, but the money was gone. Ricardo took the setback with resignation and returned to the United States a second time. When he had another thousand *pesos* saved, he and his wife went to Azteca for a month's visit with his family. There his wife had a bad attack of "colic" and Ricardo spent almost four hundred *pesos* to cure her. During the visit, Ricardo built a raised hearth of cement and adobe bricks for the kitchen so that his sister Macrina would no longer have to kneel at her cooking.

Ricardo was disturbed by the persistent poverty of his family and attributed it to his father's excessive honesty. "My family did not get ahead like others because though my *papá* was one of the municipal authorities, he never did what was possible, the way the others did. When Abraham Fuentes was president, he bought I don't know how many house sites and parcels of land which are now worth a lot. My *papá* saw all this and said that people took office for selfish reasons and not for the benefit of the village. They wanted to get what they could and set themselves up. That's why when my *papá* took office, he always did it with honor and never got anything out of it. I think he went too far in his honesty because in life it is worth while at certain times to be a little dishonest. The father is the principal axis of the home and he must know how to get on. Everything depends upon him."

Ricardo is attached to his family and enjoys his annual visits to Azteca, although so far he has resisted his father's pressure to settle there. His wife would be unable to adapt to peasant life, Ricardo thinks, nor could he again live on a low income. In the city he has a steady job as a cook's assistant at twenty-five *pesos* a day. By living very modestly, he is able to save and has, from time to time, sent as much as three hundred *pesos* to his father or to one of his brothers. Ricardo is quite contented with his life and believes he has done well.

Moisés, the youngest son, enjoyed a privileged position in the family. Protected by his father and favored by his mother, his life story has an entirely different quality from that of the others. His extended schooling provided him with experiences more typical of modern urban youth.

"My life was happy. When I was a child I had no worries. All I did was play. All I thought about was when I would go to school. I wanted to imitate my sister Conchita and become a teacher. Her books awoke in me a yearning to know everything she knew. I was happy even though I realized how poor we were. Our food was extremely scanty and my parents dressed me in *manta* cloth. When my *papá* and my brothers worked on our own cornfield there was no pay coming and my *mamá* had no money for food.

"I liked to go to the fields with my brothers even though they weren't very fond of me. I went just to play but I liked to come home with my clothing stained because then my *mamá* would keep saying I was a good little worker. When my parents went to a fair, they took me with them. My *mamá* was afraid to leave me alone with my brothers for fear they might treat me badly. Perhaps this was because my brothers held something against me; they were jealous because I was the youngest."

Moisés entered school when he was six. At eight, during a *barrio* fiesta, he was badly burned by firecrackers and was ill for seven months, losing a year of school. At ten, he spent part of the school year in the village where Conchita taught, taking care of Germán. "I liked the atmosphere in that village because everything was new to me. I enjoyed going with my sister because she had so many friends. My sister always took me along when she went to the movies and to other towns, which was a wonderful thing to me. I saw the men and women teachers having good times together and my mind became filled with dreams of becoming a teacher. I didn't think of the good of humanity then but only of my ambition to know a lot and to enjoy myself in different places, together with friends or with a girl who would share my fun. When the school year was over we went home and were received with great jubilation and pleasure by my parents."

Moisés was happy in school until his father became a councilman in the municipal administration in 1945. "That year, life for the whole family became sad. My *mamá* fell ill and there was no money to have her treated. My *papá* didn't give enough at home. I don't know whether it was because of his low salary or because he spent the money in the usual diversions of adults. My *mamá* suffered physically and morally. The family began to disintegrate because my *papá's* behavior set a bad example for my brothers. Twice they wanted to leave home and work elsewhere. We went through bitter days. I fell behind in school. My *papá* also got sick and he felt desperate, perhaps because he didn't understand his own actions. When he left his job at the town hall, we began to live better."

After completing the sixth and last grade of primary school, Moisés wanted to continue studying. His brothers opposed the idea, but his parents encouraged him to try for a scholarship to a state boarding school. "I was very sad as I thought of the coming year. I doubted that I would get a scholarship. But there were rumors that a secondary school was going to be set up in Azteca and that gave me hope. Well-intentioned persons, including my *papá*, had been struggling to get it so that boys who wanted to study wouldn't have to leave the village. They got their wish and a school was opened on March 12, 1950. I enrolled and was very happy to be able to be with my family while I studied. We were the first class to enter and we had the idea we were shining bright and there were no others in the village to compare with us. In school I almost forgot about my home. I didn't think of poverty. I began to feel a spirit of superiority. I was even bored with my family."

Moisés enjoyed school. He sometimes went without food, but he had presentable clothing and shoes. He had many friends, went swimming every day, learned to dance, and went on school excursions. Soon, however, he joined a gang of ten friends with whom he played pool and dominoes after school. They began to miss classes and did almost no studying. At the end of the first year, Moisés failed five subjects, and his father threatened to take him out of school and put him to work in the fields, reminding him how hard a peasant's life was. At about that time, too, his best friend was murdered in a quarrel over a girl. Sobered, Moisés determined to apply himself to his studies. He feared he was going to fail the second-year final examinations, but then some students bribed the school janitor to give them copies of all the exams, which Moisés saw in advance. In this way he managed to pass. He was graduated after his third year and entered the state university in Cuernavaca. His brothers helped him with his daily bus fare and with money for meals. Again he went to the movies and boxing matches every day with his friends and neglected his studies. Troubled by his own behavior, he quit school and took a road-construction job while waiting for a teaching appointment. When this came through after several months, his father accompanied him to the village to which he had been assigned. Before leaving, his father said, "God bless you. You are now taking a new path which might lead to something good if you try hard. Don't acquire vices just because you are earning a few *centavos*. Don't become a wastrel who spends even what he doesn't earn and don't take up with evil friends. Look out for your own good."

Moisés at first felt fearful and inadequate as a teacher, but after some time he began to enjoy his new position in life. Before the year was over, he had several friends and two sweethearts. In the second year, he became more serious and worked hard to get the villagers to improve the school and to build a fence around the yard. He made some enemies because of his persistence, but he felt great satisfaction when he achieved his goal. As another civic contribution, he volunteered to teach an evening class for the illiterate children of the village. In his third year, he joined a teacher's strike in which a 60 percent salary increase was demanded. As his father had done before him, Moisés marched under the union's black and red flag until the strike was won. Pleased with his own life, Moisés became increasingly concerned about the condition of his family, whom he visited during his vacations.

"I was very depressed while I was at home because of the poverty in which my family lived. My mother was ill and without money we could not cure her. There was no work for my father and brothers except in the fields. They had to wait for the rainy season to work and then for the harvest. In most cases, the harvest was very poor because the earth was sterile. And the land did not even belong to them. If they rented good land, they had to pay the owner the major part of what they produced. This was what was on my mind practically every day. Sometimes I despaired and asked myself, 'When are we going to get out of this poverty? Will my *mamá* ever get well? Can I alone do anything for my family? How can I earn a lot of money to help them? Why are we so poor, and so many others too?' The answers to these questions are difficult. Perhaps I can solve some of them. These have been some of my worries since I began to live my own life."

Moisés continued to study during vacations and finally was qualified as a federal teacher. This has made him eligible for government loans, and for the first time the family had a source of credit. With the help of periodic loans, Moisés was able to make some substantial improvements at home. Two years after his mother's death, he purchased adobe, roof tiles and other building materials to construct another house on the family site because, he said, he wanted a nicer house to live in when he came home. He also bought an iron door and windows to improve the existing house. These materials have not yet been used, but are kept piled up inside the house and in the yard. Moisés had expected his brothers to help him build the house but found that they and his father suspected him of planning to take over for himself not only the new house but also the entire property. He denied this but they did not believe him. Nevertheless, a year after he bought the building materials, he bought two beds, pillows, bed linen, a table and four chairs, a little radio, a kerosene stove, china ware and drinking glasses.

Discouraged by his family's mistrust of him, Moisés no longer tried to improve the house. Instead, he used his extra money to help Germán continue his studies. At twenty-eight Moisés' thoughts are turning more and more to the desirability of getting married, although as yet he has no particular girl in mind.

Even more than Moisés, Germán, the grandson, enjoyed a comparatively good childhood. Everyone in the family, with the exception of Esperanza, was fond of him and treated him kindly. He was obedient and co-operative at home and at school, yet quietly independent. In telling his life story, he showed himself to be thoughtful, observant, objective about himself and the other members of the family, and quite contented.

"I have never complained for lack of attention in my family. I have always felt that they cared for me. My grandma was the only one who was mean to me. She didn't like me and hit me a lot, sometimes without cause, but I didn't mind because Macrina protected me and loved me. My grandma was very choleric and would get angry over any little thing. The only time I saw her happy was when she was drinking. I don't think she was intelligent, even in the kitchen, but from what they tell me she helped my grandpa a lot in a material way. She bore a lot from him and in that sense she was very good, though I was afraid of her. When my grandpa hit me I was terribly afraid but he only beat me twice. He really loved me more than my grandma did . . .

"On the whole I can say I had a very happy childhood. I cannot say I missed my mother, because Macrina always treated me so well. My little half-brothers suffered more than I did. They had no clothes, just underpants and ragged little shirts, but Macrina made many sacrifices to buy me clothing. I noticed that she would save from the money given to her for errands and she would get together a *peso* or two to get me something to wear. In this way I lived much more happily than my half-brothers and I even pitied them . . .

"I didn't have much freedom to go out but I saw that my uncles never went out so why would I be allowed to go? My uncles have always been submissive to my grandpa. They were afraid of him and kept their distance. He never accepted their affection so they grew up like that. My grandpa was affectionate to me, but as I saw how my uncles behaved I followed their example. But there is a lot of unity in our family. I haven't seen more affection in other families here. My uncles even have more feeling for each other than is common. I know some brothers who don't speak to each other . . . Most of the families

I know don't dedicate themselves to study and education. They just work to keep alive. In our house, thanks to my grandfather, we have all received some training. Other parents say, if I suffered and didn't go to school, my children won't go either. But my grandpa was different. He was proud to send us to school and he was the first one in the *barrio* to begin. Of course, we cannot consider ourselves culturally advanced, but compared to our neighbors, yes, in a sense, we feel superior, because they know nothing. *Our* greatest lack is economic."

Germán was not hurried in his development and did not enter school until he was eight. He failed the fourth grade because he broke his hand and was kept at home by his grandfather. He also failed the fifth grade because of his irregular attendance as a result of his grandmother's illness. Germán sometimes had to do the cooking, marketing and cleaning for the entire family. He prepared the corn dough, took it to the mill, and made *tortillas* on a *tortilla* press. This machine, bought by his uncles in 1955, was the first mechanical kitchen gadget introduced in the household.

Germán was an indifferent student until he reached the sixth grade, but urged on by his grandfather and by Macrina and Moisés, he decided to continue his education. At fourteen, he entered the village secondary school. "Perhaps, too, because I was going into adolescence, I wanted to be independent. All during primary school I was withdrawn and I felt inferior because of my religion. But in the sixth grade I got along better with my companions and felt more equal. I didn't know what career I wanted to study for, but I wanted to be something, for myself, for my family and to serve society. When I went on school excursions and saw how absolutely poor some little villages were, I felt bad because I knew from the books I read that other countries had made more progress. It upset me very much that Mexico was the way it was. I wanted others to have the same idea I did, to put all my effort to improving society. At home, my family, my uncles, had only their personal, individual interests. But I listened to my grandfather and to my teachers who said, 'Mexico needs many things,' and I also dreamed that one day I would be a benefactor of my people . . .

"Just before I graduated from secondary school, my grandpa gave me a book to read. It was the Civil Code of the State of Morelos, and he said, 'Read this so that you will know how to defend yourself.' . . . I don't know whether it was his influence, because he was always talking about these things with his friends and I would listen, or whether I was born with this tendency to be concerned about social things . . . For example, take my village. It makes me sad to see the way it is. I want it to change. On the other hand, I think it should also continue its traditions. But there should be more equality. There are some who are very poor and others who are very rich, but to improve economically, it is first necessary to do away with ignorance because in ignorance it is impossible to do anything. Interest must be aroused and thoughts must be influenced . . .

"When I was about to graduate I still didn't know what I wanted to be. There was only a month to go and I was going about in a mental crisis, thinking, 'What is it I want to do? Be an engineer? a doctor? an architect? a chemist? a teacher?' I studied a book on vocational orientation and I talked it over with my friends and I decided to go to normal school to become a teacher. I would like to teach in a backward community so that I can influence it . . . We need many social changes because the Mexican Revolution isn't over, it hasn't been yet fulfilled. The first thing the candidates of the Republic do today is support the Agrarian Law, which was made because of Zapata. But they haven't carried it out well because all the land hasn't yet been divided up. There is still much to be done . . . In my opinion, I think socialism is going to dominate the world. That is my personal prophecy."

I I I

The Village Background

The study of the Martínez family grew out of my larger ethnographic study of Azteca. I hoped that an intensive study of a single village would contribute to our knowledge of some of the fundamental processes of culture change and at the same time provide government agencies and administrators working in rural areas with a better understanding of the psychology and needs of the people.

In the study of Azteca I employed quantitative procedures wherever possible, utilizing census data, local government records and documents, schedules and questionnaires. Numerous village surveys were made with the assistance of local informants and a small staff of field workers. Throughout the study, all the current anthropological field techniques were used—interviews, participant-observers, autobiographies, case studies, and psychological tests.

The *barrio* and the family were the basic units of our research. After an analysis of the population census, we began to acquire a great variety of information on every family in each of the *barrios*. Intensive case studies of three representative families in each *barrio* were then made, and finally, with the aid of student assistants who lived with each family, seven families were studied in depth.

I began the field work with several preliminary visits to Azteca and the surrounding villages of the *municipio*. On one of these visits

I brought letters of recommendation from the state Governor and others to the local municipal authorities, who were very helpful. With their aid I rented a house for my family, located informants, selected representative families, and generally prepared the way for the coming of my student assistants.

Establishing ourselves in the village presented few difficulties. Because of the frequent coming and going of tourists, the presence of a few outsiders created no particular stir. However, during the first month, rumors spread that we were U.S. spies with imperialist designs, Protestant missionaries, tax agents and, finally, army conscription officers looking for eligible youths. Fortunately for the project, the rumors never became widespread. Throughout the study, rapport with our selected families and other informants was excellent.

Azteca is supported by a household economy of small producers —peasants, artisans and merchants—whose primary motive for production is subsistence. But it is not a self-sufficient economy. The village depends heavily upon trade with nearby regions for basic elements of diet such as salt, sugar, rice and *chile*. From urban centers it obtains cloth, agricultural implements, sewing machines, Coleman lamps, kerosene, guns, patent medicines, water pipes, buses, and other manufactured goods.

The agricultural resources of Azteca are poor indeed. Only about 15 percent of the total land area is cultivable by plow and oxen and about 10 percent by the more primitive method of cutting and burning and hoe culture. Even if there were a perfectly equitable distribution of land there would be only 1.5 acres of cultivable land and about 8 acres of forest and grazing lands per capita. Furthermore, there is only one harvest a year and no irrigation.

Although 90 percent of the gainfully employed are agriculturists and the occupation of farming has high status, farming is not the sole occupation but is combined in various ways with other activities. Some Aztecans work on nearby plantations, others engage in trade or raise livestock. In 1948, there were about twenty-six nonagricultural occupations in which a total of 273 individuals took part.

The Aztecan economy, though that of a peasant society, is neither simple nor primitive. It has many elements: well-developed concepts of private property, a high degree of individualism, a free market, a definition of wealth in terms of land and cattle and other forms of property, a relatively wide range in wealth differences, the use of money, a highly developed system of marketing and trade, interest on capital, work for wages, pawning of property, renting of land, the use of plow and oxen, and specialization in part-time occupations.

Despite this roster of familiar traits, the Aztecan economic system is quite distinctive and defies easy classification in terms of such traditional categories as capitalistic or feudal. For side by side with the above traits are others—namely, communal land ownership, collective labor, hoe culture, production primarily for subsistence, barter, the absence of credit institutions, the lack of capital, the fear of displaying wealth except on ceremonial occasions, and the continued importance of religion and ritual in economic pursuits.

Three kinds of land tenure are found in Azteca: communal land holdings, *ejido* holdings, and private holdings. Communal lands comprise approximately 80 percent of the land of the *municipio* and include mountain forests for lumber, firewood and charcoal making, scrub forest on land covered with recent volcanic material, and steep hills where corn can be planted by hoe culture, grazing lands and highly eroded lands. The communal lands belong traditionally to the *municipio* and are under its control. They represent one of the oldest forms of landholding in Azteca and have remained practically intact through both the Aztec and Spanish conquests down to the present.

In theory, any individual from each of the eight villages of the *municipio* has the right to use the communal lands anywhere in the *municipio* provided he obtains permission from the municipal authorities or, as at the present time, from the forestry and *ejido* authorities. In practice, however, each of the eight villages has come to consider the lands nearest it as its own. Thus moral boundaries have developed and are recognized by all concerned.

The *ejido* holdings are a relatively recent phenomenon, dating from after the Revolution. In 1929, Azteca received 2,100 hectares of land in restitution from a nearby *hacienda*. *Ejido* holdings constitute somewhat less than 5 percent of the land within the *municipio* and consist primarily of arable land for plow agriculture. *Ejido* lands are communally owned by the *municipio* but are under the control of locally elected *ejido* authorities rather than the regular municipal authorities. *Ejido* holdings differ from communal holdings in that they are divided into small plots and assigned to individuals in accord with the rules of eligibility established by the National *Ejido* Program. Title to the *ejido* lands rests with the nation, whereas title to the municipal land rests with the *municipio*. *Ejido* holdings cannot be bought and sold, but may be passed from father to son so long as the need for the land can be satisfactorily proved. Two hundred and sixty-seven (31 percent) Aztecan families now hold *ejido* parcels, all of which are less than three hectares in size.

Private holdings consist mostly of land used for plow agriculture, and they constitute about 15 percent of the best level land in the *municipio.* Private holdings are in fee simple and ownership must be proved by legal title. It is important to remember that in Azteca all three types of land holdings are worked individually rather than collectively.

Only 36 percent or 311 of the 853 families in the village own private land. Landholdings are extremely small: over 90 percent of all holdings are less than nine hectares and 68 percent are less than four hectares. A villager with fifteen or more hectares is considered a large landowner, and only two holdings are between twenty-five and twenty-nine hectares. The large number of landless people and the small size of holdings result primarily from the poverty of resources rather than from the concentration of landownership in the hands of a few individuals.

The land problem in Azteca is not a recent one. It was at least as severe in the twenties before the *ejido* grants and it was certainly more acute before the Revolution. In 1927, 158 families who now have *ejido* parcels were landless. Thus the *ejido* program in Azteca has had at least two beneficial effects. It has reduced the number of landless families and it has helped some families who had insufficient land, to increase their holdings. But the *ejido* program has by no means solved the land problem, since 384 families still remain landless and have little prospect of becoming landowners. Nor has Azteca benefited from the great advances in agriculture which have occurred in other parts of Mexico as a result of hydroelectric projects and of mechanization. In 1950 there was not a single tractor in the village and most families continued to work their tiny subsistence holdings by means of primitive methods. By 1960 there were two tractors.

Two contrasting types of agriculture, which represent different historical and technological levels, exist side by side in Azteca. One is the primitive pre-Hispanic cutting and burning system of hoe culture; the other is the more modern post-Hispanic agriculture which uses plow and oxen. The differences between hoe culture, locally known as *tlacolol,* and plow culture are not limited to the use of different tools; each system has far-reaching social and economic implications.

In Azteca, both plow culture and hoe culture have been known since the Spanish Conquest. In hoe culture, the land used is steep and rocky, while in plow culture it is less sloping, relatively treeless, and includes the broad valley bottom in the southern part of the *municipio.* Hoe culture is practiced on communally owned land and necessitates a great deal of time and labor but very little capital. Plow culture is practiced on privately owned land and requires relatively little time and labor but considerable capital. The former depends almost exclusively on family labor; the latter depends to a greater extent on hired labor. In hoe culture the yields are much larger than in plow culture, but the amount of corn planted by each family is relatively small and never reaches the amount planted by a few of the larger operators in plow culture. In hoe culture, rotation of land is a necessity, for the fields cease to produce after the first few years; in plow culture the same fields may be planted year after year until the soil is completely exhausted.

Hoe culture is essentially geared to production for subsistence, while plow culture is better geared to production for the market. It is significant that most families who work *tlacolol* are landless and that *tlacolol* has traditionally been viewed as the last resort of the poor. Farmers who own small plots of land, however, may also work some *tlacolol* to supplement their meager income. Indeed, in recent years inflation has brought a new trend to the village. Aztecans who own considerable land now rent it out or let it rest while they work *tlacolol*. This is resented by most *tlacololeros*, who believe that the communal lands should serve the landless.

Other differences between hoe culture and plow culture include the cycles of work, the tools, the type of corn, the work techniques, and even the terminology. Generally speaking, the tools and techniques used in *tlacolol* are still known by their Nahuatl names, while in plow culture Spanish names prevail. Still another difference results from the location of the lands involved. With few exceptions the privately owned land used for plow culture is much closer to the village and some peasants take the bus to get to their fields. *Tlacololeros* usually rise at 4:00 A.M., walk for about two or three hours through the hills to reach their fields, and return home a few hours later than plow culture farmers.

In hoe culture, most of the peasants own their own tools, which are homemade except for the *machete* and the iron tip on the hoe. In plow culture, only 48 percent of the landowning families owned plows at the time of our study, and only 57 percent owned oxen. In hoe culture, it took an average of 150 man-days of work for the production of one hectare of corn, whereas in plow culture it took an average of fifty days.

In 1943, there were no clearly delineated social and economic classes in Azteca. The major bases for class stratification were largely swept away by the Mexican Revolution. Because of the limited natural resources, primitive technology and low productivity, the rate of capital accumulation was very slow. No single group controlled sufficient capital or labor to achieve wealth by its exploitation, nor did any group have a monopoly of the means of production or the sources of wealth. Agrarian reform broadened the land base somewhat and enlarged the group of small landowners and *ejidatarios*. A clearly defined rural proletariat never developed in Azteca because of the availability of the communal lands.

Nevertheless, there were significant differences in wealth, education and living standards. Aztecans are sensitive to these differences and readily classify individuals as rich or poor. Private landownership is considered the most important single form of wealth; other items frequently mentioned at the time of our study were *ejido* plots, teams of oxen, plows, urban property (the ownership of more than one house and house site in the village), sewing machines, cows, mules, horses, donkeys, hogs, and plum trees.

To rank families according to their wealth, we devised a simple point scale based on the ownership of the above items and assigned a score to every family in Azteca. Guided by the modest village standards, we estimated that a score of between forty and fifty points represented the minimum in property ownership necessary for an acceptable level of living for a family of five. The families were then classified into groups according to their scores. We found that 81 percent of the families had less than forty points and fell into the lowest group, 14 percent had between forty and ninety-nine points, forming a middle group, and 5 percent, the upper group, had from one hundred to over four hundred points.

Almost all of the landless families in the village were in the lower group; approximately one-third depended upon the communal lands and all carried on a number of activities which provided a meager income. Many burned charcoal, sold wood, worked as *peones* or small traders or had some other part-time occupation. The lower group contained ninety-two families with zero scores. These were either young married men, many of whom were living with their parents—who also had low scores—or they were widows or old men living alone.

The middle group included most of the artisans, schoolteachers and merchants, as well as better-to-do peasants, 119 families in all. This group included the more literate, better educated and more acculturated villagers. In addition to their other occupations, most of the artisans and merchants also planted their own cornfields.

The upper group consisted of thirty-eight families, all of whom had especially high scores in land and cattle. About one-half of these families inherited their land from relatives who were wealthy *caciques* before the Revolution; the other half had worked their way up to their present position. Some of the newly rich got their start in the hectic days of the Revolution by purchasing land at low prices from half-starved villagers or by more devious methods. Others became wealthy by going on dangerous cattle-buying trips to southern Morelos or Guerrero, and by selling the animals at a high profit. But the most important ways in which these families obtained wealth was through hard work, thrift and self-denial over many years. In practically all cases of better-to-do families, the wife was exceptionally industrious and economically helpful to the husband.

The heads of families in the wealthy group were elderly, mostly between fifty and sixty-nine years. There were no younger people in this group and very few in the middle group. The bulk of the younger heads of families were at the low end of the scale. But while the wealthy were of advanced age, most old people in Azteca were not wealthy. The practice of not dividing up the property until the death of the parents often resulted in married sons' with as many as five children being landless and without a house of their own. The majority of young men in the lower economic group had little prospect of substantially raising their position in the traditional manner. Convinced of the impossibility of becoming wealthy, most of these men had limited aspirations and devoted themselves to the day-to-day problems of subsistence. It was primarily the families of the middle group that strove for upward mobility.

On the whole, the people in the upper and middle groups consumed more meat, milk, eggs and bread than those in the larger lower group, their clothing was in better condition, their homes were better constructed and equipped, some even having running water. However, it was the middle group rather than the upper which most readily adopted new customs, styles and even luxuries, such as wearing shoes and factory-made clothing, eating bread instead of *tortillas,* sleeping on beds instead of on straw mats on the floor or on raised cots of wood and cane. This group, too, valued education as a means of personal advancement and sent more of its young people out of the village to attend high school.

Despite the wealth differences, the rich were not readily distinguishable from the poor. There was little ostentatious display of wealth. Both rich and poor worked the land dressed in the same white *calzones* and shirts of coarse cotton cloth, *huaraches* and wide-brimmed straw *sombreros;* both hired day laborers when necessary. Men who owned property, as well as those who did not, hired themselves out as *peones* when they needed cash. No Aztecan employed more than three or four workers and they were hired for short periods during the busy planting and harvesting season. The employer worked side by side with his workers, who were often relatives, *compadres* or friends, and there generally was a spirit of mutual co-operation and respect. In most cases, an Aztecan will work for a fellow villager only if he receives good treatment.

Full-time domestic servants in Azteca were few, though it was quite common to hire a poor relative, a widow or an orphan to help with the washing or to take care of a family when the mother was temporarily incapacitated. There was no leisure class in the village, nor was there any social stigma attached to physical labor.

In the traditional world view of Aztecan peasants there was a strong fear of natural forces and considerable anxiety about the imminence of misfortune, disaster and death. Their world was filled with hostile forces and punishing figures which had to be propitiated if their good will and protection were to be secured. The ancient village god withheld rain if he were neglected; *los aires,* the spirits who lived in the water, sent illness to those who offended them; and *nahuales,* humans in pact with the devil, could turn themselves into a pig or dog to do harm at night. Catholic figures, too, were seen as threatening. God was a punishing figure rather than one of love, and most misfortunes were ascribed to Him. He brought good fortune only rarely. The saints were seen as intermediaries between God and man, and Aztecans devoted themselves to cultivating their favor.

The profoundly practical nature of Aztecan peasants precluded much religious fantasy, mysticism or preoccupation with metaphysics. They sought from religion concrete solutions to the problems of daily life. They could understand punishment for things done or not done and the need for protection. They bowed to superior powers by doing what was expected of them or by giving or doing something that would please a particular being: lighting a candle, offering a few coins or flowers, burning incense, reciting a special prayer or performing a certain dance.

To traditional Catholic symbols the villagers imparted magical powers which gave them additional protection. They received the ash on Ash Wednesday in the belief that the cross, the formal Catholic symbol of penance and sorrow, would guard them against sorcery and enemies. Old holy images were burned to make more efficacious ashes. The palm blessed on Palm Sunday was used for protection against lightning; its ashes were used to cure headaches. Peasants trimmed their plants on Holy Saturday so they would produce more, mothers cut their daughters' hair to make it grow longer, and children were struck on the legs to make them taller. On September 28, crosses of pressed *pericón* flowers were placed on doorways and *milpas* to ward off demons and evil winds.

Aztecans viewed people, too, as potentially hostile and dangerous, and their typical reaction was a defensive one. Security in the threatening world was sought first and foremost through the economic independence of the biological family. To be able to provide one's wife and children with food, clothing and shelter was the only real assurance against want and interference. Work, industry and thrift, for the purpose of accumulating property in land and animals, were the highest, most enduring values in Azteca. So long as a man devoted himself to work, he felt secure and blameless, regardless of how little he produced. Material success was not openly admitted as an important personal goal and was not admired in others. With faith in his own effort and with the help of God, the Aztecan lived as an individualist, withdrawn, self-reliant, reluctant to seek or give economic aid or to borrow or lend. Despite the tradition of collective labor, there was a general unwillingness to co-operate with others in public and private enterprises.

The Aztecan's independence was tempered by his loyalty to and co-operation with his immediate family. The dependence of families on the communal lands and the occasional need for group effort to defend these lands and to maintain public property also modified Aztecan individualism. This individualism, however, was not competitive as in the United States. In the village, the individual did not try to win security and recognition through development of his personal talents or through self-aggrandizement but rather through conformity and submission to the needs of his family. It was an enclosing, inward-turning individualism which permitted families to live side by side in privacy and with no power over one another.

Aztecans also sought security through respect and the extension of relationships of respect, which they valued highly for the safety they promised. Persons involved in such a relationship addressed each other with the respectful *usted* rather than the intimate *tu*, and maintained a reserved, friendly attitude toward each other and fulfilled certain formal reciprocal obligations. In a relationship of respect, sexual contact, joking or drinking together or any form of aggression against the other was forbidden. Such respect might stem from a superior social, economic or political position, from advanced age, from education, or from a specific, formal relationship established between two individuals or families—for example, in-laws or *compadres*.

Aztecans tended to be reserved and guarded in most interpersonal relations, and were not an easy people to get to know. The man who spoke little, minded his own business, and maintained some distance between himself and others was considered prudent and wise. People were somber and quiet, especially in the street. Boisterousness and noise coming from a house soon earned the family an unpleasant reputation. Women and girls were expected to walk with eyes modestly downcast; those who smiled freely might be thought flirtatious or flippant. To smile very much at other peoples' babies was to be suspected of the "evil eye." Most children did not learn to smile at strangers or visitors until they attended school. Aztecan men, particularly, tended to be undemonstrative and limited in their ability to express warmth and affection and the more tender emotions.

Creativity and artistic expression were limited to the point of constriction—there were practically no handicrafts, no pottery, woodcarving, weaving, or basket making. Music and dancing were not well developed. Religious artistic expression consisted only of decorating the church at fiestas and of making costumes and masks for a few annual religious dances. Clay utensils and household articles were for the most part undecorated. The clothes of the village women were traditionally drab, although young girls were beginning to wear brighter colored dresses. Bright colors, particularly in clothing, were not in accord with Aztecan ideas of propriety, and in the past were actually believed to be dangerous because they might attract the rainbow.

Constriction was also evidenced in Aztecans' gestures and in their avoidance of bodily contact with others. Perhaps the only exceptions occur in love making and in the mother-child relationship during the nursing period; when a child reaches five, he experiences little physical contact of a tender nature. Kissing, except of infants, was not customary even in courtship. From the Spaniards, Aztecans learned the gesture of kissing the hand of the priest, parents, grandparents and godparents, but this custom was disappearing. Shaking hands and the typical Mexican double embrace were not generally practiced in Azteca. It was when Aztecans drank that their restraint relaxed; male companions might then walk arm-in-arm, and drunken men sometimes tried to hug and even kiss their children or wives.

Normally, the Aztecan showed his affection for another by fulfilling reciprocal obligations: the father expressed love for his wife and children by providing them with the necessities of life; the child showed affection by obedience, respect and diligence; *compadres* and members of the extended family demonstrated their friendship and good will by carrying out their formal duties. When these obligations were carried out, Aztecans considered that they had a satisfactory relationship with each other and demanded little more. Some of the younger people, it is true, were no longer content with formal reciprocity and sought out friends on the basis of personal interest. Younger parents were beginning to express affection for their children through gift giving and through greater indulgence and concern with their children's aspirations.

Aztecans placed value on sexual restraint not because they were puritanical or guilt-ridden but because of practical considerations of safety and self-preservation. They believed in conserving themselves for work. They also feared too strong attachments, unwanted pregnancies, and jealousy and sorcery. From childhood on, sexuality was discouraged and discussion of sex was taboo in the home; infant sexuality, masturbation and sex play among children were strictly forbidden. For women, there was little inconsistency between childhood training and acceptable adult behavior. Girls grew up with negative, prudish attitudes toward sex, marriage and childbearing; they were expected to be sexually restrained both before and after marriage. For males, however, a discontinuity existed in connection with sex. Although sexuality was inhibited all through childhood, young men were subjected to pressure from members of their age group to be sexually active; they were expected to prove their manliness through sexual conquests both before and after marriage. In practice, however, the attitudes toward sex and the slow development of boys created an aura of anxiety about sexual activity and boys were often timid in courtship. The prevailing attitude was, nevertheless, that sexual activity in men was an expression of manliness, while in women it was a form of delinquency.

Aztecans were an indirect people who relied on formality and intermediaries to facilitate interpersonal relations. Any direct expression of aggression was discouraged and competition between individuals was rare. Underlying the smooth surface, however, was a feeling of oppression, particularly for those individuals who were trying to improve themselves or who, for one reason or another, deviated from strict conformity. A good deal of suppressed hostility found indirect release in malicious gossip, stealing, secret destruction of other's property, envy, deprecation and sorcery. Assault in the form of surprise attack and murder occurred from time to time. Men in positions of wealth, power or authority often carried a gun for protection and preferred not to venture out at night. The most feared, although perhaps the least used, form of indirect aggression was sorcery.

In Azteca the motives of everyone were suspect, from the highest public officials of the nation to the local priest and even close relatives. It was assumed that anyone who had power would use it to his own advantage. Honest government or leadership was considered an impossibility; altruism was not understood. The frank, direct person, if he existed anywhere in the village, was thought to be naïve or the greatest rogue of all, so powerful or so shameless as to have no need to conceal his actions or thoughts. Friendships were few. To have friendships outside the extended family was not an Aztecan ideal, nor was there a tradition of a "best friend." Adults considered friends a source of trouble and a waste of time. Traditionally, women and girls were not supposed to have any friends whatsoever. While men may be friendly with many individuals, these relations tended to be based on a definite, limited purpose—that is, for an exchange of work or for borrowing or for drinking together.

There was a relative lack of concern for the future, and no "saving for a rainy day." Only a minority who recognized education as an important source of security saved to give a son or daughter advanced schooling. And it was among these families that one encountered the familiar urban middle-class pattern of self-denial in the present in order to gain a future reward. The rest of the villagers exercised a general thrift, but they spent when they had money and pulled in their belts when they didn't.

The majority of Aztecans seemed to lack strong drive or ambition for self-improvement. They tended to be satisfied if they had enough food and clothing from harvest to harvest. Among the young people, too, there was a general acceptance of the way of life. Young men wished to be peasants like their fathers and most young girls continued to work at home and to serve their elders. The rewards they sought were not impossible to achieve: occasional new clothes, shoes, a sweetheart, permission to attend the fiestas, and ultimately marriage, with some parental help.

Of particular interest for the understanding of the relative absence of frustration, anxiety, guilt and self-blame was the tendency to shift personal responsibility onto others or onto supernatural forces. The individual cannot help what he does, for these forces control him. Such traits as fatalism, stoicism in the face of misfortune, passivity, acceptance of things as they are, and a general readiness to expect the worst tended to free the individual from the burden of being in control of his personal fate. Even in the face of gross injustice, in which a villager could be protected by law, there might be little or no self-defense.

The patterns of child training reflected many adult attitudes and value systems. One of the underlying principles in child rearing was to develop children who were easy to control. The great amount of attention given an infant was primarily for the purpose of limiting and protecting him rather than of stimulating him. Activity, aggression, self-gratification, curiosity and independence were discouraged from infancy through young adulthood, although some children, especially boys, were occasionally indulged and permitted a greater degree of ego development. But so long as a son or daughter lived under the parental roof, he was dependent upon the parents and subject to their authority —and this situation might continue through marriage.

Although, by and large, the training the child received prepared him adequately for adult life in the village, nevertheless there were some points of conflict and inconsistency between theory and practice.

Perhaps the primary area of conflict was found in the roles of men and women and in the relations between the sexes. On the whole, men were under greater pressure than women and experienced more discontinuity in the transition from childhood to adulthood. Although boys were favored more than girls, their early training was not conducive to the development of independence or a real ability to dominate, qualities required by the ideals of a patriarchal society. Husbands frequently relied on fear to maintain authority. As the men grew older and as their sexual powers and ability to work declined, they found it more difficult to keep their position of dominance; old men in the community received little social recognition and had little power. It is interesting to note that the life cycles of men and women took an opposite course: in early life men were in a comparatively favored position but as they grew older they were weighed down by life situations. Women began with less freedom, lower aspiration levels and earlier responsibilities, but as they matured after marriage they slowly gained more freedom and often took a dominant position in the household.

Azteca is a family-centered community. Families are strong and cohesive, held together by traditional bonds of loyalty, common economic strivings, mutual dependence, the prospect of inheritance and the absence of any other social group to which the individual can turn. Co-operation within the immediate family is essential, for without a family the individual stands unprotected and isolated, a prey to aggression, exploitation and humiliation. It is within the small biological family that Aztecans seek personal security. The extended family provides some additional security, particularly in times of emergency.

The family organization is patriarchal, based on the principle of male superiority. Children bear their father's name and, at marriage, the bride goes to live with her husband's family, or, if she is lucky, the husband has his own home to which he takes her. If the young husband goes to live with his wife's family, Aztecans call him "a male daughter-in-law" and say, "He was given away like a dog." Nevertheless, over 20 percent of all married couples had matrilocal residence. Most of the husbands in these cases were poor young men, either orphans or men who had married much older women or women of higher social and economic status.

According to the ideal culture pattern for husband-wife relations in Azteca, the husband is authoritarian, he is master of the household and enjoys the highest status in it. He is responsible for the support of the family and for the behavior of its members, and he makes all major decisions. It is his prerogative to receive obedience, respect and service from his wife and children. The wife is expected to be submissive, faithful and devoted to her husband, and to ask for his advice and permission before venturing on any but the most minor enterprises. She should be industrious and manage to save money no matter how small her husband's income. She should not be critical or jealous of her husband's activities outside the home or even show any curiosity about them.

Conflicts between husbands and wives are fostered by a discrepancy between actual roles and ideal roles in the organization of the family. Although the wife is subordinate to her husband, it is she who has the central role within the house. She is responsible for planning, organizing and managing the household, and for the training and care of the children. She cooks, cleans, washes, irons, does the daily marketing, shells corn for family consumption, raises chickens, turkeys and pigs, grows fruit, herbs and flowers. She trains her daughters in woman's work and supervises them until their marriage. Aztecan women are not required to work in the fields as are the women of neighboring villages, and they have more time to devote to their families.

The husband customarily turns over all his earnings to his wife. She is thus in a position to do a great deal of spending, borrowing and paying back in secret, especially as in most cases the husband does not interfere with her handling of the money so long as she gives some to him whenever he asks for it.

The husband's actual participation in family and household affairs is minimal. His work is outside the home. The division of labor is clear-cut; except for emergencies and for such jobs as hauling water and repairing the house, the husband does not concern himself with the house or the children. He is expected to work in the fields, care for the cattle, horses or oxen, make charcoal or cut wood, trade, and practice any special occupation he may have. He may pick fruit, shell corn for storage, make his own tools or work as a *peón* for others.

The men are gone a good part of the day, sometimes for several days at a time, depending on their work and the season of the year. In the past, Aztecan men worked in distant mines or on *haciendas*, and were absent from the village for long periods; before the Revolution, large numbers of men worked on nearby *haciendas* and returned home only once every two weeks. With the husband away, the wife not only is head of the family but sometimes also has to support herself and the children.

In many homes the husband's sense of security is a function of the extent to which he can control his wife and children or make them fear him. Wife beating, more common in the past than now but still widespread, is resorted to for offenses that range from not having a good meal ready on time to suspicion of adultery. Wives are not expected to offer any resistance to the punishment. Wife beating is a recognized legal offense in the village but few wives report their husbands to the local authorities.

Aztecan women readily express hostility toward men and often characterize all men as "bad." Self-pity and a sense of martyrdom are common among married women, many of whom break down and cry when telling their life stories. As they grow older they often become more self-assertive and oppose their husbands' attempts to limit their freedom and their business ventures. The present trend in the village is for the younger women and even the unmarried girls to take on the more independent attitudes of the older women.

Women are more in conflict with traditional ways than are the men. Their standards of behavior for themselves and their husbands are changing; they veer between the old ideal roles and new needs and experiences. They readily admit to the superiority of men and tend to admire a man who is *macho*, or manly, yet they describe the "good" husband as one who is not dominating but relatively passive. They also tend to regard the very submissive wife more as a fool than as an ideal. Apparently the women do not feel inadequate when they do not achieve the ideal of feminine behavior; indeed, they seem to feel pride rather than guilt in self-assertion.

Husbands often find themselves in a defensive position. They must conserve the old order of things if they are to maintain their control in the home, but the changes within the village in the past twenty years or so make this objective difficult. In the days when young wives lived with their mothers-in-law, often for many years, husbands had little difficulty in maintaining control and they felt correspondingly more secure. Most men believe that women must be kept under strict surveillance if their good behavior is to be assured. Women are expected to discontinue all friendships when they marry, and men may drop their own friends after marriage for fear that an intimacy might develop between the wife and the friend. The majority of husbands are suspicious of any activities that take the wife out of the home. Men feel most secure when their wives are pregnant or have an infant to care for; thus, to have one child follow close upon another is a desirable state of affairs from the men's viewpoint.

In sexual relations as in social relations, the Aztecan husband is expected to take the initiative and his wife to submit to his demands. It is believed that women have less *naturaleza*—that is, that they are sexually weaker than men. Husbands do not expect their wives to be sexually demanding or passionate, nor do they consider these traits desirable in a wife. Women who "need" men are referred to as *loca* (crazy) and are thought to be in an abnormal condition which may have been brought about by black magic. Respectable women properly express negative attitudes toward sex and often do so forcefully. Some husbands deliberately refrain from arousing their wives sexually, as it is assumed that a passive or frigid wife will be more faithful. In general, sexual play is a technique men reserve for the seduction of other women.

Promiscuous sexual activity is a male prerogative in Azteca and the men feel under pressure to prove their manliness by having many affairs. Usually they have extramarital relations with widows or unmarried women, less frequently with married women. Men now go to houses of prostitution in Cuernavaca, and venereal disease is becoming more common in the village. Although male adultery is considered undesirable behavior, it is nevertheless thought to be "natural" and a good wife is not supposed to be disturbed by it. Many women are resentful, however, especially if money is involved, and some openly quarrel with their husbands and also withhold money from them. Interference by wives in such matters enrages the men and often results in wife beating.

Drunkenness is not as common in Azteca as it is in surrounding villages or in other parts of Mexico, and it is more strongly disapproved of. Most men drink a small amount of alcohol regularly, but extensive drinking is limited to Sundays, fiestas or formal occasions. Many wives resent their husbands' drunken bouts both because of the probable violence and because of the money involved, but only the most aggressive try to break their husbands of the habit.

Aztecans believe that wives who have suffered beatings or other harsh treatment may take revenge through sorcery, and Aztecan men are alert to this possibility. The most commonly feared type of sorcery is a potion made from a well-known herb called *toloache,* secretly dropped into a man's coffee or any other drink. This herb is said to contain a drug that will affect the brain if taken in large doses. In Azteca, it is also believed that it will make a man *tonto*—that is, stupid or foolish and easily managed—and that an extra large dose will make him an idiot. The most important symptom to Aztecans is that the drugged man can no longer control his wife but is dominated by her. The man's mother or sister may attempt to cure him by secretly putting a counterpotion into his coffee. It is interesting to note that there is not a single known case of *toloache* given by a man to a woman.

When I returned to the village in 1960, its physical appearance had not changed very much. The plaza and market still seemed rather desolate and unprosperous; no additional buildings had been constructed in the center. There were no new streets or paved roads, except for two long cement treads which led up a steep street to the new tourist resort run by an American family. More automobile and bus traffic entered the village, and trucks came in with such new items as purified water and tanks of cooking gas for the homes of the foreign colony.

Village men still carried water to their homes from the nearest fountain; women still queued up to have their corn ground at the mills. The older people looked much the same, but the clothes of the younger people were more varied, colorful and citified. More young women had short hair and permanent waves, and one young girl wore blue jeans. The young men wore modern trousers, shirts and jackets, and more children had shoes, sweaters and store-bought clothes. The small shops sold more canned goods and packaged foods, mostly to the employed people who live in the center. There was a small restaurant and more saloons. A blare of radios came from the houses and inside some homes one saw a new kerosene or Coleman stove, aluminum pots, forks, hand presses for shaping *tortillas,* and overstuffed furniture. Most homes in the larger *barrios* had electric lights.

But many more changes have occurred than meet the eye. As a result of the great population increase there is a shortage of house sites and housing, and Aztecans petitioned the local government to make available some of the nearby communal lands for new house sites. Several homes have been built on the outskirts of the village and in the surrounding hills. Formerly it was not customary to rent a house; if an Aztecan had an extra house he would allow another villager to use it simply for the care of it. Now rental has become quite usual.

Since the late forties Azteca has had a resident doctor, and since 1952 a doctor from Cuernavaca who formerly practiced in the village has come once a week to see his patients. The clientele of both doctors has been increasing. In 1950, the resident doctor had an average of 75 patients a month; by 1956 the average was 160. Aztecans now complain about the expense of medicines and the delay caused by having prescriptions filled in Cuernavaca; the local "druggist" cannot fill prescriptions and carries few patent medicines. The village has a free federal government health clinic which cares for children and pregnant women and administers injections. About ten patients, most of them expectant mothers, come there every day. In 1955, approximately two thousand vaccinations and revaccinations were given.

The clinic and the doctor have by no means replaced the *curanderos,* however. Most births are still attended by the native midwives. Aztecans believe that doctors can cure only certain diseases, and still frequent *curanderos* for those illnesses which they attribute to *los aires,* anger, hot or cold foods, evil eye, and sorcery. Although the villagers have substituted new terms for old concepts—for example, *los aires* are now sometimes described as tiny animals or microbes and injections are called "cleansings"—it is questionable whether this represents much of a departure from the earlier magical thinking about the causes of disease.

Like many villages in the densely populated central plateau area, Azteca has not had the benefit of the great new hydroelectric and irrigation projects. Its agricultural base has remained very much the same; there has been no mechanization and no new important cash crops have been introduced. The peasants continue to work their land as before, although a few are now using some commercial fertilizer. Because the lack of change in agriculture combined with the rapidly increasing population has forced Aztecans to seek work in nonfarm occupations, a much lower proportion of the gainfully occupied are now peasants. The federal campaign for the preservation of the forest resources sharply reduced charcoal production in the village and many families have thereby lost a traditional source of income. Some found work as agricultural laborers on the two or three nearby gladiola farms; many more found work in Cuernavaca or as day laborers on road construction.

The changes in the occupational structure of the village have accentuated earlier trends. The number of nonagricultural occupations increased from 26 in 1944 to 33 in 1956 and the number of people engaged in these occupations rose from 273 to 565. This increase has been accompanied by greater specialization and a decline in the role of agriculture in the total economy. In 1944, approximately 70 percent of those engaged in nonagricultural occupations also farmed; in 1956, the comparable figure was only 25 percent! Today there is a much greater participation of women in the nonagricultural occupations than formerly. Women still predominate as teachers, *curanderos* and corn merchants, but they now are also full-time *tortilla* makers, dressmakers and hairdressers. Other new occupations in the village are those of tailor, hog-plum merchant and milk merchant.

The most dramatic occupational change and one which has become a major new source of income to the village is the *bracero* movement. In 1948, fewer than 30 Aztecans were *braceros*—that is, temporary agricultural workers in the United States; by 1957, over 600 men had been *braceros* for periods that varied from forty-five days to over a year. This occupational change has made for other great changes in the village. In 1943, Azteca suffered from an acute land shortage. Now, because in many cases the *braceros* return to the village only to rest a few months before setting out for another period in the United States, it suffers from a shortage of manpower, and many *milpas* go uncultivated. The *braceros* earn more in some months in the United States than they could earn in almost two years in the village, and many of them have invested their savings in improvements for their houses and in land and cattle. They have brought home portable radios, mechanical toys, clothing and cloth—the village now has four full-time tailors who are kept busy providing tailor-made pants for the villagers. Although the *bracero* movement has broadened the perspective of some Aztecans, who now greet American visitors with a few words of English, most of the *braceros* in the United States are isolated in work camps or on farms, speak no English, live on a Mexican diet, and on the whole learn little about the United States and its way of life. Very few learn agricultural skills that can be applied in the village

Most of the *braceros* from Azteca are young men between the ages of twenty and thirty. They come predominantly from the upper segments of the lower economic group but also from the middle group. Few come from the poorest families and fewer from the wealthier families. This is an interesting change from the pattern in the early forties, when only individuals with political connections and with experience outside of the village became *braceros*. At that time most Aztecans feared to leave the village for a distant country or even to go to Mexico City to the government recruiting stations for *braceros*. With more education, the younger generation developed a greater readiness to explore the outside world and to dare the hazards of a long journey. The sudden spurt in *bracerismo* did not occur, however, until a schoolteacher in one of the outlying villages became a *bracero* recruiter. Aztecan men paid him a fee in the hope that he would get them longer contracts and also jobs in California rather than in Texas or Arkansas. The fees, which the recruiter purportedly shared with government authorities, ranged from 200 to 400 *pesos*, depending on the length of time of work specified in the contract. Most of the villagers who signed up had to borrow from local money lenders at the usual high rate of interest.

The *bracero* movement has served as a partial though temporary solution of the agrarian problem in the village. Azteca has become dependent on the United States economy. Were the United States suddenly to close its borders to Mexican *braceros*, there would probably be a crisis both in the village and in the nation.

Another important change in Aztecans is their greater readiness to sell their land. In 1943, it was difficult to find anyone in the village who would consider selling a house site or an agricultural plot. For example, in 1942 a banker from Mexico City who wanted to build a home in the village negotiated for over a year before he succeeded in buying a modest-sized idle plot of land. By 1956, Aztecans had sold almost forty plots to as many outsiders for building homes in the village and in the lovely valley below. Aztecan middlemen are now speculating in land because of the steadily rising prices.

Since 1943, educational facilities have been further expanded in the village. Two new schools built in the larger *barrios* gave the village a total of four elementary schools. Attendance rose from about 750 in 1950 to over 900 in 1956. In 1950, a high school was completed, and attendance rose from 54 in the first year to 110 in 1956. Boys still predominate over girls in both elementary and high schools. The surrounding villages have begun to reach out for higher education and now send their children to the central high school in Azteca. Each year a number of Aztecan high school graduates go on to the university in Mexico City.

In the past ten years, bus travel to Cuernavaca has almost doubled and travel to Mexico City also has increased. On an average week day approximately five hundred Aztecans take the bus to Cuernavaca to work, shop, study, sell produce and to find recreation.

In 1956, as part of a federal-government project to improve communications, a telephone exchange was installed in a small grocery store in Azteca. Storekeepers can now make orders, politicians can arrange meetings, and in emergencies ambulances and doctors can be reached by phone. The grocer charges fifty *centavos* to call someone to the phone, provided he lives near the center of the village. During my stay in the village in 1956 a few calls from Hollywood were received by the village government—arrangements for the filming of a movie in Azteca were in process!

Movies are now shown in Azteca on week ends from October to May, in one of the *palacio* rooms which seats about three hundred people. The movie business is an insecure one, however; it cannot always successfully compete with the fiestas. Most of the films are Mexican cowboy and war pictures which appeal to young people. Adults over forty do not frequent the movies and most of the peasants do not permit their daughters to attend.

Despite the higher educational level, greater travel, and the increase in the number of radios, there has been no increase in the number of people who read newspapers. On the contrary, there seems to have been some decline since 1943. In 1956, only about 25 individuals read a newspaper with some regularity and none of them were peasants. Magazine reading has increased, however. In 1956, about 50 villagers had magazine subscriptions. Over a third of the subscriptions were held by teachers and most of the others by persons in nonagricultural occupations. The majority of the subscribers were under fifty, and reading was predominantly done by the men. Except for schoolteachers and some officials, few people owned books. Many children, however, read comics.

Related to the developments noted above are changes in every stage of the life cycle, particularly in the rearing of children. Again, most of the changes are found in the middle economic group; changes are occurring among the tradition-oriented members of the lower groups also, but at a much slower rate.

Women still prefer to give birth on a *petate* with the help of a midwife, but a doctor is often called in for difficult cases. Many young women are rejecting some of the "Indian" customs and cures of the midwives—for example, the food taboos, the use of smoke to help labor, and the wearing of the *huipil*. Magical practices like burying the first milk or throwing it over the roof are being discarded. Because more babies are being bottle-fed, the druggist now keeps a supply of baby bottles and nipples, as well as of formula mixtures. Young women feel less need to follow such customs as sweat baths or the forty-day post-partum seclusion before going to their first Mass.

A definite trend toward greater child-orientedness on the part of both parents is evident. Parents tend to be more permissive and more demonstratively affectionate with their young children. More fathers can be seen on the street carrying small children and a few help a little with the children at home. The swaddling of infants has been completely abandoned as "cruel" by some mothers. Parents indulge their children more, especially the first-born, and openly show their pride in their infants by buying them toys, shoes and attractive clothing. This is in sharp contrast with the older attitude of guarding children from the attention of others through fear of the "evil eye." Younger and more educated parents punish more lightly, permit more play, and send their children to school for as long as possible. The period of adolescence is becoming longer and more clear-cut, and the time when youths are expected to contribute to the support of the family is often delayed by years of study.

Arranged marriages have completely disappeared and more couples are marrying for love. Church weddings have become more elaborate and expensive and are patterned after those of the urban middle class. To avoid the problems of living with mothers-in-law, newlyweds try to set up independent households immediately after marriage or as soon as it is economically feasible. Some young wives work as schoolteachers or shopkeepers, but this is still unusual. More couples are resorting to legal divorce rather than mere separation or abandonment.

A noticeable change in attitudes and values and in the quality of interpersonal relations has occurred also among the educated middle group. In 1960, Aztecans seemed on the whole more outgoing and friendly and more at ease in the presence of outsiders. Children were noisier and smiled more; they were as apt to run toward as away from a stranger. Indeed, they begged tourists for *centavos*. Small groups of unchaperoned adolescent girls laughing and talking together were not unusual sights, and occasionally a village girl might be seen walking side by side with a boy in broad daylight. In general, the villagers were more accepting of their sophisticated members and provincialism seemed to be on the wane.

It is obvious, too, that Aztecans have more drive and ambition for self-improvement. The young people are restless and are making greater demands on their parents for education. They show more ability to co-operate with people outside the family over longer periods of time and have found the courage to look for better opportunities outside the village. Friendship has become increasingly important; *compadrazgo* has assumed a new significance in providing connections and social advantages. Material success and a higher standard of living are consciously admired and worked for and the motivation to hide wealth is weaker. Respect has come to be based more and more on wealth and social status. Education imparts higher status; a young man or woman who has a teacher's certificate expects to be treated more respectfully by his or her elders. The middle class, especially, feel that status is also gained by discarding folk beliefs and practices and becoming more Catholic.

Faced with limited agricultural resources and little prospect of improving their productivity, many villagers have by-passed their agrarian problem and have instead become dependent on new occupations and on jobs outside the village. The middle economic group has doubled in size and now constitutes about 25 percent of the total population. Moreover, it is no longer merely an economic group; it is emerging rather as a true middle class, consisting of professionals, white-collar employees and self-employed artisans and shopkeepers whose values and goals have come to differ substantially from those of the peasantry. The sharpening cleavage between the middle and lower economic groups, between peasant and nonpeasant, is perhaps the most far-reaching and significant change in the village.

Although the lower economic group is proportionately smaller than it was in 1943, it still constitutes the great majority of the villagers—approximately 65 percent. Our data suggest that this group has become even poorer, both because of inflation and because its members have been deprived of a traditional source of income by the prohibiting of charcoal production. Members of the lower segments of this group have gained least from the processes set in motion by the Mexican Revolution. They have been unable or unwilling to leave the village for jobs in the cities or to work as *braceros*. They have taken least advantage of the greater educational opportunities. They continue to farm for subsistence and cling to the old ways of life largely because these are cheaper.

As Azteca moves further into the modern world, it is leaving behind its Indian language, many of its Indian customs, its local autonomy and the collective forms of pre-Hispanic times. Even the communal lands—the bulwark of the traditional order and formerly one of the most important bases for the corporate life of the community—seem destined to be divided up into *ejido* plots, and perhaps later into private holdings. With improved means of communication, greater faith in technology, greater dependence on a money economy and outside jobs, increasing occupational specialization, and a desire for a higher level of living, a corresponding change has come about in the character of the people.

ABOUT THE AUTHOR

OSCAR LEWIS was born in New York City in 1914, and grew up on a small farm in Upstate New York. He received his Ph.D. in anthropology from Columbia University, and has taught at Brooklyn College, Washington University, and now teaches at the University of Illinois, but is currently on leave, engaged in a comparative analysis of the culture of poverty in Puerto Rico and New York, under grants from the Social Security Administration, the Guggenheim Foundation, and the Research Institute for the Study of Man.

He was Field Representative in Latin America for the United States National Indian Institute, consulting anthropologist for the Ford Foundation in India, and has been the recipient of a Guggenheim fellowship. His field work has taken him from the Blackfoot Indians of Canada to Texas farmers, from a Cuban sugar plantation to Spain, and from Mexico to a village in northern India. But from his first visit to Mexico in 1943, Mexican peasants and city dwellers have been his major interest. His books on Mexico—*Life in a Mexican Village: Tepoztlán Restudied; Five Families;* and *The Children of Sánchez*—have become landmarks in anthropological studies.